Thank you

When Macromedia Flash first appeared on the Web, it fired up people's imaginations, inspiring the inner designer, animator, and programmer in each of us. Flash 8 continues that movement, delivering even more delicious multimedia capability in our hands. I hope this book unlocks Flash's potential for readers like you.

Bringing this book to you, as always, took the efforts of a team, to which I owe my gratitude. To all the editors, coordinators, and producers inside and outside of Peachpit Press, I thank you.

I want to especially thank Paul Robertson. I'm grateful for his knowledge of Flash, remarkable talent for teaching and writing, and tireless efforts. His contributions to content both new and old I'm sure will open more eyes to Flash's possibilities.

–Russell Chun

Thank you

This project ("the book," as my children refer to it) has required tremendous efforts by many people, much of which I'm certain I don't even realize, and I owe you all many thanks.

First of all, I must thank Russell Chun. It is said that the relationship between author and book is like that of parent and child. I owe you a great deal for letting me take something that is yours, and allowing me to make it partly mine, too.

Thanks to our editors Wendy and Rebecca, who are certainly two of Peachpit Press's finest, for helping bring me along through the complexities of the publishing industry while also trying to get your own work done. Thanks to the production team, especially Andrei and Pat, for making each page look so sharp and beautiful. I'm in awe when I see your work.

Special thanks to Tiffany—your incredible eye for detail and wonderful sense of clarity have certainly made this book better, and every reader owes you for it.

Thanks to Jeff for opening the door.

Thanks to the many people in the Flash community who freely share their experience, especially Aral Balkan, Jesse Warden, Peter Hall, Keith Peters, Darron Schall, and the whole OSFlash (Open Source Flash) family. You are great teachers and examples.

And finally and most especially, thanks to my dear children, Brian, Adam, and Sarah, and my precious wife—I love you all. Kelli, you have shown more patience and dedication during the course of this "little project" than I would have believed one human being could possibly possess, and I know there's no way I can thank you enough. Thanks for the hard work you do each day, and for the smiles and encouragement and love.

–H. Paul Robertson

Table of Contents

PART III: NAVIGATING TIMELINES AND COMMUNICATING 99

TABLE OF CONTENTS

INTRODUCTION

Macromedia Flash 8 is one of the hottest technologies on the Web today. Leading corporate Web sites use its streamlined graphics to communicate their brands; major motion picture studios promote theatrical releases with Flash movies; and online gaming and educational sites provide rich user experiences with Flash interactivity.

As a vector-based animation and authoring application, Flash is ideal for creating high-impact, low-bandwidth Web sites incorporating animation, text, video, sound, and database integration. With robust support for complex interactivity and server-side communication, Flash is increasingly the solution for developing Internet applications as well. From designer to programmer, Flash has become the tool of choice for delivering dynamic content across various browsers and platforms.

As the popularity of Flash increases, so does the demand for designers and developers who know how to tap its power. This book is designed to help you meet that challenge. Learn how to build complex animations; integrate sophisticated interfaces and navigation schemes; and dynamically control graphics, video, sound, and text. Experiment with the techniques discussed in this book to create the compelling media that Flash makes possible. It's not an exaggeration to say that Flash is revolutionizing the Web. This book will help you be a part of that revolution—boot up your computer and get started.

Who Should Use This Book

This book is for designers, animators, and developers who want to take their Flash skills to the next level. You've mastered the basics of tweening and are ready to move on to more complex tasks such as importing video, masking, controlling dynamic sound, or detecting movie-clip collisions. You may not be a hard-core programmer, but you're ready to learn how ActionScript can control graphics, sounds, and text. You want to integrate interactivity with your animations to create arcade-style games, to create complex user-interface elements like pull-down menus, and to learn how Flash communicates with outside applications such as Web browsers. If this description fits, then this book is right for you.

This book explores the advanced features of Flash 8, so you should already be comfortable with the basic tools and commands for creating simple Flash movies. You should know how to create and modify shapes and text with the drawing tools and be able to create symbols. You should also know how to apply motion and shape tweens and how to work with frame-by-frame animation. You should know your way around the Flash interface: how to move from the Stage to symbol-editing mode to the Timeline, and how to manipulate layers and frames. You should also be familiar with importing and using bitmaps and sounds and assigning basic actions to frames and buttons for navigation. To get yourself up to speed, review the tutorials that come with the software, or pick up a copy of *Macromedia Flash 8: Visual QuickStart Guide* by Katherine Ulrich.

Goals of This Book

The aim of this book is to demonstrate the advanced features of Flash 8 through a logical approach, emphasizing how techniques are applied. You'll learn how techniques build on each other and how groups of techniques can be combined to solve a particular problem. Each example you work through puts another skill under your belt; by the end of this book, you'll be able to create sophisticated interactive Flash projects.

For example, creating a pull-down menu illustrates how simple elements—invisible buttons, event handlers, button-tracking options, and movie clips—come together to make more complex behaviors. Examples illustrate the practical application of techniques, and additional tips explain how to apply these techniques in other contexts.

How to use this book

The concepts in this book build on each other: The material at the end is more complex than that at the beginning. If you're familiar with some of the material, you can skip around to the subjects that interest you, but you'll find it most useful to learn the techniques in the order in which they appear.

As with other books in the Visual QuickPro Guide series, tasks are presented for you to do as you read about them, so that you can see how a technique is applied. Follow the step-by-step instructions, look at the figures, and try the tasks on your computer. You'll learn more by doing and by taking an active role in experimenting with these exercises. Many of the completed tasks are provided as FLA and SWF files on the included CD-ROM; those tasks that have accompanying files are identified with this icon.

Tips follow the tasks to give you hints about how to use a shortcut, warnings about common mistakes, and suggestions about how techniques can be extended.

Occasionally, you'll see sidebars in gray boxes. Sidebars discuss related matters that aren't directly task-oriented. They include interesting and useful concepts that can help you better understand how Flash works.

What's in this book

This book is organized into five parts:

- Part I: Approaching Advanced Animation

  This part covers advanced techniques for graphics and animation, including strategies for motion tweening, shape tweening, masking, and using digital video.

- Part II: Understanding ActionScript

  This part introduces ActionScript, the scripting language Flash uses to add interactivity to a movie. You'll learn the basic components of the language and how to use the Actions panel to construct meaningful code.

- Part III: Navigating Timelines and Communicating

  This part teaches you the ways in which Flash can respond to input from the viewer and how you can create complex navigation schemes with multiple Timelines. You'll also see how Flash communicates with external files and applications such as Web browsers.

- Part IV: Transforming Graphics and Sound

  This part demonstrates how to dynamically control the basic elements of any Flash movie—its graphics and sound—through ActionScript.

- Part V: Working with Information

  The last part focuses on how to retrieve, store, modify, and test information to create complex Flash environments that can respond to changing conditions.

- Appendixes

  Two appendixes give you quick access to the standard object name extensions and key code values.

What's on the CD

Accompanying this book is a CD-ROM that contains nearly all the Flash source files for the tasks. You can see how each task was created, study the ActionScript, and use the ActionScript to do further experimentation. You'll also find a trial version of Flash 8 as well as a list of Web links to sites that are devoted to Flash and that showcase the latest Flash techniques and provide tutorials, articles, and advice.

Additional resources

Use the Web to your advantage. There is a thriving international community of Flash developers; within it, you can share your frustrations, seek help, and show off your latest Flash masterpiece. Free bulletin boards, email discussion lists, and a significant number of Flash-related weblogs exist for all levels of Flash users. Begin your search for Flash resources with the list of Web sites on the accompanying CD-ROM and with the Help panel in the Flash application, which provides a searchable ActionScript language reference and Flash manual.

Flash Basic 8 and Flash Professional 8

What's the difference between Flash Basic 8 and Flash Professional 8? And which version is right for you? Both versions are new upgrades from Flash MX 2004. Flash Basic 8 contains new features—primarily improved drawing tools such as a new object-drawing model, enhanced control over drawing strokes, and improved text display. Other new features include a new Script Assist tool to simplify programming for users who are new to ActionScript (similar to the Normal Mode in previous versions of Flash), the ability to add descriptive information to a Flash movie that will be available to Internet search engines, and numerous improvements to the Flash tools and workspace. Flash Professional 8 has all of these same new features plus significant additional tools that will interest professional graphic designers and advanced developers of Internet applications and professional video. Flash Professional 8 includes new tools such as filters and blending modes for creating advanced graphical effects. In addition, as in the previous version, Flash Professional 8 provides a forms-based environment to create applications; a slide-based environment to create presentations; additional components for database integration; and a video encoder to encode high-quality, low-bandwidth FLV files within Flash or from professional video editing tools.

If you're a casual, infrequent, or hobbyist user of Flash, and you're interested in manipulating graphics, animations, sound, text, and video, and integrating them with ActionScript, then Flash Basic 8 is for you. If you'll be using Flash on a frequent or professional basis, and you expect to design graphics with advanced visual effects or develop applications such as Internet chat rooms or e-commerce sites where connectivity to databases is essential, then Flash Professional 8 is for you.

Keep in mind that although the name of the authoring application is Flash Basic 8 or Flash Professional 8, the Web browser plug-in that plays media authored in either version is called Flash Player 8.

What's New in Flash 8

Whether you're a beginner or an advanced user, a designer or a programmer, a number of new features in Flash 8 will appeal to you. The following are just a few of the capabilities that make Flash 8 even more powerful, flexible, and easy to use.

New expressiveness capabilities

Drawing and graphics creation have received a significant facelift in Flash 8. In the new object drawing mode, tools behave like their counterparts in traditional vector illustration applications. Users can now control the styling of ends and intersections (caps and joins) of vector strokes and can apply gradient colors to strokes. In addition, Flash Professional 8 includes new capabilities for applying filters and blending to graphical content, which previously could be achieved only by creating graphics in an external graphics-editing application such as Adobe Photoshop or Macromedia Fireworks. Flash 8 also adds custom easing controls for precision control over the timing and flow of animation.

User interface improvements

A number of small but significant changes to the user interface make this the most usable and productive version of Flash yet. Macintosh users can now choose to have multiple documents open in tabs rather than separate windows. For users on any platform, document tabs can be reordered. The test-movie window appears in its own window by default, making the test, edit, and re-test process more refined. When multiple Flash documents are open, the libraries from those documents are displayed in a single Library panel; and Flash panels can be grouped together, allowing users flexibility in customizing their workspace.

Expanded interactivity

Even more ActionScript classes, properties, methods, and events help bring your Flash project to life. All the expressiveness capabilities already described plus additional filters and custom bitmap manipulation are available for use in ActionScript through new additions to the language. In addition, improvements to the Actions panel make programming with ActionScript more productive for novices and experts alike. Users with less ActionScript or programming experience will appreciate the fill-in-the-blanks Script Assist mode for writing ActionScript. Even ActionScript experts will benefit from the improved Find and Replace capabilities and the expanded help documentation.

Part I: Approaching Advanced Animation

1

Building Complexity

The key to creating complex animations in Flash is building them from simpler parts. You should think of your Flash project as being a collection of simpler motions, just as the movement of a runner is essentially a collection of rotating limbs. Isolating individual components of a much larger, complicated motion allows you to treat each component with the most appropriate technique, simplifies the tweening, and gives you better control with more refined results.

To animate a head that's turning quickly to face the camera, for example, you would first consider how to simplify the animation into separate motions. Animating the entire sequence at the same time would be difficult, if not impossible, because the many elements making up the head change in different ways as they move. The outline of the head could be a frame-by-frame animation to show the transformation from a profile to a frontal pose. Some of the features of the face could be symbol instances that you squash and stretch in a motion tween to match the turn of the head. And the hair could be a shape tween that lets you show its flow, swing, and slight bounce-back effect when the head stops.

Learning to combine different techniques and break animation into simpler parts not only solves difficult animation problems but also forces you to use multiple layers and establish symbols of the component parts. By doing so, you set up the animation so that it's easy to manage now and revise later.

This chapter describes approaches to building complex animations through layering, combining, and extending basic Flash capabilities.

Motion Tweening Strategies

Motion tweening lets you interpolate any of the instance properties of a symbol, such as its location, size, rotation, color, and transparency, as well as any filters that have been applied to the symbol instance. Because of its versatility, motion tweening can be applied to a variety of animation problems, making it the foundation of most Flash projects. Because motion tweening deals with instance properties, it's a good idea to think of the technique in terms of instance tweening. Regardless of whether actual motion across the Stage is involved, changing instances between keyframes requires motion tweening. Thinking of it as instance tweening will help you distinguish when and where to use motion tweening as opposed to shape tweening or frame-by-frame animation.

Creating seamless animated loops

Animated loops are important because they provide a way to continue motion by defining only a few keyframes. You see animated loops in interface elements such as rotating buttons and scrolling menus, as well as in cyclical motions such as a person walking, a butterfly's wings flapping, or a planet revolving. The important point in creating seamless loops is making sure the last and first keyframes are identical (or nearly identical) so that the motion is continuous.

This section shows you how to make two of the most common types of animated loops: scrolling graphics and graphics on closed motion paths. Scrolling graphics are familiar effects in interface elements such as menu options that cycle across the screen. You can also use this technique to create background animations that loop endlessly, such as a field of stars behind a spaceship.

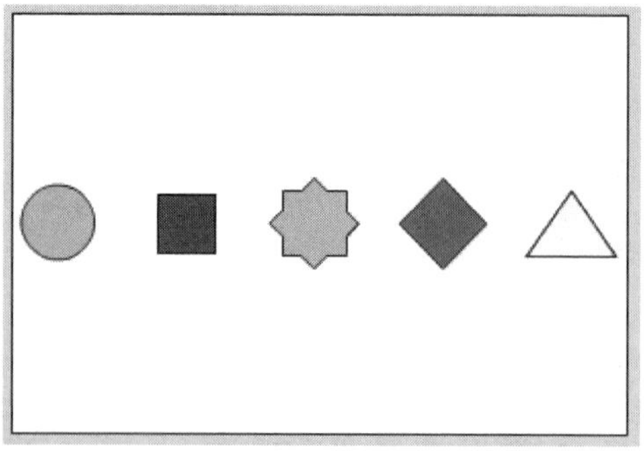

Figure 1.1 Five objects placed across the Stage as they would appear when they begin scrolling across from right to left. The objects could be buttons or simple graphics.

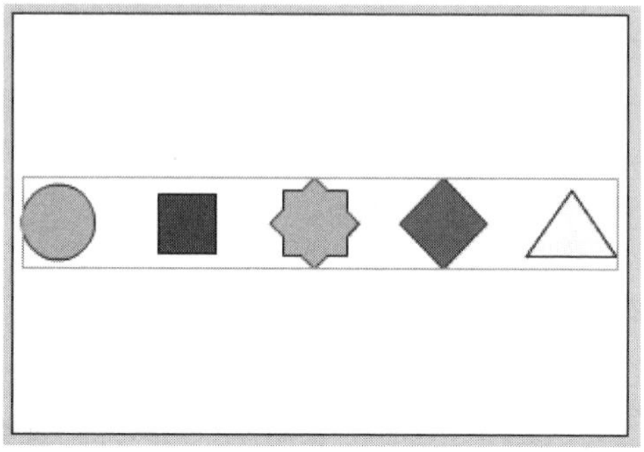

Figure 1.2 Group the objects by choosing Modify > Group.

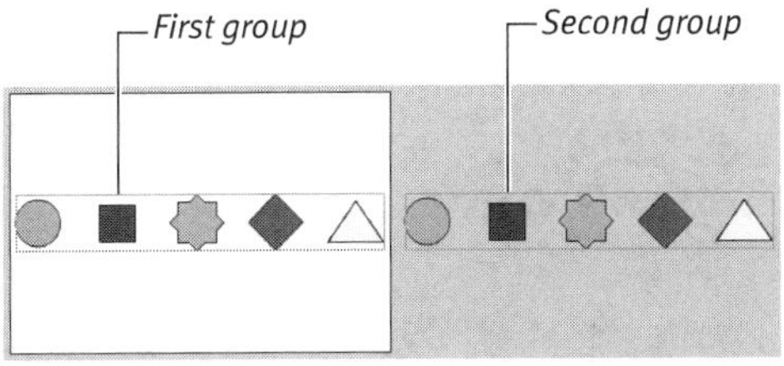

Figure 1.3 Create a pattern by copying and pasting the group.

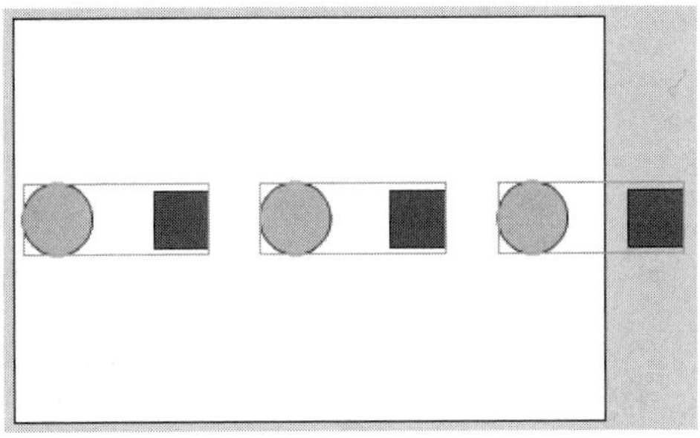

Figure 1.4 This group has only two objects. Place copies of it to extend well past the Stage.

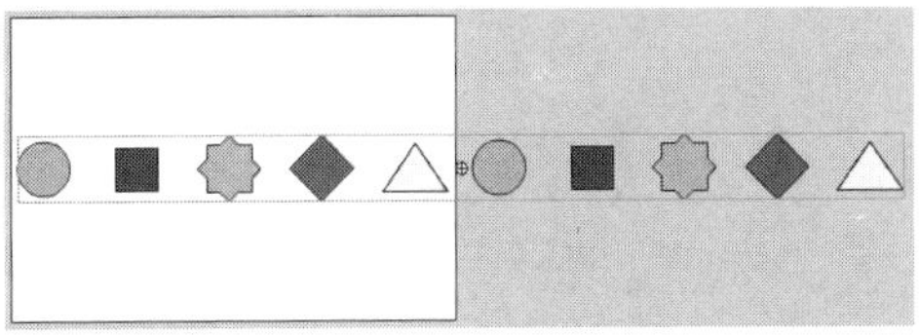

Figure 1.5 Create a graphic symbol of the entire pattern.

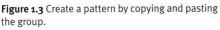

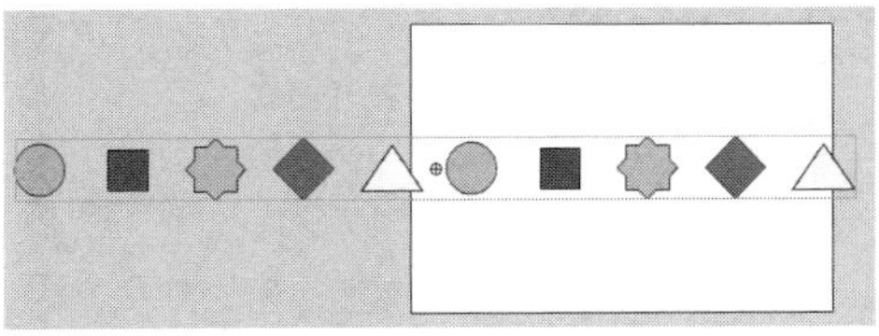

Figure 1.6 The second repeated group is moved where the first group was originally.

A motion path in a guide layer provides a way to create smooth movement along a path from the beginning point to the end point. If you make the end point of the path match the beginning point, you can create a seamless loop and effectively close the motion path.

To create a continuous scrolling graphic:

1. Create the elements that will scroll across the Stage, and place them as they would appear at any given moment (**Figure 1.1**).
2. Select all the elements, and choose Modify > Group (**Figure 1.2**).
3. Copy the group, and paste the copy next to the original group to create a long band of repeating elements.

   If your elements scroll from right to left, for example, place the second group to the right of the first group (**Figure 1.3**).

   Your scrolling elements usually will be larger than the Stage, but if your first group is smaller, you'll need to duplicate it more than once to create a repeating pattern that extends beyond the Stage (**Figure 1.4**).
4. Select all your groups, and convert your selection to a graphic symbol (**Figure 1.5**).

   An instance of the symbol remains on the Stage, allowing you to apply a motion tween.
5. Create a keyframe at a later point in the Timeline.
6. Select the instance in the last keyframe, and move it so that the second repeated group of elements aligns with the first.

   When you move your instance, use its outlines to match its previous position (**Figure 1.6**).

continues on next page

7. Apply a motion tween between the keyframes.

8. Insert a new keyframe just before the last keyframe, and remove the last frame (**Figure 1.7**).

   When you use this technique, the animation won't have to play two identical frames (the first and the last), and a smooth loop is created.

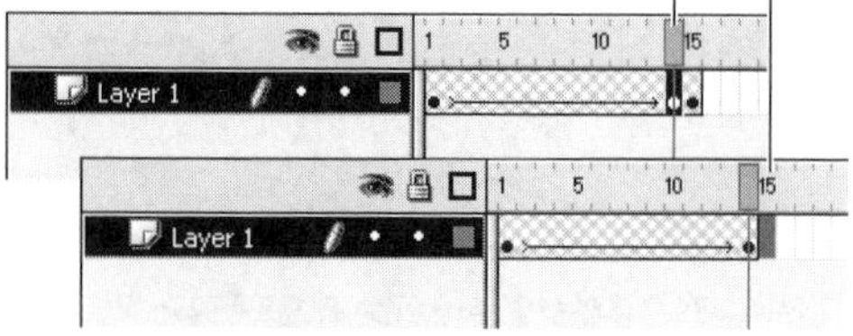

Figure 1.7 Create a new keyframe (top), and delete the last keyframe (bottom).

To make a closed motion path:

1. Create a graphic symbol, and place an instance of it on the Stage (**Figure 1.8**).

2. Create a guide layer by clicking the Add Motion Guide icon below your layers.

   A new guide layer appears above the first, and your first layer becomes a guided layer (**Figure 1.9**).

3. Draw an empty ellipse in the guide (top) layer.

4. With the Snap to Objects modifier for the Selection tool turned on, grab your instance by its registration point and place it on the path of the ellipse (**Figure 1.10**).

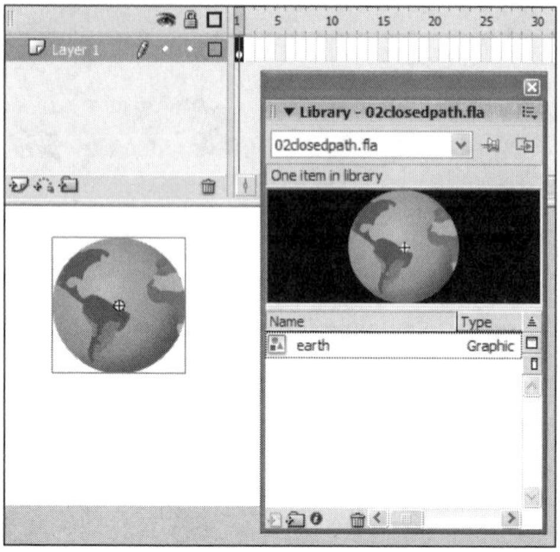

Figure 1.8 An instance of a graphic symbol is placed on the Stage for motion tweening along a path.

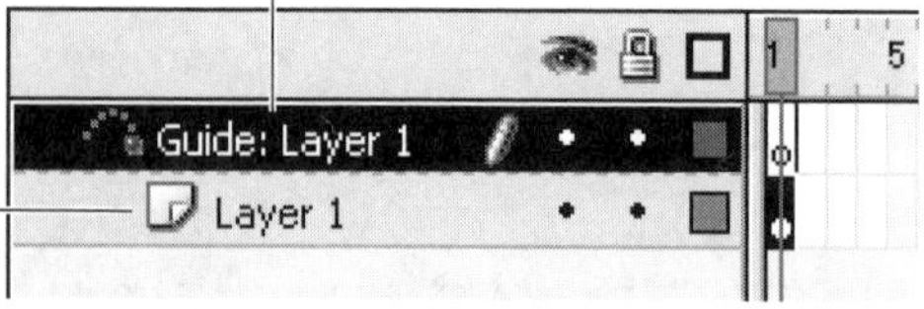

Figure 1.9 The guide layer above Layer 1 will contain the motion path.

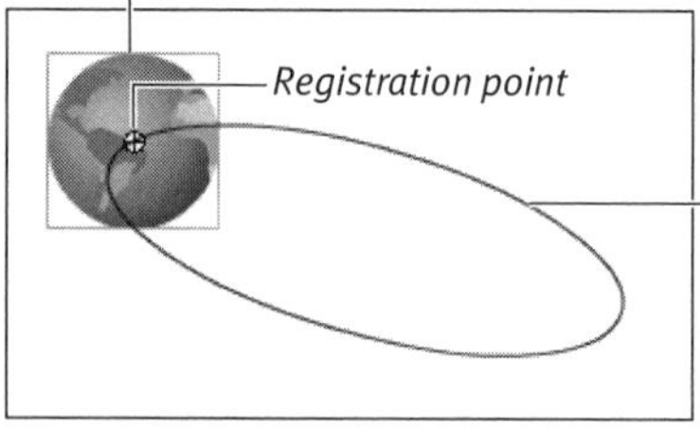

Figure 1.10 The registration point of the earth instance snaps to the motion path.

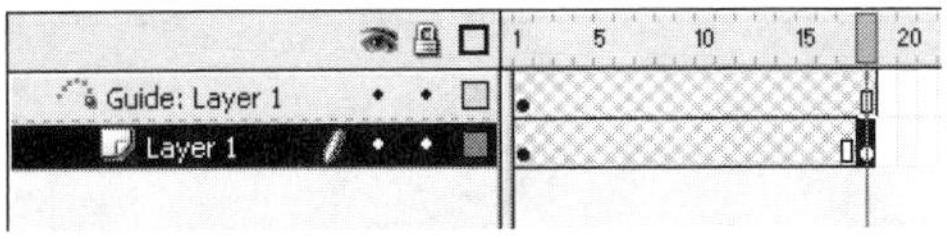

Figure 1.11 The position of the earth at keyframe 1 and at keyframe 18 in Layer 1 is the same.

5. Add frames to both layers, and create a new keyframe in the last frame of the guided (bottom) layer.

   The first and last keyframes remain the same to create the animated loop (**Figure 1.11**).

6. Select the middle frame of the guided (bottom) layer, and insert a new keyframe, moving your instance in this intermediate keyframe to the opposite side of the ellipse (**Figure 1.12**).

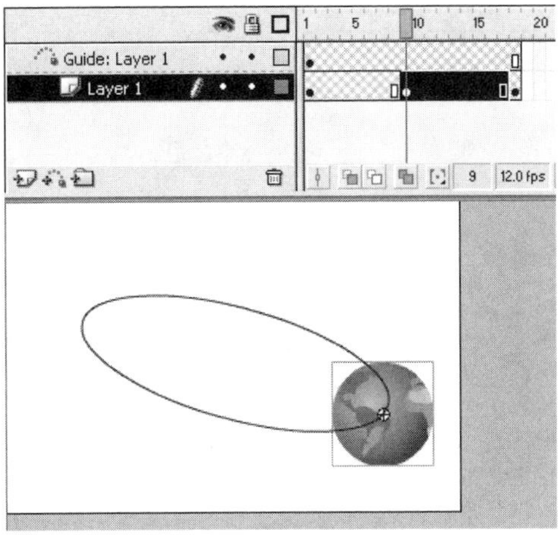

Figure 1.12 The registration point of the earth in the middle keyframe is positioned at the far side of the ellipse.

7. Select all the frames between the three keyframes. In the Property inspector, choose Motion Tween.

   Your instance now travels along the path of the ellipse, but it returns on the same segment of the ellipse rather than making a complete circuit (**Figure 1.13**).

8. Grab the instance in the last keyframe of the guided (bottom) layer, and move it slightly closer to the instance in the middle keyframe while maintaining its registration point on the path (**Figure 1.14**).

continues on next page

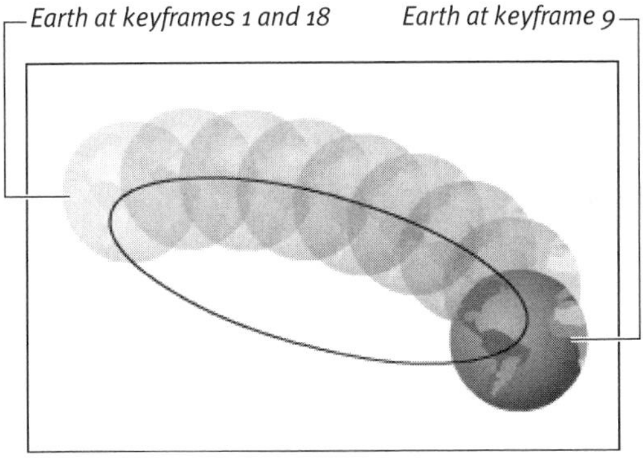

Figure 1.13 The earth bounces back and forth on the same segment of the ellipse.

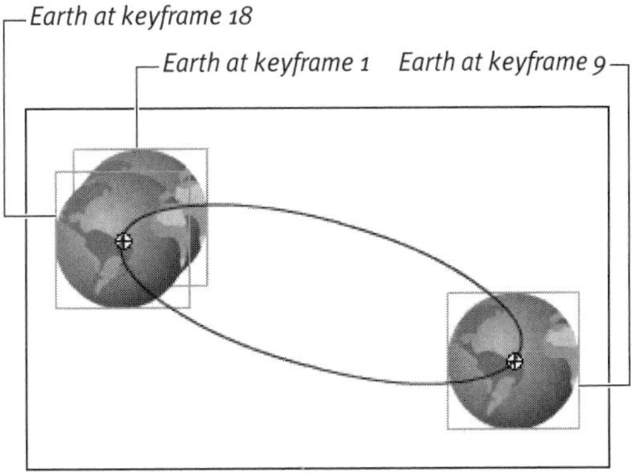

Figure 1.14 The three keyframes of the earth. The first instance is closer to the middle instance on the top path of the ellipse, and the last instance is closer to the middle instance on the bottom path of the ellipse.

Flash tweens two instances by taking the most direct path, so by shortening the distance between the last two keyframes on the bottom segment of the ellipse, you force Flash to use that segment of the ellipse.

Your instance now travels along both sides of the ellipse (**Figure 1.15**).

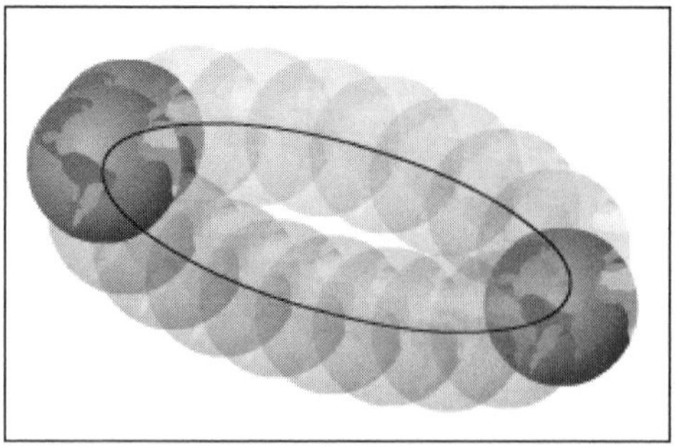

Figure 1.15 The earth moves around the closed path.

✔ Tip

- You can accomplish the same kind of looping effect by deleting a small segment of your path. When you create a gap, you essentially make an open path with beginning and end points for your instance to follow (**Figure 1.16**).

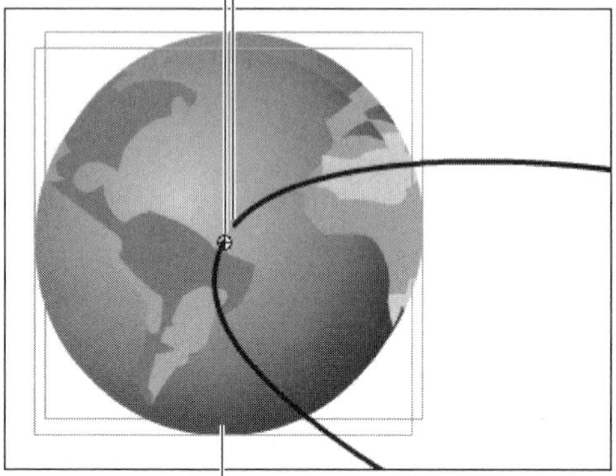

Figure 1.16 A tiny gap provides beginning and end points for your motion path.

Using multiple guided layers

A single guide layer can affect more than one guided layer, letting multiple motion tweens follow the same path. This approach is good for creating complex animations that require many objects traveling in the same direction, such as soldiers marching through a field, blood cells coursing through an artery, bullets flying through the air, or cattle stampeding in a herd. Although the individual instances may vary, you maintain control of their general direction with a single guide layer.

Several leaves blowing across the Stage could be animated to follow one guide layer, for example. The guide layer establishes the wind's general direction; the leaves could have slight individual variations by being offset in separate guided layers. Just by changing the path in the guide layer, you make all the leaves change accordingly. Using a single path to guide multiple layers this way is an example of how you build complex animations (in this case, swirling leaves) from very simple parts (one guide layer and one leaf symbol).

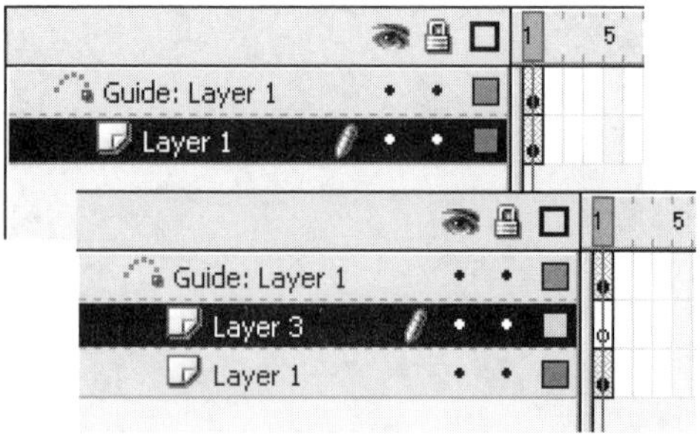

Figure 1.17 Selecting the guided layer (Layer 1) and inserting a new layer automatically modifies the new layer as a guided layer (Layer 3).

MOTION TWEENING STRATEGIES

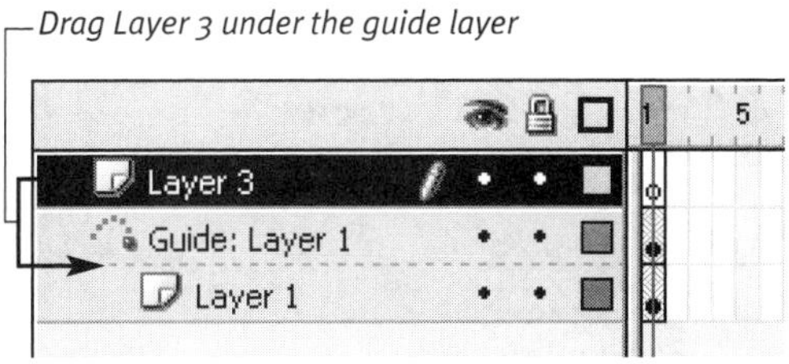

Figure 1.18 A normal layer (Layer 3) can be dragged below the guide layer to become a guided layer.

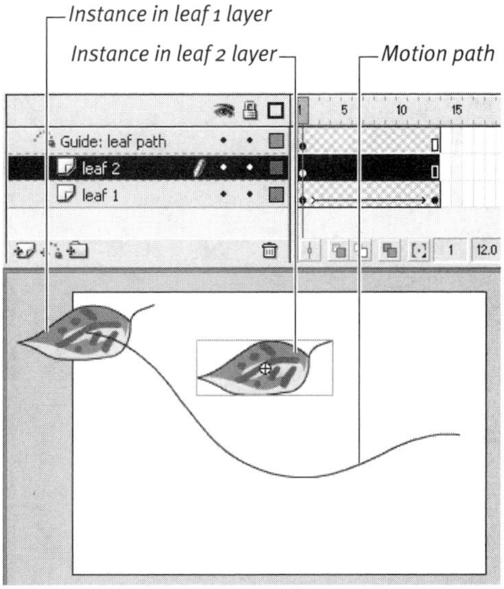

Figure 1.19 An instance on the Stage in the leaf 2 layer.

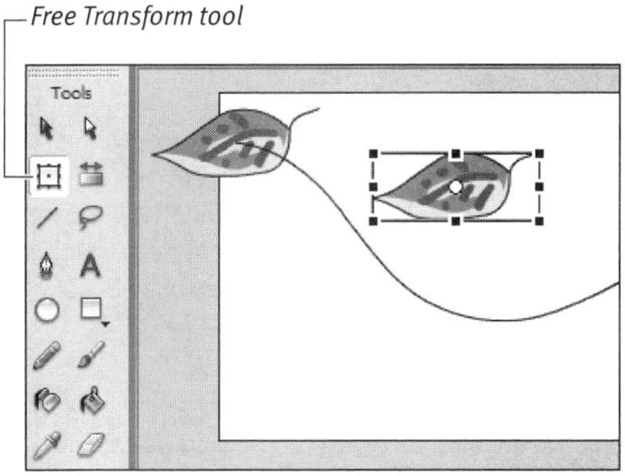

Figure 1.20 Select the instance in the second guided layer, and select the Free Transform tool in the Toolbox.

You can increase complexity by using animated graphic symbol instances along the guide layer's motion path. Animated loops within graphic symbols provide localized motion that still follows the guide layer in the main Timeline.

To assign a second guided layer to a guide layer:

- Select the first guided layer, and click the Insert Layer icon.

  A second guided layer appears above the first (**Figure 1.17**).

  or

- Drag an existing normal layer below the guide layer.

  The normal layer becomes a guided layer (**Figure 1.18**).

To offset a second guided layer:

1. Create the second guided layer as described earlier in this section, and drag in an instance that you want to tween (**Figure 1.19**).
2. Select the instance in the second guided layer, and choose the Free Transform tool in the Toolbox.

   Control handles appear around your instance, along with a white circle in the center marking the current registration point (**Figure 1.20**).

continues on next page

3. Drag the registration point to a new position.

   An instance's registration point can lie anywhere, even outside the boundaries of the Free Transform tool's control handles.

   The new registration point is set where you just placed it (**Figure 1.21**).

4. Choose the Selection tool to exit the Free Transform tool, and make sure the Snap to Objects modifier is turned on.

5. Grab the instance by its new registration point, and attach it to the beginning of the guide layer's path (**Figure 1.22**).

6. Insert a new keyframe into the last frame.

   The newly created instance in the last keyframe has the same registration point as the edited instance.

7. Attach the instance in the last keyframe to the end of the guide layer's path, and apply a motion tween between the two keyframes.

   The motion tween in the second guided layer follows the same path as the first guided layer. However, the new registration point of the instance in the second guided layer offsets the motion (**Figure 1.23**).

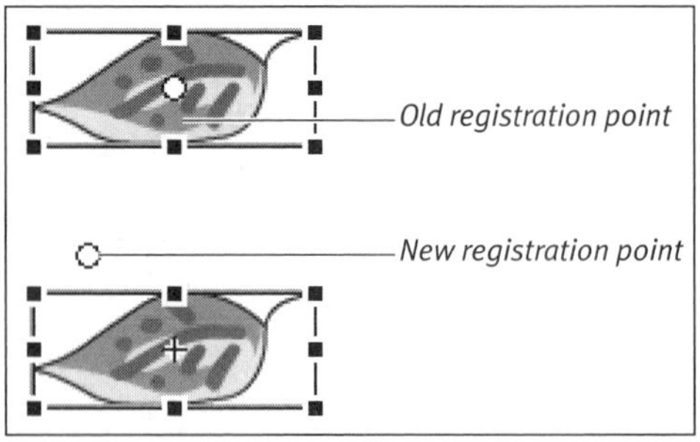

Figure 1.21 Change the registration point of your instance by moving the white circle.

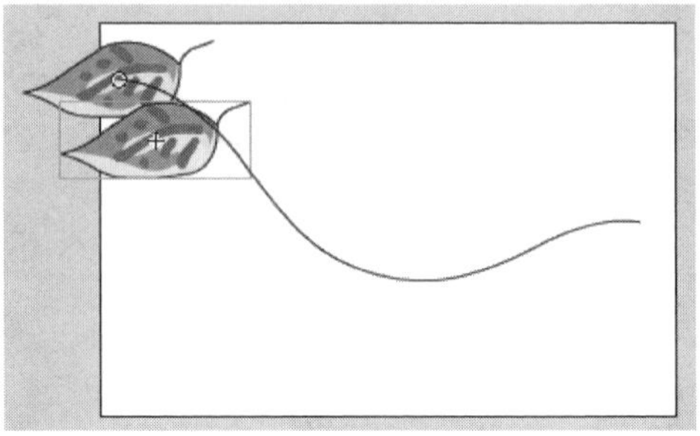

Figure 1.22 The registration point of the leaf, shown selected here, is attached to the path.

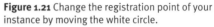

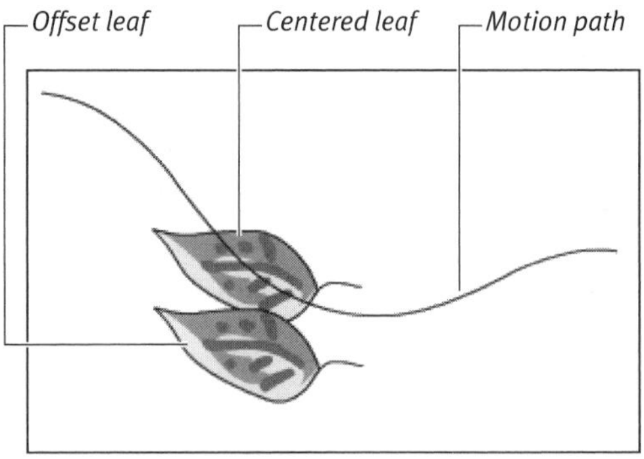

Figure 1.23 The two tweens follow the same motion path. The second leaf is offset because of its moved registration point.

Motion Tweening Strategies

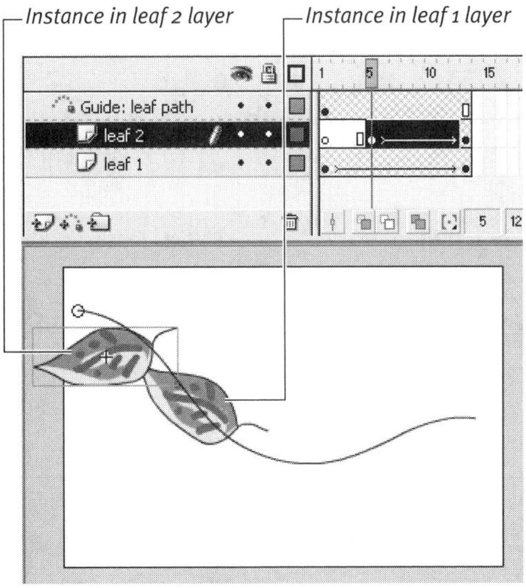

Figure 1.24 The leaf in the leaf 2 layer follows the motion path only after the one in the leaf 1 layer has already started.

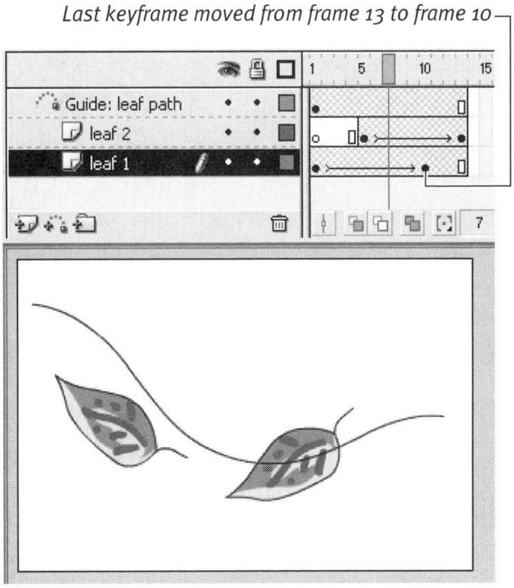

Figure 1.25 Move the last keyframe in the leaf 1 layer closer to the first keyframe.

To vary the timing of a second guided layer:

1. Continuing with the preceding example, drag the first keyframe of the second guided layer to a later point in time.

   The motion tween for that guided layer begins after the first one starts, but both animations end at the same time (**Figure 1.24**).

2. Drag the last keyframe of the first guided layer to an earlier point in time.

   The motion tweens following the path in the guide layer are staggered relative to each other (**Figure 1.25**).

3. Refine the timing of the motion tweens by moving the first and last keyframes in both guided layers.

✔ Tip

- Create variations in the second guided layer by placing the instances at any point along the path in the guide layer. The instances don't have to lie at the very beginning or end of the path for the motion tween to work.

To add local variations to multiple guided layers:

1. Enter symbol-editing mode for the graphic symbol you use on the motion path.
2. Select the contents of this symbol, and convert it to a graphic symbol.

   You create a graphic symbol within another graphic symbol, which allows you to create a motion tween within your first graphic symbol.
3. Create a looping motion tween (**Figure 1.26**).

   This type of animation ends where it begins.
4. Exit symbol-editing mode, and play the movie to see how the motion tween of the graphic symbol gets incorporated into the motion tween on the main Stage (**Figure 1.27**).

✔ Tips

- In the Property inspector, adjust the animation option and the First parameter to vary how the animated graphic instances play (**Figure 1.28**). By having your loops begin with different frames, you prevent them from being synchronized with one another (**Figure 1.29**).
- Rotating your instances at this point can produce even more complex, interesting, and seemingly random movements. Experiment with rotating your instances as they travel along the motion path.

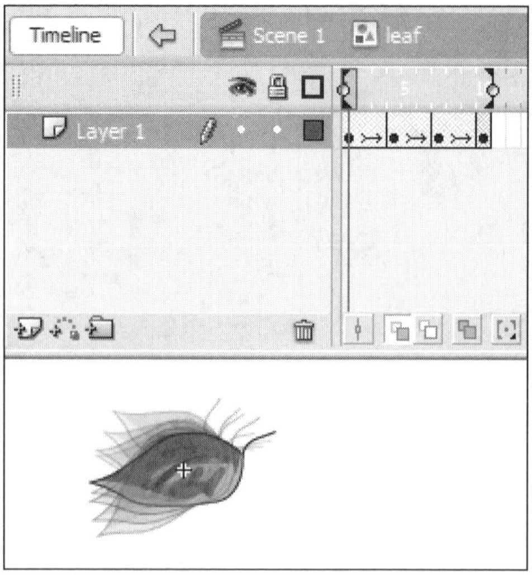

Figure 1.26 An animated graphic symbol of a leaf moving up and down.

Figure 1.27 Play the movie to see how the leaves follow the motion path while going through their own animation.

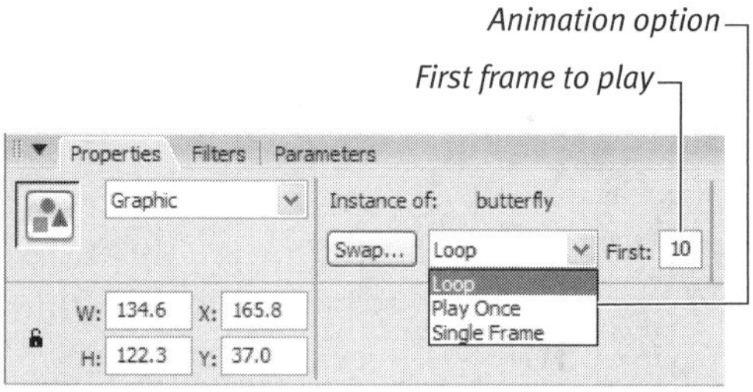

Figure 1.28 The First parameter is set to 10 so that the leaf graphic will loop beginning with frame 10. The other play mode options in the pull-down menu include Play Once and Single Frame.

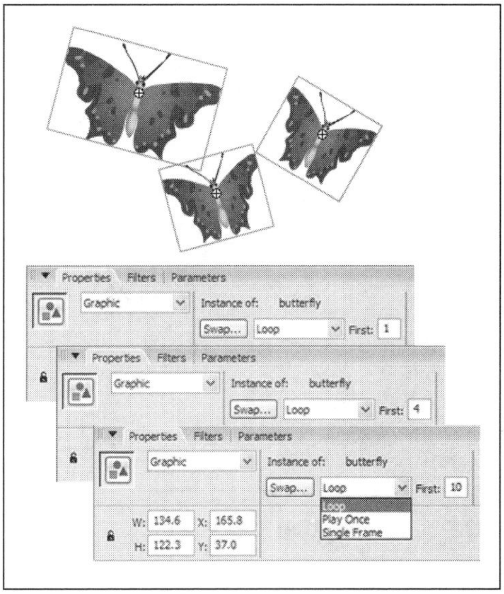

Figure 1.29 Three instances of the same graphic symbol with different first-frame play options. The left butterfly loops beginning with frame 1; its wings start to close. The middle butterfly loops beginning with frame 4; its wings are already closed and start to open. The right butterfly loops beginning with frame 10; its wings are opening.

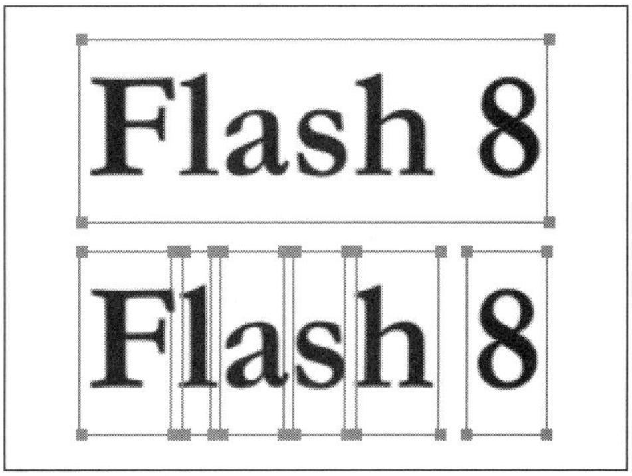

Figure 1.30 Breaking apart a block of static text (top) results in static text of the individual letters (bottom).

Animating titles

Frequently, splash screens on Flash Web sites feature animated titles and other text-related materials that twirl, tumble, and spin until they all come into place as a complete design. Several techniques can help you accomplish these kinds of effects quickly and easily. The Break Apart command, when applied to a block of static text, breaks the text into its component characters while keeping them as live, editable text. This command lets you painlessly create separate text fields for the letters that make up a word or title. You can then use the Distribute to Layers command to isolate each of those characters on its own layer, ready for motion tweening.

When you begin applying motion tweens to your individual letters or words, it's useful to think and work backward from the final design. Create an end keyframe containing the final positions of all your characters, for example. Then, in the first keyframes, you can change the characters' positions and apply as many transformations as you like, knowing that the final resting spots are secured.

To animate the letters of a title:

1. Select the Text tool, and make sure Static Text is selected in the Property inspector.
2. On the Stage, type a title you want to animate.
3. Choose Modify > Break Apart (Cmd-B for Mac, Ctrl-B for Windows).

   Flash replaces the static-text title with individual static-text letters (**Figure 1.30**).

continues on next page

4. Choose Modify > Timeline > Distribute to Layers (Cmd-Shift-D for Mac, Ctrl-Shift-D for Windows).

   Each selected item on the Stage is placed in its own layer below the existing layer. In this case, the newly created layers are named with the individual letters automatically (**Figure 1.31**).

5. Create keyframes for each layer at a later point in the Timeline.

6. In the first keyframe of each layer, rearrange and transform the letters according to your creative urges.

7. Select all the frames in the Timeline, and apply a motion tween.

   Your movie animates all these text elements coming together as a complete title (**Figure 1.32**).

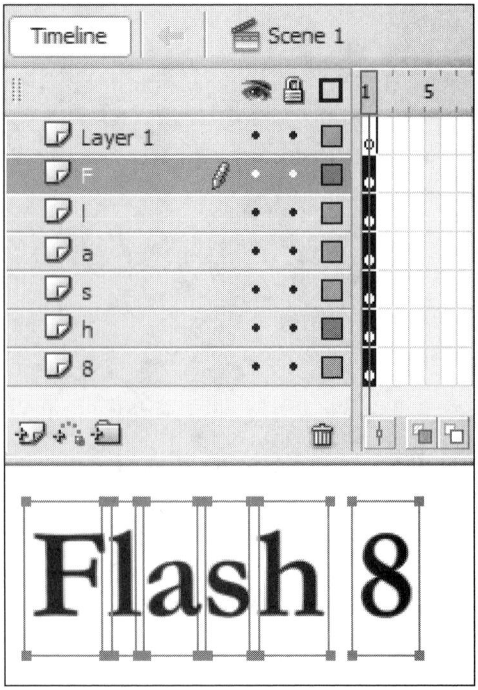

Figure 1.31 Distribute to Layers separates the selected items in their own layers.

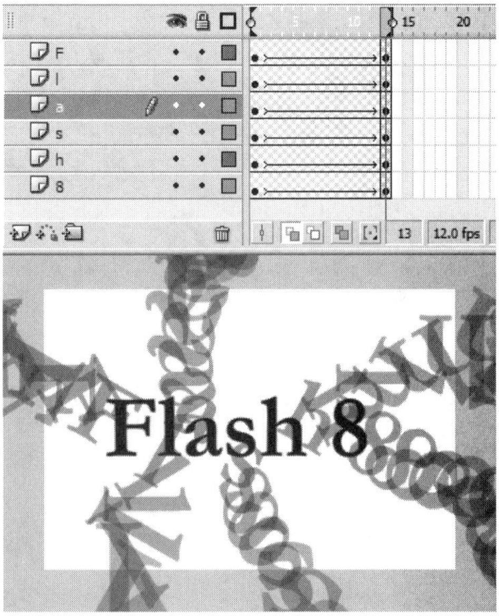

Figure 1.32 The letters tumble and fall into place at the last keyframe.

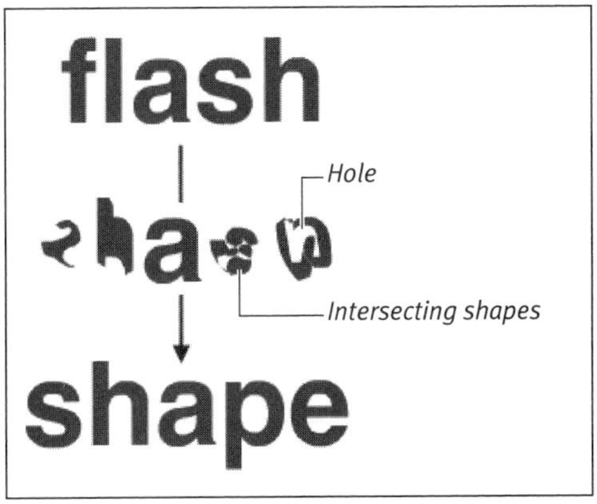

Figure 1.33 An attempt to shape tween *flash* to *shape* all at once in a single layer. Notice the breakups between the *s* and the *p* and the hole that appears between the *h* and the *e*.

Shape Tweening Strategies

Shape tweening is a technique for interpolating amorphous changes that can't be accomplished with instance transformations such as rotation, scale, and skew. Fill, outline, gradient, and alpha are all shape attributes that can be shape tweened.

Flash applies a shape tween by using what it considers to be the most efficient, direct route. This method sometimes has unpredictable results, creating overlapping shapes or seemingly random holes that appear and merge (**Figure 1.33**). These undesirable effects usually are the result of keyframes containing shapes that are too complex to tween at the same time.

As is the case with motion tweening, simplifying a complicated shape tween into more basic parts and separating those parts in layers results in a more successful interpolation. Shape hints give you a way to tell Flash what point on the first shape corresponds to what point on the second shape. Sometimes, adding intermediate keyframes helps a complicated tween by providing a transition state and making the tween go through many more-manageable stages.

Using shape hints

Shape hints force Flash to map points on the first shape to corresponding points on the second shape. By placing multiple shape hints, you can control more precisely the way your shapes will tween.

To add a shape hint:

1. Select the first keyframe of the shape tween, and choose Modify > Shape > Add Shape Hint (Cmd-Shift-H for Mac, Ctrl-Shift-H for Windows) (**Figure 1.34**).

   A letter in a red circle appears in the middle of your shape (**Figure 1.35**).

2. Move the first shape hint to a point on your shape.

   Make sure that the Snap to Objects modifier for the Selection tool is turned on to snap your selections to vertices and edges.

3. Select the last keyframe of the shape tween, and move the matching circled letter to a corresponding point on the end shape.

   This shape hint turns green, and the first shape hint turns yellow, signifying that both have been moved into place correctly (**Figure 1.36**).

4. Continue adding shape hints, up to a maximum of 26, to refine the shape tween (**Figure 1.37**).

✔ Tips

- Place shape hints in order either clockwise or counterclockwise. Flash more easily understands a sequential placement than one that jumps around.
- Shape hints need to be placed on an edge or a corner of the shape. If you place a shape hint in the fill or outside the shape, the original and corresponding shape hints will remain red, and Flash will ignore them.
- To view your animation without the shape hints, choose View > Show Shape Hints (Cmd-Option-H for Mac, Ctrl-Alt-H for Windows). Flash deselects the Show Shape Hints option, and the shape hints are hidden.

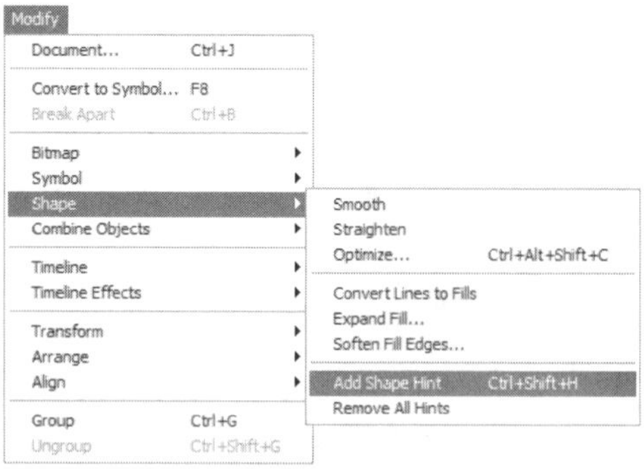

Figure 1.34 Select the first keyframe of the shape tween, and choose Modify > Shape > Add Shape Hint.

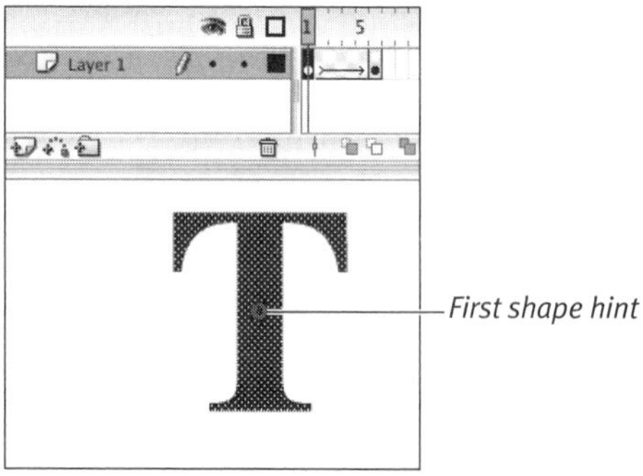

Figure 1.35 The first shape hint appears in the center of the Stage in the first keyframe.

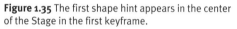

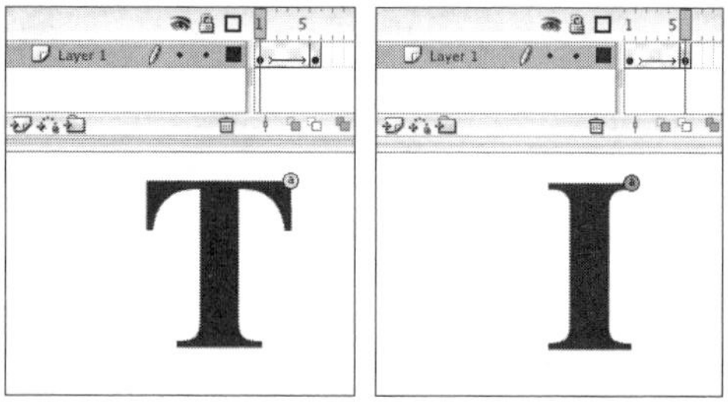

Figure 1.36 The first shape hint in the first keyframe (left) and its matching pair in the last keyframe (right).

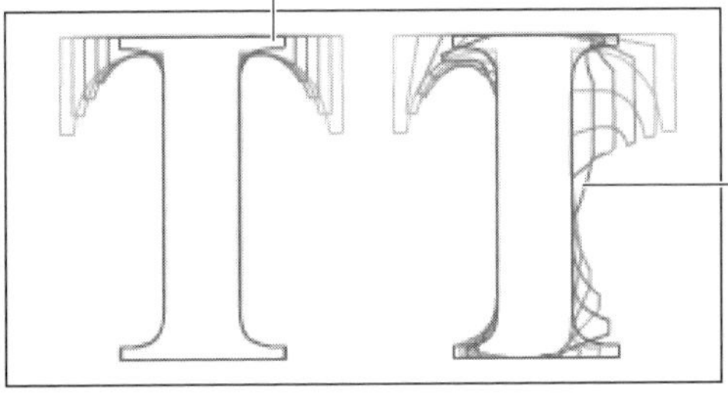

The cross of the T absorbs into the I
This T goes through some unnecessary changes to get to the I

Figure 1.37 Changing from a *T* to an *I* with shape hints (left) and without shape hints (right).

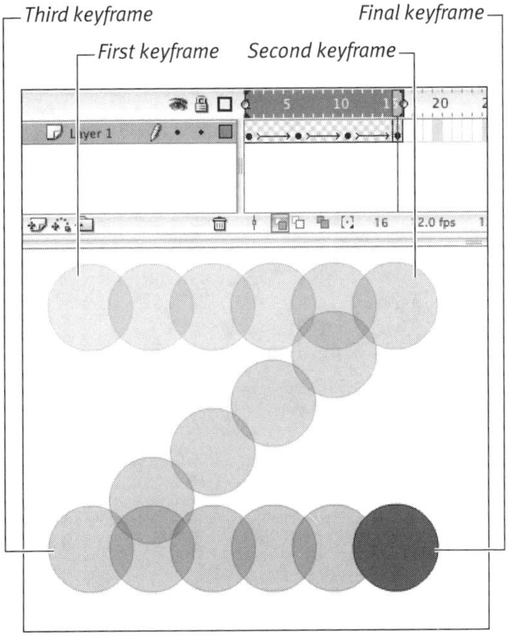

Figure 1.38 A complicated motion tween requires several intermediate keyframes.

- If you move your entire shape tween by using Edit Multiple Frames, you'll have to reposition all your shape hints. Unfortunately, you can't move all the shape hints at the same time.

To delete a shape hint:

- Drag the shape hint off the Stage.

  The matching shape hint in the other keyframe is deleted automatically.

To remove all shape hints:

- Choose Modify > Shape > Remove All Hints.

Using intermediate keyframes

Adding intermediate keyframes can help a complicated tween by providing a transition state that creates smaller changes that are more manageable. Think about this process in terms of motion tweening. Imagine that you want to create the motion of a ball starting from the top left of the Stage, moving to the top right, then to the bottom left, and finally to the bottom right (**Figure 1.38**). You can't create just two keyframes—one with the ball at the top-left corner of the Stage and one with the ball in the bottom-right corner—and expect Flash to tween the zigzag motion. You need to establish the intermediate keyframes so that Flash can create the motion in stages. The same is true with shape tweening. You can better handle one dramatic change between two shapes by using simpler, intermediate keyframes.

Sometimes, providing an intermediate keyframe isn't enough, and you need shape hints to refine the tween even more. The task "To use shape hints across multiple keyframes" shows three ways you can add shape hints to a shape tween that uses an intermediate keyframe.

To create an intermediate keyframe:

1. Study how an existing shape tween fails to produce satisfactory results when tweening the letter *Z* to the letter *S* (**Figure 1.39**).
2. Insert a keyframe at an intermediate point within the tween.
3. In the newly created keyframe, edit the shape to provide a kind of stepping stone for the final shape (**Figure 1.40**).

   The shape tween has smaller changes to go through, with smoother results (**Figure 1.41**).

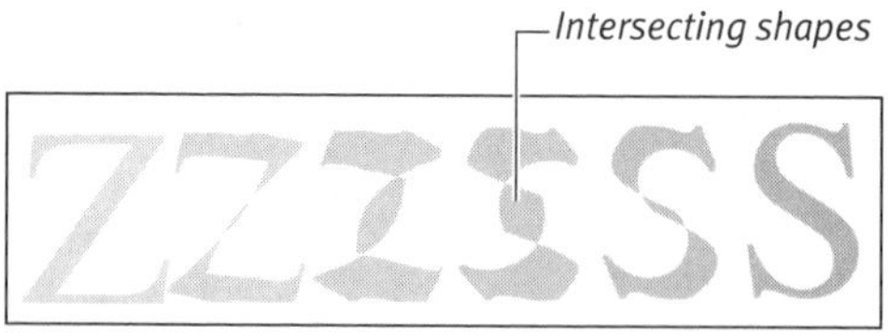

Figure 1.39 Changing a *Z* to an *S* all at once causes the shape to flip and cross over itself.

Figure 1.40 An intermediate shape.

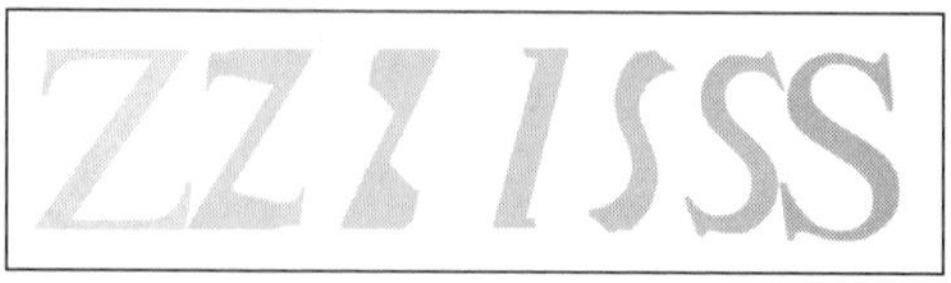

Figure 1.41 The *Z* makes an easy transition to the intermediate shape (middle), from which the *S* can tween smoothly.

To use shape hints across multiple keyframes:

- Select the intermediate keyframe, and add shape hints as though it were the first keyframe.

  Keep track of which shape hint belongs to which tween by noting their respective colors. Yellow is the shape hint for the beginning keyframe, and green is the shape hint for the ending keyframe (**Figure 1.42**).

  or

- Insert a new keyframe adjacent to the second keyframe, and begin adding shape hints.

  A new keyframe allows you to add shape hints without the confusion that overlapping shape hints from the preceding tween may cause (**Figure 1.43**).

  or

- Create a new layer that duplicates the intermediate and last keyframes of the shape tween, and begin adding shape tweens on this new layer.

  By duplicating the intermediate keyframe, you keep shape hints on separate layers, which also prevents the shape hints from overlapping (**Figure 1.44**).

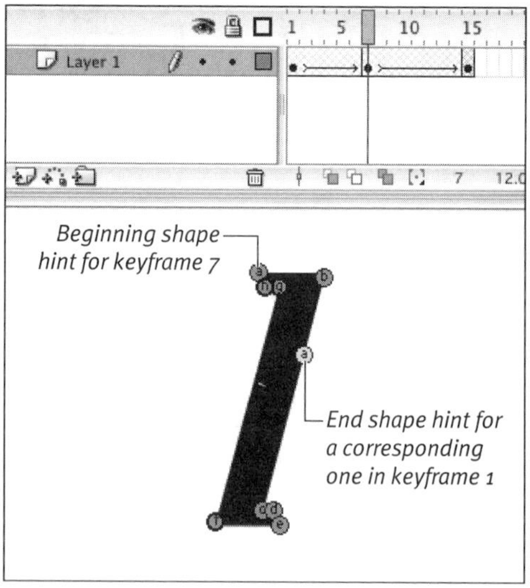

Figure 1.42 This intermediate keyframe contains two sets of shape hints. Some are the ending shape hints for the first tween; others are the beginning shape hints for the second tween.

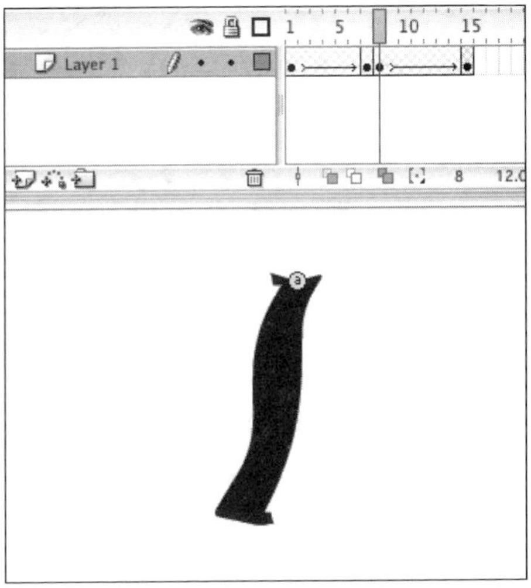

Figure 1.43 A shape hint in a new keyframe.

Using layers to simplify shape changes

Shape tweening lets you create very complex shape tweens on a single layer, but doing so can produce unpredictable results. Use layers to separate complex shapes and create multiple but simpler shape tweens.

When a shape tween is applied to change the letter *F* to the letter *D*, for example, the hole in the last shape appears at the edges of the first shape (**Figure 1.45**). Separating the hole in the *D* and treating it as a white shape allows you to control when and how it appears. Insert a new layer, and create a second tween for the hole. The compound tween gives you better, more-refined results (**Figure 1.46**).

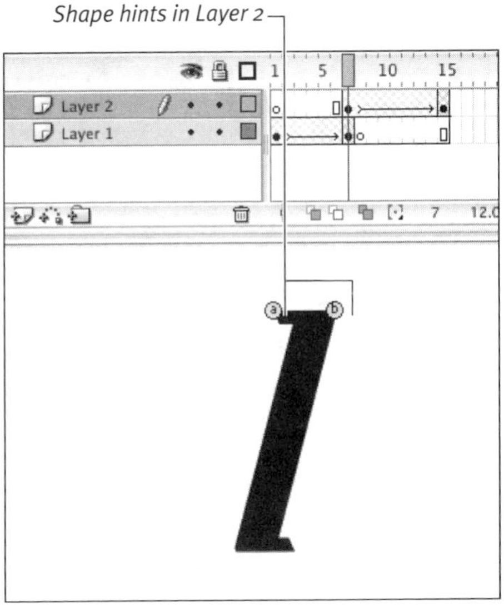

Figure 1.44 Layer 2 keeps the beginning shape hints for the tween from frames 7 to 15 separate from the end shape hints for the tween from frames 1 to 7.

Figure 1.45 A hole appears at the outline of the first shape when a shape tween is applied to change an *F* to a *D*.

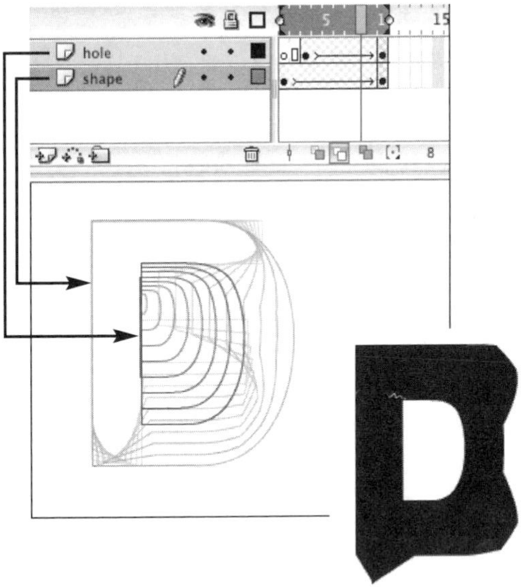

Figure 1.46 The hole and the solid shapes are separated on two layers.

Using shape tweens for gradient transitions

It helps to think about shape tweening as a technique that does more than just *morphing*, or interpolating one amorphous contour to another. After all, shape tweening can be used on any of the attributes of a shape, such as line weight; stroke color, including its alpha or gradient; and fill color, including its alpha or gradient. You can create interesting effects just by shape-tweening color gradients. For example, changing the way a gradient is applied to a particular fill using the Gradient Transform tool can be an easy way to move a gradient across the Stage; combined with changing contours, it can produce atmospheric animations like clouds or puffs of smoke.

To create a gradient transition with shape tweening:

1. Select the Rectangle tool, and draw a large rectangle on the Stage.
2. Fill the shape with a radial or linear gradient.
3. Select the Gradient Transform tool, and click the rectangle on the Stage.

   The control handles for the Gradient Transform tool appear for the gradient.
4. For this task, move the center point handle of the gradient to the left side of your rectangle (**Figure 1.47**).

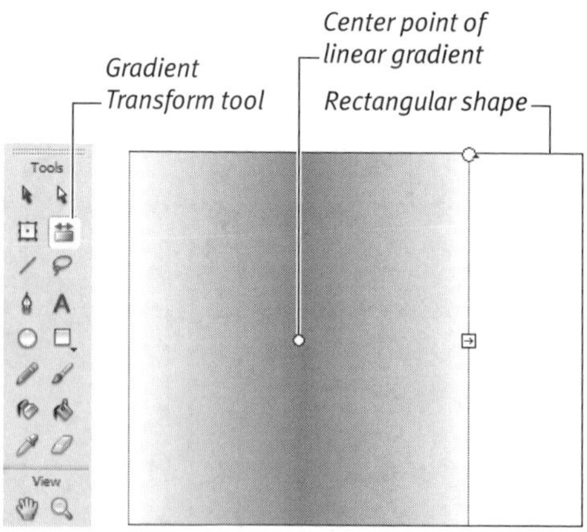

Figure 1.47 Use the Gradient Transform tool from the Toolbox to move the center point of the gradient fill to the left side of the rectangle.

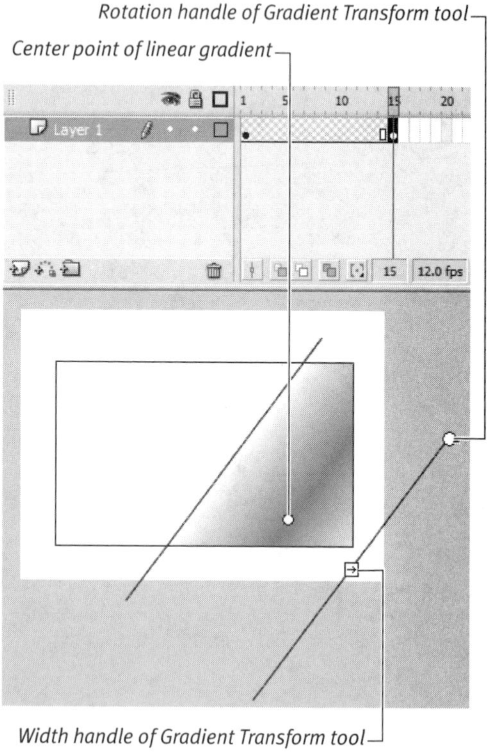

Figure 1.48 In the last keyframe, use the Gradient Transform tool to change the way the linear gradient fills the rectangle. Here, the linear gradient is moved to the far right side, tilted, and made narrower.

Figure 1.49 The final shape tween makes the gradient twist, widen, and move across the rectangle.

5. Create a new keyframe later on the Timeline.
6. Select the last keyframe, and click the rectangle with the Gradient Transform tool.

   The control handles for the Gradient Transform tool appear for the gradient in the last keyframe.
7. Move the center point handle of the gradient to the far right side of the rectangle, and change the rotation, scale, or angle of the gradient as you desire.

   Your two keyframes contain the same rectangular shape, but the gradient fills are applied differently (**Figure 1.48**).
8. Select the first keyframe and, in the Property inspector, choose Shape Tween.

   Flash tweens the transformation of the gradient fills from the first keyframe to the last keyframe. The actual contour of the rectangle remains constant.
9. Delete the outlines of the rectangle.

   The gradient moves from left to right (**Figure 1.49**).

✔ Tip

- You can't shape tween between different kinds of gradients; that is, you can't shape tween from a radial gradient to a linear gradient or vice versa.

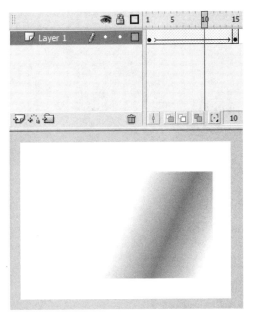

Creating Special Effects
(Flash Professional only)

Because Flash's drawing tools are vector based, you normally wouldn't think of incorporating a special effect, such as a motion blur, which is associated with bitmap applications like Adobe Photoshop and Macromedia Fireworks. But with the new filters available in Flash Professional 8, those special effects can be created directly in Flash. This technique can give your Flash movies more depth and richness by going beyond the simple flat shapes and gradients of vector drawings.

The following tasks demonstrate a blur-to-focus effect and a motion blur. A *blur* is an effect that occurs when the camera is out of focus. Blurs are particularly effective for transitions; you can animate a blurry image coming into sharp focus.

A *motion blur* is a camera artifact produced when something moves too fast for the film to capture; you see a blurry image of where the moving object used to be. Often, these images overlap, creating a streak that trails the fast-moving object. Cameras create motion blurs automatically and unintentionally; but in Flash, you must add them yourself.

To create a blur-to-focus effect:

1. In Flash, create the image you want to blur using the drawing tools or by importing an image to the Stage.
2. Convert the image to a movie clip symbol.
   In Flash, filters can only be applied to a movie clip symbol, a button symbol, or text.
3. Create a new keyframe later in the Timeline.
   This will be the in-focus instance that serves as the end of the tween.

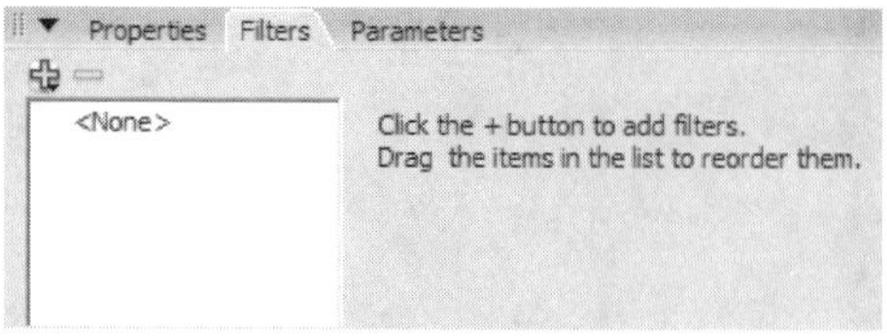

Figure 1.50 The Filters panel can be used to apply special graphical effects to movie clips, buttons, and text.

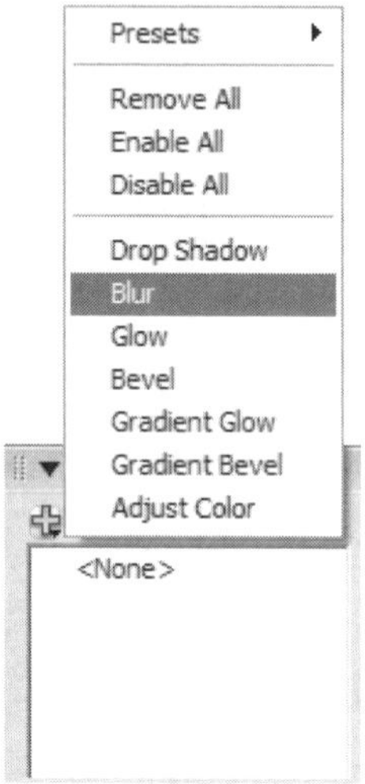

Figure 1.51 On the Add Filters pop-up menu, choose the Blur filter.

Figure 1.52 The filter properties allow you to tailor the style of the filter to your project. Each filter has specific properties you can manipulate.

Figure 1.53 The result makes an effective transition.

4. Select the instance on frame 1.
5. Open the Filters panel (**Figure 1.50**).
6. Click the Add Filter (+) button, and choose Blur (**Figure 1.51**).
7. Create the desired blur effect by adjusting the Blur X, Blur Y, and Quality properties (**Figure 1.52**).

   Blur X indicates how much blurring should be applied to the object in the x (horizontal) axis. Blur Y does the same for vertical (y-axis) blur. Because these are independent values, you can create a blur in just one direction if you choose. The Quality property controls how smooth the blur will be. A higher quality blur will be smoother and closer to what you might get using a blur filter in Photoshop; but it also makes the Flash Player work harder, so it could slow down the playback of your movie.
8. Select the keyframe on frame 1; in the Property inspector, choose Motion Tween.

   Flash creates a tween that animates your image's change from blurred to focused (**Figure 1.53**).

✔ Tips

- Try increasing the initial size of the blurry image slightly to add a subtle zoom-in effect, which enhances the blur-to-focus transition.
- You can use any filter in this manner to create a transition. Experiment with the numerous available filters to suit your movie.

To create a motion blur:

1. As in the previous task, create the image to which you want to apply a motion blur, and convert it to a movie clip symbol (**Figure 1.54**).
2. Open the Filters panel, and apply a blur filter to the symbol instance on the Stage.
3. Change the Blur X and Blur Y properties of the blur to match the direction in which your image will be moving.

   Set the Blur value to about one-tenth the overall size of your image on the axis of motion and 0 in the other direction. Set the Quality value to High (**Figure 1.55**).

   The image becomes blurry in one direction only, simulating the speed streaks from a camera.

Figure 1.54 Create a graphic symbol. This snowboarder will be moving fast enough to cause a motion blur.

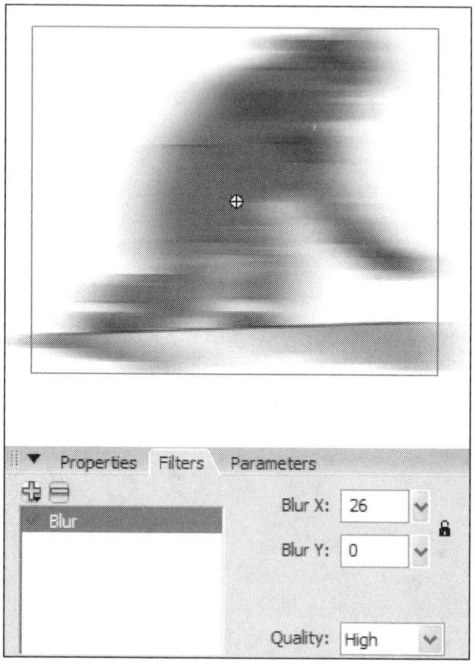

Figure 1.55 Setting a Blur value in only one direction (X or Y) makes the image blur in that direction only.

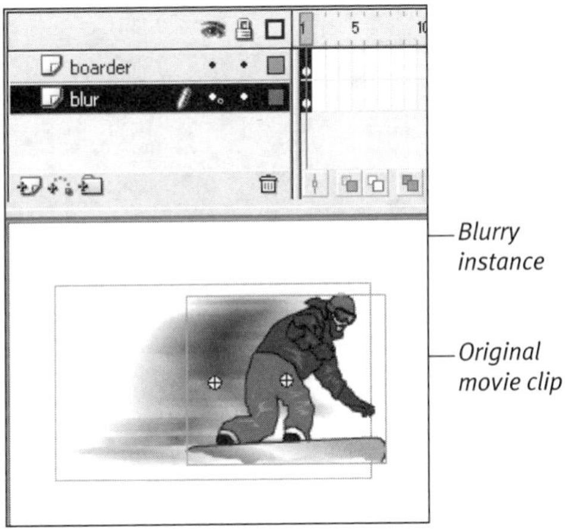

Figure 1.56 The motion blur is positioned behind the image of the snowboarder. Both instances are on separate layers, in preparation for motion tweening.

Figure 1.57 Play with the timing of the blur's motion tween so it appears when the snowboarder is in motion but disappears when he stops.

4. Create a new layer above the blurry instance, and add another instance of your movie clip symbol from the Library to the new layer (**Figure 1.56**).

5. Create keyframes for both layers later in the Timeline, move both instances across the Stage, and apply a motion tween to both layers.

   The original image and the blurred image move together, but the combined effect isn't quite convincing yet.

6. Adjust the timing of the keyframes so the blurred image starts a few frames later and the original image finishes a few frames earlier, and add an empty keyframe in the last frame for the blurred image (**Figure 1.57**).

   Having the blurred image lag behind the original graphic makes the streak more of an afterimage and completes the special effect.

Animated and Complex Masks

Masking is a simple way to reveal portions of a layer or the layers below it. This technique requires making one layer a mask layer and the layers below it the mask*ed* layers.

By adding tweening to the mask layer, the masked layers, or both, you can go beyond simple, static peepholes and create masks that move, change shape, and reveal moving images. Use animated masks to achieve such complex effects as moving spotlights, magnifying lenses that enlarge underlying pictures, or "x-ray" types of interactions that show more detail within the mask area. Animated masks are also useful for creating cinematic transitions such as wipes, in which the first scene is covered as a second scene is revealed; and iris effects, in which the first scene collapses in a shrinking circle, leaving a second scene on the screen.

You can add even more complexity to animated masks by inserting layers above and below them. A shape filled with an alpha gradient, for example, can make the hard edges of a mask fade out slowly for a subtle spotlight.

In the mask layer, Flash sees all fills as opaque shapes, even if you use a transparent solid or gradient. As a result, all masks have hard edges. To create a softer edge, place a gradient with a transparent center either under or over the mask to hide the edges. Creating soft edges with radial transparent gradients works well with circular masks; but if the shapes of your masks are more complicated, you'll need to resort to customizing the fades of your edges.

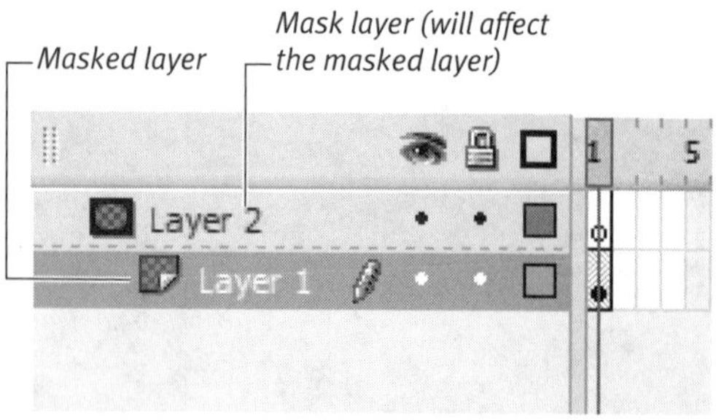

Figure 1.58 Layer 2 is the mask layer, and Layer 1 is the masked layer.

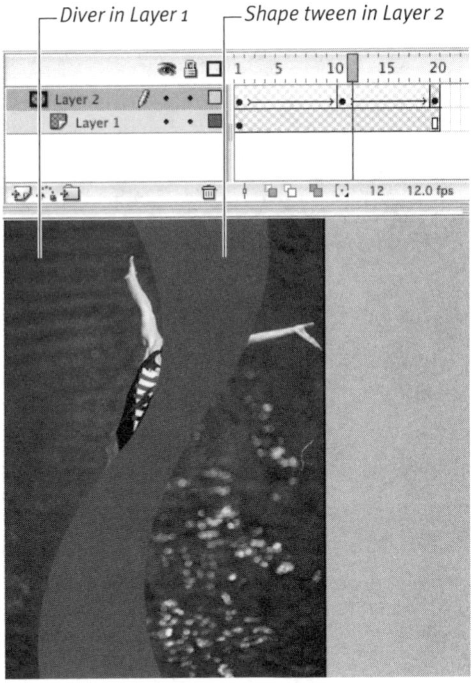

Figure 1.59 A shape tween of a moving vertical swirl is on the mask layer. The diver image is on the masked layer.

Figure 1.60 The shape tween uncovers the image of the diver. Only the part of the photo that is under the mask is revealed.

Using movie clips in mask layers provides more possibilities, including multiple masks, masks that move on a motion guide, and even dynamically generated masks that respond to the user. Because dynamic masks rely on ActionScript, however, they'll be covered in detail later (in Chapter 7) after you've learned more about Flash's scripting language.

To tween the mask layer:

1. In Layer 1, create a background image or import a bitmap.
2. Insert a new layer above the first layer.
3. Select the top layer, and choose Modify > Timeline > Layer Properties.

   or

   Double-click the layer icon in the top layer.

   The Layer Properties dialog box appears.
4. Select Layer Type: Mask.
5. Select the bottom layer, and choose Modify > Timeline > Layer Properties.
6. Select Layer Type: Masked.

   The top layer becomes the mask layer, and the bottom layer becomes the masked layer (the layer that is affected by the mask) (**Figure 1.58**).
7. Create a shape tween or a motion tween in the mask layer (the top layer) (**Figure 1.59**).
8. Insert sufficient frames into your masked layer (the bottom layer) to match the number of frames in the mask layer tween.
9. Lock both layers to see the effects of your animated mask on the image in the masked layer (**Figure 1.60**).

✔ Tips

- Use two images that vary slightly, one in the masked layer and one in a normal layer under the masked layer. This technique makes the animated mask act as a kind of filter that exposes the underlying image. For example, add a bright image in the masked layer and a dark version of the same image in a normal layer under the masked layer. The mask creates a spotlight effect on the image (**Figure 1.61**).
- Explore other duplicate-image combinations, such as a sharp image and a blurry image, a grayscale image and a color image, or an offset image (**Figure 1.62**).
- Place a tween of an expanding box in the mask layer that covers the Stage to simulate cinematic wipes between images (**Figure 1.63**).

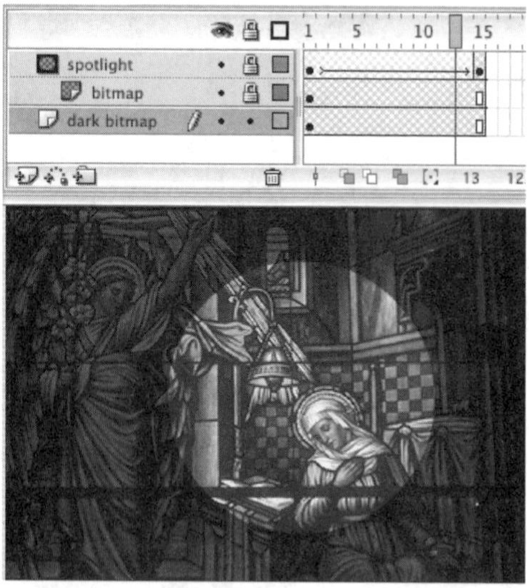

Figure 1.61 The moving spotlight in the mask layer (spotlight) uncovers the stained-glass image in the masked layer (bitmap). A duplicate darker image resides in the bottom, normal layer (dark bitmap).

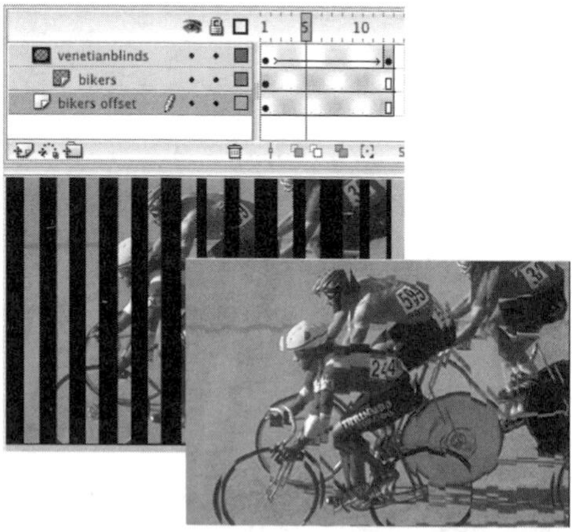

Figure 1.62 The moving vertical shapes in the mask layer (venetianblinds) uncover the image of bicyclists in the masked layer (bikers). A duplicate image in the bottom normal layer (bikers offset) is shifted slightly to create the rippling effect.

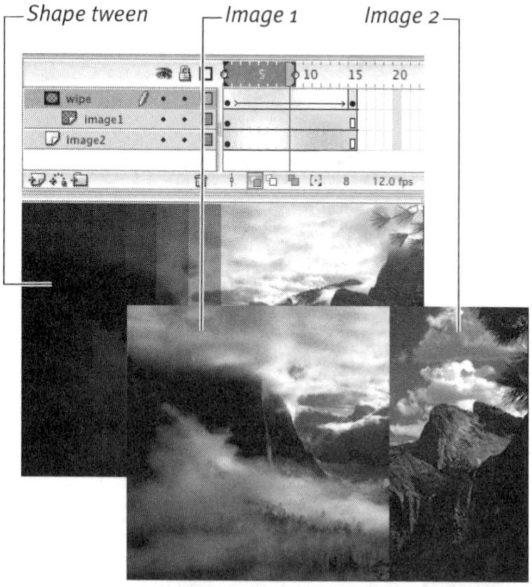

Figure 1.63 The mask layer contains a large shape tween that covers the entire Stage. This technique creates a cinematic wipe between an image in the masked layer (image 1) and an image in the bottom, normal layer (image 2).

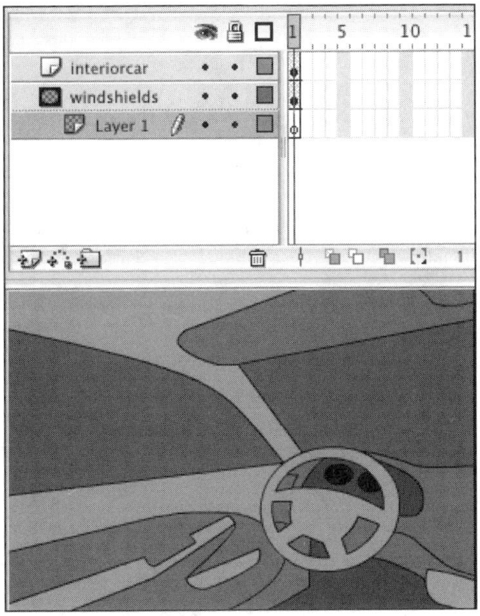

Figure 1.64 The windshield shapes are in the mask layer called windshields. The drawing of the car interior is in a normal layer above the windshields layer.

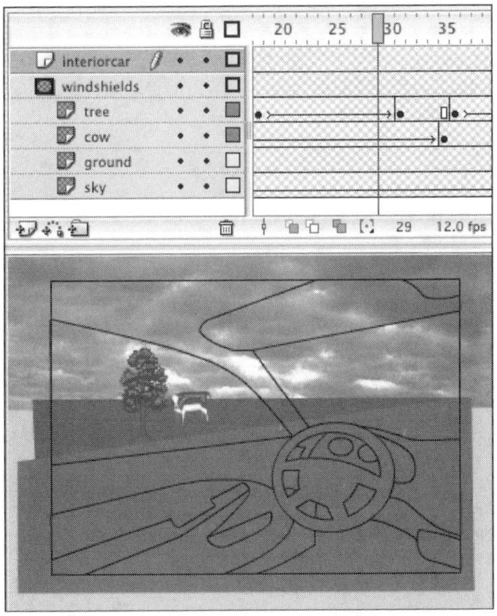

Figure 1.65 Several motion tweens in masked layers (tree, cow, ground, and sky) move under the windshield shapes in the mask layer.

To tween the masked layer:

1. Beginning with two layers, modify the top to be the mask layer and the bottom to be the masked layer.
2. Draw a filled shape or shapes in the mask layer (the top layer) (**Figure 1.64**).

   This area becomes the area through which you see your animation on the masked layer.
3. Create a shape tween or a motion tween in masked layers (the bottom layers) that pass under the shapes in the mask layer. You can have as many masked layers as you want under a single mask layer (**Figure 1.65**).
4. Lock both layers to see the effects of your animated masked layers as they show up behind your mask layer (**Figure 1.66**).

Figure 1.66 The images of the tree, cow, ground, and sky move under the mask, creating the illusion of the car's forward motion.

✔ Tip

- This approach is a useful alternative to using shape tweens to animate borders or similar types of objects that grow, shrink, or fill in. Imagine animating a fuse that shortens to reach a bomb (**Figure 1.67**). Create a mask of the fuse, and animate the masked layer to become smaller slowly, making it look like the fuse is shortening (**Figure 1.68**). Other examples that could benefit from this technique include trees growing, pipes or blood vessels flowing with liquid, and text that appears as it's filled with color. Just remember that Flash doesn't recognize strokes in the mask layer; if you want to create thin lines in the mask layer, use fills only.

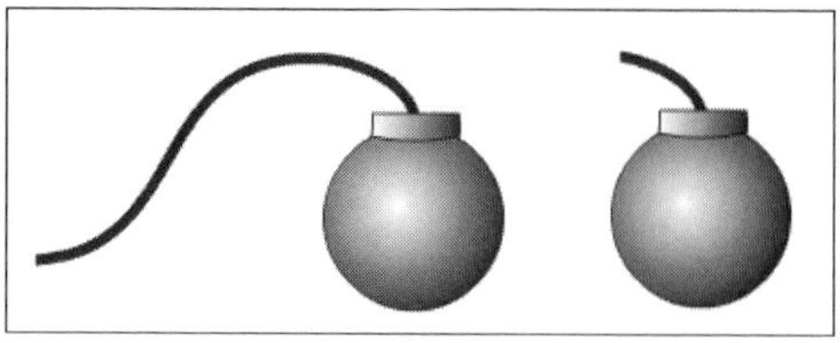

Figure 1.67 The fuse of a bomb shortens.

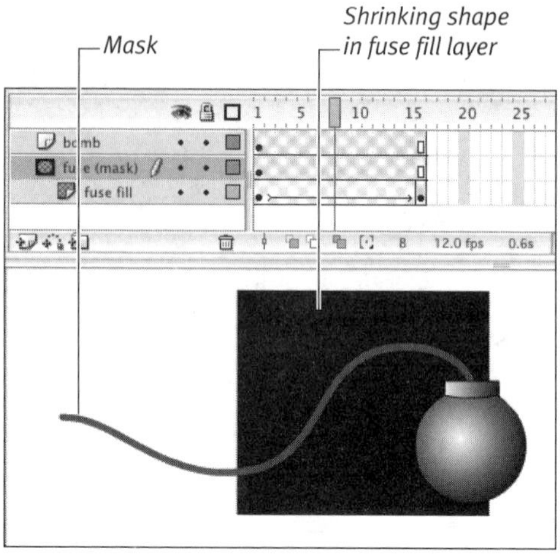

Figure 1.68 The bomb's fuse is a thin shape in the mask layer. The rectangular tween in the masked layer shrinks, making the fuse appear to be shortening.

To create a soft-edged mask:

1. Create a mask layer and a masked layer.
2. Place or draw a background image in the masked layer (the bottom layer).
3. Draw an ellipse in the mask layer (the top layer).
4. Copy the ellipse.
5. Insert a new layer between the mask layer and the masked layer.
   Your new layer will become a masked layer.
6. Choose Edit > Paste in Place (Cmd-Shift-V for Mac, Ctrl-Shift-V for Windows).
   An ellipse appears in the new masked layer, right under the ellipse in the top mask layer (**Figure 1.69**).

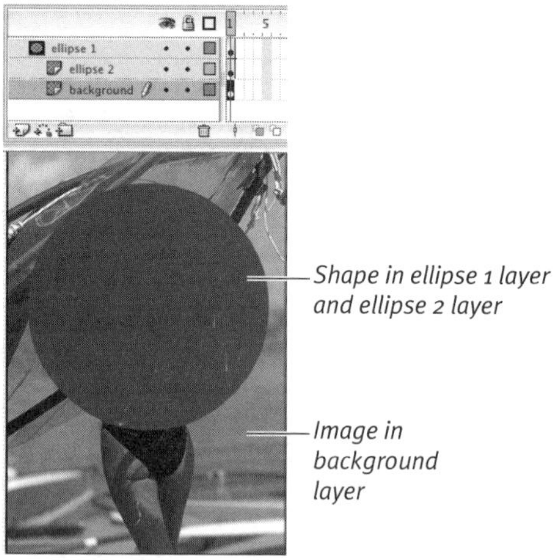

Figure 1.69 The same ellipse appears in both the mask layer (ellipse 1) and the top masked layer (ellipse 2). The image of the windsurfer is in the bottom masked layer (background).

Figure 1.70 A radial gradient with a transparent center in the top masked layer.

Figure 1.71 The resulting soft-edged mask.

7. Fill the pasted ellipse with a radial gradient, defined with a transparent center to an opaque perimeter, in the same color as the Stage (**Figure 1.70**).

8. Lock all three layers to see the effects of the mask (**Figure 1.71**).

   The mask layer lets you see through an elliptical area. The top masked layer hides the edges of the ellipse by creating a gradual fade toward the center. The bottom masked layer holds the contents of your background image (**Figure 1.72**).

To create a soft-edged mask with an irregular shape:

1. Create a mask layer and a masked layer.
2. Place or draw an image in the masked layer (the bottom layer).
3. Draw an irregular shape in the mask layer (the top layer).

continues on next page

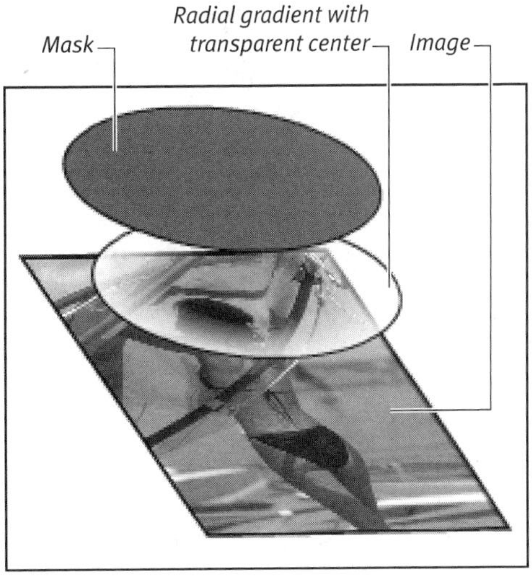

Figure 1.72 The soft-edged mask is the combination of the mask in the top layer (mask layer), a radial gradient in the middle layer (top masked layer), and the background image in the bottom layer (bottom masked layer).

4. Copy the shape.
5. Insert a new masked layer between the mask layer and the first masked layer.
6. Choose Edit > Paste in Place (Cmd-Shift-V for Mac, Ctrl-Shift-V for Windows).

   Your irregular shape appears in the new masked layer right under the original shape in the top mask layer (**Figure 1.73**).
7. With the Oval or Rectangle tool, draw an outline around your shape (**Figure 1.74**).
8. Fill the area between your shape and the outline with the background color, and delete the fill in the original shape.

   Your irregular shape is now the "hole" of a larger shape (**Figure 1.75**).

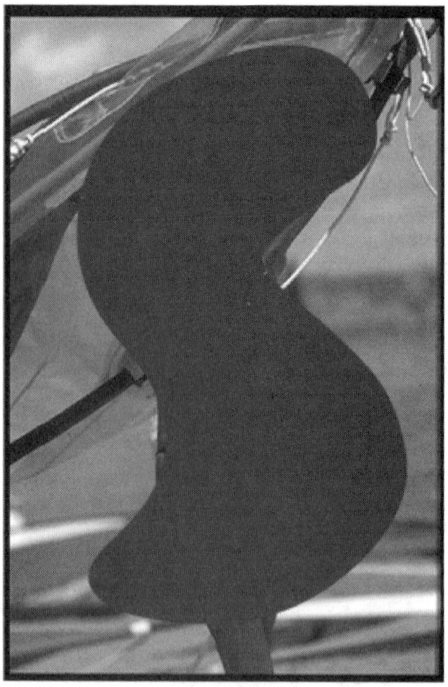

Figure 1.73 An irregular shape in the top masked layer above an image in the bottom masked layer.

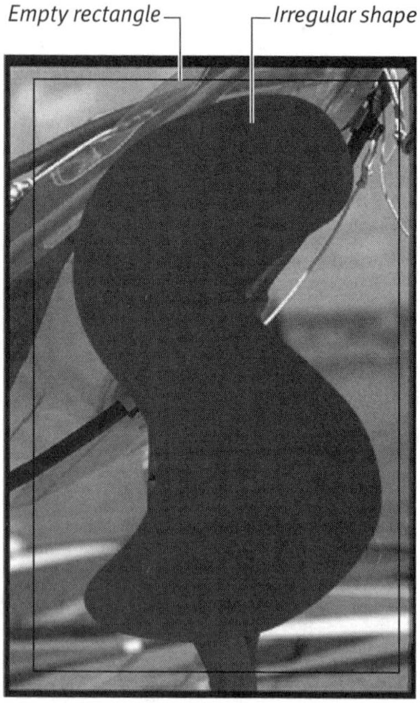

Figure 1.74 An empty rectangle drawn around the irregular shape.

Figure 1.75 By filling the area between the shape and the rectangle and then deleting the shape, you create a hole.

9. Select the entire shape, and choose Modify > Shape > Soften Fill Edges (**Figure 1.76**).

   The Soften Fill Edges dialog box appears (**Figure 1.77**). The Distance option determines the thickness of the soft edge. The "Number of steps" option determines how gradual the transition from opaque to transparent will be. The Direction option determines which way the edge softening will take place.

10. Enter the distance (in pixels) and the number of steps, and choose Expand for the direction.

    All the edges around your shape soften. Because the entire shape expands, the hole shrinks (**Figure 1.78**).

11. Lock all three layers to see the effects of the mask (**Figure 1.79**).

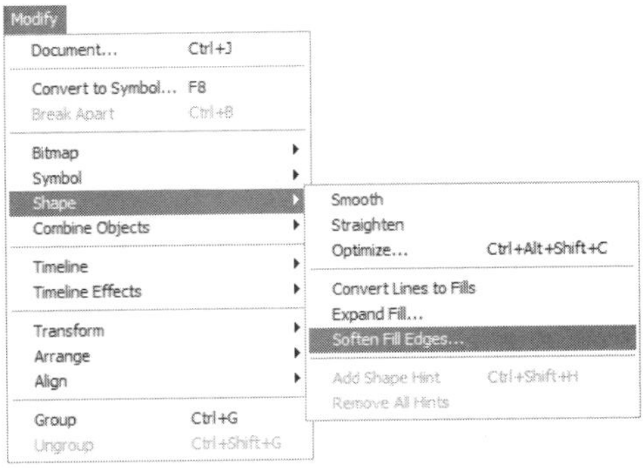

Figure 1.76 Choose Modify > Shape > Soften Fill Edges.

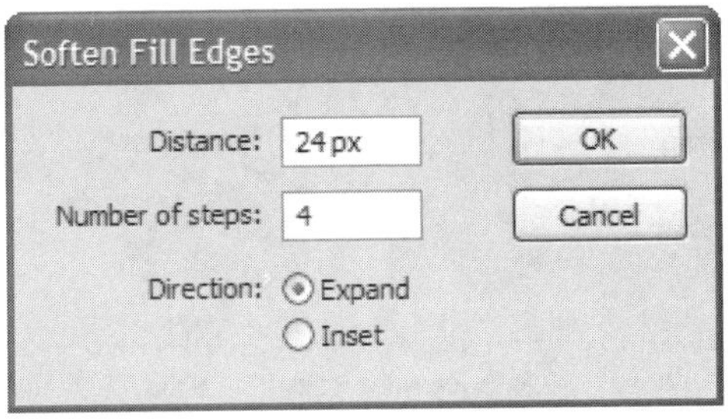

Figure 1.77 The Soften Fill Edges dialog box.

Figure 1.78 The softened edges expand into the hole, where the image is visible through the mask in the top mask layer.

Figure 1.79 The soft edges of an irregular mask created with Modify > Shape > Soften Fill Edges.

Creating multiple masks

Although Flash allows multiple masked layers under a single mask layer, you can't have more than one mask layer affecting any number of masked layers (**Figure 1.80**). To create more than one mask, you must use movie clips. Why would you need multiple masks? Imagine creating an animation that has two spotlights moving independently on top of an image (**Figure 1.81**). Because the two moving spotlights are tweened, they have to be on separate layers. The solution is to incorporate the two moving spotlights into a movie clip and place the movie clip on the mask layer.

Putting a movie clip instance inside the mask layer not only makes multiple masks possible but also provides a way to have a mask follow a motion guide. Build your tween that follows a motion guide inside a movie clip. Place that movie clip in a mask layer on the main Stage, and voilà—you have a mask that follows a path.

You'll learn much more about movie clips in Chapters 4 and 7. If you'd like, skip ahead to read about movie clips and return when you feel comfortable.

To create multiple masks:

1. Create a mask layer and a masked layer.
2. Place your image on the masked layer (the bottom layer).
3. Choose Insert > New Symbol (Cmd-F8 for Mac, Ctrl-F8 for Windows).

   The Create New Symbol dialog box appears.
4. Enter a descriptive name, and choose Movie Clip (**Figure 1.82**); then click OK.

   Flash creates a movie clip symbol, and you enter symbol-editing mode for that symbol.

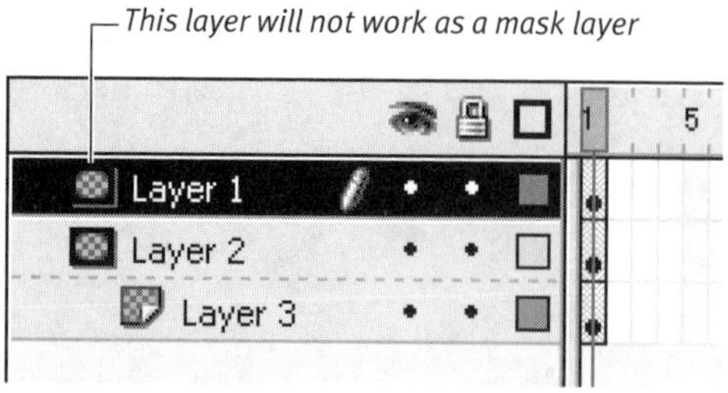

Figure 1.80 Layer 1 and Layer 2 are both defined as mask layers, but only Layer 2 affects Layer 3—the masked layer.

Figure 1.81 Two independent spotlights moving, each uncovering portions of the image.

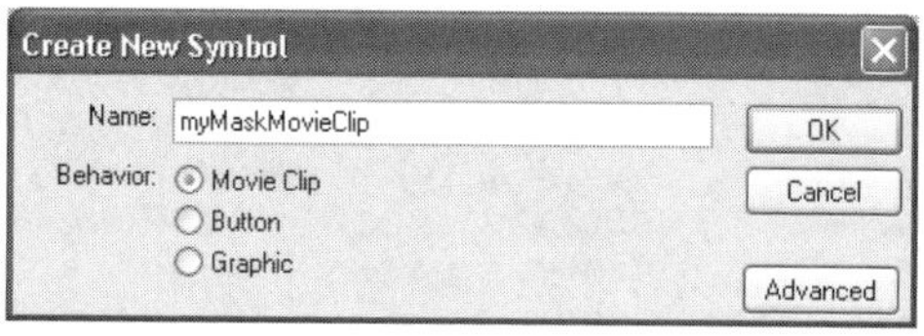

Figure 1.82 Choose Movie Clip to create a new movie clip symbol.

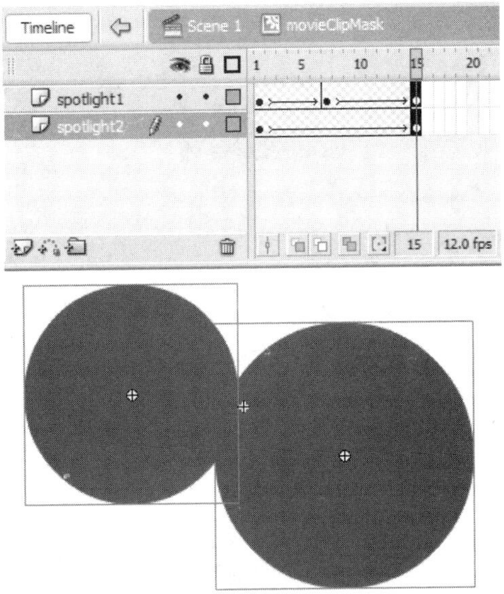

Figure 1.83 The two moving spotlights are motion tweens inside a movie clip.

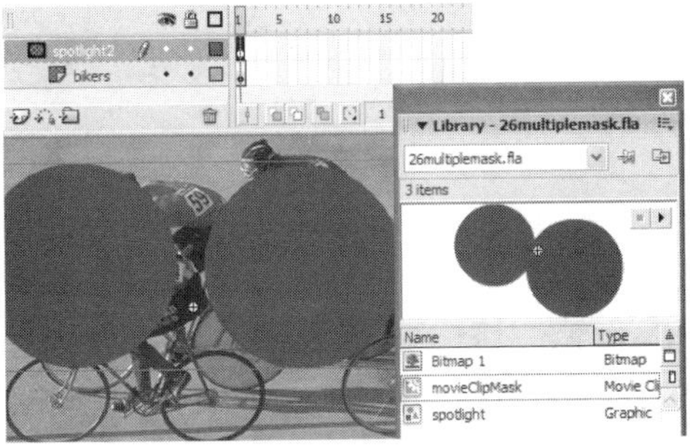

Figure 1.84 An instance of the movie clip is in the top (mask) layer, and the image of the bikers is in the bottom (masked) layer.

5. Create two motion tweens of spotlights moving in different directions on the Timeline of your movie clip symbol (**Figure 1.83**).
6. Return to the main Stage, and drag an instance of your movie clip symbol into the mask layer (the top layer) (**Figure 1.84**).
7. Choose Control > Test Movie to see the effects of the movie clip mask.

   The two motion tweens inside the movie clip both mask the image on the masked layer.

continues on next page

✔ Tips

- To see what your masks are uncovering, use a transparent fill or choose the View Layer as Outlines option in the Layer Properties dialog box (**Figure 1.85**).
- To prevent the animation inside the movie clip from looping constantly, add a keyframe to its last frame and add a `stop` action.

To guide a mask on a path:

1. Create a mask layer and a masked layer.
2. Place your image on the masked layer (the bottom layer) (**Figure 1.86**).
3. Create a new movie clip symbol.

Figure 1.85 Viewing your masks as outlines lets you see the image underneath. Choose the View Layer as Outlines option in the Layer Properties dialog box, or click the Show as Outlines icon in your layer.

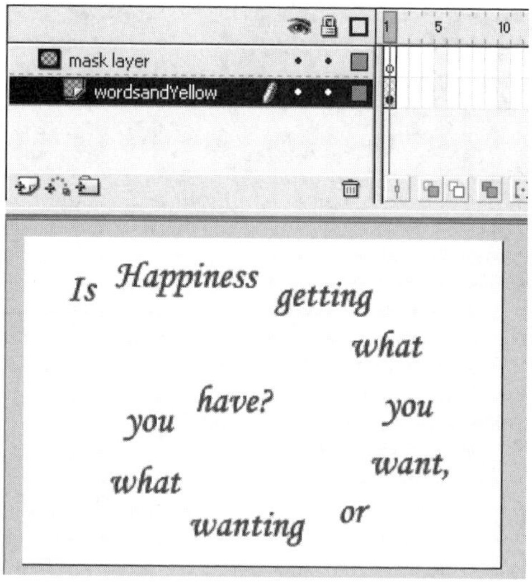

Figure 1.86 The words of this interesting question and a background fill are on the bottom (masked) layer.

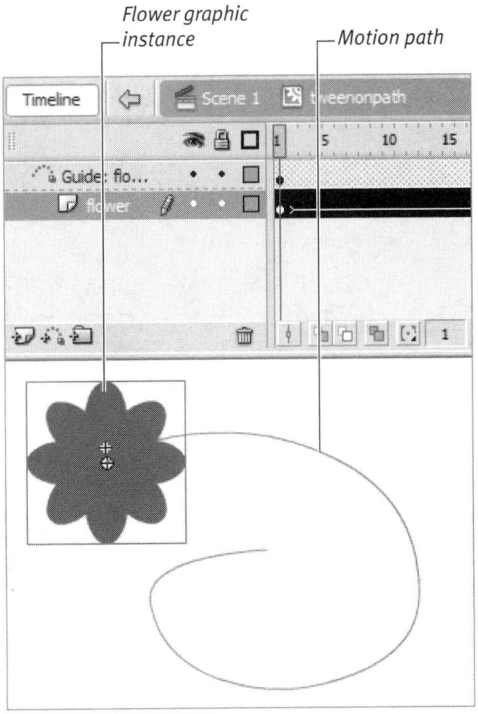

Figure 1.87 Inside a movie clip, the flower graphic instance follows a motion path.

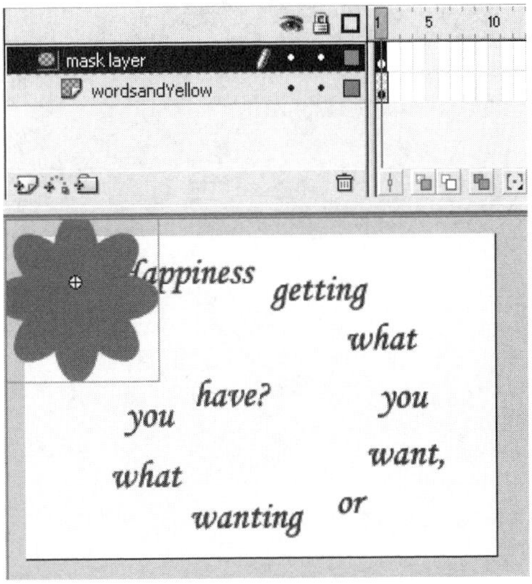

Figure 1.88 The movie clip containing the moving flower is in the mask layer and positioned over the words.

4. Inside your movie clip symbol, create a motion tween that follows a motion guide (**Figure 1.87**).

5. Return to the main Stage, and drag an instance of your movie clip into the mask layer (the top layer) (**Figure 1.88**).

continues on next page

6. Edit the motion path to get it exactly the way you want, relative to the other graphics on the Stage, by choosing Edit > Edit in Place or by double-clicking the instance (**Figure 1.89**).

   Flash dims all graphics except the instance you're editing.

7. Choose Control > Test Movie to see the effect of your movie clip on the mask layer.

   The animation follows its path in the motion guide; at the same time, it masks the image in the masked layer on the main Stage (**Figure 1.90**).

Figure 1.89 Edit in Place allows you to make changes in your movie clip symbol and see the graphics on the main Stage at the same time.

Figure 1.90 The moving flower exposes the question as it moves along its motion path.

Animated and Complex Masks

2

Working with Video

This chapter explores the exciting possibilities of integrating video in your Flash project. Flash makes importing video easy with the Video Import wizard, which takes you step by step through the process and gives you options for editing, cropping, changing color balances, and setting levels of compression.

When you combine digital video with Flash, you can develop imagery with all the interactivity of Flash ActionScript but without the limitations of the Flash drawing or animation tools. You can create truly interactive movies, for example, by importing your videos into Flash and then adding buttons and hotspots, sounds, and vector graphics. You can export this combination of video and Flash as either a Flash movie or a QuickTime file. You can also create streaming movies with Flash so your audience can watch video as it downloads. The Video Import wizard guides you through this process and provides ready-made player interfaces. Finally, for a unique effect, consider rotoscoping, a technique that uses video as a guide for your Flash animation. Use this effect to give hand-drawn frame-by-frame animated sequences a live-motion feel.

Importing Video into Flash

Everybody loves movies. So when you can add video to your Flash Web site, you'll likely create a richer and more compelling experience for your viewers. Several popular formats for digital video are QuickTime, MPEG, AVI, and DV. Fortunately, Flash supports all of them. Flash also supports its own video format, the Flash Video (FLV) format. In Flash 8, the FLV format has been updated with a new codec (the part of the program used to compress the video during authoring and decompress it during playback), making Flash Video a strong competitor for best image quality and lowest file size for Internet video.

You can import any of these digital video formats into Flash; you can add any effects such as Flash graphics, animation, masking, and interactivity, and you can even apply motion tweens to your imported video.

You can use video in Flash by embedding it directly into the Flash document or, with the FLV or QuickTime format, linking to an external video file. Embedding puts the video file inside your Flash document, increasing the document's file size just as importing a bitmap does. Linking, on the other hand, maintains your video as a separate file outside Flash. Flash keeps track of the video with a path to the filename.

You have several ways to acquire digital video. You can shoot your own footage using a digital video camera, or you can shoot with an analog video camera and convert the video using a digitizing board that you install in your computer. Alternatively, you can use copyright-free video clips that have already been digitized and are available on CD-ROM from commercial image stock houses. Any way you go, adding digital video is an exciting way to enrich a Flash Web site.

To embed a digitized video in Flash:

1. From the File menu, choose Import > Import Video.

   The Video Import wizard appears (**Figure 2.1**).
2. Click the Browse button; in the dialog box that appears, select the file you want to import and click Open.
3. Back in the Video Import wizard, click Next (Win) or Continue (Mac).

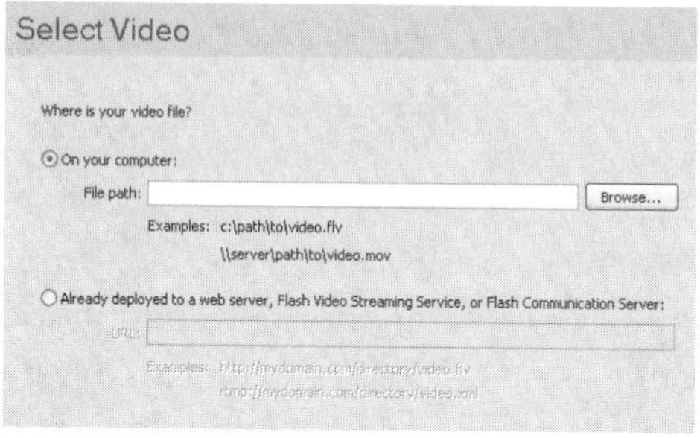

Figure 2.1 The Video Import wizard prepares the video you choose to embed in the document or link to it.

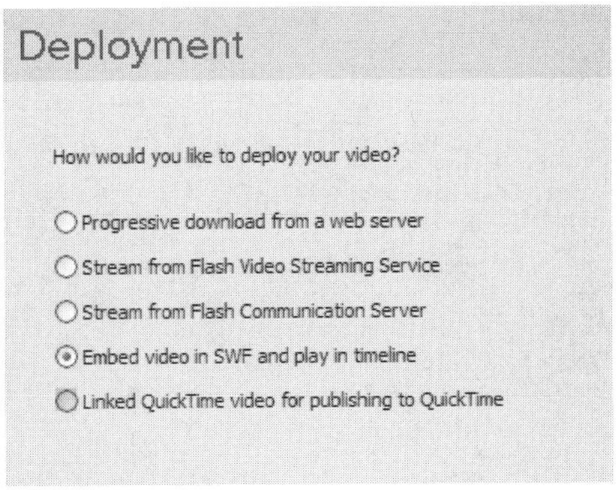

Figure 2.2 You can choose to embed the video or link to it in several ways.

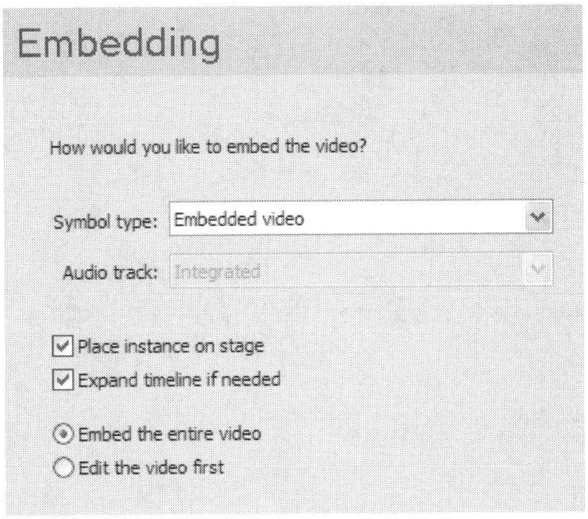

Figure 2.3 The Embedding step lets you choose settings for embedding your video.

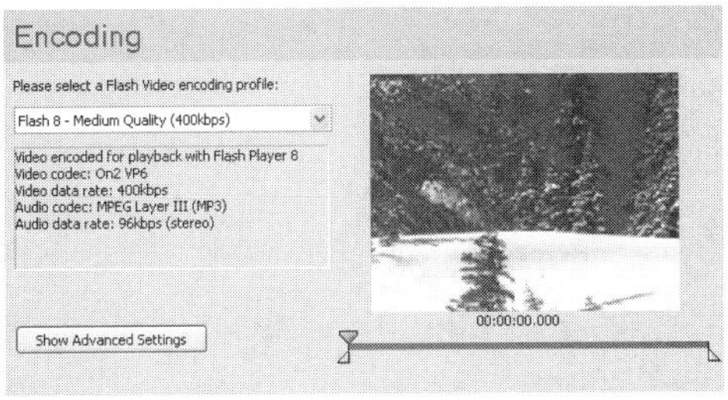

Figure 2.4 In the Encoding step, you can choose an encoding profile, preview your video, or use advanced settings for greater control over how your video is compressed.

4. For the Deployment option (**Figure 2.2**), choose "Embed video in SWF and play in timeline"; click Next/Continue.
5. In the Embedding options (**Figure 2.3**), set the Symbol type to "Embedded Video," select "Place instance on stage," select "Expand timeline if needed," select "Embed the entire video," and click Next/Continue.
6. The Video Import wizard proceeds to the Encoding options (**Figure 2.4**), giving you the option to set the Flash Video encoding profile, where you set the trade-offs between image quality and file size and the minimum Flash Player version (7 or 8) viewers will need to play back your video. You can also view the advanced settings, where you can crop your video or fine-tune the settings for compressing your video.

continues on next page

Choose an encoding profile setting to best match your file needs (**Figure 2.5**). **Table 2.1** lists the video data rates of the various encoding profiles, together with the minimum Internet connection speeds for those profiles.

Flash uses the one of two codecs (*co*mpression-*dec*ompression schemes) to import and display video: either the new On2 VP6 codec, which requires Flash Player 8, or the Sorenson Spark codec, which requires Flash Player 7 or higher. These codecs are *lossy*, meaning some (usually less important or less visible) video information is discarded in order to make the file smaller. The rebuilt movie appears similar to the original but not exactly the same. The encoding profiles are based on bandwidth, in kilobits per second (Kbps), which is a measure of how much data can download per second. Flash may alter the quality of individual frames in order to keep the download at a consistent speed. Remember, the higher the Kbps of your chosen setting, the larger the file size and the higher the quality of your video.

7. Click Next/Continue, and then click Finish.

   Flash embeds the video in your document, putting a video symbol in your Library and an instance of the video on the Stage in the active layer (**Figure 2.6**).

✔ Tips

- Macintosh users can import a file quickly by dragging the video file from the Desktop to the Stage.

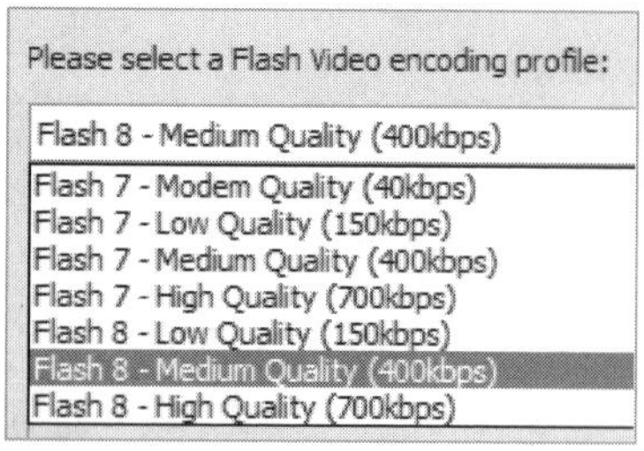

Figure 2.5 The predefined encoding profiles have settings matching common playback scenarios.

Figure 2.6 Importing a video puts a video symbol in the Library and an instance of the movie on the Stage in the active layer.

Table 2.1

Encoding Profiles and Internet Connection Speeds

Profile Quality	Video Data Rate	Internet Connection
Modem Quality	40 kbps	56 kbps modem
Low Quality	150 kbps	Corporate LAN
Medium Quality	400 kbps	DSL/Cable 512 kbps
High Quality	700 kbps	DSL/Cable 786 kbps

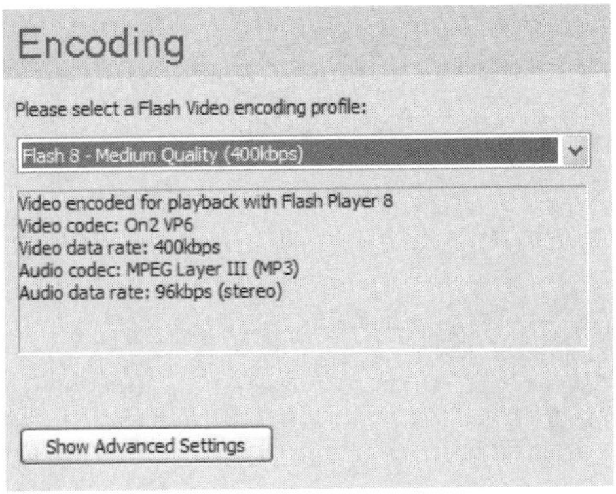

Figure 2.7 Click the Show Advanced Settings button to customize your compression settings.

- Flash can't display the soundtrack of imported videos, so if your original video file has sound, you won't hear it within the Flash authoring environment. When you publish your Flash movie or test it by choosing Control > Test Movie, the sound will be audible again.
- If you have more frames than are needed in a layer containing an embedded video, Flash displays the last frame of the video until the end of the Timeline. To make the end of the Timeline match up with the end of the video, select the excess frames and choose Edit > Timeline > Remove Frames.

To select your own compression settings:

1. On the Encoding options screen of the Video Import wizard, click the Show Advanced Settings button (**Figure 2.7**).

   Several compression settings options appear in the bottom half of the screen (**Figure 2.8**).

continues on next page

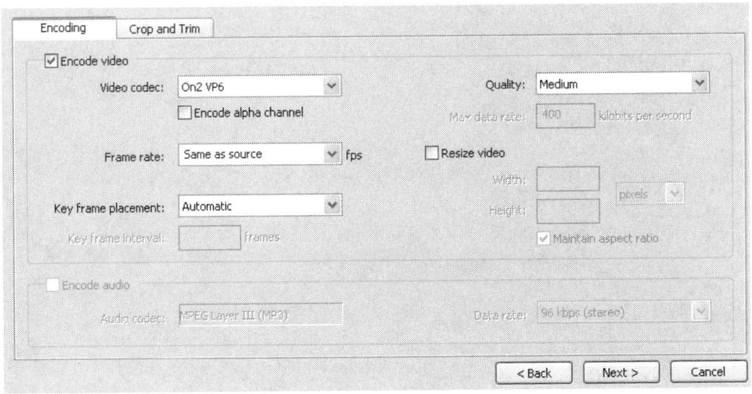

Figure 2.8 With the advanced compression settings, you can more precisely control the quality and file size of your video by tailoring the options to work with your video.

2. Choose the video settings that will give the best tradeoff between video file size and image quality for your movie:

   Video codec. Indicates which of the two available codecs will be used to compress your video.

   Frame rate. Lets you choose whether to match the frame rate of your video to the frame rate of your Flash movie. For embedded video, you'll usually choose Same as FLA (**Figure 2.9**). This choice ensures that an embedded video plays at its intended speed even if its frame rate is different than that of the Flash document. However, this usually causes video frames to be removed from the video. With the "Same as source" setting, a video shot at 30 frames per second (fps) and brought into a Flash movie running at 15 fps will last twice as long (and play twice as slowly) as the original source video. You should usually choose "Same as source" or one of the other specific frame rates (10, 12, 15, and so on) when creating an external video (described later in this chapter).

   Key frame placement. Determines the *keyframe interval*, or how frequently complete frames of your video are stored. The frames between keyframes (known as *delta frames*) store only the data that differs between the delta frame and the preceding keyframe. A keyframe interval of 24, for example, stores the complete frame every twenty-fourth frame of your video. If your video contains the action of someone raising his hand between frames 17 and 18, only the portion of the image where his hand is being raised is stored in memory until frame 24, when the full frame is stored. The lower you set the keyframe interval, the more keyframes are stored and the larger the file.

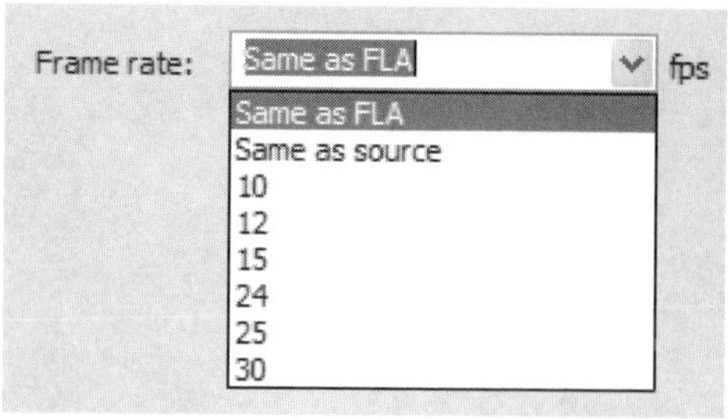

Figure 2.9 You can choose to match the frame rate to your Flash document or use one of several common presets.

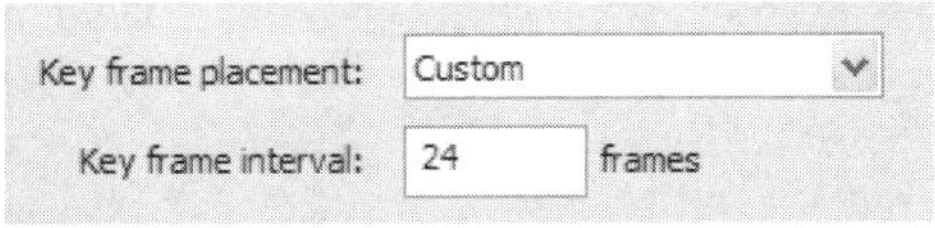

Figure 2.10 Adjust the "Key frame placement" option based on how often significant visual changes occur in your video.

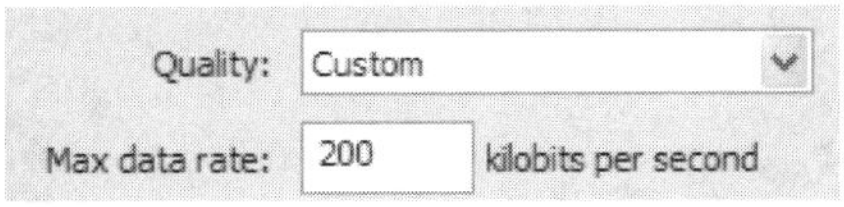

Figure 2.11 Video quality determines the bandwidth required to download the video.

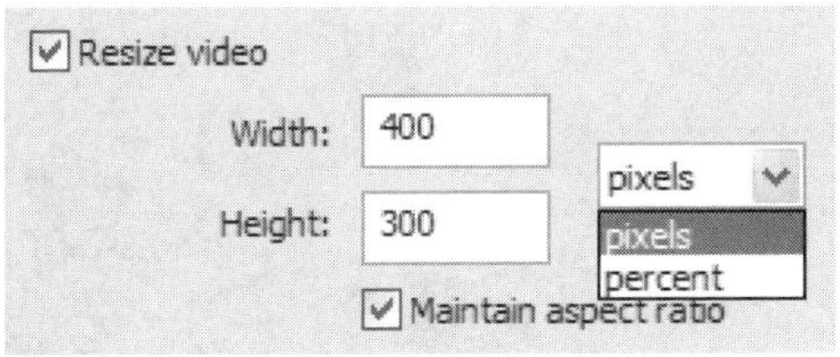

Figure 2.12 The "Resize video" option lets you set how your video's size will be scaled.

For video where the image doesn't change much (such as a talking head in front of a solid background), a higher keyframe interval works well. For video with lots of movement and changing images, a lower keyframe interval is necessary to keep the image clear (**Figure 2.10**).

Quality. Determines the *bit rate*, which is the quality of video based on download speeds measured in Kbps (**Figure 2.11**).

Resize video. Lets you change the image size (width and height) of the video. You can set a fixed width and height in pixels, or scale the video using a percent value (**Figure 2.12**). Normally, you should leave the "Maintain aspect ratio" check box selected; it prevents the image from being squashed or stretched by keeping the width and height proportional. Reducing the image size can significantly reduce the file size of your video, but doing so also reduces the visible detail of the image.

continues on next page

What Makes a Good Video?

We all know a good video when we see one. But how do you create and prepare digitized videos so they play well and look good within Flash? Knowing a little about the video compression that is built into Flash will help.

The On2 VP6 and Sorenson codecs compress video both spatially and temporally. *Spatial compression* happens within a single frame, much like JPEG compression on an image. *Temporal compression* happens between frames, so the only information that is stored is the differences between two frames. Therefore, videos that compress well contain localized motion or very little motion (such as a talking head), because the differences between frames are minimal. (In a talking-head video, only the mouth is moving.) For the same reasons, transitions, zooms, and fades don't compress or display well—stick with quick cuts if possible.

Here are a few other tips, not related to compression, for making a good embedded video:

- Keep the size small (320 by 240 maximum) and the length of the video short. Often, a few well-placed moments of video are enough to heighten the drama of your Flash movie.
- Maintain reasonable frame rates. Although video may run at about 30 fps, use 12 to 15 fps.
- Shoot in digital. You'll get a cleaner image by using a digital source rather than filming in analog and then converting to digital.

3. Click Next (Win) or Continue (Mac).

   The Video Import wizard proceeds to the Finish Video Import screen. The wizard will remember your custom settings the next time you use it to import a video.

Adjusting video length and cropping options

In some situations, you may want to crop away the edges of a video to remove unsightly background or to display your video in an unconventional format. Or, you may decide to use just a portion of the video rather than all of it. Using the Video Import wizard, you can make the necessary adjustments to crop the video frame or change the starting and ending points of the video. These options are available from the Crop and Trim tab, which is found in the advanced settings in the Encoding stage of the video import process.

To change video length or cropping:

1. From the Encoding options of the Video Import wizard, click the Show Advanced Settings button.

   The Advanced Settings tabs appear.

2. Click the Crop and Trim tab to see the options for cropping and shortening your video (**Figure 2.13**).

3. Adjust the Crop and Trim options settings. Each adjustment can be viewed in the preview window:

   Crop. Sets the top, bottom, left, and right pixel dimensions of the amount of video information to crop. Guide lines in the preview window show the cropped image area (**Figure 2.14**).

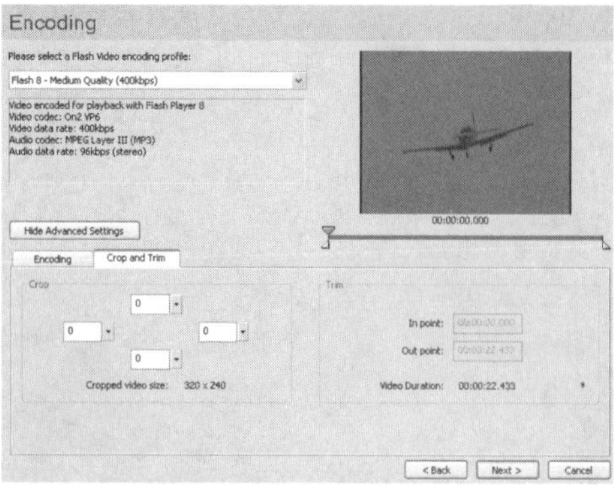

Figure 2.13 The Crop and Trim tab gives you control over cropping and adjusting the length of your video. The preview window to the right shows the effects of your changes.

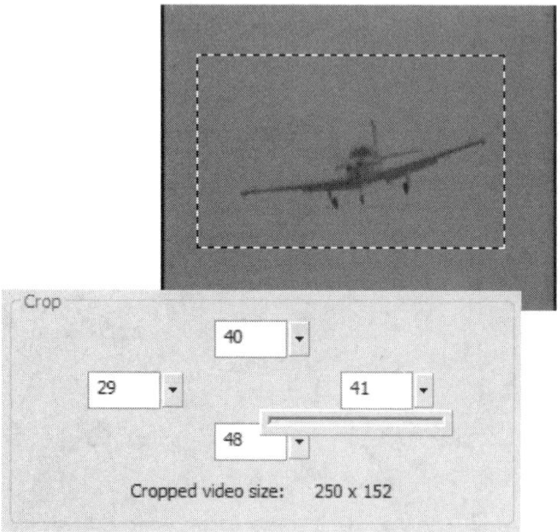

Figure 2.14 Adjust the crop sliders to cut out unwanted material from the edges of the video. The preview window shows the cropped size.

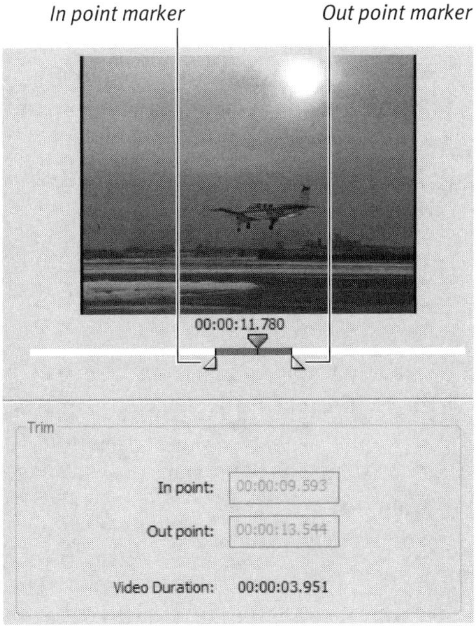

Figure 2.15 To trim extra footage off the ends of your video, slide the In and Out point markers.

Trim. Indicates the start (*In*) and end (*Out*) points for your video. The values are shown as points in time in hours, minutes, seconds, and fractions of seconds. To adjust the In and Out points, slide the In and Out point markers on the scrubber bar below the preview window (**Figure 2.15**).

4. Click Next (Win) or Continue (Mac).

   The Video Import wizard proceeds to the Finish Video Import screen.

✔ **Tip**

- To precisely adjust the In and Out point markers, select a marker and use the left and right arrow keys to adjust its position.

Creating a streaming external video

So far, you've learned how to embed and play video from a variety of formats (AVI, MOV, MPEG) in Flash. However, embedded video has a length restriction (16,000 frames, or approximately 8.5 minutes of 30 fps video). Also, embedded video doesn't truly stream (start playing before it's completely downloaded). It streams only if it's placed on the main Timeline, because the main Timeline of a SWF streams. If an embedded video is inside a movie clip symbol, the entire movie clip must download before playing. By dynamically loading external video, you can bypass these problems. Using external video is also free from the restriction that embedded video must have the same frame rate as its container Flash movie. By loading an external video, you can have a 12 fps Flash movie but still be able to show a 30 fps video.

Loading external video requires that your video be in the FLV file format. The FLV format was previously used exclusively with communication applications, such as the Flash Communication Server. Beginning with Flash Player 7 and now with Flash Player 8, you have the ability to progressively download an external FLV file without needing a special streaming video server such as the Flash Communication Server.

To create an FLV file, you convert an existing video file to FLV in one of three ways: from within Flash, from within Sorenson Squeeze, or from a third-party video application using the FLV plug-in that is included with Flash Professional 8.

The simplest way to include an FLV file in your Flash document is to use the Video Import wizard (the same one you've been using to embed video) to create the external video file. As part of the wizard, a special video playback component is added to your Flash file, giving you a video player built into your document. Chapter 6 looks at more advanced ways to load and control external video using ActionScript.

To create an external video:

1. Choose File > Import > Import Video to open the Video Import wizard.
2. Use the Browse button to select the video file that you want to convert to FLV format, and click Next (Win) or Continue (Mac).

   The Deployment step of the wizard appears, just as it does when you're embedding a video into a FLA.
3. Select "Progressive download from a web server," and click Next/Continue (**Figure 2.16**).

   Progressive download is a type of video streaming that allows the video to start playing as soon as video information reaches the Flash Player rather than wait to download the entire video file.

   For long videos, you may want to use *true video streaming*, which lets viewers jump to any point in the video even if it hasn't downloaded yet. However, true video streaming requires a special video streaming server. You can use Macromedia's Flash Communication Server or one of the commercial Flash Video Streaming Services. In either case, in this step you'd select the corresponding option instead of choosing "Progressive download from a web server."
4. On the next screen, adjust the video encoding settings or crop or trim the video. These are the same options that were described earlier in the chapter. Click Next/Continue.
5. On the Skinning screen, choose a player skin for your video from the menu, and click Next/Continue (**Figure 2.17**).

   The player skin provides a viewing window and playback controls for your video. The different skins use different colors and include different sets of playback controls; in the preview window, you can see what the different skins look like. The player you choose will be added to your Flash document by the wizard. You will then be able to position the controls wherever you want the video window to appear in your SWF file.

   To encode the video as an FLV file without adding playback controls to your Flash document, choose None from the menu.

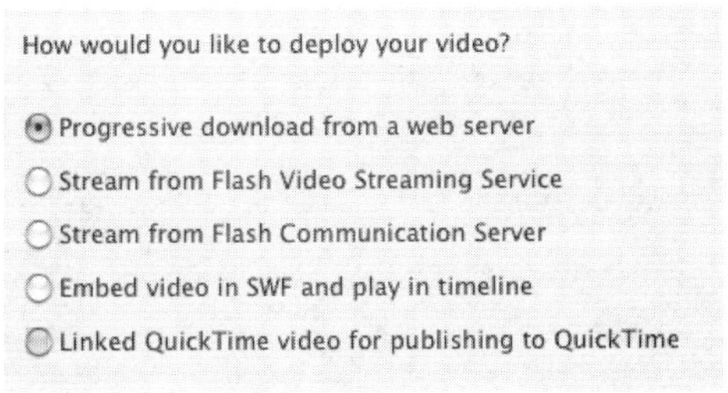

Figure 2.16 To create an external video file, choose one of the first three Deployment options.

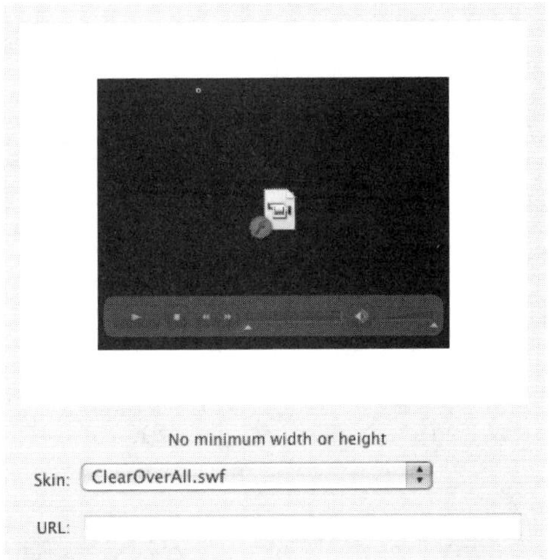

Figure 2.17 Select a video player skin from the list. You can use the preview window to see how the controls will appear with your video (represented by the black square).

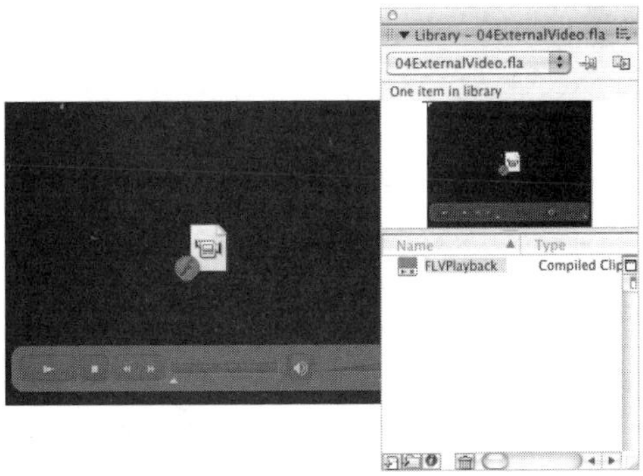

Figure 2.18 After encoding the file, your selected skin will be added to your Flash document.

6. On the final screen, click Finish.

   Flash converts your video file to FLV format and saves the FLV file and the SWF file for the player skin you selected in the same folder as your Flash document.

   If you didn't save your Flash document before opening the Video Import wizard, you're prompted to save it at this point so that Flash knows where to put the FLV and player skin SWF.

7. The player skin appears on the Stage of your Flash document and in the document's Library (**Figure 2.18**).

✔ Tips

- Because the FLV file you create is stored as an external file, separate from your Flash document, you can use it in multiple projects without needing to encode it as an FLV file each time. If you select an FLV file in the first step of the Video Import wizard, the wizard skips straight to the Skinning step, allowing you to choose a player skin and add it to your document without needing to recompress the video.
- In addition to the predefined player skins, you can create your own custom skin by either modifying parts of a predefined skin or creating your own skin from scratch. However, to do this you need to write some simple ActionScript. For details, see the Flash Help topic Components Language Reference > FLVPlayback Component > Customizing the FLVPlayback Component.

Batch-processing external video (Flash Professional only)

If you want to convert several video files to FLV format, you may find it tedious to have to use the Video Import wizard within Flash Professional 8 to encode one file at a time. Or perhaps you want to encode an FLV file without having to create a new Flash document just for that purpose. In either case, you can use the stand-alone Flash 8 Video Encoder that comes with Flash Professional 8 to encode an FLV format video file without opening Flash.

To create multiple external videos:

1. Open the Macromedia Flash 8 Video Encoder, which is installed in the same location as Flash Professional 8 (**Figure 2.19**).

2. Click the Add button. In the dialog that appears, you can browse to select a video file.

   Repeat this step to add all the video files you want to encode.

3. Select a file in the list, and click the Settings button to adjust the compression settings for that video file.

   The Flash Video Encoding Settings dialog box that appears provides the same encoding options available in the Video Import wizard that is built into Flash (**Figure 2.20**).

   In addition, the "Output filename" field in this dialog allows you to specify a different name for the FLV file that the encoder will create.

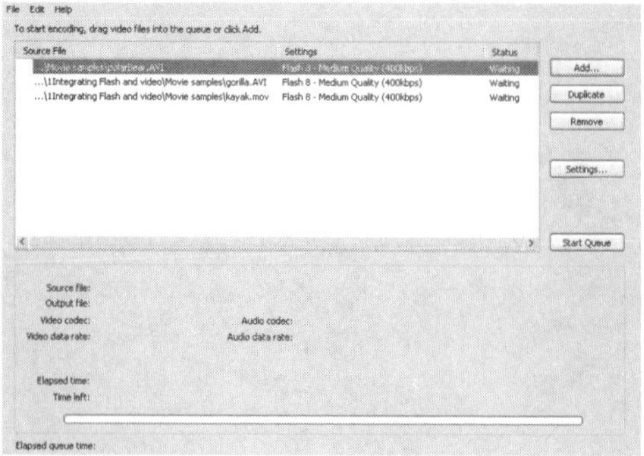

Figure 2.19 The Flash Video Encoder is a stand-alone tool that lets you create several external video files at one time.

Figure 2.20 For each video file, you can choose an encoding profile or advanced compression settings.

Figure 2.21 As each video is encoded, its progress is displayed in the bottom half of the window.

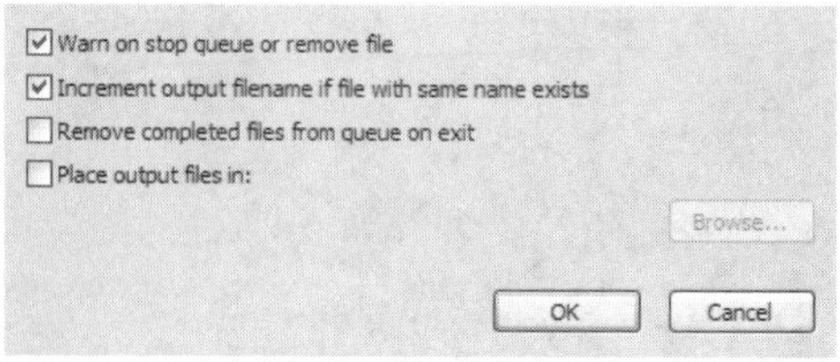

Figure 2.22 Frequent users of the Flash Video Encoder will appreciate being able to set a single output location and other preferences.

Other Ways to Create FLV Files

You can create FLV files in a variety of ways. Using the Video Import wizard to encode the video as described in this chapter is the easiest, most basic method. However, video professionals can also create FLV files using specialized tools or many of the video products they already use.

These are some stand-alone tools that create FLV files:

- On2 Flix (www.on2.com)
- Sorenson Squeeze (www.sorensonmedia.com)

Alternatively, if you're using Flash Professional 8 and have QuickTime 6.1.1 installed on your machine, you can use the Flash FLV QuickTime Export plug-in, which enables many third-party video applications to export the FLV format. You can use the professional video-editing tools in these applications to prepare your video and then export an FLV file directly from your application for use as streaming video in a Flash movie.

You can use the Flash FLV QuickTime Export plug-in from within these applications:

- Adobe After Effects (www.adobe.com)
- Apple Final Cut Pro (www.apple.com)
- Apple QuickTime Pro (www.apple.com)
- Avid Xpress DV (www.avid.com)

4. Click OK to close the dialog box.
5. To start the encoding process, click Start Queue.

   The bottom half of the window shows file details, a progress bar, and a preview of each video as it's encoded (**Figure 2.21**). As each file is encoded, its status in the file list changes from Waiting to Encoding to, finally, the Encoding Complete icon (a green circle with a check mark, indicating the file was encoded successfully).

   Each new FLV file is saved in the same location as its source video file.

✔ Tips

- To encode the same video file with different settings (for example, to create two versions of the same video with different sizes or quality settings), select the video in the list and click Duplicate. The video is added to the list again, and you can change the settings for the new listing.
- To specify a single output location for all your files, choose Flash Video Encoder > Preferences (Mac) or Edit > Preferences (Win). In the Preferences dialog, select the "Place output files in" check box (**Figure 2.22**) and choose a folder in the dialog box that appears.

Updating and Replacing Videos

When you make changes in your original video file, you'll want those changes to be reflected in your Flash movie as well. Luckily, Flash makes updating your imported videos easy, whether the videos are embedded into the Flash document or encoded as external FLV files. For an embedded video, you can update it or re-import it to modify the compression settings.

To update an external (FLV) video file, you can re-encode the file. Because the file is separate from the Flash document, the SWF file will use the updated FLV file the next time it loads. However, if you want to modify the SWF file to point to a different FLV file (in a different location or with a different filename) you can change the path to the file in your playback skin using the Parameters panel in Flash.

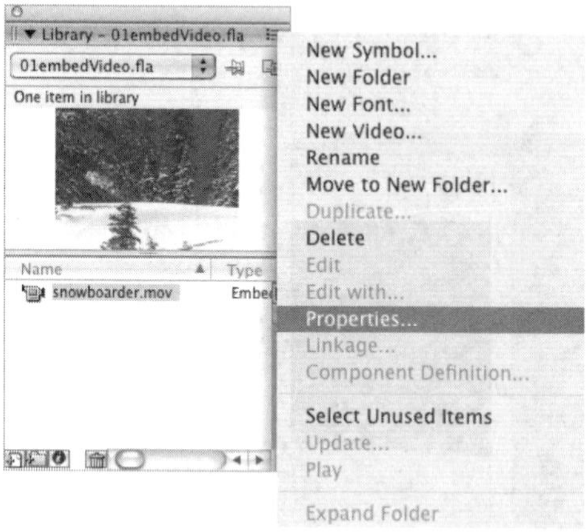

Figure 2.23 Choose Options > Properties in the Library panel to get information about the selected symbol.

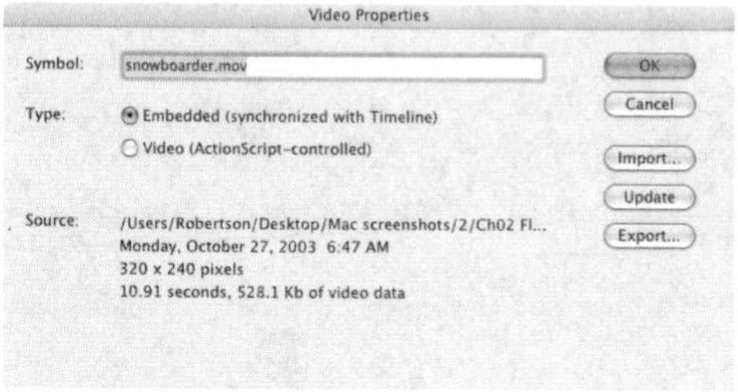

Figure 2.24 The Video Properties dialog box shows the name of the symbol and the location of the original video file, as well as the properties of the compressed video (dimensions, time, and size).

To update an embedded video:

1. Double-click the video icon or the preview window in your Library.

   or

   Click the video symbol in the Library; then, from the Library window's Options menu, choose Properties (**Figure 2.23**).

   The Video Properties dialog box appears, showing the symbol name and the original video file's location (**Figure 2.24**).

2. Click Update.

   Flash opens the file and shows a dialog, allowing you to change the compression settings. Flash then re-encodes the video and embeds it into your document. The video must be in the same file path as the original video you imported. If it isn't, you can't use the Update button to update the video.

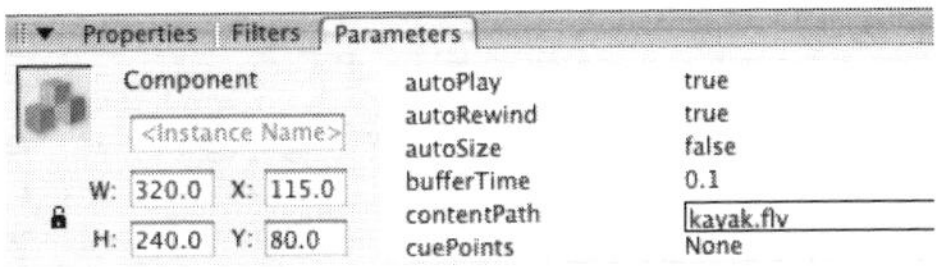

Figure 2.25 The Parameters panel lets you set options for your video player skin and other Flash components.

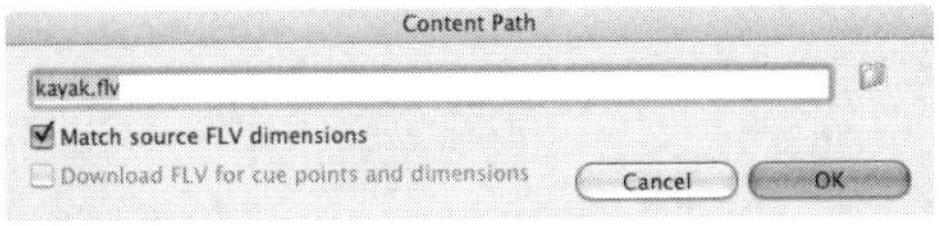

Figure 2.26 In the Content Path dialog box, you can change the name or location of the file that the video player loads.

To set a new path for an external video:

1. Select the video player skin (the FLVPlayback component instance) on the Stage.
2. Activate the Parameters panel, which is grouped with the Property inspector (**Figure 2.25**).

   The Parameters panel shows parameters (user-configurable options) for a Flash component on the Stage.
3. Select the contentPath parameter, and click again anywhere in the value (where the FLV file name is shown) to change the value.

   The Content Path dialog box appears (**Figure 2.26**).
4. In this dialog box, you can type the name of a FLV file or click the folder icon to browse to the new FLV file; click OK to confirm your choice.

   When you publish your Flash document, the SWF that is created will load the new FLV file.

Adding Flash Elements to Your Video

After you've imported your video into Flash, you can add Flash elements such as titles, labels, and animated special effects over the movie. Add graphics next to a talking-head video to mimic a newscast, for example, or use labels to point out important features as they appear in an instructional video on fixing a bicycle.

Put your embedded video inside a graphic symbol, and you can also apply motion tweens to create transitions with the alpha or color effect or create funky rotations, skewing, scaling, and even horizontal or vertical flips.

Add interactivity by integrating buttons or frame actions that control the playback of the video content. Create your own Pause, Stop, Play, Fast Forward, and Rewind buttons to customize the video-playback interface. You can even convert your video to a movie clip symbol and have at your disposal the methods, properties, and events of the `MovieClip` class. Create drag-and-drop video puzzle pieces as a twist on standard puzzles, for example. You'll learn much more about the `MovieClip` class in later chapters, so be sure to return here after reading about it to see how you can incorporate it into imported videos.

Figure 2.27 Add Flash graphics and animation over your imported video. This example shows two animated titles, a mask that uncovers a border, and the special effect of the shape-tweened smoke behind the skateboarder's foot.

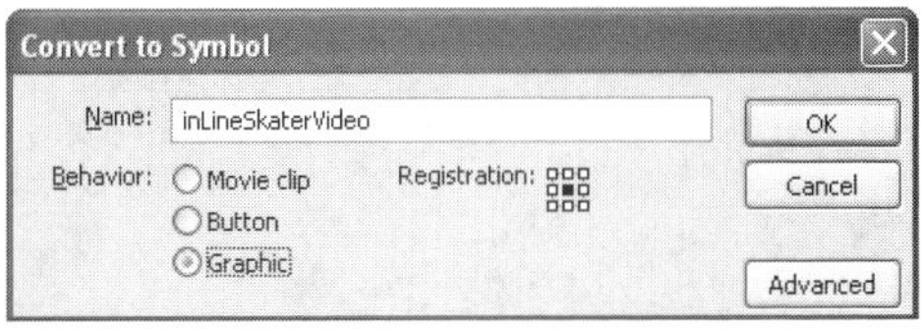

Figure 2.28 Convert your embedded video to a graphic symbol so you can apply motion tweens.

To overlay Flash elements on a video:

1. For this task, set the Stage to the same size as the imported video file (320 by 240 pixels), and position an imported movie to cover the Stage exactly.
2. Lock the layer that contains the video to prevent it from being moved accidentally.
3. Add separate layers over the video layer to create animated titles, graphics, or special effects.

   Figure 2.27 shows a few animated elements superimposed on the imported video file. Check out the Flash and video files provided on the CD.

To apply a motion tween to an embedded video:

1. Select the video instance on the Stage.
2. Choose Modify > Convert to Symbol (F8).

   The Convert to Symbol dialog box appears.
3. Enter a descriptive name, choose the Graphic option in the Behavior section, and click OK (**Figure 2.28**).

   A warning dialog box appears, asking whether you want to insert enough frames into the new graphic symbol to accommodate the length of your video.
4. Click Yes.

   The video on the Stage is now an instance of a graphic symbol to which you can apply motion tweens.

continues on next page

5. Create new keyframes along the Timeline, and modify the instance by changing its color effect, position, scale, rotation, or skew.

6. Apply motion tweens between the keyframes (**Figure 2.29**).

✔ Tips

- You can always add layers and drag out more instances of the graphic symbol containing your video; your video will play in all the instances. Be aware, however, that new keyframes of the same instance will make your file larger.

- The First parameter in the Property inspector, which normally establishes which frame of a graphic instance begins playing, doesn't affect the playback of the video.

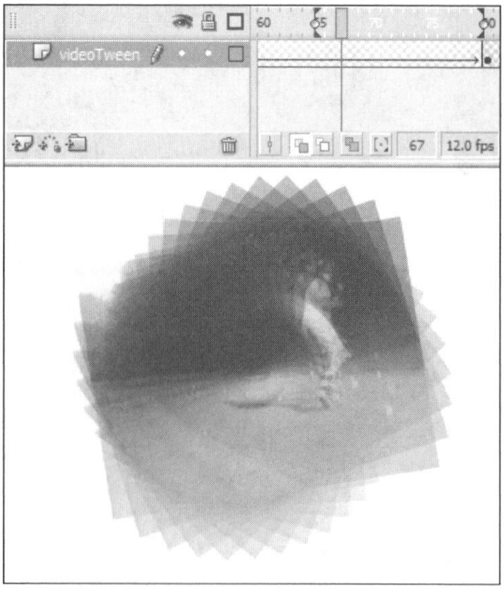

Figure 2.29 This video of an inline skater coming toward the viewer is given a motion tween that rotates and enlarges it, enhancing the excitement.

To create interactive controls for a video:

1. Create four buttons: a Play button, a Pause button, a Skip to End button, and a Skip to Beginning button.

2. Place your four button instances in a new layer above the layer containing an imported video file (**Figure 2.30**).

3. Add a third layer, and insert a keyframe at the last frame of the Timeline.

Four button instances placed on a layer above the video

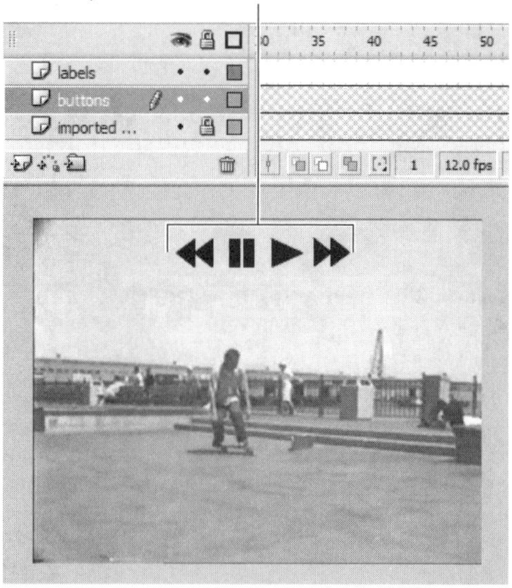

Figure 2.30 Add button instances to let your users navigate the video. These buttons are placed on a separate layer.

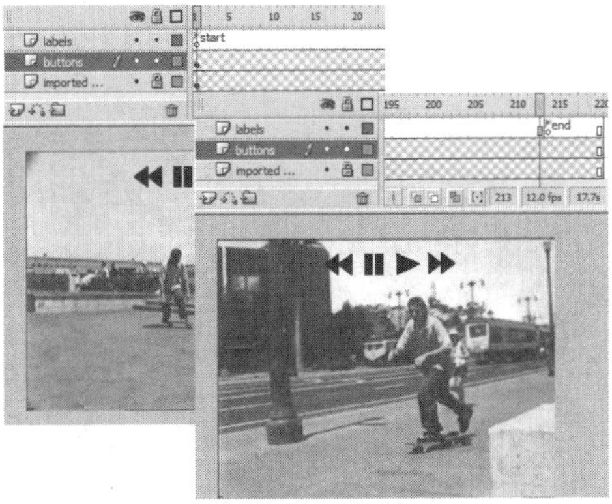

Figure 2.31 In another layer, label the start of the Timeline `start` (top) and the end of the Timeline `end` (bottom). This method makes assigning frame destinations for your buttons easier.

Figure 2.32 The published SWF file plays your video, and buttons and actions you've customized control its playback.

4. Label the first keyframe `start`, and label the last keyframe `end` (**Figure 2.31**).
5. To give each button instance an instance name, select the instance on the Stage and enter its name in the Instance Name field of the Property inspector:
   - Give the Play button the name `play_btn`.
   - Give the Pause button the name `pause_btn`.
   - Give the Skip to End button the name `end_btn`.
   - Give the Skip to Beginning button the name `start_btn`.
6. Assign actions to all four button instances by selecting frame 1 of the top layer of the main Timeline and then adding the following lines in the Actions panel:

```
play_btn.onRelease = function() {
    play();
};
pause_btn.onRelease = function() {
    stop();
};
end_btn.onRelease = function() {
    gotoAndStop("end");
};
start_btn.onRelease = function() {
    gotoAndStop("start");
};
```

   For more information about the Actions panel, see Chapter 3.
7. Test your movie to see how your custom Flash buttons let you navigate to different spots on the Timeline and control the playback of the video (**Figure 2.32**).

Rotoscoping

Rotoscoping is a traditional animator's technique that involves tracing live-motion film to create animation. This process is named after an actual machine, the Rotoscope, which projected live-action film onto an animation board. There, an animator could easily trace the outline of an actor frame by frame to get natural motion that would be too difficult to animate by hand. The old Disney animators often used rotoscoping to do studies, and feature movies and commercials rely on rotoscoping even today.

You can use Flash to import and display digitized videos of actors or moving objects and then do the rotoscoping yourself.

To copy the motion in an imported video:

1. Import a video as described earlier in this chapter (**Figure 2.33**).
2. Lock the layer that contains the video.
3. Add a new layer above the layer that contains your video.
4. Begin tracing the actors or the action in the new layer in keyframe 1 with any of the drawing tools (**Figure 2.34**).

video
1
12.0 fps
0.0s

Figure 2.33 A video that is good for rotoscoping contains dramatic or interesting motion with a clear distinction between background and foreground.

Lock the layer containing the video to prevent you from moving it accidentally
tracings
video
58
12.0 fps
4.8s
A simple tracing of this gorilla was made with the Pencil tool set on the Smooth modifier

Figure 2.34 Zoom in to the area you want to trace, and use the imported video file as your guide.

Figure 2.35 Rotoscoping this gorilla results in a layer of keyframes with drawings that follow its gait.

Figure 2.36 When you play the finished rotoscoped animation, see how natural the animation appears even if the tracings are very simple.

5. Add a blank keyframe by choosing Insert > Timeline > Blank Keyframe.

   An empty keyframe appears in frame 2.

6. Trace the actors or action in the empty keyframe you just created.

7. Continue the process of adding blank keyframes and tracing until your sequence is complete (**Figure 2.35**).

8. Delete the layer that contains the imported video to see the final rotoscoped animation (**Figure 2.36**).

   In this example, rotoscoping produces a very simple outline of the action, but you can trace any level of detail depending on the desired effect.

✔ Tips

- To make it easier to see the video below your tracings, you can use the Show Layers As Outlines option in your active layer, or you can use a semitransparent color until you finish the entire sequence.
- Use the Onion Skin buttons (**Figure 2.37**) to help you see your drawings in the previous keyframes.
- Use the comma (,) and period (.) keys to move back or forward on the Timeline in one-frame increments. This technique helps you go back and forth rapidly between two frames to test the differences between your drawings, much like a traditional animator flips between two tracings.

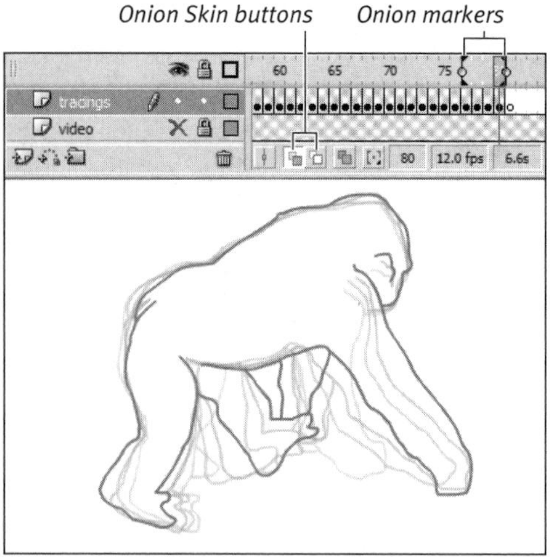

Figure 2.37 Use the Onion Skin buttons below the Timeline to show multiple frames in front of or behind the current frame. Move the onion skin markers to show fewer or more frames. This onion-skin shows three frames behind the current frame 80.

Part II: Understanding ActionScript

Getting a Handle on ActionScript

3

ActionScript is Flash's scripting language for adding interactivity to your graphics and movies. You can use ActionScript to create anything from simple navigation within your Flash movie to complex interfaces that react to the location of the viewer's pointer, arcade-style games, and even full-blown e-commerce sites with dynamically updating data. In this chapter, you'll learn how to construct ActionScript to create effective Flash interaction. Think of the process as learning the grammar of a foreign language: First, you must learn how to put nouns and verbs together and integrate adjectives and prepositions; then you can expand your communication skills and have meaningful conversations by building your vocabulary. This chapter will give you a sound ActionScripting foundation upon which you can build your Flash literacy.

If you're familiar with JavaScript, you'll notice some similarities between it and ActionScript. In fact, ActionScript is based on the same standard as JavaScript, which is a popular object-oriented programming language for adding interactivity to a Web page. Whereas JavaScript is intended to control the Web browser, ActionScript controls the interactivity within Flash content, so the two scripting languages have slight differences. But the basic syntax of scripts and the handling of objects—reusable pieces of code—remain the same.

Even if you've never used JavaScript, you'll see in this chapter that Flash makes basic scripting easy. You'll learn about the logic of objects and how the Actions panel can automate much of the scripting process while giving you the flexibility to build more sophisticated interaction as your skills improve.

About Objects and Classes

At the heart of ActionScript are objects and classes. *Objects* are data types—such as sound, graphics, text, and numeric values—that you create in Flash and use to control the movie. A date object, for example, retrieves information about the time and the date, and an array object manipulates data stored in a particular order.

All the objects you use and create belong to a larger collective group known as a *class*. Flash provides certain classes for you to use in your movie. These built-in classes handle a wide range of Flash elements such as data (`Array` class, `Math` class) and sound and video (`Sound` class, `Video` class).

Learning to code in ActionScript centers on understanding the capabilities of objects and their classes and using them to interact with one another and with the viewer.

In the real world, you're familiar with objects such as a cow, a tree, and a person (**Figure 3.1**). Flash objects range from visible things, such as a movie clip of a spinning ball, to more abstract concepts, such as the date, pieces of data, or the handling of keyboard inputs. Whether concrete or abstract, however, Flash objects are versatile because after you create them, you can reuse them in different contexts.

Before you can use objects, you need to be able to identify them, and you do so by name just as you do in the real world. Say you have three people in front of you: Adam, Betty, and Zeke. All three are objects that can be distinguished by name. All three belong to the collective group known as *humans*. You can also say that Adam, Betty, and Zeke are all *instances* of the Human class (**Figure 3.2**). In ActionScript, *instances* and *objects* are synonymous, and the terms are used interchangeably in this book.

Figure 3.1 Objects in the real world include things like a cow, a tree, and a person.

Figure 3.2 Adam, Betty, and Zeke are three objects of the Human class. Flash doesn't have such a class, but this analogy is useful for understanding objects.

Figure 3.3 Adam, Betty, and Zeke are human objects with different properties. Properties differentiate objects of the same class.

✔ Tip

- It helps to think of objects as nouns, properties as adjectives, and methods as verbs. Properties describe their objects, whereas methods are the actions that the objects perform.

About Methods and Properties

Each object of a class (Zeke of the humans, for example) differs from the others in its class by more than just its name. Each person is different because of several defining characteristics, such as height, weight, gender, and hair color. In object-oriented programming, you say that objects and classes have properties. Height, weight, sex, and hair color are all properties of the Human class (**Figure 3.3**).

In Flash, each class has a predefined set of properties that lets you establish the uniqueness of the object. The `Sound` class has just two properties: `duration`, which measures the length of a sound; and `position`, which measures the time the sound has been playing. The `MovieClip` class, on the other hand, has many properties, such as `_height`, `_width`, and `_rotation`, which are measures of the dimensions and orientation of a particular movie clip object. By defining and changing the properties of objects, you control what each object is like and how each object appears, sounds, and behaves.

Objects also do things. Zeke can run, sleep, and talk. The things that objects can do are known as *methods*. Each class has its own set of methods. The `Sound` class, for example, has a `setVolume` method that plays its sound louder or softer, and the `Date` class has a `getDay` method that retrieves the day of the week. When an object does something by using a method, you say that the method is called or that the object calls the method.

Understanding the relationships between objects, classes, properties, and methods is important. Putting objects together so that the methods and properties of one influence the methods and properties of another is what drives Flash interactivity. The key to building your ActionScript vocabulary is learning the properties and methods of different classes.

Writing with Dot Syntax

As with other foreign languages, you must learn the rules of grammar to put words together. *Dot syntax* is the convention that ActionScript uses to put objects, properties, and methods together into statements. You connect objects, properties, and methods with dots (periods) to describe a particular object or process. Here are two examples:

```
Zeke.weight = 188
```

```
Betty.weight = 135
```

The first statement assigns the value `188` to the weight of Zeke. The second statement assigns the value `135` to the weight of Betty. The dot separates the object name (`Zeke`, `Betty`) from the property (`weight`) (**Figure 3.4**).

Betty.weight = 135
Zeke.weight = 188

Figure 3.4 The hypothetical `weight` property describes Betty and Zeke. In Flash, many properties of objects can be both read and modified with ActionScript.

In this statement, the object `Betty` is linked to the object `shirt`:

```
Betty.shirt.color = "gray"
```

The object `shirt`, in turn, has the property `color`, which is assigned the value `gray`. Notice that with dot syntax, you use multiple dots to maintain object hierarchy. When you have multiple objects linked in this fashion, it's often easier to read the statement backward. So you could read it as "Gray is the color of the shirt of Betty."

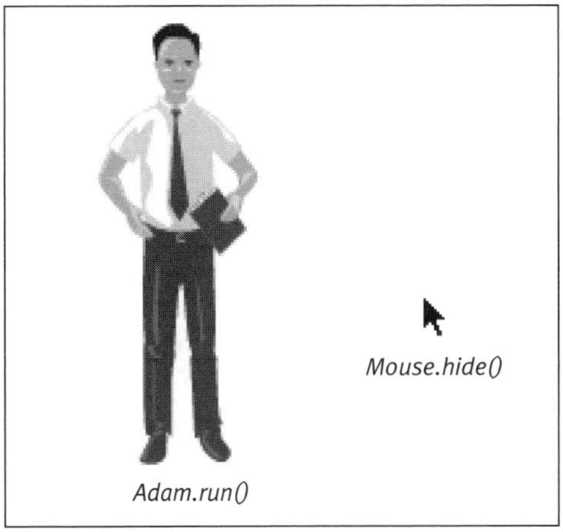

Figure 3.5 Dot syntax lets you make objects call methods. Just as the hypothetical method `run()` could make the Adam object begin to jog, the real Flash method `hide()`, when applied to the `Mouse` object, makes the pointer disappear.

Symbols and Classes

Symbols aren't classes. Symbols aren't even objects. It's true that most types of symbols (like movie clips, buttons, bitmaps, and video) have an associated class, which is perhaps the source of some confusion. The symbols that appear in the Library aren't objects or classes because they don't have methods and properties that you can control with ActionScript.

Some parallels exist between classes and symbols. Symbols are reusable assets, like blueprints, created in or imported to the Library. You create instances, or copies, of the symbols to use in your movie. As you have seen, you can also create instances of classes to use in your movie. When you place an instance of a button or a movie clip symbol on the Stage and give it a name, it becomes an instance of the corresponding class (`Button` or `MovieClip`) that you can manipulate using ActionScript.

Now consider the following statement:

```
Zeke.run()
```

This statement causes the object `Zeke` to call the method `run()`. The parentheses after `run` signify that `run` is a method and not a property. You can think of this construction as noun-dot-verb (**Figure 3.5**). Methods often have *parameters,* or arguments, within the parentheses. These parameters affect how the method is executed.

For example, both of these statements will make the `Zeke` and `Adam` objects call the `run()` method, but because each method contains a different parameter, the way the run is performed is different—Zeke runs fast, and Adam runs slowly:

```
Zeke.run(fast)
```

```
Adam.run(slow)
```

Each method has its own set of parameters that you must learn. Consider the basic Flash action `gotoAndPlay("Scene 1", 20)`. `gotoAndPlay` is a method of the `MovieClip` class. The parenthetical parameters, `("Scene1", 20)`, refer to the scene and the frame number, so calling this method makes the playhead of the object jump to scene 1, frame 20, and begin playing.

✔ Tip

- The dot syntax replaces the slash syntax used in previous versions of Flash. Although you can still use the slash syntax, the dot syntax is recommended because it's more compatible with all the new actions. Use slash syntax only if you're authoring for the Flash 4 Player or earlier, or for the Flash Lite Player 1.1 (the Flash player that is installed on many handheld devices such as cell phones).

More on Punctuation

Dot syntax allows you to construct meaningful processes and assignments with objects, properties, and methods. Additional punctuation symbols let you do more with these single statements.

The semicolon

To terminate individual ActionScript statements and start new ones, you use the semicolon (`;`). The semicolon functions as a period does in a sentence—it concludes one idea and lets another one begin. Here are two examples:

```
stopAllSounds();
```

```
play();
```

The semicolons separate the statements so that all the sounds stop first, and then the movie begins to play. Each statement is executed in order from the top down, like a set of instructions or a cookbook recipe.

✔ Tip

- Flash will still understand ActionScript statements even if you don't use semicolons to terminate each one. It's good practice, however, to include them in your scripts.

Curly braces

Curly braces (`{}`) are another kind of punctuation that ActionScript uses frequently. Curly braces group related blocks of ActionScript statements. When you assign actions to a button, for example, those actions appear within curly braces in the `onRelease` statement:

```
myButton.onRelease = function() {
    stopAllSounds();
    play();
};
```

In this case, both the `stopAllSounds` action and the `play` action are executed when the mouse button is released. Notice how the curly braces are separated on different lines to make the related ActionScript statements easier to read.

Commas

Commas (`,`) separate the parameters of a method. A method can take many parameters. The `gotoAndPlay()` method, for example, can take two: a scene name and the frame number. With commas separating the parameters, the ActionScript code looks like this:

```
gotoAndPlay("Scene 1", 20);
```

Some methods may have three, four, or perhaps even ten parameters, but as long as you separate the parameters with commas, Flash knows how to handle the code.

Capitalization

ActionScript 2 is case sensitive. That is, it knows the difference between lowercase letters and uppercase letters, so you must be very careful and conscientious about capitalizations in all your code.

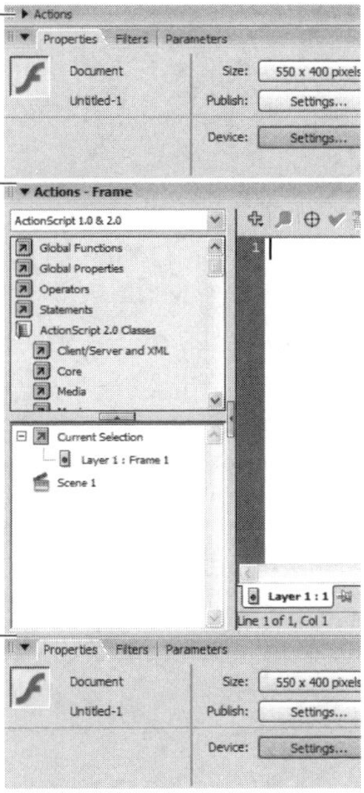

Figure 3.6 Click the triangle in the Actions bar to expand or collapse the Actions panel.

The Actions Panel

The Actions panel is a Flash dialog box that lets you access all the actions that control your Flash movie. Depending on your level of expertise, you can write ActionScript by choosing commands from a hierarchical list and filling in dialogs to specify parameters, or you can write the ActionScript code directly.

If you're uncomfortable with the ActionScript rules of grammar, several tools are available to help you. The Script Assist tool lets you choose commands and use a fill-in-the-blanks style to write those commands. Even if you're writing your own ActionScript, the Actions panel provides hints as you enter code and also automates some of the formatting. The Actions panel can also give you anytime access to the ActionScript Reference Guide.

In Flash, the name of the Actions panel appears as Actions-Frame, Actions-Button, or Actions-Movie Clip, depending on which element you have selected. The panel's contents remain the same, so this book always refers to the panel as the Actions panel.

To open the Actions panel:

- From the Windows menu, choose Actions (Option-F9 on Mac, F9 on Windows).

  or

  Click the right-facing triangle in the Actions bar.

  The Actions panel expands, and the triangle points downward (**Figure 3.6**).

  or

  Alt-double-click (Win) or Option-double-click (Mac) an instance on the Stage or a keyframe in the Timeline.

  The Actions panel appears so that you can attach actions to either the keyframe or the instance.

To undock the Actions panel:

1. Hover your cursor over the Actions panel's gripper (the two lines of dots in the top-left corner).

   Your pointer changes (hand for Mac, arrow for Windows), indicating that you can undock the Actions panel (**Figure 3.7**).

2. Click to grab the panel, and drag it to a new location.

To redock the Actions panel:

1. Grab the Actions panel by the gripper, and drag it over the different panels on your desktop.

   Those areas highlight with a bold outline.

2. Drop the Actions panel.

   The Actions panel docks with the highlighted panels. In Mac OS X, the Actions panel can't dock with the Property inspector or the Timeline.

✔ Tip

- You can group the Actions panel with another panel or group of panels by opening the Actions panel Options menu (in the upper-right corner of the Actions panel) and choosing "Group Actions with > [your chosen panel]".

Area to grab to dock or redock Actions panel

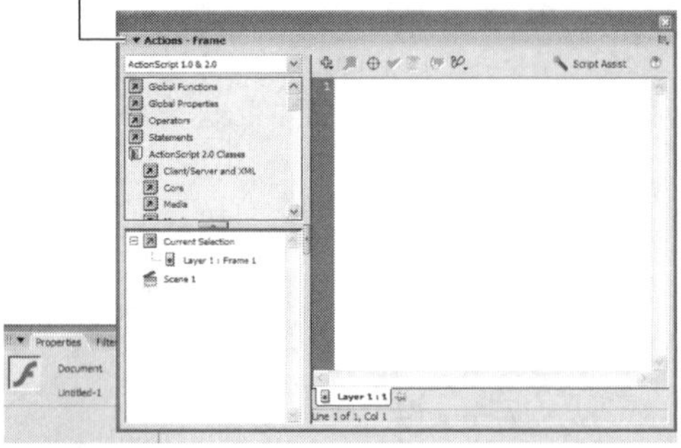

Figure 3.7 The Actions panel can be undocked from the Property inspector (Windows only).

Actions panel layout

The Actions panel features several sections and multiple ways to enter ActionScript statements (**Figure 3.8**). The Actions toolbox on the left side displays all the available commands, organized in logical categories. At the bottom of the categories, an index lists all the ActionScript commands in alphabetical order. You can choose actions from this categorized list. You can use the Script navigator in the lower-left portion of the Actions panel to navigate to different scripts within your Flash movie. In the right section, your completed script appears in the Script pane. This part of the Actions panel also offers additional functions when the panel is in the special Script Assist mode.

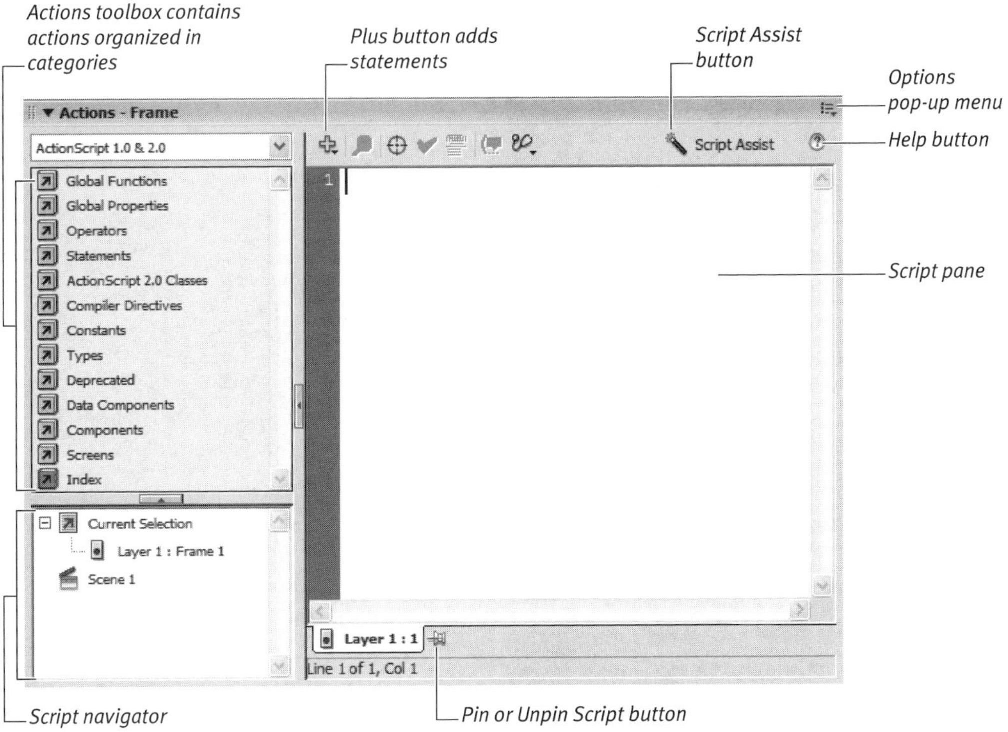

Figure 3.8 The Actions panel.

Using Script Assist to ease into ActionScript

If you're new to programming or to ActionScript, you may find it difficult to remember the rules of ActionScript and the various objects, methods, and properties. Flash 8 includes a feature known as Script Assist that can help you write scripts more easily.

Script Assist is similar to what was known as Normal Mode for writing ActionScript in versions of Flash through Flash MX. With Script Assist mode turned on, you don't type in ActionScript directly. Instead, you choose objects, statements, and so forth from a hierarchical menu. The top half of the Actions panel becomes a data-entry form where you fill in the blanks to provide any information necessary to complete the ActionScript code you're writing. In this way, although you still need to be familiar with the various objects and what they're used for, you don't have to be concerned about the intricacies of ActionScript syntax. In addition, with Script Assist mode turned on, you can easily view a description of any ActionScript element.

There are several ways to add an action to the Script pane. In addition to typing the action in directly, you can choose from menus and click or drag actions into your script. All of these methods also work in Script Assist mode.

To turn on Script Assist:

1. Open the Actions panel.
2. Click the Script Assist button.

   The Actions panel switches to Script Assist mode. The Script pane splits into two parts: a code pane on the bottom and a space on top that is used to modify actions (**Figure 3.9**).

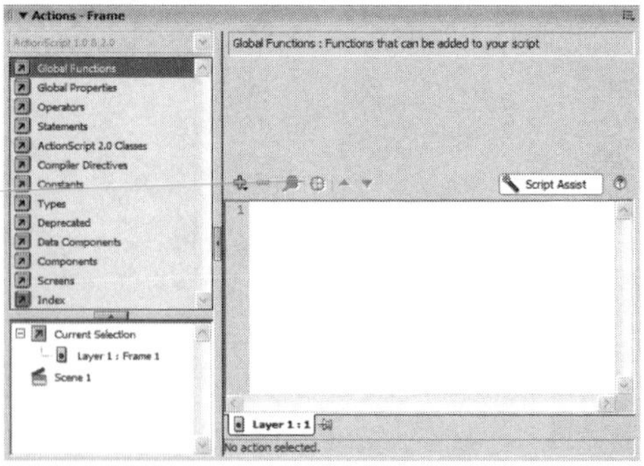

Figure 3.9 With Script Assist mode turned on, the top half of the Script pane displays information and options for the selected ActionScript element.

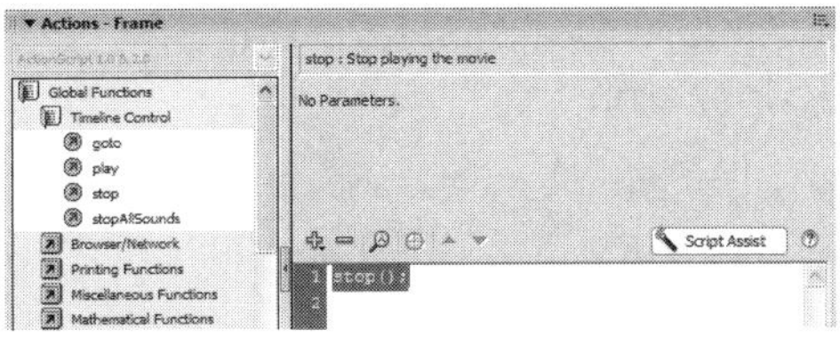

Figure 3.10 Add an action by choosing a statement from the Actions toolbox. Here, the action `stop()` has been added to the Script pane.

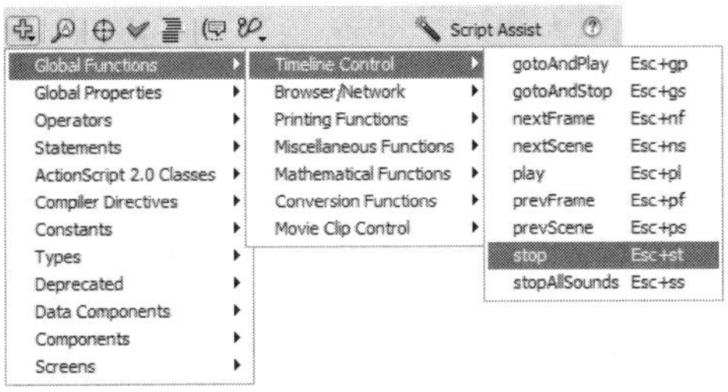

Figure 3.11 Add an action by choosing it from the plus button's pull-down menus.

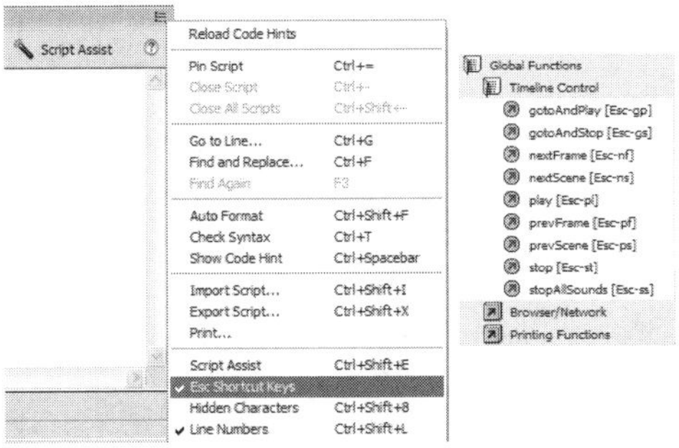

Figure 3.12 Choosing Esc Shortcut Keys from the Actions panel's Options pop-up menu displays the shortcut keys for many actions in the Actions toolbox.

✔ Tip

- While making your selection in the Actions toolbox, you can use the arrow keys, the Page Up and Page Down keys, or the Home and End keys to navigate through the list. Press Enter or the spacebar to open or close categories or to choose an action to put in the Script pane.

To add an action in the Script pane:

1. Select the instance or frame where you want to assign an action.

   In the Actions toolbox, expand an action category by clicking it.
2. Double-click the desired action.

   The action appears in the Script pane (**Figure 3.10**).

   or

1. Select the instance or frame where you want to assign an action.

   In the Actions toolbox, expand an action category by clicking it.
2. Select the action, and drag it into the Script pane.

   The action appears in the Script pane.

   or

1. Select the instance or frame where you want to assign an action.
2. Click the plus button above the Script pane, and choose the action from the pull-down menus (**Figure 3.11**).

   The action appears in the Script pane.

   or

1. Select the instance or frame where you want to assign an action, put your pointer in the Script pane of the Actions panel, and press the Esc key.
2. Type the two-letter code corresponding to the action you want.

   The action appears in the Script pane.

   Choose Esc Shortcut Keys from the Actions panel's Options menu (**Figure 3.12**) to display shortcut keys in the Actions toolbox.

To edit actions in the Script pane:

- Highlight the action, and then click and drag it to a new position in the Script pane.

  or

- In Script Assist mode, select the action, and click the up- or down-arrow button above the Script pane to move the line up or down.

✔ Tip

- You can use familiar editing commands such as Copy, Cut, and Paste to create and rearrange lines of ActionScript.

To remove an action from the Script pane:

- Highlight the action, and use the Delete key to remove it from the Script pane.

  or

- In Script Assist mode, select the action, and click the minus button above the Script pane to remove the code.

To modify the Actions panel display:

- Drag or double-click the vertical splitter bar, or click the arrow button that divides the Actions toolbox and Script pane, to collapse or expand an area (**Figure 3.13**).
- Drag or double-click the horizontal splitter bar, or click the arrow button that divides the Actions toolbox and Script navigator, to collapse or expand an area (Figure 3.13).

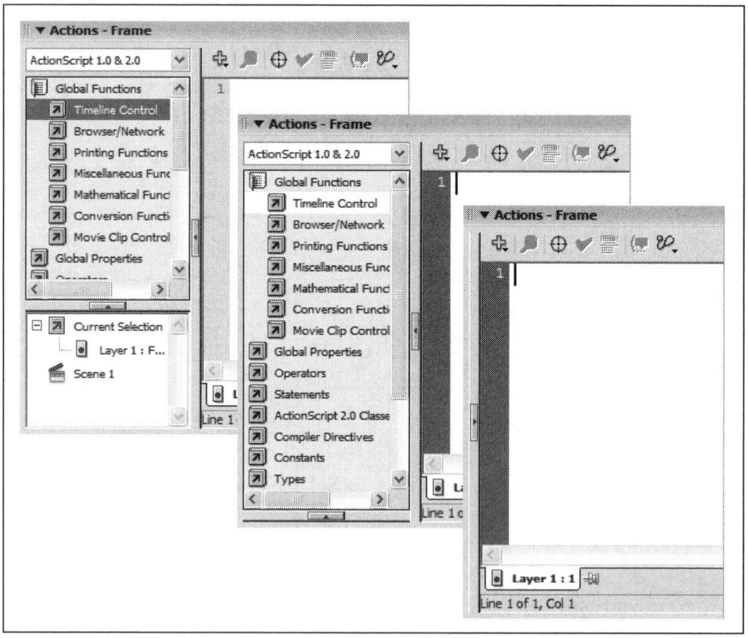

Figure 3.13 Resize the Actions panel by dragging or clicking the vertical or horizontal splitter bars that separate the Actions toolbox, the Script navigator, and the Script pane. The Script navigator can be completely collapsed (middle) and the Actions toolbox can be completely collapsed as well, leaving just the Script pane (bottom).

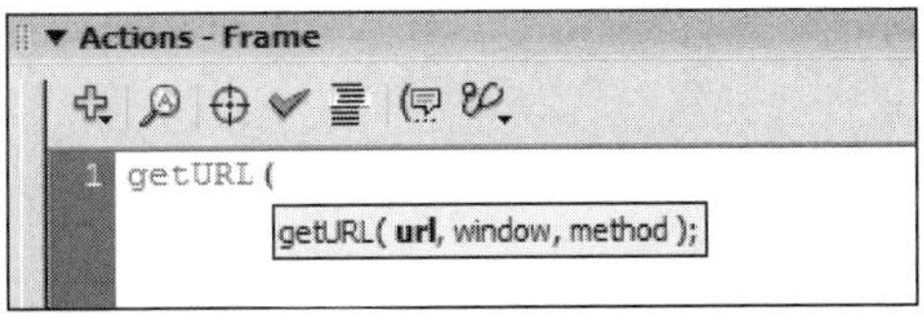

Figure 3.14 A code hint guides you as you enter ActionScript. The first required parameter for this action is the URL.

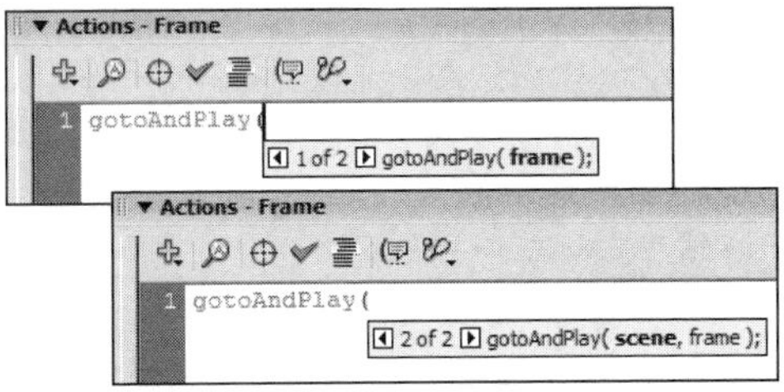

Figure 3.15 The action `gotoAndPlay` can be used with one or two parameters. The code hint shows you both ways, using only one parameter for `frame` (top) or using two parameters for `scene` and `frame` (bottom).

Actions panel options

The Actions panel provides many features that can help you write reliable code quickly and easily. Chapter 13 explains many of the debugging tools in detail.

When you're writing ActionScript in the Script pane, you can use *code hints*, which appear as you type. Code hints recognize what kind of action you're typing and offer choices and prompts on how to complete it. Flash makes it easy to be an expert! You can also customize the format options so that your code looks just the way you want it for ease of reading and understanding.

Coding help is always available in the Actions panel. The Help button, for example, calls up the Help panel and sends you directly to the description and usage of any action selected in the Actions toolbox, in case you have trouble remembering what a particular action does or how it's used.

If you want to keep an ActionScript visible as you select other elements in your Flash movie, you can do so by pinning your script. *Pinning* makes your script "stick" in the Script pane until you unpin it. This technique is useful if you've forgotten the name of a text box or a movie clip and need to reference it in an ActionScript statement. You can pin your current script and then go look for your text box or movie clip. Your script remains in place so that you can make the necessary edits.

To use code hints:

1. Enter an action in the Script pane, and then type the opening parenthesis.

   Flash detects the action and anticipates that you will enter its parameters. A code hint appears to guide you (**Figure 3.14**). If an action has different ways of handling parameters, the tool tip shows those options (**Figure 3.15**).

continues on next page

2. Enter the first parameter and then a comma.

   The bold in the code hint advances to highlight the next required parameter (**Figure 3.16**).

3. Continue entering the required parameters, and type a closing parenthesis to finish the action.

   The code hint disappears (**Figure 3.17**).

   or

1. Enter an object target path and then a period.

   Flash anticipates that you will enter a method or property of the particular object that appears before the period. A menu-style code hint appears to guide you (**Figure 3.18**).

2. Choose the appropriate method or property from the menu.

   The method or property appears in the Script pane after the dot. Another code hint appears to guide you, providing the parameters of the method (**Figure 3.19**).

3. Enter the parameters of the method, and type a closing parenthesis to finish.

   The code hint disappears (**Figure 3.20**).

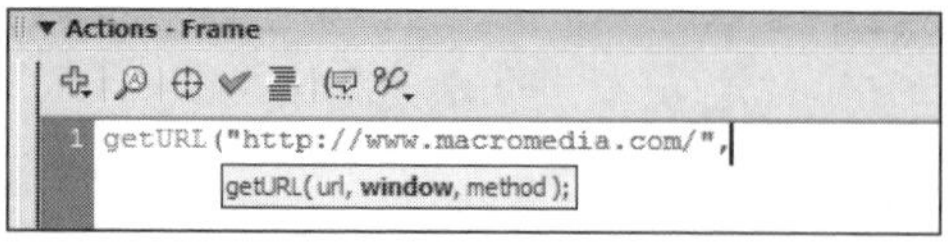

Figure 3.16 After you enter the first parameter, the code hint directs you to the next parameter. The next parameter for this action is `window`.

Figure 3.17 When you enter the closing parenthesis, the code hint disappears. The `getURL` action shown here doesn't require the last parameter (the method).

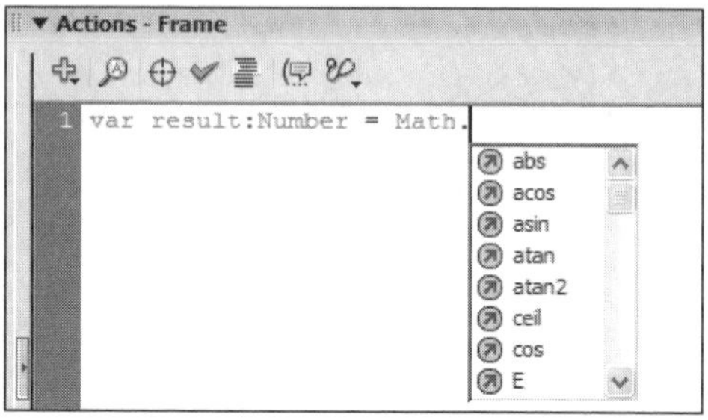

Figure 3.18 The code hint provides a scrolling list of methods and properties for each object. This list contains the methods and properties of the `Math` object.

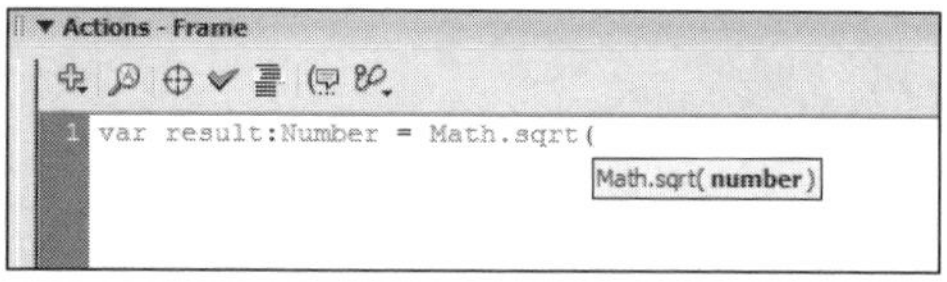

Figure 3.19 The `sqrt()` method of the `Math` object requires a number for its parameter.

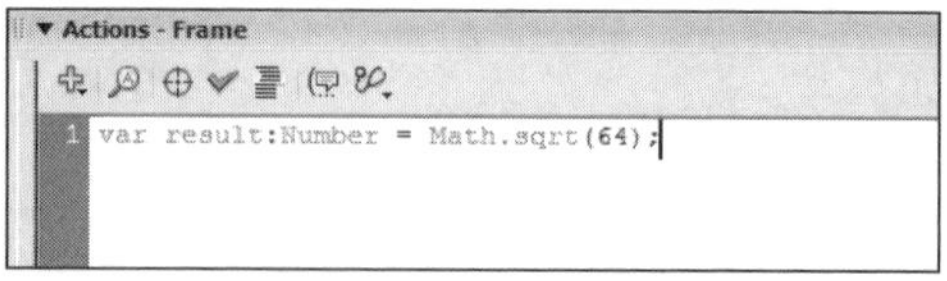

Figure 3.20 When you complete the method, the code hint disappears.

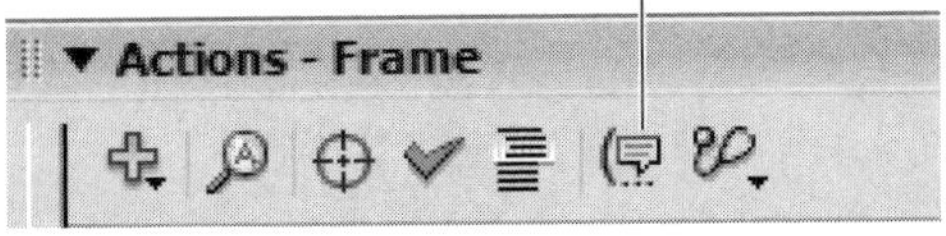

Figure 3.21 The Show Code Hint button is above the Script pane.

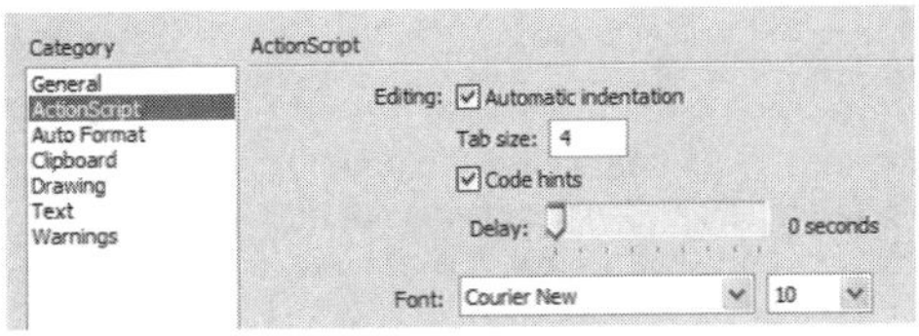

Figure 3.22 In the Preferences dialog box, you can change the time that it takes for code hints to appear.

✔ Tips

- There are two ways to trigger code hints for object methods and properties. You can trigger code hints by giving your object a name that ends with a recognizable suffix. Flash provides code hints for a button, for example, if the name of the button ends with `_btn`. In addition, Flash gives code hints for objects if you specify the data type of the object when you first define it. Learn more about defining and naming variables later in this chapter, and see Appendix A for a full list of name suffixes that trigger code hints.
- Dismiss a code hint by pressing the Esc key or clicking a different place in your script.
- Navigate the menu-style code hints by using the arrow keys, the Page Up and Page Down keys, or the Home and End keys. You can also start typing, and the entry that begins with the letter you type will appear in the code hint. Press Enter or the key that will follow the method or property (for example a space, comma, or parenthesis) to choose the selection.
- You can call up code hints manually by pressing Ctrl-Spacebar or by clicking the Show Code Hint button above the Script pane when your pointer is in a spot where code hints are appropriate (**Figure 3.21**).
- Change the delay time for code hints to appear or turn off code hints by choosing Preferences from the Actions panel's Options menu. When the Preferences dialog box appears, change your preferences in the ActionScript options category (**Figure 3.22**).

To set formatting options:

1. From the Actions panel's Options menu, choose Preferences.

   The Flash Preferences dialog box appears.

2. Choose the Auto Format category.

3. Set the different formatting options, and specify the way a typical block of code should appear (**Figure 3.23**); then click OK.

4. Choose Auto Format from the Actions panel's Options menu (Ctrl-Shift-F for Windows, Cmd-Shift-F for Mac), or click the Auto Format button above the Script pane.

   Flash formats your script in the Script pane according to the preferences you set in the Auto Format category of the Flash Preferences dialog box.

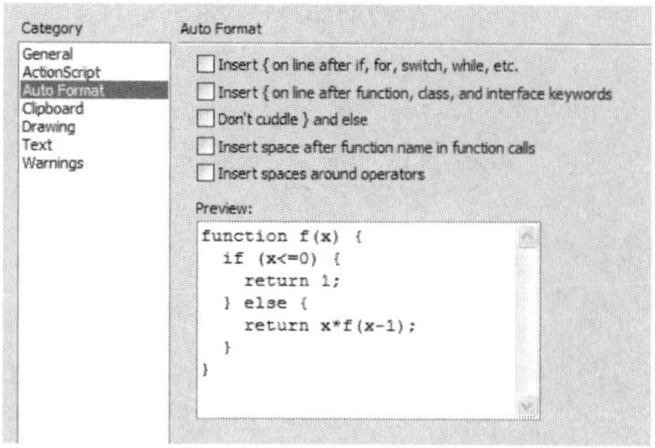

Figure 3.23 The Auto Format category in the Flash Preferences gives you a preview of how a typical block of code will look with the selections you make.

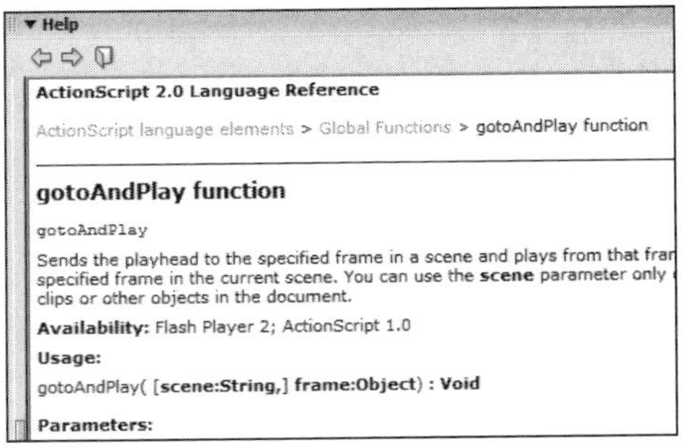

Figure 3.24 The entry for the `gotoAndPlay` action in the Help panel.

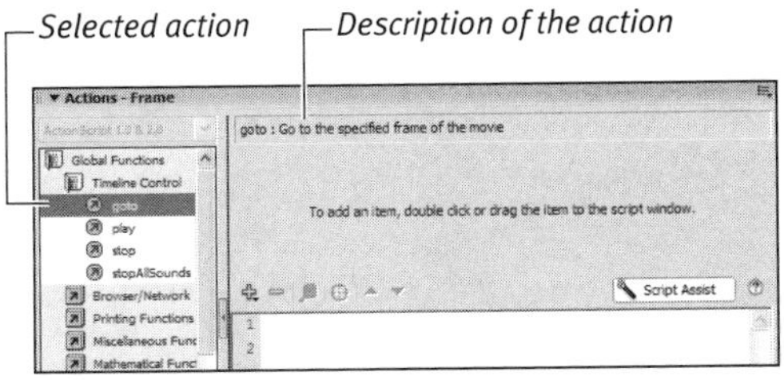

Figure 3.25 Script Assist mode provides a description of any action selected in the Actions toolbox or the Script pane.

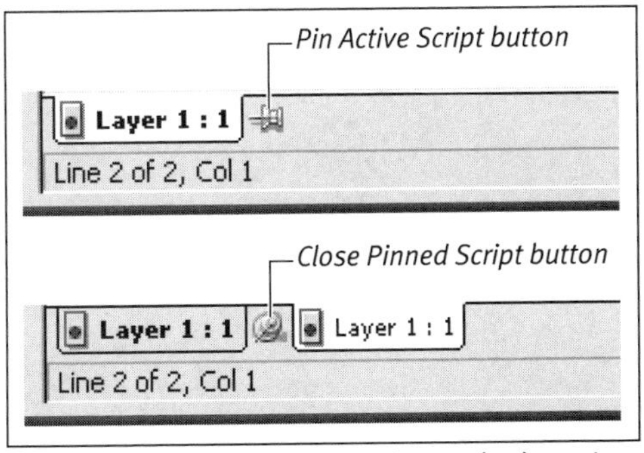

Figure 3.26 The Pin Active Script button (top) toggles to Close Pinned Script (bottom).

To get information about an action:

- Select an ActionScript term in the Actions toolbox or in the Script pane, and click the Help button above and to the right of the Script pane.

  or

- Right-click (Win) or Ctrl-Click (Mac) an action in the Actions toolbox or in the Script pane, and select View Help from the context menu that appears.

  The Help panel opens to the selected ActionScript term. The typical entry in the Help panel contains information about usage and syntax, lists parameters and their availability in various Flash versions, and shows sample code (**Figure 3.24**).

  or

- In Script Assist mode, select an ActionScript element in the Actions toolbox or in the Script pane.

  A short description of the action is displayed at the top of the Script pane (**Figure 3.25**).

To pin or unpin a script in the Script pane:

- With ActionScript visible in the Script pane, click the Pin Active Script button at the bottom of the Actions panel (**Figure 3.26**).

  To unpin the script, click the button again.

Editing ActionScript

When the code in the Script pane of the Actions panel becomes long and complex, you can check, edit, and manage it using the Options menu of the Actions panel. There are menu options for searching and replacing words, importing and exporting scripts, and printing your scripts as well as for different ways to display your script, such as using word wrap (**Figure 3.27**).

You can use the Find and Replace functions in the Actions panel to quickly change variable names, properties, or even actions. For example, if you create a lengthy script involving the variable `redTeamStatus` but change your mind and want to change the variable name, you can replace all instances of `redTeamStatus` with `blueTeamStatus`. You can find all the occurrences of the property `_x` and replace them with `_y`, or you can locate all the occurrences of the action `gotoAndStop` and replace them with `gotoAndPlay`.

The Import Script and Export Script functions of the Actions panel let you work with external text editors.

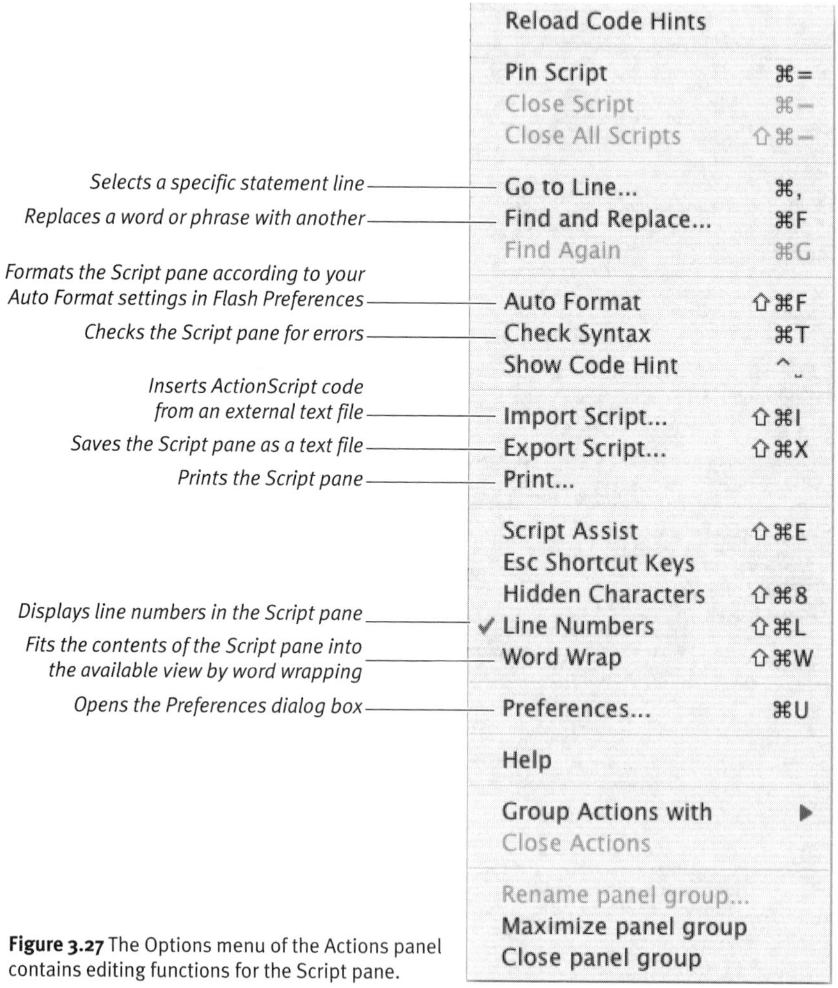

Figure 3.27 The Options menu of the Actions panel contains editing functions for the Script pane.

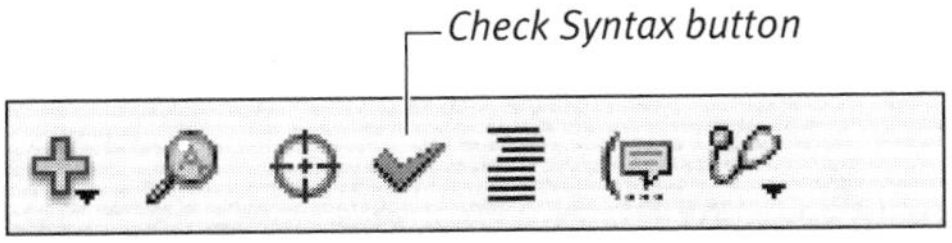

Figure 3.28 The Check Syntax button is the check mark icon above the Script pane.

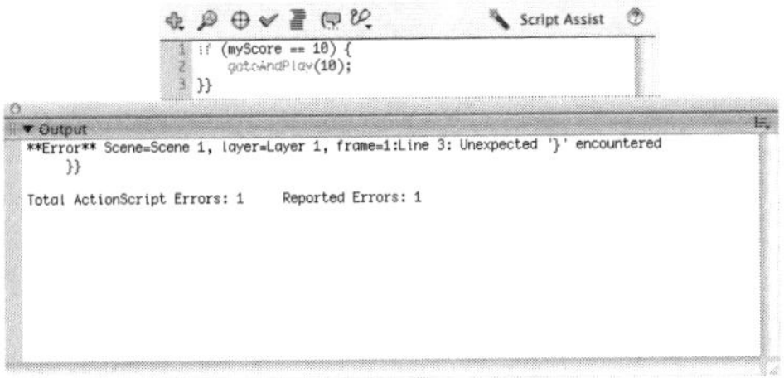

Figure 3.29 The Script pane (top) contains an extra closing curly brace. Flash notifies you of the nature and location of the error in the Output window (bottom).

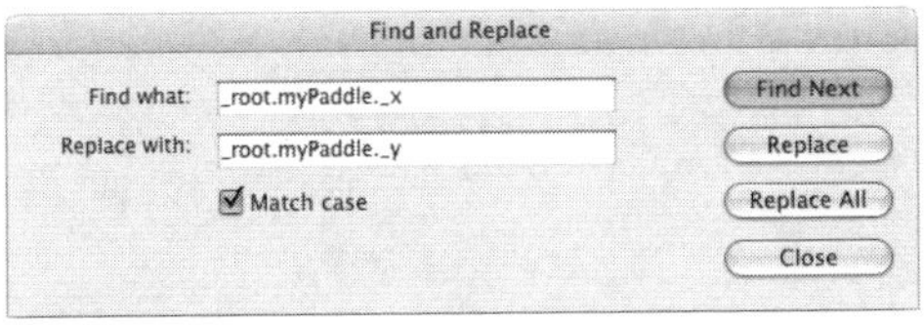

Figure 3.30 Every occurrence of `_root.myPaddle._x` will be replaced with `_root.myPaddle._y`.

✔ Tip

- The Replace dialog box replaces all the occurrences of a particular word or phrase only in the current Script pane of the Actions panel. To replace every occurrence of a certain word in the whole movie, you need to go to each script and repeat this process.

To check the syntax in the Script pane:

- In the Actions panel, choose Options > Check Syntax (Command-T for Mac, Ctrl-T for Windows). You can also click the Check Syntax button above the Script pane (**Figure 3.28**).

  Flash checks the script in the Script pane for errors in syntax. If it finds an error, it displays a warning dialog box and reports any errors in an Output window (**Figure 3.29**). Use the information provided in the Output window to locate the error and correct the syntax.

✔ Tip

- Check Syntax only reports the errors in the current Script pane, not for the entire movie.

To find and replace ActionScript terms in the Script pane:

1. In the Actions panel, choose Options > Find and Replace (Command-F for Mac, Ctrl-F for Windows).

   The Find and Replace dialog box appears.

2. In the "Find what" field, enter a word or words that you want Flash to find. In the "Replace with" field, enter a word or words that you want the found words to be replaced with. Select the "Match case" check box to make Flash distinguish between upper- and lowercase letters (**Figure 3.30**).

3. Click Replace to replace the first instance of the found word, or click Replace All to replace all instances of the found word.

To import an ActionScript:

1. Select Options > Import Script (Command-Shift-I for Mac, Ctrl-Shift-I for Windows).
2. In the dialog box that appears, choose the text file that contains the ActionScript you wish to import, and click Open.

   Flash inserts the ActionScript contained in the text file into the current Script pane at the insertion point. (Note that this works differently from some earlier versions of Flash, where the entire contents of the Script pane would be replaced.)

To export an ActionScript:

1. Select Options > Export Script (Command-Shift-X for Mac, Ctrl-Shift-X for Windows).
2. Enter a destination filename, and click Save.

   Flash saves a text file that contains the entire contents of the current Script pane. The recommended extension for external ActionScript files is *.as*, as in myCode.as.

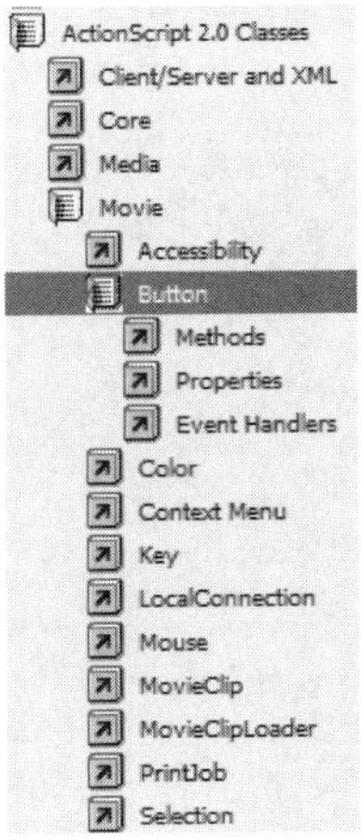

Figure 3.31 Flash's built-in classes control different kinds of information. The ActionScript 2.0 Classes category in the Actions toolbox is divided into more categories. Here, you see the `Button` class and the contents of its folder.

Using Objects

Now that you know what objects are and how to operate the Actions panel, you can begin to script with objects and call their methods or evaluate and assign new properties.

Flash provides existing classes that reside in the ActionScript 2.0 Classes category in the Actions toolbox (**Figure 3.31**). These Flash classes have methods and properties that control different elements of your Flash movie, such as graphics, sound, data, time, and mathematical calculations. You can also build your own classes using ActionScript 2.0, a topic that is not covered in this book.

In ActionScript, like most programming languages, you access and manipulate objects using variables. *Variables* are containers that hold information. You can create, change the contents of, and discard variables at any time. In ActionScript 2.0, it's necessary to define the existence of a variable, known as *declaring* the variable, before you use it. To declare a variable, you use the ActionScript keyword `var` followed by the name of the variable, which is followed in turn by a colon and the type of information the variable will be used to store. The different kinds of information that variables can contain are known as *data types*.

The Rules of Naming

Although you're free to make up descriptive names for your objects, you must adhere to the following simple rules. If you don't, Flash won't recognize your object's name and will ignore your commands to control the object with ActionScript:

1. Don't use spaces or punctuation (such as slashes, dots, and parentheses), because these characters often have a special meaning to Flash.
2. You can use letters, numbers, and underscore characters, but you must not begin the name with a number.
3. You can't use certain words for variable names because they are reserved for special functions or for use as keywords in ActionScript. If you try to use then as variables, Flash will display an error message when you test your movie. The complete list of these words can be found in the Flash Help under Learning ActionScript 2.0 in Flash > Best Practices and Coding Conventions for ActionScript 2.0 > Naming conventions > Avoiding reserved words or language constructs.

Those are the only three rules. Some additional general naming strategies, however, can make your scripts easier to understand, debug, and share:

1. Variable names should describe the information that the variables hold. The variable names `playerScore` and `spaceshipVelocity`, for example, are appropriate and will cause fewer headaches than something like `xyz` or `myVariable`.
2. Use a consistent naming practice. A common method is to use multiple words to describe an object and to capitalize the first letter of every word except the first. The names `spinningSquare1`, `spinningSquare2`, and `leftPaddle`, for example, are intuitive, descriptive, and easy to follow in a script. Remember that ActionScript 2 is case sensitive! Using a consistent naming practice will help you avoid mismatches between your object name and your ActionScript code due to capitalization.
3. Get in the habit of adding suffixes to your names to describe the object type. Using the standard suffix `_mc` for movie clips and `_btn` for buttons readily identifies the objects. It also helps the ActionScript panel recognize the object type so it brings up the appropriate code hints. For example, if you begin typing `leftPaddle_mc` and then a dot, the code hint that appears will display a list of the movie clip methods and events because the ActionScript panel knows that `leftPaddle_mc` is a movie clip. In this book, all names have the standard suffixes for objects found in Appendix A.

Variables, data types, and strict typing

Examples of typical types of variables are a user's score (`Number` data type), an Internet address (`String` data type), a date object (`Date` data type), and the on/off state of a toggle button (`Boolean` data type). In ActionScript 2.0, you specify the data type of your variable when you create it; Flash will allow only values of that data type to be stored in the variable. This is called *strict typing.* Strict data-typing prevents you from accidentally assigning the wrong type of data to a variable, which can cause problems during the playback of your movie. Strict data-typing involves adding a colon (`:`) and the data type after the name of your variable—for example, `var myScore:Number = 20`. In this statement, the variable called `myScore` is strictly typed to hold only a numerical value.

Table 3.1 lists the most basic data types that variables can hold. However, a variable can be declared with any ActionScript class as its data type, including any of the built-in classes and classes you create yourself.

Once you declare a variable, you *initialize* it, or put information into the variable for the first time (usually a default value). Initializing a variable in the Actions panel involves using the equals sign (=), which assigns a value to a variable. The name of the variable that receives the value goes on the left side of the equals sign, and a value to be assigned goes on the right side. This point is crucial; the expression `a = b` is *not* the same as `b = a`. When you initialize a variable at the same time you declare the variable, it's clear which part of the statement is the variable and which part is the new value, as in the following example:

```
var myPassword:String = "hocusPocus";
```

If you no longer need a variable, it's a good idea to delete it so you can free memory. To remove a variable, use the `delete` action.

Table 3.1

Basic Data Types

DATA TYPE	DESCRIPTION	EXAMPLE
`Number`	A numeric value.	`var myScore:Number = 24`
`String`	A sequence of characters, numbers, or symbols. A string is always contained within quotation marks.	`var yourEmail:String = "johndoe@domain.com"`
`Boolean`	A value of either true or false. The words aren't enclosed in quotation marks.	`var buttonPressed:Boolean = true`
`Object`	A generic object to which you can add properties or methods. Used in cases where a simple object is needed.	`var myObj:Object = new Object()`

To declare and initialize a variable:

1. Select the first frame of the root Timeline, and open the Actions panel.
2. Click the Script Assist button to activate Script Assist mode if it isn't already turned on.
3. In the Script pane, choose Statements > Variables > var.
4. In the Variables field, enter a descriptive name for your variable.
5. If you want to initialize your variable, in the Variables field to the right of the variable name you just added, type an equals sign and the initial value to assign to the variable. If the value is a string, remember to put quotation marks around it.
6. Choose the data type your variable will hold from the Type menu.

   The value on the right side of the equals sign is assigned to the variable on the left side (**Figure 3.32**).

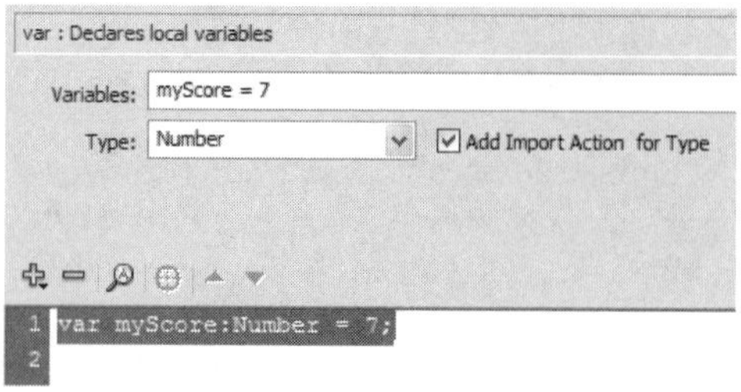

Figure 3.32 Variables can be initialized to hold different kinds of information. The word `var` indicates that `myScore` is a variable, and the equals sign assigns the numerical value 7 to the variable.

✔ Tips

- It's good practice to initialize your variables in the first frame of your Timeline. That way, you keep them all in the same place and can edit their initial values easily.
- When you assign a value that is one of the intrinsic data types (`Number`, `String`, `Boolean`) to a variable, even if you're assigning to one variable the value in another, Flash determines the value and puts it in your variable at that moment. If the property or the referenced variable subsequently changes, the value of your variable won't change unless you reassign it. Consider this example: `var xPosition:Number = _xmouse;`. When you initialize the variable called `xPosition` in the first frame of your movie, it holds the x-coordinate of the pointer. As you move the pointer around the screen, the property `_xmouse` changes but the variable `xPosition` does not. The variable `xPosition` still holds the original x coordinate from when it was initialized. To have a variable updated continually, you must put it within a function that is triggered continuously (such as an `onEnterFrame` event handler or a function called by a `setInterval` action).

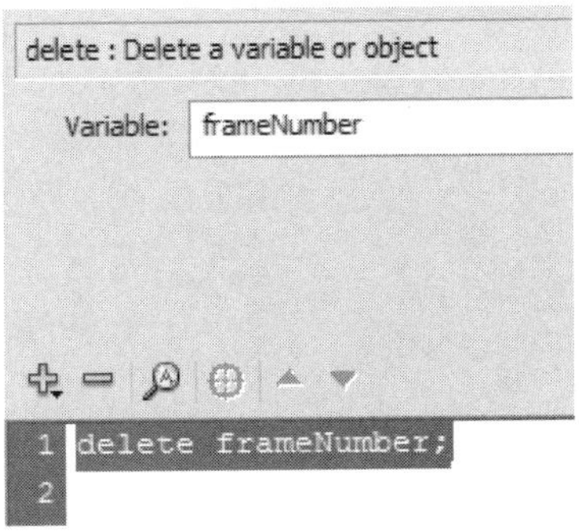

Figure 3.33 This statement deletes the variable called `frameNumber`.

To delete a variable:

- In the Script pane, choose Statements > Variables > delete; then, in the Variable field, type the name of the variable you want to remove.

  When this statement is executed, the variable is deleted (**Figure 3.33**).

Expressions and strings

Using expressions and using strings are two important ways to describe data. An *expression* is a statement that may include variables, properties, and objects and must be resolved (figured out) before Flash can determine its value. Think of an expression as being an algebraic formula, like $a^2 + b^2$. The value of the expression has to be calculated before it can be used (**Figure 3.34**).

A *string*, on the other hand, is a statement that Flash uses *as is* and considers to be a collection of characters. The string "$a^2 + b^2$" is literally a sequence of seven characters (including the spaces around the plus sign but not the quotation marks). When you initialize a variable with a literal string value, you must enclose the characters in quotation marks.

```
var myArea:Number = myLength * myWidth;
dogYears = 7 * Age;
downloadProgress = _root._framesloaded / _root._totalframes;
```

Figure 3.34 Some examples of expressions. The variable names are on the left side of the equals signs, and the expressions are on the right.

Expressions and strings aren't mutually exclusive—that is, sometimes you can have an expression that includes strings! For example, the statement `"Current frame is " + _root._currentframe` is an expression that puts together a string and the frame number of the main Timeline. You'll learn more about this kind of operation, called *concatenation*, in Chapter 11.

✔ Tip

- If quotation marks always surround a string, how do you include quotation marks in the actual string? You use the backslash (\) character before including a quotation mark. This technique is called *escaping* a character. The string `"The line \"Call me Shane\" is from a 1953 movie Western"` produces the following result: *The line "Call me Shane" is from a 1953 movie Western.* **Table 3.2** lists a few common escape sequences for special characters.

Table 3.2

Common Escape Sequences

Sequence	Character
\b	Backspace
\n	New line
\t	Tab
\"	Quotation mark
\'	Single quotation mark
\\	Backslash

Creating objects

Before you can use one of the existing classes, you must create an instance of the class by assigning it to a variable. The process is similar to creating an instance of, or *instantiating*, a symbol. Once you have declared a variable and specified its data type as the name of the class, you create an instance of the class to store in the variable using the keyword new followed by the of the class and a pair of parentheses:

```
var Adam:Human = new Human();
var myData_array:Array = new Array();
```

Where do you find the keyword new? In the ActionScript 2.0 Classes category of the Actions toolbox, the classes that require you to make new instances include the command new (**Figure 3.35**).

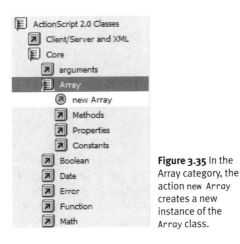

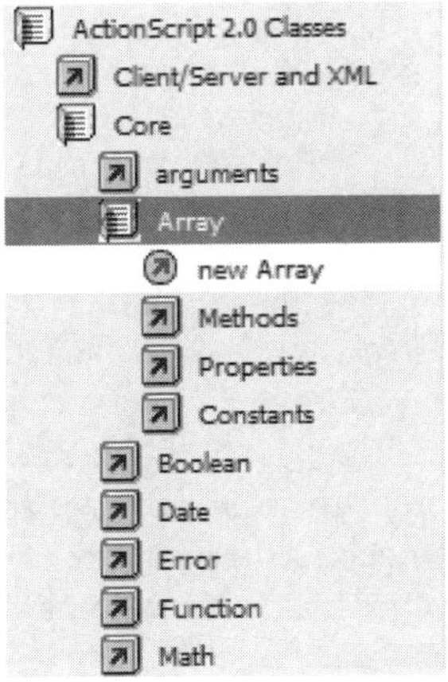

Figure 3.35 In the Array category, the action new Array creates a new instance of the Array class.

The previous two ActionScript statements create two new objects that you can manipulate. The first example is a hypothetical statement that makes a new object called Adam, an instance of the Human class. The second is an actual ActionScript statement that makes a new Array instance called myData_array. The statement that contains the new operator in front of the class is called a *constructor.* Most classes have a constructor method, a special method that creates new instances of that class.

The following task demonstrates how to create an instance of the Date class, but the general technique works for instantiation of all objects.

To instantiate an object:

1. Select the first frame on the main Timeline, and open the Actions panel with Script Assist mode turned on.
2. In the Script pane, choose Statements > Variables > var to declare the variable that will hold the new instance.

   The var keyword appears in the Script pane with the variable name not_set_yet.
3. In the Variables field, enter a name for your new object.
4. In the Type field, choose Date.
5. Choose Statements > Variables > set variable.
6. In the Variable field, enter the name of your Date object.

continues on next page

USING OBJECTS

7. Place the cursor in the Value field; using the plus button, choose ActionScript 2.0 Classes > Core > Date > "new Date".
8. Select the Expression check box next to the Value field.

   By default, Flash considers the text you enter in the Value field to be a literal string of text and surrounds it with quotation marks. Selecting the Expression check box tells Flash to treat the text as an expression (such as a variable or calculation) instead.

   The full statement creates a new `Date` object with the name you entered. Your `Date` object is instantiated and ready to use (**Figure 3.36**).

✔ Tips

- When you're adding an ActionScript statement into one of the Script Assist fields (as in step 7), it's easiest to use the plus button to add the code. If instead you click in the Actions toolbox to select the item to add, the Script pane hides the Script Assist field and shows the description of the selected item. You then need to reselect the relevant line in the Script pane to add the action into the field.
- If you prefer to declare your variable and assign a value to it on a single line, instead of steps 4–7 enter `= new Date()` after your variable name in the Variables field (**Figure 3.37**).

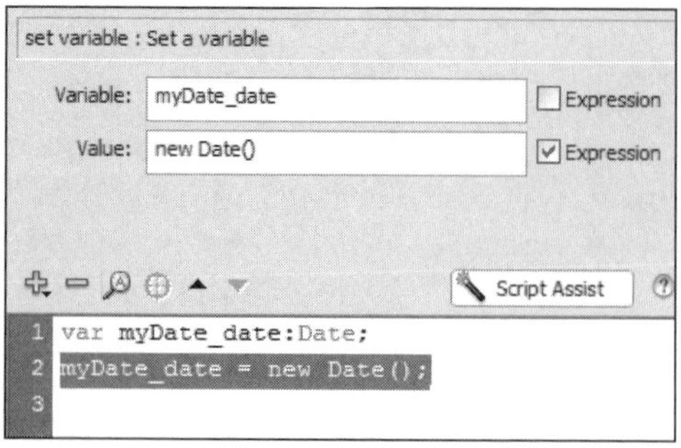

Figure 3.36 The finished statement creates an object called `myDate_date` from the `Date` class.

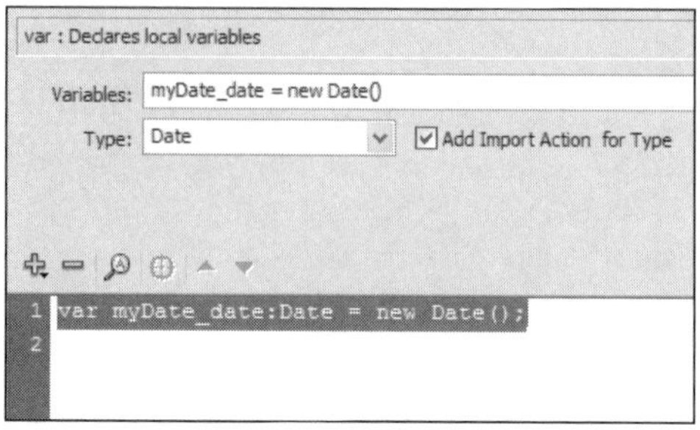

Figure 3.37 If you prefer, you can assign a value as part of the variable declaration.

- Some of the Flash classes—such as `Key`, `Math`, and `Mouse`—don't require you to create an instance of the class to use them. You can use their methods and properties immediately without having a named object. This practice makes sense because only one unique instance can exist for these special objects. (The `Mouse` class, for example, can have only one instance because there is only one mouse per computer.) You can tell which Flash objects don't require you to create instances by looking in the ActionScript 2.0 Classes category in the Actions toolbox. Objects that don't allow you to create instances don't have the command `new` listed among their methods and properties.

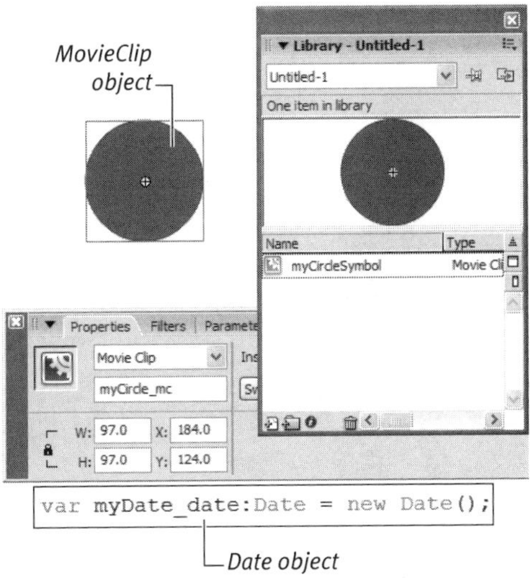

Figure 3.38 Instantiation of a movie clip symbol (called `myCircle_mc`) versus instantiation of a date object (called `myDate`).

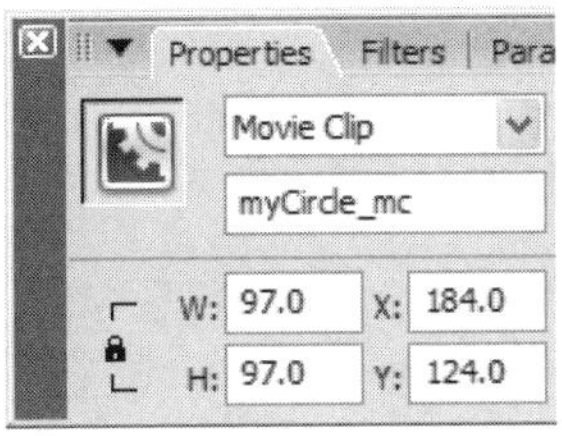

Figure 3.39 The Property inspector for a selected movie clip. The name of this movie clip object is `myCircle_mc`.

Creating instances on the Stage

A few types of ActionScript objects, such as movie clips, buttons, and text fields, are unique because you often create them visually by adding an instance from the library (for button and movie clip symbols) or using the drawing tools (for text fields). Instantiation of these objects involves two steps: placing an instance on the Stage, and naming that instance in the Property inspector. These two steps accomplish the same task that the constructor function performs for other Flash classes (**Figure 3.38**). The result is the same: A named object, or an instance, of a class is created. You can manipulate that object by calling its methods or evaluating its properties.

Later in the book, you'll learn how to create `MovieClip` instances (Chapter 7) and `TextField` instances (Chapter 11) and place them on the Stage using only code.

To name a movie clip instance or a button instance:

1. Create a movie clip symbol or a button symbol.
2. Drag an instance of the symbol from the Library to the Stage.
3. Select the instance.
4. In the Property inspector, below the pull-down menu for the symbol type, enter a unique name for your instance (**Figure 3.39**).

   Now you can use this name to refer to your movie clip instance or your button instance with ActionScript.

✔ Tip

- The name of your symbol (the one that appears in the Library) and the name you give it in the Property inspector are two different identifiers (**Figure 3.40**). The name that appears in the Library is a symbol property and basically is just an organizational reminder. The name in the Property inspector is more important because it's the actual name of the object and will be used in targeting paths. End your movie clip instance name with `_mc` so that the Actions panel can identify it as a movie clip.

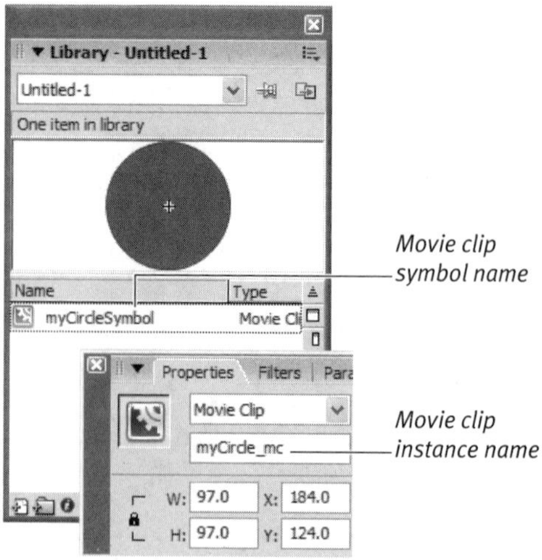

Figure 3.40 The name of the movie clip symbol appears in the Library (`myCircleSymbol`), and the name of the movie clip instance appears in the Property inspector (`myCircle_mc`).

Calling methods

The next step after creating a new object involves calling the object's methods. Recollect that you can call a method by using an object's name followed by a period and then the method with its parameters within parentheses. All the methods of a particular class can be found in the Methods category of that class category in the Actions toolbox (**Figure 3.41**).

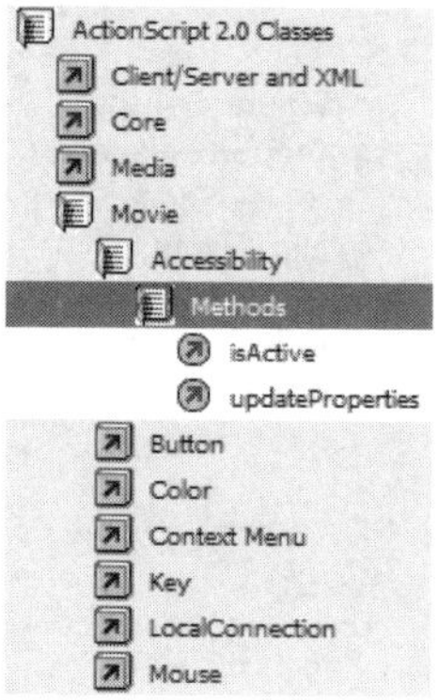

Figure 3.41 Below every class category, a Methods folder lists the methods you can choose to use. The methods of the `Accessibility` class are shown here.

There are three ways to enter a method in the Script pane; but, ultimately, your final ActionScript will look the same no matter which method you use. Your code in the Script pane will look something like this:

```
myData_array.join("-");
```

This statement calls the method `join()` of the `Array` object. The parameter is the string `"-"`.

Your ActionScript could also look something like this:

```
currentDate = myDate_date.getDate()
```

This statement calls the method `getDate()` from the `myDate_date` object and puts the information it retrieves into the variable `currentDate`.

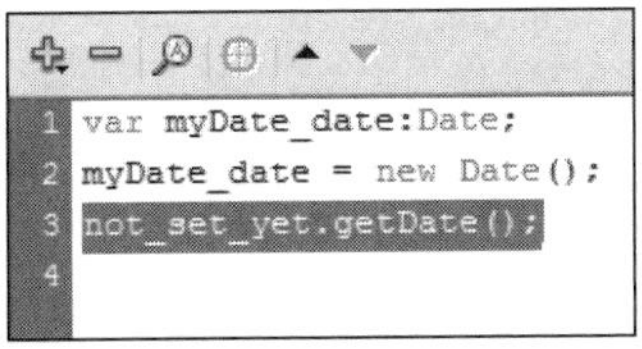
var myDate_date:Date;
myDate_date = new Date();
not_set_yet.getDate();

Figure 3.42 The placeholder `not_set_yet` that appears before the method should be replaced by the name of your `Date` object.

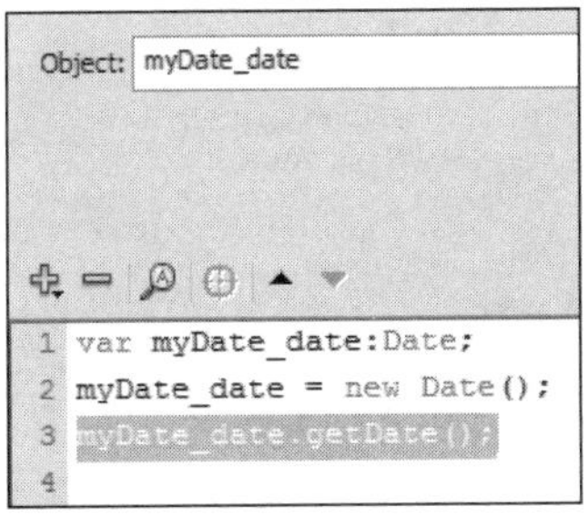
Object: myDate_date
var myDate_date:Date;
myDate_date = new Date();
myDate_date.getDate();

Figure 3.43 The `Date` object called `myDate_date` retrieves the current date from your computer's internal clock.

The following task continues the task "To instantiate an object" and calls a method of your newly created `Date` object. Later chapters introduce specific classes, provide more information about the `Date` class, and show you how to use methods to control your Flash movie.

In the following task, Flash calls the `getDate()` method, which retrieves the current date. The information that a method gets is called the *returned value*. In order for the user to see the returned value and verify that the method works, you must put that information in a variable and display it in a dynamic text field. You'll learn more about text fields in Chapter 11.

To call a method of an object:

1. Continuing with the task "To instantiate an object," choose ActionScript 2.0 Classes > Core > Date > Methods > getDate.

   The `getDate()` method appears with a placeholder `not_set_yet` before it (**Figure 3.42**).

2. In the Object field, enter the name of your `Date` object.

   The completed statement, consisting of the object name followed by a dot and the method, appears in the Script pane (**Figure 3.43**).

To display the results of the getDate method:

1. Continue with the previous task. Select the last line of the script, which reads `myDate_date.getDate();`, and click the "Delete action" (minus) button.

2. Choose Statements > Variables > "set variable" to add a `set variable` action.

3. In the Variable field, enter `myTextField_txt` and then a period (.), and choose "text" from the code hint menu that appears (**Figure 3.44**).

4. In the Value field, enter `myDate_date` and then a period (.), and choose getDate from the code hint menu. Also select the Expression check box next to the Value field.

   The returned value of the method will be displayed in the text field called `myTextField_txt` (**Figure 3.45**).

5. Select the Text tool, and drag out an empty text field on the Stage.

6. In the Property inspector, choose Dynamic Text from the pull-down menu, and in the <Instance Name> field, enter `myTextField_txt` (**Figure 3.46**).

7. Test your movie by choosing Control > Test movie.

   Flash instantiates a `Date` object and then calls the `getDate()` method. The returned value (the day of the month) is put in the `text` property of your text field on the Stage.

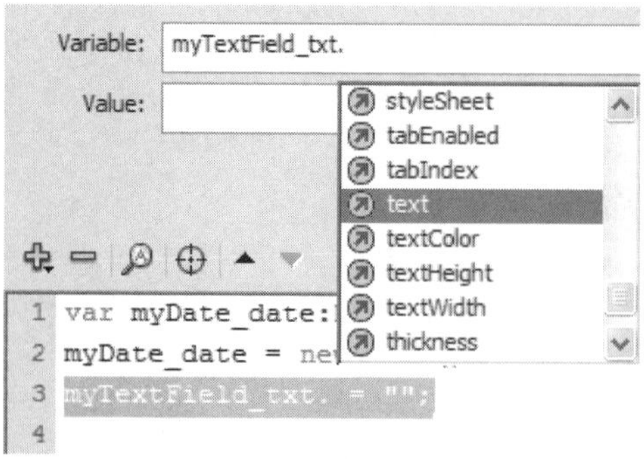

Figure 3.44 Select the desired property from the code hint pull-down menu for your object. Here, the properties of the `TextField` class appear.

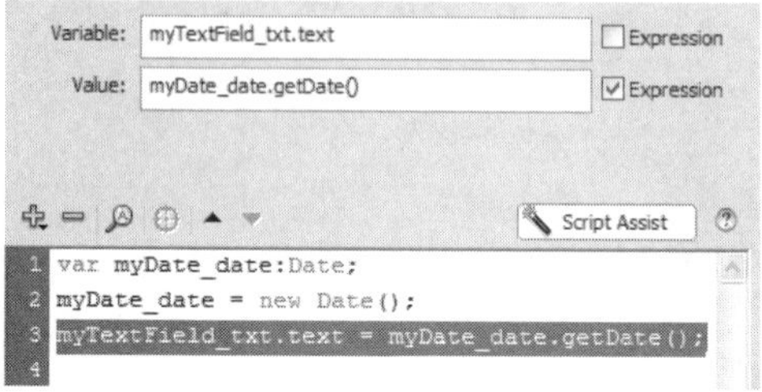

Figure 3.45 Assign the results of the `getDate()` method to the `text` property of a text field called `myTextField_txt`.

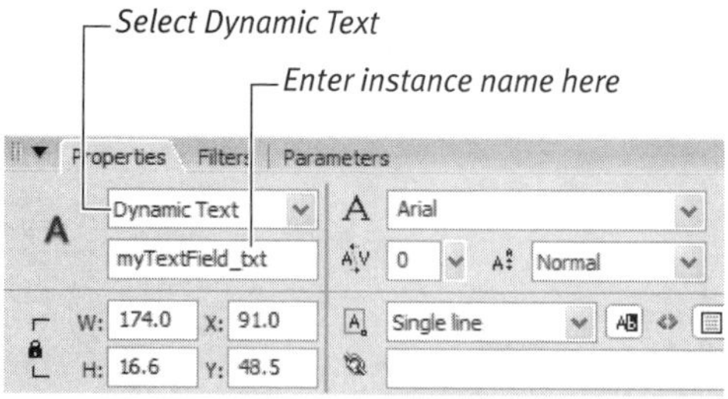

Figure 3.46 Your text field on the Stage should be set to Dynamic Text with `myTextField_txt` entered as the instance name.

Assigning properties

Just as you have multiple ways to call a method, you have multiple ways to assign properties in the Actions panel. No matter which way you go, in the end, keep in mind that you want the Script pane to display your object name followed by a dot and then the property name. If you want to assign a value to a property, that value goes on the right side of an equals sign.

This statement assigns the word *hello* to the `text` property of the object called `myTextField_txt`:

```
myTextField_txt.text = "hello";
```

If you want to read the value of a property and put it in a variable to use later, the object-dot-property construction goes on the right side of an equals sign.

The following statement puts the value of the `text` property of the object called `myTextField_txt` in the variable called `myText`:

```
var myText:String =
myTextField_txt.text;
```

To assign a value to a property:

1. In the Script pane, choose Statements > Variables > "set variable". In the Variable field, enter the name of your object, followed by a period.

   The code hint pull-down menu appears, displaying a list of choices available to the particular object.

2. Select the desired property.

   The statement consisting of the object name, a dot, and the property appears.

continues on next page

3. In the Value field, enter a value for the property.

   If the new value is not a literal text value, select the Expression check box next to the Value field.

   A new value is assigned to the property (**Figure 3.47**).

   or

1. In the Script pane, choose Statements > Variables > "set variable". In the Variable field, enter the name of your object.
2. With the cursor still in the Variable field, choose a property using the "Add item" (plus) button.

   Properties are located inside each class's folder in the ActionScript 2.0 Classes folder.

   The statement consisting of the object name, a dot, and the property appears.
3. In the Value field, enter a property value.

   If the new value is not a literal text value, select the Expression check box next to the Value field.

   A new value is assigned to the property.

   or

1. Choose a property from the Actions toolbox.

   Properties are located inside each class's folder in the ActionScript 2.0 Classes folder.

   The statement consisting of a placeholder name, a dot, and the property appears (**Figure 3.48**).
2. In the Expression field, replace the placeholder `not_set_yet` with the name of your object.
3. In the same field, enter an equals sign and then a value for the property.

   A new value is assigned to the property (**Figure 3.49**).

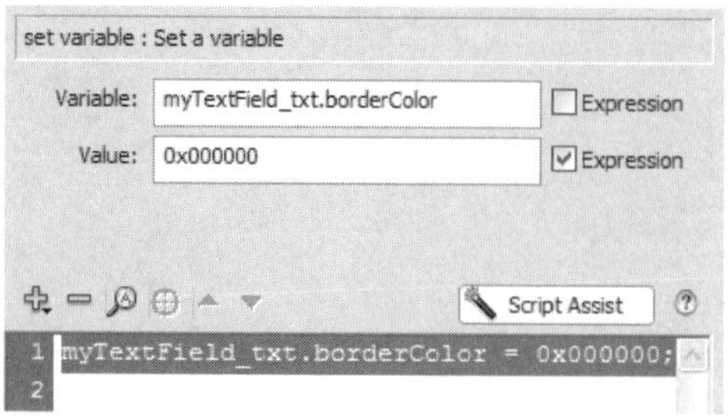

Figure 3.47 The `borderColor` property takes a hex number as its value. The final statement makes the border color of the text field called `myTextField_txt` black.

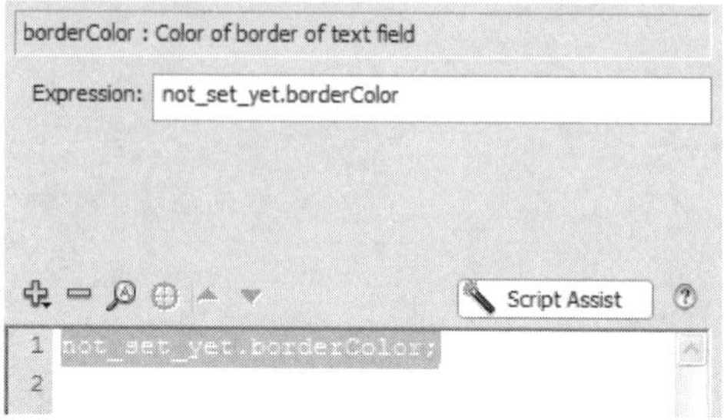

Figure 3.48 The placeholder `not_yet_set` that appears before the property should be replaced by the name of your own object.

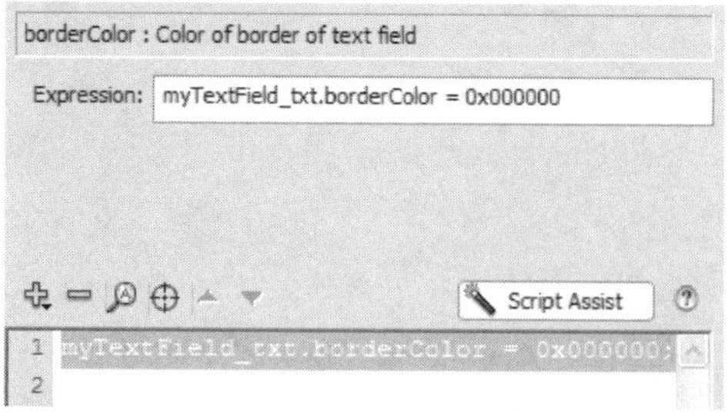

Figure 3.49 Assigning a value to a property using the Expression field gives you more free-form control for writing your actions.

About Functions

If objects and classes are at the heart of ActionScript, functions must lie in the brain. Functions are the organizers of ActionScript. Functions group related ActionScript statements to perform a specific task. Often, you need to write code to do a certain thing over and over. Functions eliminate the tedium of manually duplicating the code by putting it in one place where you can call on it to do its job from anywhere and at any time, as many times as necessary.

As you learned earlier in this chapter, the objects Adam, Betty, and Zeke can perform certain tasks, called methods. If these objects were to put on a dinner party, they could organize themselves and do the following:

```
Adam.answerDoor();
Betty.serveDinner();
Zeke.chitChat();
```

But every Friday night when they have a dinner party, you'll have to write the same three lines of code—not very efficient if these objects plan to entertain often. Instead, you can write a function that groups the code in one spot:

```
function dinnerParty() {
    Adam.answerDoor();
    Betty.serveDinner();
    Zeke.chitChat();
}
```

Now, every Friday night, you can invoke the function by name and write the code `dinnerParty()`. The three statements inside the function's curly braces will be executed. You can add a function by choosing Statements > User-Defined Functions > function (Esc-fn).

You'll also be using *anonymous functions*. As their name suggests, anonymous functions aren't named. Anonymous functions don't work alone and must be assigned to another object:

```
myButton_btn.onPress = function() {
    Adam.answerDoor();
    Betty.serveDinner();
    Zeke.chitChat();
};
```

Now your three friends perform their jobs when the object called `myButton_btn` is clicked.

You'll learn much more about named functions and anonymous functions in the upcoming chapters, after you have a few more actions and concepts under your belt. Anonymous functions are important for handling events (Chapter 4). Named functions are important for building reusable code (Chapter 12).

Using Comments

After you've built a strong vocabulary of Flash actions and are constructing complex statements in the Actions panel, you should include remarks in your scripts to remind yourself and your collaborators of the goals of the ActionScript. Comments help you keep things straight as you develop intricate interactivity and relationships among objects (**Figure 3.50**).

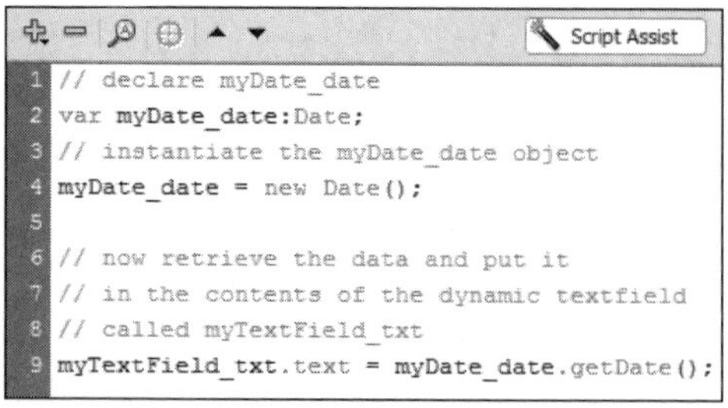

Figure 3.50 Comments interspersed with ActionScript statements help make sense of the code.

To create a comment:

- In Script Assist mode only, in the Script pane, choose Global Functions > Miscellaneous Functions > comment. Enter your comments in the Comment field.

  or

- In the Script pane, type two slashes (//) followed by your comments.

  Comments appear in a different color than the rest of the script, making them easy to locate.

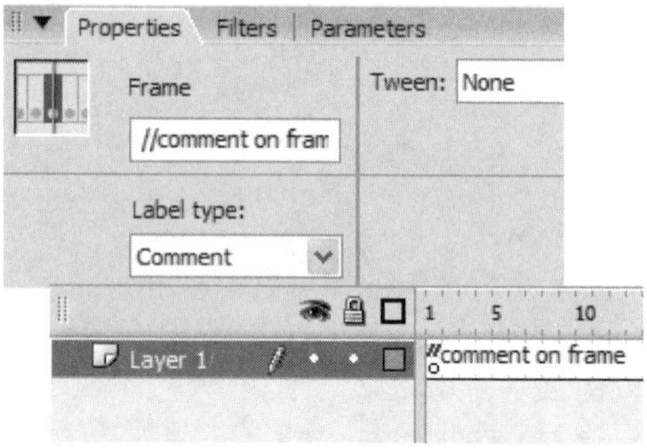

Figure 3.51 In the Property inspector, double slashes indicate a comment in a frame label.

✔ Tips

- If you have a long comment, break it up with multiple comment statements. That way, you'll have separate lines and you won't have to scroll the Script pane horizontally to see the end of a long remark.
- If a long comment spans multiple lines, you can select the Multiline check box in Script Assist mode. Or, if you're typing, use a slash and an asterisk (/*) to mark the beginning of a comment block and an asterisk and a slash (*/) to mark the end, as in the following examples:

```
/* This begins the comment. Even text in between is considered part of the comment.

This is the end of the comment.

*/
```

- Don't worry about creating too many comments. Comments aren't compiled with the rest of the script, so they won't bog down performance. Also, because they aren't included in the exported SWF file, they don't increase the final file size.
- The slash convention for creating comments in ActionScript is the same for creating them in keyframes. When you choose Comment in the "Label type" pull-down menu in the Property inspector, the name in the <Frame Label> field automatically begins with two slashes (//). You can also enter two slashes manually to begin a frame comment (**Figure 3.51**).

Part III: Navigating Timelines and Communicating

Advanced Buttons and Event Detection

4

Creating graphics and animation in Flash is only half the story. You can incorporate interactivity via buttons, the keyboard, and the mouse to give the viewer control of those graphics and animation. Interactivity is essential for basic site navigation and e-commerce interfaces on the Web, as well as for game development, online tutorials, or anything else that requires the viewer to make choices.

What makes a movie interactive? Interactivity is the back-and-forth communication between the user and the movie. In a Flash movie, the user might react to something that's going on by moving the pointer, clicking the mouse button, or pressing a key on the keyboard. That reaction may trigger a response from the Flash movie, which in turn prompts the user to do something else. The things that the user does—mouse movements, button clicks, or keyboard presses—are part of things that happen, called *events*. Events form the basis of interactivity. There are many kinds of events, even events that happen without the user knowing about them. You'll learn to detect these events and create the responses to events in statements conveniently known as *event handlers*.

This chapter first introduces events, event handlers, and anonymous functions used for event handling. Next, it explores the simplest class that handles events: the `Button` class. You'll learn how to extend its functionality by creating invisible buttons, tweening button instances, and creating fully animated buttons. You'll tackle the issues involved in creating a more complex button, such as a pull-down menu, which includes different button events, tracking options, and movie clips. You'll also learn about the `Key` class, the `Mouse` class, and the classes that control the contextual menu, as well as how to create actions that run continuously. Understanding these classes and event handling is essential to creating Flash interactivity because these elements are the scaffold on which you'll hang virtually all your ActionScript.

Events and Event Handlers

Events are things that happen that Flash can recognize and respond to. A button click is an event, as are button rollovers, mouse movements, and keypresses on the keyboard. Events can also be things that the user can't control. The completion of a sound, for example, is an event. Events can even occur regularly.

With all these events happening, you need a way to detect and respond to them. Event handlers are statements that perform this task. *Event handlers* perform certain actions as a response to events. You can create an event handler to detect a click of a button, for example. In response, you can make Flash go to another frame in a different scene.

Event handlers are associated with particular Flash classes. Button presses, rollovers, and releases are associated with the `Button` class. The pressing of a key is associated with the `Key` class. And the completion of a sound is associated with the `Sound` class. You'll learn about all these events as you learn about the classes themselves. Let's begin with the `Button` class.

The Button Class

The `Button` class handles the events involving how the pointer interacts with a button; to a limited extent, it also handles keyboard presses. To assign an event handler to a button, you first give your button an instance name in the Property inspector. Then you write ActionScript on a frame on the main Timeline that references that button instance name. In the Actions panel, you start by entering the instance name of your button followed by a dot and then an event that is assigned an anonymous function. If your button were named `myButton_btn`, then your code would look similar to this:

```
myButton_btn.onRelease = function() {
};
```

where `onRelease` represents a specific kind of button event. Other kinds of button events are possible.

You then add ActionScript between the curly braces of the event handler. Those actions will be performed whenever the event happens.

The `onRelease` button event is the typical trigger for button interactivity. The event is triggered when the mouse button is released inside the area defined by the `Hit` state of a button symbol. This setup allows viewers to change their minds and release the mouse button over a safe spot outside the hit area even after they've already clicked a button. Other types of button events make possible a range of interactions. **Table 4.1** lists all the button events.

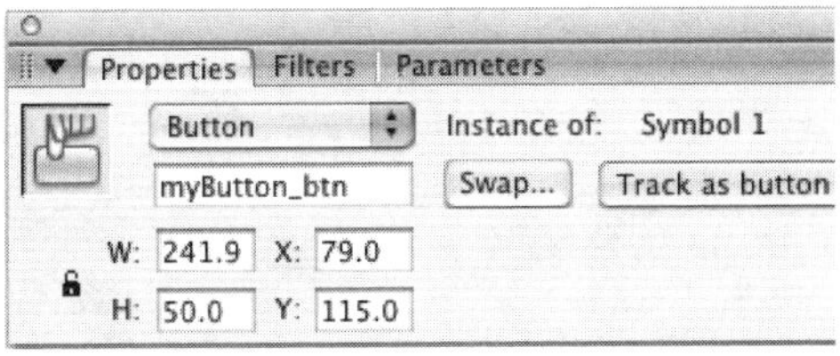

Figure 4.1 The button instance is called `myButton_btn` in the Property inspector.

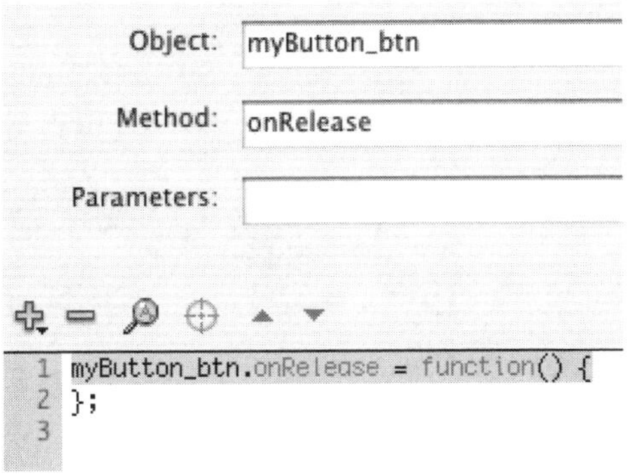

Figure 4.2 The response to the button click hasn't yet been added to the event handler.

To assign an event handler on the Timeline:

1. Create a button symbol, and place an instance of the button on the Stage.
2. Select the button instance, and enter a descriptive name in the Property inspector. Make sure to add the suffix `_btn` to the name (**Figure 4.1**).

   This name is the name of your button object; you'll use it to reference the button from ActionScript. This name is *not* the same one that appears in your Library.
3. Select the first frame of the main Timeline, and open the Actions panel.
4. In the Actions toolbox or using the Add Action (+) button, choose an event from ActionScript 2.0 Classes > Movie > Button > Event Handlers. Enter the instance name of your button in the Object field.

   An anonymous function is assigned for the event (**Figure 4.2**).

continues on next page

Table 4.1

Button Events

Button Event	Triggered When...
`onPress`	The pointer is over the hit area and the mouse button is pressed.
`onRelease`	The pointer is over the hit area and the mouse button is pressed and released.
`oReleaseOutside`	The pointer is over the hit area and the mouse button is pressed, and then the pointer is dragged and released outside the hit area.
`onRollover`	The pointer moves over the hit area.
`onRollOut`	The pointer moves from the hit area off the hit area.
`onDragOver`	The pointer is over the hit area and the mouse button is pressed, and then the pointer is moved off the hit area and back over the hit area while the button remains pressed.
`onDragOut`	The pointer is over the hit area and the mouse button is pressed, and then the pointer is moved off the hit area while the button remains pressed.
`onKeyDown`	The button has keyboard focus and a keyboard key is pressed.
`onKeyUp`	The button has keyboard focus and a keyboard key is released.
`onSetFocus`	The button receives keyboard focus through the Tab key. (The button is highlighted by a yellow rectangle when the Tab key is used to select a button on the Stage.)
`onKillFocus`	The button loses keyboard focus through the Tab key. (The button is highlighted by a yellow rectangle when the Tab key is used to select a button on the Stage.)

5. With the line selected that contains the `function()` declaration, choose an action as the response to the event (**Figure 4.3**).

✔ Tips

- As described in Chapter 3, it's recommended that you end all instance names for buttons with `_btn` so that Flash can provide the appropriate code hints in the Script pane.
- When you create your event handler on the main Timeline, your button must be present on the Stage at the same time to receive its instructions. If you create the event handler in keyframe 1, for example, but your button doesn't appear until keyframe 10, your button won't respond to the event handler.

To select different button events:

1. Highlight the existing button event, and press the Delete key (**Figure 4.4**).
2. Type in the name of the event that should trigger the actions.

✔ Tips

- If you want to assign more than one event by using an anonymous function, you can create separate function statements or you can assign one event handler to the other using a `set variable` action. The code looks like this:

```
myButton_btn.onPress = function() {};
myButton_btn.onRelease =
myButton_btn.onPress;
```

  The second line essentially duplicates the anonymous function from the `onPress` event handler to the `onRelease` handler, so that they both call the same anonymous function (**Figure 4.5**).

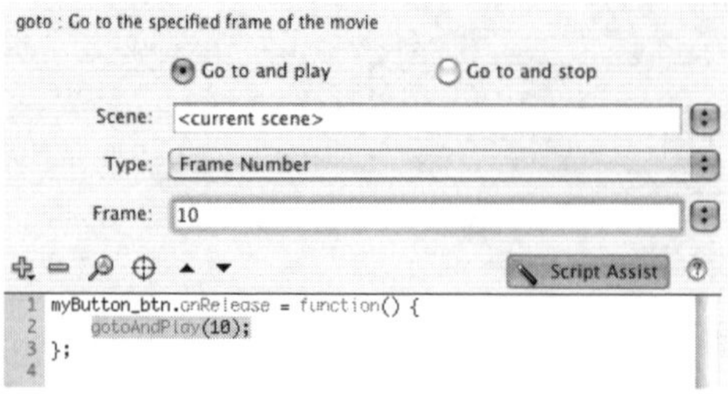

Figure 4.3 When the viewer presses and releases the button called `myButton_btn`, Flash goes to frame 10 and begins playing. Compare this script with the one in Figure 4.2.

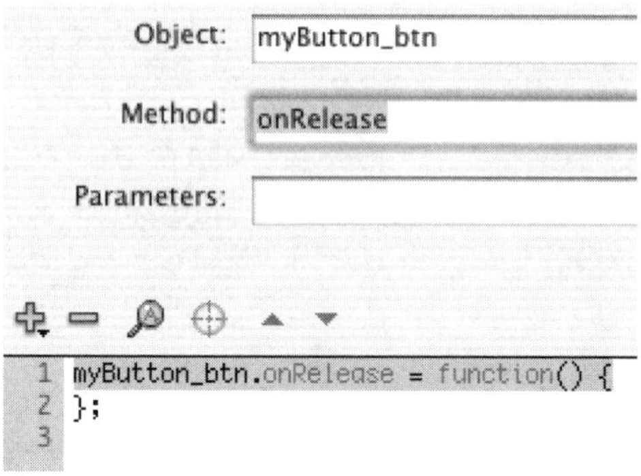

Figure 4.4 Change the button event by highlighting it and choosing another.

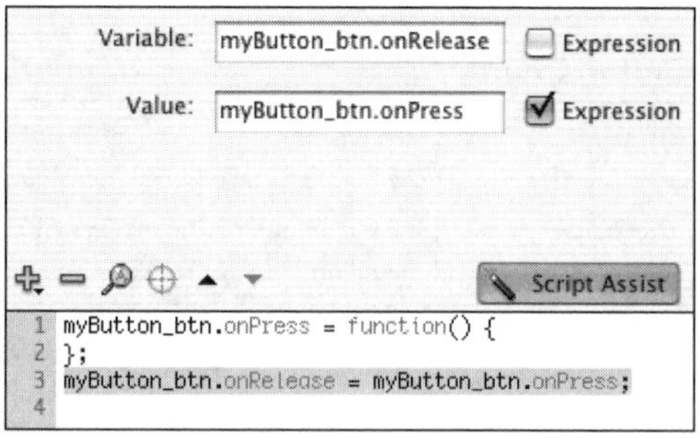

Figure 4.5 If either the `onPress` or `onRelease` event happens, Flash performs the same actions.

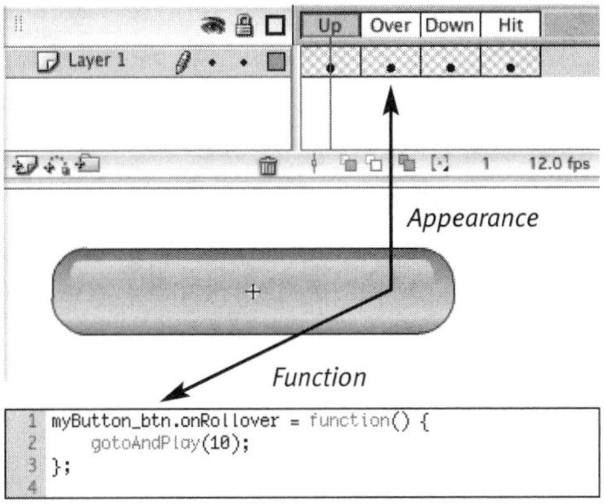

Figure 4.6 The `Over` state of the button symbol (top) defines how the button looks when the pointer is over the `Hit` state. An `onRollOver` event handler (bottom) defines what the button does when the pointer is over the `Hit` state.

- Within one button instance, if you want one event to have a different consequence than another event has, you must create separate anonymous function statements. To have the `onRollOver` event make your movie play and the `onRollOut` event make your movie stop, your actions look like this:

```
myButton_btn.onRollOver = function() {
 play();
};
myButton_btn.onRollOut = function() {
    stop();
};
```

- Don't confuse the `onRollover` button event with the `Over` keyframe of your button symbol. Both involve detecting when the pointer is over the hit area; but the `Over` state describes how your button looks when the mouse is over the hit area, whereas the `onRollover` event assigns an action when that event occurs. The keyframes of a button symbol define how it looks, and the event handler defines what it does (**Figure 4.6**).

onPress or on (press)?

So far, you've seen only one way to assign event handlers to buttons: by assigning an anonymous function in code on the main Timeline. There is another way to assign an event handler to a button. This older technique involves attaching the event handler code directly to the button instance by selecting the button before typing in the code. You use a special event handler syntax known as an `on (event)` statement to define the event handler code. For example, the following code, attached directly to a button instance on the Stage, would achieve the same functionality as the code in Figure 4.3:

```
on (release) {
    gotoAndPlay(10);
}
```

Experienced ActionScript developers as well as Macromedia's documentation say that it's better practice to assign event handlers on the main Timeline. This method keeps all your ActionScript code in one place rather than scattered among individual buttons on the Stage. As your movie becomes more complex and you have more buttons to deal with, you'll find it easier to isolate and revise button events. Putting the event handler on the main Timeline also forces you to name your button instances so that you can target and control their properties with ActionScript.

Assigning event handlers directly to button instances is required, however, if you're creating a Flash document that will be published for Flash Player 4 or for Flash Lite 1.1 or earlier. (Flash Lite is the version of the Flash Player that is used on many portable devices such as cell phones.) If you plan to target one of those players, you'll want to be comfortable using both `on (press)` and `onPress`.

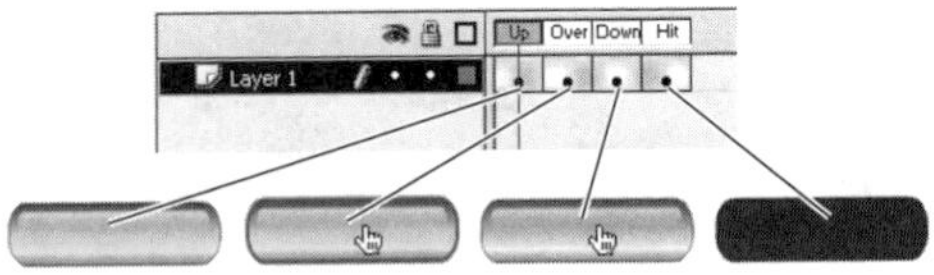

Figure 4.7 The four keyframes of a button symbol.

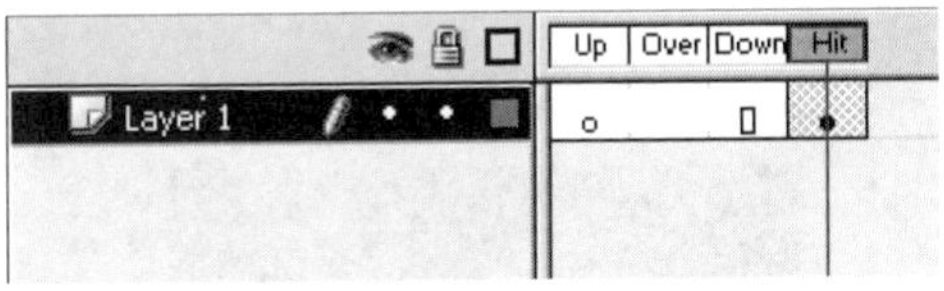

Figure 4.8 An invisible button has only the `Hit` keyframe defined.

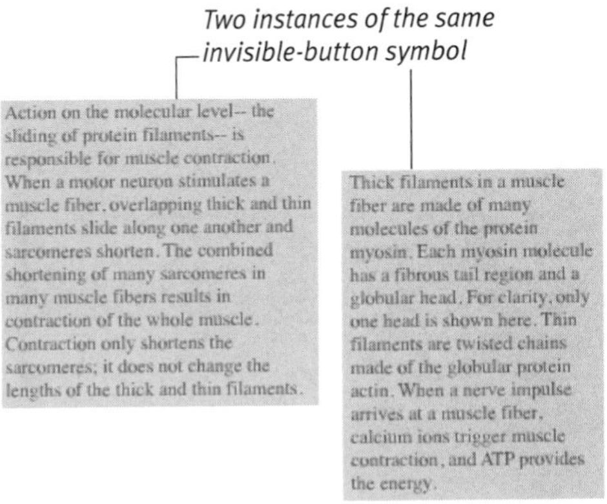

Figure 4.9 Invisible-button instances over text blocks.

Invisible Buttons

Flash lets you define four special keyframes of a button symbol that describe how the button looks and responds to the mouse: the `Up`, `Over`, `Down`, and `Hit` states. The `Up` state shows what the button looks like when the pointer isn't over the button. `Over` shows what the button looks like when the pointer is over the button. `Down` shows what the button looks like when the pointer is over the button with the mouse button pressed. And `Hit` defines the actual active, or *hot*, area of the button (**Figure 4.7**).

You can exploit the flexibility of Flash buttons by defining only particular states. If you leave empty keyframes in all states except for the `Hit` state, you create an invisible button (**Figure 4.8**). Invisible buttons are extremely useful for creating multiple generic hotspots to which you can assign actions. By placing invisible button instances on top of graphics, you essentially have the power to make anything on the Stage react to the mouse pointer. If you want the user to read several blocks of text in succession, you can have the user click each paragraph to advance to the next one. Instead of creating separate buttons out of each text block, make just one invisible button and stretch instances to fit each block. Assign actions to each invisible-button instance that covers the paragraphs (**Figure 4.9**).

When you drag an instance of an invisible button onto the Stage, you see the hit area as a transparent blue shape, which allows you to place the button precisely. When you choose Control > Enable Simple Buttons (Ctrl-Alt-B for Windows, Cmd-Option-B for Mac), the button disappears to show you its playback appearance.

To create an invisible button:

1. Choose Insert > New Symbol (Cmd-F8 for Mac, Ctrl-F8 for Windows).

   The Symbol Properties dialog box appears.

2. Type the symbol name of your button, choose Button as the behavior, and click OK.

   A new button symbol is created in the Library, and you enter symbol-editing mode.

3. Select the `Hit` keyframe.

4. Choose Insert > Timeline > Keyframe (F6).

   A new keyframe is created in the `Hit` state.

5. With the `Hit` keyframe selected, draw a generic shape that serves as the hotspot for your invisible button (**Figure 4.10**).

6. Return to the main Timeline.

7. Drag an instance of the symbol from the Library onto the Stage.

   A transparent blue shape appears on the Stage, indicating the `Hit` state of your invisible button.

8. Move, scale, and rotate the invisible-button instance to cover any graphic.

   When you choose Control > Enable Simple Buttons, the transparent blue area disappears, but your pointer changes to a hand to indicate the presence of a button.

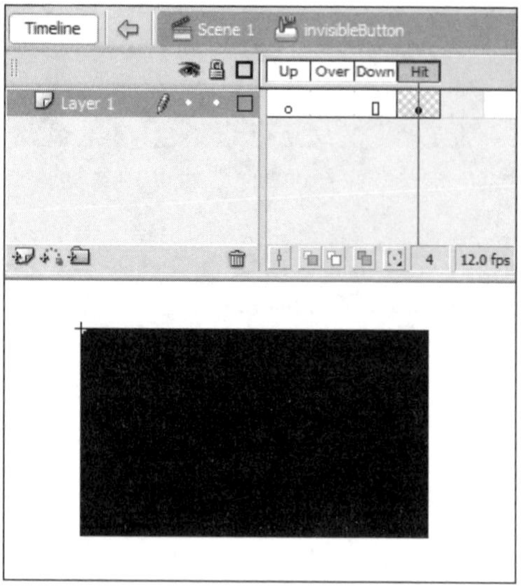

Figure 4.10 An invisible-button symbol. The rectangle in the `Hit` keyframe defines the active area of the button.

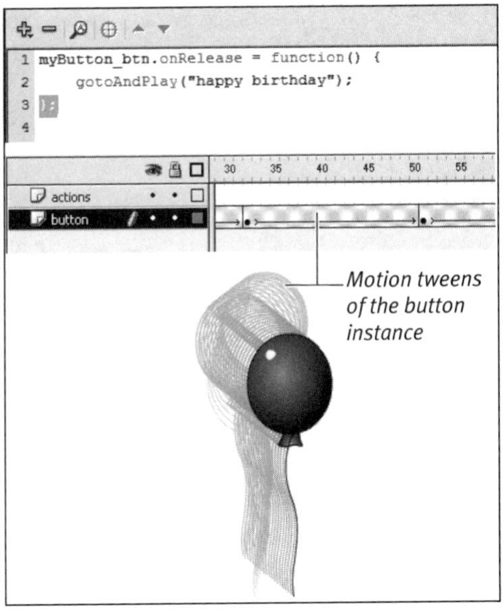

Figure 4.11 This balloon is a button that floats up and down in a motion tween. The event handler for this button is assigned on the main Timeline (top). When the user clicks the moving balloon, Flash sends the user to a frame label called "happy birthday" (not shown here).

Tweening Buttons

You can tween buttons just as you do any other kind of symbol instance. This allows you to create menus and interfaces that move and still respond to the pointer and carry out actions assigned to them.

To apply a motion tween to a button:

1. Choose Insert > New Symbol, and create a button symbol.
2. Return to the main movie Timeline, and drag an instance of the button symbol onto the Stage. In the Property inspector, give a name to your button instance.
3. Create a motion tween as you normally would for a graphic instance.

   Insert new keyframes, move or transform each instance, and then choose Motion Tween in the Property inspector.
4. Create a new Layer, select the first keyframe, and open the Actions panel.
5. Assign an event handler to the button as previously described, coding in this form:

   ```
   myButton_btn.onRelease = function() {
       // add your actions here
   };
   ```
6. Test your movie.

   Throughout its tween, the button instance is active and responds to your pointer (**Figure 4.11**).

Animated Buttons and the Movie Clip Symbol

Animated buttons display an animation in any of the first three keyframes (`Up`, `Over`, and `Down`) of the button symbol. A button can spin when the pointer rolls over it, for example, because you have an animation of the spinning button in the `Over` state. How do you fit an animation into only one keyframe of the button symbol? Use a movie clip.

A *movie clip* is a special kind of symbol that allows you to have animations that run regardless of where they are or how many actual frames the instance occupies. This feature is possible because a movie clip's Timeline runs independently of any other Timeline, including other movie clip Timelines and the main movie Timeline in which the movie clip resides. This independence means that as long as you establish an instance on the Stage, a movie clip animation plays all its frames regardless of where it is. Placing a movie clip instance in a keyframe of a button symbol makes the movie clip play whenever that particular keyframe is displayed. That is the basis of an animated button.

An animation of a butterfly flapping its wings, for example, may take 10 frames in a movie clip symbol. Placing an instance of that movie clip on the Stage in a movie that has only one frame still lets you see the butterfly flapping its wings (**Figure 4.12**). This functionality is useful for cyclical animations that play no matter what else may be going on in the current Timeline. Blinking eyes, for example, can be a movie clip placed on a character's face. No matter what the character does—whether it's moving or static in the current Timeline—the eyes blink continuously.

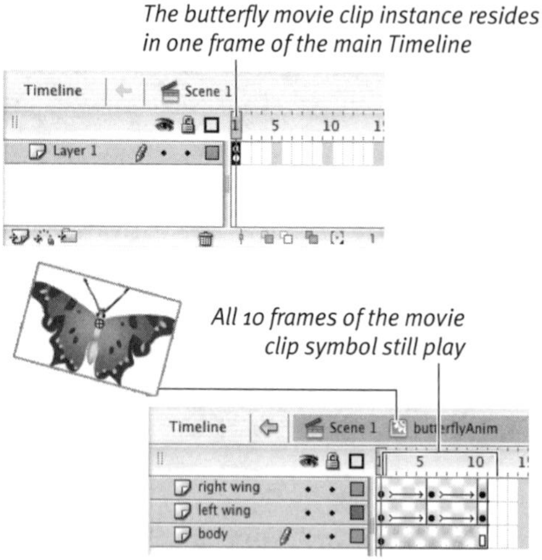
The butterfly movie clip instance resides in one frame of the main Timeline
Timeline
Scene 1
Layer 1
All 10 frames of the movie clip symbol still play
Timeline
Scene 1
butterflyAnim
right wing
left wing
body

Figure 4.12 Movie clips have independent Timelines.

Comparing a Movie Clip Instance with a Graphic Instance

How does a movie clip instance differ from a graphic instance? If you create the same animation in both a movie clip symbol and a graphic symbol and then place both instances on the Stage, the differences become clear. The graphic instance shows its animation in the authoring environment, displaying however many frames are available in the main Timeline. If the graphic symbol contains an animation lasting ten frames and the instance occupies four frames of the main Timeline, you see only four frames of the animation. Movie clips, on the other hand, don't work in the Flash authoring environment. You need to export the movie as a SWF file to see any movie clip animation or functionality. When you export the movie (you can do so by choosing Control > Test Movie), Flash plays the movie clip instance continuously regardless of the number of frames the instance occupies and even when the movie itself has stopped.

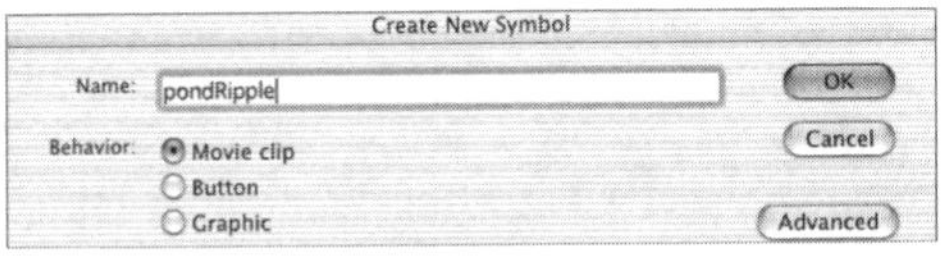

Figure 4.13 Create a new movie clip symbol by naming it and selecting the Movie Clip behavior.

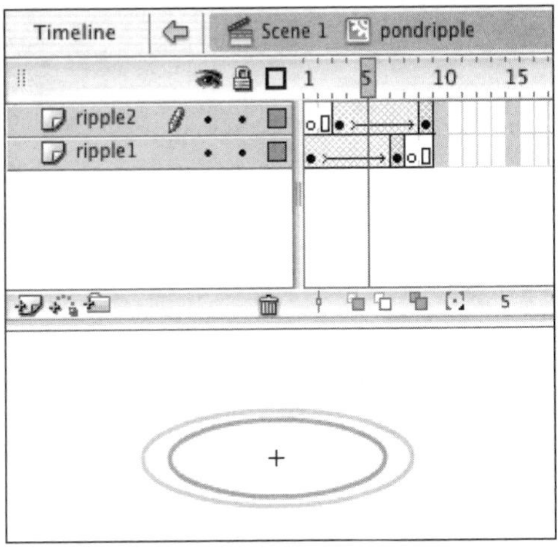

Figure 4.14 The `pondRipple` movie clip symbol contains two tweens of an oval getting bigger and gradually fading.

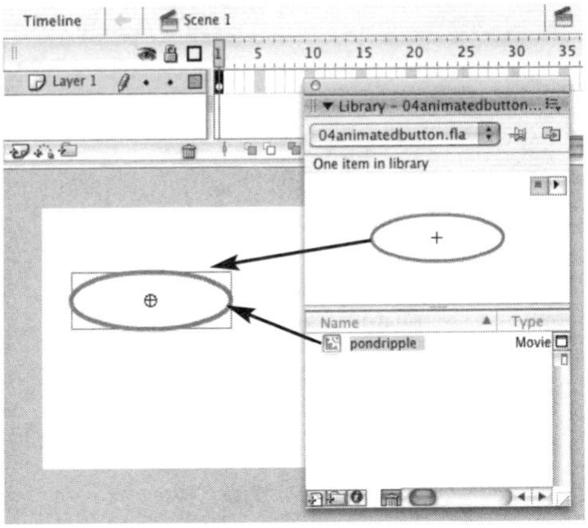

Figure 4.15 Bring an instance of a movie clip symbol onto the Stage by dragging it from the Library.

To create a movie clip:

1. Choose Insert > New Symbol.

   The Symbol Properties dialog box appears.

2. Type a descriptive name for your movie clip symbol, choose Movie Clip as the behavior, and click OK (**Figure 4.13**).

   You now enter symbol-editing mode.

3. Create the graphics and animation on the movie clip Timeline (**Figure 4.14**).

   Notice how the path above the Timeline tells you that you're currently editing a symbol.

4. Return to the main Stage.

   Your movie clip is stored in the Library as a symbol, available for you to bring onto the Stage as an instance (**Figure 4.15**).

✔ Tip

- New instances of movie clips begin playing automatically from the first frame, as do instances in different scenes. Imagine that you build a movie clip animation of a clock whose hand makes a full rotation starting at 12 o'clock. If you place an instance in scene 1 and continue your movie in scene 2, Flash considers the instance in scene 2 to be new; it resets the movie clip animation and begins playing the clock animation at 12 o'clock.

To create an animated button:

1. Create a movie clip symbol that contains an animation, as described in the preceding task.
2. Create a button symbol, and define the four keyframes for the `Up`, `Over`, `Down`, and `Hit` states (**Figure 4.16**).
3. In symbol-editing mode, select the `Up`, `Over`, or `Down` state for your button, depending on when you would like to see the animation.
4. Place an instance of your movie clip symbol on the Stage inside your button symbol (**Figure 4.17**).
5. Return to the main movie Timeline, and drag an instance of your button to the Stage.
6. Choose Control > Test Movie.

   Your button instance plays the movie clip animation continuously as your pointer interacts with the button (**Figure 4.18**).

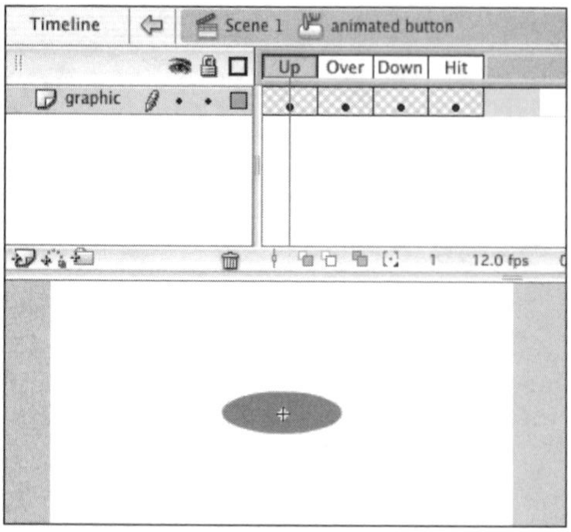

Figure 4.16 A simple button symbol with ovals in all four keyframes.

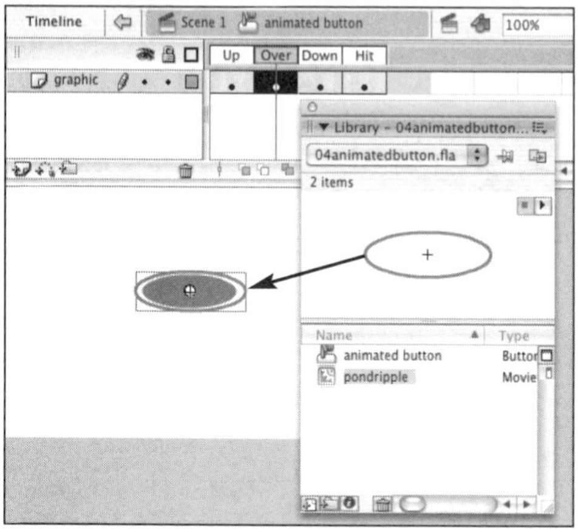

Figure 4.17 The `Over` state of the button symbol. Place an instance of the `pondRipple` movie clip in this keyframe to play the pond-ripple animation whenever the pointer moves over the button.

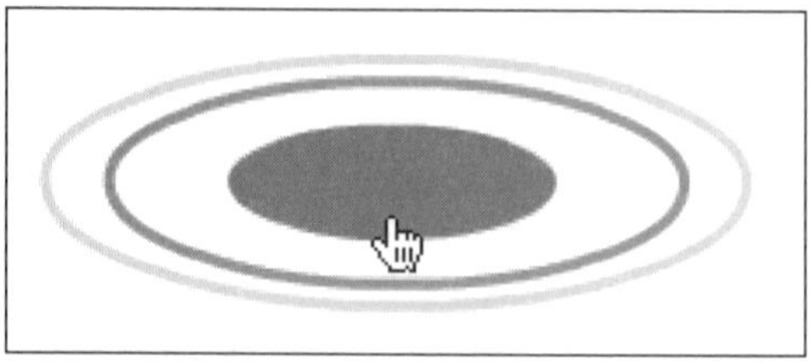

Figure 4.18 The completed animated button. When the pointer passes over the button, the pond-ripple movie clip plays.

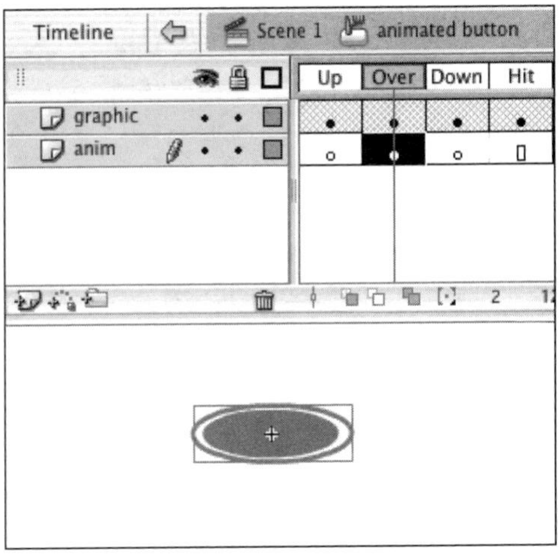

Figure 4.19 A new layer in the button symbol Timeline helps organize the animation.

✔ Tips

- Stop the continuous cycling of your movie clip by placing a `stop` action in the last keyframe of your movie clip symbol. Because movie clips have independent Timelines, they respond to frame actions. Graphic symbols don't respond to any frame actions.
- To better organize animated buttons, it's useful to create a new layer in the Timeline of your button symbol and reserve it specifically for the animation (**Figure 4.19**).

Complex Buttons

You can use a combination of invisible buttons, tweening buttons, animated buttons, and movie clips to create complex buttons such as pull-down menus. The pull-down (or pop-up) menu is a kind of button that is common in operating systems and Web interfaces and is useful for presenting several choices under a single heading. The functionality consists of a single button that expands to show more buttons and collapses when a selection has been made (**Figure 4.20**).

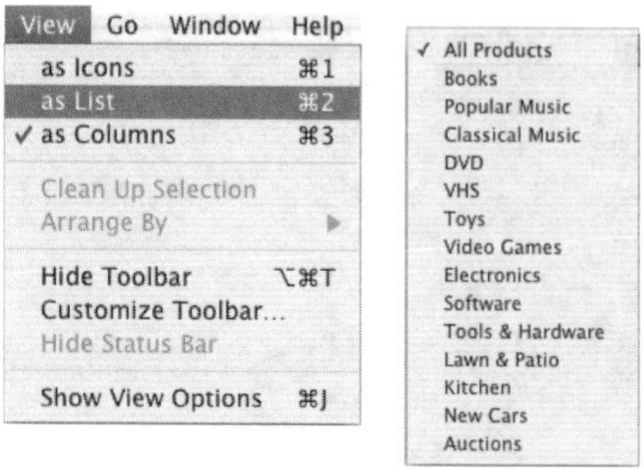

Figure 4.20 Typical pull-down menus: a Mac OS system menu (left) and a Web menu (right).

To build your own pull-down menu, the basic strategy is to place buttons inside a movie clip. The buttons specify which frames within the movie clip Timeline to play. Whether the menu is expanded or collapsed is determined within the movie clip. Placing an instance of this movie clip on the Stage allows you to access either the expanded or collapsed state independently of what's happening in your main movie.

When you understand the concept behind the simple pull-down menu, you can create menus that are more elaborate by adding animation to the transition between the collapsed state and the expanded state. Instead of having the expanded state suddenly pop up, for example, you can create a tween that makes the buttons scroll down gently.

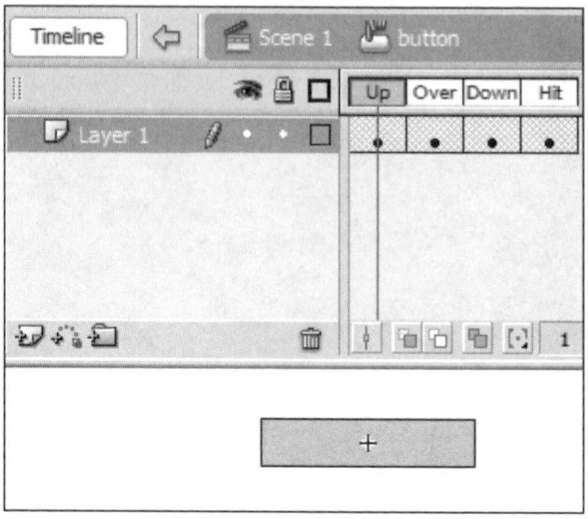

Figure 4.21 A generic button with the four keyframes defined.

To create a simple pull-down menu:

1. Create a button symbol that will be used for the top menu button as well as the choices in the expanded list.
2. Add a filled rectangle to the `Up`, `Over`, `Down`, and `Hit` keyframes (**Figure 4.21**).
3. Create a new movie clip symbol.
   Enter symbol-editing mode for the movie clip.

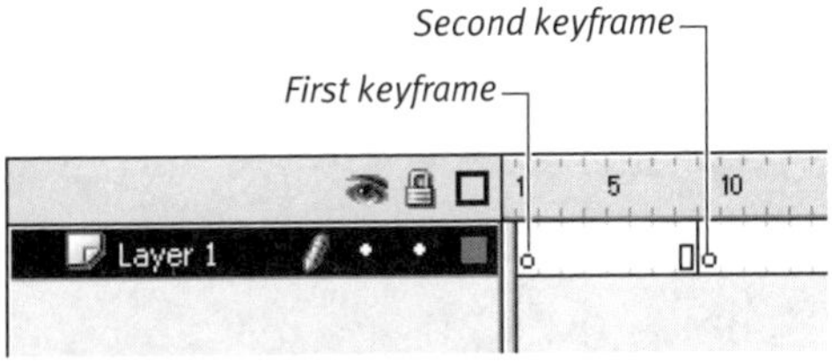

Figure 4.22 The pull-down menu movie clip Timeline contains two keyframes: one at frame 1 and another at frame 9.

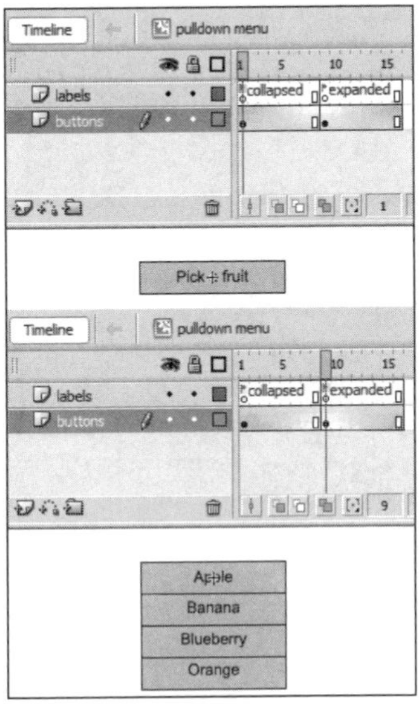

Figure 4.23 The two states of your pull-down menu. The collapsed state is in the first keyframe (top); the expanded state is in the second keyframe (bottom). The expanded state contains four button instances that represent the menu choices.

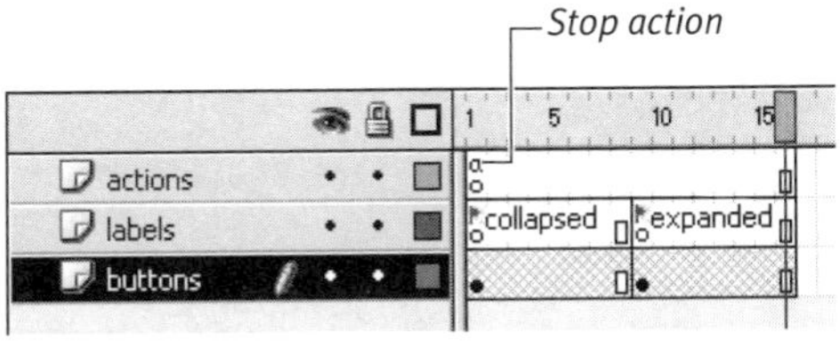

Figure 4.24 The completed movie clip Timeline for the pull-down menu. A `stop` action is assigned to the first frame in the top layer.

4. Insert a new keyframe at a later point in the movie clip Timeline.

   You now have two keyframes. The first one will contain the collapsed state of your menu, and the second one will contain its expanded state (**Figure 4.22**).

5. Drag one instance of your button symbol into the first keyframe, and add text over the instance to describe the button.

   This is the collapsed state of your menu.

6. Drag several instances of your button symbol into the second keyframe, align them with one another, and add text over these instances to describe the buttons.

   This is the expanded state of your menu.

7. Add a new layer, and place labels to mark the collapsed and expanded keyframes (**Figure 4.23**).

   In the Frame Label field of the Property inspector, enter `collapsed` for the first keyframe and `expanded` for the second keyframe.

   The labels let you see clearly the collapsed and expanded states of your movie clip and let you use the `gotoAndStop` action with frame labels instead of frame numbers.

8. Select the button instance in the first keyframe, and give it an instance name.

9. Add a new layer; select the first keyframe in that layer, and open the Actions panel.

10. Add the action `stop` by choosing Global Functions > Timeline Control > stop.

    Without this `stop` in the first frame of your movie clip, the menu would open and close repeatedly because of the automatic cycling of movie clips. The `stop` action ensures that the movie clip stays on frame 1 until you click the menu button (**Figure 4.24**).

continues on next page

11. In the Script pane, add an `onRelease` event handler to the first button by using its instance name followed by the code `.onRelease = function()` (ActionScript 2.0 Classes > Movie > Button > Event Handlers > onRelease).

12. After the first line of the event handler, add the `gotoAndStop` action by choosing Global Functions > Timeline Control > gotoAndStop.

    The `gotoAndStop` action appears inside the event handler.

13. In the Type field, choose Frame Label. Choose "expanded" in the Frame field, to tell the Flash Player that you want Flash to stop at the frame with the label `expanded` (**Figure 4.25**).

    If you're typing in the code directly rather than using Script Assist, be sure to include the quotation marks around the frame label name.

14. Select the first button instance on the last keyframe, and give it an instance name.

15. In the layer with your ActionScript, select the frame above the `expanded` keyframe, and add a new keyframe.

    In this keyframe, you'll add the code for the buttons in the expanded menu. Just like content that you draw on the Stage, ActionScript on the Timeline must be placed on a keyframe.

    You have to put more code here because you can't add event handler code to buttons until they're present on the Stage. Otherwise, Flash won't find the button instances and won't attach the code to them (**Figure 4.26**).

16. With your new keyframe selected, open the Actions panel and add an `onRelease` event handler for the button you just named.

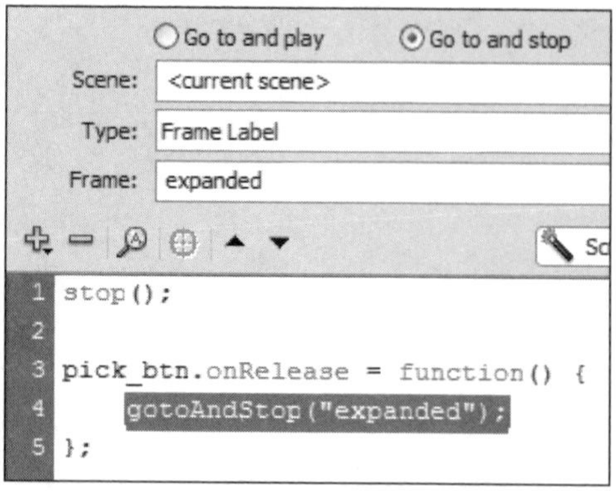

Figure 4.25 This button sends the Flash playhead to the frame labeled `expanded` and stops there.

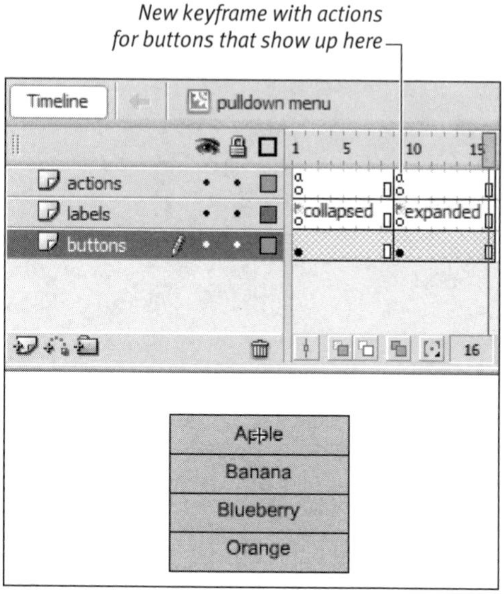

Figure 4.26 When buttons appear on a later frame, add a new keyframe at the same frame number with event handler code for those buttons.

Figure 4.27 This button sends the Flash playhead to the frame labeled `collapsed` and stops there.

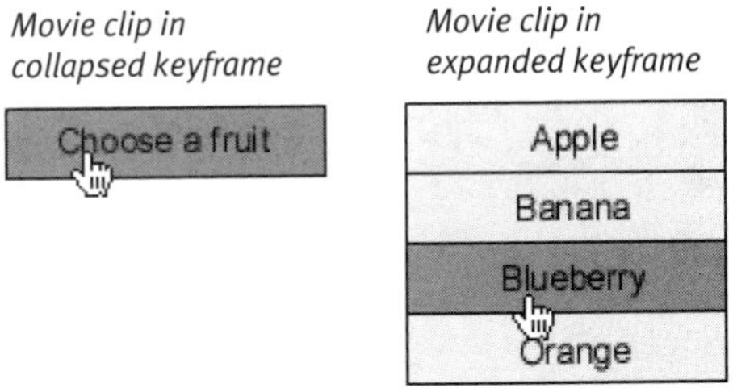

Figure 4.28 The two states of the pull-down menu work independently of the main Timeline.

✔ Tip

- Even in Script Assist mode, you can select one or more lines of code and use edit commands such as Copy and Paste to create similar blocks of code such as event handlers for several buttons. Once you paste in a copy of the code, don't forget to change the name of the button to which the event handler is assigned.

17. Inside the curly braces of the event handler, add a `gotoAndStop` command by selecting Global Functions > Timeline Control > gotoAndStop.

The `gotoAndStop` action appears inside the event handler.

18. Just as you did before, make the action target a frame label; choose `collapsed` as the label of the frame at which you want Flash to stop (**Figure 4.27**).

19. Assign instance names to each of the remaining button instances on this keyframe, and repeat steps 16–18 to add event handler code for each of them.

20. Return to the main movie Timeline, and place an instance of your movie clip on the Stage.

21. Choose Control > Test Movie to see how your pull-down menu works.

When you click the first button, the buttons for your choices appear because you direct the playhead to go to the `expanded` keyframe on the movie clip Timeline. When you click one of the buttons in the expanded state, the buttons disappear, returning you to the `collapsed` keyframe of the movie clip Timeline. All this happens independently of the main movie Timeline, where the movie clip instance resides (**Figure 4.28**).

At this point, you've created a complex button that behaves like a pull-down menu but doesn't actually do anything (except modify itself). In Chapter 5, you'll learn how to make Timelines communicate with one another, which enables you to create complex navigation systems.

To create an animated pull-down menu:

1. Create a simple pull-down menu, as described in the preceding task.
2. Enter symbol-editing mode for your movie clip.
3. Change the actions in the event handler for the button in the first keyframe from `gotoAndStop` to `gotoAndPlay`:

   `gotoAndPlay("expanded");`

   This action makes the playhead go to the label `expanded` and begin playing.
4. Create motion tweens for your button instances in the last keyframe (**Figure 4.29**).

   You must assign instance names to the buttons and add the event handlers to them in the first frame of the tween.
5. In the last frame of the movie clip, insert a keyframe and assign a `stop` action (Global Functions > Timeline control > stop).
6. Return to the main movie Timeline, and place an instance of your movie clip on the Stage.
7. Choose Control > Test Movie to see how your pull-down menu works.

   When you click the first button, the playhead jumps to the label `expanded` in the movie clip and begins playing, showing the motion tweening of your button choices.

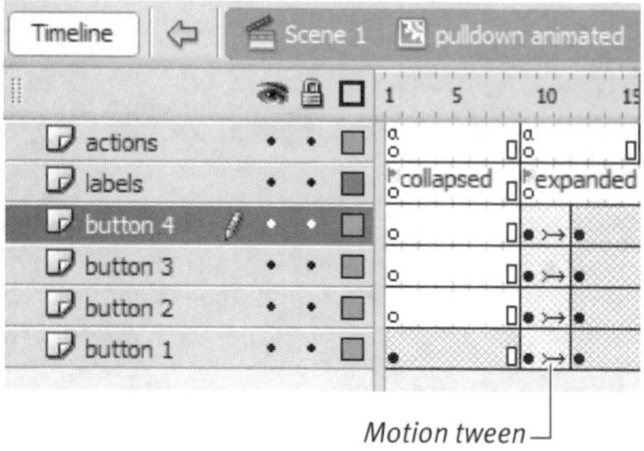

Figure 4.29 The pull-down-menu movie clip. The expanded-menu buttons are separated on different layers so you can motion tween them.

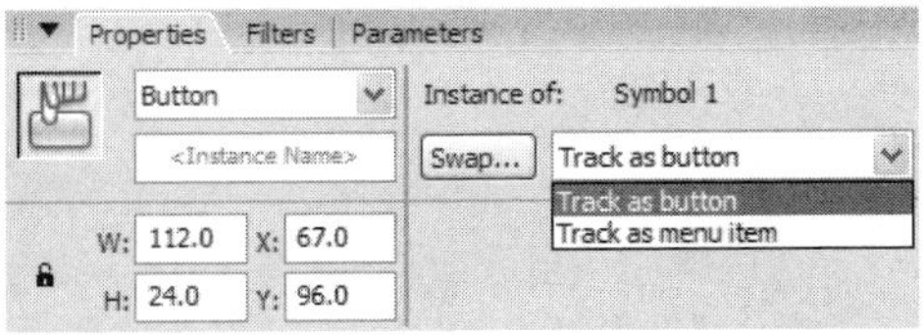

Figure 4.30 The button-tracking options in the Property inspector.

Button-Tracking Options

You can define a button instance in the Property inspector in one of two ways: "Track as button" or "Track as menu item" (**Figure 4.30**). These two tracking options determine whether button instances can receive a button event even after the event has started on a different button instance. The "Track as menu item" option allows this to happen; the "Track as button" option doesn't. The default option, "Track as button," is the typical behavior for buttons; it causes one button event to affect one button instance. More-complex cases, such as pull-down menus, require multiple button instances working together.

Imagine that you click and hold down the menu button to see the pop-up choices, drag your pointer to your selection, and then release the mouse button. You need Flash to recognize the `onRelease` event in the expanded menu even though the `onPress` event occurred in the collapsed menu for a different button instance (in fact, in a different frame altogether). Choosing "Track as menu item" allows these buttons to receive these events and gives you more flexibility to work with combinations of button events.

You can refine the pull-down menu with an `onDragOver` event so that the menu collapses even if no selection is made. This technique is important to keep pull-down menus expanded only when your viewer is making a choice from the menu.

To set "Track as menu item" with the onPress event:

1. Create a pull-down menu, as described in the preceding task.
2. Go to symbol-editing mode for the movie clip.
3. Select the keyframe on frame 1 containing the event handler actions for the button instance in the first keyframe, and change the mouse event to `onPress` (**Figure 4.31**).
4. Select each button instance in the expanded keyframe.
5. In the Property inspector, choose "Track as menu Item" (**Figure 4.32**).

   The button instances in the expanded menu will now trigger an `onRelease` event even if the `onPress` event occurs on a different instance.
6. Return to the main Timeline, and test your movie.

   You now click and hold down the mouse button to keep the menu open.

✔ Tip

- When you set "Track as menu item" for this pull-down menu, the expanded button instances display their `Down` state as you move your pointer over them. This display occurs because your mouse button is, in fact, pressed, but that event occurred earlier on a different instance.

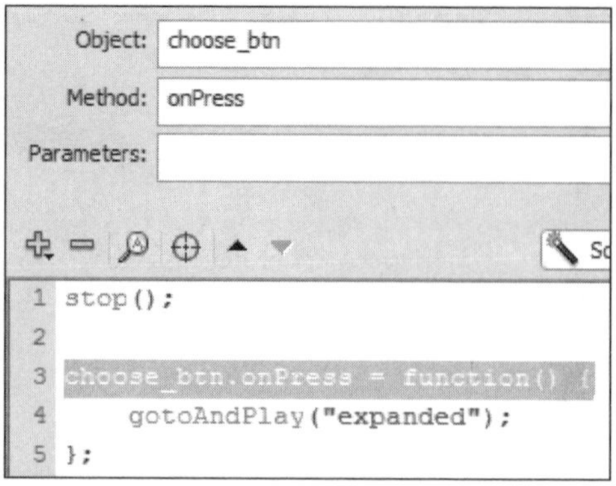

Figure 4.31 The collapsed-menu button is assigned the `onPress` event.

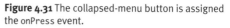

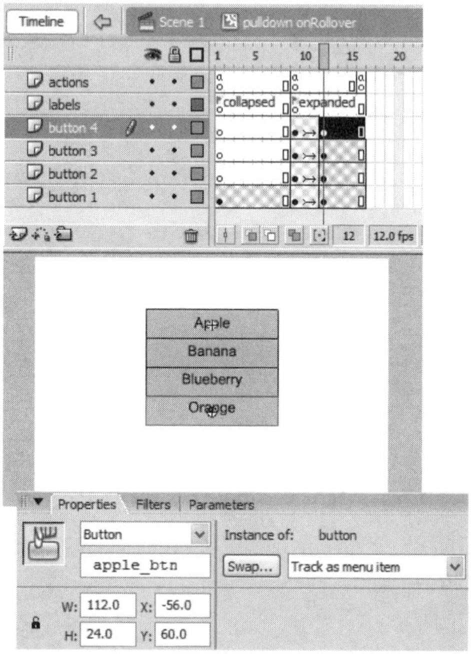

Figure 4.32 You need to change the setting for each button instance in the expanded section of the Timeline to "Track as menu item," including all the buttons in both starting and ending keyframes if you have tweened buttons.

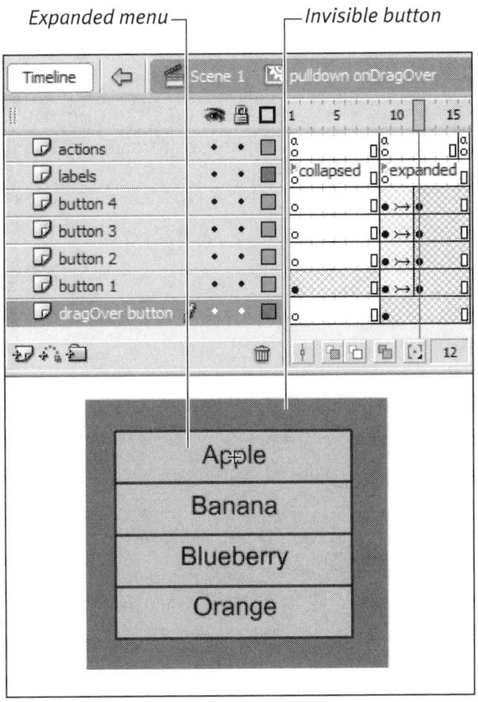

Figure 4.33 When the pointer leaves one of the buttons in the expanded state of the menu, it's dragged over the invisible button that sits in the bottom layer.

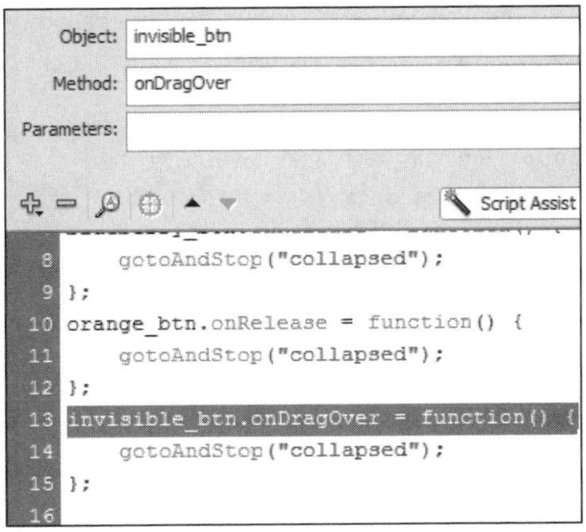

Figure 4.34 The `onDragOver` event is detected in the invisible button, signaling the playhead to jump to the keyframe labeled `collapsed`.

To set "Track as menu item" with the onDragOver event:

1. Continuing with the pull-down menu constructed in the preceding tasks, go to symbol-editing mode for the movie clip.
2. Add a new layer under the existing layers.
3. In the new layer, create an invisible button, and place an instance in a new keyframe corresponding to the expanded keyframe.

   Your invisible-button instance should be slightly larger than the expanded menu (**Figure 4.33**).
4. Select the invisible-button instance.
5. In the Property inspector, choose the "Track as menu item" option, and give the invisible button an instance name.
6. Select the keyframe containing the event handler actions for your expanded menu buttons. In the Actions panel, assign an `onDragOver` event handler to your invisible button with a `gotoAndStop` action (**Figure 4.34**).
7. Return to the main Timeline, and test your movie.

   The invisible-button instance under the expanded menu detects whether the pointer leaves any of the other button instances. If it does, Flash sends the movie clip back to frame 1 and collapses the menu.

Button-Tracking Options

Button Properties

Because the buttons you create are objects of the Button class, you can control their properties by using dot syntax. Many button properties control the way a button looks (such as its width, height, and rotation) as well as the way the button behaves (such as its button tracking). **Table 4.2** summarizes the properties of the Button class. Many of these properties are also properties of the MovieClip class (see Chapter 7).

Table 4.2

Button Properties

Property	Value	Description
_alpha	A number from 0 to 100	Specifies the alpha transparency; 0 is transparent, and 100 is opaque.
_visible	True or false	Specifies whether a button can be seen.
_name	A string	Gets the instance name of the button or sets a new instance name.
_rotation	A number	Specifies the degree of rotation in a clockwise direction from the 12 o'clock position. A value of 45, for example, tips the button to the right.
_width	A number, in pixels	Specifies the horizontal dimension.
_height	A number, in pixels	Specifies the vertical dimension.
_x	A number, in pixels	Specifies the horizontal position of the button's registration point.
_y	A number, in pixels	Specifies the vertical position of the button's registration point.
_xscale	A number	Specifies the percentage of the original button symbol's horizontal dimension.
_yscale	A number	Specifies the percentage of the original button symbol's vertical dimension.
blendMode	A number or string	Indicates which blend mode to use to visually combine the button with other visual objects. (See Chapter 7.)
cacheAsBitmap	True or false	Indicates whether to redraw the contents of the button every frame (false) or use a static bitmap of the button's contents (true). (See Chapter 7.)
filters	An Array of filter objects	Specifies the set of graphical filters to apply to this button instance. (See Chapter 7.)
scale9Grid	A Rectangle object	Defines the nine regions that control how the button distorts when scaling. (See Chapter 7.)
_target	A string	Gets the target path of the button, using slash syntax.
useHandCursor	True or false	Determines whether the pointer changes to a hand icon when hovering over a button.
enabled	True or false	Determines whether the button can receive events.
menu	A ContextMenu object	Associates a button with a ContextMenu object.
trackAsMenu	True or false	Determines whether the button will track as a button or track as a menu item.
_focusRect	True or false	Determines whether a yellow rectangle appears around the button as you use the Tab key to select it.
tabEnabled	True or false	Determines whether the button can receive keyboard focus when you use the Tab key to select objects.
tabIndex	A number	Determines the order of focus when you use the Tab key to select objects. The tab order uses tabIndex in ascending order.

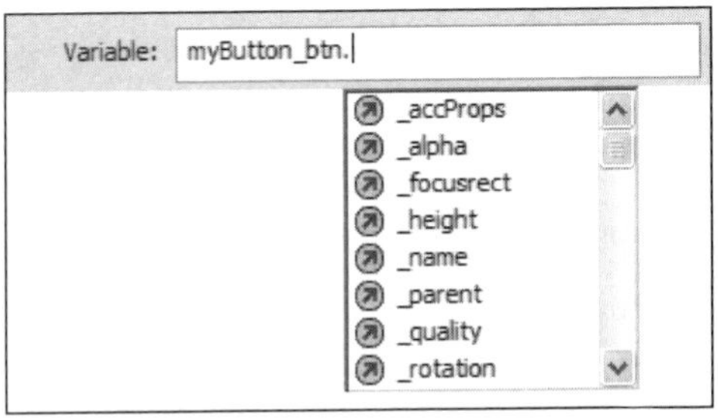

Figure 4.35 Use the code hint pull-down menu to select a property for your button called `myButton_btn`.

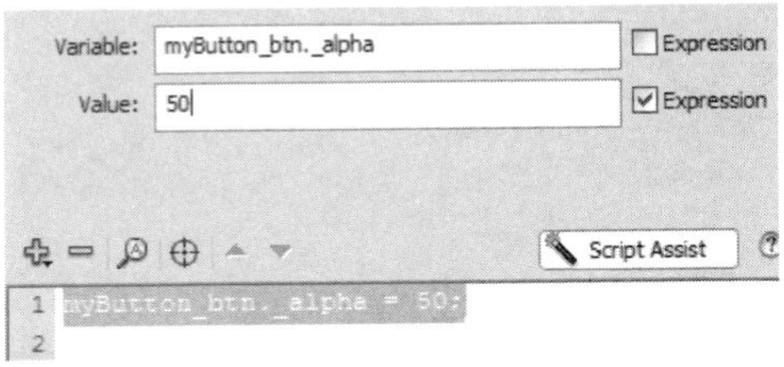

Figure 4.36 The value 50 is assigned to the `_alpha` property of the button called `myButton_btn`.

To change a property of a button:

1. Create a button, and drag an instance of it to the Stage.
2. In the Property inspector, give the button an instance name.
3. Select the first frame of the main Timeline, and open the Actions panel.
4. In the Script pane, choose Statements > Variables > "set variable". In the Variable field, enter the instance name of the button followed by a period.

   If your instance name ends with `_btn`, the code hint pull-down menu appears (Win only).
5. Select the property to change from the pull-down menu (**Figure 4.35**).

   or

   With the cursor in the Variable field, use the add action (+) button to choose the property to change from ActionScript 2.0 Classes > Movie > Button > Properties, and add the name of your button instance before the period.
6. In the Value field, enter a value for the property (**Figure 4.36**). If the value isn't a literal string, select the Expression check box for the Value field.

   The completed statement assigns a new value to the property of your button.

✔ Tip

- The code-hint pull-down menu in steps 4–5 should appear as long as you use one of the prescribed suffixes for your instance name. Due to a bug in the Mac OS X version of Flash, at the time this chapter is being written these code hints don't appear in the fields in Script Assist mode. With Script Assist off, code hints work as they should on both Windows and Mac OS.

To disable a button:

- Set the `enabled` property to false.

  If you name your button instance `myButton_btn`, enter the following statement:

  ```
  myButton_btn.enabled = false;
  ```

  Your button will no longer receive any events.

To disable the hand pointer:

- Set the `useHandCursor` property to false (**Figure 4.37**).

  If you name your button instance `myButton_btn`, enter the following statement:

  ```
  myButton_btn.useHandCursor = false;
  ```

Figure 4.37 The hand pointer is disabled for the button called `myButton_btn`. Only the arrow pointer will show up.

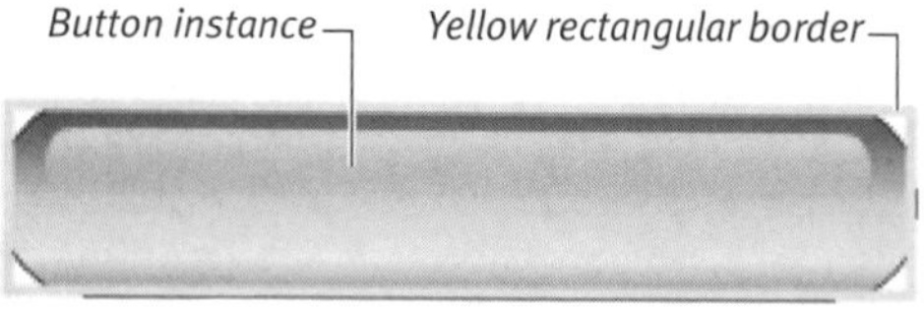

Figure 4.38 When you use the Tab key, buttons show their focus with a yellow rectangular border in their `Over` state.

Changing button focus with the Tab key

The last several properties listed in Table 4.2—`_focusRect`, `tabEnabled`, and `tabIndex`—deal with controlling the button focus. The *button focus* is a way of selecting a button with the Tab key. When a Flash movie plays within a browser, you can press the Tab key and navigate between buttons, text fields, and movie clips. The currently focused button displays its `Over` state with a yellow rectangular border (**Figure 4.38**). Pressing the Enter key (or Return key on the Mac) is equivalent to clicking the focused button. The button property `_focusrect` determines whether the yellow rectangular border is visible. If `_focusrect` is set to false, a focused button displays its `Over` state but doesn't display the yellow rectangular highlight. The property `tabEnabled`, if set to false, disables a button's capability to receive focus from the Tab key.

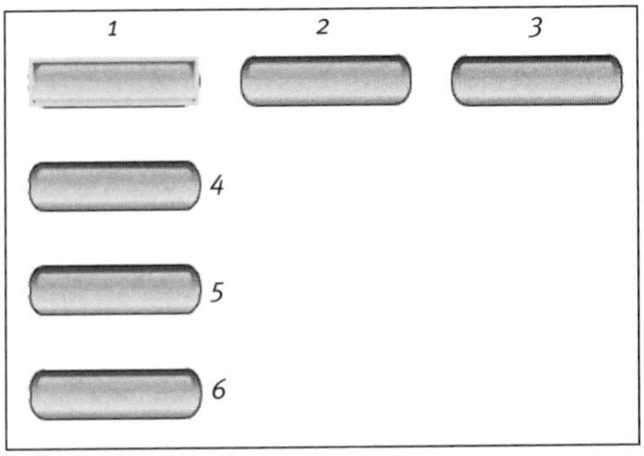

Figure 4.39 The automatic order of button focusing with the Tab key is by position. The numbers show the order in which the buttons will receive focus.

The order in which a button, movie clip, or text field receives its focus is determined by its position on the Stage. Objects focus from left to right and then from top to bottom. So, if you have a row of buttons at the top of your movie and a column of buttons on the left side below it, the Tab key will focus each of the buttons in the top row first and then focus on each of the buttons in the column (**Figure 4.39**). After the last button receives the focus, the tab order begins again from the top row.

You can set your own tab order with the button property `tabIndex`. Assign a number to the `tabIndex` for each button instance, and Flash will organize the tab order using the `tabIndex` in ascending order. Take control of the tab order to create more helpful forms, allowing the user to use the Tab and Enter keys to fill out multiple text fields and click multiple buttons.

To hide the yellow rectangular highlight over focused buttons:

◆ Set the `_focusrect` property to false.

  If you name your button instance `myButton_btn`, for example, use the statement `myButton_btn._focusrect = false`.

✔ Tip

■ You can also hide the yellow rectangular highlight for all your buttons in one statement. Set the `_focusrect` property to false, and target the main Timeline by using the keyword `_root`. Use the statement `_root._focusrect = false`.

To disable focusing with the Tab key:

- Set the `tabEnabled` property to false.

  If you name your button instance `myButton_btn`, for example, use the statement `myButton_btn.tabEnabled = false`.

To change the tab order of button focus:

1. Give each button instance a name in the Property inspector.
2. Select the first frame of the main Timeline, and open the Actions panel.
3. Create a `set variable` statement (Statements > Variables > "set variable"). In the Variable field, enter your first button's instance name followed by a dot.
4. Select `tabIndex` from the code hint pull-down menu (Win), or type `tabIndex` after the dot (**Figure 4.40**).
5. For the value to assign to the variable, you must indicate where in the tab order this object should be when the user presses the Tab key. In the Value field, enter a numerical value; then, select the Expression check box (**Figure 4.41**).

   This button instance will be in the tab order in the specified index.

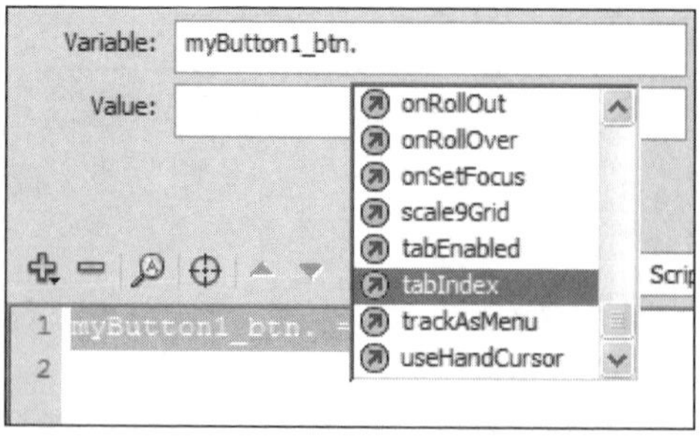

Figure 4.40 Use the code hint pull-down menu to select the `tabIndex` property.

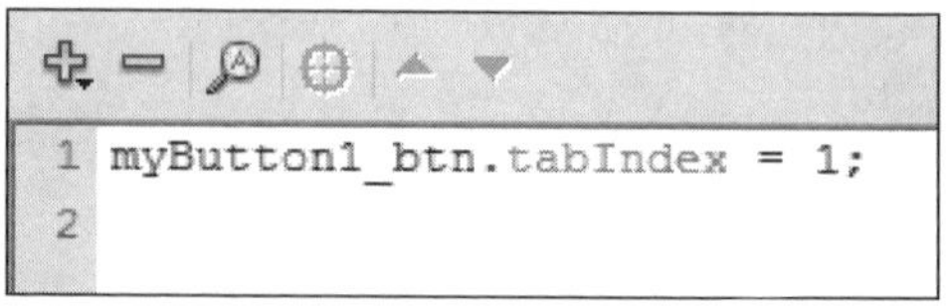

Figure 4.41 The button called `myButton1_btn` will receive the first focus with the Tab key.

```
myButton1_btn.tabIndex = 1;
myButton2_btn.tabIndex = 2;
myButton3_btn.tabIndex = 3;
myButton4_btn.tabIndex = 4;
myButton5_btn.tabIndex = 5;
myButton6_btn.tabIndex = 6;
```

Figure 4.42 This block of code declares the `tabIndex` properties for `myButton1_btn` through `myButton6_btn`.

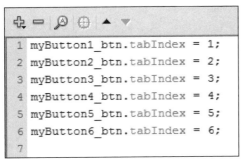

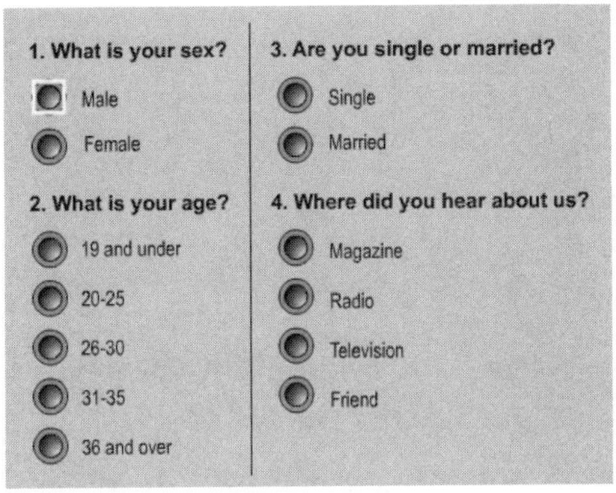

Figure 4.43 Control the order of button focusing to provide easier tab navigation through forms and questionnaires. This movie focuses buttons in columns to follow the question numbers rather than rely on Flash's automatic ordering.

6. Repeat steps 3–5 for each of your button instances. Continue to assign numbers in sequence to the `tabIndex` property of each button instance (**Figure 4.42**).

7. Choose Publish Preview > Default-(HTML) to view your movie in a browser.

   When you press the Tab key, Flash follows the `tabIndex` in ascending order for button focusing (**Figure 4.43**).

✔ Tip

- Some browsers intercept keypresses, so you may have to click the Flash movie in your browser window before you can use the Tab key to focus on buttons.

The Movie Clip as a Button

Movie clips are objects that have their own Timeline in which animations play independently from the main Timeline. This fact lets you put movie clips inside button symbols to create animated buttons, as described earlier in this chapter. But movie clips can also behave like buttons all by themselves. You can assign many of the same event handlers to movie clips that you assign to buttons. Assign an `onRelease` event handler to a movie clip, for example, and the event will respond when the viewer clicks the movie clip instance.

Within the movie clip Timeline, you can assign the frame labels `_up`, `_over`, and `_down`, and those keyframes will behave like the `Up`, `Over`, and `Down` keyframes of a button symbol (**Figure 4.44**). The `_up` label identifies the state of the movie clip when the pointer isn't over the hit area. The `_over` label identifies the state of the movie clip when the pointer is over the hit area. And the `_down` label identifies the state of the movie clip when the pointer is over the hit area and the mouse button is pressed. The hit area of a movie clip is, by default, the shape of the movie clip. You can define a different hit area by assigning another movie clip to the property `hitArea`.

Beware—actions assigned to movie clips behave quite differently from those assigned to buttons. An event handler on a movie clip belongs to that movie clip's Timeline, whereas an event handler on a button belongs to the Timeline on which it's sitting. Consider this simple code:

```
myObject.onRelease = function() {
    gotoAndStop(10);
};
```

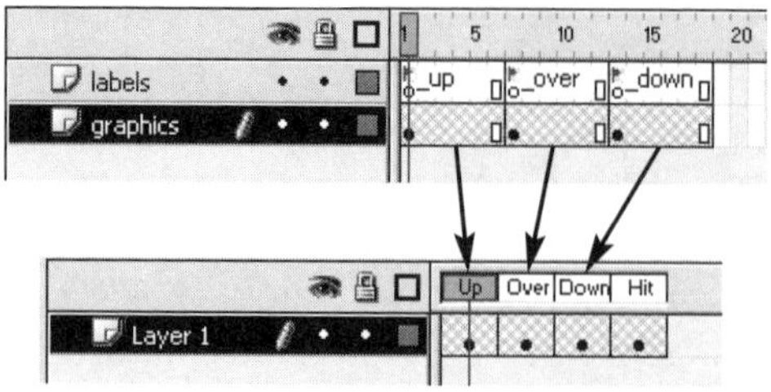

Figure 4.44 The `_up`, `_over`, and `_down` labels of a movie clip symbol correspond to the `Up`, `Over`, and `Down` keyframes of a button symbol.

Why Have Movie Clips Behave Like Buttons?

Why would you want to use a movie clip as a button? Why not just use a regular button? Movie clips offer you more power and greater flexibility to deal with dynamic situations. Using movie clips as buttons lets you create more complex and sophisticated buttons. Because you can define the hit area of a movie clip yourself, you can shrink, grow, move, and change it dynamically by using ActionScript. You can't do that with buttons. Using movie clips as buttons also makes it easier to combine the methods of movie clips with the events of buttons. The `startDrag()` movie clip method, for example, can be tied to the `onPress` event handler on a single movie clip.

This doesn't mean that you shouldn't use buttons at all. It does mean you have more options for your creative toolkit.

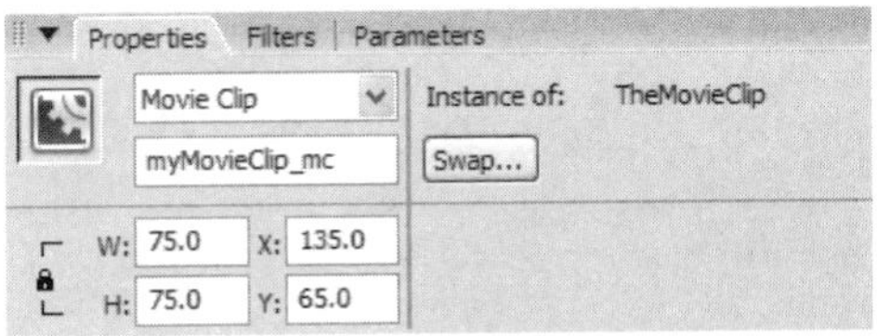

Figure 4.45 This movie clip instance has been named `myMovieClip_mc` in the Property inspector.

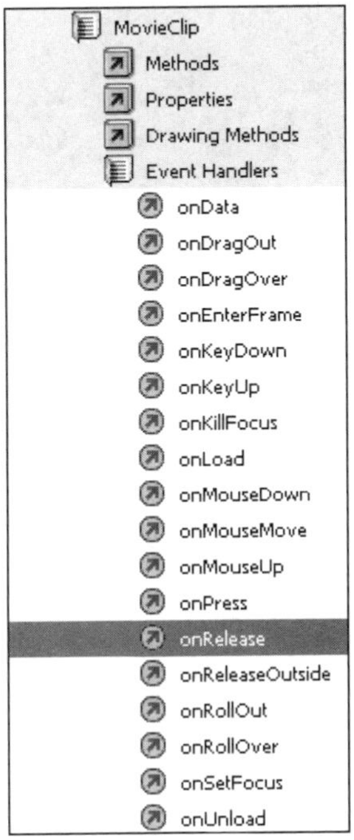

Figure 4.46 The `onRelease` event is one of several event handlers that can be assigned to a movie clip.

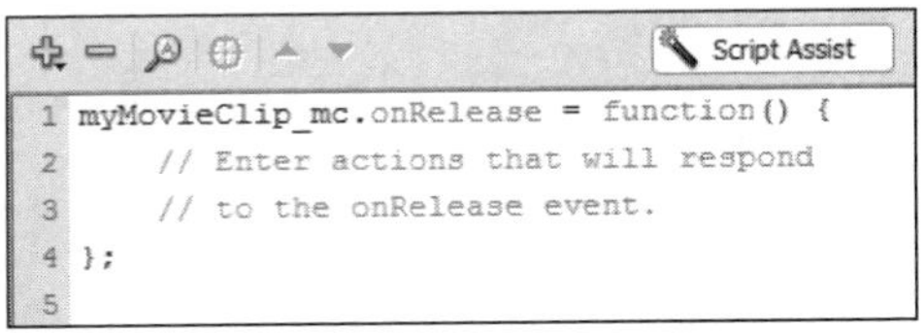

Figure 4.47 An anonymous function is created that responds to a click on the movie clip called `myMovieClip_mc`.

When this action is assigned to a movie clip on the main Timeline, Flash moves the playhead of the *movie clip's* Timeline to frame 10. When the code is assigned to a regular button on the main Timeline, Flash moves the playhead of the *main* Timeline to frame 10. You'll learn more about navigating different Timelines in Chapter 5.

To assign a button event handler to a movie clip:

1. Create a movie clip symbol, drag an instance of it to the Stage, and give the instance a name in the Property inspector (**Figure 4.45**).
2. Select the first frame of the main Timeline, and open the Actions panel.
3. In the Script pane, choose the event you want to respond to under ActionScript 2.0 Classes > Movie > MovieClip > Event Handlers (**Figure 4.46**).
4. In the Object field, enter the instance name of the movie clip.
5. Between the curly braces of the function, add an action to perform in response to the event (**Figure 4.47**).

To define the Up, Over, and Down keyframes of a movie clip:

1. Create a movie clip symbol, and enter symbol-editing mode for it.
2. Insert a new layer.
3. Choose Insert > Keyframe twice along the Timeline.

   Two more keyframes are created in the movie clip Timeline (**Figure 4.48**).
4. Select the first keyframe, and type `_up` as its label in the Property inspector.
5. Select the second keyframe, and type `_over` as its label in the Property inspector.
6. Select the last keyframe, and type `_down` as its label in the Property inspector.

   The three keyframes define the `Up`, `Over`, and `Down` states of your movie clip (**Figure 4.49**).
7. In the layer containing your graphics, create keyframes corresponding to the labeled keyframes you just created, and alter your graphics for the `Up`, `Over`, and `Down` states (**Figure 4.50**).
8. Insert another new layer.
9. Select the first frame of the new layer, and open the Actions panel.
10. Choose Global Functions > Timeline Control > stop.

    The `stop` action prevents the movie clip from playing automatically.
11. Exit symbol-editing mode.
12. Drag an instance of your movie clip symbol to the main Stage.
13. Assign a button event handler to your movie clip instance.

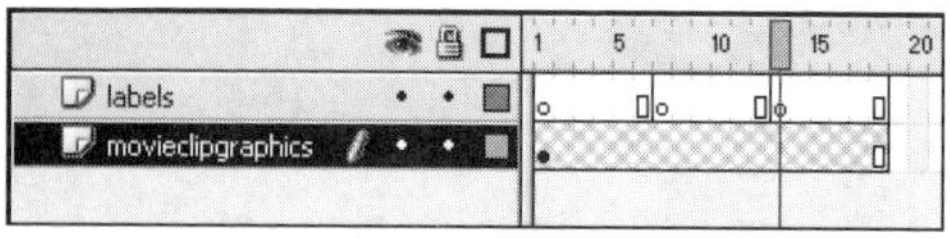

Figure 4.48 Two additional keyframes, at frames 7 and 13, are created in a new layer.

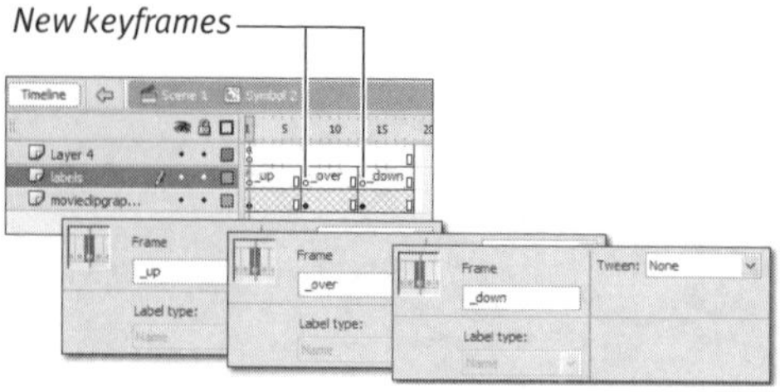

Figure 4.49 Label the three keyframes in the Property inspector.

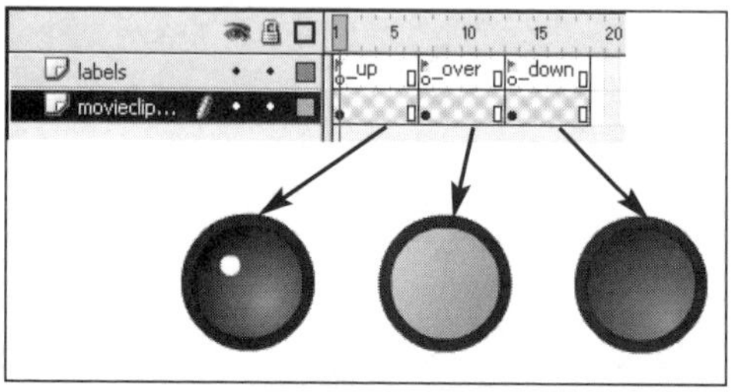

Figure 4.50 The three keyframes contain the `Up`, `Over`, and `Down` states of your movie clip.

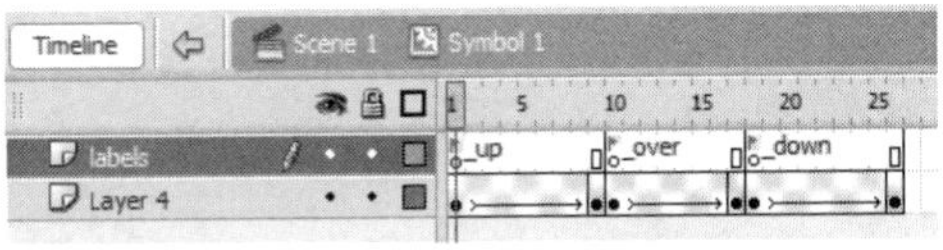

Figure 4.51 Create animations for the `Up`, `Over`, and `Down` states in the `_up`, `_over`, and `_down` keyframes.

14. Test your movie.

Flash uses the `_up`, `_over`, and `_down` keyframes for the `Up`, `Over`, and `Down` states of the movie clip. You must have a button event handler such as `onPress` or `on (press)` assigned to the movie clip to make it behave like a button and recognize the labeled keyframes.

To create an animated button by using a movie clip:

1. Choose Insert > New Symbol.
2. Select Movie Clip, and click OK.

   A new movie clip symbol is created in your Library, and you're put in symbol-editing mode.
3. Insert a new layer, and define the `_up`, `_over`, and `_down` labels for three separate keyframes, as described in the preceding task.
4. In the first layer, create keyframes corresponding to the labeled keyframes you just created.
5. For each keyframe in the first layer, create a motion or shape tween that you want to play for the `Up`, `Over`, and `Down` states of the button (**Figure 4.51**).
6. Insert another new layer, and create keyframes corresponding to the beginning and end of each labeled state.
7. Select each beginning keyframe, and, in the Actions panel, choose Global Functions > Timeline Control > Play.
8. Select each ending keyframe, and, in the Actions panel, choose Global Functions > Timeline Control > gotoAndPlay.

continues on next page

9. For each gotoAndPlay action, choose Frame Label in the Type field; in the Frame field, choose the frame label name corresponding to each ending keyframe.

   For the Up, Over, and Down states, the ending keyframe sends the playhead back to the beginning keyframe, creating a loop for each of your tweens (**Figure 4.52**).

10. Exit symbol-editing mode.

11. Drag an instance of your movie clip to the Stage.

12. Assign a button event handler to your movie clip instance.

13. Test your movie.

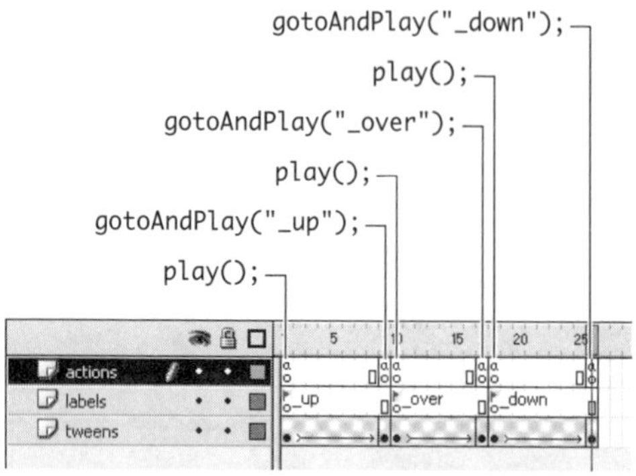

Figure 4.52 The actions in the top layer play and repeat the tweens in each labeled keyframe.

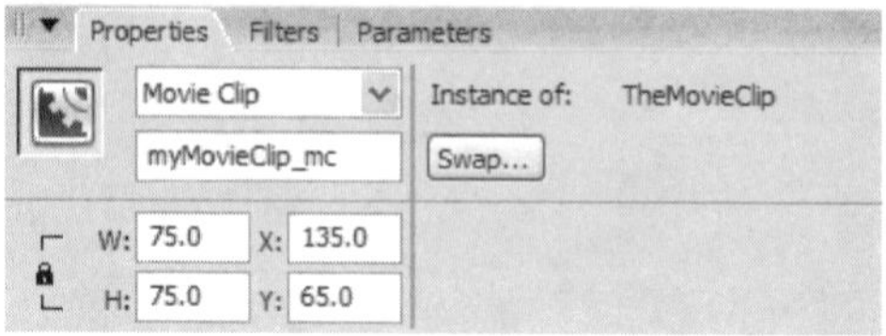

Figure 4.53 A new movie clip has been created and assigned an instance name of myMovieClip_mc.

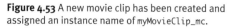

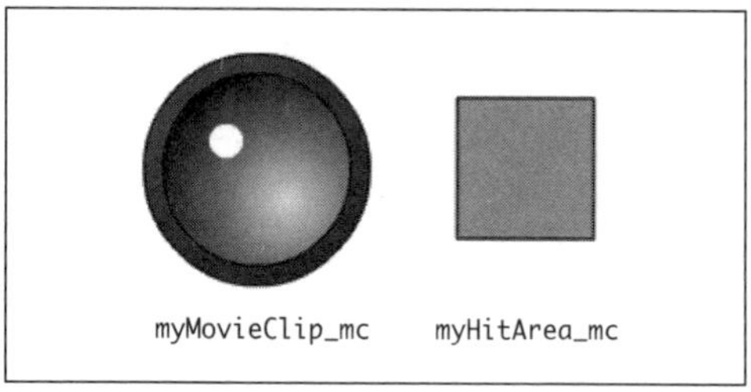

Figure 4.54 The movie clip called myMovieClip_mc will use the movie clip called myHitArea_mc as its hit area.

✔ Tip

- You can assign a stop action instead of a gotoAndPlay action to the end keyframes of the Up, Over, and Down states. Doing so makes the movie clip play the tween only once.

To define the hit area of a movie clip:

1. Create a movie clip symbol, place an instance of it on the Stage, and name it in the Property inspector (**Figure 4.53**).

   This instance is the movie clip to which you'll assign a button event handler.

2. Create another movie clip symbol, place an instance of it on the Stage, and name it in the Property inspector.

   This instance is the movie clip that will act as the hit area for the first movie clip (**Figure 4.54**).

3. Select the first frame of the main Timeline, and open the Actions panel.

4. Assign a button event handler to the first movie clip instance.

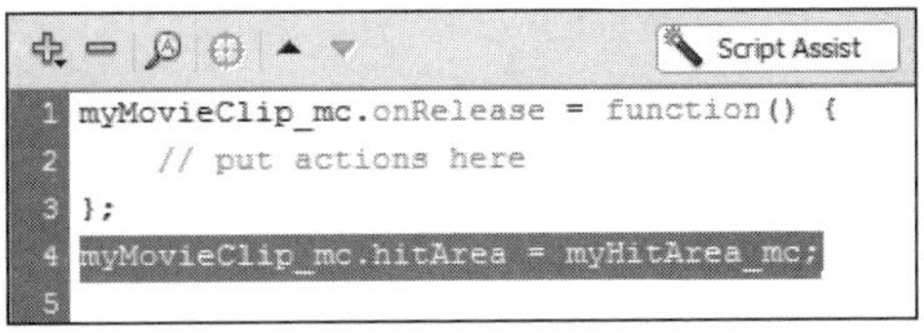
Script Assist
myMovieClip_mc.onRelease = function() {
// put actions here
};
myMovieClip_mc.hitArea = myHitArea_mc;

Figure 4.55 The completed statement in the Script pane.

5. In the Script pane, create a `set variable` statement (Statements > Variables > "set variable"); in the Variable field, enter the name for the first movie clip instance followed by a period.

   The code hint pull-down menu appears.

6. Select `hitArea` from the code hint pull-down menu.

7. For the value to assign to the `hitArea` property, enter the name of the second movie clip instance (**Figure 4.55**).

   The completed statement assigns the second movie clip as the hit area for the first movie clip.

8. Test your movie.

   The `Up`, `Over`, and `Down` states of your first movie clip respond to the shape of the second movie clip. You can use any movie clip as the hit area for another movie clip, and you can place it anywhere, even inside the movie clip that's acting as a button. As long as you name it, you can target it and assign it to the `hitArea` property of another.

✔ Tip

- The movie clip assigned to the `hitArea` property doesn't need to be visible to work. You can change its alpha transparency in the Property inspector to be clear, or you can set its `_visible` property to `0`. See Chapter 7 for more information on modifying movie clip properties.

Movie clip properties that affect button behavior

Like buttons, movie clips have properties that affect their button behavior. **Table 4.3** summarizes these properties. Use these properties as you would for buttons to control whether a movie clip is enabled or whether the hand pointer is visible or to control the tab ordering for the focusing of movie clips. The following code disables the hand pointer on a movie clip called `myMovieClip_mc` that is behaving as a button:

```
MyMovieClip_mc.useHandCursor = false;
```


Table 4.3

Movie Clip Properties That Affect Button Behavior

Property	Value	Description
`hitArea`	Movie clip instance name	Defines the hit area of a movie clip.
`useHandCursor`	True or false	Determines whether the pointer changes to a hand icon when hovering over a movie clip.
`enabled`	True or false	Determines whether the movie clip can receive button events.
`trackAsMenu`	True or false	Determines whether the movie clip will track as a button or track as a menu item.
`_focusrect`	True or false	Determines whether a yellow rectangle appears around objects as you use the Tab key to select them.
`tabEnabled`	True or false	Determines whether the movie clip can receive keyboard focus when you use the Tab key to select objects. Movie clips (children) within a movie clip (parent) may still receive focus even if the parent can't.
`tabIndex`	A number	Determines the order of focus when you use the Tab key to select objects. The `tabIndex` is in ascending order.
`tabChilden`	True or false	Determines whether movie clips inside movie clips can receive focus when you use the Tab key.
`focusEnabled`	True or false	Determines whether the movie clip can receive focus even when it isn't acting as a button.

Keyboard Detection

The keyboard is just as important an interface device as the mouse, and Flash lets you detect events occurring from single keypresses. This arrangement opens the possibility of having navigation based on the keyboard (using the arrow keys or the number keys, for example) or having keyboard shortcuts that duplicate mouse-based navigation schemes. Flash even lets you control live text that the viewer types in empty text fields in a movie; these text fields merit a separate discussion in Chapter 10. This section focuses on single or combination keystrokes that trigger things to happen using the Key class.

Figure 4.56 The Key class is under ActionScript 2.0 Classes > Movie.

The Key class

The Key class handles the detection of keypresses on the keyboard (**Figure 4.56**). In Chapter 3, you learned that you must instantiate a class before you can use it. The Key class, however, is one of a few classes that don't require you a to create an instance or call a constructor function before you can use it. To call one of its methods, you use the class name itself (Key).

The Key class has methods that allow you to retrieve the key that was pressed most recently or to test whether a certain key was pressed. The most common method is `isDown()`, which takes a single parameter—a specific key on the keyboard. This method checks whether that key has been pressed; if so, it returns a value of true.

All keys in Flash have a specific number associated with them; this number is known as the *key-code value* (see Appendix B). You use these codes in conjunction with the `isDown()` method to construct a conditional statement that detects the keyboard interaction. `Key.isDown(32)` for example, returns true or false, depending on whether the spacebar (whose key-code value is 32) is pressed.

Fortunately, you don't have to use clumsy numeric key codes all the time. The most common keys are conveniently assigned as properties of the Key class. These properties are constants that you can use in place of the key codes. The statement `Key.isDown(32)`, for example, is the same as `Key.isDown(Key.SPACE)`.

To detect a keypress by using the Key class's isDown() method:

1. Select the first keyframe in the Timeline, and open the Actions panel.
2. Choose Statements > Conditions/ Loops > if.

   The incomplete `if` statement appears in the Script pane, with the placeholder text `not_set_yet` for the missing condition parameter (**Figure 4.57**).
3. Put the cursor in the Condition field; using the add script (+) button, choose ActionScript 2.0 Classes > Movie > Key > Methods > isDown.

   The `isDown()` method appears as the condition parameter. The key code parameter is required for this method (**Figure 4.58**).
4. Place the cursor between the parentheses of the `Key.isDown()` method call.
5. Use the add script (+) button to choose ActionScript 2.0 Classes > Movie > Key > Constants, and select a keyboard key from the list (**Figure 4.59**).

   or

   Type `Key` followed by a period, and select a keyboard key from the code hint menu that appears.

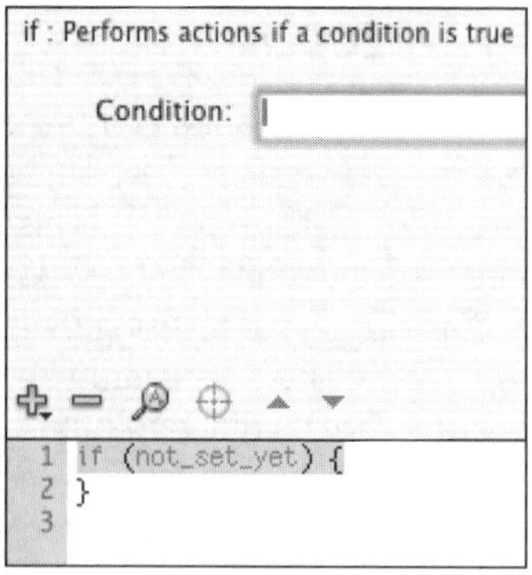

Figure 4.57 The `if` statement has a condition that it tests. If that condition is true, the actions within the curly braces are carried out.

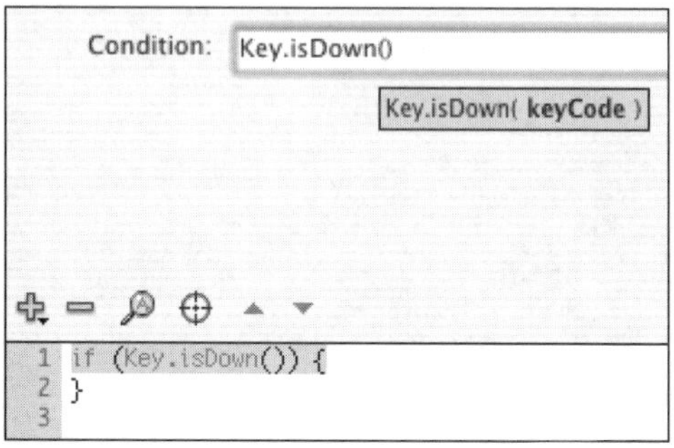

Figure 4.58 The method `isDown()` expects a key code value, as suggested by the code hint.

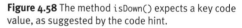

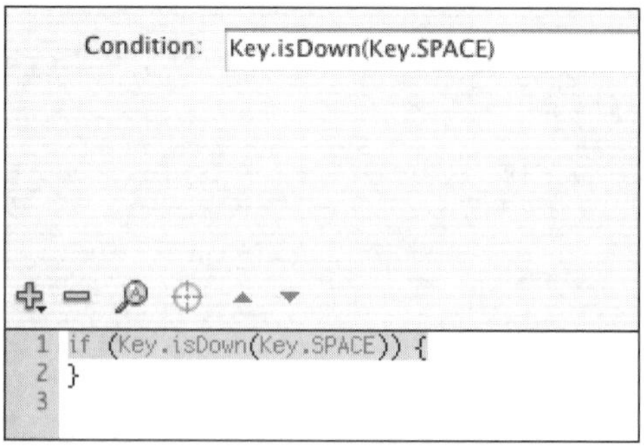

Figure 4.59 The property `Key.SPACE` is in place as the key code parameter for the method `isDown()`.

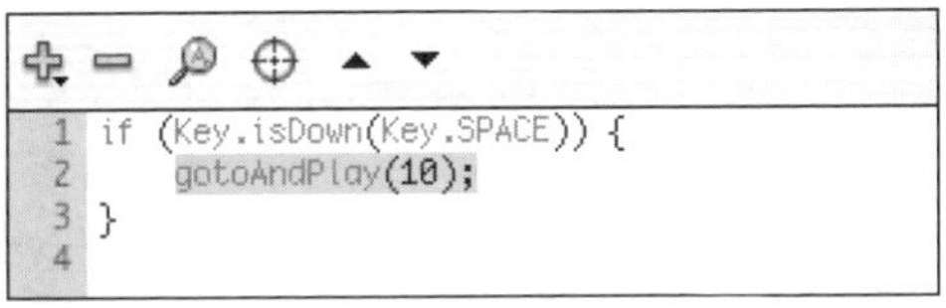

Figure 4.60 If the spacebar is pressed, Flash goes to frame 10.

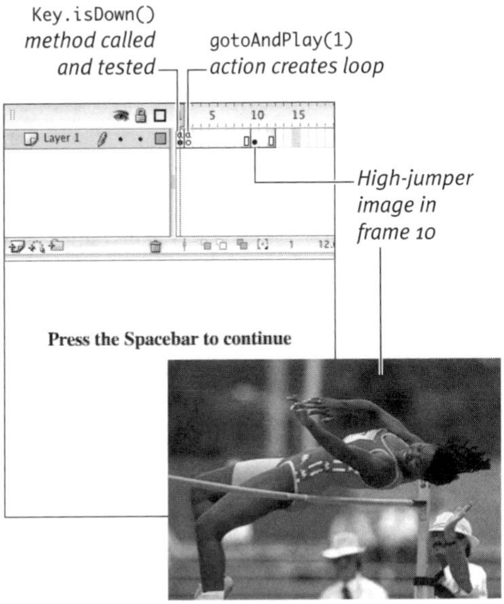

Figure 4.61 This movie loops between frames 1 and 2 until the spacebar is pressed.

6. Choose a basic action to be performed when the condition is true, and add it between the curly braces of the `if` statement (**Figure 4.60**).

7. Insert a new keyframe after the first one, and assign the frame action `gotoAndPlay(1);`.

   The second keyframe loops back to the first so that the conditional statement is checked continuously. This method, known as a *frame loop*, is the simplest way to have the `if` statement tested repeatedly (**Figure 4.61**).

   We'll explore more-refined ways of dealing with conditionals and action loops later in this chapter. For now, you can use this basic loop to test the `isDown()` method and different `Key` class properties.

To create key combinations with the Key class isDown() method:

1. Select the first keyframe from the preceding task, and open the Actions panel.

2. Place your pointer at the end of the method call in the Condition field of the `if` statement.

3. Select Operators > Logical Operators > &&, or enter two ampersands (&&) manually.

   The logical and operator `&&` joins two statements so that both must be true for the entire statement to be true. You can think of the operator as being the word *and*.

4. Put the cursor at the end of the Conditions field, if necessary; select ActionScript 2.0 Classes > Movie > Key > Methods > isDown.

   The `isDown()` method appears after the `&&` operator. Another parameter is required for this method.

continues on next page

5. With the cursor between the parentheses of the second `Key.isDown()` statement, select ActionScript 2.0 Classes > Movie > Key > Constants > CONTROL.

   The property `Key.CONTROL` appears as the parameter for the second `isDown()` method (**Figure 4.62**). The `if` statement will perform the action within its curly braces only if both the spacebar and the Ctrl key are pressed together.

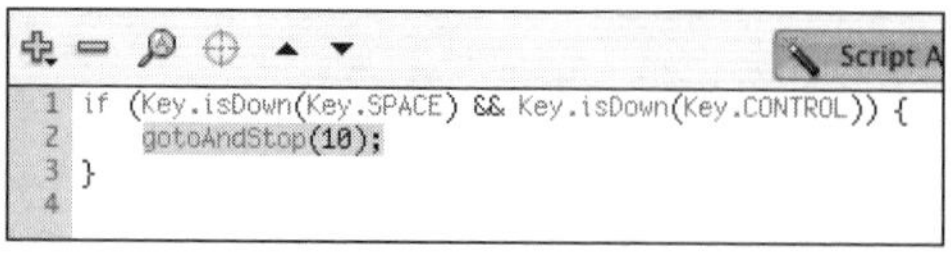

Figure 4.62 The operator && connects two statements, requiring both to be true.

Creating listeners for key events

In the preceding section, you had to create a two-frame loop on the main Timeline to test the `isDown()` method. You can eliminate that loop and detect events of the `Key` class by creating an event listener object. A *listener object* is an object (often an instance of the generic `Object` class) that "listens for" events from an object that broadcasts events, such as the `Key` class. The listener object has event handler methods defined with specific names that match the events that the broadcaster object sends.

You can create an object called `myListener` with this statement:

```
var myListener:Object = new Object();
```

Then you add an anonymous function to your listener object with the same name as the event you want to respond to. If you want your listener to listen for the `Key` class's `onKeyDown` event and respond by going to frame 10, you create the following function:

```
myListener.onKeyDown = function() {
    gotoAndStop(10);
};
```

When your event handler method has been defined on your listener object, you must register your listener with the Key class. Do so by using the addListener() method of the Key class, as follows:

```
Key.addListener(myListener)
```

From that point on, whenever the specified event occurs, your listener object is notified. The two events that are broadcast by the Key class are onKeyDown and onKeyUp. The onKeyDown event happens when a key on the keyboard is pressed. The onKeyUp event happens when a key is released.

Listeners are required for the events of the Key, Selection, TextField, and Stage classes. They're available for the Mouse class but aren't required except for the onMouseWheel event.

You can combine a Key listener with the Key.isDown() method to make Flash respond only to certain keypresses. First, your listener detects whether any key is pressed. Then you can use the if statement to test whether a certain key has been pressed.

The Key Class and the keyPress Event

Using the events and methods of the Key class is the most common way to create keyboard interaction, but it isn't the only way. For Flash Player versions 6 and earlier, the Key class was not a part of ActionScript. Instead, to detect whether a key was pressed, you could define event handlers for the onKeyDown and onKeyUp events of a movie clip or button on the Stage. A common approach was to create an invisible button or movie clip symbol placed outside of the visible Stage and assign the event handlers to that button or movie clip. The event handler code, which was usually attached directly to the instance (because that was the only option at that time) looks like this:

```
on (keyPress "<Right>") {
    // actions for right arrow
}
```

In some ways, the keyPress event is easier to use than the Key class, and it's perfectly valid, if not common. If you're targeting one of the older Flash Player versions (Flash Player 5 or 4; or Flash Lite 1.1 or earlier), if your Flash movie doesn't require much in terms of keyboard interaction, or if you want to have a keyboard shortcut accompany a button event, you can use the on(keyPress) action or the onKeyDown and onKeyUp event handlers of the Button and MovieClip classes.

Why would you use the Key class and a listener instead of a button with a keyPress event? It's really a matter of sophistication versus ease of use and simplicity. Using a listener and the Key class to detect keypresses is much more powerful than using a button instance because you can construct ActionScript code that's more complex around the Key class. You can test for key combinations, for example, by requiring two isDown() methods to be true before performing certain actions as a response. Using key-code values also opens virtually the entire keyboard. For instance, the function keys and the Esc key have key-code values, so they're available to the Key class.

To create a listener for a key event:

1. Select the first frame of the main Timeline, and open the Actions panel.
2. In the Script pane, declare your listener object using the `var` statement (Statements > Variables > var). Enter a name for your listener object, and set its type to `Object`.
3. Instantiate your `Object` instance using a `set variable` statement (Statements > Variables > "set variable"). For the value on the right side of the equal sign, select ActionScript 2.0 Classes > Core > Object > "new Object".

   The completed statement creates a new, named object (**Figure 4.63**).
4. On the next line, define the `onKeyDown` function on your listener object by selecting ActionScript 2.0 Classes > Movie > Key > Listeners > onKeyDown.
5. Type the name of the listener object that you declared in step 2 as the object to be assigned the function.

   Flash creates an anonymous function that will be called when the `onKeyDown` event is triggered (**Figure 4.64**).
6. Between the curly braces of the event handler, choose an action as the response to the `onKeyDown` event (**Figure 4.65**).
7. On the line following the closing bracket of the anonymous function, choose ActionScript 2.0 Classes > Movie > Key > Methods > addListener.

   The `addListener` method appears. It requires a listener object as its parameter to be complete.
8. Enter the name of the listener object that you created.

   Your listener is registered to the `Key` class and will now respond to the `onKeyDown` event (**Figure 4.66**).

```
var myListener:Object;
myListener = new Object();
```

Figure 4.63 The object called `myListener` will be your listener to detect events of the `Key` class. It's created from the `Object` class.

```
var myListener:Object;
myListener = new Object();
myListener.onKeyDown = function() {
};
```

Figure 4.64 The `onKeyDown` event is assigned to your listener object.

```
var myListener:Object;
myListener = new Object();
myListener.onKeyDown = function() {
    gotoAndStop(5);
};
```

Figure 4.65 When the listener detects a key being pressed, Flash goes to frame 5 and stops there.

```
1 stop();
2 var myListener:Object;
3 myListener = new Object();
4 myListener.onKeyDown = function() {
5     gotoAndStop(5);
6 };
7 Key.addListener(myListener);
8
```

Figure 4.66 The final step in using this listener is registering it to the `Key` class. The `stop` action in line 1 has been added here to keep the movie at frame 1 until the key is pressed.

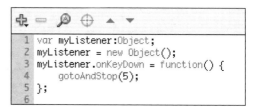

```
stop();
var myListener:Object;
myListener = new Object();
myListener.onKeyDown = function() {
    if (not_set_yet) {
    }
};
Key.addListener(myListener);
```

Figure 4.67 An `if` statement has been placed inside of the onKeyDown event handler.

```
stop();
var myListener:Object;
myListener = new Object();
myListener.onKeyDown = function() {
    if (Key.isDown(Key.SPACE)) {
        gotoAndStop(5);
    }
};
Key.addListener(myListener);
```

Figure 4.68 The completed script. The `stop` action has been added at the top to keep the movie at frame 1 until the spacebar is pressed.

To listen for a specific keypress:

1. Continuing with the preceding task, select the first frame of the Timeline, and open the Actions panel.
2. Delete the `gotoAndStop(5)` action in the Script pane.
3. Within the `onKeyDown` event listener function, Choose Statements > Conditions/Loops > if.

   The `if` statement appears within the `onKeyDown` event handler (**Figure 4.67**).
4. For the if statement's condition, select ActionScript 2.0 Classes > Movie > Key > Methods > isDown.

   The `isDown()` method is set as the condition parameter of the `if` statement.
5. Between the parentheses of the `isDown()` method call, Enter the key code for the specific key you want to detect, or select the code from ActionScript 2.0 Classes > Movie > Key > Constants.
6. Add back the `gotoAndStop(5)` action within the `if` statement.

   The final script (**Figure 4.68**) creates and registers a listener to detect any key that is pressed with the `onKeyDown` event. The `if` statement within the event handler makes sure that there is a response only if a certain key is pressed.

Mouse Detection

The Mouse class, like the Key class, is one of the few ActionScript classes that doesn't need to be instantiated before you can use it. Its properties are available immediately, and its methods are called with the class name (Mouse). You'll learn about its methods and properties in Chapter 7 when you learn more about the movie clip. Here, you'll learn about the mouse events and how to detect them.

You can detect four mouse events:

- onMouseMove happens whenever the user moves the mouse pointer.
- onMouseDown happens when the mouse button is pressed.
- onMouseUp happens when the mouse button is released.
- onMouseWheel happens when the user scrolls the mouse wheel.

To detect onMouseMove, onMouseDown, or onMouseUp, you can assign an anonymous function to a MovieClip instance, like this (_root is an ActionScript word that refers to the MovieClip instance that is the main Timeline):

```
_root.onMouseMove = function() { };
```

Used in this way, you're creating an event handler for a MovieClip event, just as you used anonymous functions as event handlers for MovieClip and Button events such as onRelease earlier in this chapter. Unlike the events you've worked with previously, such as onPress, onRelease, and onDragOver, these events are triggered no matter where on the Stage they take place. That is, if a MovieClip instance named myClip_mc has an onMouseDown event handler defined, that function will be called every time the mouse button is pressed, whether or not the mouse cursor is over myClip_mc at the time the button is pressed.

Another way to detect any of the mouse events is to create a listener object, just as you do to detect key events. Create a listener object from the generic Object class. Define a function on the listener object with the same name as the event you want to listen for, and then register your listener object with the Mouse class, using the method Mouse.addListener().

Figure 4.69 An onMouseMove MovieClip event handler.

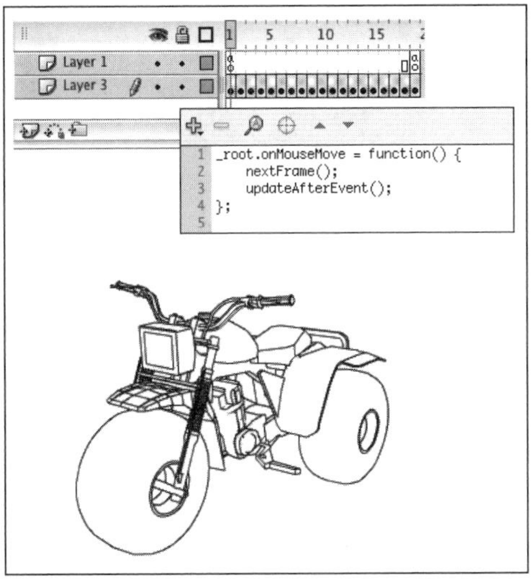

Figure 4.70 This movie contains a frame-by-frame animation of a three-wheeler that rotates. Any time the mouse pointer moves, Flash advances to the next frame.

To detect mouse movement using MovieClip mouse events:

1. Select the first frame of the main Timeline, and open the Actions panel.
2. Choose ActionScript 2.0 Classes > Movie > MovieClip > Event Handlers > onMouseMove (**Figure 4.69**).
3. By default, no instance is specified. In the Object field, enter `_root`, which refers to the main Timeline.

   The `onMouseMove` event handler is assigned to the main Timeline.
4. Choose an action as a response to this event.

   Whenever the mouse moves, Flash performs the actions listed within the `onMouseMove` event handler (**Figure 4.70**).
5. As the final action within the curly braces of the event handler function, choose Global Functions > Movie Clip Control > updateAfterEvent.

   The `updateAfterEvent` action forces Flash to refresh the display. For certain events, such as `onMouseMove`, `updateAfterEvent` makes certain that the graphics are updated according to the event, not the frame rate.

To create a listener to detect a mouse press:

1. Select the first frame of the main Timeline, and open the Actions panel.
2. Declare a variable of type `Object`, which will be your listener object.
3. Add a `set variable` action by choosing Statements > Variables > "set variable". The variable that is assigned the value is your listener object. For the value to assign, choose ActionScript 2.0 Classes > Core > Object > "new Object".

   The constructor function `new Object()` appears. Flash instantiates a new generic object, using the name you entered for your listener (**Figure 4.71**).
4. On the next line, choose ActionScript 2.0 Classes> Movie > Mouse > Listeners > onMouseDown. Complete the handler by assigning it to the listener object you just created.

   The `onMouseDown` event handler for your listener is created (**Figure 4.72**).
5. Now choose an action as the response to the `onMouseDown` event (**Figure 4.73**).
6. After the event handler block, choose ActionScript 2.0 Classes > Movie > Mouse > Methods > addListener.
7. Enter the name of your listener object so that it appears between the opening and closing parentheses (**Figure 4.74**).

   Your listener is registered and will now listen and respond to the `onMouseDown` event.

```
var myListener:Object;
myListener = new Object();
```

Figure 4.71 A listener called `myListener` has been created.

```
var myListener:Object;
myListener = new Object();
myListener.onMouseDown = function() {
};
```

Figure 4.72 The `onMouseDown` event is assigned to your listener.

```
var myListener:Object;
myListener = new Object();
myListener.onMouseDown = function() {
    nextFrame();
};
```

Figure 4.73 When the listener detects the mouse button being pressed, Flash goes to the next frame.

```
stop();
var myListener:Object;
myListener = new Object();
myListener.onMouseDown = function() {
    nextFrame();
};
Mouse.addListener(myListener);
```

Figure 4.74 The final step in using this listener is registering it with the `Mouse` class. The `stop` action has been added here to keep the movie at frame 1 until the event happens.

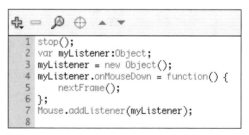

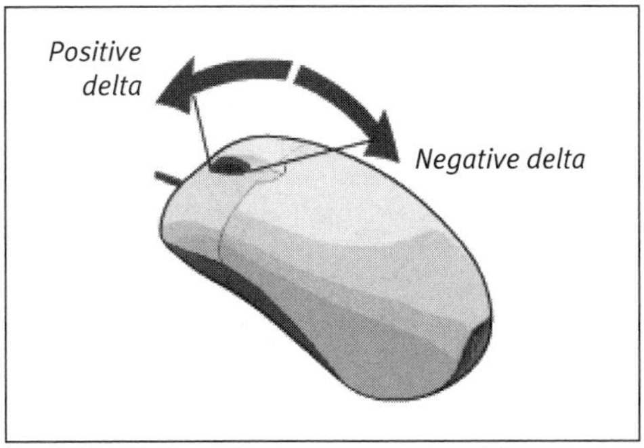

Figure 4.75 The mouse wheel returns a positive delta when it rolls forward and a negative delta when it rolls backward.

The mouse wheel

The now-commonplace mouse wheel is a third button that is nestled between the left and right mouse buttons and spins forward or backward like a wheel. By assigning the mouse event `onMouseWheel` to a listener, you can detect and respond to the mouse wheel motion. For example, you can connect the forward or backward motion of the mouse wheel to the up or down scrolling of text or to the selection of items in a pull-down menu. Although you can use Flash on Macintosh or Windows to create SWF files that use the `onMouseWheel` event, the Flash Player only triggers this event on Windows machines.

The `Mouse` class passes along two parameters when it calls the function you define for the `onMouseWheel` event: `delta` and `scrollTarget`. The parameter `delta` is a number that indicates how quickly the user spins the mouse wheel. A positive (+) delta refers to a forward motion of the mouse wheel (**Figure 4.75**). A negative (–) delta refers to a backward motion.

Often, more than one object on the Stage can respond to the mouse wheel. In those cases, the object that is directly under the mouse pointer is usually the one that responds. For example, in a browser window, the mouse wheel controls text scrolling only in the frame that is under the pointer. The `onMouseWheel` event provides the parameter `scrollTarget`, which returns the name of the object that is under the mouse pointer. Knowing the name of the object lets you control it according to the motion of the mouse wheel.

To detect mouse wheel motion:

1. Select the first frame of the main Timeline, and open the Actions panel.
2. Declare your listener object using the `var` statement, specifying its type as `Object`.
3. Add a `set variable` action to instantiate your listener object. For the value to assign, choose ActionScript 2.0 Classes > Core > Object > "new Object".

   A listener object is instantiated.
4. On the next line, choose ActionScript 2.0 Classes> Movie > Mouse > Listeners > onMouseWheel. In the Object field, enter the name for the listener object that you just created.
5. In the Parameters field, enter the following:

   `delta, scrollTarget`

   This declares the two parameters as variables that exist within the function as though you had declared them using the `var` statement.

   The `onMouseWheel` event handler for your listener is created (**Figure 4.76**).
6. Inside of the function (between the opening and closing curly braces), enter an action that will respond to the motion of the scroll wheel (**Figure 4.77**).

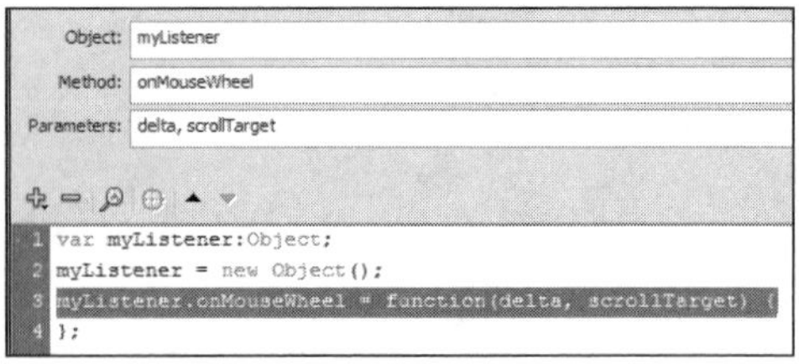

Figure 4.76 The `onMouseWheel` event is assigned to your listener called `myListener`.

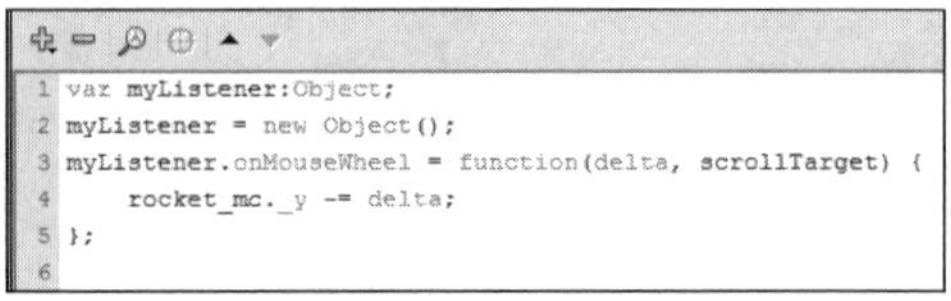

Figure 4.77 For each notch that the user scrolls on the mouse wheel, Flash will move the movie clip called `rocket_mc` up or down on the y-axis.

7. On the line after the function's closing curly brace, select ActionScript 2.0 Classes > Movie > Mouse > Methods > addListener.

8. As the parameter of the `addListener` method, enter the name of the listener object you wish to register.

   Your listener is registered and will now listen and respond to the motion of the mouse wheel (**Figure 4.78**).

To target an object to respond to mouse wheel motion:

1. Create multiple movie clip symbols, and place them on the main Stage.

2. Select the first frame of the main Timeline, and open the Actions panel.

3. Use the `var` action to declare your listener object; set its data type to `Object`.

continues on next page

```
var myListener:Object;
myListener = new Object();
myListener.onMouseWheel = function(delta, scrollTarget) {
    rocket_mc._y -= delta;
};
Mouse.addListener(myListener);
```

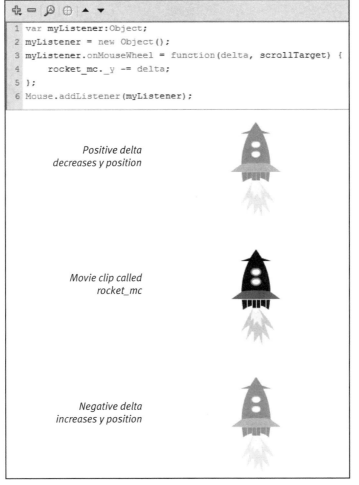

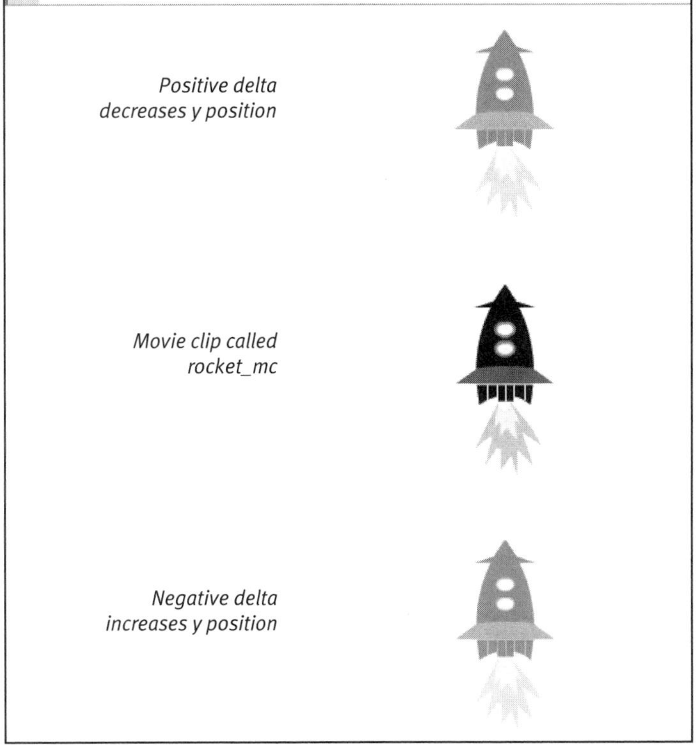

Figure 4.78 The completed code allows the user to decrease the y position of the movie clip called `rocket_mc` by rolling the mouse wheel forward or increase the y position by rolling the mouse wheel backward.

MOUSE DETECTION

4. Use the `set variable` action to instantiate your listener object. To set the value, choose ActionScript 2.0 Classes > Core > Object > "new Object".

   Your listener object is instantiated.

5. On the next line, choose ActionScript 2.0 Classes> Movie > Mouse > Listeners > onMouseWheel. In the Object field, enter the name for the listener object that you just created.

6. Enter `delta, scrollTarget` as the function's parameters.

   The `onMouseWheel` event for your listener is created.

7. Inside the function (between the opening and closing curly braces), enter an action that tells the parameter `scrollTarget` to respond to the motion of the mouse wheel.

   In this example (**Figure 4.79**), the `_rotation` property of the object directly under the mouse pointer changes according to the mouse wheel motion.

8. On the line after the function block, select ActionScript 2.0 Classes > Movie > Mouse > Methods > addListener.

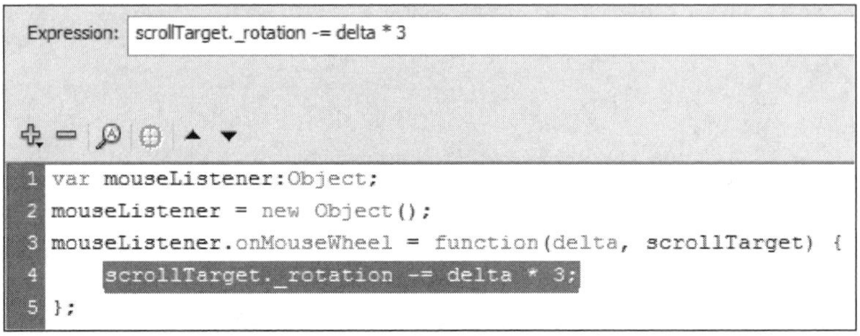

Figure 4.79 The `scrollTarget` returns the name of the movie clip directly under the mouse pointer. Line 3 in this Script pane allows the mouse wheel to change the rotation of any movie clip that is under the mouse pointer.

9. As the parameter of the `addListener` method, enter the name of the listener object you created in step 3 (**Figure 4.80**).

   Your listener is registered and will now listen and respond to the motion of the mouse wheel.

✔ Tip

- Multiline text fields (discussed in Chapter 11) automatically scroll in response to the mouse wheel. You can, however, disable the mouse wheel with the text field property `mouseWheelEnabled`. Set the `mouseWheelEnabled` property of any text field to false like this: `myTF_txt.mouseWheelEnabled = false;`. The text field called `myTF_txt` will no longer respond to the mouse wheel.

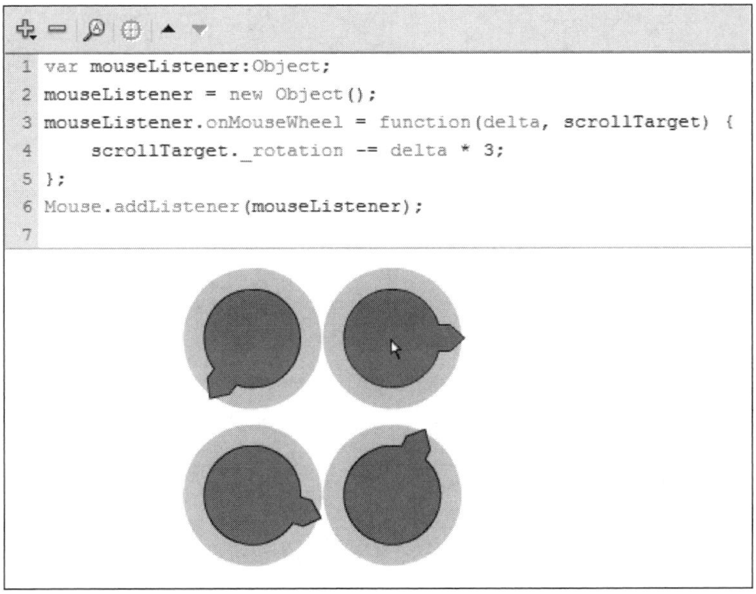

Figure 4.80 Here, because the mouse is over the top-right dial, that's the movie clip whose rotation property can be currently affected by the mouse wheel.

The Contextual Menu

In the playback of any Flash movie, a contextual menu appears when you right-click (Windows) or Ctrl-click (Mac) on the movie. There are three different types of contextual menus: a standard menu that appears over any part of the Stage, an edit menu that appears over text fields, and an error menu (**Figure 4.81**). You can customize, to a certain extent, the items that appear in the standard and edit menus through the `ContextMenu` class. You can disable certain items or create your own custom items with the related `ContextMenuItem` class. You can even make different contextual menus appear over different buttons, movie clips, or text fields.

Manipulating the contextual menu first requires that you instantiate a new instance of the `ContextMenu` class, like so:

```
var myMenu_cm:ContextMenu = new
ContextMenu();
```

After you have a new `ContextMenu` object, you can call its methods or set its properties to customize the items that appear. All the default menu items are properties of the object `builtInItems`. Setting each property to true or false enables or disables that particular item in the menu. For example, the following statement disables the print item in the `ContextMenu` object called `myMenu_cm`:

```
myMenu_cm.builtInItems.print = false;
```

See **Table 4.4** for the properties of the `builtInItems` object of the `ContextMenu` class.

Finally, you must associate your `ContextMenu` object with the `menu` property of another object, such as the `_root` Timeline, or a specific movie clip, like so:

```
_root.menu = myMenu_cm;
```

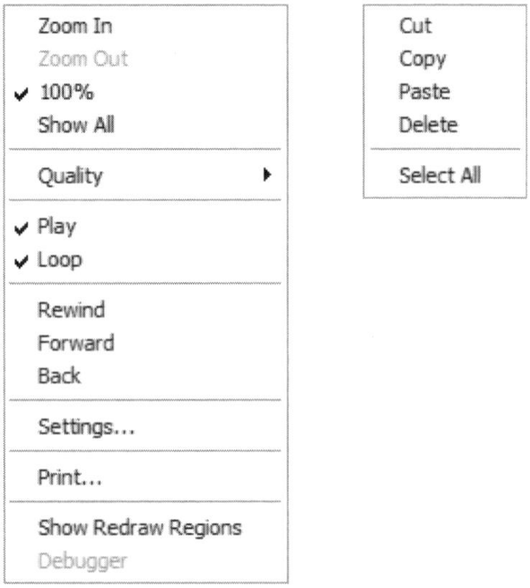

Figure 4.81 The standard contextual menu (left), and the edit contextual menu that appears over selectable text fields (right).

Table 4.4

BuiltInItems Properties

Property	Value	Menu Items
`forward_back`	True or false	Forward, Back
`save`	True or false	Save
`zoom`	True or false	Zoom in, Zoom out, 100%, Show all
`quality`	True or false	Quality
`play`	True or false	Play
`loop`	True or false	Loop
`rewind`	True or false	Rewind
`print`	True or false	Print

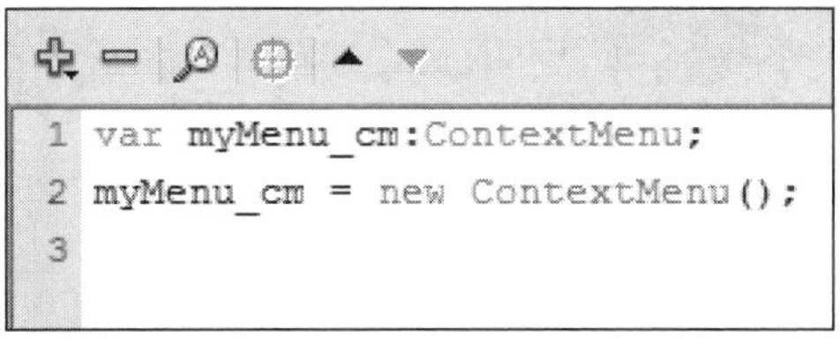
var myMenu_cm:ContextMenu;
myMenu_cm = new ContextMenu();

Figure 4.82 A new `ContextMenu` object called `myMenu_cm` is instantiated.

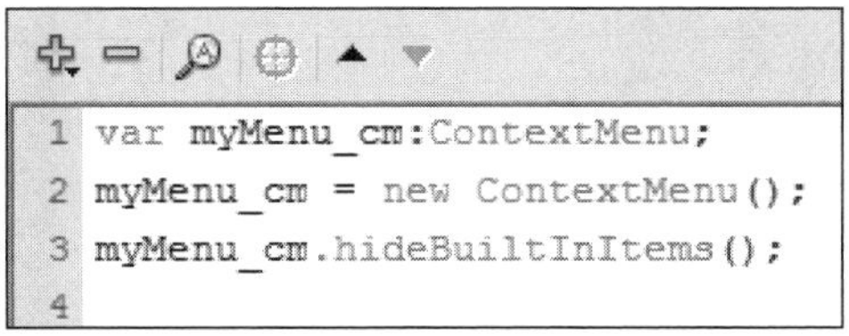
var myMenu_cm:ContextMenu;
myMenu_cm = new ContextMenu();
myMenu_cm.hideBuiltInItems();

Figure 4.83 By using the `hideBuiltInItems` method, you disable all built-in (default) items of the contextual menu.

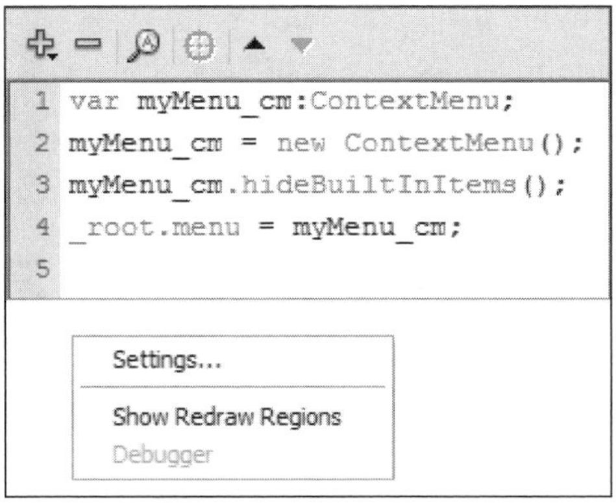
var myMenu_cm:ContextMenu;
myMenu_cm = new ContextMenu();
myMenu_cm.hideBuiltInItems();
_root.menu = myMenu_cm;
Settings...
Show Redraw Regions
Debugger

Figure 4.84 The final code (top) hides the all the default items except for the Settings and Debugger items (bottom). The Show Redraw Regions item appears only in debugger versions of the Flash Player and won't appear for regular users.

If you associate your `ContextMenu` object with a specific button or movie clip, your custom contextual menu will appear when the user activates the contextual menu while the mouse pointer is over that object. For example, a particular movie clip of a map can have the Zoom item in its contextual menu enabled, whereas other objects may have the Zoom item in their contextual menu disabled.

To disable the contextual menu:

1. Select the first frame of the main Timeline, and open the Actions panel.
2. Declare a variable for your new `ContextMenu` object using the `var` statement. Set its type to `ContextMenu`.
3. Instantiate your `ContextMenu` variable using the `set variable` action. For the value, choose ActionScript 2.0 Classes > Movie > Context Menu > ContextMenu > "new ContextMenu".

   A new `ContextMenu` object is named and created (**Figure 4.82**).
4. On the next line of the Script pane, choose ActionScript 2.0 Classes > Movie > Context Menu > ContextMenu > Methods > hideBuiltInItems; add the name of your `ContextMenu` object (**Figure 4.83**).

   This method sets all the properties of the `builtInItems` object of the `ContextMenu` class to false, which hides the items of the contextual menu.
5. On the third line of the Script pane, use a `set variable` action to set the main Timeline's menu property (`_root.menu`) equal to your `ContextMenu` object.

   The `ContextMenu` object now becomes associated with the `_root` Timeline, so the default items of the main Timeline's contextual menu are hidden. The only items that remain are Settings and Debugger (**Figure 4.84**).

To associate custom contextual menus with different objects:

1. Continue with the preceding task. Starting on the next available line in the Script pane, declare another `ContextMenu` object and instantiate the object using the constructor function, `new ContextMenu()`.

   A second `ContextMenu` object is named and created (**Figure 4.85**).

2. Add a call to the `hideBuiltInItems` method for your new `ContextMenu` instance (choose ActionScript 2.0 Classes > Movie > Context Menu > ContextMenu > Methods > hideBuiltInItems).

   The items of your second `ContextMenu` object, like the first, are disabled.

3. Add a `set variable` action (Statements > Variables > "set variable").

   This will be used to make the Zoom items visible only on your new `ContextMenu` instance.

4. For the variable that will be assigned the value, enter the name for the second `ContextMenu` object that you created, followed by a period.

5. Choose `builtInItems.zoom` from the code hint menu that appears (Win).

   or

   With the cursor after the period, select ActionScript 2.0 Classes > Movie > Context Menu > ContextMenu > Objects > builtInItems > Properties > zoom.

6. Set the property to the value true.

   The completed statement, `zoom_cm.builtInItems.zoom = true`, tells Flash to enable the Zoom item in the contextual menu.

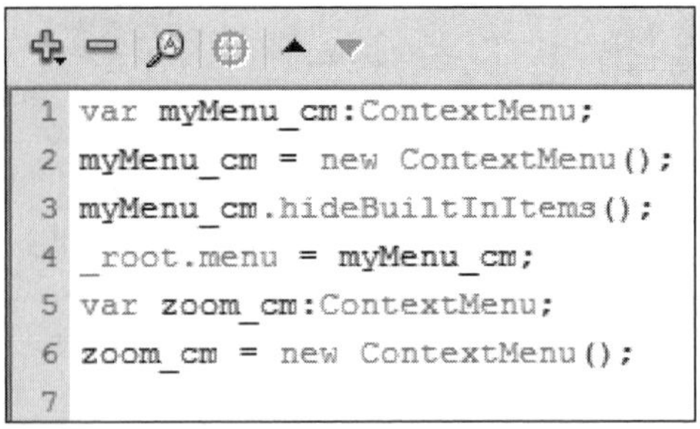
var myMenu_cm:ContextMenu;
myMenu_cm = new ContextMenu();
myMenu_cm.hideBuiltInItems();
_root.menu = myMenu_cm;
var zoom_cm:ContextMenu;
zoom_cm = new ContextMenu();

Figure 4.85 A new `ContextMenu` object named `zoom_cm` has been created.

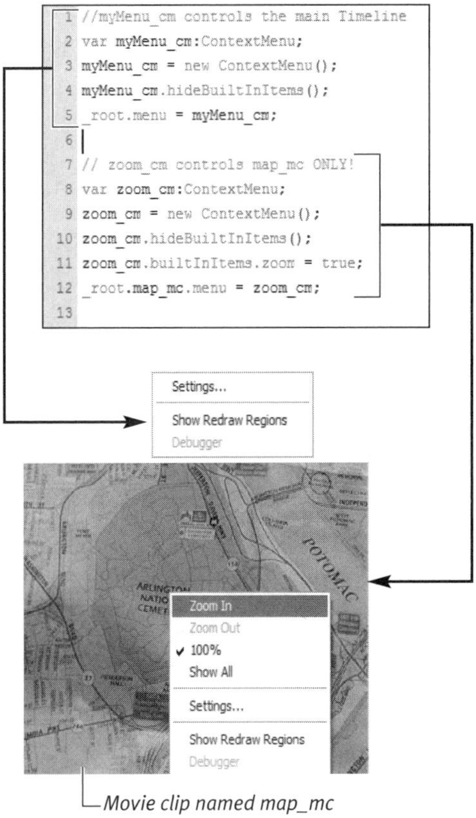
//myMenu_cm controls the main Timeline
var myMenu_cm:ContextMenu;
myMenu_cm = new ContextMenu();
myMenu_cm.hideBuiltInItems();
_root.menu = myMenu_cm;
// zoom_cm controls map_mc ONLY!
var zoom_cm:ContextMenu;
zoom_cm = new ContextMenu();
zoom_cm.hideBuiltInItems();
zoom_cm.builtInItems.zoom = true;
_root.map_mc.menu = zoom_cm;
Settings...
Show Redraw Regions
Debugger
POTOMAC
Zoom In
Zoom Out
100%
Show All
Settings...
Show Redraw Regions
Debugger
Movie clip named map_mc

Figure 4.86 The completed script (top). The contextual menu that is attached to the main Timeline has its default items hidden (middle). The contextual menu that is attached to the movie clip called `map_mc` contains the Zoom In item (bottom).

7. On next line, add a `set variable` action to assign your second contextual menu to the `menu` property of a movie clip or button. For the variable to receive the value, enter `_root.` followed by the instance name of the object you wish to associate with your second contextual menu, then another period, and the property `menu`. For the value to assign, enter the name of your second `ContextMenu` item that you created in the beginning of this task.

The completed statement associates the second `ContextMenu` object with the movie clip instance only (**Figure 4.86**).

Creating new contextual menu items

You can add your own items in the contextual menu by creating new objects from the `ContextMenuItem` class. Each new item requires that you instantiate a separate `ContextMenuItem` object, as in the following code:

```
var myFirstItem_cmi:ContextMenuItem =
new ContextMenuItem("First Item",
myFirstItemHandler);
```

The first parameter of the constructor function is a string value that represents the text that will be displayed for the item in the contextual menu. Because it's a string, use quotation marks around the first parameter to display the enclosed text. The second parameter represents the name of a function that will be invoked when the user selects the item. Create the function to respond to the item selection, like so:

```
function myFirstItemHandler() {
    // place actions here
}
```

Finally, you must add your new ContextMenuItem object to the customItems property of your ContextMenu object. However, the customItems property is different than the builtInItems property you learned about in the preceding section. The customItems property is an array, which is an ordered list of values or objects. (You can learn more about arrays in Chapter 11.) In order to add your new ContextMenuItem object to the customItems array, use the array method push(), as in the following code:

```
my_cm.customItems.push(myFirstItem_cmi);
```

In this statement, my_cm is the name of the ContextMenu object, and myFirstItem_cmi is the name of the ContextMenuItem object.

To create a new item for the contextual menu:

1. Select the first frame of the main Timeline, and open the Actions panel.
2. In the Script pane, create a new ContextMenu object as in previous tasks. The completed code looks like this:
   ```
   var my_cm:ContextMenu;
   my_cm = new ContextMenu();
   ```
3. Starting on the next line, declare and instantiate a new ContextMenuItem object.
   This is identical to declaring and instantiating a ContextMenu object, except for the data type and constructor function (in this case, ActionScript 2.0 Classes > Movie > Context Menu > ContextMenuItem > "new ContextMenuItem").
   A new ContextMenuItem is instantiated.
4. Between the parentheses of the constructor function, enter an item name for the first parameter and a function name for the second parameter.
   Be sure to enclose the first parameter in quotation marks and to separate your parameters with a comma (**Figure 4.87**).
5. On the next line, add a call to the Array class's push method by choosing ActionScript 2.0 Classes > Core > Array > Methods > push.
6. For the Array whose method you're calling (the Object field), enter the name of your ContextMenu object followed by a period.

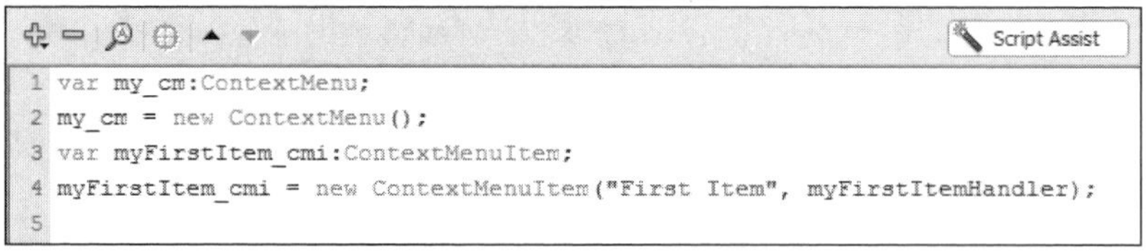

Figure 4.87 A new ContextMenuItem object called myFirstItem_cmi is created with two parameters: the name of the item ("First Item") and the name of a function that will be invoked when the item is selected (myFirstItemHandler).

7. In the code hint pull-down menu that appears, choose customItems (Win).

or

Choose ActionScript 2.0 Classes > Movie > Context Menu > ContextMenu > Properties > customItems.

8. Between the parentheses of the push() method (in the "value" field in Script Assist mode), enter the name of your ContextMenuItem object.

The completed statement adds your ContextMenuItem object to the customItems array of your ContextMenu object (**Figure 4.88**).

9. On the following line, create the function that will respond to the selection of your ContextMenuItem by choosing Statements > User-Defined Functions > function. Set the function's name (the Name field) to the name that is passed to the ContextMenuItem's constructor in step 4 (**Figure 4.89**).

The actions that should happen when the user selects your custom item in the contextual menu go inside the function's curly braces.

continues on next page

| Object: | my_cm.customItems |
| value: | myFirstItem_cmi |

```
1  var my_cm:ContextMenu;
2  my_cm = new ContextMenu();
3  var myFirstItem_cmi:ContextMenuItem;
4  myFirstItem_cmi = new ContextMenuItem("First Item", myFirstItemHandler);
5  my_cm.customItems.push(myFirstItem_cmi);
6
```

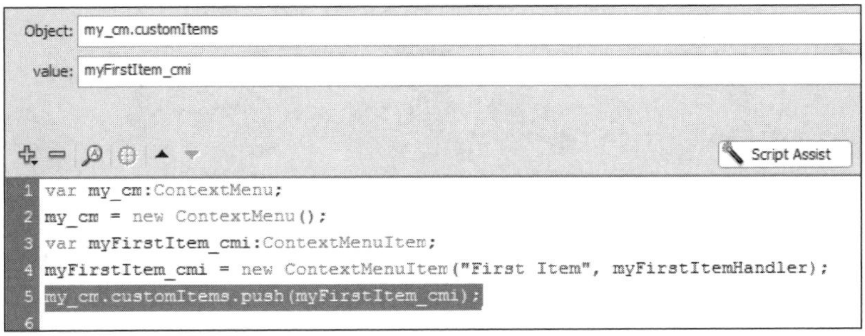

Figure 4.88 The ContextMenuItem called myFirstItem_cmi is put into the customItems array.

Name:	myFirstItemHandler
Parameters:	
Type:	<Type> ☑ Add Import Action for Type

```
1  var my_cm:ContextMenu;
2  my_cm = new ContextMenu();
3  var myFirstItem_cmi:ContextMenuItem;
4  myFirstItem_cmi = new ContextMenuItem("First Item", myFirstItemHandler);
5  my_cm.customItems.push(myFirstItem_cmi);
6  function myFirstItemHandler() {
7  }
8
```

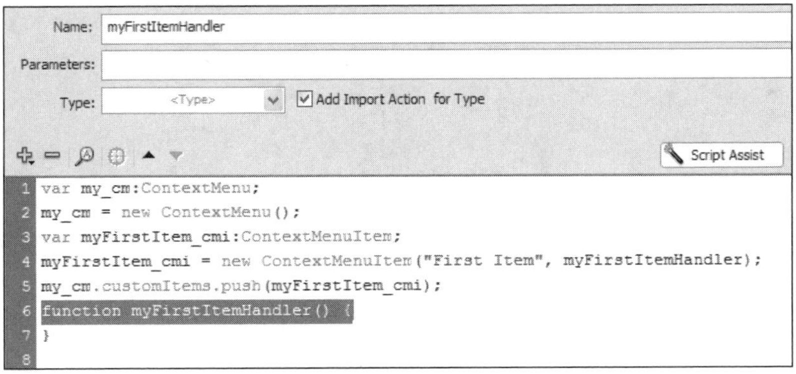

Figure 4.89 The function that will respond to the selection of the item is defined in myFirstItemHandler.

10. On the line after the end of the function, assign the ContextMenu object as the _root movie clip's menu, just as you did in the previous tasks (use a set variable action with _root.menu as the Variable and the name of your ContextMenu object as the Value expression).

The ContextMenu object now becomes associated with the _root Timeline (**Figure 4.90**).

✔ Tips

- If you have multiple custom items in your contextual menu, you may want to organize them by separating them into groups. An optional third parameter in the ContextMenuItem constructor function adds a horizontal separator above the item if it's set to true (**Figure 4.91**).
- The function that is defined as the second parameter of the new ContextMenuItem is required. Without it, your item won't show up in the contextual menu.

```
var my_cm:ContextMenu;
my_cm = new ContextMenu();
var myFirstItem_cmi:ContextMenuItem;
myFirstItem_cmi = new ContextMenuItem("First Item", myFirstItemHandler);
my_cm.customItems.push(myFirstItem_cmi);
function myFirstItemHandler() {
}
_root.menu = my_cm;
```

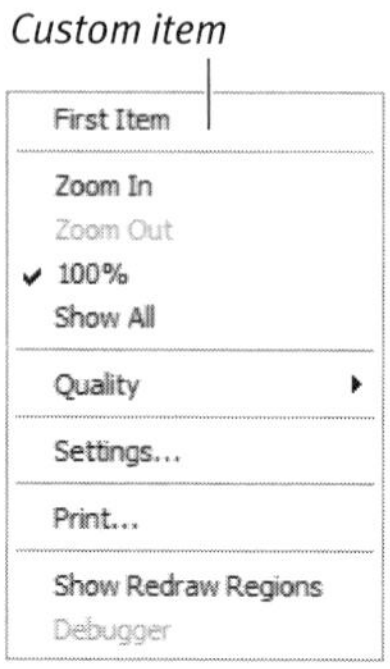

Figure 4.90 The final code (left) makes the custom item show up at the top of the contextual menu (right).

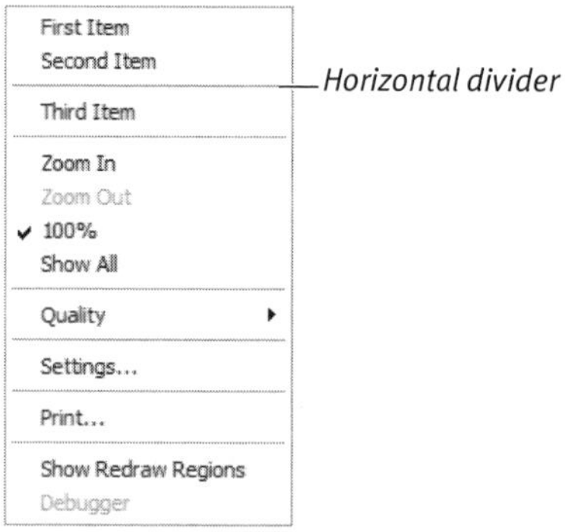

Figure 4.91 The custom item called Third Item has been defined with a horizontal divider above it.

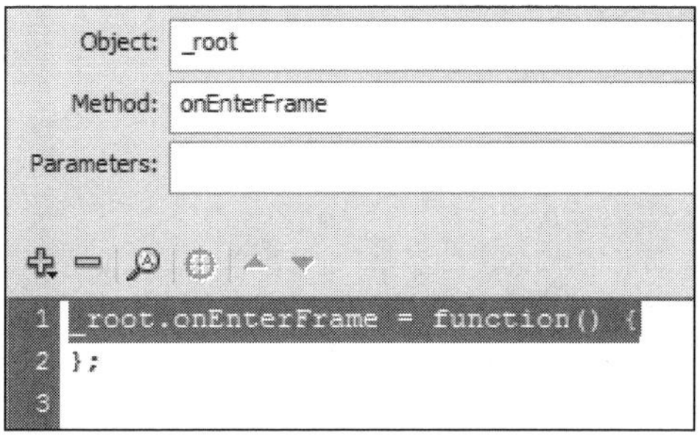

Figure 4.92 The `onEnterFrame` event handler.

Creating Continuous Actions with onEnterFrame

So far, you've learned ways to execute an action in response to events that happen when the user does something. But on many occasions, you'll want to perform an action continuously. An `if` statement, for example, often needs to be performed continuously to check whether conditions in the movie have changed. And often, the command that changes the position of a movie clip needs to be performed continuously to animate it across the Stage.

The movie clip event `onEnterFrame` happens continuously. The event is triggered at the frame rate of the movie, so if the frame rate is set to 12 frames per second, the `onEnterFrame` event is triggered 12 times per second. Even when the `onEnterFrame` event is assigned to a movie clip whose Timeline is stopped, the event continues to happen. This setup is an ideal way to make actions run on automatic pilot; they will run as soon as the `onEnterFrame` event handler is established and stop only when the `onEnterFrame` event handler is deleted or the movie clip on which the `onEnterFrame` is defined is removed.

To create continuous actions with onEnterFrame:

1. Select the first frame of the main Timeline, and open the Actions panel.
2. In the Script pane, choose ActionScript 2.0 Classes > Movie > MovieClip > Event Handlers > onEnterFrame.
3. Enter `_root` as the object to which the method is assigned (the Object field in Script Assist mode) (**Figure 4.92**).

continues on next page

4. Between the function's curly braces, choose Statements > Conditions/Loops > if.

5. For the `condition` parameter (the expression that goes between the opening and closing parentheses of the `if` statement), enter this statement:

   `Key.getCode() == Key.SPACE`

   The `getCode()` method of the `Key` class retrieves the key code of the last key pressed. Flash checks to see whether that key matches the one you specify after the double equals signs. The double equals signs (==) tell Flash to compare two items to determine if they're equal.

   Flash tests the condition continuously at the frame rate of the main Timeline. This test happens even if the Timeline is stopped.

6. Choose an action as the consequence of this `if` statement, and add it between the curly braces of the `if` statement (**Figure 4.93**).

```
stop();
_root.onEnterFrame = function() {
    if (Key.getCode() == Key.SPACE) {
        gotoAndStop(5);
    }
};
```

Figure 4.93 Flash continuously monitors whether the last key pressed was the spacebar. If so, it moves the playhead to frame 5 and stops there.

✔ Tips

- Here's a preview of the kind of dynamic updates you can do with the `onEnterFrame` clip event by combining it with movie clip properties. Replace the `if` statement in the preceding task with the statement `ball_mc._xscale += 1;`. Now, add a movie clip instance to the Stage, and name it `ball_mc` in the Property inspector. The Script pane should look like this:

```
_root.onEnterFrame = function() {
    ball_mc._xscale += 1;
};
```

  The statement `ball_mc._xscale += 1` adds 1 percent to the horizontal width of your movie clip. Because the action is triggered continuously by the `onEnterFrame` event, the movie clip keeps growing.

- Be careful of over-using the `onEnterframe` event handler, because it can be processor-intensive. After you no longer need the event handler, it's good practice to use the `delete` statement to remove the event handler from the movie clip that is associated with it. Doing so prevents Flash from having to execute the event needlessly.

Creating Continuous Actions with setInterval

The `onEnterFrame` event, although easy to use and effective for creating most continuous actions, is limited to the frame rate of your Flash movie. If you want to perform an action on a continuous basis but do so at specific intervals, you should use the action `setInterval` instead.

You can use the `setInterval` action in two basic ways. In the first way, you provide two parameters: a function that is invoked on a continuous basis, and the interval (in milliseconds) that separates the function invocation. If you want the function called `blinkingLight` to be called every 5 seconds, you can write the statement `setInterval(blinkingLight, 5000)`. Then you then must define the `blinkingLight` function.

The second way to use `setInterval` is to provide an object, its method, and an interval. Instead of calling a function at a periodic interval, Flash calls the method of the object at a periodic interval. This method can be one that already exists or one that you define yourself. You can call the `nextFrame()` method on the main Timeline every second with this statement:

```
setInterval(_root, "nextFrame", 1000)
```

Notice that the method name is in quotation marks.

To create continuous actions with setInterval (first way):

1. Select the first frame of the main Timeline, and open the Actions panel.
2. Choose Global Functions > Miscellaneous Functions > setInterval.
3. Between the parentheses, enter the name of a function followed by a comma and then an interval (in milliseconds) (**Figure 4.94**).

   The function will be called continuously at the specified interval.

continues on next page

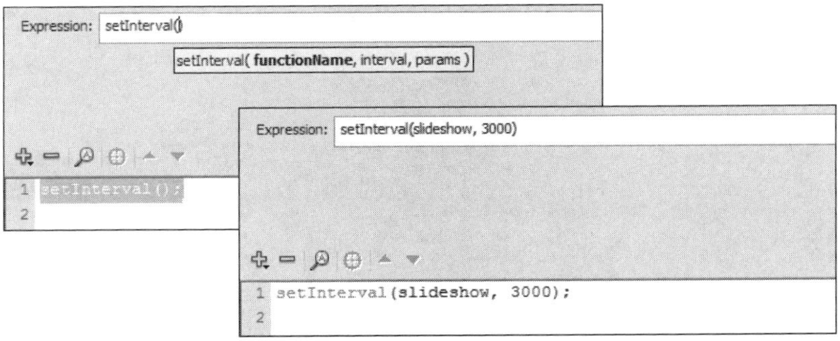

Figure 4.94 The function called `slideshow()` will be called every 3 seconds.

4. On the next line, choose Statements > User-Defined Functions > function (Esc + fn).

5. Enter a name for the function.

   This name is the same one that you used in the `setInterval` action (**Figure 4.95**).

6. Add actions inside your function that you want to execute at the periodic interval (**Figure 4.96**).

✔ Tip

- Add the action `updateAfterEvent` (Global Functions > Movie Clip Control > updateAfterEvent) to your function if you're modifying graphics at a smaller interval than your movie frame rate. This method forces Flash to refresh the display, providing smoother results.

To create continuous actions with setInterval (second way):

1. Select the first frame of the main Timeline, and open the Actions panel.

2. Choose Global Functions > Miscellaneous Actions > setInterval.

3. Between the parentheses for `setInterval()`, enter the name of an object followed by the name of its method in quotation marks and then an interval (in milliseconds), separating your parameters with commas (**Figure 4.97**).

   The method will be called continuously at the specified interval. This example uses a method of the `MovieClip` class, but you can define and use your own method.

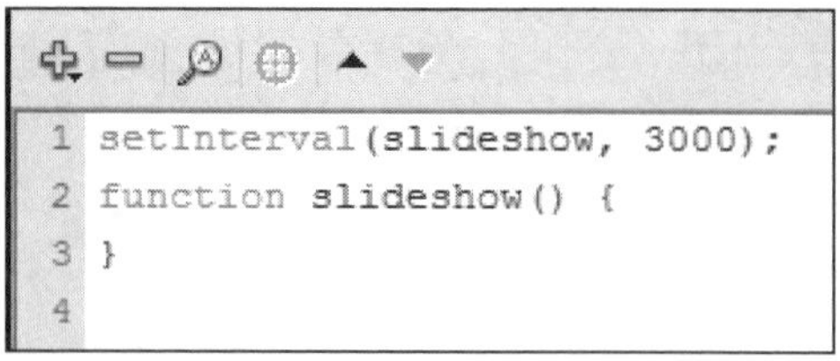
setInterval(slideshow, 3000);
function slideshow() {
}

Figure 4.95 A new function named `slideshow()` has been created.

setInterval
Layer 5
slides
stop();
setInterval(slideShow, 3000);
function slideShow() {
nextFrame();
}

Figure 4.96 This movie contains images from a recent trip to the zoo. The images are in separate keyframes. The `setInterval` action advances to the next image every 3 seconds automatically. The `stop` action has been added to prevent the images from playing until `setInterval` calls the `slideshow` function.

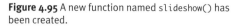

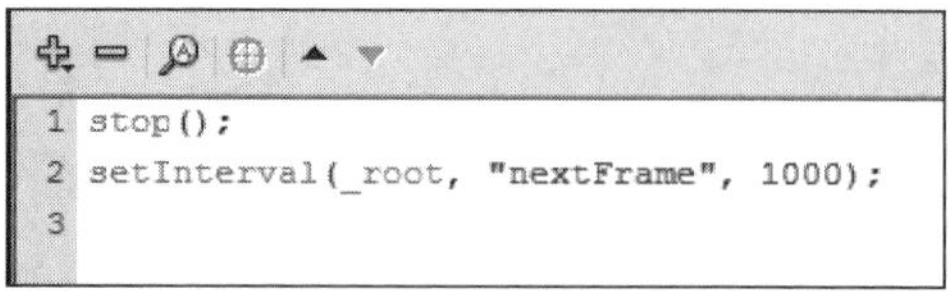
stop();
setInterval(_root, "nextFrame", 1000);

Figure 4.97 This `setInterval` does the same job as in the preceding example, except that it advances every second.

✔ Tips

- In both ways of using the `setInterval` action, you can pass parameters. The first way, you can pass parameters to your function; the second way, you can pass parameters to your method. If the method you define in `setInterval` requires parameters, you must provide them at the end of the parameters for `setInterval`, as in this example:

  ```
  setInterval(myObject, "myMethod",
  1000, parameter1, parameter2);
  ```

  This `setInterval` statement causes `myObject.myMethod(parameter1, parameter2)` to be called every second.

- Although `setInterval` uses milliseconds to determine when to trigger a function or a method, it must do so during frame transitions set by the movie frame rate. This setup makes the interplay between `setInterval` and the frame rate a little tricky and makes exact timing less direct than you'd expect. At 10 frames per second, for example, a frame transition occurs every 100 milliseconds. If you define an interval of 200 milliseconds, Flash waits two frames (200 ms) until the interval passes; then it triggers the method or function on frame 3. It waits two more frames (another 200 ms) and then triggers on frame 6. Finally, after two more frames, it triggers on frame 9.

  If you change your movie to play at 20 frames per second, a frame transition occurs every 50 milliseconds. Flash waits four frames (200 ms) and triggers the method or function on frame 5. It waits another four frames and triggers on frame 10. It continues to trigger on every fifth frame—at frame 15 and frame 20. If you compare the two movies, the one at 10 fps gets triggered three times in the first second (frames 3, 6, and 9), whereas the one at 20 fps gets triggered four times in the first second (frames 5, 10, 15, and 20). Even though they both have the same 200 ms interval defined in `setInterval`, frame rates can have significant effects.

Stopping a setInterval action

The `setInterval` action continues to call the function or method at regular intervals until the movie ends or until you remove the `setInterval` action with `clearInterval`. The action `clearInterval` requires one parameter, which is a numerical ID that Flash assigns to each `setInterval` action. Flash passes back the ID when you call the `setInterval` action, allowing you to store it in a variable. In the preceding tasks, you didn't save the ID returned by the `setInterval` action because you had no intention of stopping it. In this next task, you'll store the ID of your `setInterval` action in a variable. Then, you can clear it by using the `clearInterval` action.

To clear a setInterval action:

1. Select the first frame of the main Timeline, and open the Actions panel.
2. Declare a variable with a data type of `Number`.

   This variable will keep track of the ID of the `setInterval` action.
3. Add a `set variable` action, which will be used to call the `setInterval` action and store the ID in your variable.
4. Add your variable's name to the left side of the equals sign (the Variable field in Script Assist mode).
5. On the right side of the equals sign (the Value field in Script Assist mode), choose Global Functions > Miscellaneous Actions > setInterval.
6. Between the parentheses for `setInterval()`, enter the name of the object followed by the name of its method in quotation marks and then the interval (in milliseconds). Remember to separate your parameters with commas (**Figure 4.98**).

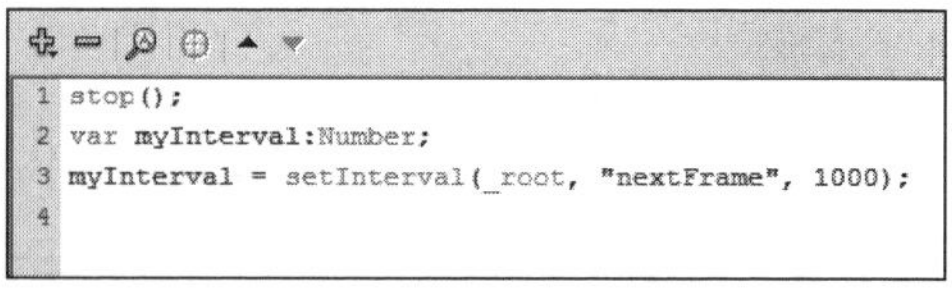
stop();
var myInterval:Number;
myInterval = setInterval(_root, "nextFrame", 1000);

Figure 4.98 A variable name has been assigned to the `setInterval` so that you can identify and clear the interval.

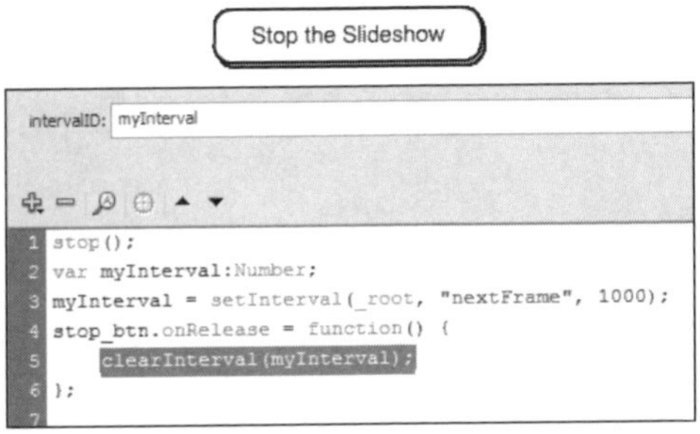

Figure 4.99 When the `clearInterval` action is assigned to a button named `stop_btn` (top), it removes the `setInterval` identified as `myInterval`. The movie no longer advances to the next frame continuously, and the slideshow stops.

7. At a later point in your Flash movie when you want to stop the `setInterval`, such as on a later frame or in an event handler function, choose Global Functions > Miscellaneous Functions > clearInterval.

8. Enter the name of your interval ID variable as the `intervalId` parameter (between the parentheses) of the `clearInterval` action.

   When Flash encounters the `clearInterval` action, it removes the `setInterval` and stops the continuous actions (**Figure 4.99**).

A Summary of Events and Event Handlers

Table 4.5 organizes and compares the many ways you can create event handlers to detect and respond to events.

Table 4.5

A Summary of Events and Event Handlers

Object	Event Handler	Anonymous Function Assigned To
Button	onPress	button instance
	onRelease	
	onReleaseOutside	
	onRollover	
	onRollOut	
	onDragOver	
	onDragOut	
	onSetFocus	
	onKillFocus	
Mouse	onMouseUp	Listener
	onMouseDown	
	onMouseMove	
	onMouseWheel	
Key	onKeyUp	Listener
	onKeyDown	
MovieClip (may also receive Button events)	onLoad	MovieClip instance
	onUnload	
	onData	
	onEnterFrame	
	onMouseDown	
	onMouseUp	
	onMouseMove	
	onKeyUp	
	onKeyDown	

5 Controlling Multiple Timelines

To create interactivity and direct your users to see, hear, and do exactly what you want, you have to know how to control the Flash playhead on different Timelines. The playhead displays what is on the Stage at any time, plays back any sound, and triggers any actions attached to the Timeline. Jumping from frame to frame on the main movie Timeline is simple enough; you use basic actions you should be familiar with, such as `gotoAndPlay`, `gotoAndStop`, `play`, and `stop`. But when you include movie clip symbols in your movie, you introduce other independent Timelines that can be controlled individually. Your main Timeline can control a movie clip's Timeline; a movie clip's Timeline can, in turn, control the main Timeline. You can even have the Timeline of one movie clip control the Timeline of another. Handling this complex interaction and navigation between Timelines is the subject of this chapter.

Navigating Timelines with Movie Clips

The independent Timelines of movie clip symbols make complicated navigation schemes possible (**Figure 5.1**). While the main Timeline is playing, other Timelines of movie clips can be playing as well, interacting with one another and specifying which frames to play or when to stop. It's quite common to have enough movie clips on the Stage all talking to one another that the main movie Timeline need be only a single frame for the entire movie to work. Driving all this navigation between Timelines is, of course, ActionScript. The basic actions used to navigate within the main Timeline (`gotoAndStop`, `gotoAndPlay`, `stop`, `play`, `nextFrame`, and `prevFrame`) can also be used to navigate the Timeline of any movie clip. This navigation is possible because you can give a name to every movie clip instance on the Stage. As you've seen in previous chapters, you name a movie clip instance in the Property inspector. When an instance is named, you can identify its particular Timeline and give instructions on where you want to move its playhead.

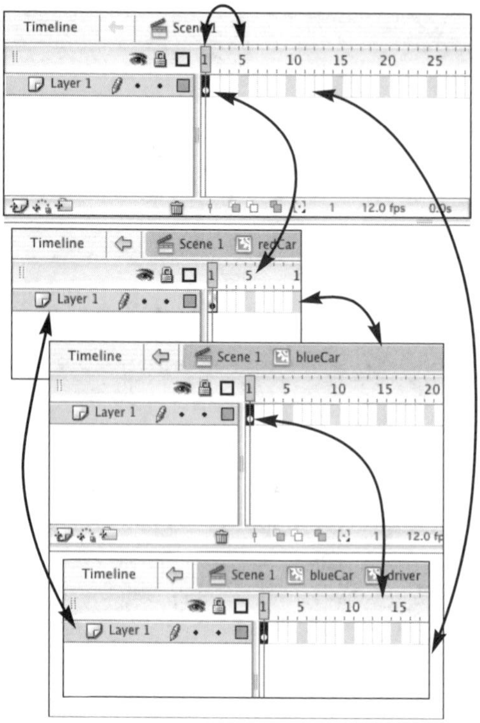

Figure 5.1 A movie can contain many Timelines that interact with one another. This example shows Scene 1 as the main Timeline; it contains two movie clips. One of the movie clips contains another movie clip. The arrows show just a few of the possible lines of communication.

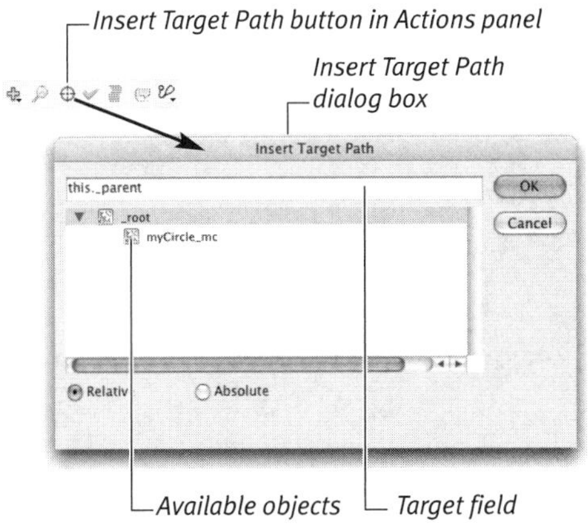

Figure 5.2 The Insert Target Path dialog box allows you to choose a target path by clicking a movie clip, button, or text field within the hierarchy.

Target Paths

A *target path* is essentially an object name, or a series of object names separated by dots, that tells Flash where to find a particular object. To control movie clip Timelines, you specify the target path for a particular movie clip followed by the method you want to call. The target path tells Flash which movie clip instance to look at, and the method tells Flash what to do with that movie clip instance. The methods of the `MovieClip` class that control the playhead are `gotoAndStop()`, `gotoAndPlay()`, `play()`, `stop()`, `nextFrame()`, and `prevFrame()`. If you name a movie clip instance `myClock_mc`, for example, and you write the ActionScript statement `myClock_mc.gotoAndStop(10)`, the playhead within the movie clip instance called `myClock_mc` will move to frame 10 and stop there. `myClock_mc` is the target path, and `gotoAndStop()` is the method.

The Insert Target Path button at the top of the Script pane of the Actions panel opens the Insert Target Path dialog box, which provides a visual way to insert a target path (**Figure 5.2**). All named movie clip instances, button instances, and text fields are shown in a hierarchical fashion in the display window. You can select individual objects, and the correct target paths appear in the Target field.

To target a movie clip instance from the main Timeline:

1. Create a movie clip symbol that contains an animation on its Timeline, and place an instance of it on the Stage.
2. In the Property inspector, give the instance a name (**Figure 5.3**).
3. Select a keyframe of the main Timeline, and open the Actions panel.

   You'll assign an action to the main Timeline that will control the movie clip instance.
4. Choose ActionScript 2.0 Classes > Movie > MovieClip > Methods > stop.

   The placeholder text `not_set_yet` appears in the Script pane, followed by a `stop()` action (**Figure 5.4**).
5. Select the text `not_set_yet` in the Actions panel, and replace it with the instance name of the movie clip symbol.

   or

   In Script Assist mode, enter the instance name of the movie clip symbol in the Object field (**Figure 5.5**).
6. Test your movie (Control > "Test movie").

   Your movie clip would normally play its animation on the main Stage. The action you assign on the main Timeline, however, targets your movie clip and tells the playhead to stop.

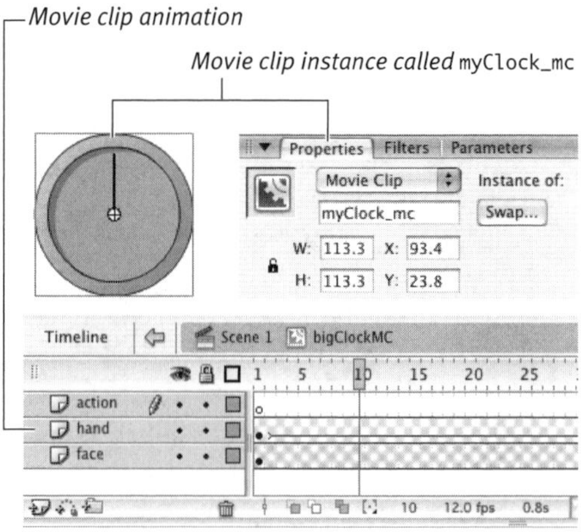

Figure 5.3 The movie clip instance called `myClock_mc` is on the main Timeline. The movie clip contains an animation (below) of the hand rotating.

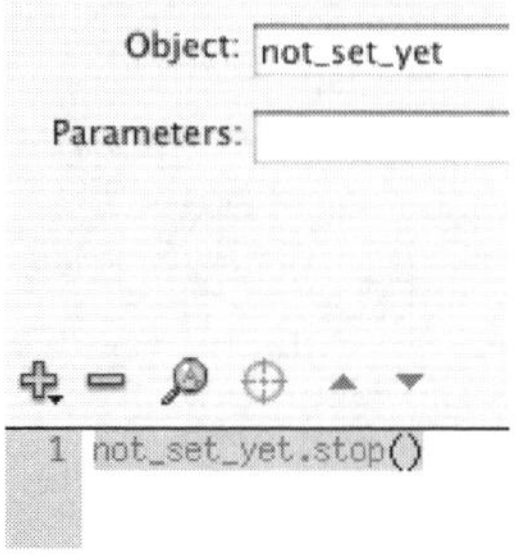

Figure 5.4 A default placeholder named `not_set_yet` (selected) appears in the Script pane, followed by a `stop()` action.

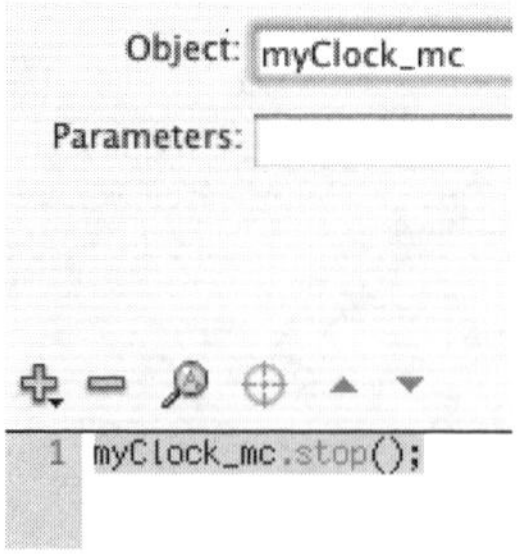

Figure 5.5 The target path is `myClock_mc`, and the method is `stop()`. The playhead of the `myClock_mc` Timeline stops when this action is triggered.

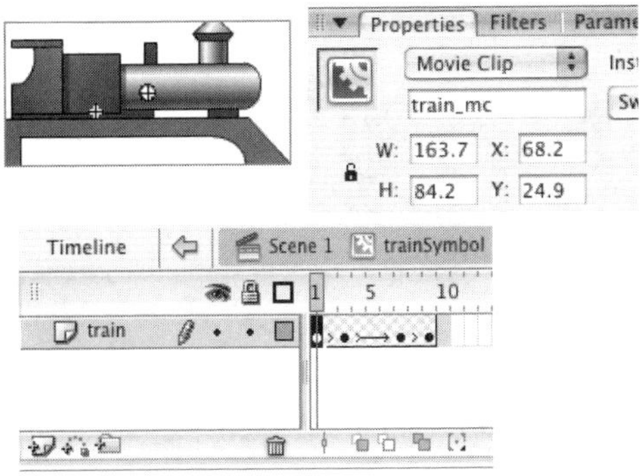

Figure 5.6 The movie clip instance called `train_mc` is on the main Timeline. The movie clip contains an animation (below) of the train shaking back and forth.

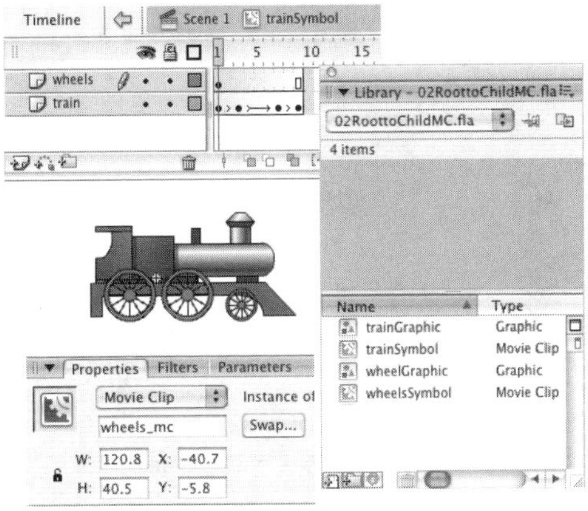

Figure 5.7 Place an instance of a movie clip inside the train movie clip. Name the child movie clip instance `wheels_mc`.

Target paths for nested movie clips

You can have a movie clip within another movie clip. The outer movie clip is the parent, and the one that's nested inside it is the child. Because the child clip is part of the parent, any transformations you do to the parent also affect the child. To control the Timeline of a child movie clip from the main Timeline, use the parent name followed by the child name, separated by a period, to form the target path. In the following task, the parent movie clip is a train (`train_mc`), and the child movie clip is its wheels (`wheels_mc`).

To target a child of a movie clip instance from the main Timeline:

1. Create a movie clip symbol that contains an animation on its Timeline, place an instance on the Stage, and name it in the Property inspector (**Figure 5.6**).
2. Create another movie clip symbol that contains an animation on its Timeline.
3. Go to symbol-editing mode for the first movie clip, and drag an instance of your second movie clip to the Stage.
4. In the Property inspector, give the second movie clip instance a name (**Figure 5.7**).

   You now have a parent movie clip on the main Stage. The parent movie clip contains a child movie clip.
5. Exit symbol-editing mode, and return to the main Stage.
6. Select a keyframe in the main Timeline, and open the Actions panel.
7. Choose ActionScript 2.0 Classes > Movie > MovieClip > Methods > stop.

continues on next page

8. Select the placeholder `not_set_yet`, and then click the Insert Target Path button.

   or

   In Script Assist mode, place the cursor in the Object field, and click the Insert Target Path button.

   The Insert Target Path dialog box opens.

9. Choose Relative from the radio buttons at the bottom of the Insert Target Path dialog box.

10. In the display window, click the triangle (Mac) or the plus sign (Windows) in front of the parent movie clip.

    The hierarchy expands, showing the child movie clip within the parent (**Figure 5.8**).

11. Select the child movie clip as the target path, and click OK.

    The target path, in the form `this.Parent.Child`, appears before the method.

12. Test your movie.

    The animation of the wheels turning plays within the movie clip of the train, which is bobbing up and down. The action you assign on the main Timeline, however, targets the movie clip of the wheels that is inside the movie clip of the train and tells its playhead to stop. The animation of the train continues (**Figure 5.9**). Despite the parent-child relationship, the Timelines remain independent.

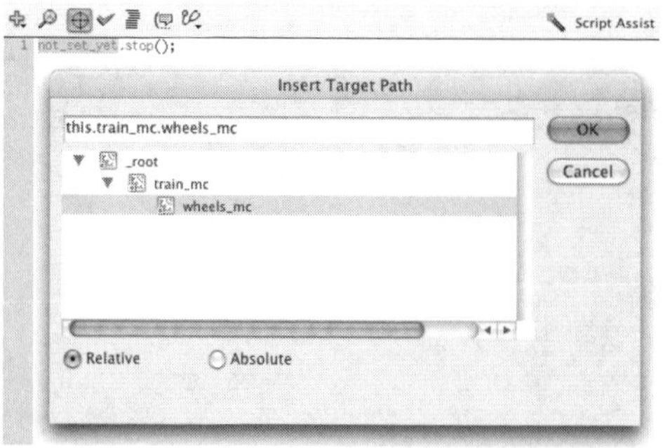

Figure 5.8 The display window of the Insert Target Path dialog box. The hierarchy shows parent-child relationships.

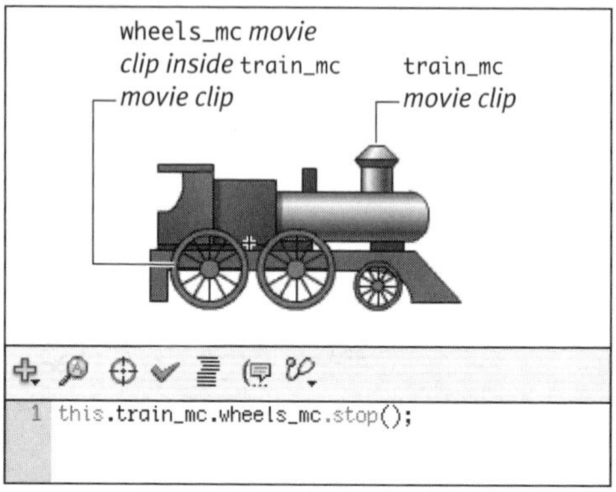

Figure 5.9 The ActionScript statement on the main Timeline tells the `wheels_mc` movie clip inside the `train_mc` movie clip to stop.

Why Relative Paths?

Why use relative paths at all? Absolute paths seem to be a safer construction because they identify an object explicitly no matter where you are.

Relative paths, however, are useful in at least two cases:

- If you create a movie clip that contains actions that affect other movie clips relative to itself, you can move the entire ensemble and still have the target paths work by using relative terms. This method makes it easier to work with complex navigation schemes because you can copy, paste, and move the pieces without having to rewrite the target paths.

  A direct parallel is managing a Web site and maintaining its links. If you were to create absolute paths to links to your résumé and then move your home page to a different server, you'd have to rewrite your links. The more practical method would be to establish relative links within your home page.

- Relative paths are also useful when you create movie clips dynamically. You'll learn how to create movie clip objects and name them on the fly with ActionScript. In these cases, movie clips aren't static, and relative target paths are required to follow them around.

Absolute and Relative Paths

Flash gives you two path type options in the Insert Target Path dialog box: relative and absolute. In the preceding example, the method `this.train_mc.wheels_mc.stop()` originated from the main Timeline. When Flash executes that method, it looks within its own Timeline for the object called `train_mc` that contains another object called `wheels_mc`. This is an example of a relative path. Everything is relative to where the ActionScript statement resides—in this case, the main Timeline. An alternative way of inserting a target path is to use an absolute path, which has no particular frame of reference. You can think of relative target paths as being directions given from your present location, as in "Go two blocks straight; then turn left." Absolute target paths, on the other hand, are directions that work no matter where you are, as in "Go to 555 University Avenue."

Why would you use one type of path instead of the other? If you need to target a Timeline that sits at a higher level than the Timeline you're working in, you can use an absolute path. Imagine that a movie clip sits on the main Timeline. You want to have this movie clip control the main Timeline. In relative mode, you see only the Timelines that are inside the current one. In absolute mode, you see all the Timelines no matter where you are. Absolute mode is like having a bird's-eye view of all the movie clips on the Stage at the same time.

Using this and _root

In relative mode, the current Timeline is called `this`. The keyword `this` means *myself.* All other Timelines are relative to the `this` Timeline. In absolute mode, the path starts with the main movie Timeline, which is called `_root`. All other Timelines are organized relative to the `_root` Timeline (**Figure 5.10**).

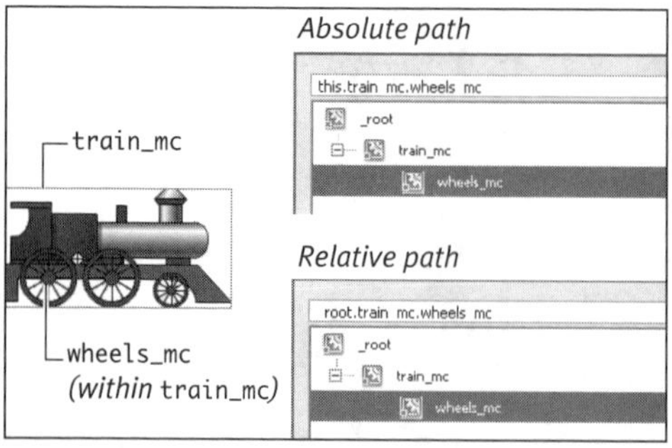

Figure 5.10 Absolute mode versus relative mode of target paths. This example shows the `wheels_mc` movie clip inside the `train_mc` movie clip. When you assign actions on the train Timeline, `this` in the relative path refers to `_root` in the absolute path.

To target the main Timeline from a movie clip instance:

1. Create a movie clip symbol that contains an animation on its Timeline, place an instance of it on the Stage, and give it an instance name in the Property inspector.
2. Go to symbol-editing mode for your movie clip.
3. Select a keyframe on the movie clip's Timeline, and open the Actions panel.

   You'll assign ActionScript to the movie clip's Timeline to control the main Timeline (**Figure 5.11**).
4. Choose ActionScript 2.0 Classes > Movie > MovieClip > Methods > gotoAndStop.

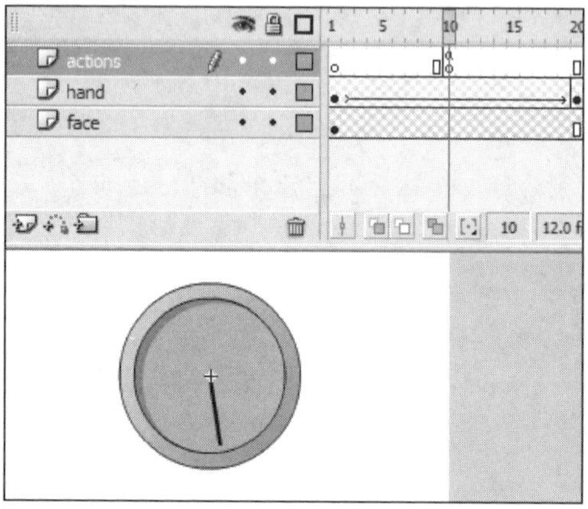

Figure 5.11 This movie clip contains an animation. At keyframe 10, you'll assign an action to move the playhead of the main Timeline.

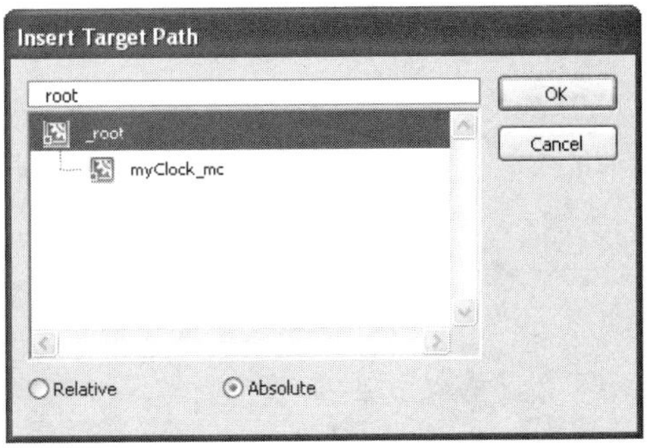

Figure 5.12 An absolute path, selected in the Insert Target Path dialog box, is a top-down address to a Timeline.

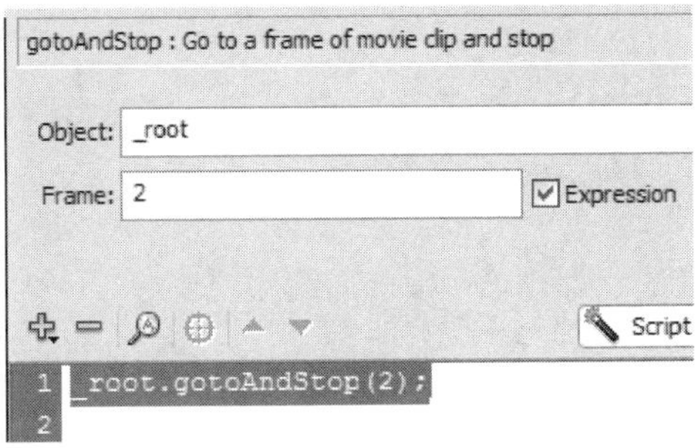

Figure 5.13 The target `_root` inside the Script pane.

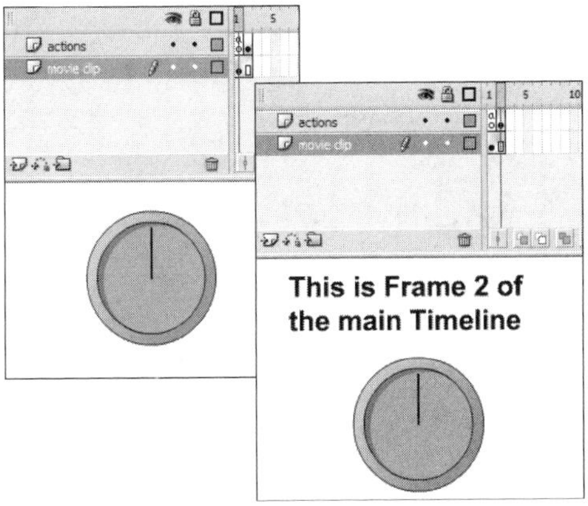

Figure 5.14 The action on the `myClock_mc` Timeline moves the playhead on the main Timeline to frame 2. There is a `stop` action on the main Timeline at frame 1.

5. Select the `not_set_yet` placeholder text.

   or

   In Script Assist mode, click in the Object field.

6. Click the Insert Target Path button to open the Insert Target Path dialog box. Select the Absolute path type.

7. Select `_root`, and click OK (**Figure 5.12**).

   The target path `_root` appears in the Script pane (**Figure 5.13**).

8. With your pointer located between the parentheses (in the Frame field in Script Assist mode), enter a frame number as the main Timeline destination.

9. Test your movie.

   When the ActionScript statement on the movie clip Timeline is executed, Flash jumps outside that Timeline and looks up to the `_root` Timeline to perform the method there (**Figure 5.14**).

To target a movie clip instance from another movie clip instance:

1. Create a movie clip symbol that contains an animation, place an instance of it on the Stage, and give it an instance name in the Property inspector.
2. Create two more movie clip symbols that contain animation.
3. Go to symbol-editing mode for the first movie clip, place instances of the second and third movie clips on the Stage, and give names to both instances in the Property inspector (**Figure 5.15**).

   You now have a parent movie clip on the main Timeline. The parent movie clip contains two child movie clips.
4. Go to symbol-editing mode for the first movie clip (`wheels_mc` in this example).
5. Select a keyframe on the movie clip's Timeline, and open the Actions panel.

   You'll assign ActionScript on the first clip's Timeline to control the Timeline of the second movie clip (`smoke_mc` in this example).
6. Choose ActionScript 2.0 Classes > Movie > MovieClip > Methods > stop.
7. Select the placeholder text `not_set_yet`, and click the Insert Target Path button.

   or

   In Script Assist mode, place the cursor in the Object field, and click the Insert Target Path button.

   The Insert Target Path dialog box opens.
8. Select Absolute as the path type.
9. Select your second movie clip instance (`smoke_mc`), and click OK.

   The target path `_root.train_mc.smoke_mc` appears in the Script pane (**Figure 5.16**).

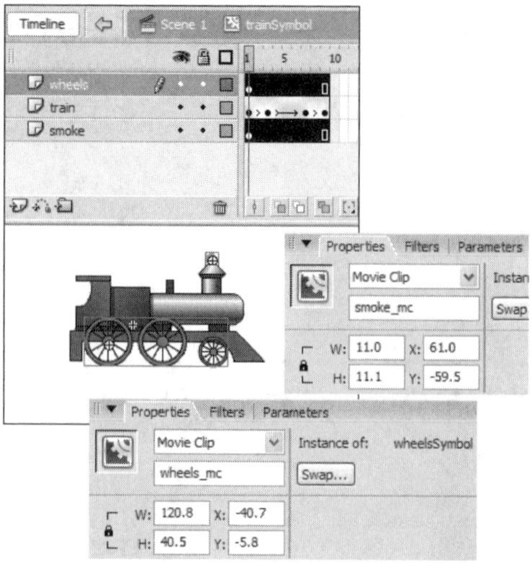

Figure 5.15 The `smoke_mc` movie clip and the `wheels_mc` movie clip are dragged into the movie clip symbol called `trainSymbol`. The instance of `trainSymbol` on the Stage is called `train_mc` (not shown).

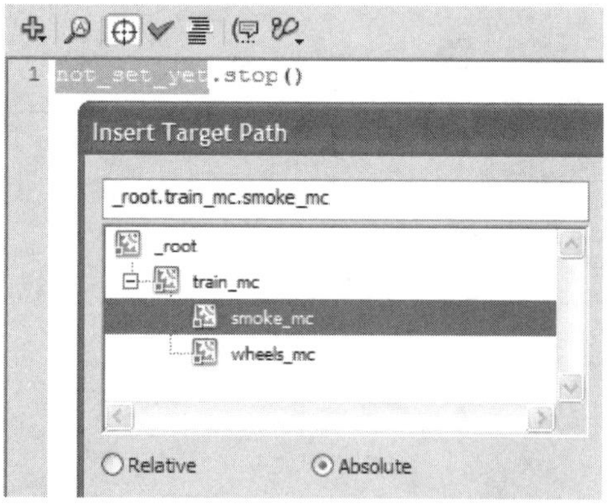

Figure 5.16 Choosing the `smoke_mc` movie clip in the Insert Target Path dialog box and clicking OK replaces the placeholder text (top) with the full target path for the `stop()` method.

Figure 5.17 The animation in the `wheels_mc` movie clip plays. When the clip hits frame 9 of its Timeline (bottom), the ActionScript there tells the `smoke_mc` movie clip to stop playing. The smoke animation has a chance to play only nine frames of itself.

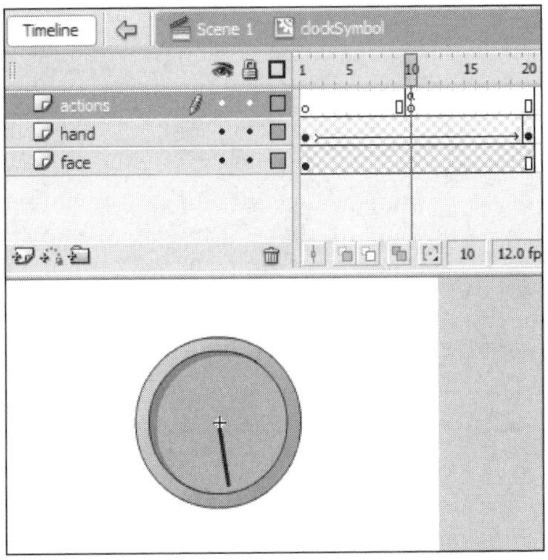

Figure 5.18 This movie clip contains an animation of the hand rotating. The action you'll assign on keyframe 10 will make it stop, so the hand barely makes it to 6 o'clock.

10. Test your movie.

When the ActionScript statement on the `wheels_mc` movie clip Timeline is executed, Flash starts looking from the `_root` Timeline, drills down through the object called `train_mc` to the object called `smoke_mc`, and performs the method on that object (**Figure 5.17**).

To target a movie clip's own Timeline:

1. Create a movie clip symbol that contains an animation, place an instance of it on the Stage, and give the instance a name in the Property inspector.
2. Go to symbol-editing mode for your movie clip.
3. Select a keyframe on the movie clip's Timeline, and open the Actions panel.

   You'll assign ActionScript to the movie clip Timeline that controls its own Timeline (**Figure 5.18**).
4. Choose ActionScript 2.0 Classes > Movie > MovieClip > Methods > stop.
5. Select the placeholder `not_set_yet`, and click the Insert Target Path button.

   or

   In Script Assist mode, click in the Object field, and click the Insert Target Path button.

continues on next page

6. Select Absolute or Relative as the target path mode. In the Target Path dialog box, select the movie clip that you want to target.

   or

   Don't click the Insert Target Path button; instead, delete the placeholder `not_set_yet` and period entirely (**Figure 5.19**).

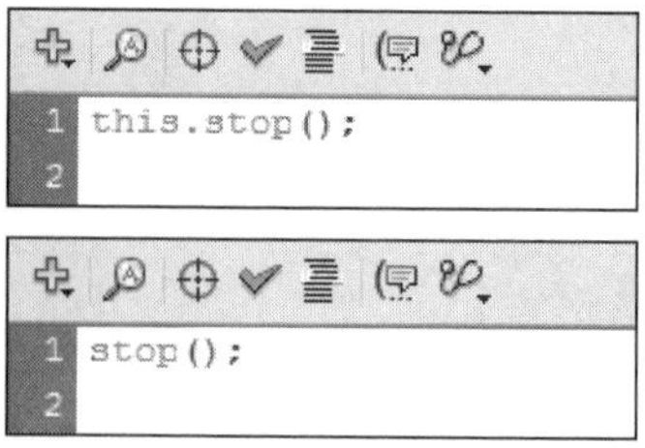

Figure 5.19 Two equivalent statements to target the `myClock` Timeline from within `myClock` itself.

✔ Tip

- Using `this` or an absolute path to target a movie clip's own Timeline is unnecessary, just as it's unnecessary to use `this` or `_root` when navigating within the main Timeline. It's understood that actions residing in one movie clip pertain, or are scoped, to that particular movie clip.

Using _parent in target paths

You may find that you want to use a relative path, but you need to target a movie clip that is above the current Timeline on the hierarchy (or contained within one that is higher on the hierarchy). In that case, you can choose Relative in the Insert Target Path dialog box, and you'll see the special term `_parent`. Use `_parent` to create a relative path to the movie clip at the next-higher level from the current Timeline.

To target the parent of a movie clip:

1. Create a movie clip symbol that contains an animation, place an instance of it on the Stage, and give the instance a name in the Property inspector.
2. Create another movie clip symbol that contains an animation.
3. Go to symbol-editing mode for the first movie clip, place an instance of the second movie clip on the Stage, and give the instance a name in the Property inspector.

   You now have a parent movie clip on the main Timeline. The parent movie clip contains a child movie clip (**Figure 5.20**).

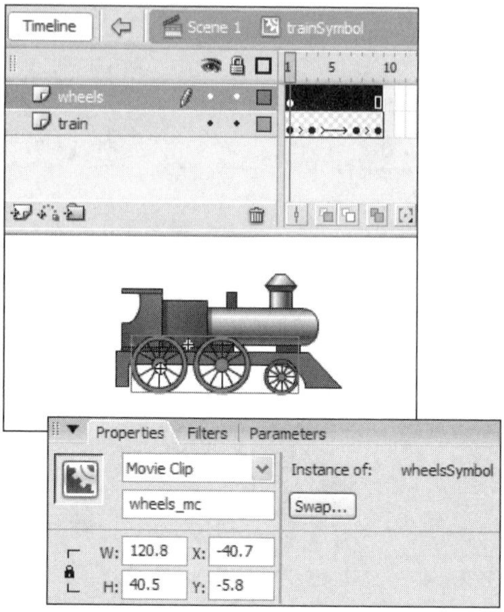

Figure 5.20 Place an instance of a movie clip inside the `train_mc` movie clip. This child movie clip is called `wheels_mc`.

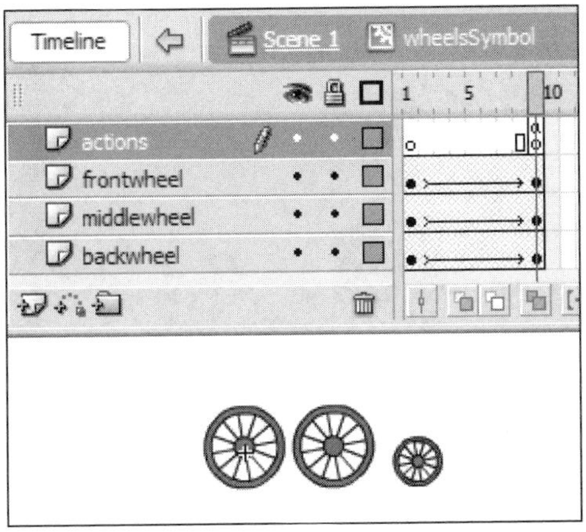

Figure 5.21 The `wheels_mc` movie clip contains an animation of the wheels rotating.

Figure 5.22 The completed code as seen in the Script pane.

4. Go to symbol-editing mode for the child movie clip.
5. Select a keyframe on the child movie clip's Timeline, and open the Actions panel.

   You'll assign ActionScript to the child movie clip's Timeline to control the parent movie clip's Timeline (**Figure 5.21**).
6. Choose ActionScript 2.0 Classes > Movie > MovieClip > Methods > stop.
7. Select the placeholder text `not_set_yet`, and click the Insert Target Path button.

   or

   In Script Assist mode, put the cursor in the Object field, and click the Insert Target Path button.
8. Set the path type to Relative, and select the instance name of the first instance created (the outer movie clip).

   or

   Skip step 7 (opening the Target Path dialog box); select the placeholder `not_set_yet` (or click in the Object field in Script Assist mode), and type `this._parent` (**Figure 5.22**).

continues on next page

9. Test your movie.

When the ActionScript statement on the wheels_mc movie clip Timeline is executed, Flash looks up to its parent—the train_mc movie clip Timeline—and performs the method there (**Figure 5.23**).

Table 5.1 and **Figure 5.24** summarize the ways you can use absolute and relative paths to target different movie clips.

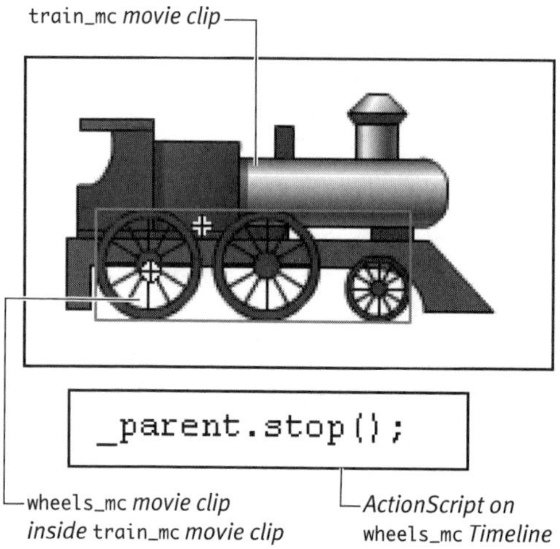

Figure 5.23 The action on the wheels_mc Timeline targets its parent, which is the train_mc Timeline. The action makes the train stop shaking.

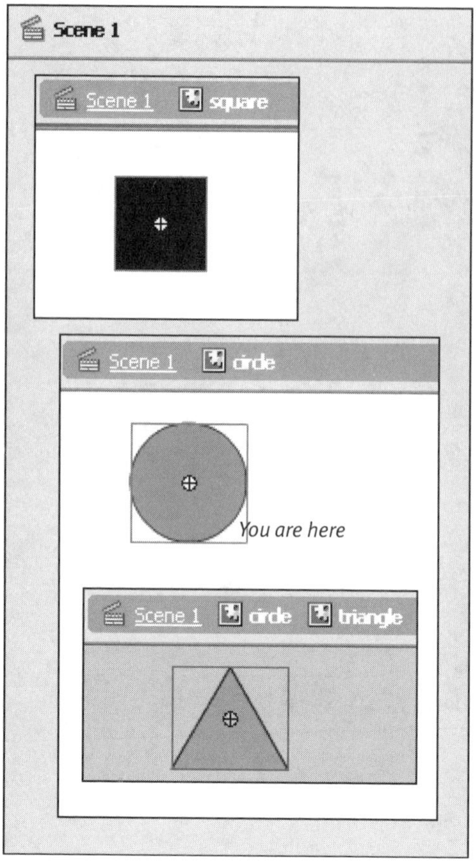

Figure 5.24 A representation of a movie with multiple movie clips. The main Timeline (Scene 1) contains the square movie clip and the circle movie clip. The circle movie clip contains the triangle movie clip. These names represent instances. Table 5.1 summarizes the absolute and relative target paths for calls made within the circle movie clip (you are here).

Table 5.1

Absolute vs. Relative Target Paths

To Target... (From Circle)	Absolute Path	Relative Path
Scene 1	_root	_parent
square	_root.square	_parent.square
circle	_root.circle	this
triangle	_root.circle.triangle	triangle

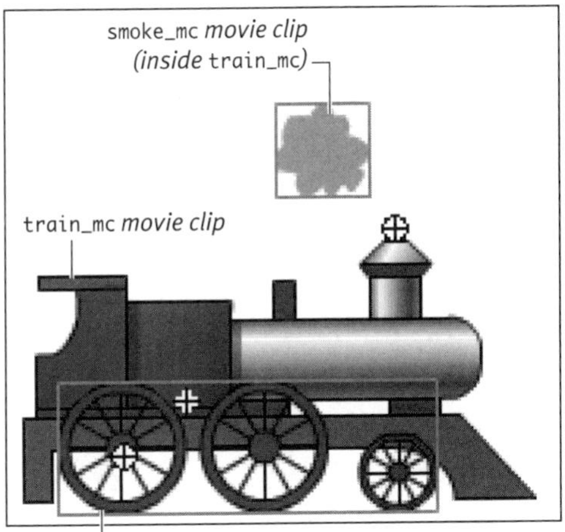

Figure 5.25 `with` statements are an alternative to multiple repeated target paths.

Using the with Action to Target Movie Clips

An alternative way to target movie clips is to use the action `with`. Instead of creating multiple target paths to the same movie clip, you can use the `with` action to target the movie clip only once. Imagine creating these statements to make the `wheels_mc` movie clip inside a train movie clip stop and shrink 50 percent:

```
train_mc.wheels_mc.stop();
train_mc.wheels_mc._xscale = 50;
train_mc.wheels_mc._yscale = 50;
```

You can rewrite those statements with the `with` statement, like this:

```
with (train_mc.wheels_mc) {
    stop();
    _xscale = 50;
    _yscale = 50;
}
```

This `with` action temporarily sets the target path to `train_mc.wheels_mc` so that the method and properties between the curly braces affect that particular target path (**Figure 5.25**). When the `with` action ends, any subsequent statements refer to the current Timeline.

To use the with action:

1. In a keyframe or within an event handler, open the Actions panel.
2. Choose Statements > Variables > with (Esc + wt).
3. Select the placeholder `not_set_yet` between the parentheses (or click in the Object field in Script Assist mode); enter the target path directly or using the Insert Target Path button (**Figure 5.26**).
4. Between the curly braces of the `with` action, create your statements for the targeted object.

   Remember, you don't need to specify a target path or put a dot before the method name (**Figure 5.27**).

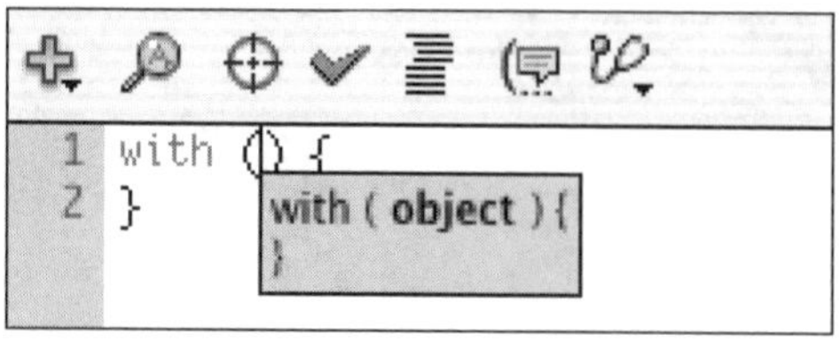

Figure 5.26 The `with` action in the Actions panel. The code hints help you determine the proper code to put between the parentheses.

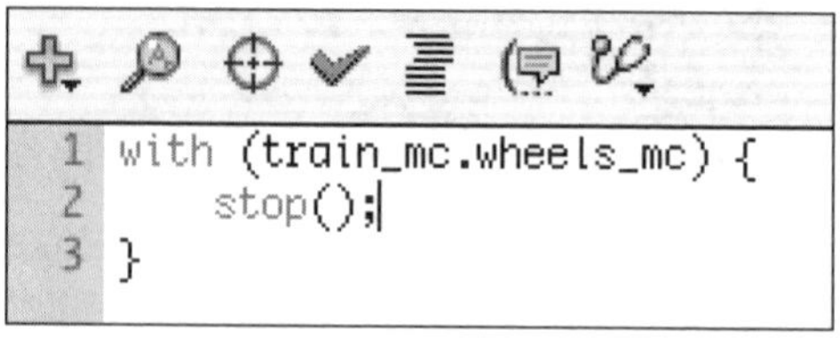

Figure 5.27 The action `stop()` and any other actions between the curly braces apply to the target path `train_mc.wheels_mc`.

Scope

You've learned that to direct an ActionScript statement to affect a different Timeline, you need a target path that defines the *scope*. Without a target path, the ActionScript would affect its own Timeline. An ActionScript statement belongs, or is *scoped*, to a particular Timeline or a particular object where it resides. Everything you do in ActionScript has a scope, so you must be aware of it. You could be giving the correct ActionScript instructions, but if they aren't scoped correctly, nothing—or, worse, unexpected things—could happen.

When you assign ActionScript to a frame of the `_root` Timeline, the statement is scoped to the `_root` Timeline. When you assign ActionScript to a frame of a movie clip Timeline, the statement is scoped to that movie clip Timeline. When you create an ActionScript object by using the constructor function `new`, that object is scoped to the Timeline where it was created. If you create a `date` object (as you did in Chapter 3) on the main Timeline with the statement

```
var myDate:Date = new Date();
```

the object `myDate` is scoped to the `_root` Timeline. You can target the `myDate` object with the target path `_root.myDate`.

The scope of buttons, movie clips, and functions

Keeping track of the scope of ActionScript assigned to a Timeline is a straightforward matter. When you assign ActionScript to buttons, movie clips, and functions, however, you need to keep an important detail in mind:

ActionScript assigned to a function is scoped to the Timeline on which it was created. If the following event handler is on the main Timeline for a movie clip or a button, the playhead on the main Timeline will move to frame 10:

```
myInstance.onRelease = function() {
    // moves the current Timeline
    gotoAndStop(10);
    // moves myInstance's Timeline
    this.gotoAndStop(10);
    // rotates myInstance
    this._rotation = 45;
};
```

The keyword `this` refers to the object the function is assigned to, however, so in this example, `this` refers to `myInstance`. The statement `this._rotation = 45` rotates `myInstance` whether it's a button or a movie clip. The statement `this.gotoAndStop(10)` moves the playhead of `myInstance` only if it's a movie clip. Buttons don't have Timelines that can be navigated.

When you use the older on(event) style of defining events, the scope issues become even more complex—which is a good reason to avoid that style of event handling. However, if you're publishing your movie for Flash 4 or for Flash Lite 1.1 or earlier, you'll want to keep the following points in mind:

- ActionScript assigned to a button with the on action is scoped to the Timeline where the button lies. If a button is on the main Timeline, the event handler

```
on(release) {
    // moves the parent Timeline
    gotoAndStop(10);
    // moves the parent Timeline
    this.gotoAndStop(10);
    // rotates the parent movie clip
    this._rotation = 45;
}
```

  will send the playhead of the main Timeline to frame 10. The keyword this refers to the main Timeline, so this.gotoAndStop(10) is synonymous with the preceding statement, and this._rotation = 45 rotates the main Stage, *not* the button.

- ActionScript assigned to a movie clip with the on action (so that it behaves like a button) is scoped to the movie clip's Timeline. If a movie clip is on the main Timeline, the event handler

```
on(release) {
    // moves the current Timeline
    gotoAndStop(10);
    // moves the current Timeline
    this.gotoAndStop(10);
    // rotates the current instance
    this._rotation = 45;
}
```

  will send the playhead of the movie clip Timeline to frame 10. The keyword this refers to the movie clip, so this.goto AndStop(10) is synonymous with the preceding statement, and this._rotation = 45 rotates the movie clip. Notice how the scope of the on action is different depending on whether it's assigned to a button or to a movie clip.

- ActionScript assigned to a movie clip with the onClipEvent action is scoped to the movie clip's Timeline. If a movie clip is on the main Timeline, the event handler

```
onClipEvent(mouseDown) {
    // moves the current Timeline
    gotoAndStop(10);
    // moves the current Timeline
    this.gotoAndStop(10);
    // rotates the current instance
    this._rotation = 45;
}
```

  will send the playhead of the movie clip Timeline to frame 10. The keyword this refers to the movie clip, so this.goto AndStop(10) affects the movie clip's Timeline. The statement this._rotation = 45 rotates the movie clip.

Table 5.2 reviews the scope of different event handlers for buttons, movie clips, and functions.

Finding target paths

Sometimes, you'll want to target an object or a movie clip Timeline, but you don't know the target path. This happens when movie clips are generated dynamically and are given names automatically. If you want the target path of any movie clip, button, or other object at run time, you can use the property `_target` or the function `targetPath`.

The property `_target` returns the absolute target path in slash notation. If a movie clip called `child_mc` is inside a movie clip called `parent_mc`, the `_target` property of the child is `/parent_mc/child_mc`.

Slash notation is considered a deprecated syntax, meaning that it's no longer supported. However, you can use the `eval()` function (Global Functions > Miscellaneous Functions > eval) to convert a target path written in slash notation to a target path written in dot syntax. For instance, the statement `eval(this._target)` returns the target path of the current Timeline in dot syntax.

The function `targetPath` returns the absolute target path in dot notation. It starts the target path with the level designation. (Chapter 6 covers levels.) `_level0`, for example, refers to the `_root` Timeline in a movie that has no other loaded movies. If a movie clip called `child_mc` is inside a movie clip called `parent_mc`, the `targetPath` function returns `_level0.parent_mc.child_mc`.

In the following tasks, you'll use the `trace` command to display the target path in the Output panel. This technique is useful for debugging code, but you can also integrate `_target` and `targetPath` into expressions when you need the absolute target path of an object.

SCOPE

Table 5.2

Scope of Event Handlers

ActionScript Assigned To	Event Handler	Scope
Button	`on(event)`	Timeline where button instance sits. Keyword `this` refers to the Timeline where the button instance sits.
Movie clip	`on(event)` `onClipEvent(event)`	Movie clip Timeline. Keyword `this` refers to the movie clip instance.
Function on the Timeline	`myInstance.onEvent = function()`	Timeline where the function is created. Keyword `this` refers to the object of the function (`myInstance`).

To find the target path with _target:

1. Create a movie clip symbol, place it on the main Stage, and give it an instance name in the Property inspector.
2. Create another movie clip symbol, place it inside the first movie clip, and give it an instance name in the Property inspector.

   Now you have a parent movie clip that contains a child movie clip. The parent movie clip sits on the main Timeline.
3. Select a keyframe on the parent movie clip's Timeline, and open the Actions panel.
4. Define an `onRelease` event handler for the child movie clip by choosing ActionScript 2.0 Classes > Movie > MovieClip > Event Handlers > onRelease and putting your child movie clip's instance name in the placeholder.
5. For the event handler's action, choose Global Functions > Miscellaneous Functions > trace (**Figure 5.28**).

   The `trace` command appears within the `onRelease` event handler. The `trace` command displays messages in the Output panel when you test a movie for debugging purposes. You'll display the target path in the Output panel.
6. With your pointer between the parentheses of the `trace` command, type `this`, or click the Insert Target Path button.

   or

   In Script Assist mode, type `this` into the Message field, and select the Expression check box.
7. After the word `this`, enter a dot, and then choose ActionScript 2.0 Classes > Movie > MovieClip > Properties > _target (**Figure 5.29**).

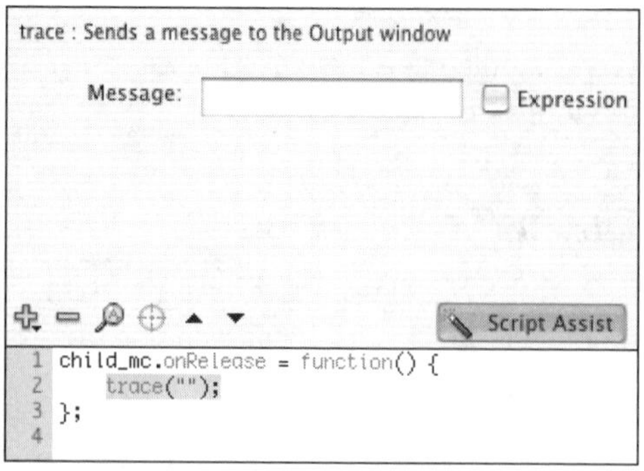

Figure 5.28 The `trace` action displays messages in the Output panel.

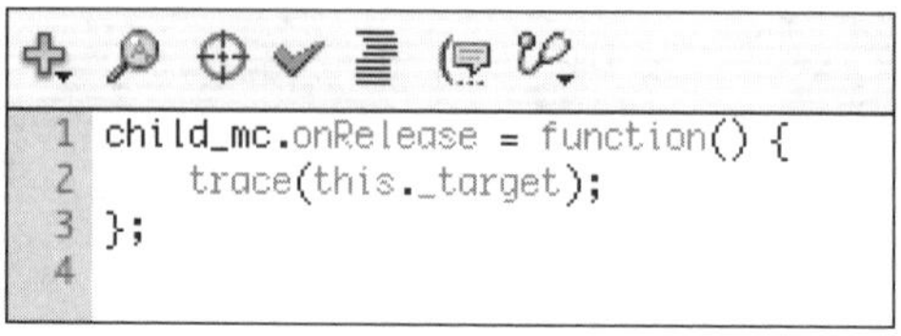

Figure 5.29 This `trace` action displays the target path of the current movie clip in slash notation (shown in Figure 5.30).

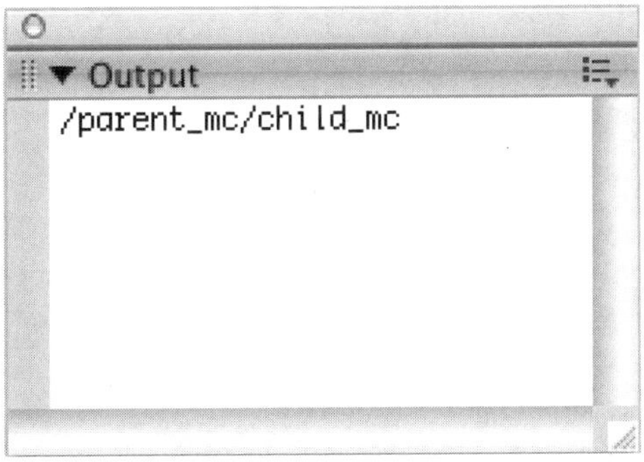

Figure 5.30 The Output panel for the `_target` trace.

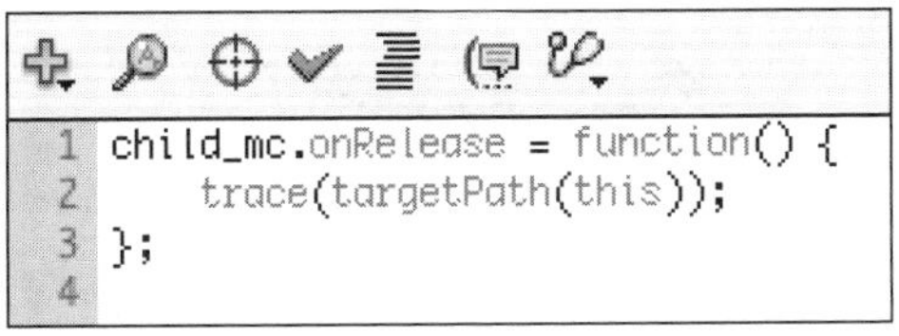

Figure 5.31 This `trace` action will display the target path of the current movie clip in dot notation (shown in Figure 5.32).

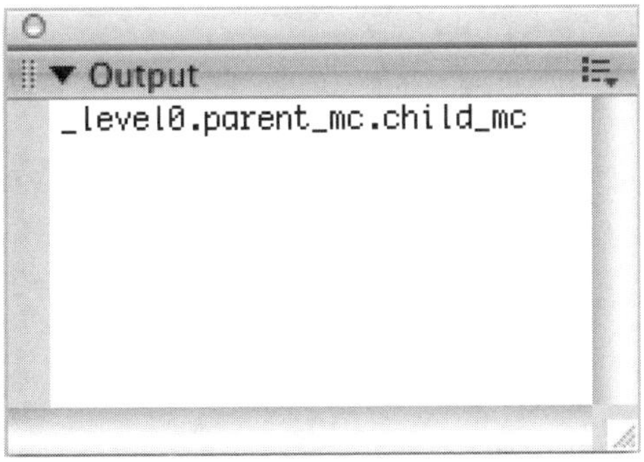

Figure 5.32 The Output panel for the `targetPath` trace.

8. Test your movie.

   When you click the child movie clip, the Output panel appears and displays its target path (**Figure 5.30**).

To find the target path with targetPath:

1. Continue with the file you created in the preceding task.
2. Select the keyframe inside the parent movie clip that contains your Action-Script, and open the Actions panel.
3. Place your pointer inside the parentheses for the `trace` statement in the Script pane.

   or

   In Script Assist mode, select the trace line, and place your pointer in the Message field.
4. Delete the current contents located between the parentheses.
5. Choose Global Functions > Movie Clip Control > targetPath.
6. Between the parentheses of the `targetPath` function, enter the keyword `this` (**Figure 5.31**).
7. Test your movie.

   When you click the child movie clip, the Output panel appears and displays its target path using dot syntax (**Figure 5.32**).

Movie Clips as Containers

So far in this chapter, you've learned how to name your movie clip objects, target each one, and navigate within their Timelines from any other Timeline in your movie. But how does the ability to control movie clip Timelines translate into meaningful interactivity for your Flash project? The key is to think of movie clips as containers that hold stuff: animation, graphics, sound, and even data. By moving the playhead back and forth or playing certain parts of a particular movie clip Timeline, you can access those items whenever you want, independently of what else is going on (**Figure 5.33**).

For example, movie clips are commonly used to show objects with different states that toggle from one to the other; the different states are contained in the movie clip's Timeline. When you built pull-down menus in Chapter 4, you used movie clips to serve that purpose. The pull-down menu is essentially a movie clip object that toggles between a collapsed state and an expanded state. The buttons inside the movie clip control which of those two states you see while also providing navigation outside the movie clip's Timeline (**Figure 5.34**).

Another example is using different keyframes of a movie clip to hold different states of a main character in a game. Depending on the circumstances, you can tell the playhead to go to a certain frame of the movie clip to display the character in a sad state, in a happy state, or in a sleepy state.

The following task demonstrates how to create a toggle button with a movie clip. Building a toggle button is a matter of defining two different keyframes that toggle between an on state and an off state.

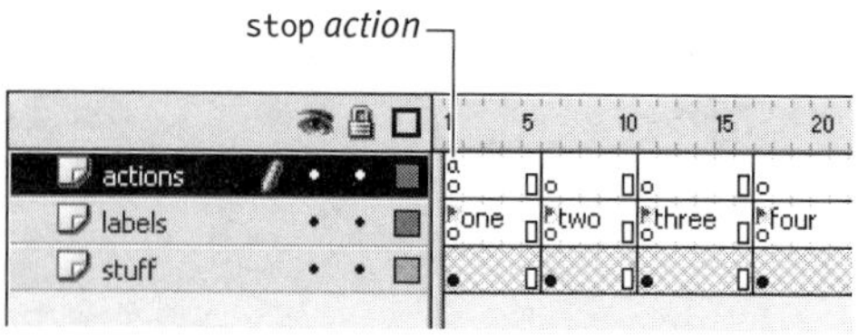

Figure 5.33 The movie clip as a container. This movie clip has a stop action in the first keyframe. The other labeled keyframes can contain buttons, graphics, animations, or any other kind of Flash information, which you can access by targeting the movie clip and moving its playhead to the appropriate keyframe.

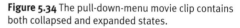

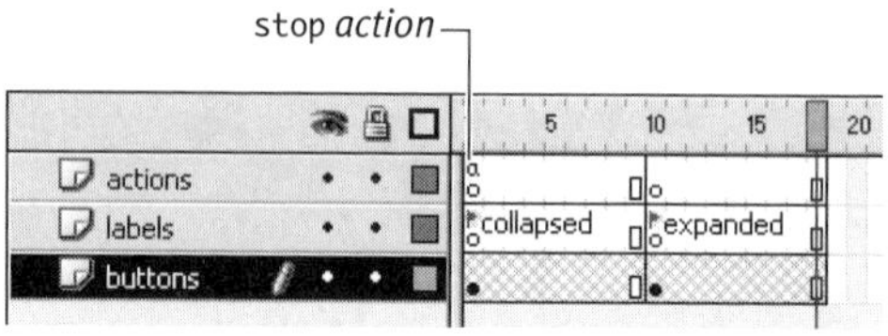

Figure 5.34 The pull-down-menu movie clip contains both collapsed and expanded states.

Movie Clips as Containers

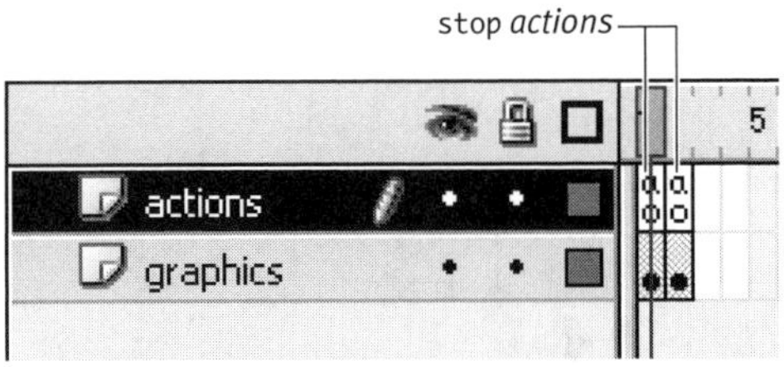

Figure 5.35 The toggle-button movie clip contains a stop action in both keyframes and two different states that toggle. The graphics represent the two different states of the toggle button.

To create a toggle button:

1. Create a movie clip symbol.
2. Go to symbol-editing mode for the movie clip, and insert a new keyframe.
3. In the first keyframe, add a `stop` action (Global Functions > Timeline Control > stop).
4. Insert another keyframe, and in this second keyframe, add another `stop` action.

   The `stop` action in both keyframes will prevent this movie clip from playing automatically and will stop the playhead on each keyframe.
5. Insert another new layer.
6. Create graphics that correspond to the off state in the first keyframe and graphics that correspond to the on state in the second keyframe (**Figure 5.35**).
7. Exit symbol-editing mode, and return to the main Stage.
8. Place an instance of your movie clip on the Stage, and give it an instance name in the Property inspector.
9. Create a new layer, select the keyframe on frame 1 of this layer, and open the Actions panel.
10. Add an `onPress` event handler declaration (ActionScript 2.0 Classes > Movie > MovieClip > Event Handlers > onPress).
11. Replace the placeholder instance name with the instance name of your movie clip.

    or

    In Script Assist mode, enter your movie clip's instance name in the Object field.

continues on next page

12. Inside the curly braces of the `onPress` event handler function, add a `play` method call (ActionScript 2.0 Classes > Movie > MovieClip > Methods > play). Enter the word `this` as the movie clip calling the method (in place of the `not_set_yet` text, or in the Object field in Script Assist mode).

    Remember, when you define an event handler method, the word `this` inside the event handler function refers to the instance to which you're assigning the function.

13. Test your movie.

    When you click the movie clip, the playhead moves to the next keyframe and stops. Each click toggles between two different states, just like a toggle button (**Figure 5.36**).

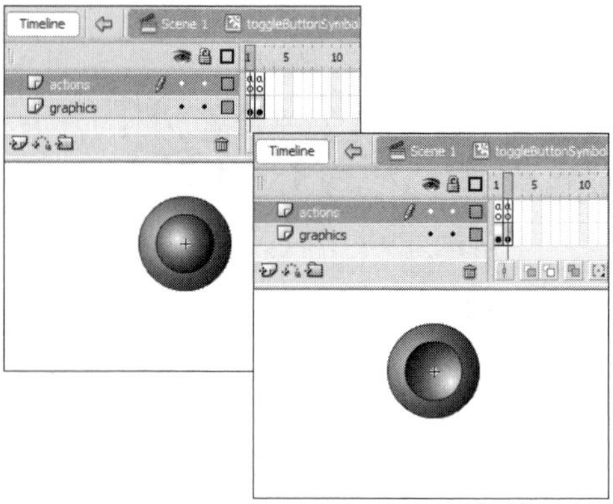

Figure 5.36 The movie clip in the first keyframe (top) sends the playhead to the second keyframe (bottom), and vice versa.

Creating a movie clip with hidden contents

You can do the same thing to a movie clip that you do to a button to make it invisible—that is, leave the first keyframe that is visible to the user blank so that the instance is invisible on the Stage initially. If the first keyframe of a movie clip is blank and contains a `stop` frame action to keep it there, you can control when to expose the other frames inside that movie clip Timeline. You could create a movie clip of an explosion but keep the first keyframe blank. Then, you could place this movie clip on a graphic of a submarine and, at the appropriate time, advance to the next frame to reveal the explosion.

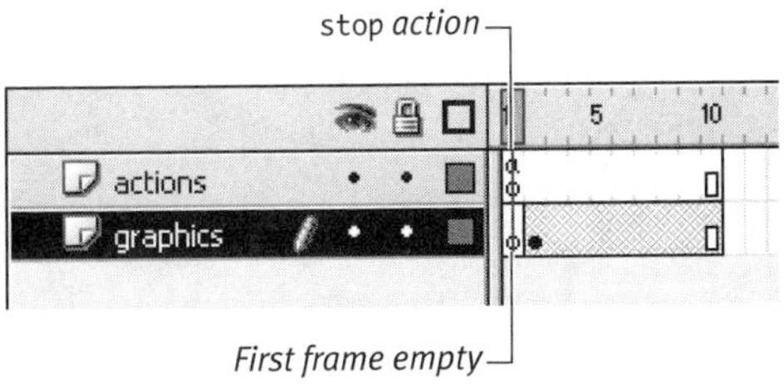

Figure 5.37 A movie clip with an empty first keyframe is invisible on the Stage. This movie clip has a `stop` action in the top layer and graphics in the bottom layer starting in keyframe 2.

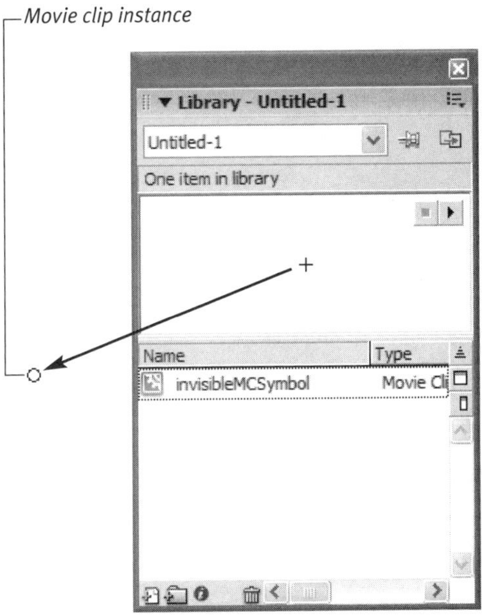

Figure 5.38 An instance of a movie clip with an empty first frame appears as an empty circle.

Note that you have other ways of using ActionScript to hide or reveal the contents of a movie clip or to place a movie clip on the Stage dynamically; you'll learn about these possibilities in upcoming chapters. But being aware of both the simple (frame-based, as described here) and sophisticated (purely ActionScript-based) approaches will help you tackle a broader range of animation and interactivity challenges.

To create an "invisible" movie clip:

1. Create a movie clip symbol.
2. Go to symbol-editing mode for the movie clip, and insert a new keyframe into its Timeline.

   This layer will hold the content of the movie clip.
3. Add a new layer to hold ActionScript. Select the first keyframe of this layer, and open the Actions panel.
4. Add a `stop` action (Global Functions > Timeline Control > stop).
5. Leave the first keyframe of the content layer empty, and begin placing graphics and animations in the second keyframe (**Figure 5.37**).
6. Exit symbol-editing mode, and return to the main Timeline.
7. Drag an instance of the movie clip from the Library to the Stage.

   The instance appears on the Stage as an empty circle (**Figure 5.38**). The empty circle represents the registration point of the instance, allowing you to place the instance exactly where you want it.

Managing Outside Communication

6

Flash provides powerful tools to communicate with other applications and external data, scripts, and files to extend its functionality. By using Flash to link to the Web, you can build sites that combine Flash animation and interactivity with non-Flash media supported by the browser. Use Flash to make your browser link to PDF documents, RealMedia files, or even Java applets. Use Flash to send email, communicate with JavaScript, or relay information to and from servers with the CGI `GET` and `POST` methods, as well as with Cold Fusion, PHP, ASP.NET, and more. Flash also supports XML, allowing you to create customized code for data-driven e-commerce solutions. This chapter introduces you to some ways Flash can communicate with HTML, JavaScript, and CGI.

You can also work with external images, video, and Flash movies. Load one or more Flash movies into another Flash movie to create modular projects that are easier to edit and have smaller file sizes. Your main Flash movie might serve simply as an interface that loads your portfolio of Flash animations when the viewer selects them. Learn to communicate from the main Flash movie to its loaded movie or even between two different Flash movies in separate browser windows.

In this chapter, you'll also learn about stand-alone Flash players called *projectors*, and you'll see how specialized commands affect the way they appear, function, and interact with other programs. Because they don't require a browser to play, projectors are ideal for distributing Flash content on CD-ROM or other portable media.

Finally, you'll learn to communicate with your movie's playback environment. Learn to detect your viewers' system capabilities, Stage size, or Flash Player version so that you can better cater your content to them. Check the amount of data that has downloaded to users' computers so you can tell them how much longer they have to wait before your movie begins. Keeping track of these external factors will help you provide a friendlier and customized user experience. Flash can also serve as a key component of dynamic, commercial, and entertainment applications.

Communicating through the Web Browser

Flash links to the Web browser through the action `getURL` in the Actions panel. This action is very similar to the HTML tag `<a href>`, in which the URL of a Web site is specified in the form http://www.domain-name.com/directory/. Use an *absolute URL* (a complete address to a specific file) to link to any Web site, or use a *relative URL* (a path to a file that's described in relation to the current directory) to link to pages in the same Web site or local files contained on your hard drive or a CD-ROM. The `getURL` action also provides ways to target different frames you create within the browser window or in new browser windows. You can create Flash movies that navigate between these frames and windows and control what loads in each one.

Linking to the Web

Use the `getURL` action to link to the Web with the standard scheme http:// followed by the rest of the Web address. Use different schemes to request different protocols, such as `mailto:` for email.

If you test your Flash movie by choosing Control > Test Movie or play it in Flash Player, the action `getURL` automatically launches the default browser and loads the specified Web address in a new window.

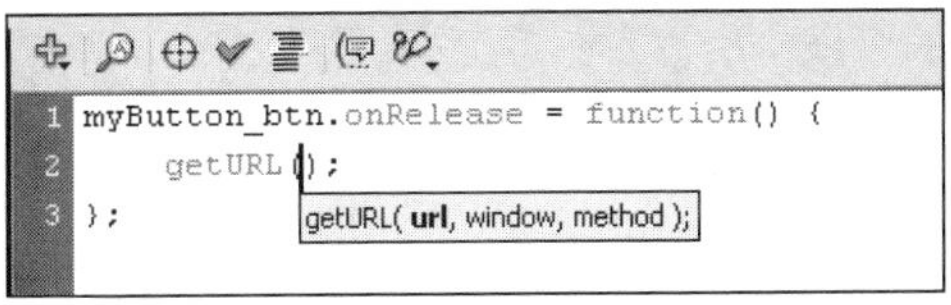
myButton_btn.onRelease = function() {
getURL ();
};
getURL(url, window, method);

Figure 6.1 The getURL action has parameters for a URL, a window name, and a method of sending variables.

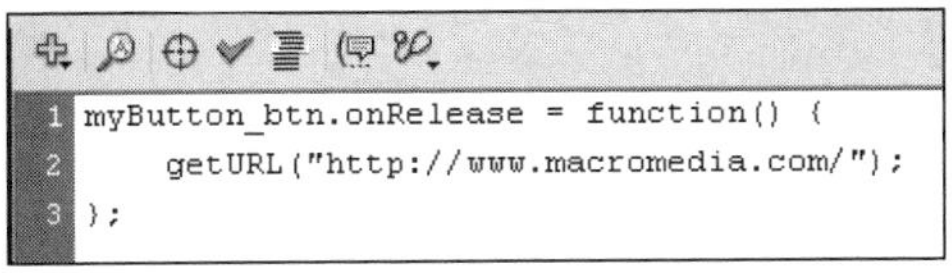
myButton_btn.onRelease = function() {
getURL("http://www.macromedia.com/");
};

Figure 6.2 Enter a URL between the parentheses for the `getURL` action.

To link to a Web site with the getURL action:

1. Create a button symbol, drag an instance from the Library to the Stage, and give it a name in the Property inspector.

   You'll assign the `getURL` action to this button.

2. Select the first frame of the main Timeline, and open the Actions panel.

3. Enter the name of your button followed by a period.

4. Choose ActionScript 2.0 Classes > Movie > Button > Events > onRelease.

   or

   Choose `onRelease` from the code hint menu, and complete the event handler by entering `= function() {};`.

   The `onRelease` event handler for your button is created.

5. Inside the curly braces of the `onRelease` event handler, choose Global Functions > Browser/Network > getURL (Esc + gu).

   The `getURL` action is added to the `onRelease` event handler (**Figure 6.1**).

6. With your pointer between the parentheses, enter the full address of a Web site surrounded by quotation marks (**Figure 6.2**).

   or

   In Script Assist mode, enter the Web site address in the URL field of the `getURL` action.

7. Choose File > Publish Settings.

   The Publish Settings dialog box opens.

continues on next page

8. In the Flash tab, under the "Local playback security" option, choose "Access network only" (**Figure 6.3**). Click OK.

   This will prevent you from getting a security error message when you test your SWF file and the file, which will play locally from your hard drive, tries to access a Web site on the Internet.

9. Publish your Flash movie, and play it in either the Flash Player or a browser.

   When you click the button you created, the Web site loads in the same window as your Flash movie (**Figure 6.4**). Click the Back button in your browser to return to your Flash movie.

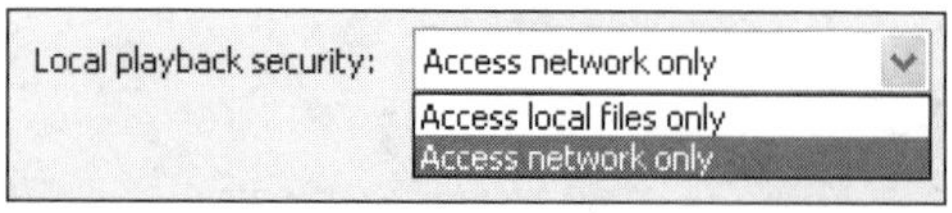

Figure 6.3 In the Publish Settings dialog box, set your SWF file to allow remote (network only) access.

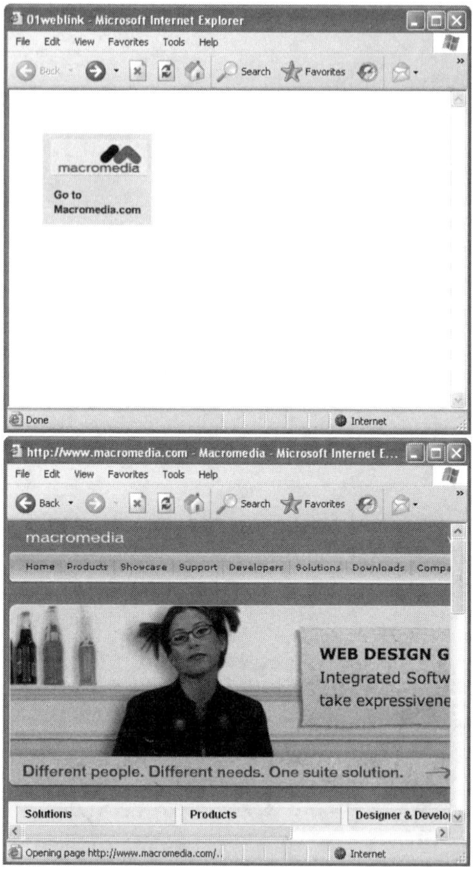

Figure 6.4 The Flash movie (top) links to the Macromedia site in the same browser window (bottom) when the window parameter isn't provided.

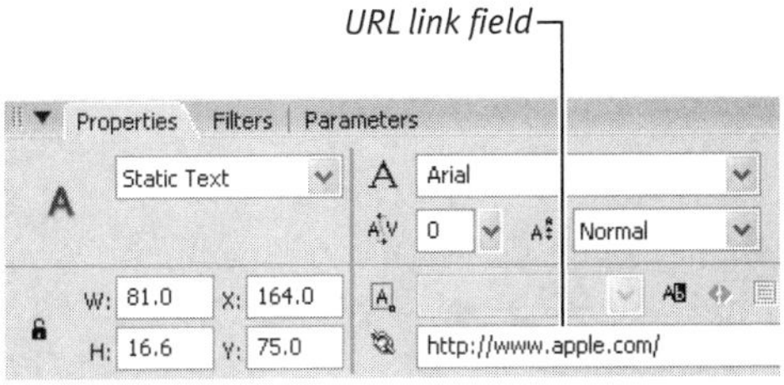

Figure 6.5 A Web address in the link field of the Property inspector makes the entire static text link to the site.

✔ Tips

- If you skip steps 7–8 (changing the Publish Settings) and then test the movie in a browser from your hard drive, you may see a security warning when you click the button that calls the `getURL` action. For more about working around this issue, see the sidebar "Flash Player Security: Mixing Local and Remote Content." However, testing the movie within Flash or over the internet in a Web browser won't cause the security warning to appear.
- You can link to the Web from a static horizontal text field. Create static text with the Text tool, and, in the Property inspector, enter the address of the Web site in the link field (**Figure 6.5**). Your static text will display a dotted underline to show that it's linked to a URL. When your viewers click the text, the Web site will load in the same browser window as your Flash movie.
- In addition to button instances, the `getURL` action can be assigned to a keyframe. If assigned to a keyframe, `getURL` links to the URL when the play-head enters that particular frame. This method is effective for loading Web links automatically—perhaps after an introductory splash animation.

Flash Player Security: Mixing Local and Remote Content

In Flash Player 8, a new security feature has been added that protects users from the possibility of a SWF file secretly loading a file from the user's hard drive and sending it over the Internet. Users who view your Flash content in a Web site won't run into this security restriction, because it only applies to SWF files that are running locally—that is, running directly from the user's hard drive rather than playing in a Web browser and loading from a Web site.

However, Flash authors who test files on their own computer will see a security warning message if the locally running SWF file tries to access any network resource (**Figure 6.6**). This includes the `getURL` action and many of the other actions we'll discuss in this chapter.

One way to prevent the warning is to change the "Local playback security" setting in the Publish Settings dialog from "Local only" to "Remote only," as explained in the task "To link to a Web site with the getURL action." However, you'll have to remember to change this setting for each Flash document you test locally that accesses a remote resource.

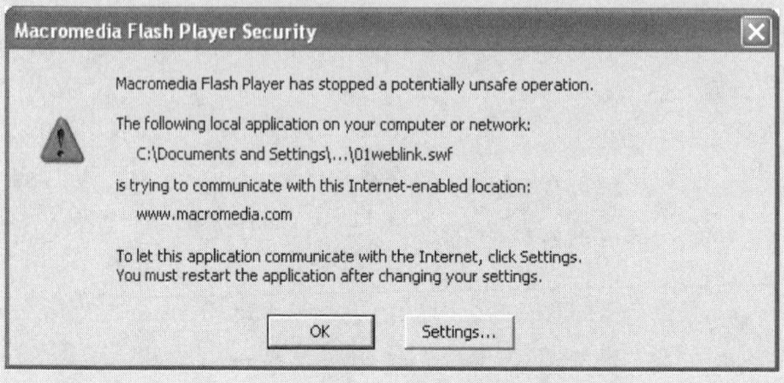

Figure 6.6 The Flash Player Security dialog indicates that a SWF has tried to access the network and isn't allowed to. Click the Settings button to create a trusted location on your computer, which prevents this warning.

You can make a single change to resolve this issue for all your Flash documents. The simplest way is to specify a *trusted* location on your computer—a folder within which any Flash movies are trusted by the Flash Player and don't cause this security warning.

To designate a trusted location on your computer:

1. Create a Flash document containing ActionScript that will cause the security warning. For example, add a `getURL` action with an absolute URL to a frame on the main Timeline.
2. Test the file in a browser by choosing File > Publish Preview > HTML. Do whatever is necessary to trigger the getURL action.
3. In the error dialog box that appears (Figure 6.6), click the Settings button.

   A new browser window opens to the Flash Player Settings Manager page on Macromedia's Web site.

continues on next page

Flash Player Security: Mixing Local and Remote Content *(continued)*

Macromedia Flash Player™ Settings Manager
Global Security Settings
Some websites may access information from other sites using an older system of security. This is usually harmless, but it is possible that some sites could obtain unauthorized information using the older system. When a website attempts to use the older system to access information:
Always ask
Always allow
Always deny
Always trust files in these locations:
Edit locations...
Add location...
Edit location...
Delete location
Delete all locations

Figure 6.7 You can specify a location on your computer whose contents are trusted by the Flash Player.

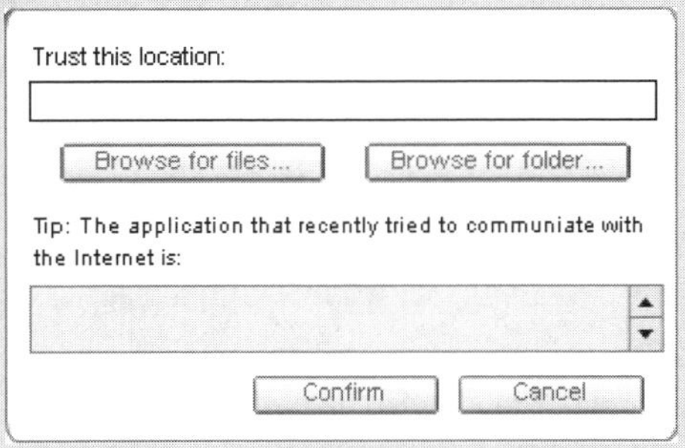
Trust this location:
Browse for files...
Browse for folder...
Tip: The application that recently tried to communiate with the Internet is:
Confirm
Cancel

Figure 6.8 Choose a single SWF file or a folder to designate as trusted.

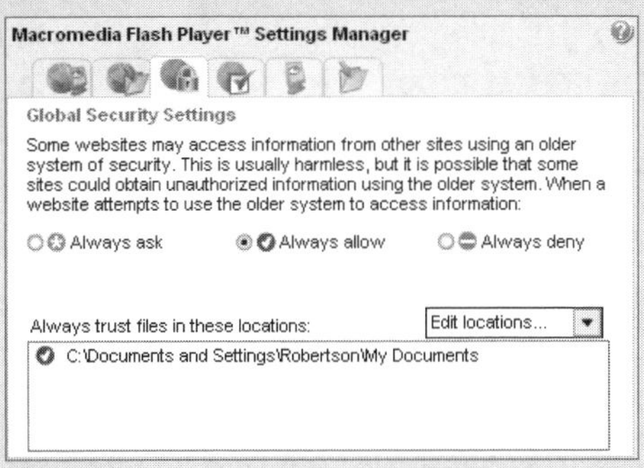
Macromedia Flash Player™ Settings Manager
Global Security Settings
Some websites may access information from other sites using an older system of security. This is usually harmless, but it is possible that some sites could obtain unauthorized information using the older system. When a website attempts to use the older system to access information:
Always ask
Always allow
Always deny
Always trust files in these locations:
Edit locations...
C:\Documents and Settings\Robertson\My Documents

Figure 6.9 Choose the permission setting to apply to this location (in this case, "Always allow").

4. In the Settings Manager, click the "Edit locations" menu, and choose "Add location" (**Figure 6.7**).

5. In the dialog that appears, click the "Browse for folder" button (**Figure 6.8**); another dialog will allow you to choose a folder whose contents will always be trusted by the Flash Player.

   In general, you should choose a folder that contains your Flash projects (subfolders of this folder are trusted as well). You also need to use caution to never place in that folder any SWF files that you don't completely trust.

6. Click the Confirm button. The dialog closes, and you return to the Settings Manager.

7. With your newly added location selected, choose the "Always allow" radio button (**Figure 6.9**).

   With this setting, the Flash Player will no longer trigger the error message when you test local SWF files that are in the trusted location.

8. Close the browser window that triggered the error message, and then reopen it to test your project.

   For more information about this error and some alternative ways of working around it, see the Flash Help section Learning ActionScript 2.0 in Flash > Understanding Security > "About local file security and Flash Player."

To preaddress an email:

1. Create a button symbol, drag an instance from the Library to the Stage, and give it a name in the Property inspector.
2. Select the first frame of the main Timeline, and open the Actions panel.
3. Enter the name of your button followed by a period.
4. Choose ActionScript 2.0 Classes > Movie > Button > Events > onRelease.

   or

   From the code hint menu, choose `onRelease`; complete the event handler by entering `= function() {};`.

   The `onRelease` event handler for your button is created.
5. Within the body of the `onRelease` event handler function, choose Global Functions > Browser/Network > getURL.

   The `getURL` action is added to the `onRelease` event handler.
6. With your pointer between the parentheses of the `getURL` statement, enter `mailto:` followed by the email address of the person who should receive the email (**Figure 6.10**).

   The entire statement must be surrounded by quotation marks.

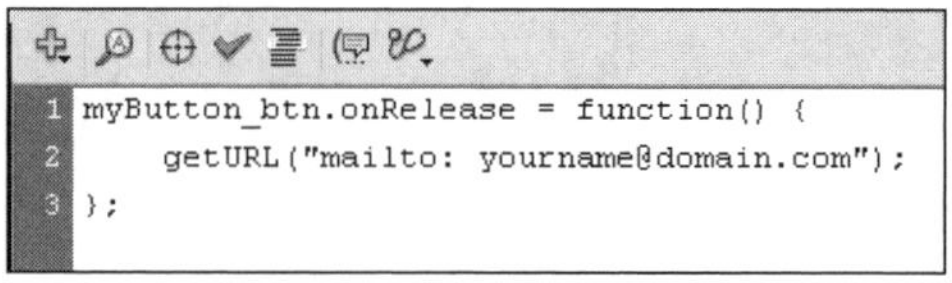
myButton_btn.onRelease = function() {
getURL("mailto: yourname@domain.com");
};

Figure 6.10 Enter email recipients after `mailto:` for the URL parameter. Separate additional email addresses with semicolons.

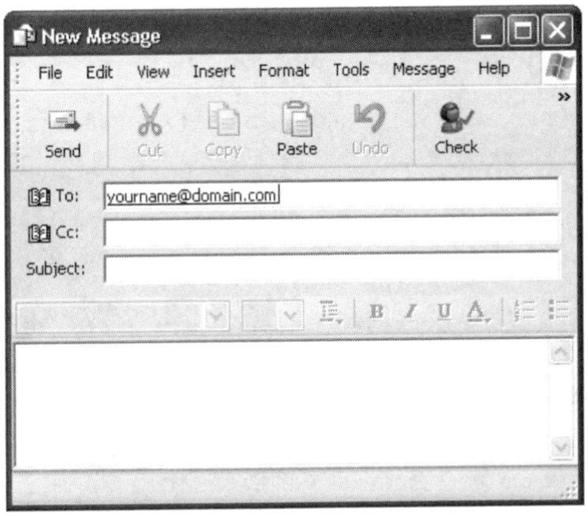

Figure 6.11 A new email message appears in your default mail program.

7. Test your Flash movie.

   When you click the button you created, an email form appears with the recipient's email address already filled in (**Figure 6.11**). The viewer then types a message and clicks Send. Use `getURL` to preaddress email that viewers can use to contact you about your Web site or to request more information.

✔ Tip

- It's a good idea to spell out the email address of the `getURL mailto:` recipient in your Flash movie (**Figure 6.12**). If a person's browser isn't configured to send email, an error message appears instead of an email form. By spelling out the address, you allow users to enter it in their email applications themselves.

Linking using a relative path

Just as you can with images or hyperlinks in a Web page, you can use relative paths rather than absolute URLs to link to other content. In addition, you can use relative paths rather than complete URLs to specify local files instead of files on the Web. This method lets you distribute your Flash movie on a CD-ROM or DVD without requiring an Internet connection. Instead of using the complete URL http://www.myServer.com/images/photo.jpg, for example, you can specify just images/photo.jpg, and Flash will have to look only inside the folder called images to find the file called photo.jpg.

To link to a file using a relative path:

1. Create a button symbol, drag an instance from the Library to the Stage, and give it a name in the Property inspector.
2. Select the first frame, and open the Actions panel; create an `onRelease` event handler function assigned to your button.
3. Inside the curly braces of the `onRelease` event, add a `getURL` statement (Global Functions > Browser/Network > getURL).
4. With your pointer between the parentheses, enter the relative path to the desired file, surrounded by quotation marks.

   Use a slash (/) to separate directories and two periods (..) to move up one directory (**Figure 6.13**).
5. Publish your Flash movie, and place it and your linked file in the correct level in the folder hierarchy (**Figure 6.14**).

Figure 6.12 This email address is also a button that links to the browser via `mailto:`.

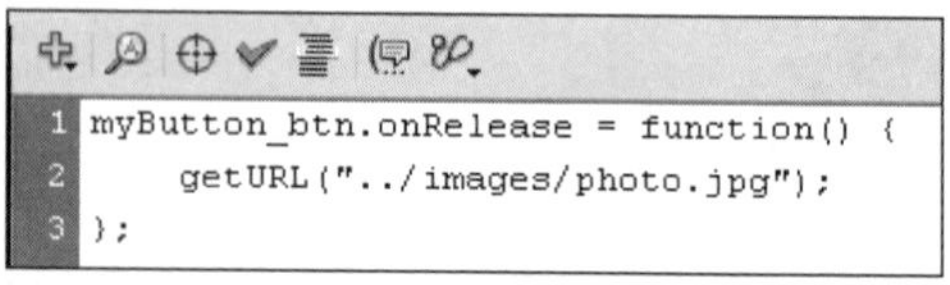

Figure 6.13 This relative URL goes up one directory level and looks for a folder called images, which contains a file called photo.jpg.

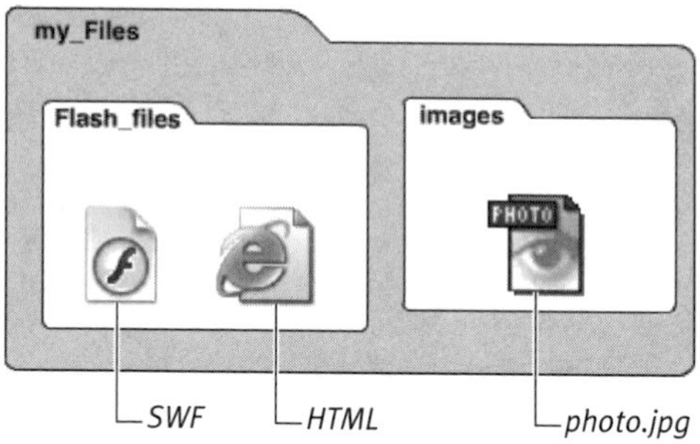

Figure 6.14 Your Flash movie (SWF) and its accompanying HTML file are in a directory that's at the same level as the directory that contains the file photo.jpg.

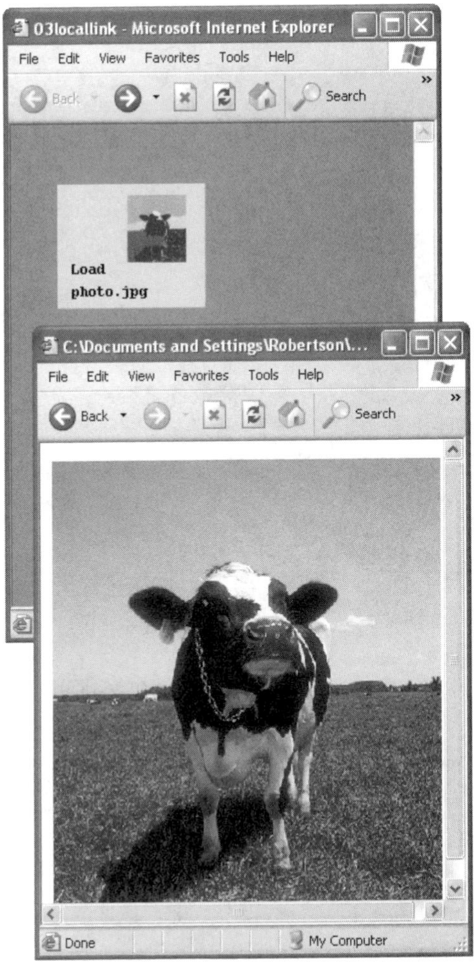

Figure 6.15 The Flash movie (top) links to the local file in the same browser window (bottom).

6. Play the movie in either the Flash Player or a browser.

   When you click the button you created, Flash looks for the file using the relative path and loads it into the same browser window (**Figure 6.15**).

✔ Tip

- Any file type can be targeted in the URL field of the `getURL` action. You can load HTML, JPEG, GIF, QuickTime, and PDF files and even other Flash movies. Just keep in mind that the viewer's browser must have the required plug-ins to display these different media types.

Working with browser framesets and windows

When you play your Flash movie in a browser window, the `getURL` action loads the new Web address in the same window, replacing your Flash movie. To make it load into a new window or a different frame of your window so that your original Flash movie isn't replaced, enter a second parameter in the `getURL` action for the window, as defined in **Table 6.1.**

What's the difference between a window and a frame? Browser windows can be divided into separate areas, or *frames,* that contain individual Web pages. The collection of frames is called a *frameset,* and the frameset HTML file defines the frame proportions and the name of each frame (**Figure 6.16**).

The `getURL` action's `window` parameter can use the name that the frameset HTML file assigns to a frame to load a URL directly into that specific frame. This method is similar to using the HTML `<a href>` tag attribute `target`. If you divide a Web page into two frames, for example, you can call the left frame *navigator* and the right frame *contents.* Place a Flash movie in the navigator frame with buttons assigned the `getURL` action. By entering the frame name contents as the `window` parameter of `getURL`, you target the right frame to load the URL. **Figure 6.17** depicts how each page loads into a frameset.

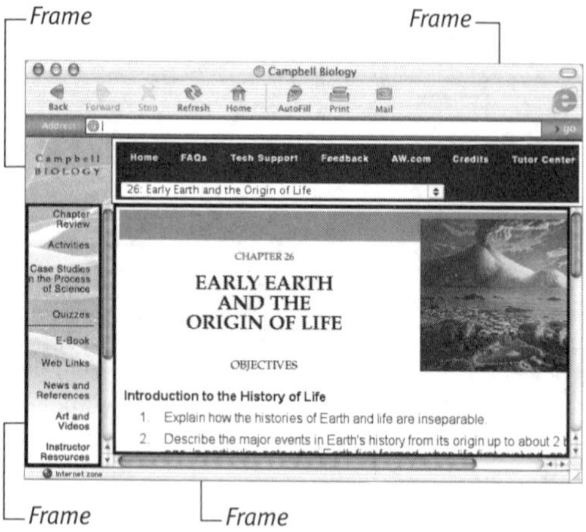

Figure 6.16 A Web site using frames to divide content. The window is divided horizontally into two frames. The bottom and top frames are divided vertically into two more frames. Ad banners, navigation bars, and content usually are separated in this way.

Table 6.1

Window Parameters for getURL

WINDOW NAME	EXPLANATION
`_self`	Current frame of the current browser window; default behavior when no `window` parameter is specified
`_blank`	New browser window
`_parent`	Frameset that contains the current frame
`_top`	Top-level frameset in the current browser window

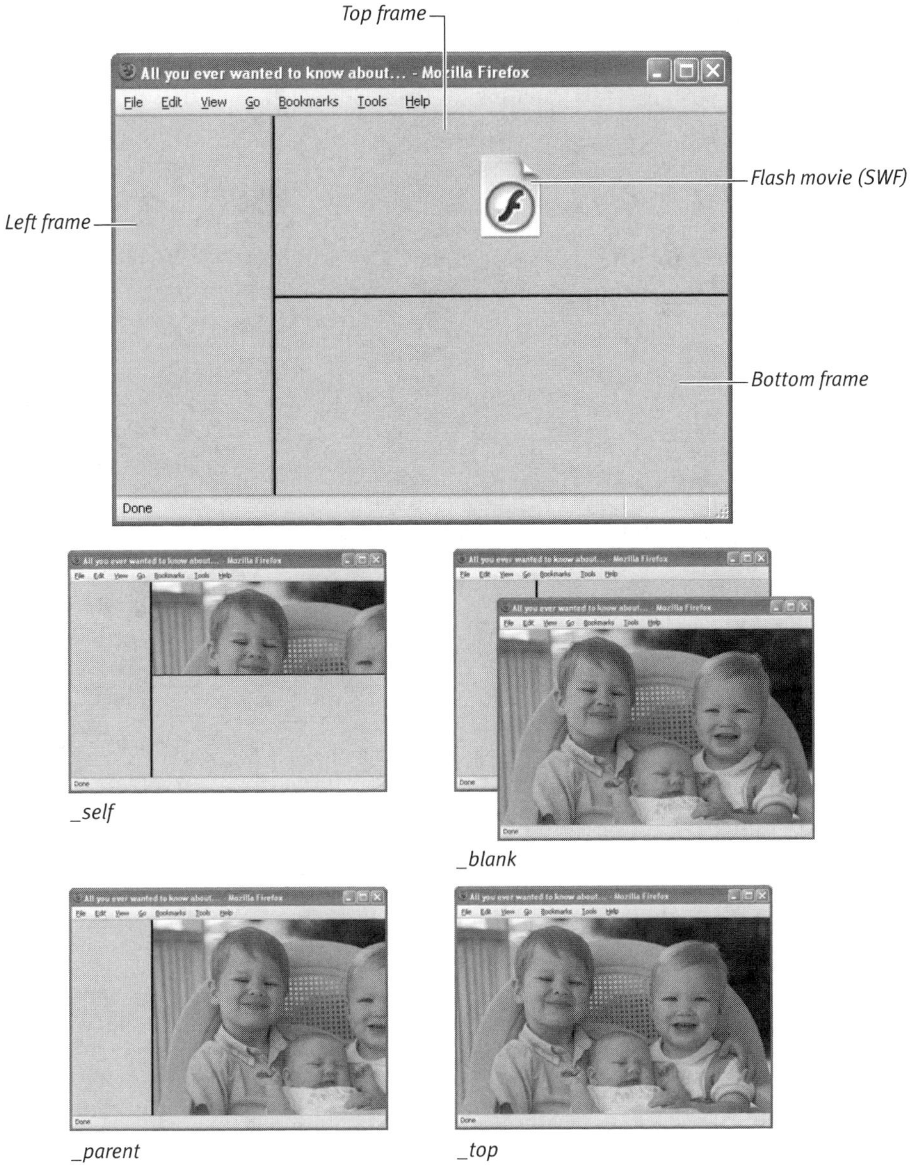

Figure 6.17 At top, a frameset divides a window into a left and a right frame. The right frame contains another frameset that divides itself into top and bottom frames. The Flash movie (SWF) plays in the top frame of the second frameset. The window names specify where the URL loads.

To open a Web site in a named frame:

1. In an HTML editor such as Macromedia Dreamweaver, create an HTML frameset with two frames and unique names for both.

   Your Flash movie will play in one frame, and the Web site links will be loaded into the other frame (**Figure 6.18**).

2. In Flash, create a button symbol, drag an instance from the Library to the Stage, and give it a name in the Property inspector.

3. Select the first frame of the main Timeline, and open the Actions panel.

4. As you have done in previous tasks, create an `onRelease` event handler function for your button (ActionScript 2.0 Classes > Movie > Button > Events > onRelease).

5. Add a `getURL` statement as the action to be performed by the `onRelease` event (Global Functions > Browser/Network > getURL).

6. For the `url` parameter of the `getURL` statement, enter `http://` and then the address of a Web site; the `http://` and the address must be surrounded by quotation marks.

7. To add a `window` parameter, after the closing quotation mark for the Web site address, enter a comma and then enter the name of the frame established in the HTML frameset (**Figure 6.19**).

   or

   In Script Assist mode, enter the name of the frame in the Window field.

   The second parameter, which tells Flash where to load the Web address, must also be surrounded by quotation marks.

```
<!DOCTYPE HTML PUBLIC "-//W3C//DTD HTML 4.01 Frameset//EN" "http://www.w3.org/TR/html4/frameset.dtd">
<html>
<head>
<title>Untitled Document</title>
<meta http-equiv="Content-Type" content="text/html; charset=UTF-8">
</head>
<frameset rows="8" cols="130,*" framespacing="8" frameborder="yes" border="8" bordercolor="#999999">
<frame src="navigator.html" name="navigator" scrolling="NO" noresize>
<frame src="contents.html" name="contents" scrolling="NO">
</frameset>
</html>
```

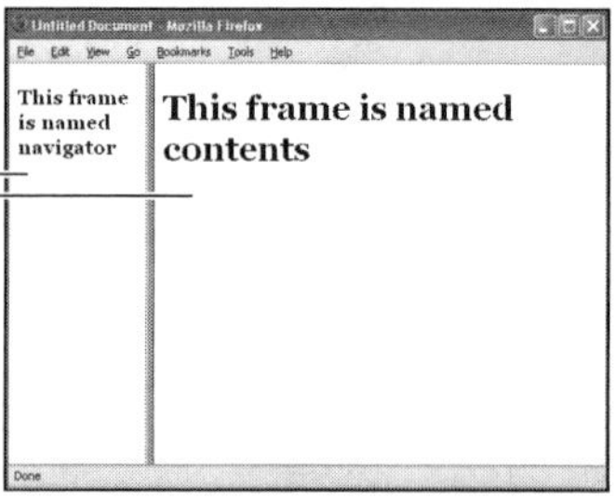

Figure 6.18 The frameset file (top) divides this window into a left column named navigator, which is 20 percent of the browser width, and a right column named contents, which is 80 percent of the browser width (bottom).

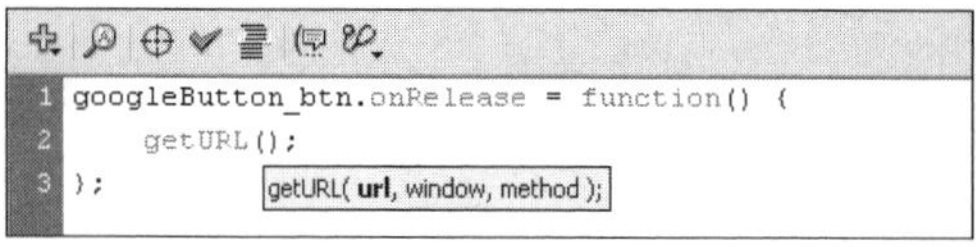

Figure 6.19 The parameters of the `getURL` action specify the Google Web site to load in the contents frame (right). The code hints that appear after the opening parenthesis (left) remind you of the parameters the action can take.

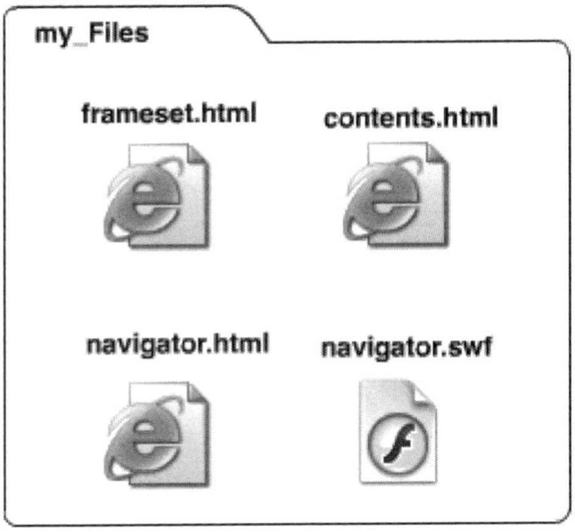

Figure 6.20 The frameset.html file puts the contents.html file in the contents frame and the navigator.html file in the navigator frame. The navigator.html file embeds the Flash movie (navigator.swf).

```
googleButton_btn.onRelease = function() {
    getURL("http://www.google.com", "contents");
};
yahooButton_btn.onRelease = function() {
    getURL("http://www.yahoo.com", "contents");
};
exciteButton_btn.onRelease = function() {
    getURL("http://www.excite.com", "contents");
};
```

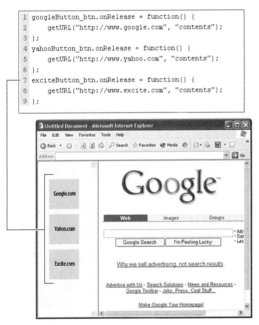

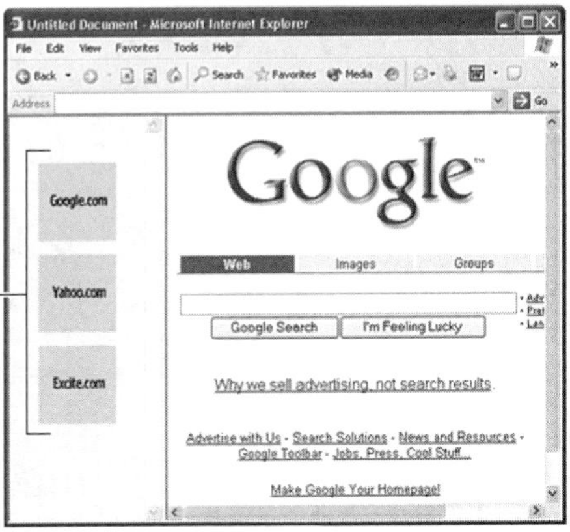

Figure 6.21 The ActionScript for the buttons in the navigator frame is shown. The Google, Yahoo, and Excite sites load in the other frame, keeping the left frame (which contains your Flash movie) intact.

8. To prevent a security warning when testing your movie, Choose File > Publish Settings; in the Flash tab, set the "Local playback security" field to "Access network only."

   or

   Be sure to test your project from a trusted location on your computer (as described in the sidebar "Flash Player Security: Mixing Local and Remote Content").

9. Publish your Flash movie with its accompanying HTML file.

10. Create another HTML file for the other frame in the frameset.

11. Name both HTML files according to the `<frame src>` tags in the frameset document, and place all files in the same folder (**Figure 6.20**).

12. Open the frameset document in a browser.

    Your Flash movie plays in one frame. The button loads a Web site in the other frame (**Figure 6.21**).

To open a Web site in a new window:

1. Create a button symbol, drag an instance from the Library to the Stage, and give it a name in the Property inspector.
2. Select the first frame of the main Timeline, and open the Actions panel.
3. Create an `onRelease` event handler for your button.
4. Within the `onRelease` event handler's curly braces, add a `getURL` action (as you have done in the preceding tasks).
5. With your pointer between the parentheses, enter a Web site address in quotation marks followed by a comma.
6. Enter `_blank` surrounded by quotation marks (**Figure 6.22**).

   The first parameter for the `getURL` action is the Web address. The second parameter tells Flash to load that Web address in a new browser window.
7. Publish your Flash movie, and play it in the Flash Player or a browser.

   When you click the button you created, a new window appears, and the Web site loads in it.

   As with the previous task, in order to avoid a security warning message, you must change the Publish Settings or test the SWF from a trusted folder on your computer.

```
myButton_btn.onRelease = function() {
    getURL("http://www.peachpit.com", "_blank");
};
```

Figure 6.22 When you enter `_blank` as the second parameter, the Peachpit Press Web site will load in a new, unnamed window.

Figure 6.23 Multiple `getURL` actions with the second parameter set to `_blank` (top) and set to a unique name (bottom). This behavior happens on all platforms except when Internet Explorer is used on Windows.

✔ Tip

- There is a crucial difference between opening a new window by using the term `_blank` and opening a new window by using a name that you enter yourself. If you use `_blank`, each time you click your button to link to a Web site, a new window is created. If you use a name in the Window field, the first click opens a new window. Subsequent clicks find the newly created window you named, so Flash reloads the Web site into that existing window (**Figure 6.23**). Both methods are useful, depending on whether you want your Web links to be in separate windows or to replace each other in a single new window.

Using JavaScript to control new window parameters

The `window` parameter in the `getURL` action is useful for directing Web links to new browser windows, but the appearance and location of these new windows are set by the browser's preferences. If you play a Flash movie in a browser that shows the location bar and the toolbar, for example, and you open a new window, the new window also has a location bar and a toolbar. You can't control these `window` parameters directly with Flash, but you can control them indirectly with JavaScript.

In the HTML page that holds your Flash movie, you can define JavaScript functions that control the opening and even closing of new browser windows. In your Flash movie, you can call on these JavaScript functions by using the `getURL` action. Instead of entering a Web address in the URL field, enter `javascript:` followed by the name of the function. Flash finds the JavaScript in the HTML page, and the browser calls the function.

You can use JavaScript to control several window properties. These properties specify the way the window looks, how it works, and where it's located on the screen (**Figure 6.24**). These properties can be defined in the `getURL` action in your Flash movie and passed to the JavaScript function in the HTML page. When you define these window properties, use `yes` (`1`), `no` (`0`), or a number specifying pixel dimensions or coordinates. **Table 6.2** lists the most common window properties that are compatible with all major Web browsers.

Table 6.2

JavaScript Window Properties

Property	Description
`height`	Vertical dimension, in pixels
`width`	Horizontal dimension, in pixels
`left`	X-coordinate of left edge
`top`	Y-coordinate of top edge
`resizable`	Resizable area in the bottom-right corner that allows the window to change dimensions (yes/no or 1/0)
`scrollbars`	Vertical and horizontal scroll bars (yes/no or 1/0)
`directories`	Also called links, where certain bookmarks are accessible (yes/no or 1/0)
`location`	Location bar, containing URL area (yes/no or 1/0)
`menubar`	Menu bar, containing drop-down menus such as File and Edit; works only in the Windows operating system (yes/no or 1/0)
`status`	Status bar in the bottom-left corner, containing browser status and security (yes/no or 1/0)
`toolbar`	Toolbar, containing the back and forward buttons and other navigation aides (yes/no or 1/0)

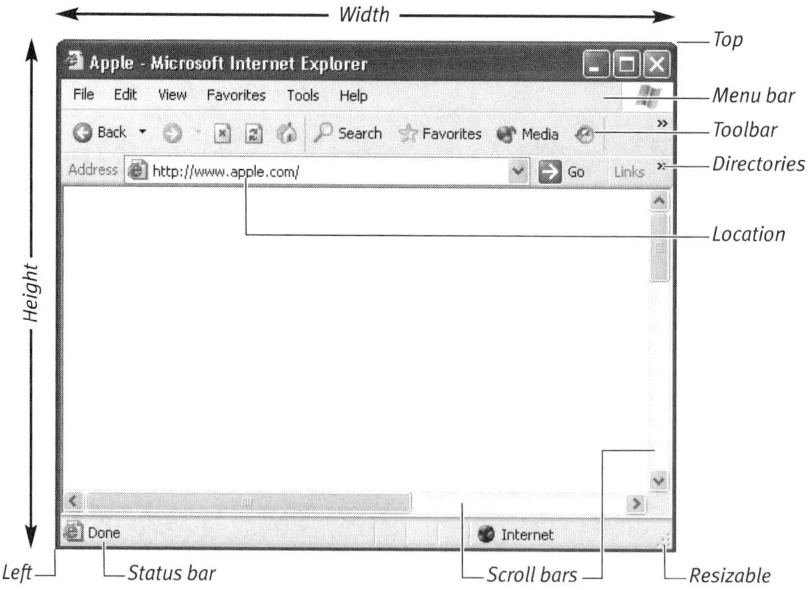

Figure 6.24 You can set the properties of a browser window with JavaScript.

To open a new window with JavaScript:

1. Create a button, name it, and attach the `getURL` action to an `onRelease` event handler as described in the preceding tasks.

   This button will communicate with a JavaScript function in the HTML page.

2. With your pointer between the parentheses for `getURL`, enter the following for the `url` parameter:

   ```
   "javascript:openWindow('http://www.
   peachpit.com','newWin','left=80,
   top=180,toolbar=0,scrollbars=0,
   height=250,width=200')"
   ```

   When the `getURL` action sends this statement to the browser, it will instruct the browser to call a JavaScript function named `openWindow`, which you'll define in the container Web page.

   The information that you enter in single quotation marks between the parentheses is parameters that get passed to the JavaScript function called `openWindow`. You don't have to define all the window properties (**Figure 6.25**).

3. Publish your Flash movie with its associated HTML file.

4. Open the HTML page in a text- or HTML-editing application.

continues on next page

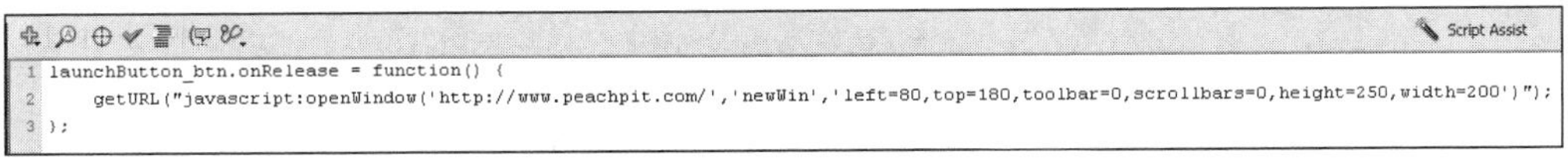
Script Assist
launchButton_btn.onRelease = function() {
getURL("javascript:openWindow('http://www.peachpit.com/','newWin','left=80,top=180,toolbar=0,scrollbars=0,height=250,width=200')");
};

Figure 6.25 The `javascript:` statement calls the `openWindow` function in the HTML page that embeds the Flash movie. Note the use of single quotation marks inside double quotation marks. You can also use escape sequences for the quotation marks. Use \" in place of the single quotation marks. Escape sequences are described in Chapter 3.

5. To define the JavaScript openWindow function in the HTML page, add the following script to the head of the HTML page:

```
<script language="JavaScript">
<!-- Code for Flash JS Pop-up Window
function openWindow(URL, windowName,
windowFeatures) {
     newWindow = window.open(URL,
windowName, windowFeatures);
}
// End -->
</script>
```

The openWindow function has three parameters: URL, windowName, and windowFeatures. When this function is called, the object newWindow is created and receives the three parameters from the Flash movie. The HTML page should be similar to **Figure 6.26**.

6. Save the modified HTML page, and open it in a browser.

When you click the button that you created, Flash passes the Web address, the window name, and the window properties to the JavaScript function called openWindow. Then JavaScript creates a new window with the new properties (**Figure 6.27**).

✔ Tips

- When you use getURL to call a JavaScript function in a SWF file that is running locally and isn't in a trusted folder, the Flash Player ignores the getURL action regardless of the "Local playback security" setting in the Publish Settings of your Flash document. To make this task work, you must test the file from a trusted folder, as described in the sidebar "Flash Player Security: Mixing Local and Remote Content."
- This method of using Flash to talk to JavaScript won't work with older versions of Internet Explorer (version 3 or earlier) or Internet Explorer 4.5 or earlier for the Macintosh.
- If you're using getURL to call JavaScript functions in Netscape browsers older than version 6.2, you may need to add the following attribute to the <embed> tag in your HTML page in order to enable JavaScript communication using getURL:

  ```
  swliveconnect="true"
  ```

- More JavaScript window properties are available, but many of them work in only one or some of the most popular browsers. The properties innerHeight and innerWidth, for example, define the dimensions of the actual window content area, but these properties are unique to Mozilla-based browsers such as Netscape Navigator and Firefox. You're safe if you stick to the properties listed in Table 6.2.

JavaScript

```
<!DOCTYPE html PUBLIC "-//W3C//DTD XHTML 1.0 Transitional//EN"
"http://www.w3.org/TR/xhtml1/DTD/xhtml1-transitional.dtd">
<html xmlns="http://www.w3.org/1999/xhtml" xml:lang="en" lang="en">
<head>

<script language="javaScript">

<!-- Code for Flash JS Pop-up Window

function openWindow(URL, windowName, windowFeatures){
        newWindow = window.open(URL, windowName, windowFeatures)
}

// End -->
</script>
```

Figure 6.26 JavaScript code in the head of an HTML document. The Flash movie embedded in this HTML document will call the function `openWindow`.

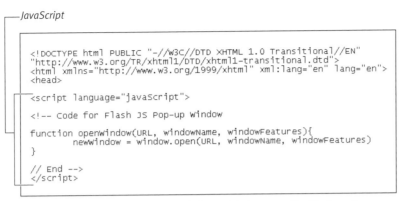

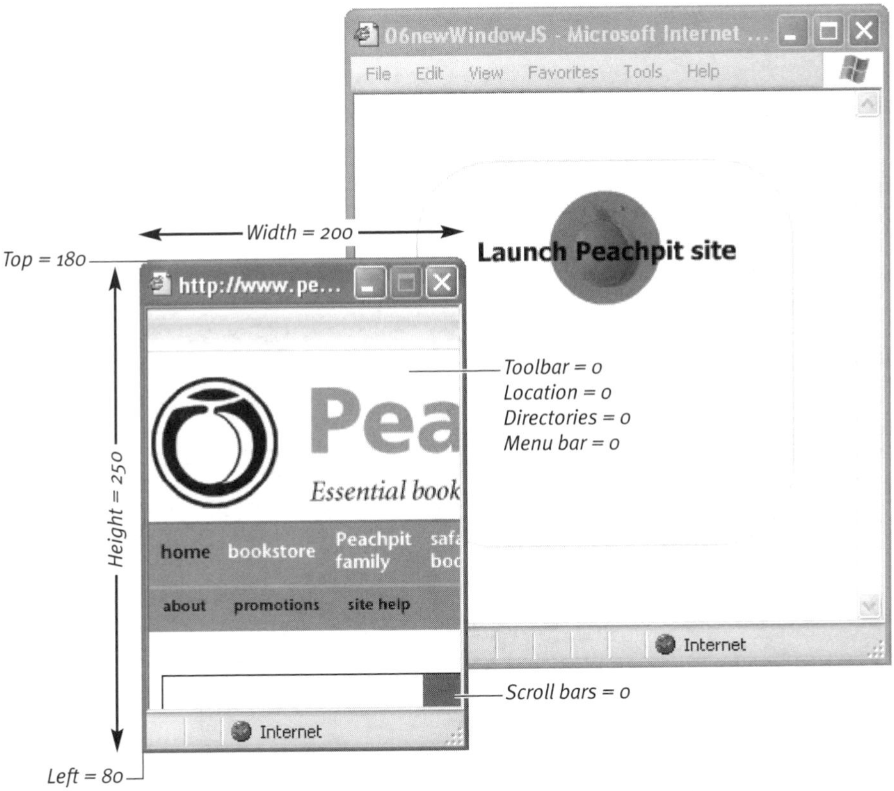

Figure 6.27 The new window created by the JavaScript function is a customized window without most features. The status bar and resize control are still visible because those properties aren't specified in the `getURL` action.

To close a window with JavaScript:

1. In your Flash movie, create a second button, and assign the `getURL` action to an `onRelease` event handler.
2. With your pointer between the parentheses for `getURL`, enter the following (**Figure 6.28**):

   `"javascript:closeWindow('newWin')"`
3. Publish your Flash movie, and open the HTML document in a text editor program.
4. In the JavaScript portion of your HTML page, add the new `closeWindow` function after the `openWindow` function, as follows:

   ```
   function closeWindow(windowName) {
       newWindow.close(windowName);
   }
   ```

   The function `closeWindow` calls the method `close()`. The parameter `windowName` is the name of the window you want to close (**Figure 6.29**).
5. Save your modified HTML page, and open it in a browser.

   When you click the first button, Flash tells JavaScript to create a new window called newWin. When you click the second button, Flash tells JavaScript to close the window called newWin.

```
closeButton_btn.onRelease = function() {
    getURL("javascript:closeWindow('mynewWindow')");
};
```

Figure 6.28 The `getURL` action calls the JavaScript `closeWindow` function. The window object called `newWin` closes.

```
<!DOCTYPE html PUBLIC "-//W3C//DTD XHTML 1.0 Transitional//EN"
"http://www.w3.org/TR/xhtml1/DTD/xhtml1-transitional.dtd">
<html xmlns="http://www.w3.org/1999/xhtml" xml:lang="en" lang="en">
<meta http-equiv="Content-Type" content="text/html; charset=iso-8859-1">
<title>07CloseWindowJS</title>

<head>

<script language="javaScript">

<!-- Code for Flash JS Pop-up Window

function openWindow(URL, windowName, windowFeatures){
newWindow = window.open(URL, windowName, windowFeatures)
}

function closeWindow(windowName){
newWindow.close(windowName)
}


// End -->
</script>

</head>
```

JavaScript

Figure 6.29 JavaScript code in the header of an HTML document. Both the `openWindow` and `closeWindow` functions are defined here.

Communicating between Flash and the Web Browser

In these tasks, you've used the `getURL` action and JavaScript to open and close new browser windows. However, this technique isn't limited to using JavaScript to manipulate browser windows—it can be used to call any JavaScript function defined in the Web page, meaning the actions that can be performed are only limited to the capabilities of JavaScript.

This technique has a limitation: the browser can't communicate back to the SWF file. The function can't pass back values in response to the function call, and the browser can't send actions to the SWF. Macromedia has developed two solutions that allow true two-way communication between the browser's JavaScript and Flash.

In Flash 8, new functionality known as the *External API* handles all the complications of two-way communication between the Flash Player and the browser. The function calls are *synchronous* (meaning they happen directly, just like function calls within Flash), and a function call to Flash or to JavaScript can return a value back to the other. In order to use the External API, you must publish the SWF for Flash Player 8.

If you want your Flash movie to be viewable by users with earlier Flash Player versions, you can use the Flash / JavaScript Integration Kit, a freely available set of ActionScript and JavaScript code that Macromedia has created. This technique is more complicated to use but doesn't require Flash Player 8.

To learn more about the External API, see the Flash Help section Learning ActionScript 2.0 in Flash > Working with External Data > "Sending messages to and from Flash Player" > About the External API.

You can get information about and download the Flash / JavaScript Integration Kit from http://weblogs.macromedia.com/flashjavascript/.

Using CGI and the GET and POST methods

An optional third parameter for the `getURL` action lets you specify whether to send information via the `GET` or `POST` method. These methods send variables that you define in your Flash movie to a server-side application (such as a CGI or PHP application) for processing. These methods are most commonly used by Web browsers to send information such as keywords to a search engine or data in a form on a Web page.

The difference between `GET` and `POST` is simple:

- `GET` appends the variables to the URL in the `getURL` action. It's used for few variables and for those that contain only a small amount of information. The variables `term=CGI`, `category=All`, and `pref=all` are put at the end of this URL as follows:

  ```
  http://search.domain.com/cgi-bin/
  search?term=CGI&category=All&pref=all
  ```

  You've probably seen this type of long URL after you've requested information from a search engine.

- `POST` sends the variables in the HTTP header of the user's browser, as though it were submitted by a form in an HTML page. Use `POST` for more security or to send long strings of information in the `getURL` operation. A message board, for example, would do better with a `POST` method.

When the Flash Player reaches your `getURL` action, any variables defined on the same Timeline as the `getURL` command are automatically sent to the server. The variables are sent to the CGI script on the Web server, which can retrieve them from the URL or HTTP headers. These server-side scripts are handled by your Internet service provider or your Webmaster, so you should contact them for more information.

To send information by using GET:

1. Select the text tool, and drag out a text field on the Stage.
2. In the Property inspector, choose Input Text from the pull-down menu.

   This option lets you use the text field you created to enter information.
3. In the Property inspector, give the text field an instance name.

   Whatever you enter in that text field will be assigned to its `text` property.
4. Create a button, place an instance of it on the Stage, and name the button in the Property inspector.
5. Select a keyframe on the Timeline, and open the Actions panel.
6. Declare a variable that will contain the data to send along with the `getURL` action.

   This variable's name should ultimately match the variable retrieved in the CGI script so that the entered data can be sent.

7. Create an `onRelease` event handler for the button.

8. Inside the curly braces of the event handler function, enter the name of the variable you declared in step 6 followed by an equals sign.

9. After the equals sign, type the instance name of your text field followed by a period. Choose the `text` property from the code hint menu that appears.

   This statement gets the contents of the text field and stores it in your variable. The value of the variable will be sent to the server automatically as part of any `getURL` action.

10. On the next line of the event handler function, add a `getURL` action.

11. For the `url` parameter of the `getURL` statement, enter the address to the server-side script (such as `"http://www.myserver.com/cgi-bin/list.cgi"`).

12. After the `url` parameter, add comma and then a `window` parameter of `"_self"`.

13. Enter `"GET"` for the third (`method`) parameter.

    Your Script pane should look like **Figure 6.30**.

    When a viewer enters an email address in the text field and then clicks the button, the email address is added to the end of the URL and is sent to the CGI script.

    You'll learn more about input text in Chapter 11.

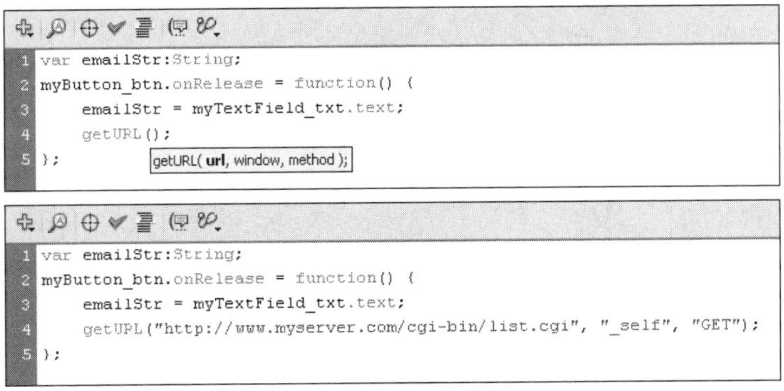

Figure 6.30 Using the code hints inside the `getURL` method (top), enter the `url`, `window`, and `method` parameters (bottom).

Loading External Flash Movies

You've learned how a Flash movie can use the action `getURL` to link to any file, including another Flash movie. This action loads the new SWF file into the same browser window, replacing the original movie, or into a new browser window.

Another way to communicate with external Flash movies and combine them with the original Flash movie is to use the actions `loadMovie` and `loadMovieNum`. Both actions allow you to bring in another SWF and integrate it with the current content. The original Flash movie establishes the frame rate, the Stage size, and the background color, but you can layer multiple external SWF files and even navigate in their Timelines. In Chapter 5, you learned to navigate the Timelines of movie clips in a single Flash movie. Now imagine the complexity of navigating multiple Timelines of multiple Flash movies!

One of the benefits of loading external Flash movies is that doing so lets you keep your Flash project small and maintain quick download times. If you build a Web site to showcase your Flash animation work, for example, you can keep all your individual animations as separate SWF files. Build the main interface so that your potential clients can load each animation as they request it. That way, your viewers download only the content that's needed, as it's needed. The main interface doesn't become bloated with the inclusion of every one of your Flash animations (**Figure 6.31**).

You can load external SWF files into another Flash movie in two ways. One way is to load a SWF into a level with `loadMovieNum`; the other is to load a SWF into a movie clip instance with `loadMovie`.

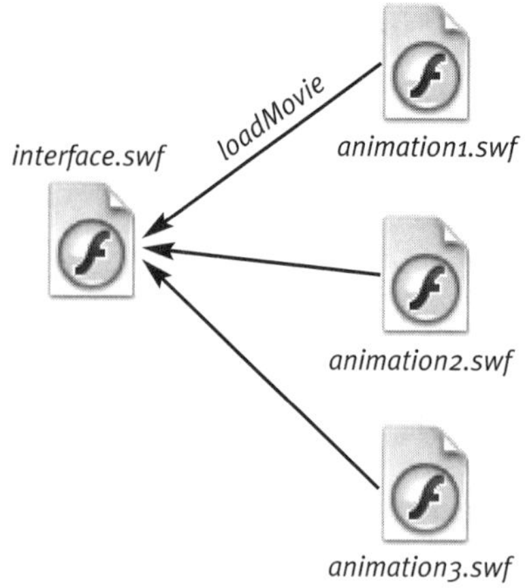

Figure 6.31 You can keep data-heavy content separate by maintaining external SWF files. Here, the interface.swf movie loads the animation files one by one as they're requested.

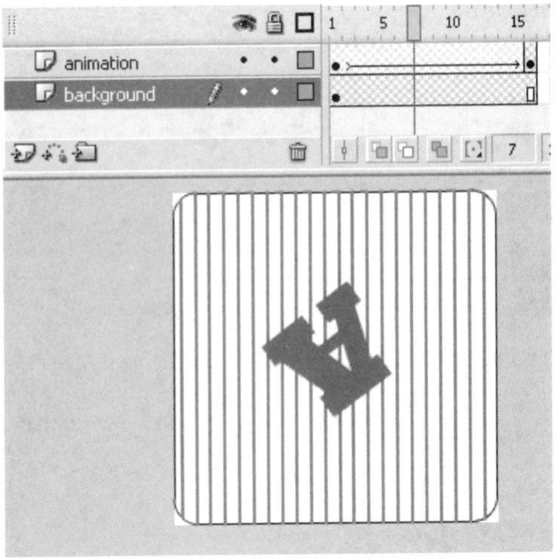

Figure 6.32 An animation of the letter *A* spins on a vertical grid.

Working with levels

Levels hold individual SWF files in a Flash movie. The original Flash movie is always at level 0, and subsequent Flash movies are kept at higher levels. You can have only one movie per level. Higher-level numbers overlap lower-level numbers, so loaded movies always appear above your original movie on the screen. To unload a movie, specify the level number; the movie in that level is purged with the action `unloadMovieNum`. Another way to remove a movie in a particular level is to replace it with a new movie. If you load a new movie into a level already occupied by another movie, the old one is replaced.

To load an external movie into a level:

1. Create the external movie you want to load.

   For this example, keep the animation at a relatively small Stage size (**Figure 6.32**).
2. Publish your external movie as a SWF file.
3. Open a new Flash document to create the main movie that will load your external movie.
4. Create a button symbol, drag an instance of it from the Library to the Stage, and give it a name in the Property inspector.
5. Select the first frame of the main Timeline, and create an `onRelease` event handler for your button.
6. Inside the `onRelease` event handler, choose Global Functions > Browser/ Network > loadMovieNum (Esc + ln).

   The `loadMovieNum` action appears within the `onRelease` event handler.

continues on next page

7. With your pointer between the parentheses, enter the name of your external SWF file surrounded by quotation marks and followed by a comma.

   Here, you enter a relative path so Flash looks in the same directory for the SWF file. You can also change directories by using the slash (/) or double periods (..), or you can enter an absolute path if your SWF file resides on a Web site.

8. For the second parameter of the `loadMovieNum` action, enter a number higher than zero representing the level in which your movie will load (**Figure 6.33**). Ignore the optional third parameter.

9. Publish your movie.

10. Place the SWF file, its HTML file, and the external SWF file in the same directory.

11. Play the main movie in Flash Player or a browser.

    When you click the button, Flash loads the external movie, which sits on top of your original movie and begins playing (**Figure 6.34**).

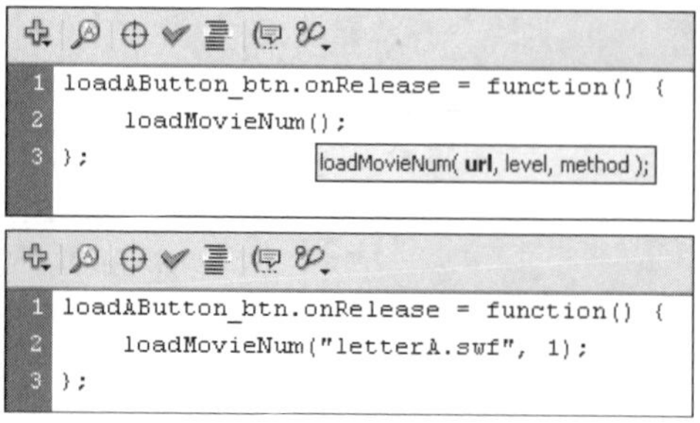

Figure 6.33 The `loadMovieNum` action has parameters for a `url` (its target path), for `level` (its destination), and for `method` (for variables). The `method` parameter isn't used in this example.

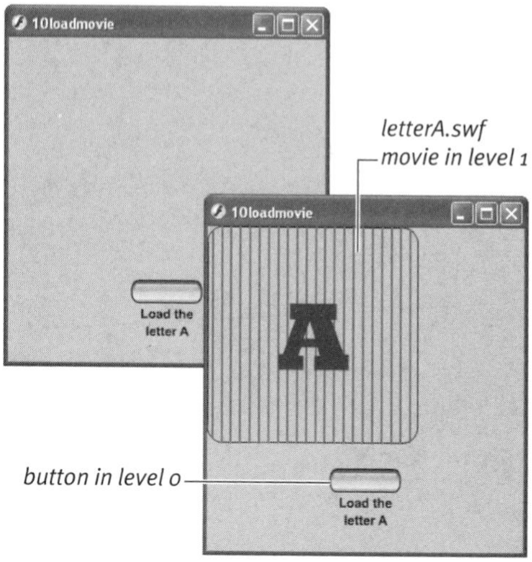

Figure 6.34 The original movie in level 0 (top) and the loaded movie in level 1 (bottom).

Characteristics of Movies Loaded into Levels

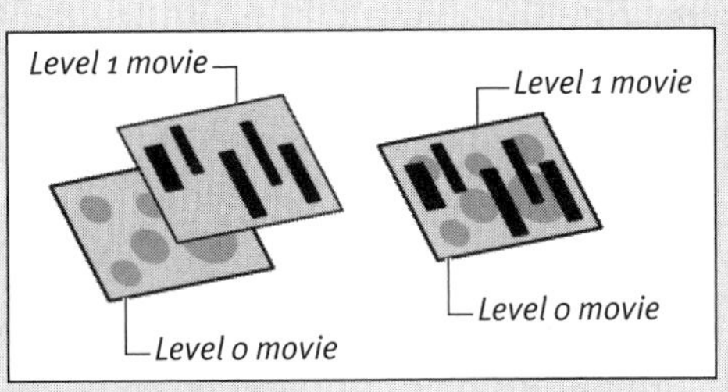

Figure 6.35 The Stage of an external SWF becomes transparent when the SWF is loaded on top of the level o movie.

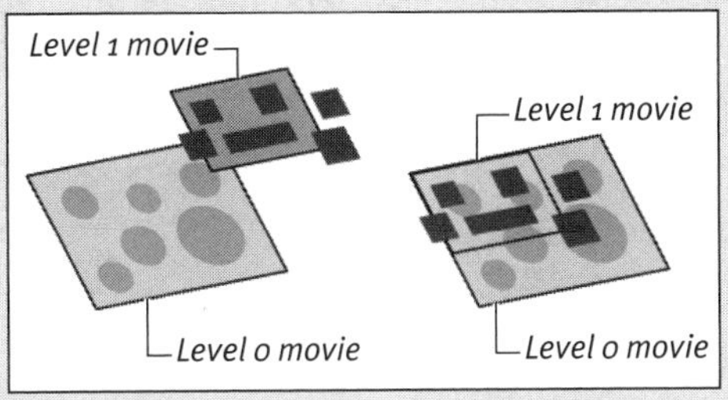

Figure 6.36 Smaller external SWFs are aligned at the top-left corner and display the work area off their Stages. Consider using masks or external SWFs with the same Stage dimensions.

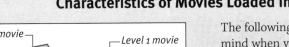

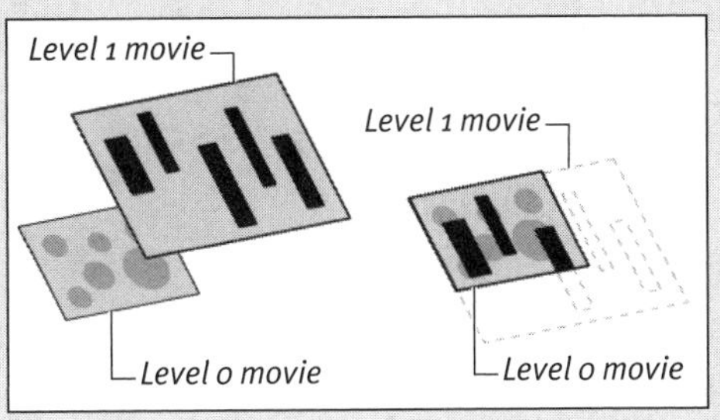

Figure 6.37 Larger external SWFs get cropped when they're loaded on top of the level o movie.

The following is a list of things to keep in mind when you're working with movies loaded into levels:

- You can have only one movie per level.
- Loaded movies in higher levels overlap loaded movies in lower levels.
- Loaded movies have transparent Stages. To have an opaque Stage, create a filled rectangle in the bottom layer of your loaded movie (**Figure 6.35**).
- Loaded movies are aligned with the level 0 movie at their registration points. That means loaded movies are positioned from their top-left corner (x = 0, y = 0) to the top-left corner of the original movie (x = 0, y = 0). So, loaded movies with smaller Stage sizes still show objects that are off their Stage (**Figure 6.36**). Create a mask to block objects that may go beyond the Stage and that you don't want your audience to see. Likewise, loaded movies with larger Stage sizes are cropped at the bottom and right boundaries (**Figure 6.37**).
- Movies loaded into level 0 replace the original movie, but the Stage size, frame rate, and background color are still set by the original movie. If the loaded movie has a different Stage size than the original, it's centered and scaled to fit.

To unload a movie in a level:

1. Using the files from the preceding task, create another instance of the button in the original movie, and give it a name in the Property inspector.
2. In the first frame of the main Timeline, create an `onRelease` event handler for the second button.
3. Within the `onRelease` event handler, choose Global Functions > Browser/Network > unloadMovieNum (Esc + un).

   The `unloadMovieNum` action appears within the `onRelease` event handler.
4. With your pointer between the parentheses, enter the number that you entered for the `level` parameter in the `loadMovieNum` action (**Figure 6.38**).
5. Publish your movie, and place it in the same directory as your external SWF file.
6. Play your movie in Flash Player or in a browser.

   The first button loads your external movie in the specified level. The second button unloads that movie from that level.

```
loadAButton_btn.onRelease = function() {
    loadMovieNum("letterA.swf", 1);
};
unloadAButton_btn.onRelease = function() {
    unloadMovieNum(1);
};
```

Figure 6.38 The `unloadMovieNum` action has only one parameter for level. Any movie in level 1 will be removed.

```
loadAButton_btn.onRelease = function() {
    loadMovieNum("letterA.swf", 1);
};
unloadAButton_btn.onRelease = function() {
    unloadMovieNum(1);
};
loadBButton_btn.onRelease = function() {
    loadMovieNum("letterB.swf", 1);
};
```

Figure 6.39 The `loadMovieNum` action assigned to the button called `loadBButton_btn` loads the movie letterB.swf into level 1, replacing anything currently occupying that level.

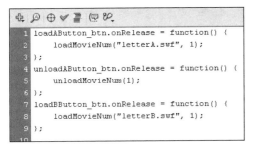

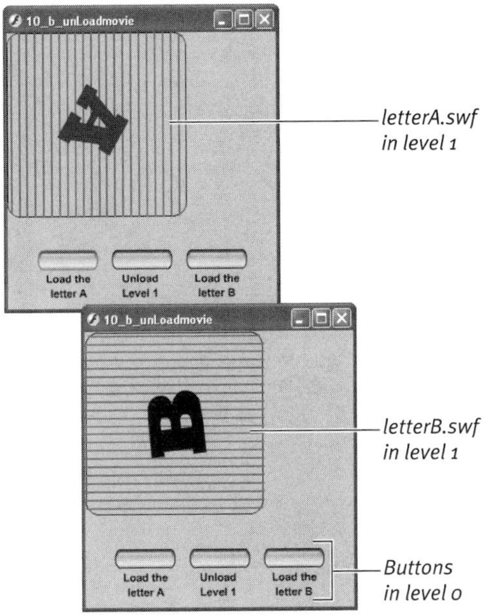

Figure 6.40 Initially, the letterA.swf movie occupies level 1 (top). Loading another movie in the same level replaces letterA.swf.

To replace a movie loaded in a level:

1. Open a new Flash document, and create another small Flash animation to serve as a second external movie.
2. Using the Flash document that you used as the container movie in the preceding tasks, add a third instance of your button, and give it a name in the Property inspector.
3. In the first frame of the main Timeline, create an `onRelease` event handler for the third button.
4. Within the `onRelease` event handler, choose Global Functions > Browser/Network > loadMovieNum.

   The `loadMovieNum` action appears below the `onRelease` event handler.
5. With your pointer between the parentheses, enter the name of the second external movie surrounded by quotation marks and followed by a comma.
6. For the second parameter, enter the same level number that you used for the first `loadMovieNum` action (**Figure 6.39**).
7. Publish your movie, and place both the container SWF file and the two external SWF files in the same directory.
8. In the Flash Player or a browser, play the original movie, which contains the three buttons.

   When you click the first button, Flash loads the first external movie, which sits on top of your original movie. When you click your newly created third button, Flash loads the second external movie in the same level, replacing the first (**Figure 6.40**).

Loading Flash movies into movie clips

Loading external movies into levels is somewhat restricting because the default placement of those movies is at the top-left corner of the original Stage. You can work with that positioning by shifting the elements in your external movie relative to where you know it will appear, or you can change all your external movies so that their Stage sizes correspond to the original Stage size.

A better solution is to load those movies into movie clip instances instead of levels with the `MovieClip` class's `loadMovie` method. This method places the top-left corner of the loaded movie (x=0, y=0) at the registration point of the targeted movie clip (x=0, y=0) (**Figure 6.41**). Because you can place movie clips anywhere on the Stage, you effectively have a way to position your loaded movie where you want. The loaded movie takes over the movie clip; the Timeline and content of the movie clip are replaced by the Timeline and content of the loaded movie. However, the movie clip maintains its instance name. In addition, all movie clip property changes such as scaling, rotation, skewing, and alpha effects that have been applied to the movie clip instance are applied to the loaded movie (**Figure 6.42**).

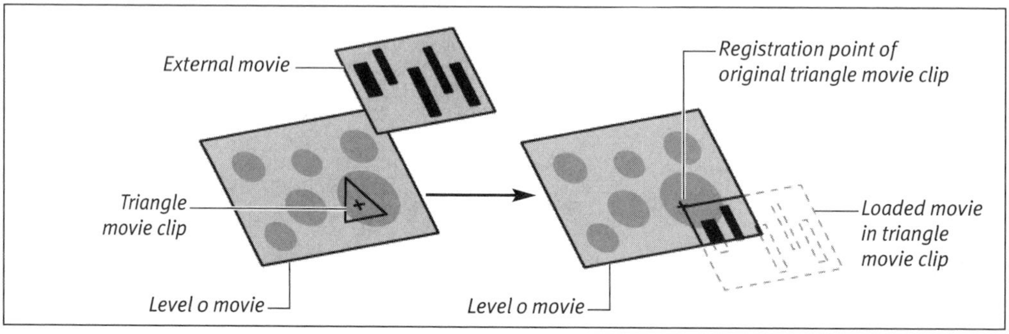

Figure 6.41 The loaded movie's top-left corner is aligned with the registration point of the target movie clip.

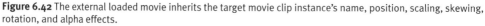

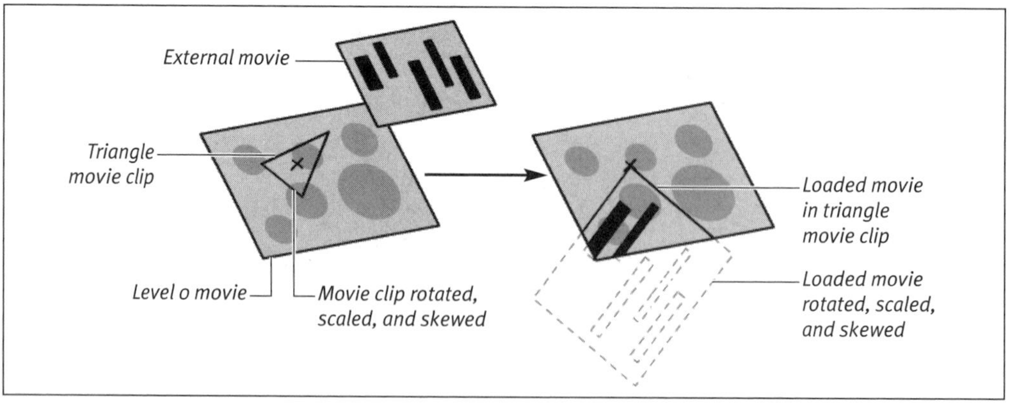

Figure 6.42 The external loaded movie inherits the target movie clip instance's name, position, scaling, skewing, rotation, and alpha effects.

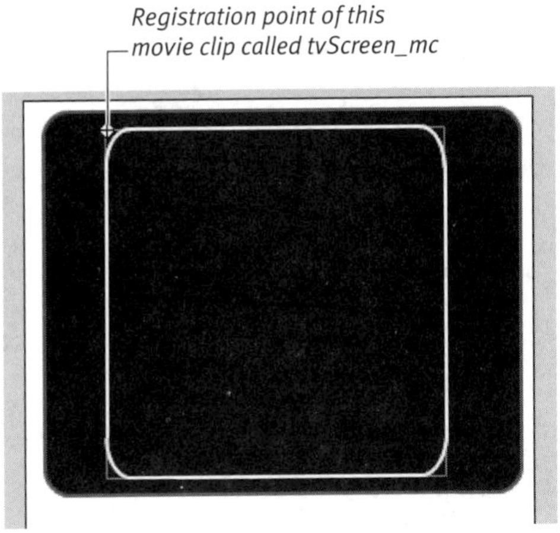

Figure 6.43 A movie clip instance is the future destination for a loaded movie.

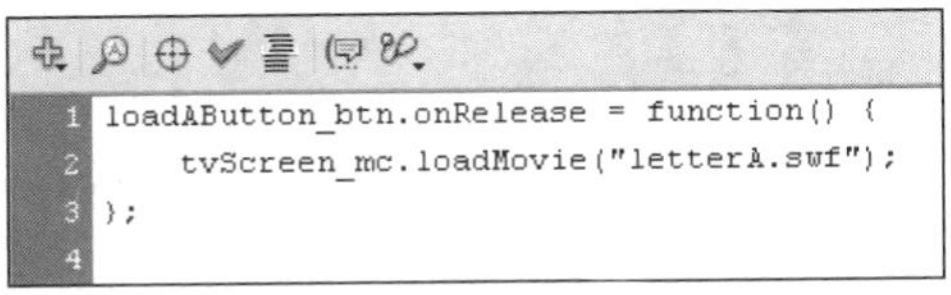

loadAButton_btn.onRelease = function() {
tvScreen_mc.loadMovie("letterA.swf");
};

Figure 6.44 When the button called `loadAButton_btn` is clicked, letterA.swf will load into the movie clip called `tvScreen_mc`.

To load an external Flash movie into a movie clip:

1. Create a movie clip symbol with the registration point set to the upper-left corner, and drag an instance of it from the Library to the Stage (**Figure 6.43**).
2. Select the instance, and give it a name in the Property inspector.
3. Create a button symbol, drag an instance of it from the Library to the Stage, and give it a name in the Property inspector.
4. In the first frame of the main Timeline, create an `onRelease` event handler for the button.
5. Within the `onRelease` event handler, type the name of your movie clip instance; choose ActionScript 2.0 Classes > Movie > MovieClip > Methods > loadMovie.

   The `loadMovie` method call appears within the `onRelease` event handler.
6. With your pointer between the parentheses, enter the name of an external SWF file surrounded by quotation marks (**Figure 6.44**).

continues on next page

Flash Player Security: Loading Movies Across Domains

Loading external SWFs introduces data security issues and some restrictions you should be aware of. Because SWFs published on the Internet can be loaded into any Flash movie, the potential exists for private information and sensitive data held in variables in the SWF to be accessed. To prevent this abuse, Flash movies operate in their own secure space, called a *sandbox*. Only movies playing in the same sandbox can access and/or control each other's variables and other Flash elements. The sandbox is defined by the domain in which the Flash movie resides. So, a movie on www.macromedia.com can access other movies on www.macromedia.com without restriction, because they're in the same domain.

If you need to access data in SWFs that reside in different domains, you can call the ActionScript method `System.security.allowDomain("domainName")` within those SWFs, and movies from the specified domain can access their variables. For more specific information and details about domain-based authentication and granting access, see the Flash Help topic Learning ActionScript 2.0 in Flash > Understanding Security. Current information is also available at the Macromedia Developer Center Security site: http://www.macromedia.com/devnet/security/.

7. Publish your movie, and place the SWF file, its HTML file, and the external SWF file in the same directory.

8. Play the original movie in the Flash Player or a browser.

   When you click the button that you created, Flash loads the external movie into the movie clip. The loaded movie inherits all the characteristics of the movie clip, such as position, scale, and rotation, but the Timeline of the movie clip is now the Timeline of the loaded movie (**Figure 6.45**).

✔ Tips

- In the next chapter, you'll learn to dynamically create an empty movie clip with the movie clip method `createEmptyMovieClip`. You can use that method to create a movie clip to act as your placeholder, load an external SWF into that movie clip, and then set its `_x` and `_y` properties to position it where you want.

- You can also load an external SWF into a movie clip by using the global function `loadMovie`. Type `loadMovie()` (with no object name before it). Between the parentheses, enter two parameters: the name of the external file you want to load (in quotation marks) and the instance name of the instance that will be replaced by the loaded movie.

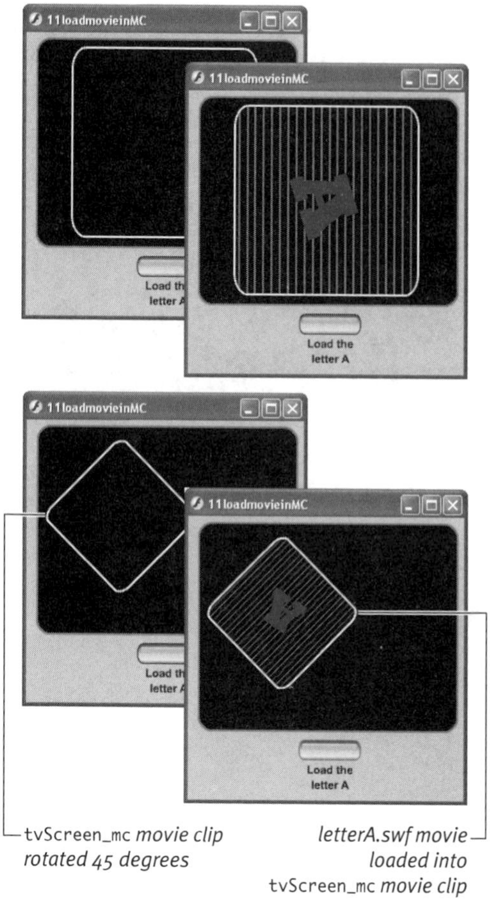

Figure 6.45 The letterA.swf movie loads into the `tvScreen_mc` movie clip (top). When the `tvScreen_mc` movie clip rotates and shrinks, so does letterA.swf (bottom).

Navigating Timelines of loaded movies

After external movies are loaded into your original movie, you can access their Timelines and control when and where the playhead moves. If you thought navigation between movie clip Timelines was complex, just think how intricate navigation can become with multiple movies, each containing its own movie clips!

To minimize confusion, Flash provides a straightforward way of targeting loaded movies and their Timelines. Because movies loaded with `loadMovieNum` reside on different levels, Flash uses the term `_level1` to refer to the movie in level 1, `_level2` to refer to the movie in level 2, and so on. Movies that are loaded into movie clips can be accessed using their instance name, so targeting those loaded movies means targeting movie clip instances. If loaded movies have movie clips themselves, use dot syntax to drill down the Timeline hierarchy as you do with movie clips on the root Timeline. For example, `_level2.train_mc.wheels_mc` is the target path for the movie clip named `wheels_mc` inside the movie clip named `train_mc` that resides in the loaded movie on level 2.

To target a movie loaded into a level:

1. As in the preceding tasks, create an animation to serve as an external Flash movie, and export it as a SWF file.
2. Open a new Flash document.
3. Create a button, drag an instance of it from the Library to the Stage, and give it an instance name in the Property inspector.
4. In the first frame of the main Timeline, create an `onRelease` event handler for the button.

continues on next page

5. Assign the action `loadMovieNum` to the button event handler, specifying the external SWF file and a number higher than zero for its level (**Figure 6.46**).

6. Drag another instance of the button onto the Stage, and give it an instance name.

   This button will control the Timeline of the loaded movie.

7. In the first frame of the main Timeline, create an `onRelease` event handler for this second button.

8. Within the `onRelease` event handler, enter `_level` and then the level number followed by a period.

9. From the code hint menu that appears, choose `stop` (**Figure 6.47**).

   Clicking the button stops the playhead of the movie in the specified level.

10. Publish your movie, and place the SWF and its HTML in the same directory as the external SWF file.

11. Play the movie containing the buttons in Flash Player or a browser.

    The first button loads the external SWF in the specified level. The second button targets that level and stops the playhead.

```
loadAButton_btn.onRelease = function() {
    loadMovieNum("letterA.swf", 1);
};
```

Figure 6.46 The `loadMovieNum` action assigned to the button called `loadAButton_btn` puts letterA.swf in level 1.

```
loadAButton_btn.onRelease = function() {
    loadMovieNum("letterA.swf", 1);
};
controlAButton_btn.onRelease = function() {
    _level1.stop();
};
```

Figure 6.47 The `stop()` method acts on the movie in level 1.

Defining the root Timeline for loaded movies

When you're working with loaded movies, understanding which Timeline the word `_root` refers to is crucial to constructing accurate target paths. In Chapter 5, you learned that to target a movie clip on the main Timeline from within another movie clip on the main Timeline, you write `_root.instanceName`. That target path tells Flash to jump out of the movie clip's Timeline to the root Timeline and find the `instanceName` instance. If this movie is played on its own, everything will work as you would expect. However, once you begin working with multiple movies using `loadMovie` or `loadMovieNum`, you may come across multiple `_root` references. Imagine that this movie is now loaded into a movie clip in a new file named main.swf. The `_root` in its target path now refers to the main Timeline of main.swf, and many of its actions that include `_root` in the target path will fail.

The answer to this problem is to force `_root` to refer to the main Timeline of the loaded movie as opposed to the real root (level 0) Timeline. This is achieved by using the `_lockroot` property. If you set a movie clip's `_lockroot` property to true, that movie clip's Timeline acts as the root Timeline for any movies loaded into it.

In the following task, you'll load an external movie into a movie clip. The external movie contains ActionScript that refers to the root Timeline, so you'll use the `_lockroot` property to force the external movie to reference the movie clip as the root Timeline to preserve its functionality.

To identify a movie clip as the root for loaded external SWF files:

1. Create a new movie with multiple movie clips on the main Timeline. In this example, the movie clips contain animation (**Figure 6.48**).

   This movie will be your external SWF that you'll load into another Flash movie.

continues on next page

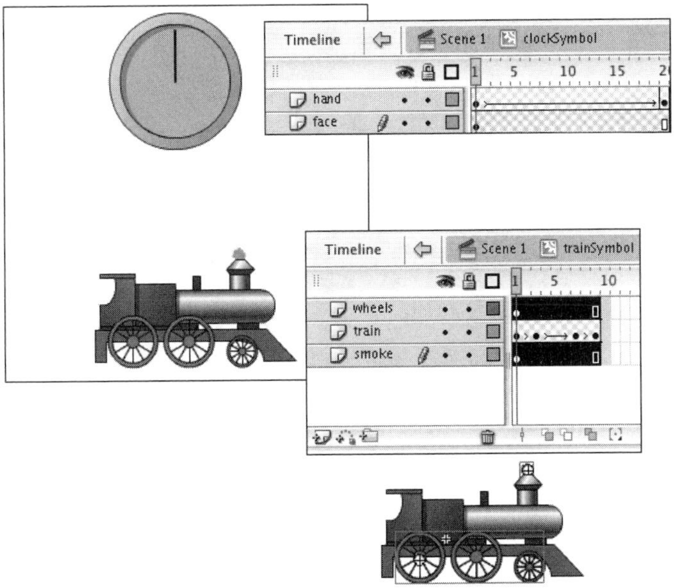

Figure 6.48 The `clock_mc` movie clip has an animation on its Timeline. The `train_mc` movie clip contains two nested movie clips, `smoke_mc` and `wheels_mc`.

2. In the Property inspector, give a name to each of your movie clips.

3. On the main Timeline, select the first frame, and open the Actions panel.

4. Assign an `onRelease` event handler to one of your movie clips. Within the `onRelease` event handler, target the other movie clip to stop its animation, using `_root` in the target path (**Figure 6.49**).

5. Publish your external movie as a SWF file.

6. In a new Flash document, create a movie clip with the registration point in the upper-left corner, place an instance of it on the Stage, and give it a name in the Property inspector (**Figure 6.50**).

   This movie clip will be the placeholder into which the external SWF will load.

7. Create a button symbol, drag an instance from the Library to the Stage, and give it a name in the Property inspector.

   This button will load the external SWF into your placeholder movie clip.

8. In the first frame of the main Timeline, create an `onRelease` event handler for the button.

9. Within the `onRelease` event handler, enter the target path of the movie clip instance on the Stage. Choose Action-Script 2.0 Classes > Movie > MovieClip > Methods > loadMovie.

```
clock_mc.onRelease = function() {
    _root.train_mc.wheels_mc.stop();
};
```

Figure 6.49 When you click the `clock_mc` movie clip, the animation on the `train_mc.wheels_mc` movie clip Timeline stops. Note that the target path before the `stop` action includes the `_root` keyword.

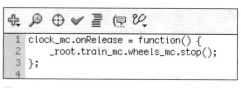

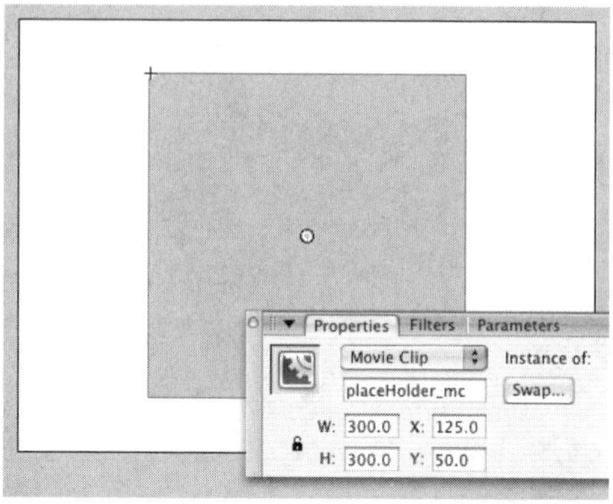

Figure 6.50 The registration point is at the upper-left corner for the movie clip named `placeHolder_mc`.

```
loadButton_btn.onRelease = function(){
    placeHolder_mc.loadMovie("anim.swf");
};
```

Figure 6.51 When the `loadButton_btn` is clicked, the external SWF file called anim.swf will load into the movie clip called `placeHolder_mc`.

```
loadButton_btn.onRelease = function(){
    loadMovie("anim.swf", "placeHolder_mc");
};
placeHolder_mc.onLoad = function() {
    this._lockroot = true;
```

Figure 6.52 Declaring `_lockroot` to be true for the `placeHolder_mc` movie clip forces it to be the `_root` Timeline for all movies loaded into it.

10. With your pointer between the parentheses of the `loadMovie` method call, enter the name of the external SWF file surrounded by quotation marks (**Figure 6.51**).

11. On the next line (inside the `onRelease` event handler function), type the instance name of the placeholder movie clip.

12. Choose ActionScript 2.0 Classes > Movie > MovieClip > Properties > _lockroot, and assign it a Boolean value of `true` (**Figure 6.52**).

Any movie clips loaded into this movie clip can now use `_root` to refer to their own root Timeline.

13. Publish your movie into the same directory as the external SWF you created in step 1, and play it.

When you click the button, the external SWF loads into your placeholder movie clip. The functionality in the external SWF remains intact because you defined the placeholder movie clip to act as the root Timeline.

✔ Tip

- In this task, you defined the placeholder movie clip to act as the root Timeline for loaded SWFs. If you have access to the FLA file of the loaded SWF, you can also add ActionScript to its main Timeline to force Flash to use it as the root Timeline. On the first keyframe, enter `this._lockroot = true`. The term `_root` will always refer to the main Timeline no matter what it's loaded into.

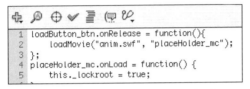

Loading External Images

Using the same actions that load external SWF files into your movie dynamically, you can load images dynamically, including JPEG, progressive JPEG, GIF, and PNG images. Use the `loadMovie` method or the `loadMovieNum` action to pull images into your movie at run time to reduce the size of your Flash movie and save download time. As is the case with external SWFs, keeping images separate from your Flash movie makes revisions quicker and easier because you can swap or change the images without needing to open the actual Flash file.

Loaded images follow many of the same rules that loaded movies do, and those rules are worth repeating here:

- You can have only one image per level.
- Higher levels overlap lower levels.
- Images loaded into level 0 replace the original movie.
- The top-left corner of an image aligns with the top-left corner of the Stage or the registration point of a movie clip.
- An image loaded into a movie clip inherits its instance name and transformations.

To load an image in a level:

1. Create a button symbol, drag an instance to the Stage, and give it an instance name.

   This button will load an image file into your movie dynamically.
2. Select the first frame of the main Timeline, and open the Actions panel.
3. Create an `onRelease` event handler for your button.
4. Within the `onRelease` event handler, choose Global Functions > Browser/ Network > loadMovieNum.

   The `loadMovieNum` action appears within the `onRelease` event handler.
5. With your pointer between the parentheses, enter the path to the external image file followed by a comma.

   The URL can be a relative path (such as images/mypet/dog.jpg), so that Flash looks for the file relative to the current directory; or the URL can be an absolute path (such as http://www.mydomain.com/images/mypet/dog.jpg), so that Flash retrieves the file from any Web site.

```
loadImageButton_btn.onRelease = function() {
    loadMovieNum("myPhoto.jpg", 1);
};
```

Figure 6.53 The `loadMovieNum` action can also be used to load image files. Here, myPhoto.jpg is loaded in level 1 when the button is clicked.

Figure 6.54 The buttons on the bottom row load images that are kept external to your Flash movie. The top-left corner of each image aligns with the top-left corner of the Stage.

6. For the second parameter, enter a number higher than zero (**Figure 6.53**).

7. Publish your movie, and place your image in the correct directory so your Flash movie can find it.

   When you click the button, Flash loads the external image into the designated level. The top-left corner of the JPEG aligns with the top-left corner of the Stage (**Figure 6.54**).

To load an image in a movie clip:

1. Create a movie clip symbol, drag an instance of it from the Library to the Stage, and give it an instance name in the Property inspector.

2. Create a button symbol, drag an instance of it from the Library to the Stage, and give it an instance name.

   This button will load an image file into your movie clip dynamically.

3. In the first frame of the main Timeline, create an `onRelease` event handler for the button.

4. Inside the event handler function, enter the instance name of your movie clip on the Stage; choose ActionScript 2.0 Classes > Movie > MovieClip > Methods > loadMovie.

   The `loadMovie` method appears within the `onRelease` event handler.

continues on next page

5. With your pointer between the parentheses, enter the path to the external image file (**Figure 6.55**).

6. Publish your movie, and place your image in the correct directory so your Flash movie can find it.

   When you click the button that you created, Flash loads the external image into the movie clip. The top-left corner of the image aligns with the registration point of the movie clip. The image replaces all the movie clip graphics and inherits all the characteristics of the movie clip, such as position, scale, and rotation, and can be accessed using the same instance name (**Figure 6.56**).

To remove or replace a loaded image:

- To remove an image, use the action `unloadMovieNum` and choose a level, or use the MovieClip class's `unloadMovie` method with the instance name of the movie clip containing the image.

- To replace an image, use the `loadMovie` method or `loadMovieNum` action, and load another image file into the same level or movie clip instance. The new image will replace the old one.

✔ Tip

- Flash Player 7 and earlier can only load standard (not progressive) JPEG files and can't load GIF or PNG files at all.

```
loadImageButton_btn.onRelease = function() {
    target_mc.loadMovie("myPhoto.jpg");
};
```

Figure 6.55 The file myPhoto.jpg will be loaded into the movie clip called `target_mc` when the button is clicked.

Figure 6.56 For precise placement of your loaded image files, load them into movie clips, which you can position. This movie clip is empty, meaning that it contains no graphics or animation and simply acts as a shell to receive your loaded images.

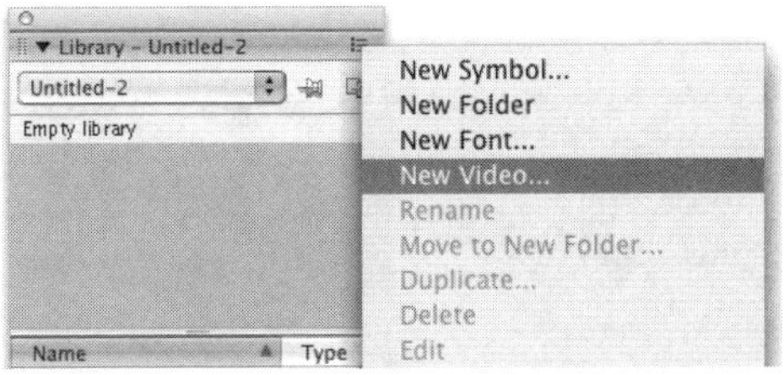

Figure 6.57 Choose New Video from the Library panel's Options menu.

Communicating With External Video

In Chapter 2, you learned how to embed video in a SWF file and also how to create an external Flash Video (FLV) file that loads into a player skin in a SWF file. In addition to using the player skin to control the loading and playback of an FLV file, you can also control both loading and playback of external video directly using ActionScript. As described previously, one of the key advantages of using an external FLV file is that you can *stream* the video—begin playing the video file before the entire file has downloaded.

Once you have an FLV file, use a `NetConnection` object and a `NetStream` object to load the video stream into Flash. The `NetConnection` object provides the measures to play back an FLV file from your local drive or Web address, whereas the `NetStream` object makes the actual connection and tells Flash to play the video. In order to receive the streaming video, you must also create a video symbol in your Library and place an instance on the Stage where you want the video to appear.

To dynamically load external video:

1. Convert your video file to an FLV file, as described in Chapter 2.
2. Open a new Flash document, with its Stage size large enough to accommodate the FLV file.
3. Open the Library. From the Library panel's Options menu, choose New Video (**Figure 6.57**).

   The Video Properties dialog box appears.
4. Give your symbol a name in the Symbol field; in the Type field, choose Video (ActionScript-controlled).

   A new video symbol appears in the library.

continues on next page

5. Place an instance of the video symbol on the Stage.

6. Modify its width and height to match the external FLV file that will be loaded in, and give it an instance name in the Property inspector (**Figure 6.58**).

   Your external FLV will play inside this video instance.

7. Create a button symbol, drag an instance of it from the Library to the Stage, and give it an instance name in the Property inspector.

   You'll assign actions to this button to load the FLV during playback.

8. In the first frame of the main Timeline, create an `onRelease` event handler for the button.

9. Inside the curly braces of the `onRelease` event, declare and instantiate a new `NetConnection` instance.

   Reminder: to do this, enter `var` followed by a variable name and then `:NetConnection` followed by an equals sign; choose ActionScript 2.0 Classes > Media > NetConnection > "new NetConnection" (**Figure 6.59**).

   A new `NetConnection` object is instantiated.

10. On the next line, enter the name of the `NetConnection` object you just created followed by a period; choose ActionScript 2.0 Classes > Media > NetConnection > Methods > connect.

11. With your pointer between the parentheses, enter the keyword `null`.

    The parameter `null` tells Flash that it isn't connecting through the Flash Communication Server but instead to expect a download from the local hard drive or a Web address.

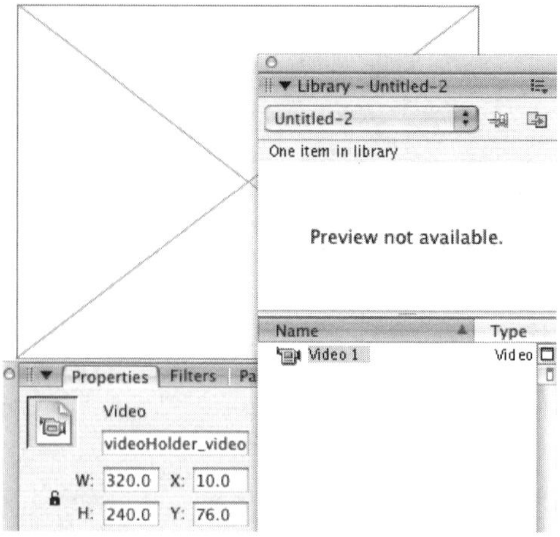

Figure 6.58 A video symbol placeholder named `videoHolder_video` is placed on the Stage. The instance looks like a square with an x inside of it.

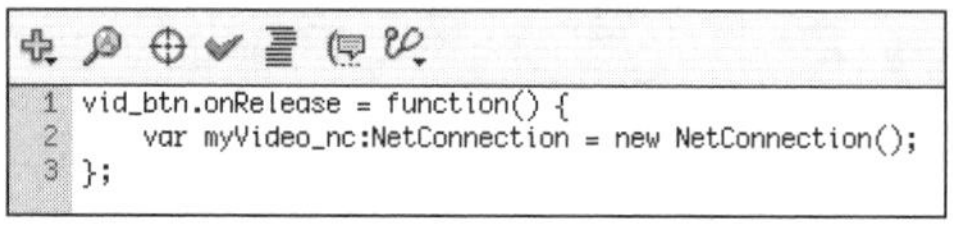

Figure 6.59 A new `NetConnection` object named `myVideo_nc` is created.

```
vid_btn.onRelease = function() {
    var myVideo_nc:NetConnection = new NetConnection();
    myVideo_nc.connect(null);
    var newStream_ns = new NetStream(myVideo_nc);
};
```

Figure 6.60 The NetConnection object is used as the parameter for the instantiation of a new NetStream object.

```
vid_btn.onRelease = function() {
    var myVideo_nc:NetConnection = new NetConnection();
    myVideo_nc.connect(null);
    var newStream_ns:NetStream = new NetStream(myVideo_nc);
    videoHolder_video.attachVideo(newStream_ns);
    newStream_ns.play("kayak.flv");
};
```

Figure 6.61 The external FLV file named kayak.flv (top) loads into the videoHolder_video instance on the Stage and plays.

12. On the next line, declare and instantiate a new NetStream variable (ActionScript 2.0 Classes > Media > NetStream > new NetStream).

13. With your pointer between the parentheses for the NetStream object, enter the name of the NetConnection object you created in step 9 (**Figure 6.60**).

    A new NetStream object is instantiated using your NetConnection object as its parameter.

14. Enter the instance name of the video symbol instance you placed on the Stage, followed by a period.

15. Choose ActionScript 2.0 Classes > Media > Video > Methods > attachVideo.

16. Between the parentheses of the attachVideo method call, enter the video source parameter. In this case, enter the name of the new NetStream object created in step 12.

17. On the next line, enter the name of the NetStream object created in step 12, followed by a period.

18. Choose ActionScript 2.0 Classes > Media > NetStream > Methods > play.

19. As the parameter for the play() method, enter the name of the external FLV file that you wish to play on the Stage (**Figure 6.61**).

    Make sure the FLV filename is surrounded by quotation marks.

20. Publish your movie, and place the SWF file in the same directory as the FLV file whose name you entered.

    When you click the button, Flash attaches your external FLV file to the instance of the video symbol on the Stage begins to stream the video.

Communicating between two movies

So far, you've learned how a single Flash movie can communicate outside itself—to retrieve a link on the Web, to incorporate another SWF, or to load an image or video. But can one Flash movie communicate with another entirely independent Flash movie? The answer is yes, with the help of a `LocalConnection` object. A `LocalConnection` object enables communication between two separate Flash movies as long as they're running from the same machine (server). Instructions from one movie can control the appearance, behavior, or interactivity of another. Imagine, for example, creating a frameset that contains a Flash movie in a top frame and a Flash movie in a bottom frame. The movie in the top frame can have buttons or pull-down menus that control the movie in the bottom frame. You can also build a Flash-based laboratory simulation in one browser window and keep a Flash lab notebook in another. Information from the simulation can be sent to the notebook and recorded automatically as the experiment progresses.

Using `LocalConnection` requires that you create a `LocalConnection` object in the sender movie as well as the receiver movie. Create the new object in both movies with the `new` constructor function, as follows:

```
var myLC_lc:LocalConnection = new
LocalConnection();
```

Next, in the sender movie, use the `send()` method to send the name of your message and the name of a function you want the receiver movie to perform:

```
myLC.send("incomingMessage",
"onReceive");
```

Finally, close the connection:

```
myLC_lc.close();
```

In the receiver movie, you must define a function that will be performed when that movie receives the message from the sender movie. After the function is established, use the `connect()` method to listen for the name of the message. In the receiver movie, the code will look something like this:

```
var myLC_lc:LocalConnection = new
LocalConnection();
myLC_lc.onReceive = function() {
    animation_mc.play();
};
myLC_lc.connect("incomingMessage");
```

When this receiver movie receives the message called `incomingMessage`, the movie clip called `animation_mc` plays.

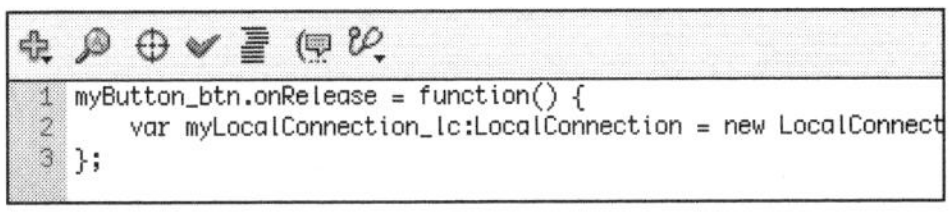

myButton_btn.onRelease = function() {
var myLocalConnection_lc:LocalConnection = new LocalConnect
};

Figure 6.62 The name of your `LocalConnection` object is `mySender_lc`.

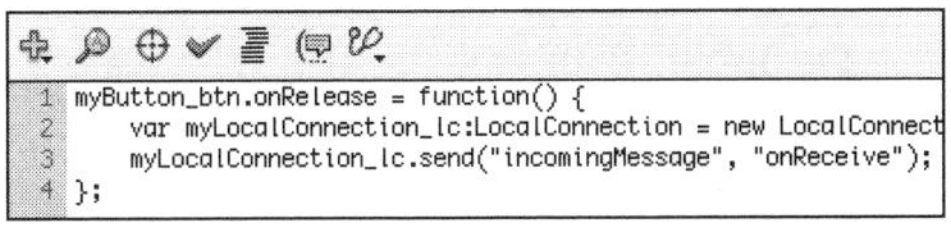

myButton_btn.onRelease = function() {
var myLocalConnection_lc:LocalConnection = new LocalConnect
myLocalConnection_lc.send("incomingMessage", "onReceive");
};

Figure 6.63 This `send()` method sends the message identified as `incomingMessage` and makes the receiver movie perform the function assigned to `onReceive`.

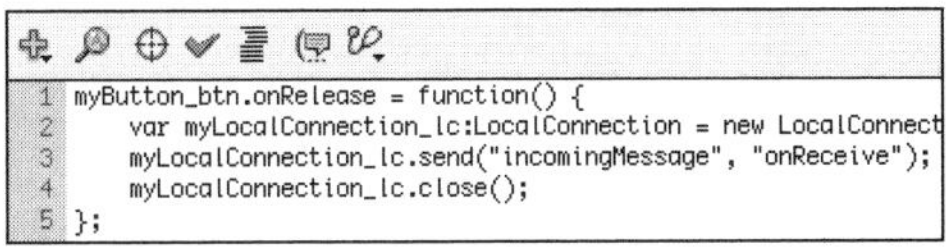

myButton_btn.onRelease = function() {
var myLocalConnection_lc:LocalConnection = new LocalConnect
myLocalConnection_lc.send("incomingMessage", "onReceive");
myLocalConnection_lc.close();
};

Figure 6.64 Close the connection.

To create the sender movie:

1. Create a button symbol, place an instance of it on the Stage, and give it a name in the Property inspector.
2. In the first frame of the main Timeline, create an `onRelease` event handler for the button.

   This button will tell a movie clip in another Flash movie (the receiver movie) to play.
3. Declare and instantiate a new `LocalConnection` object by entering `var`, then a name, and then `:LocalConnection` followed by an equals sign; choose ActionScript 2.0 Classes > Movie > LocalConnection > new LocalConnection (**Figure 6.62**).
4. On the next line, enter the name of your `LocalConnection` object followed by a period. Choose ActionScript 2.0 Classes > Movie > LocalConnection > Methods > send.
5. For the parameters of the `send()` method, enter `"incomingMessage"` and `"onReceive"`. Put quotation marks around both parameters, and separate them with a comma (**Figure 6.63**).
6. On the next line, enter the name of your `LocalConnection` object followed by a period. Choose ActionScript 2.0 Classes > Movie > LocalConnection > Methods > close (**Figure 6.64**).

   After sending a connection, you should close it, thereby disconnecting the `LocalConnection` object.

To create the receiver movie:

1. In a new Flash document, create a movie clip symbol that contains an animation.

   The movie clip should have a `stop` action in the first frame of its Timeline.

2. Drag an instance of the movie clip to the Stage, and name it in the Property inspector.

   This movie clip will be the target of a function in this movie. When the incoming message is received, the function will instruct the movie clip to play.

3. Select the first frame of the main Timeline, and open the Actions panel.

4. In the Script pane, use the `var` statement to declare and instantiate a new `LocalConnection` object.

5. Enter the name of your `LocalConnection` object, then a period, and then the name of the incoming message from the sender movie. Enter an equals sign, and then choose Statements > User-Defined Functions > function (Esc + fn) (**Figure 6.65**).

   You can think of the name of the incoming message as being similar to the name of an event. When the message is received, the function is executed. The final form of the function statement is identical to an event handler.

6. Within the function statement's curly braces, enter the name of your movie clip, a period, and then the method `play()`.

   This is the receiver movie's response to the incoming message (**Figure 6.66**).

7. On a new line outside the function statement, enter the `LocalConnection` object's name and a period, and then choose ActionScript 2.0 Classes > Movie > LocalConnection > Methods > connect.

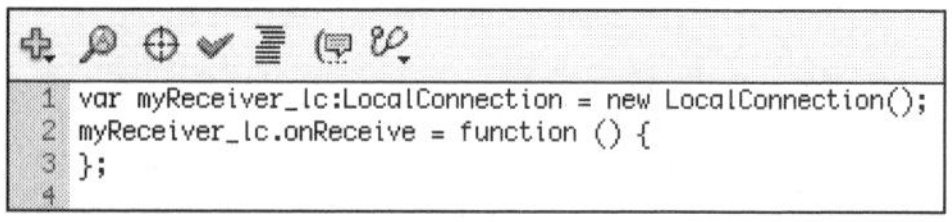
var myReceiver_lc:LocalConnection = new LocalConnection();
myReceiver_lc.onReceive = function () {
};

Figure 6.65 Create the function that responds to the incoming message.

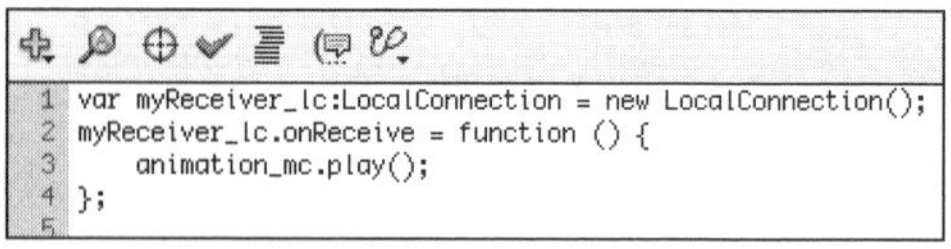
var myReceiver_lc:LocalConnection = new LocalConnection();
myReceiver_lc.onReceive = function () {
animation_mc.play();
};

Figure 6.66 When this receiver movie gets the message from the sender, it plays the movie clip called `animation_mc`.

```
var myReceiver_lc:LocalConnection = new LocalConnection();
myReceiver_lc.onReceive = function () {
    animation_mc.play();
};
myReceiver_lc.connect("incomingMessage");
```

Figure 6.67 The `connect()` method opens the connection for the message called `incomingMessage` from the sender movie.

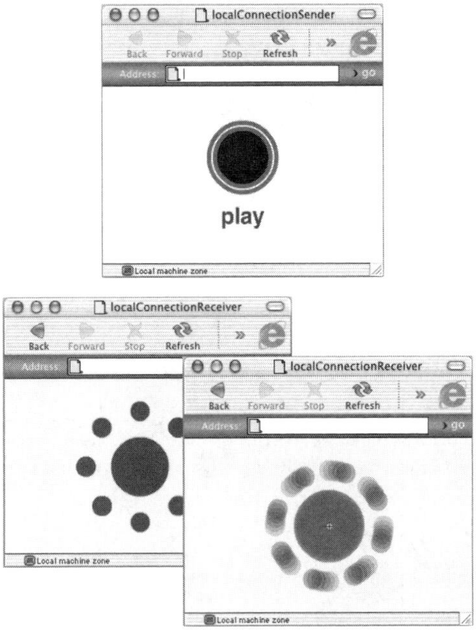

Figure 6.68 The sender movie (top) sends a message when the user clicks the button. The receiver movie in a separate browser window (bottom) responds by playing the animation.

8. Between the parentheses of the method, enter the name of the incoming message specified in your sender movie within quotation marks. In this example, the parameter is `"incomingMessage"` (**Figure 6.67**).

   The `connect()` method opens the connection for your `LocalConnection` object.

To test communication between the sender and receiver movies:

- Publish both movies, and play them in separate browser windows.

  When you click the button in the sender movie, a `LocalConnection` object is created and a message is sent. The receiver movie connects to the message and, as instructed by the sender movie, executes the function. As a result, the animation in the receiver movie plays (**Figure 6.68**).

Passing parameters between movies

Making a sender movie instruct a receiver movie to perform a function is useful, but it's even more useful to make the sender movie instruct a receiver movie to perform a function with certain parameters. Passing parameters between two independent movies is not only possible but also allows customized communication. Parameters determine the way the function is performed, much as they determine the way methods are performed. (Learn more about functions and parameters in Chapter 12, and return here to see how they're used with the `LocalConnection` object.) Sending parameters from the sender movie can make the response in the receiver movie vary according to the interaction in the sender movie.

In this task, you'll create an input text field in the sender movie and a dynamic text field in the receiver movie. You can make the sender movie pass text entered in its input text field to the receiver movie, which displays the text in its dynamic text field.

To pass parameters from the sender to the receiver movie:

1. Using the sender and receiver movies you created in the preceding tasks, delete the button in the sender movie and the movie clip in the receiver movie.
2. In both movies, select the Text tool and create a text field on the Stage.
3. In the Property inspector, choose Input Text for the sender movie and Dynamic Text for the receiver movie, and give them instance names (**Figure 6.69**).

   The name of a text field, like the names of buttons and movie clips, lets you target the text field and control it.
4. In the sender movie, change the `onRelease` event handler to an `onEnterFrame` event handler scoped to the main Timeline (**Figure 6.70**).
5. Place your cursor after the last parameter in the parentheses of the `send()` method. Add a comma, and then enter `myInputText_txt.text` (**Figure 6.71**).

   This parameter and any additional parameters in the `send()` method are sent to the receiver movie. Here, the contents of the text field called `myInputText_txt` are sent as a parameter to the receiver movie.

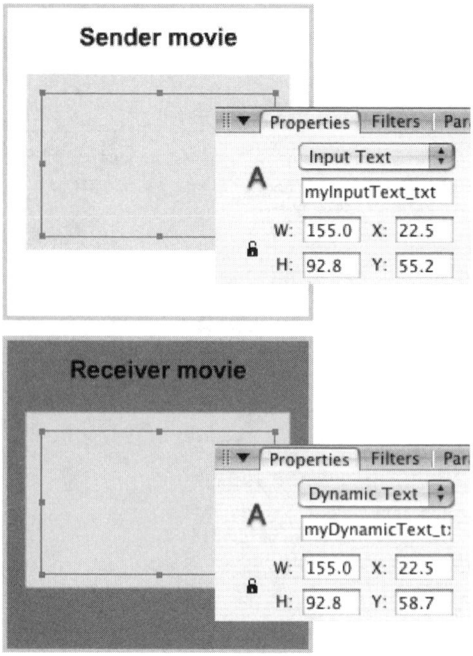

Figure 6.69 The input text field in the sender movie is called `myInputText_txt`. The dynamic text field in the receiver movie is called `myDynamicText_txt`.

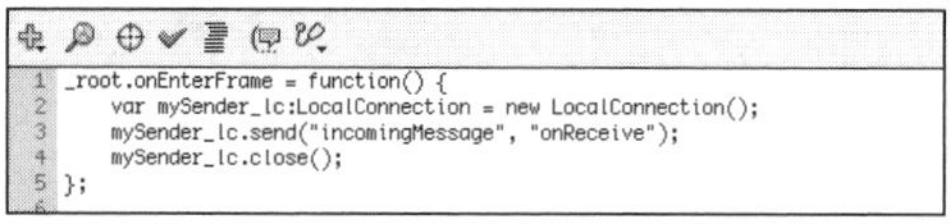

_root.onEnterFrame = function() {
var mySender_lc:LocalConnection = new LocalConnection();
mySender_lc.send("incomingMessage", "onReceive");
mySender_lc.close();
};

Figure 6.70 The `onEnterFrame` event is triggered continuously, so this message is sent to the receiver movie continuously.

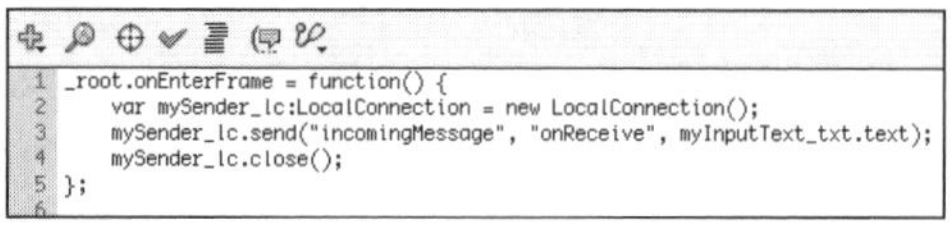

Figure 6.71 Flash passes the parameter `myInputText_txt.text` with its message.

```
var myReceiver_lc:LocalConnection = new LocalConnection();
myReceiver_lc.onReceive = function(myParameter:String) {
    myDynamicText_txt.text = myParameter;
};
myReceiver_lc.connect("incomingMessage");
```

Figure 6.72 In the receiver movie, the function's parameter is called `myParameter`.

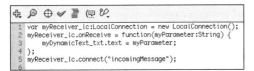

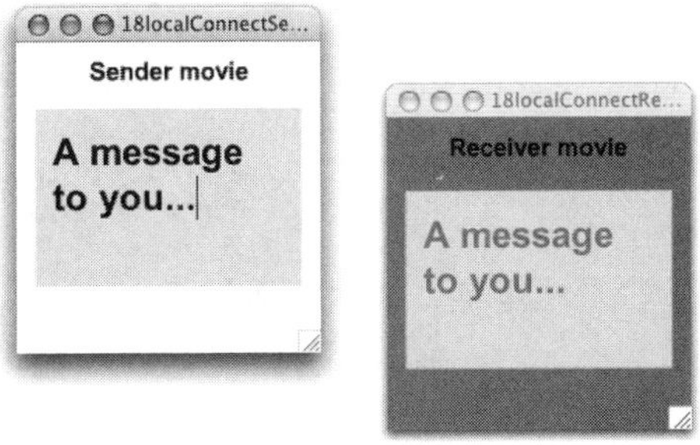

Figure 6.73 The results for the sender movie (top) and receiver movie (bottom). Text in the sender movie's input text field appears in the receiver movie's dynamic text field.

6. Open the receiver movie, and delete the action in the current function statement.

7. Within the parentheses of the function statement, enter `myParameter:String` as a name to identify the incoming parameter.

8. In a new line within the function's curly braces, enter the following:

   `myDynamicText_txt.text = myParameter;`

   `myParameter` is the name you entered in step 7, and `myTextField_txt` is the name of the dynamic text field on the Stage (**Figure 6.72**).

   The receiver movie receives a single parameter called `myParameter`, used in the actions within the function. Here, the value in the parameter is assigned to the contents of the dynamic text field called `myDynamicText_txt`.

9. Test your movies by playing them in separate browser windows.

   When you enter text in the sender movie, it's also displayed in the receiver movie because the text is being passed as a parameter (**Figure 6.73**).

Using Projectors and the fscommand Action

Most of the time, you'll play Flash movies in a browser over the Web. Flash was conceived and developed to deliver content this way. But Flash also provides a way to create *projectors*—self-executable applications that don't require the browser or Flash Player for playback. On either a Windows or Mac system, you can publish projectors for either platform. When you create a Windows projector, the projector's file extension is .exe. For a Mac projector, the word *projector* is appended to the filename if it's created on a Mac, or the file is given an .hqx extension if published in Windows. These projector files are larger than the normal exported SWF files, but they contain everything you need to play the content you create, including graphics, animation, sound, and interactivity. Use projectors to deliver your Flash content on transportable media such as CD-ROMs—an ideal scenario for portfolios, presentations, or marketing material.

Playback of Flash content through projectors is different from playback in a Web browser in one respect: Projectors don't use an HTML page that contains tags or instructions to tell it how to be displayed. Will playback be full screen? Can the window be scalable? You have to give the projector answers to these playback questions rather than rely on an accompanying HTML page. To set or change these kinds of display parameters, use the `fscommand` action, which has a few simple parameters for projectors, as detailed in **Table 6.3**.

Table 6.3

fscommand Parameters for Projectors

Command	Description and Parameters
`fullscreen`	Allows playback at full screen and prevents resizing (true/false).
`allowscale`	Makes the graphics scale when the window is resized (true/false). The scaling mode is always set to `showAll`.
`trapallkeys`	Allows the movie, rather than the Flash Player, to capture keypresses (true/false)
`showmenu`	Displays the top menu bar. Also shows the control menu when you Control-click (Mac) or right-click (Windows) the movie (true/false).
`exec`	Opens an executable file (path to file). The target file must be in a folder called fscommand for security reasons.
`quit`	Quits the projector.

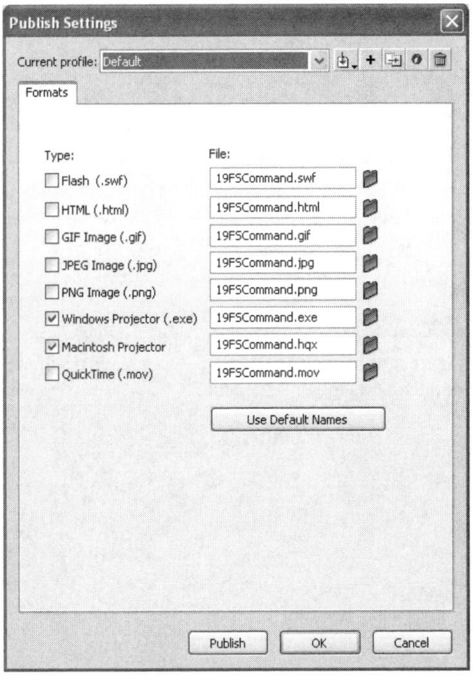

Figure 6.74 The Formats tab of the Publish Settings dialog box. Select the check boxes to choose the Windows and/or Macintosh projectors.

To publish a projector:

1. Open your Flash file.
2. Choose File > Publish Settings (Opt-Shift-F12 Mac, Ctrl-Shift-F12 Windows).

   The Publish Settings dialog box appears.
3. In the Formats tab, deselect all the check boxes except the Macintosh Projector and/or Windows Projector check boxes (**Figure 6.74**).
4. To name your projector something other than the default name, change the name in the field provided.

   Clicking the Use Default Names button restores all the filenames to their defaults.
5. Click Publish.

   Your projector file is saved in the same folder as the Flash file.

or

1. Open your SWF file in the stand-alone Flash Player.
2. Choose File > Create Projector.
3. Choose a filename and destination, and click Save.

   If you choose to create a projector from Flash Player, you can create projectors only for the operating system in which Flash Player is opened.

✔ Tips

- The `getURL` action, when used in a projector, launches your default browser to open any Web link.
- The preferred way to create projectors is through the Publish Settings command (File > Publish Settings). Flash won't compress the projector if you make it from Flash Player. In larger files, you can see a big difference.

To use fscommand to define playback options in a projector:

1. Select the first keyframe of a Flash movie you want to publish as a projector, and open the Actions panel.
2. Choose Global Functions > Browser/Network > fscommand (Esc + fs).

   The `fscommand` action appears in the Script pane (**Figure 6.75**).
3. With your pointer between the parentheses, enter `fullscreen` surrounded by quotation marks; then, enter a comma and the value `true` (**Figure 6.76**).

   The first parameter of the `fscommand` action is the command, and the second parameter is its parameters. This statement sets `fullscreen` to `true`.
4. On the next line, again choose Global Functions > Browser/Network > fscommand (Esc + fs).
5. With your pointer between the parentheses, enter `showmenu` surrounded by quotation marks; then, enter a comma and the value `false`.

   The `showmenu` command is set to `false`.
6. Create a button, place an instance of that button on the Stage, and give it an instance name in the Property inspector.
7. Select the first frame of the main Timeline, and open the Actions panel.
8. Create an `onRelease` event handler for your button.
9. Within the `onRelease` event handler, choose Global Functions > Browser/Network > fscommand.

fscommand();
fscommand(command, parameters);

Figure 6.75 The parameters for the `fscommand` action.

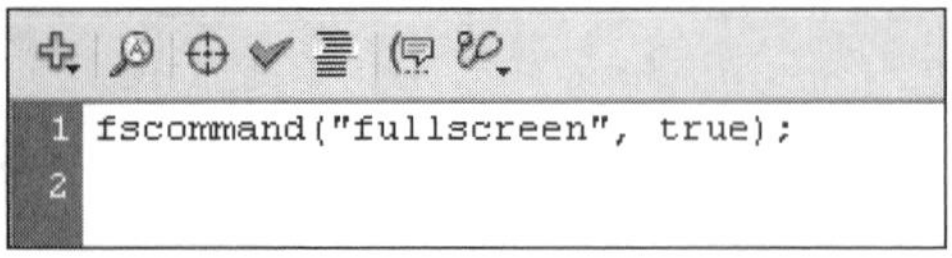
fscommand("fullscreen", true);

Figure 6.76 When `fullscreen` is `true`, playback of the projector fills the entire monitor.

```
fscommand("fullscreen", true);
fscommand("showmenu", false);
quitButton_btn.onRelease = function() {
    fscommand("quit");
};
```

Figure 6.77 The command `fscommand("quit")` assigned to a button closes the projector.

10. With your pointer between the parentheses, enter `quit` surrounded by quotation marks (**Figure 6.77**).

    When you click this button, the projector will quit.

11. Publish your movie as a projector.

12. Double-click your projector to play it.

    The Flash projector plays at full screen, effectively preventing the window from being scaled. The menu options are disabled when you right-click or Control-click (Mac) the movie. When you click the button, the projector quits.

✔ Tip

- You can also use the Stage properties (discussed later in this chapter) to define some of the ways a projector displays its Flash content. You can define the scale mode for your projector, for example, by setting the `Stage.scaleMode` property. However, `fscommand` always overrides the Stage properties if a conflict occurs.

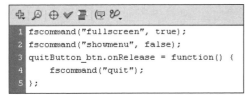

Communicating with the Printer

Flash can send information directly to a printer to output text and graphics, circumventing the Web browser's print function. Printing Flash content is handled by the `PrintJob` class. With the `PrintJob` class, you can specify a level or movie clip to print, and you can also control which areas should be printed for the specific level or movie clip. The printable areas don't even have to be visible on the Stage. Graphics and text in any frame in the main Timeline of the movie or any frame of a movie clip's Timeline are available to the printer, making the `PrintJob` object more than a simple tool for making hard copies of what is visible on the computer screen.

Imagine, for example, that you have documents in external SWF files. You can easily load a particular movie into a movie clip or into another level with the action `loadMovie` and then print selected frames from that loaded movie.

In Chapter 11, you'll learn about input text and dynamic text; you can enter information on the keyboard and display text dynamically. You can combine this capability with order forms or receipts, resulting in customized documents that you can send to the printer.

The first step in printing requires that you instantiate a new `PrintJob` object. Then, you can call the `start()` method. The `start()` method spools the print job and opens the print dialog box. The *spooler* is the part of your computer's operating system that manages printing. The next step is to identify the content you wish to print with the method `addPage()`.

The `addPage()` method takes four parameters, but only the first is required. The parameters appear in the method as `addPage(target, printArea, options, frameNumber)`:

- `target` identifies the level or the movie clip to print.
- `printArea` defines the printable area.
- `options` specifies whether you want to print bitmaps.
- `frameNumber` identifies a specific frame to print.

Finally, you must call the `send()` method, which sends the spooled pages to the printer.

Specifying the target to print

The first parameter of the `addPage()` method identifies the target to print. The target can be either a level or a movie clip. Enter a number to specify the level number, or enter the target path in quotation marks to specify a named movie clip on the Stage. In either case, if no other parameters of `addPage()` are defined, the entire Stage of the current frame prints.

To print all content in a specific level:

1. In a new Flash document, create the graphics you want to be available to the printer on keyframe 1 (**Figure 6.78**).
   You can use multiple layers; all layers will print.
2. Create a button, drag an instance of this button to the Stage, and name it in the Property inspector.
   You'll assign ActionScript to this button to print the contents of the Stage.
3. Create an `onRelease` event handler for your button.

Figure 6.78 Content (this bicycle picture and label) is placed on frame 1 of the root Timeline.

```
printAll_btn.onRelease = function() {
    var myPrintJob_pj:PrintJob = new PrintJob();
};
```

Figure 6.79 A new `PrintJob` object named `myPrintJob_pj` is created.

```
printAll_btn.onRelease = function() {
    var myPrintJob_pj:PrintJob = new PrintJob();
    myPrintJob_pj.start();
};
```

Figure 6.80 The `start()` method opens the printer dialog box.

4. Within the `onRelease` event handler, declare and instantiate a `PrintJob` variable: enter `var`, a variable name, and then `:PrintJob` followed by an equals sign. Choose ActionScript 2.0 Classes > Movie > PrintJob > "new PrintJob" (**Figure 6.79**).

   A new `PrintJob` object is instantiated.

5. On the next line, enter the name of your `PrintJob` object followed by a period.

6. Choose ActionScript 2.0 Classes > Movie > PrintJob > Methods > start (**Figure 6.80**).

   This action spools the print job to the user's operating system and also opens the print dialog box. Your ActionScript pauses until the user confirms or cancels the print dialog box.

7. On the next line, enter the `PrintJob` object's name followed by a period.

8. Choose ActionScript 2.0 Classes > Movie > PrintJob > Methods > addPage.

   Each printed page requires a separate `addPage()` method statement.

9. Between the parentheses for `addPage()`, enter `0`.

   The first parameter of the `addPage()` method identifies the target to print. The number 0 refers to the level, so this statement prints all the content on level 0.

continues on next page

10. On the next line, enter the name of the `PrintJob` object followed by a period. Choose ActionScript 2.0 Classes > Movie > PrintJob > Methods > send.

    The `send()` method sends the pages from the spooler to the printer.

11. On the next line, enter the keyword `delete` followed by a space and your `PrintJob` object name (**Figure 6.81**).

    As the last line of the script, make sure to delete the `PrintJob` object to free up memory.

12. Test your movie.

    When the button is clicked, Flash spools everything that resides on level 0 and sends it to the printer.

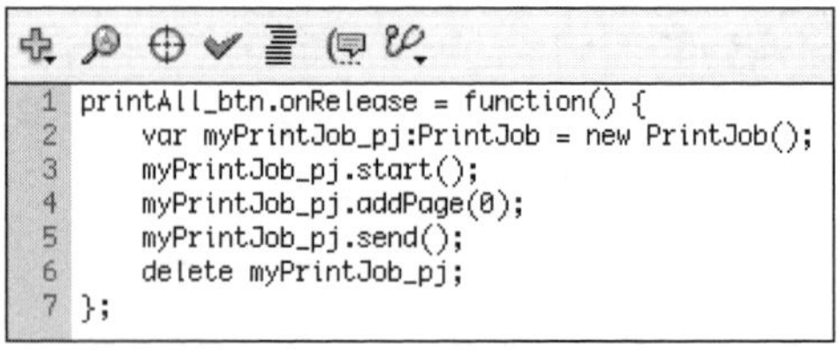

```
printAll_btn.onRelease = function() {
    var myPrintJob_pj:PrintJob = new PrintJob();
    myPrintJob_pj.start();
    myPrintJob_pj.addPage(0);
    myPrintJob_pj.send();
    delete myPrintJob_pj;
};
```

Figure 6.81 After the `PrintJob` object spools the requested page and sends it to the printer, the object is deleted to free up memory.

✔ Tips

- When the `PrintJob` object's `start` method is called (step 6), it sends back a true or false value indicating whether the user accepts or cancels the print job in the print dialog box. You can capture that value by assigning the result of the `start()` method call to a Boolean variable, like this:

  ```
  var doJob:Boolean =
  myPrintJob_pj.start();
  ```

  It's a good idea to retrieve this value and, using an `if` statement, add pages and send the print job only if the user accepts the print job (the result of the `start()` method is `true`). If you don't, and the user chooses to cancel the print job, the `addPage()` and `send()` method calls will be ignored by the system; but this still causes the Flash Player to do unnecessary work. Use the `delete` statement to delete the `PrintJob` action regardless of whether the user accepts the print job.

  The `if` statement is explained in Chapter 10.

- To calculate how the area of a graphic translates to the size of the printed piece, multiply the pixel dimensions by the screen resolution, which is 72 ppi (pixels per inch). An 8.5-by-11-inch sheet of paper is equivalent to a Stage size of 612 pixels (8.5 inches x 72 ppi) by 792 pixels (11 inches x 72 ppi). Also take into account the margins for the actual printable area.

Specifying the printable area

The addPage() method can also control what areas of the Stage you want to print. Its first parameter controls the target, and its second parameter, printArea, controls the x- and y-coordinates of the Stage to print. The second parameter for addPage() is in the form {xMin: value, xMax: value, yMin: value, yMax: value}. You provide coordinates for each of the values. For the printable area, xMin represents the left edge, xMax represents the right edge, yMin represents the top edge, and yMax represents the bottom edge. For example, the statement

```
myPrintJob_pj.addPage(0, {xMin: 50,
xMax: 150, yMin: 10, yMax: 110});
```

identifies a 100-by-100-pixel area at level 0 to print with the top-left corner at (50,10) (**Figure 6.82**). If the printArea parameter isn't defined, then the default is to print the entire contents of the target.

✔ Tip

- Any objects outside the Stage show up on print. To restrict the print area to the size of the default Stage, provide xMin, xMax, yMin, and yMax parameters similar to the following:

```
myPrintJob_pj.addPage(0, {xMin: 0,
xMax: 550, yMin: 0, yMax: 400});
```

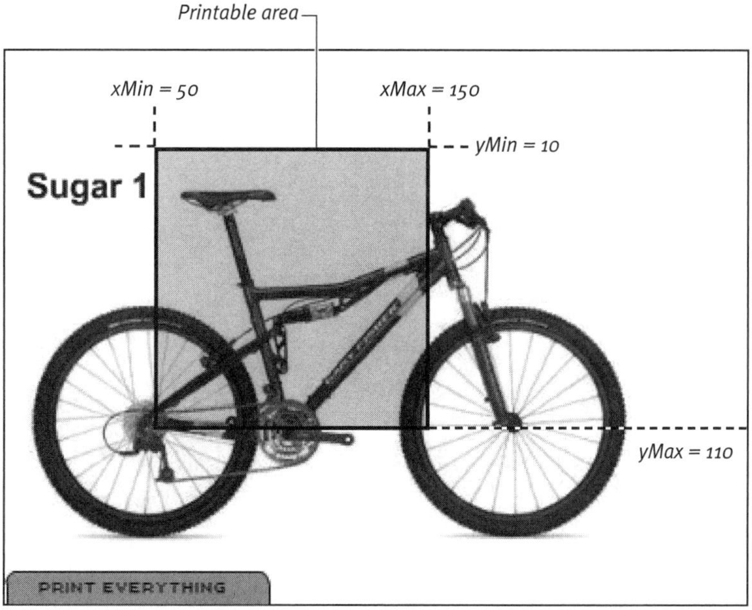

Figure 6.82 The gray square marks the printable area. This is defined in the second parameter for the addPage() method.

Printing bitmap graphics with transparencies or color effects

Graphics that contain bitmaps with alpha or color effects won't print properly unless you identify them to print as bitmaps. To do so, you must specify a third parameter for the `addPage()` method. The third parameter takes the form `{printAsBitmap: Boolean}`, where `Boolean` is either `true` or `false`. For example, the statement

```
myPrintJob_pj.addPage(0, {xMin: 50,
xMax: 150, yMin: 10, yMax: 110},
{printAsBitmap:true});
```

identifies a specific area on level 0 to print as a bitmap. Bitmap printing preserves alpha and color effects but results in a lower print quality.

Printing selected frames

If you specify a target path for the first parameter of the `addPage()` method instead of a level, then Flash prints the current frame of the targeted movie clip. The statement `myPrintJob_pj.addPage(myMC_mc)` identifies the current frame of the movie clip called `myMC_mc` to print. To print only a selected frame of your movie clip, you must specify a frame number as the fourth parameter of the `addPage()` method.

If you want to specify a frame number as the fourth parameter but not have to specify the second or third parameters (and leave them at their default settings), then you can use the keyword `null`. The statement `myPrintJob_pj.addPage(myMC_mc, null, null, 4)` identifies frame 4 of the movie clip `myMC_mc` to print.

To print a selected frame in a movie clip:

1. Continuing with the file from the preceding task, create a new movie clip symbol that contains graphics and text in its second keyframe. Keep the first keyframe empty, and add a `stop()` action to it (**Figure 6.83**).

   The movie clip's contents appear on its second frame, hidden from the viewer.

2. Return to the main Timeline, drag an instance of your movie clip to the Stage, and give the instance a name in the Property inspector.

3. Create another button, drag an instance of it to the Stage, and give it an instance name.

   This button will print the second (hidden) frame of your movie clip.

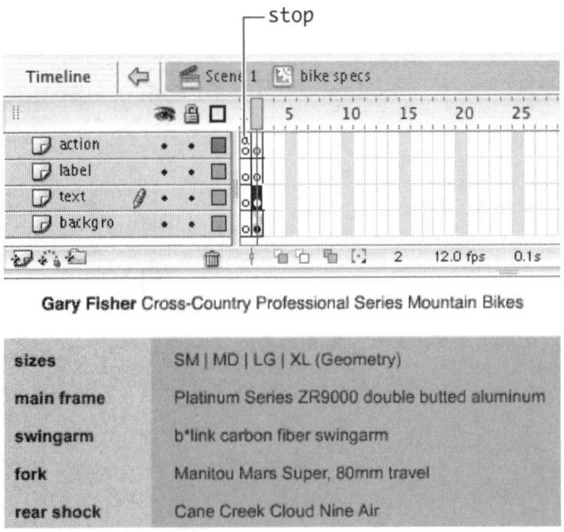

Figure 6.83 The new movie clip, called `bikespecs_mc`, contains the technical specs for the bike on its second keyframe. The `stop` action on the first frame of the Timeline keeps the contents hidden.

```
specsButton_btn.onRelease = function() {
    var myPrintJob_pj:PrintJob = new PrintJob();
    myPrintJob_pj.start();
    myPrintJob_pj.addPage("bikespecs_mc", null, null, 2);
    myPrintJob_pj.send();
    delete myPrintJob_pj;
};
```

Figure 6.84 The addPage() method targets the second frame of the bikespecs_mc movie clip to print.

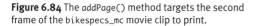

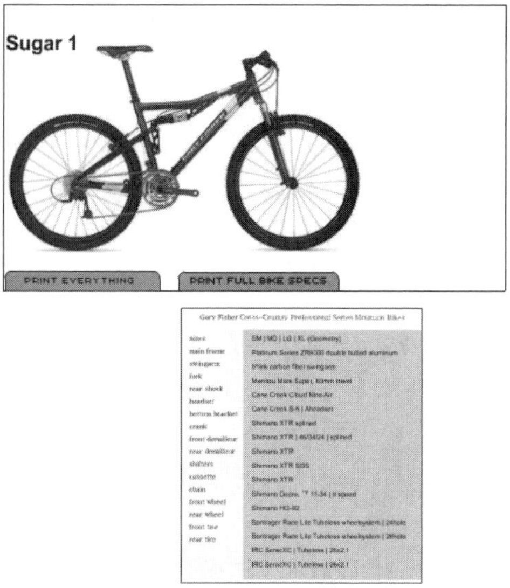

Figure 6.85 The bike specs are invisible to the user on the Stage (top) because the movie clip's first frame is empty. When the second button is clicked, the contents of the movie clip's second frame are sent to the printer (bottom).

4. Create an `onRelease` event handler for this button.

5. Within the `onRelease` event handler, add actions that instantiate a new `PrintJob` object, call the `start()` method, and call the `addPage()` method as described in the previous task.

6. For the parameters of the `addPage()` method, enter the target path of the movie clip in quotation marks, the keyword `null`, another keyword `null`, and finally the number 2. Separate the parameters with commas (**Figure 6.84**).

   Flash identifies the second frame of the movie clip to print and uses default values for the second and third parameters.

7. Call the `send()` method, and then delete your `PrintJob` object as described in the previous task.

8. Test your movie.

   When the button is clicked, Flash retrieves the graphics, text, and any other information residing on the second keyframe of your movie clip and sends it to the printer (**Figure 6.85**).

✔ Tips

- You can print more than one page under a single print dialog box. Add a separate `addPage()` method for each page. The order in which you add the methods in the Script pane is the order in which they will print.

- You can use looping statements to easily print multiple frames of a Timeline. Substitute the `frameNumber` parameter in the `addPage()` method for a variable, and increase its value each time you loop. You'll learn more about looping statements in Chapter 10.

Printing in Flash Player 6

The `PrintJob` class makes customized printing easy. However, it was added in Flash Player 7. If you're authoring for Flash Player 6 or earlier, you must use the older actions `print`, `printNum`, `printAsBitmap`, and `printAsBitmapNum` to print.

The actions `print` and `printNum` take two parameters. The first is the target path of a movie clip you wish to print (for `print` and `printAsBitmap`) or the level of the movie you wish to print (for `printNum` and `printAsBitmapNum`). The second is a modifier that determines how the content will print. The second parameter can be one of the following (be sure to include the quotation marks) (**Figure 6.86**):

- `"bmovie"` makes the print area the bounding box of the frame marked with the frame label #B.
- `"bframe"` scales each printable item to fit the maximum print area.
- `"bmax"` makes a composite bounding box of all the printable items and uses that area to print.

To print multiple frames of your Timeline, mark each keyframe to print by adding the label #P (**Figure 6.87**).

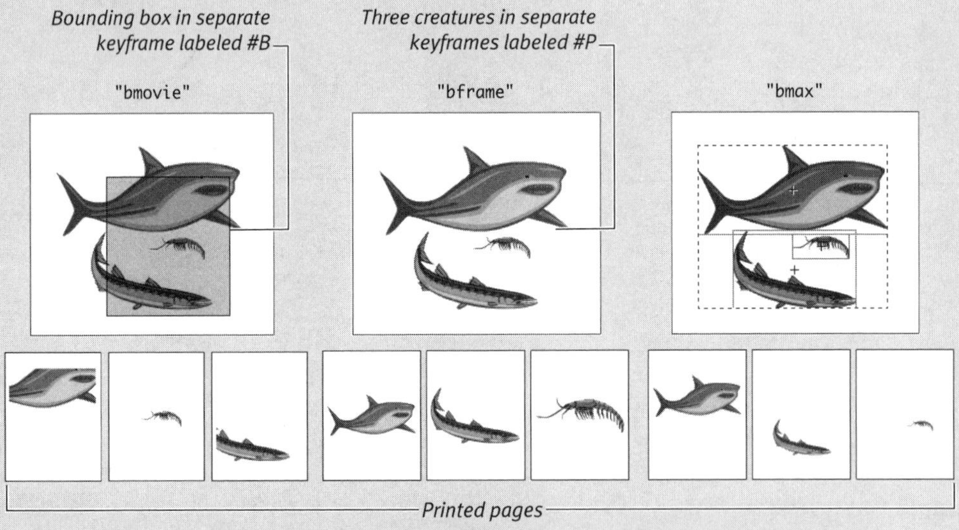

Figure 6.86 The three options for the second parameter of the `print`, `printNum`, `printAsBitmap`, and `printAsBitmapNum` actions. `"bmovie"` (left) prints the marked frames within a defined bounding box in a frame labeled #B. `"bframe"` (center) prints the marked frames to fit the paper. `"bmax"` (right) prints the marked frames based on the composite sizes of all the objects.

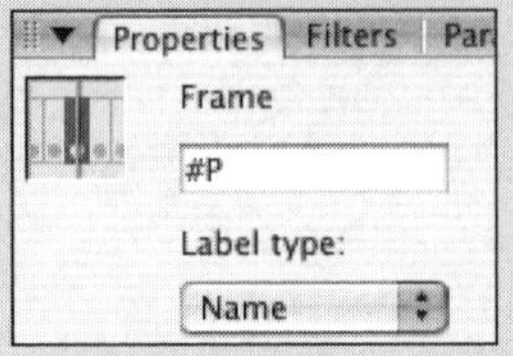

Figure 6.87 The #P label identifies individual keyframes to print.

Detecting the Movie's Playback Environment

Communicating with a movie's playback environment is important for knowing how your Flash movie will play and be seen by your audience. With that information, you can tailor the movie's display or provide warnings and recommendations to your viewers so they can better enjoy your movie. A viewer might have a lower screen resolution than you require to display the entire Stage of your movie, for example. You can load a different movie that fits, or you can modify the movie's display settings to allow it to be scaled down. Detecting system capabilities and the kind of player hosting the movie is especially important as Flash content becomes more prevalent in devices such as cell phones, PDAs, and television set-top boxes.

Two classes can help you gather information about the playback environment: the `System.capabilities` class and the `Stage` class. The `System.capabilities` class can tell you about screen resolution, the operating system, the color capabilities, and many other useful properties. **Table 6.4** summarizes the `System.capabilities` properties.

Table 6.4

Properties of the `System.capabilities` Class

PROPERTY	DESCRIPTION
`language`	Language that Flash Player supports, indicated by a two-letter code (`en` = English)
`os`	Operating system
`manufacturer`	Manufacturer of the Flash Player
`serverString`	All `System.capabilities` properties in a single string that could be sent to a server
`isDebugger`	Is a debugger version of the player
`version`	Flash Player version
`playerType`	Type of player playing the movie (stand-alone, plug-in, and so on)
`hasAudio`	Audio capability
`hasMP3`	MP3 decoder capability
`hasAudioEncoder`	Audio encoder capability
`hasEmbeddedVideo`	Embedded video support
`hasPrinting`	Printing support
`hasVideoEncoder`	Video encoder capability
`screenResolutionX`	Horizontal size of screen, in pixels
`screenResolutionY`	Vertical size of screen, in pixels
`screenDPI`	Screen resolution, in dots per inch
`screenColor`	Color capability (color, grayscale, or black and white)
`pixelAspectRatio`	Pixel aspect ratio of the screen
`hasAccessibility`	Accessibility capability

The `Stage` class can tell you about the display and layout of the movie, detect whether the Stage is resized, and modify the movie's properties in response. **Table 6.5** summarizes the properties of the `Stage` object.

The properties and methods of both the `System.capabilities` class and the `Stage` classes can be used without creating an instance of the class.

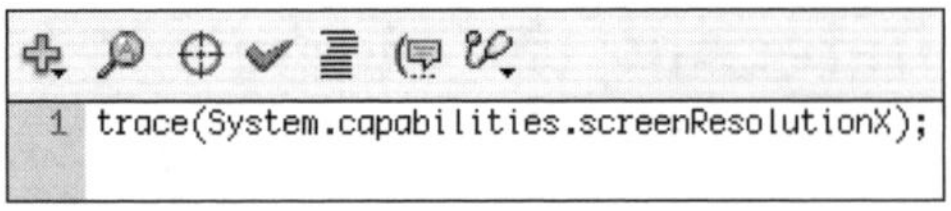

Figure 6.88 The `trace` statement returns the horizontal size of the computer screen in pixels.

To retrieve the properties of the user's system:

1. Select the first frame in the main Timeline of a new Flash document, and open the Actions panel.
2. Choose Global Functions > Miscellaneous Functions > trace.

   You'll use the `trace` action to display information about your own system in the Output window in test mode.
3. Put your pointer between the parentheses, and choose ActionScript 2.0 Classes > Core > System > Objects > Capabilities > Properties > screenResolutionX (**Figure 6.88**).

   The `trace` action will display the horizontal resolution of your computer screen.
4. On the next line, create another `trace` action.

Table 6.5

Properties of the `Stage` Class

Property	Description
`align`	Alignment of the Flash content ("T" = top, "B" = bottom, "R" = right, "L" = left, "TR" = top right, "TL" = top left, "BR" = bottom right, "BL" = bottom left, "C" = center)
`height`	Height of the Stage, in pixels (read-only)
`width`	Width of the Stage, in pixels (read-only)
`scaleMode`	Type of scaling display ("showAll", "noBorder", "exactFit", or "noScale")
`showMenu`	Whether to show the default menu items when you Control-click (Mac) or right-click the movie (true/false)

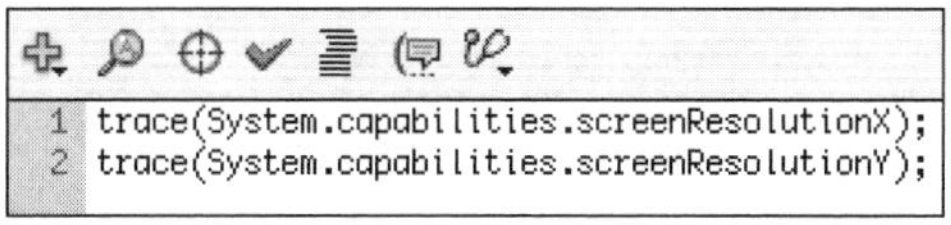

Figure 6.89 The `trace` statement returns the vertical size of the computer screen in pixels.

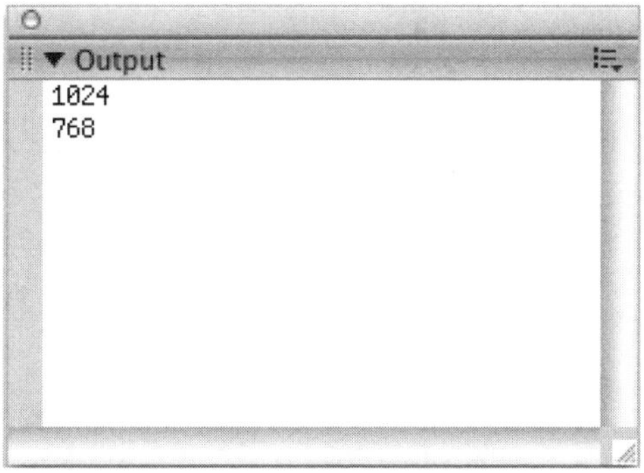

Figure 6.90 The Output window displays the `trace` actions. The monitor for this computer is 1024 x 768 pixels.

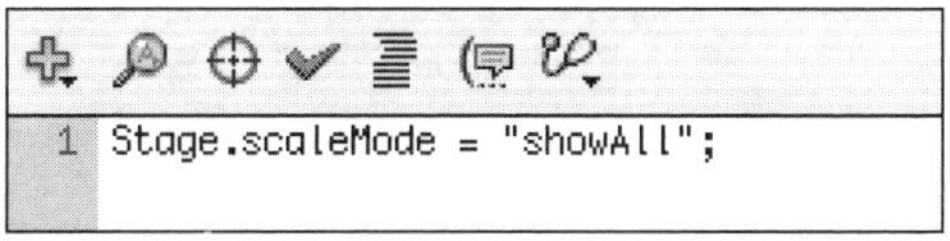

Figure 6.91 The `scaleMode` property controls how your Flash movie reacts to resizing. "`showAll`" displays all the content with no distortions or cropping.

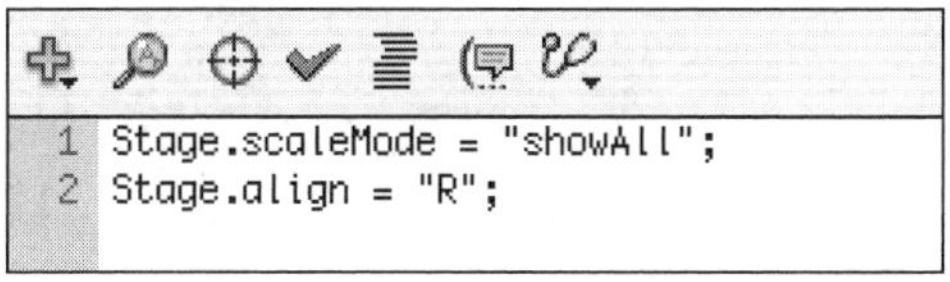

Figure 6.92 The `align` property controls where your Flash content appears in the window. "R" puts the movie flush against the right edge.

5. Between the parentheses, choose ActionScript 2.0 Classes > Core > System > Objects > Capabilities > Properties > screenResolutionY (**Figure 6.89**).

   The trace will display the vertical resolution of your computer screen.

6. Test your movie.

   In the Output window that appears, the screen resolution of your monitor displays (**Figure 6.90**).

✔ Tip

- Instead of `System.capabilities.version`, you can use the global variable `$version`. Both properties report the Flash Player version. The `$version` property is always listed in the Output window when you choose Debug > List Variables while testing a movie.

To modify the display mode of the movie:

1. Open an existing Flash movie that contains graphics on the Stage.
2. Select the main Timeline, and open the Actions panel.
3. Choose ActionScript 2.0 Classes > Movie > Stage > Properties > scaleMode.

   The `Stage.scaleMode` property appears in the Script pane.
4. Place your pointer after `Stage.scaleMode`, and enter an equals sign followed by `"showAll"` (**Figure 6.91**).
5. Choose ActionScript 2.0 Classes > Movie > Stage > Properties > align.

   The `Stage.align` property appears in the Script pane.
6. Place your pointer after `Stage.align`, and enter an equals sign followed by `"R"` (**Figure 6.92**).

continues on next page

7. Test your movie.

   When you resize the test movie window, the graphics on the Stage resize so that one dimension (either height or width) always fills the window. This is the result of the `Stage.scaleMode = "showAll"` statement. The graphics are also aligned to the right side of the window as a result of the `Stage.align = "R"` statement. For a summary of the `scaleMode` property, see **Figure 6.93**.

✔ Tips

- Remember to include the quotation marks for the `align` and `scaleMode` properties, but don't include them for the `height`, `width`, and `showMenu` properties.
- The `width` and `height` properties of the Stage object report different values depending on how `Stage.scaleMode` is defined. When `Stage.scaleMode = "noScale"`, `Stage.width` and `Stage.height` report the size of the window that contains the Flash movie. This result could be the size of the browser window, the projector, or the window in test movie mode. When `Stage.scaleMode` is set to `"exactFit"`, `"showAll"`, or `"noBorders"`, `Stage.width` and `Stage.height` report the size of the Flash Stage when it was created. The default scaling mode for all Flash movies is `"noScale"`.
- Avoid using the HTML page to hold your movie if you're going to modify the Stage properties to prevent conflicts with alignments and `scaleMode` settings.

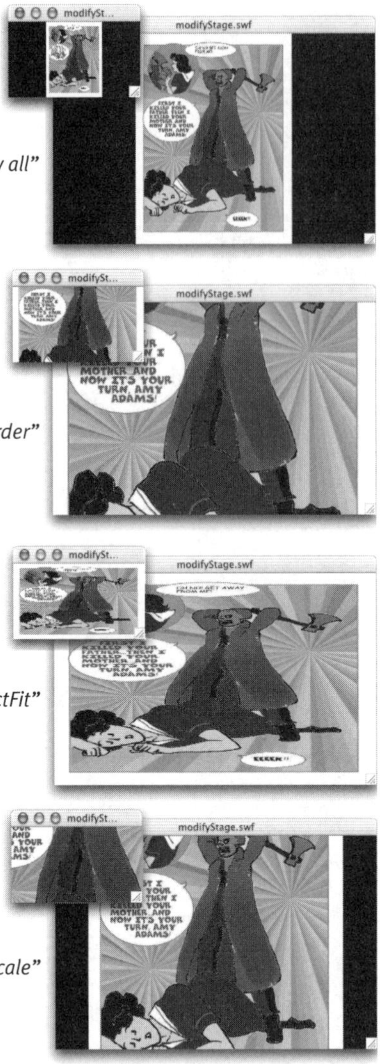

"show all"

"noBorder"

"exactFit"

"noScale"

Figure 6.93 The `scaleMode` options. `"showAll"` (top) scales the movie to fit the window without any distortions or cropping to show all the content; this is the default mode. `"noBorder"` (top middle) scales the movie to fit the window without any distortions but crops content to fill the window. In this mode, none of the background color shows. `"exactFit"` (bottom middle) scales the movie to fill the window on both the horizontal and vertical dimensions. In this mode, none of the background color shows but the content is distorted. `"noScale"` (bottom) keeps the movie at 100% no matter how big or small the window is. In this mode, the content is cropped if the window is too small, and the background color shows if the window is too big.

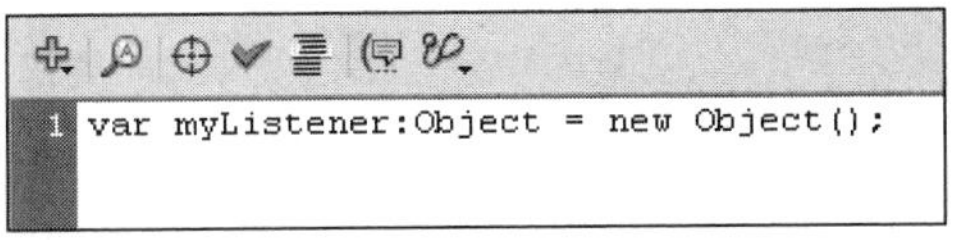
var myListener:Object = new Object();

Figure 6.94 Create a new listener object called `myListener`.

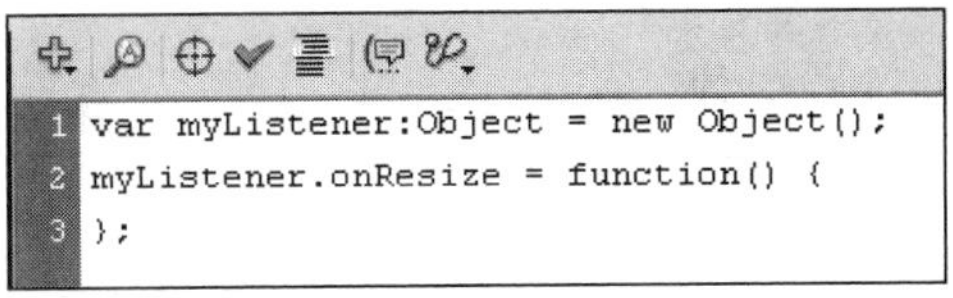
var myListener:Object = new Object();
myListener.onResize = function() {
};

Figure 6.95 The `onResize` event handler.

Detecting Stage resizing

In order to detect the resizing of the Stage, you create a listener object, just as you do to detect the events of the `Key` class. Create a listener object from the generic `Object` data type, and create the event `onResize` with an anonymous function assigned to it. After you register the listener with the `Stage` class using the method `addListener()`, you can detect and respond to Stage resizing.

To detect when the Stage is resized:

1. Select the first frame of the main Timeline, and open the Actions panel.
2. Declare your listener object by typing `var`, the name of your listener object, `:Object`, and then an equals sign.
3. Choose ActionScript 2.0 Classes > Core > Object > "new Object".

   A new object is instantiated for you to use as a listener (**Figure 6.94**).
4. On the next line, enter the name of your listener object followed by a period.
5. Choose ActionScript 2.0 Classes > Movie > Stage > Events > onResize, and add an equals sign.
6. Choose Statements > User-Defined Functions > function (**Figure 6.95**).

   or

   Add this code after the equals sign:

   ```
   function() {
   };
   ```

   The `onResize` event handler is completed and assigned to your listener object.

continues on next page

7. Between the curly braces of the function, assign actions that will be performed when the `onResize` event occurs (**Figure 6.96**).

   In this example, when the viewer resizes the window, Flash checks whether the size is smaller than the default Stage size. If so, Flash scales the main Stage proportionately according to the smaller of the horizontal and vertical window dimensions. Resizing the window bigger, however, doesn't make the Flash content scale with the window. The result: you can shrink the window to accommodate smaller monitors and still see the content, but you can't enlarge the Stage more than its normal size.

8. On the next line outside the `onResize` event handler, choose ActionScript 2.0 Classes > Movie > Stage > Methods > addListener.

9. With your pointer between the parentheses, enter the name of your listener object.

   The listener is registered with the Stage class to listen for the `onResize` event.

10. Test your movie.

11. Resize the movie window.

   Resizing the window triggers the `onResize` event, which calls the function on the listener object (**Figure 6.97**).

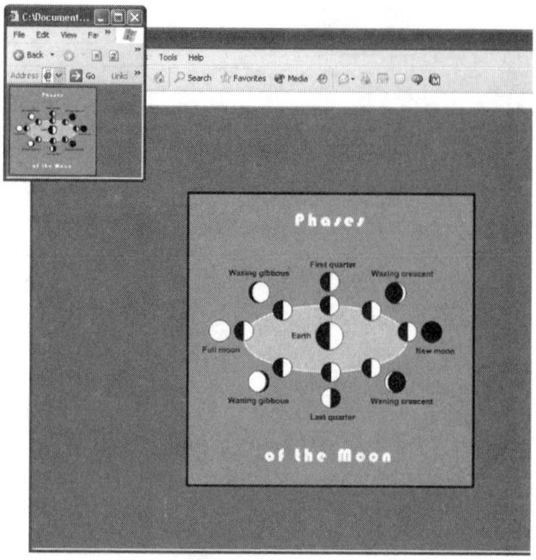

Figure 6.97 Decreasing the size of the window scales the movie so that all its content is still visible (top). Increasing the size of the window scales the movie only to 100%, at which point it maintains its size. This technique is useful if you want viewers to be able to see your movie on smaller monitors but you want to prevent other users from enlarging your movie to the point that bitmaps and videos are jagged and lose resolution.


```
var myListener:Object = new Object();
myListener.onResize = function() {
    Stage.align = "C";
    if (Stage.height < 499 || Stage.width < 499) {
        Stage.align = "TL";
        _root._xscale = Math.min(Stage.width, Stage.height) / 500 * 100;
        _root._yscale = Math.min(Stage.width, Stage.height) / 500 * 100;
    }
};
Stage.addListener(myListener);
```

Figure 6.96 The full ActionScript for this example. The Stage for this movie is 500 x 500. If its window is resized smaller, the content is aligned to the top-left corner. The `Math.min()` method decides which dimension (horizontal or vertical) of the window is smaller and scales the movie proportionately according to that size.

Detecting Download Progress: Preloaders

All the hard work you put into creating complex interactivity in your movie will be wasted if your viewer has to wait too long to download the movie over the Web and leaves. You can avoid losing viewers by creating short animations that entertain them while the rest of your movie downloads. These diversions, or *preloaders*, tell your viewer how much of the movie has downloaded and how much longer they have to wait. When enough data has been delivered over the Web to the viewer's computer, you can trigger your movie to start. In effect, you hold back the playhead until you know that all the frames are available to play. Only then do you send the playhead to the starting frame of your movie.

Preloaders must be small because you want them to load almost immediately, and they should be informative, letting your viewers know what they're waiting for.

Flash provides many ways to monitor the state of the download progress. You can test for the number of frames that have downloaded with the Timeline properties `_framesloaded` and `_totalframes`. You can also test for the amount of data that has downloaded with the movie clip methods `getBytesLoaded()` and `getBytesTotal()`. Testing the amount of data is a more accurate gauge of download progress because the frames of your movie most likely contain data that aren't evenly spread.

If you're loading data-intensive images or movies (SWFs) into your Flash movie, then you can use the `MovieClipLoader` class to detect their download progress. The `MovieClipLoader` class provides powerful events, such as `onLoadStart` and `onLoadProgress`, that give you a finer degree of control over the download progress.

All the approaches use the same basic concept. You tell Flash to compare the number of frames or the amount of data loaded with the total frames or data in the movie. As this ratio changes, you can display the percentage numerically with a dynamic text field or represent the changing ratio graphically, such as with a growing progress bar. Because they often show the progress of the download, these preloaders are known as *progressive preloaders*.

To create a progressive preloader that detects data:

1. Create a long rectangular movie clip symbol.

   Make sure its registration point is at its far-left edge (**Figure 6.98**).

2. Place an instance of the symbol on the Stage, and give it an instance name (this example uses `bar_mc`).

   Your preloader is a rectangle that grows longer according to the percentage of downloaded frames. You'll change the properties of the rectangular movie clip to stretch it dynamically. Because the bar should grow from left to right, the registration point is placed on the left edge.

3. Select the first frame of the main Timeline, and open the Actions panel.

4. Choose Global Functions > Timeline Control > stop.

   The `stop` action prevents your movie from playing until it has downloaded completely.

5. On the next line, use the `var` statement to declare a variable of type `Number` followed by an equals sign.

6. Choose Global Functions > Miscellaneous Functions > setInterval.

7. For the parameters of the `setInterval` action, enter a name of a function followed by the interval 10 (**Figure 6.99**).

   The `setInterval` action calls the specified function every 10 milliseconds.

8. To create the function, on a new line, choose Statements > User-Defined Functions > function.

9. Place your pointer before the opening parenthesis for the function, and enter the name you gave the function in the `setInterval` action (**Figure 6.100**).

Registration point

Figure 6.98 A rectangular movie clip with its registration point on the far-left edge can be used as a graphical representation of download progress.

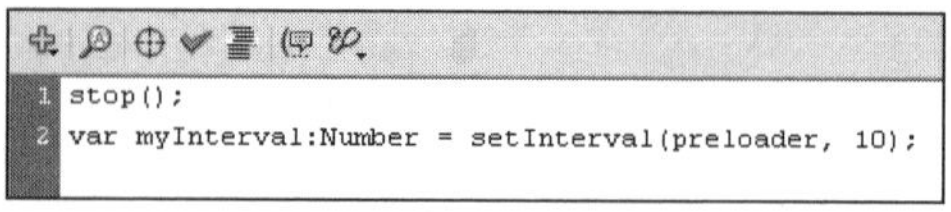
stop();
var myInterval:Number = setInterval(preloader, 10);

Figure 6.99 Create the `setInterval` action to monitor the download progress continuously.

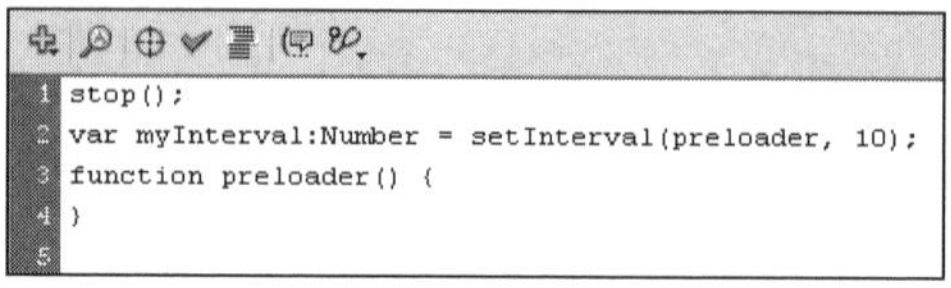
stop();
var myInterval:Number = setInterval(preloader, 10);
function preloader() {
}

Figure 6.100 The function called `preloader` is invoked at regular intervals by the `setInterval` action. The function will contain the actions to test and display the download progress.

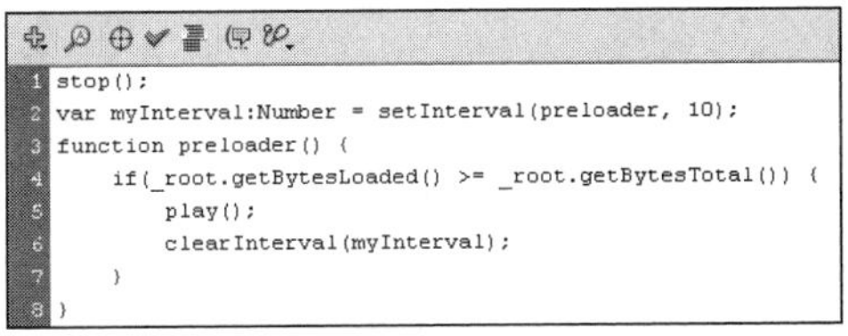
stop();
var myInterval:Number = setInterval(preloader, 10);
function preloader() {
if(_root.getBytesLoaded() >= _root.getBytesTotal()) {
play();
clearInterval(myInterval);
}
}

Figure 6.101 When the number of bytes downloaded is greater than or equal to the total number of bytes, the actions between the curly braces of the `if` statement are executed. Flash begins playing the main Timeline and removes the `setInterval` action.

10. With your pointer inside the curly braces of the function, choose Statements > Conditions/Loops > if.

11. Inside the parentheses of the `if` statement, enter the following condition to test:

```
_root.getBytesLoaded() >=
_root.getBytesTotal()
```

Flash checks whether the number of bytes (data) that have been loaded is greater than or equal to the total number of bytes in the SWF file. You can find the `getBytesLoaded()` and `getBytesTotal()` methods by choosing ActionScript 2.0 Classes > Movie > MovieClip > Methods.

12. Inside the curly braces of the `if` statement, choose Global Functions > Timeline Control > play.

If the condition between the parentheses of the `if` statement is `true`, the movie begins to play.

13. On the next line, choose Global Functions > Miscellaneous Functions > clearInterval.

14. With your pointer between the parentheses for the `clearInterval` statement, enter the variable that was assigned the interval ID of the `setInterval` action (**Figure 6.101**).

Once the download is complete, you no longer need to check its progress, so the `clearInterval` statement deletes the initial `setInterval`.

15. Place your pointer after the closing curly brace for the `if` statement, and press Enter to make a new line.

continues on next page

16. Enter the following line of code (**Figure 6.102**):

```
bar_mc._xscale =
(_root.getBytesLoaded() /
_root.getBytesTotal()) * 100;
```

The horizontal dimension of the movie clip called `bar_mc` now stretches based on the percentage of bytes loaded.

17. Begin the actual content of your Flash document from keyframe 2 (**Figure 6.103**).

18. Test your movie with the Bandwidth Profiler and with Show Streaming on.

The Bandwidth Profiler is an information window above your movie in Test Movie mode; it displays the number of frames and the amount of data in each frame as vertical bars. If the vertical bars extend over the bottom of the red horizontal line, there is too much data to be downloaded at the bandwidth setting without causing a stutter during playback. The Show Streaming option simulates actual download performance (**Figure 6.104**). The green bar at the top shows the download progress. The triangle marks the current location of the playhead. The playhead remains in frame 1 until the green progress bar reaches the end of the Timeline. Only then does the playhead begin moving.

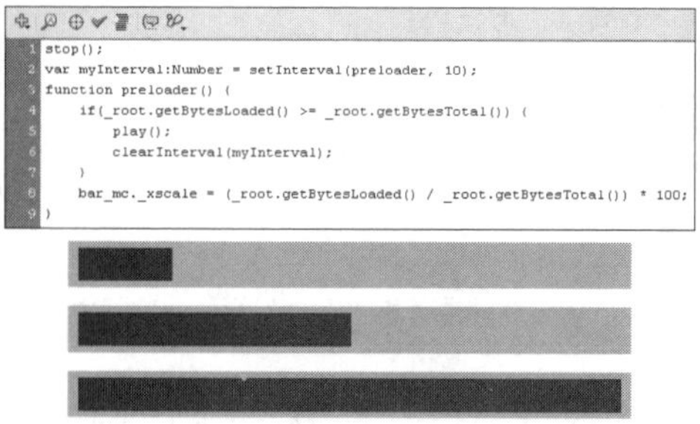
stop();
var myInterval:Number = setInterval(preloader, 10);
function preloader() {
if(_root.getBytesLoaded() >= _root.getBytesTotal()) {
play();
clearInterval(myInterval);
}
bar_mc._xscale = (_root.getBytesLoaded() / _root.getBytesTotal()) * 100;
}

Figure 6.102 The complete code (above) and the progress bar movie clip as it grows steadily during the download process (bottom).

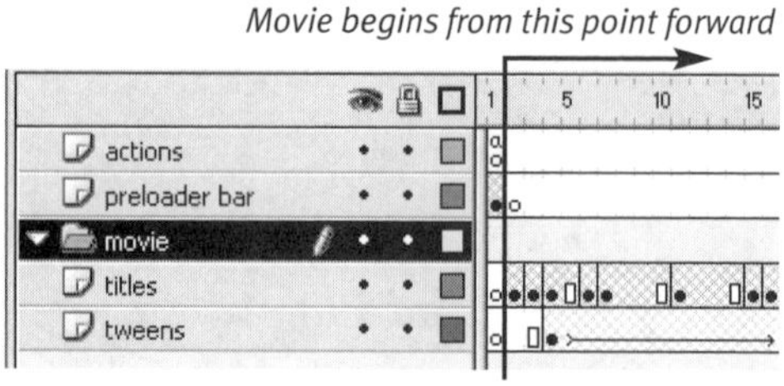
Movie begins from this point forward
actions
preloader bar
movie
titles
tweens

Figure 6.103 The real movie begins at keyframe 2, after the rectangular movie clip is removed.

✔ Tips

- You won't see your preloader working unless you build an animation with many frames containing fairly large graphics that require lengthy download times. If your animation is small, you'll see your preloader whiz by because all the data will download quickly and begin playing almost immediately.
- Explore other graphical treatments of the download progress. Stretching the length of a movie clip is just one way to animate the download process. With subtle changes to your ActionScript, you can apply a variety of animated effects to your preloader.

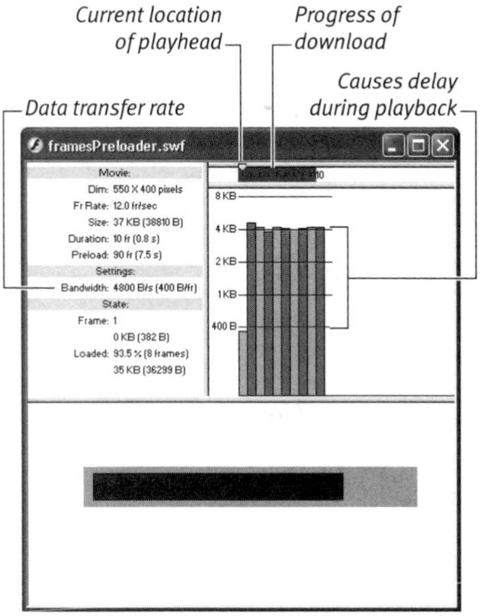

Figure 6.104 The Bandwidth Profiler shows the individual frames that cause pauses during playback because the amount of data exceeds the data transfer rate. The alternating light and dark bars represent different frames. Notice how the progress of the download (about 8 out of 10 frames have loaded completely) affects the proportion of the movie clip (about 80%).

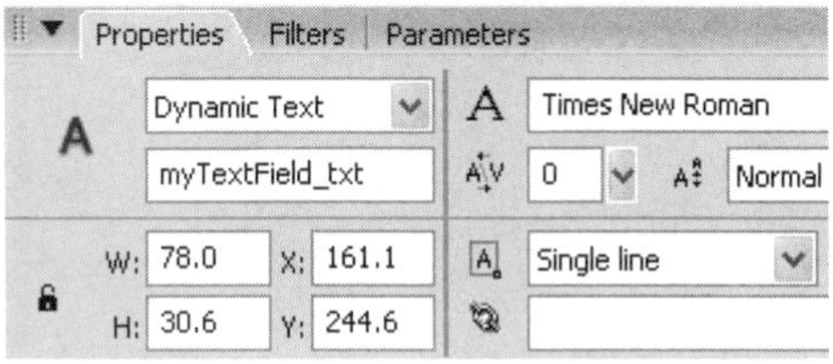

Figure 6.105 This dynamic text field is called `myTextField_txt`.

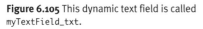

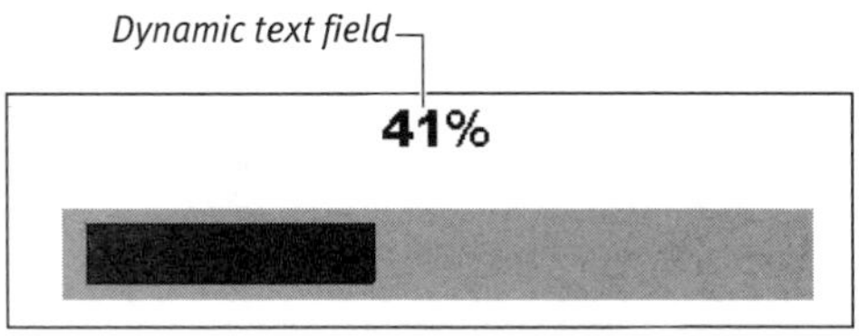

Figure 6.106 The dynamic text field displays the percentage of the download progress along with the graphical representation.

Showing numeric download progress

Often, a preloader has an accompanying display of the percentage of download progress. This display is accomplished with a dynamic text field placed on the Stage. You'll learn more about dynamic text in Chapter 11, but you can use the steps in the following task now to add a simple numeric display.

To add a numeric display to the progressive preloader:

1. Continuing with the file from the preceding task, select the Text tool, and drag out a text field on the Stage.
2. In the Property inspector, choose Dynamic Text, and give the text field an instance name (**Figure 6.105**).

   As with buttons and movie clip symbols, the instance name of the text field lets you target the text field and control it using ActionScript.
3. Select the first frame of the main Timeline, and open the Actions panel.
4. Create a new line before the closing curly brace for the function.
5. Enter the following script:

   ```
   myTextField_txt.text = Math.round
   (_root.getBytesLoaded() /
   _root.getBytesTotal() * 100) + "%";
   ```

   The percentage of download progress is rounded to a whole number by the `Math.round()` method. The percent (%) character is appended to the end, and the result is assigned to the `text` property of your text field, displaying it on the Stage (**Figure 6.106**).

The Bandwidth Profiler

The Bandwidth Profiler is a handy option to see how data is distributed throughout your Flash movie and how quickly (or slowly) it will download over the Web. In Test Movie mode, choose View > Bandwidth Profiler (Command-B for Mac, Ctrl-B for Windows) to see this information.

The left side of the Bandwidth Profiler shows movie information, such as Stage dimensions, frame rate, file size, total duration, and preload time in frames and seconds. It also shows the Bandwidth setting, which simulates actual download performance at a specified rate. You can change that rate in the Debug menu and choose the Internet connection speed that your viewer is likely to have. Flash gives you options for 28.8 and 56 K modems, for example.

The bar graph on the right side of the Bandwidth Profiler shows the amount of data in each frame of your movie. You can view the graph as a streaming graph (choose View > Streaming Graph) or as a frame-by-frame graph (choose View > Frame by Frame Graph). The streaming graph indicates how the movie downloads over the Web by showing you how data streams from each frame, whereas the frame-by-frame graph indicates the amount of data in each frame. In Streaming Graph mode, you can tell which frames will cause hang-ups during playback by noting which bar exceeds the given Bandwidth setting.

To watch the actual download performance of your movie, choose View > Simulate Download. Flash simulates playback over the Web at the given Bandwidth setting. A green horizontal bar at the top of the window indicates which frames have been downloaded, and the triangular playhead marks the current frame.

Detecting download progress of external images and movies

Using the `MovieClipLoader` class is an ideal way to monitor the loading of external images or movies into Flash. This class lets you create listeners that return information about the download progress of loading SWF or image files, and it provides many events that are triggered at various points of the download process. Imagine that you have multiple images on a Web server and you want to load them into a Flash photo album movie. Using the `MovieClipLoader` class, you can load each image into a movie clip and detect their initial download, progress, completion, or even errors in their loading. Similarly, this method can be used with external SWF files.

Creating a preloader for loaded images or SWFs first requires that you instantiate a `MovieClipLoader` object and a listener object. Next, you define event handler functions on your listener object. These events are broadcast by the `MovieClipLoader` object to your listener object in the order listed:

- `listenerObject.onLoadStart`: The event is triggered when the first bytes of the downloaded file have been transferred to the movie.
- `listenerObject.onLoadProgress`: The event happens repeatedly during the loading process, each time more data from the loading object arrives at the Flash Player. This event can pass three important parameters: the movie clip target (the movie clip in which the image or SWF will load), the number of bytes loaded, and the total number of bytes.
- `listenerObject.onLoadComplete`: The event is triggered when the entire file has been transferred to the movie but before it's initialized (available to be manipulated by ActionScript).
- `listenerObject.onLoadInit`: The event happens when the downloaded file is initialized and its first frame actions have been executed.

It isn't always necessary to create listener functions for all four of these events in every movie.

After your listener functions are created, register your listener object with the `MovieClipLoader` object and then begin loading your external file with the method `loadClip()`. The `loadClip()` method is part of the `MovieClipLoader` class and functions much like the `MovieClip` method `loadMovie()`. However, you must use the `loadClip()` method in order to use the event handlers of the `MovieClipLoader` class.

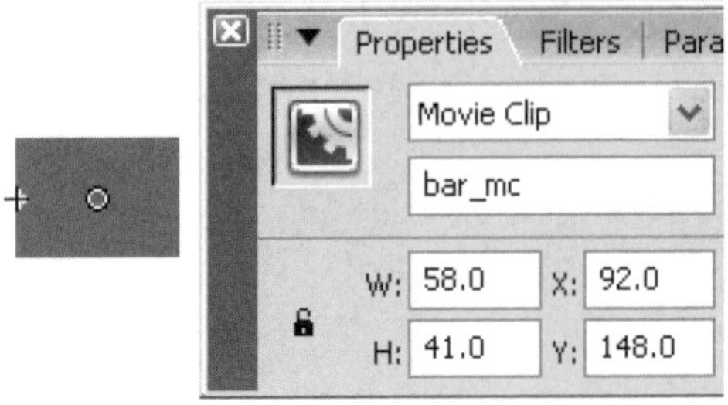

Figure 6.107 A new rectangular movie clip is given an instance name of `bar_mc`.

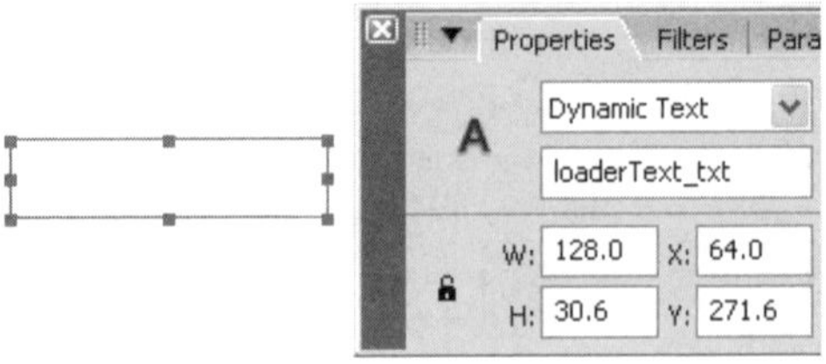

Figure 6.108 A dynamic text field is given an instance name of `loaderText_txt`.

To create a progressive preloader for external images or movies:

1. Create a small rectangular movie clip symbol.

   Make sure its registration point is at the far-left edge.

2. Place an instance of the symbol on the Stage, and give it a name in the Property inspector (**Figure 6.107**).

   The properties of the rectangle will change in proportion to the number of bytes that are downloaded. This will act as a visual indicator to the audience that the movie is loading.

3. Create a movie clip symbol, and drag an instance of it from the Library to the Stage.

   This will act a placeholder into which external movies or images will load.

4. Select the instance, and give it a name in the Property inspector.

5. Select the Text tool, and drag out a text field on the Stage. In the Property inspector, select Dynamic Text from the drop-down list, and give the field an instance name (**Figure 6.108**).

   The dynamic text field will display the percentage of download progress.

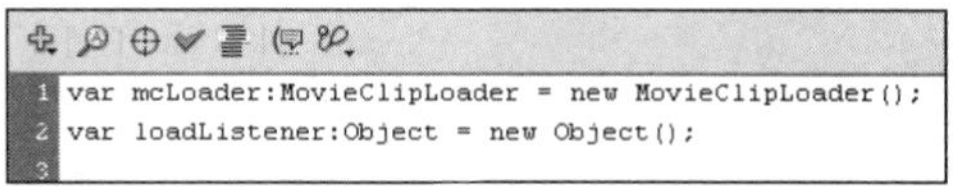

```
var mcLoader:MovieClipLoader = new MovieClipLoader();
var loadListener:Object = new Object();
```

Figure 6.109 A `MovieClipLoader` instance and a listener object are created.

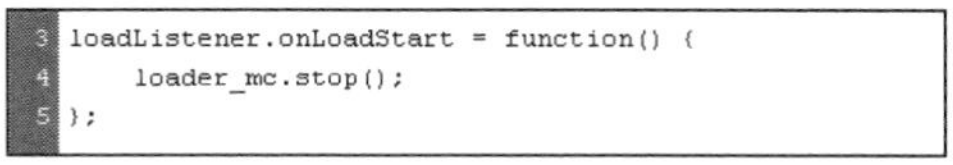

```
loadListener.onLoadStart = function() {
    loader_mc.stop();
};
```

Figure 6.110 When the movie begins to load the external SWF into the movie clip called `loader_mc`, the animation it contains stops.

6. Select the first frame of the main Timeline, and open the Actions panel.

7. Declare a variable with the data type `MovieClipLoader`, followed by an equals sign. Choose ActionScript 2.0 Classes > Movie > MovieClipLoader > "new MovieClipLoader".

   A new `MovieClipLoader` object is instantiated.

8. On the next line, declare another variable to be the listener object, and set its type to Object. Add an equals sign, and choose ActionScript 2.0 Classes > Core > Object > "new Object" (**Figure 6.109**).

9. On the next line, enter the name of your listener followed by a period. Choose ActionScript 2.0 Classes > Movie > MovieClipLoader > Listeners > onLoadStart.

10. Between the curly braces of this function, add a call to the `stop()` method of your movie clip placeholder (**Figure 6.110**).

    As soon as the external movie begins to load, it will stop. This ensures that all its data is loaded before playing, preventing the stuttering that often happens when a movie plays while downloading. If you're loading an image, you won't need this step.

11. On a new line after the end of the `onLoadStart` function, enter the name of your listener object followed by a period. Choose ActionScript 2.0 Classes > Movie > MovieClipLoader > Listeners > onLoadProgress.

continues on next page

12. Between the parentheses of the function, add three variable names separated by commas, with the data types shown in **Figure 6.111**.

    The `onLoadProgress` event is triggered as data is downloaded. The three parameters passed to the function are the movie clip target, the bytes currently loaded, and the total bytes of the external file.

13. Enter the following code between the curly braces for the `onLoadProgress` handler:

    ```
    var preloaded:Number = Math.floor
    (loadedBytes / totalBytes * 100);
    loaderText_txt.text =
    preloaded.toString() + "% loaded";
    bar_mc._xscale = preloaded;
    ```

    Your script for the `onLoadProgress` function should resemble **Figure 6.112**.

    During the download progress, the percentage of total bytes downloaded is displayed in the text field on the Stage, and the rectangular movie clip is stretched accordingly.

14. On a new line outside the function, enter the name of your listener object followed by a period. Choose ActionScript 2.0 Classes > Movie > MovieClipLoader > Listeners > onLoadInit.

```
loadListener.onLoadProgress = function(target:MovieClip, loadedBytes:Number, totalBytes:Number) {
};
```

Figure 6.111 The `onLoadProgress` handler passes three parameters: the target movie clip (called `target` here), the number of bytes loaded (called `loadedBytes` here), and the total number of bytes to be loaded (called `totalBytes` here).

```
loadListener.onLoadProgress = function(target:MovieClip, loadedBytes:Number, totalBytes:Number) {
    var preloaded:Number = Math.floor(loadedBytes / totalBytes * 100);
    loaderText_txt.text = preloaded.toString() + "% loaded";
    bar_mc._xscale = preloaded;
};
```

Figure 6.112 During the loading progress, Flash updates the contents of the text field called `loaderText_txt` and stretches the rectangular movie clip called `bar_mc` in proportion to the percentage of downloaded bytes.

```
loadListener.onLoadInit = function() {
    loaderText_txt._visible = false;
    bar_mc._visible = false;
    loader_mc.play();
};
```

Figure 6.113 When loading is finished and the loaded movie has initialized, the text field and the elongated rectangle disappear and the loaded movie plays.

```
mcLoader.addListener(loadListener);
```

Figure 6.114 The listener is registered to the `MovieClipLoader`.

15. Between the curly braces of the function, add the following code (**Figure 6.113**):

    ```
    loaderText_txt._visible = false;
    bar_mc._visible = false;
    loader_mc.play();
    ```

    The `onLoadInit` event is triggered when all the data has downloaded and the movie clip is ready to be controlled using ActionScript. When this happens, the text field and rectangular movie clip disappear and the downloaded movie plays.

16. On the next line, enter the name of the `MovieClipLoader` object followed by a period. Choose ActionScript 2.0 Classes > Movie > MovieClipLoader > Methods > addListener.

17. With your pointer between the parentheses, enter the name that you assigned to the listener object (**Figure 6.114**).

    The listener object is now registered with the `MovieClipLoader` object.

18. On the next line, enter the name that you assigned to the `MovieClipLoader` object, followed by a period. Choose ActionScript 2.0 Classes > Movie > MovieClipLoader > Methods > loadClip.

19. With your pointer between the parentheses, enter the absolute or relative URL of the SWF file or image you want to load. Make sure the address is between quotation marks and followed by a comma.

    Absolute URLs must include the protocol reference, such as http:// or file:///.

continues on next page

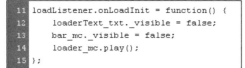

20. For the loadClip() method's second parameter, enter the target path of the movie clip into which you want the SWF or JPG to load. (**Figure 6.115**).

21. Test your movie.

    As your external movie or image loads into your placeholder movie clip, the text field displays the percentage of total bytes downloaded, and the rectangular movie clip grows longer. When the entire movie or image has loaded, the text field and elongated rectangular movie clip disappear (**Figure 6.116**).

✔ Tip

- The same security restrictions apply to external movies loaded with the method `loadClip()` as they do for `loadMovie()` and `loadMovieNum()`. See the sidebar "Flash Player Security: Loading Movies Across Domains" earlier in this chapter for details.


```
mcLoader.loadClip("http://www.someDomain.com/movie.swf", loader_mc);

```

Figure 6.115 The method `loadClip()` loads an external SWF file that resides at http://www.someDomain.com/movie.swf into the movie clip named `loader_mc`.

```
var mcLoader:MovieClipLoader = new MovieClipLoader();
var loadListener:Object = new Object();
loadListener.onLoadStart = function() {
    loader_mc.stop();
};
loadListener.onLoadProgress = function(target:MovieClip, loadedBytes:Number, totalBytes:Number) {
    var preloaded:Number = Math.floor(loadedBytes / totalBytes * 100);
    loaderText_txt.text = preloaded.toString() + "% loaded";
    bar_mc._xscale = preloaded;
};
loadListener.onLoadInit = function() {
    loaderText_txt._visible = false;
    bar_mc._visible = false;
    loader_mc.play();
};
mcLoader.addListener(loadListener);
mcLoader.loadClip("http://www.someDomain.com/movie.swf", loader_mc);
```

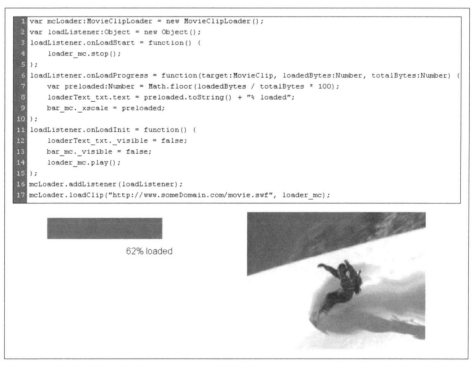

Figure 6.116 The completed code (top) provides a progress bar and text updates (bottom left) until all the data for the external SWF (bottom right) loads.

Part IV: Transforming Graphics and Sound

7 Controlling the Movie Clip

The movie clip is a powerful object. Its power comes from the myriad of properties, methods, and events that are available to it. Essentially, Flash lets you control the way movie clips look and behave. Movie clip properties such as position, scale, rotation, transparency, color, and even instance name can all be changed with ActionScript. As a result, you can create arcade-style interactivity, with characters changing in response to viewer input or conditions. Imagine a game of Tetris created entirely in Flash. Each geometric shape could be a movie clip, and the viewer would control its rotation and position with the keyboard. A game of Asteroids could feature an alien ship that moves in response to the viewer's position. This kind of animation isn't based on tweens you create while authoring the Flash movie. Rather, this is dynamic animation that is essentially created during playback.

Flash also gives you powerful methods to control a movie clip's behavior. You can make movie clips draggable so that viewers can pick up puzzle pieces and put them in their correct places, or you can develop a more immersive online shopping experience in which viewers can grab merchandise and drop it into their shopping carts. You'll learn how to detect where draggable movie clips are dropped on the Stage, as well as control collisions and overlaps with other movie clips. And you'll learn how to generate movie clips dynamically, so that new instances appear on the Stage during playback. You can use movie clips to create moving masks and even to create drawings—lines, curves, fills, and gradients.

Learning to control movie clip properties, methods, and events is your first step in understanding how to animate entirely with ActionScript.

Dragging the Movie Clip

Drag-and-drop behavior gives the viewer one of the most direct interactions with the Flash movie. Nothing is more satisfying than grabbing a graphic on the screen, moving it around, and dropping it somewhere else. It's a natural way of interacting with objects, and you can easily give your viewers this experience. Creating drag-and-drop behavior in Flash involves two basic steps: creating the movie clip and then assigning ActionScript to an event handler that triggers the drag action.

Usually, during drag-and-drop interactivity, the dragging begins when the viewer presses the mouse button with the pointer over the movie clip. When the mouse button is released, the dragging stops. Hence, the action to start dragging is tied to an `onPress` event handler, and the action to stop dragging is tied to an `onRelease` event handler.

In many cases, you may want the movie clip to snap to the center of the user's pointer as it's being dragged rather than wherever the user happens to click, described in the task "To center the draggable movie clip," or you may want to limit the area where viewers can drag movie clips, as described in the task "To constrain the draggable movie clip."

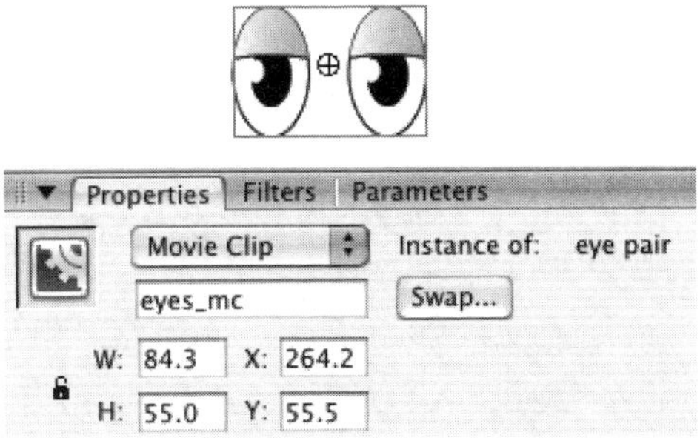

Figure 7.1 The movie clip instance of these cartoon eyes is given the name eyes_mc in the Property inspector.

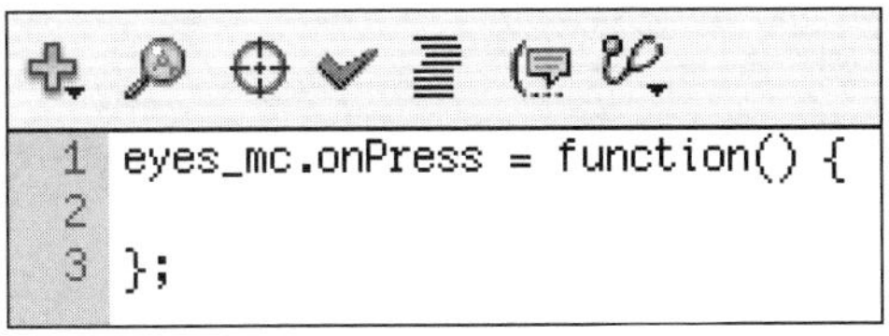

Figure 7.2 The `onPress` event handler is created with an anonymous function.

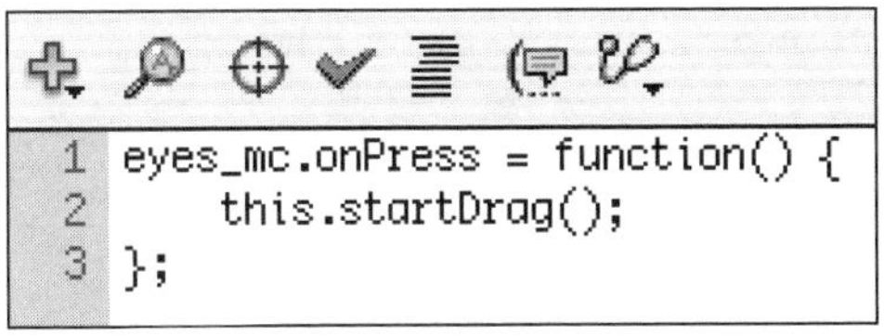

Figure 7.3 The target path `this` makes the `startDrag` method affect the movie clip `eyes_mc`.

To start dragging a movie clip:

1. Create a movie clip symbol, place an instance of it on the Stage, and name it in the Property inspector (**Figure 7.1**).
2. Select the first frame of the root Timeline, and open the Actions panel.
3. Enter the instance name for the movie clip that you just created, followed by a period.
4. Choose ActionScript 2.0 Classes > Movie > MovieClip > Events > onPress (**Figure 7.2**).

   The completed statement creates an `onPress` event handler for your movie clip.
5. Inside the event handler function, enter the keyword `this`, followed by a period.

   The keyword `this` refers to the movie clip on which the event handler function is defined.
6. Choose ActionScript 2.0 Classes > Movie > MovieClip > Methods > startDrag (**Figure 7.3**). The `startDrag` action appears between the function's curly braces.
7. Test your movie.

   When your pointer is over the movie clip and you press your mouse button, you can drag the clip around.

To stop dragging a movie clip:

1. Using the file you created in the preceding task, create a new line after the closing curly brace for the `onPress` event.
2. Enter the instance name of the movie clip followed by a period and `onRelease`. Complete the handler by entering `= function() {` followed by a closing curly brace and semicolon on the next line.

   The `onRelease` event handler is completed for your movie clip.

continues on next page

3. Choose ActionScript 2.0 Classes > Movie > MovieClip > Methods > stopDrag.

   The `stopDrag` statement appears, with no parameters.

4. Test your movie.

   When your pointer is over the movie clip and you press your mouse button, you can drag it. When you release your mouse button, the dragging stops (**Figure 7.4**).

✔ Tip

- Only one movie clip can be dragged at a time. For this reason, the `stopDrag` action doesn't need any parameters; it stops the drag action on whichever movie clip is currently draggable.

To center the draggable movie clip:

1. Place your pointer inside the parentheses for the `startDrag` method, and click the Show Code Hint button (Cmd-spacebar for Mac, Ctrl-spacebar for Windows) (**Figure 7.5**).

   The code hint for the `startDrag` method appears.

2. Enter the Boolean value `true`.

   The `startDrag` method's first parameter, `lockCenter`, is set to `true`. After you press the mouse button when your pointer is over the movie clip to begin dragging, the registration point of your movie clip snaps to the mouse pointer.

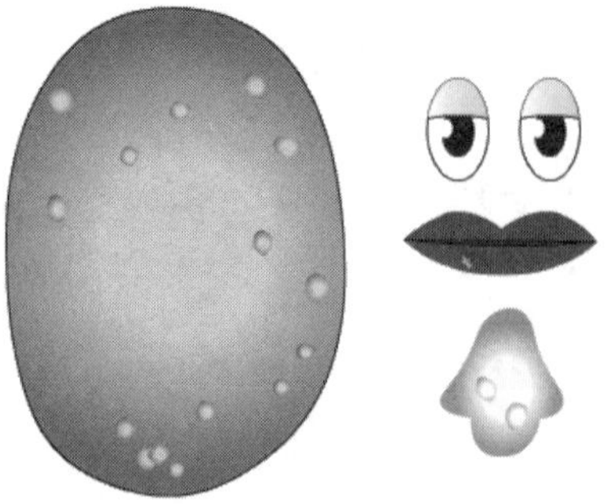

```
eyes_mc.onPress = function() {
    this.startDrag();
}
eyes_mc.onRelease = function(){
    stopDrag();
}
```

Figure 7.4 Each of the three facial features is a movie clip that can be dragged to the potato face and dropped into position.

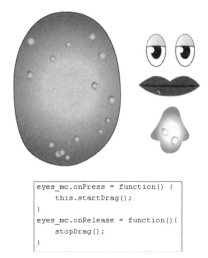

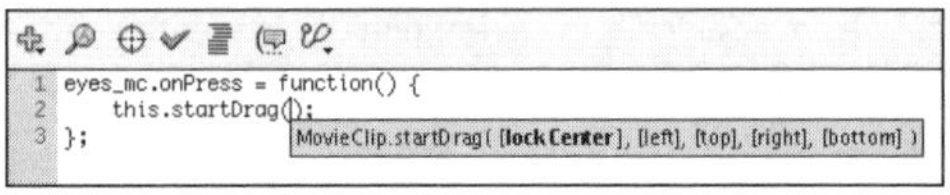

1 eyes_mc.onPress = function() {
2 this.startDrag();
3 };
MovieClip.startDrag([lockCenter], [left], [top], [right], [bottom])

Figure 7.5 The `lockCenter` parameter forces the viewer to drag the movie clip by its registration point.

✔ Tip

- If you set the `lockCenter` parameter to `true`, make sure the hit area of your movie clip covers its registration point. (By default, the hit area of your movie clip is the graphics it contains.) If it doesn't, then after the movie clip snaps to your mouse pointer, your pointer will no longer be over any hit area and Flash won't be able to detect when to stop the drag action.

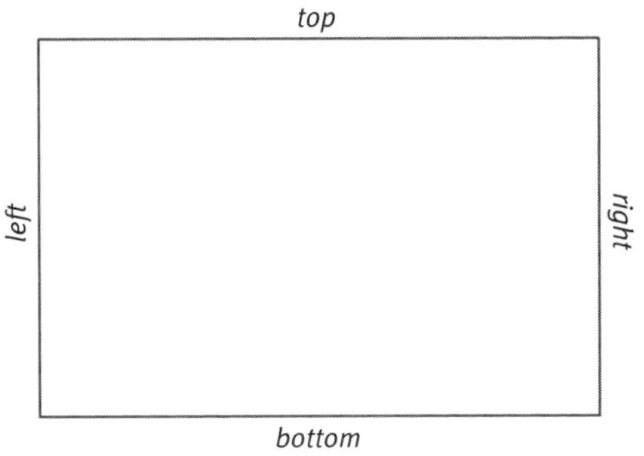

Figure 7.6 The parameters to constrain the drag motion define the left, right, top, and bottom boundaries.

- In order to define the `left`, `right`, `top`, and `bottom` parameters to constrain the draggable motion, you must also set the `startDrag` method's first parameter (`lockCenter`) to `true` or `false`.

To constrain the draggable movie clip:

1. Place your pointer inside the parentheses for the `startDrag` method, and click the Show Code Hint button (Cmd-spacebar for Mac, Ctrl-spacebar for Windows).

   The code hint appears.

2. Using the code hint to help guide you, enter pixel coordinates for each of the four fields representing the maximum and minimum limits for the registration point of your draggable movie clip (**Figure 7.6**):

   Left: The leftmost margin (minimum x position) where the registration point of the movie clip can go

   Right: The rightmost margin (maximum x position) where the registration point of the movie clip can go

   Top: The topmost margin (minimum y position) where the registration point of the movie clip can go

   Bottom: The bottommost margin (maximum y position) where the registration point of the movie clip can go

   The pixel coordinates are relative to the Timeline in which the movie clip resides. If the draggable movie clip sits on the root Timeline, the pixel coordinates correspond to the Stage, so `left=0`, `top=0` refers to the top-left corner. If the draggable movie clip is within another movie clip, `left=0`, `top=0` refers to the registration point of the parent movie clip.

✔ Tips

- You can use the `left`, `right`, `top`, and `bottom` parameters to force a dragging motion along a horizontal or a vertical track, as in a scroll bar. Set the `left` and `right` parameters to the same number to restrict the motion to up and down, or set the `top` and `bottom` parameters to the same number to restrict the motion to left and right.

Setting the Movie Clip Properties

Many movie clip properties—`size`, `transparency`, `position`, `rotation`, and `quality`—define how the movie looks. By using dot syntax, you can target any movie clip and change any of those characteristics during playback. **Table 7.1** summarizes properties that are available. A few of these properties affect the entire movie, not just a single movie clip.

In the task "To change the position of a movie clip," you will assign ActionScript to a button that changes a property of a movie clip.

Table 7.1

Movie Clip Properties

Property	Value	Description
`_alpha` (Alpha)	Number from 0 to 100	Alpha (transparency), where 0 is totally transparent and 100 is opaque.
`_visible` (Visibility)	`true` or `false`	Whether a movie clip can be seen.
`_name` (Name)	String-literal name	New instance name of the movie clip.
`_rotation` (Rotation)	Number	Degree of rotation in a clockwise direction from the 12 o'clock position. A value of 45, for example, tips the movie clip to the right.
`_width` (Width)	Number in pixels	Horizontal dimension.
`_height` (Height)	Number in pixels	Vertical dimension.
`_x` (X Position)	Number in pixels	Horizontal position of the movie clip's registration point.
`_y` (Y Position)	Number in pixels	Vertical position of the movie clip's registration point.
`_xscale` (X Scale)	Number	Percentage of the original movie clip symbol's horizontal dimension.
`_yscale` (Y Scale)	Number	Percentage of the original movie clip symbol's vertical dimension.
`blendMode`	Number or string	Which blend mode to use to visually combine the movie clip with other visual objects.
`cacheAsBitmap`	`true` or `false`	Whether to redraw the contents of the movie clip every frame (`false`) or use a static bitmap of the movie clip's contents (`true`).
`opaqueBackground`	Numeric color value	Nontransparent background color for the instance.
`scrollRect`	`Rectangle` object	Window of visible content of the movie clip, which can be changed to efficiently simulate scrolling.
`filters`	`Array` of filter objects	Set of graphical filters to apply to this movie clip instance.
`scale9Grid`	`Rectangle` object	Nine regions that control how the movie clip distorts when scaling.
`transform`	`Transform` object	Values representing color, size, and position changes applied to the instance.
`_focusrect` (Show focus rectangle)	`true` or `false`	Whether a yellow rectangle appears around objects as you use the Tab key to select objects.
`_quality` (Quality)	`LOW`, `MEDIUM`, `HIGH`, `BEST`	Level of anti-aliasing for playback of the movie. `BEST` = anti-aliasing and bitmap smoothing. `HIGH` = anti-aliasing and bitmap smoothing if there is no animation. `MEDIUM` = lower-quality anti-aliasing. `LOW` = no anti-aliasing. This is a global property that affects the entire movie rather than a single movie clip.
`_soundbuftime` (Sound buffer time)	Number	Number of seconds of audio that must be downloaded before the movie begins to stream sound. The default value is 5. This is a global property that affects the entire movie rather than a single movie clip.

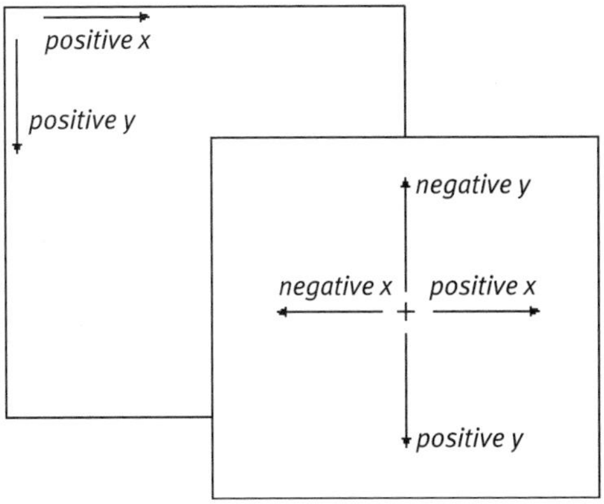

Figure 7.7 The x, y coordinates for the root Timeline (top) are centered at the top-left corner of the Stage. The x, y coordinates for movie clips (bottom) are centered at the registration point.

✔ Tips

- There is a difference between an `alpha` of `0` and a visibility of `false`, although the result may look the same. When the `_visible` property is `false`, the movie clip literally can't be seen. Mouse events in the movie clip and buttons within the movie clip don't respond. When `_alpha` is `0`, on the other hand, mouse events and buttons within the movie clip still function.
- The x- and y-coordinate space for the root Timeline is different from movie clip Timelines. In the root Timeline, the x-axis begins at the left edge and increases to the right; the y-axis begins at the top edge and increases to the bottom. Thus, x = 0, y = 0 corresponds to the top-left corner of the Stage. For movie clips, the coordinates x = 0, y = 0 correspond to the registration point (the crosshair). The value of x increases to the right of the registration point and decreases into negative values to the left of the registration point. The value of y increases to the bottom and decreases into negative values to the top (**Figure 7.7**).
- The `_xscale` and `_yscale` properties control the percentage of the original movie clip symbol, which is different from what may be on the Stage. For example, if you place an instance of a movie clip on the Stage and shrink it 50 percent, and then you apply an X Scale setting of 100 and a Y Scale setting of 100 during playback, your movie clip will double in size.

To change the position of a movie clip:

1. Create a movie clip symbol, place an instance of it on the Stage, and give it an instance name in the Property inspector.
2. Create a button symbol, place an instance of it on the Stage, and give it an instance name.
3. Select the first frame of the root Timeline, and open the Actions panel.
4. Enter the instance name of your button followed by a period.
5. Choose ActionScript 2.0 Classes > Movie > Button > Event Handlers > onRelease. (**Figure 7.8**).
6. Inside the function body, enter the instance name of the movie clip to which you would like to assign actions, followed by a period.
7. After the period, enter the property _x (X Position), followed by an equals sign and a number for the x position (**Figure 7.9**).
8. On the next line, enter the movie clip's instance name, a period, and the property _y (Y Position) followed by an equals sign and a numerical value for its position on the Stage (**Figure 7.10**).
9. Test your movie. When you click the button that you created, your movie clip jumps to the new position defined by the two property assignment statements (**Figure 7.11**).

```
placeEyes_btn.onRelease = function() {

};
```

Figure 7.8 The onRelease event handler for the placeEyes_btn button is added. In this example, this button will modify the x and y positions of a movie clip.

```
placeEyes_btn.onRelease = function() {
    eyes_mc._x = 122;
};
```

Figure 7.9 The x position of the movie clip eyes_mc on the root Timeline is set to 122.

```
placeEyes_btn.onRelease = function() {
    eyes_mc._x = 122;
    eyes_mc._y = 93;
};
```

Figure 7.10 The y position of the movie clip eyes_mc on the root Timeline is set to 93.

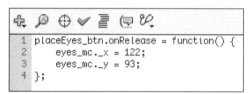

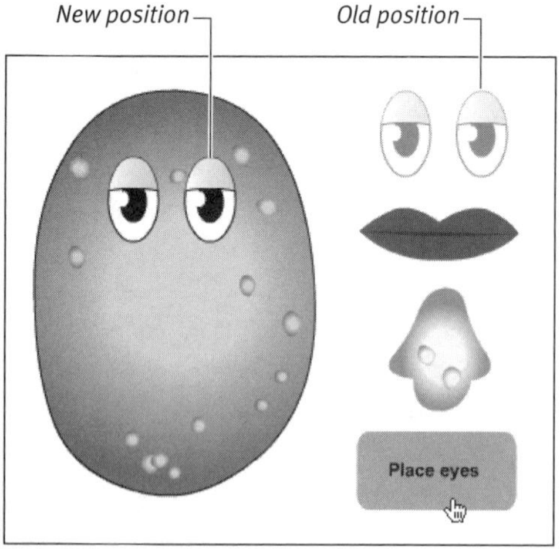

Figure 7.11 The button sets the movie clip of the eyes_mc into its new position on the potato.

Getting the Movie Clip Properties

Very often, you'll want to change a movie clip's property relative to its current value. You may want to rotate a cannon 10 degrees each time your viewer clicks a button, for example. How do you find the current value of a movie clip's property? By writing the target path and property in dot syntax, just as you did to set properties. To change a movie clip's property based on its current value, you can write the expression

```
cannon_mc._rotation += 10;
```

This expression adds 10 degrees to the current angle of the movie clip `cannon_mc`.

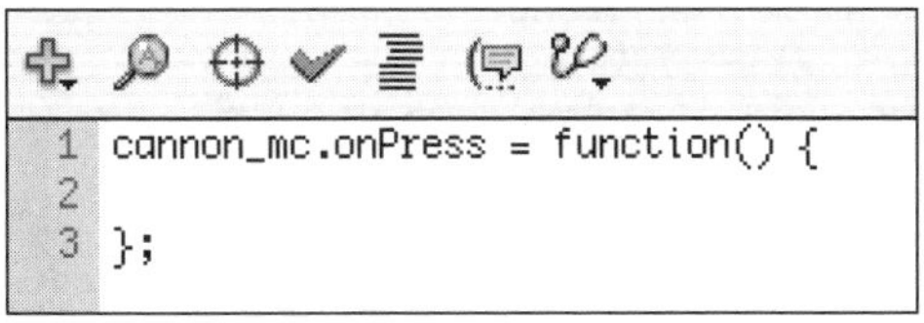
cannon_mc.onPress = function() {
};

Figure 7.12 The `onPress` event handler for the cannon movie clip is added.

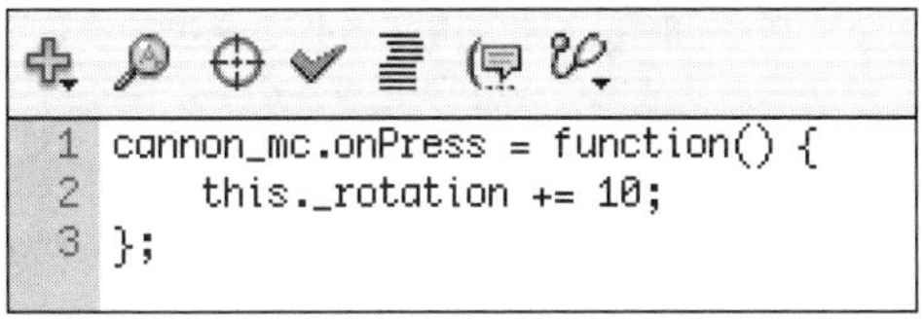
cannon_mc.onPress = function() {
this._rotation += 10;
};

Figure 7.13 The numeric value 10 is added to the current rotation of the movie clip `cannon_mc`.

To get a property of a movie clip:

1. Create a movie clip, place an instance on the Stage, and give it an instance name in the Property inspector.

   In this task, you'll get the rotation property of this movie clip and change it so that 10 degrees are added each time you click the movie clip.

2. Select the first frame of the root Timeline, and open the Actions panel.

3. Enter the instance name of the movie clip you just created.

4. Choose ActionScript 2.0 Classes > Movie > MovieClip > Event Handlers > onPress. (**Figure 7.12**).

5. On the next line, enter the target path `this` followed by a period.

6. Choose ActionScript 2.0 Classes > Movie > MovieClip > Properties > _rotation.

7. On the same line, choose Operators > Assignment > +=.

   An addition assignment operator is added to the statement. It will read the value of the `_rotation` property, add to it the amount written to the right of the operator, and store the result back in the property's value.

8. Enter the numeric value `10` (**Figure 7.13**).

   Each time the movie clip is clicked, Flash will get the current value of `cannon_mc` and rotate the cannon 10 degrees clockwise.

✔ Tip

- You can use shortcuts to add and subtract values by using combinations of the arithmetic operators. You'll learn about these combinations in Chapter 10.

Modifying the Movie Clip Color

One conspicuous omission from the list of movie clip properties is color. But you can use the `ColorTransform` class to change the color of movie clips.

New in Flash 8, each movie clip object has a `transform` property, which is an instance of the `Transform` class. This `Transform` object contains a snapshot of all the transformations that have been applied to the movie clip, including color changes, scaling, rotation, and more. Each of these transformations is stored in the `Transform` object as an object itself—an instance of a particular class that represents that type of transformation. For example, the `Transform` class has a property, `colorTransform`, which is an instance of the `ColorTransform` class. The first step in modifying a movie clip's color is instantiating a new `ColorTransform` object in which you define color changes that will eventually be applied to the movie clip. You create a `ColorTransform` instance with a constructor function such as this:

```
import flash.geom.ColorTransform;

var myCT:ColorTransform = new
ColorTransform();
```

In this example, `myCT` is the name of your new `ColorTransform` object. The `import` statement is a special command that tells Flash where to find the `ColorTransform` class. The full name of the `ColorTransform` class is `flash.geom.ColorTransform`. The `flash.geom` part of the name is what's known as the class's *package*. Packages are a way of organizing ActionScript code by grouping related classes together. All the Flash classes you've worked with up to this point, such as `MovieClip`, `Button`, and so on, are in the top-level package (and consequently have no package prefix). However, many of the classes added in Flash 8 are organized into packages. Packages are also commonly used by developers who create their own ActionScript classes.

Because the `ColorTransform` class is defined in a package, to create a `ColorTransform` instance, you'd normally have to use this line of ActionScript:

```
var myCT:flash.geom.ColorTransform = new
flash.geom.ColorTransform();
```

Notice that the full class name including its package name, `flash.geom`, is used in both places where the class name is specified (in the data type of the variable after the colon, and in the name of the constructor function). This ends up making the code quite long; so, to shorten the code, you use the `import` statement to define a shortcut name. The `import` statement tells Flash that any time you use the class name `ColorTransform` in your code, you really mean `flash.geom.ColorTransform`.

Once you have a `ColorTransform` instance, the next step is to set the RGB values that you want to apply to the movie clip by using the `rgb` property. To define your new color, use the hexadecimal equivalents of each color component (red, green, and blue) in the form 0x*RRGGBB*. You may have seen this six-digit code in HTML to specify the background color of a Web page. You can find these values for a color in the Color Mixer panel. Choose a color in the color spectrum, and the hexadecimal value for that color appears in the display to the left (**Figure 7.14**).

Finally, once you've defined the color changes you want to apply in your `ColorTransform` instance, you define your `ColorTransform` instance as the movie clip's color transformation by setting the `colorTransform` property of the movie clip's `transform` property, like this:

```
my_mc.transform.colorTransform = myCT;
```

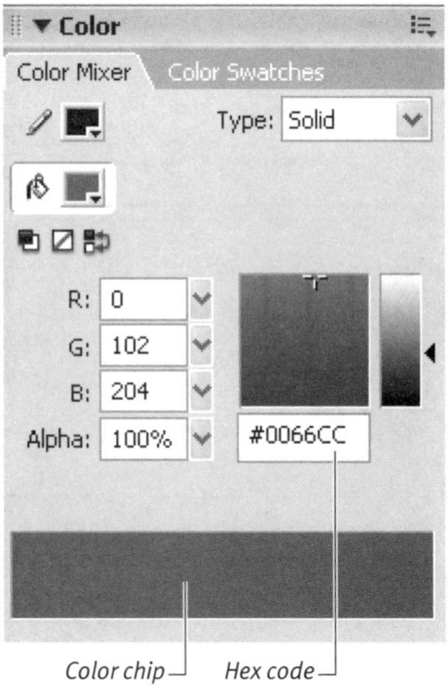

Figure 7.14 The Color Mixer panel has a display window to show the selected RGB color in hexadecimal code.

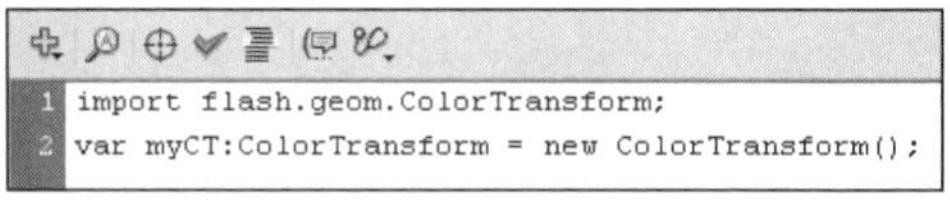

```
import flash.geom.ColorTransform;
var myCT:ColorTransform = new ColorTransform();
```

Figure 7.15 The new `ColorTransform` object is `myCT`. The `import` statement makes it so that you can use the class name without specifying the package each time.

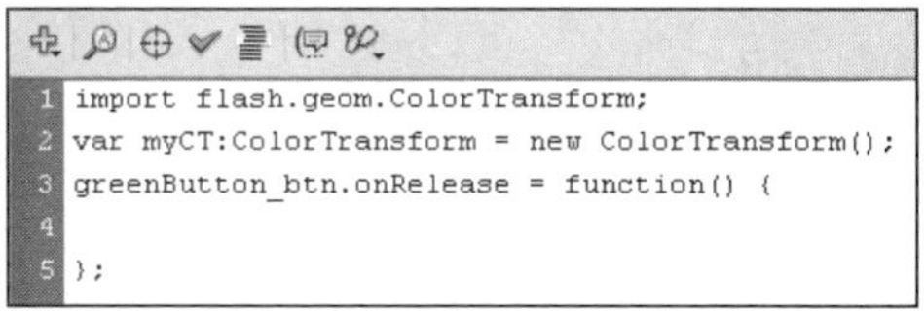

```
import flash.geom.ColorTransform;
var myCT:ColorTransform = new ColorTransform();
greenButton_btn.onRelease = function() {

};
```

Figure 7.16 The `onRelease` event handler is defined for the `greenButton_btn` button.

In this line, `my_mc` is the name of the movie clip. You get its transform property using `my_mc.transform`. Because that value is an instance of the `Transform` class, you can in turn target the color transformation property specifically by adding `.colorTransform`. Then you assign your `ColorTransform` object to that property.

To set the color of a movie clip:

1. Create a movie clip symbol whose color you want to modify, place an instance of it on the Stage, and name it in the Property inspector.
2. Create a button symbol, place an instance of it on the Stage, and name it in the Property inspector.

   You'll use this button to define the `colorTransform` property of your movie clip's transform object.
3. Select the first frame of the root Timeline, and open the Actions panel.
4. Add the following import statement: `import flash.geom.ColorTransform`.
5. To declare your `ColorTransform` instance, enter `var`, a name for your new color object, and then `:ColorTransform` and an equals sign.
6. Choose ActionScript 2.0 Classes > "flash.geom package" > ColorTransform > "new ColorTransform" (**Figure 7.15**).

   The completed statement instantiates a new `ColorTransform` object that is ready to be used.
7. On the next line, enter the instance name of your button.
8. Choose ActionScript 2.0 Classes > Movie > Button > Event Handlers > onRelease (**Figure 7.16**).

continues on next page

9. Inside the event handler function, choose ActionScript 2.0 Classes > "flash.geom package" > ColorTransform > Properties > rgb.

   The `rgb` property appears within your button event handler with a placeholder named `not_set_yet`.

10. Replace `not_set_yet` with the name of your `ColorTransform` object.

11. For the value of the `rgb` property, enter `0x` followed by the six-digit hexadecimal code for the new color.

12. On the following line, enter the name of your movie clip. Choose ActionScript 2.0 Classes > Movie > MovieClip > Properties > transform.

13. On the same line, choose ActionScript 2.0 Classes > "flash.geom package" > Transform > Properties > colorTransform. Enter an equals sign and the name of your `ColorTransform` object (**Figure 7.17**).

14. Test your movie.

   In the first frame, a `ColorTransform` object is instantiated. When you click your button, that `ColorTransform` object's `rgb` property is set to a color, and the object is then attached to the movie clip.

✔ Tip

- The `ColorTransform` class and the movie clip's `transform` property are new as of Flash 8. For previous versions of the Flash Player (back to version 5), you can use the `Color` class to change a movie clip's color.

```
import flash.geom.ColorTransform;
var myCT:ColorTransform = new ColorTransform();
greenButton_btn.onRelease = function() {
    myCT.rgb = 0x009900;
    shirt_mc.transform.colorTransform = myCT;
};
```

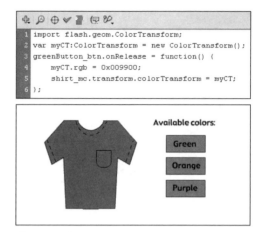

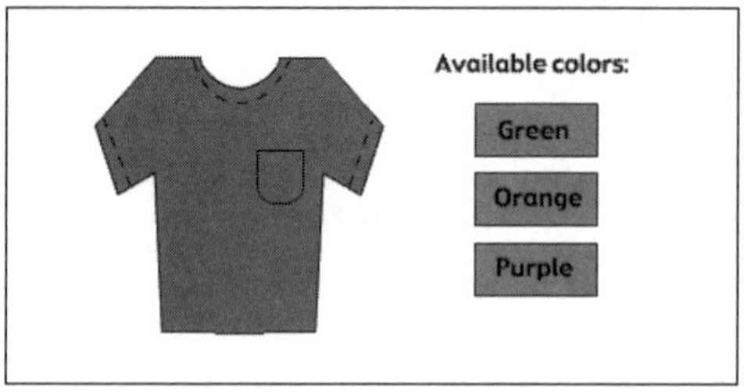

Figure 7.17 The `rgb` property takes a number value. It's easiest to use the form `0xRRGGBB`, which is the hex code for a color. Use `rgb` with different hex codes to change the color of this movie clip, `shirt_mc`.

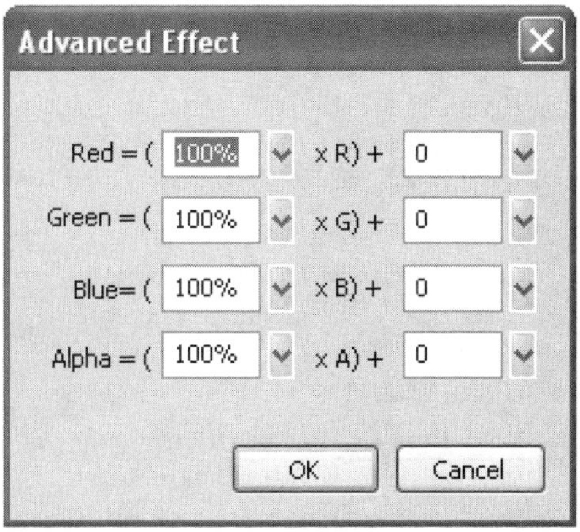

Figure 7.18 The options for advanced effects in the Property inspector control the RGB and alpha percentages and the offset values for any instance.

Table 7.2

ColorTransform Properties

Property	Value
redMultiplier	Decimal number to multiply by the red component
redOffset	Offset (–255 to 255) of the red component
greenMultipler	Decimal number to multiply by the green component
greenOffset	Offset (–255 to 255) of the green component
blueMultiplier	Decimal number to multiply by the blue component
blueOffset	Offset (–255 to 255) of the blue component
alphaModifier	Decimal number to multiply by the alpha (transparency)
alphaOffset	Offset (–255 to 255) of the alpha (transparency)

Making advanced color transformations

The property `rgb` lets you change only a movie clip's color. To change its brightness or its transparency, you must specify multiplier and offset properties. There is one property to define a multiplier and one to specify an offset value for each of the RGB components as well as the alpha (transparency). These properties are the same as those in the Advanced Effect dialog box that appears when you apply an advanced color effect to an instance (**Figure 7.18**). The only difference is that in the dialog box, you specify the multiplier as a percentage (0–100); but in ActionScript, the multiplier properties are set as decimal numbers. A multiplier is usually in the range 0–1, which corresponds to 0–100% (for example, 25% is specified as `.25`). However, the multiplier can be any decimal number (such as `2` to double the value, for instance).

You can specify multiplier and offset properties in two ways. The `ColorTransform` class has individual multiplier and offset properties for each color channel, described in **Table 7.2**. To change just one of these properties, assign a new value to the appropriate property.

You may want to set several of the multiplier or offset properties for a `ColorTransform` instance, which is cumbersome to do one property at a time. As an alternative, you can specify the multiplier and offset values as parameters when you call the constructor function to create your `ColorTransform` instance. To set the properties as parameters in the constructor function, you must specify all eight in the following order: red multiplier, green multiplier, blue multiplier, alpha multiplier, red offset, green offset, blue offset, alpha offset.

When you call the `ColorTransform` constructor without parameters as you did previously, the `ColorTransform` object is created with the default parameters that maintain the movie clip's color—1 for each multiplier and 0 for each offset.

To transform the color and alpha of a movie clip:

1. Create a movie clip symbol whose color or transparency you want to modify, place an instance of it on the Stage, and name it in the Property inspector.
2. Create a button symbol, place an instance of it on the Stage, and name it in the Property inspector.

   You'll use this button to create a `ColorTransform` object with specified multiplier and offset parameters.
3. Select the first frame of the root Timeline, and open the Actions panel.
4. Add an `import` statement for the `flash.geom.ColorTransform` class.
5. As before, to declare and instantiate a new `ColorTransform` object, enter `var`, then the name, and then `:ColorTransform` and an equals sign.
6. On the end of that line, add the `ColorTransform`'s constructor by choosing ActionScript 2.0 Classes > "flash.geom package" > ColorTransform > "new ColorTransform" (**Figure 7.19**).
7. Inside the parentheses of your `ColorTransform` object's constructor, enter the eight transform parameters (RGBA multipliers, then RGBA offsets) (**Figure 7.20**).

   The properties for the color transformation are defined in the parameters of your `ColorTransform` constructor call.
8. On the next line, enter the name of your button.
9. Choose ActionScript 2.0 Classes > Movie > Button > Event Handlers > onRelease.
10. Between the curly braces of your button's event handler, enter the name of your movie clip.
11. Choose ActionScript 2.0 Classes > Movie > MovieClip > Properties > transform, and then choose ActionScript 2.0 Classes > "flash.geom package" > Transform > properties > colorTransform.

```
import flash.geom.ColorTransform;
var myCT:ColorTransform = new ColorTransform();
```

Figure 7.19 A new `ColorTransform` object is created.

```
import flash.geom.ColorTransform;
var myCT:ColorTransform = new ColorTransform(1, 1, 1, .5, 75, 90, 255, 0);
```

Figure 7.20 The red, green, blue, and alpha multiplier and offset values are set with a series of parameters of the `ColorTransform` object constructor function.

12. On the same line, enter an equals sign followed by the name of your `ColorTransform` object.

    The full script should look like the one in **Figure 7.21**.

13. Test your movie.

    First, a `ColorTransform` object is instantiated, with the specified transformation values. When you click the button that you created, the `ColorTransform` object is assigned into the movie clip's `transform` property. The movie clip associated with the `ColorTransform` object changes color and transparency.

To change the brightness of a movie clip:

◆ Increase the offset parameters for the red, green, and blue components equally, but leave the other parameters unchanged.

If your `ColorTransform` object is called `myCT`, for example, set its properties individually as follows:

```
myCT.redMultiplier = 1;
myCT.greenMultiplier = 1;
myCT.blueMultiplier = 1;
myCT.alphaMultiplier = 1;
myCT.redOffset = 125;
myCT.greenOffset = 125;
myCT.blueOffset = 125;
myCT.alphaOffset = 0;
```

Or, instantiate your `ColorTransform` object with these parameters:

```
new ColorTransform(1, 1, 1, 1, 125,
125, 125, 0)
```

A color object using these parameters will increase the brightness of a movie clip to about 50 percent. You can set the offset parameters of red, green, and blue to their maximum (255), as follows:

```
myCT.redMultiplier = 1;
myCT.greenMultiplier = 1;
myCT.blueMultiplier = 1;
myCT.alphaMultiplier = 1;
myCT.redOffset = 255;
myCT.greenOffset = 255;
myCT.blueOffset = 255;
myCT.alphaOffset = 0;
```

A color object using these parameters will increase the brightness of a movie clip completely so that it will turn white.

To change the transparency of a movie clip:

◆ Decrease either the offset or the percentage parameter for the alpha component, and leave the other parameters unchanged.

Decrease `alphaMultiplier` to 0 or decrease `alphaOffset` to –255 for total transparency.


```
import flash.geom.ColorTransform;
var myCT:ColorTransform = new ColorTransform(1, 1, 1, .5, 75, 90, 255, 0);
transformButton_btn.onRelease = function() {
    shirt_mc.transform.colorTransform = myCT;
};
```

Figure 7.21 The full ActionScript changes the color and alpha of the movie clip `shirt_mc` with a button event.

Creating Color Interactions

If you've used a graphics manipulation program such as Photoshop or Fireworks, you've likely seen a *blend mode* option, which is a way to control how the colors of overlapping objects interact. Normally, when one object overlaps another, the object is opaque and completely blocks the object below from view. By applying a blend mode to the top object, you can change this behavior and show a blend of the colors of the two objects rather than just the color of the top object.

The ability to apply blend modes to movie clips has been added in Flash 8, meaning these creative effects are now available directly in Flash. If you have Flash Professional 8, you can apply a blend mode to a movie clip from within the authoring tool by selecting an instance on the Stage and choosing the desired mode from the Blend menu in the Property inspector (**Figure 7.22**). You can also select a blend mode for a movie clip using ActionScript by setting a value for the movie clip's `blendMode` property.

Each of the blend modes works by examining the overlapping portions of graphical objects. The color value of each pixel from the top (or *blend*) movie clip is taken together with the color of the pixel directly below it in the bottom (or *base*) movie clip. The two color values are then plugged into a mathematical formula to determine the resulting color displayed in that pixel location on the screen. The blend mode you choose determines the mathematical formula that's used (and hence the output color). **Table 7.3** describes the blend modes available in Flash.

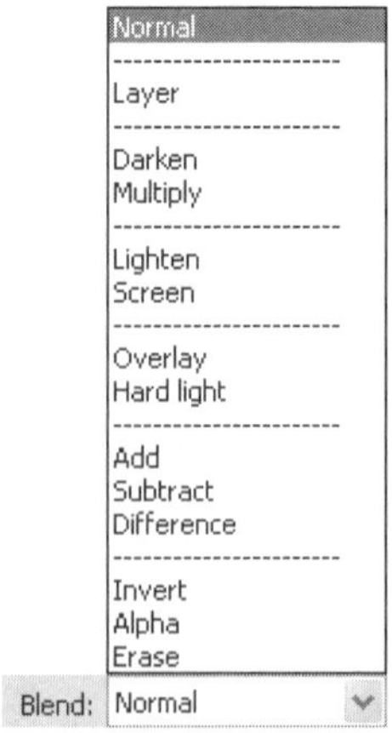

Figure 7.22 Using the Blend menu in Flash Professional 8, you can easily apply a blend mode to a movie clip.

Figure 7.23 In this example, the colored squares are a movie clip that overlaps a photo, which is also a movie clip.

To designate a blend mode for a movie clip instance, set the `blendMode` property of the movie clip to the appropriate string or number value for the blend mode, as in these two examples:

```
myMovieClip.blendMode = 6;
```

```
myMovieClip.blendMode = "darken";
```

To change color blending between movie clips:

1. Create two movie clip symbols whose colors will be blended, using the drawing tools or by importing images.
2. Put one instance of each symbol on the Stage, overlapping as desired. Give the top (blend) movie clip an instance name in the Property inspector (**Figure 7.23**).
3. If you'll be applying an Alpha or Erase blend mode, select the two instances on the Stage, choose Modify > "Convert to symbol", and give the new symbol an instance name as well.

   This creates a parent movie clip that contains the movie clips to be blended.
4. Select the first keyframe, and open the Actions panel.

continues on next page

Table 7.3

Movie Clip Blend Modes

Blend Mode	ActionScript Value	Description
Darken	6 or "darken"	Color values are compared and the darker of the two is displayed, resulting in a darker image overall. Often used to create a background for (light) text.
Lighten	5 or "lighten"	Lighter of the two color values is displayed, leading to a lighter image overall. Often used to create a background for (dark) text.
Multiply	3 or "multiply"	Color values are multiplied to get the result, which is usually darker than either value.
Screen	4 or "screen"	Opposite of multiply; the result is lighter than either original color. Typically used for highlighting or flare effects.
Overlay	13 or "overlay"	Uses Multiply if the base color is darker than middle gray or Screen if it's lighter.
Hard light	14 or "hardlight"	Opposite of overlay; uses Screen if the base color is darker than middle gray or Multiply if it's lighter.
Add	8 or "add"	Adds the two colors together, making a lighter result. Often used for a transition between images.
Subtract	9 or "subtract"	Subtracts the blend color from the base color, making the resulting color darker. Often used as a transition effect.
Difference	7 or "difference"	Darker color is subtracted from the lighter one, resulting in a brighter image, often with unnatural results.
Invert	10 or "invert"	Displays the inverse of the base color anywhere the blend clip overlaps.
Alpha	11 or "alpha"	Creates an alpha mask. The blend clip doesn't show, but any alpha values of the blend clip are applied to the base clip, making those areas transparent. The clips must be inside another clip with Layer mode applied.
Erase	12 or "erase"	Inverse of Alpha mode. the blend clip doesn't show. Under opaque areas on the blend clip, the base clip becomes transparent; beneath transparent areas on the blend image, the base clip is visible, creating a stencil or cookie-cutter effect. The clips must be inside a Layer mode clip.
Layer	2 or "layer"	Special container blend mode in Flash. Any blends inside a movie clip set to Layer don't affect images outside the layer clip.
Normal	1 or "normal"	Blend image is opaque (no blending takes place).

5. Enter the target path of your blend clip (including the parent clip's name if applicable). Choose ActionScript 2.0 Classes > Movie > MovieClip > Properties > blendMode.

6. Continuing on the same line, enter an equals sign followed by the number or string value for the desired blend mode (**Figure 7.24**).

   The blend mode is applied to the blend clip, altering the color interaction between the two movie clips.

7. If you chose the Alpha or Erase blend mode, on the next line, enter the name of the parent movie clip and add a statement to assign the Layer blend mode to the parent clip's `blendMode` property as described in steps 5–6.

8. Test your movie.

   The colors of the movie clips on the Stage blend together according to the blend mode selected (**Figure 7.25**).

✔ Tips

- Blend modes can also be applied to button instances, both in the authoring environment and using ActionScript.
- It's helpful to use the Flash authoring environment to experiment with different blend modes using the images you want to combine, even if you ultimately plan to apply the effect using ActionScript.

```
squares_mc.blendMode = "invert";
```

Figure 7.24 The `blendMode` property of the squares movie clip is set to `invert`.

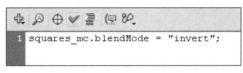

Figure 7.25 In the resulting image, the blend mode causes the colors in the photo to be inverted.

Applying Movie Clip Filter Effects

Flash graphics can look nice, but it's the little finishing touches that make a good graphic into a great one. These finishing touches are usually subtle—the soft glow of light emanating from a mysterious orb or the drop shadow behind an object that creates a sense of depth. As mentioned in Chapter 1, Flash 8 includes a number of filter effects that can be used to create these finishing touches as well as complex graphic manipulation. These filter effects are built into the Flash Player, so using them adds nothing to the download size of your SWF file. Because this is Flash, you can add these effects not only within the authoring environment but also dynamically using ActionScript. In fact, in addition to the filters available with the drawing tools, two filters, the Convolution filter and the Displacement Map filter, can only be applied using ActionScript.

Each filter is represented as a class in ActionScript. These classes are all found in the `flash.filters` package (**Table 7.4**). To apply a filter effect to a movie clip, you first create an instance of the filter you want. Each filter can be customized with several values, which are usually set as parameters of the constructor function that is called to create the filter object, like this:

```
import flash.filters.BlurFilter;
var myBlur:BlurFilter;
myBlur = new BlurFilter(3, 0, 1);
```

Once you have one or more filter objects, you can apply them to a movie clip or button instance. The `MovieClip` class has a `filters` property that takes an `Array` (an object that is a set of objects or values) containing one or more filter objects. (You'll learn more about the `Array` class in Chapter 11.) Most often, you can create the `Array` instance and assign it to the filters property in a single statement by calling the `Array` class's constructor function and passing your filter object or objects as parameters, like this:

```
my_mc.filters = new Array(myBlur);
```


Table 7.4

Filter Classes

Filter Class Name	Description
`BevelFilter`	Adds a beveled edge to an object, making it look three-dimensional
`BlurFilter`	Makes an object looked blurred
`ColorMatrixFilter`	Performs complex color transformations to an object
`ConvolutionFilter`	A highly customizable filter that can be used to create unique filter effects beyond those included with Flash by combining pixels with neighboring pixels in various ways
`DisplacementMapFilter`	Shifts pixel values according to values in a map image to create a textured or distorted effect
`DropShadowFilter`	Adds a drop-shadow to an object
`GlowFilter`	Adds a colored halo around an object
`GradientBevelFilter`	Like the Bevel filter, with the additional ability to specify a gradient color for the bevel
`GradientGlowFilter`	Like the Glow filter, with the additional ability to specify a gradient color for the glow

When you pass objects as parameters to the `Array` constructor, those objects are automatically added into the `Array` object; in this example, the `new Array()` constructor function creates a new `Array` object, and the object passed as a parameter (the filter object) is added into the array. The `Array` instance is then stored in the movie clip's `filters` property, causing any filter objects it contains (just one, in this case) to be applied to the movie clip.

In the next task, you'll see how to apply a drop-shadow filter to a movie clip. The procedure for applying any other filter to a movie clip is the same; the only difference is that with each one, you use the specific parameters for that filter when calling the constructor function to create the filter object.

To dynamically add a drop-shadow filter effect:

1. Create a movie clip symbol; place an instance on the Stage, and give it an instance name in the Property inspector.
2. Select the first keyframe, and open the Actions panel.
3. Add an `import` statement with the full class name of the filter including package (`flash.filters.DropShadowFilter`).

   The `import` statement allows you to refer to the filter class using only the class name.
4. Declare a variable for your filter object by entering `var` and then the variable name, followed by a colon and the filter's class name (`DropShadowFilter`), and then an equals sign.
5. Add the constructor function call by choosing ActionScript 2.0 Classes > "flash.filters package" > DropShadowFilter > "new DropShadowFilter" (**Figure 7.26**).

   The filter's constructor function is added without parameters.

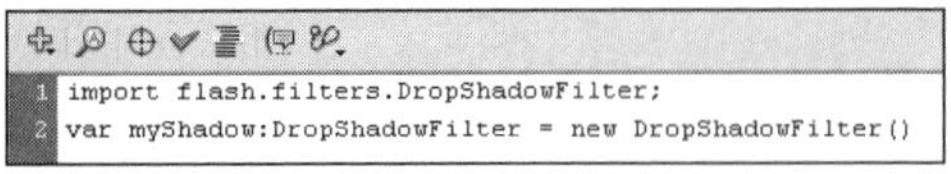

Figure 7.26 This ActionScript creates a new `DropShadowFilter` with all the default properties.

6. Between the parentheses, enter values separated by commas as parameters for the constructor function (**Figure 7.27**).

   The `DropShadowFilter` constructor takes up to eleven parameters, which match different options. However, they're all optional, and you can specify just some of them if you wish. To get you started, the first five are the offset distance (a number of pixels), the shadow angle (a number of degrees), the shadow color (a hexadecimal numeric color value), and `blurX` and `blurY` (both numbers).

7. On the next line, choose ActionScript 2.0 Classes > Movie > MovieClip > Properties > filters, and replace the placeholder `not_set_yet` with the name of your movie clip.

8. At the end of the same line, enter an equals sign; then choose ActionScript 2.0 Classes > Core > Array > "new Array".

   This creates a new `Array` object.

9. Between the parentheses of the `Array` constructor, enter the name of your filter object.

   Your filter object is added into the new `Array` as it's created; consequently, it's applied to the movie clip as the array is assigned to the `filters` property.

10. Test your movie.

    Your movie clip instance on the Stage has a drop shadow applied with the properties you specified (**Figure 7.28**).

```
import flash.filters.DropShadowFilter;
var myShadow:DropShadowFilter = new DropShadowFilter(5, 75, 0x000000, 10, 10);
```

Figure 7.27 Add parameters when calling the filter object's constructor function to modify the filter's properties. Here the parameters are offset distance 5, shadow angle 75 degrees, shadow color black (`0x000000`), horizontal blur 10, and vertical blur 10.

```
import flash.filters.DropShadowFilter;
var myShadow:DropShadowFilter = new DropShadowFilter(5, 75, 0x000000, 10, 10);
myWindow_mc.filters = new Array(myShadow);
```

Figure 7.28 The complete code creates a drop-shadow filter object (`myShadow`) and applies it to a movie clip (`myWindow_mc`).

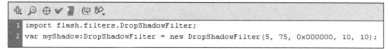

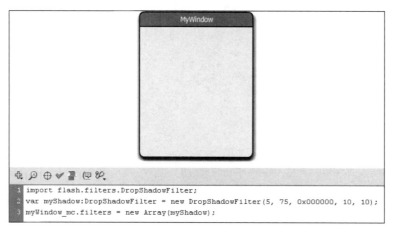

✔ Tips

- Because the filters property accepts an Array, you can apply multiple filters to a movie clip. To add multiple filters to a movie clip, instantiate all the filter objects first, and then add them all as parameters to the new Array() constructor that is assigned to the filters property (steps 8–9). For instance, if you create two filter objects named filter1 and filter2, this line of code applies both filters to a movie clip named myClip_mc:

```
myClip_mc.filters = new
Array(filter1, filter2);
```

- Use a drop-shadow filter to enhance a drag-and-drop interaction. In the onPress event handler, in addition to calling the startDrag method, add a drop shadow to the dragged movie clip. When the mouse button is released and dragging stops, remove the filter by assigning an empty Array (created by calling the new Array() constructor with no parameters) to the filters property.

- When the Flash Player is drawing a movie clip to the Stage, any filters are applied to the movie clip before transformations (such as scale or rotation) are calculated. Thus if you apply a drop-shadow filter to a movie clip that is also rotated 90 degrees, the shadow that appears is the shadow of the original clip—not the shadow of the rotated version of the clip that appears on the screen. However, if a filter is applied to a bitmap graphic that has a transformation applied, the filter is applied to the transformed graphic (see the next chapter).

Controlling Movie Clip Stacking Order

When you have multiple draggable movie clips, you'll notice that the objects maintain their stacking order even while they're being dragged, which can seem a little odd. Each movie clip instance is placed on its own *depth* (or stacking order) within its parent container, and dragging the movie clip doesn't change its depth.

In a drag-and-drop interaction, you expect that the item you pick up will come to the top. You can make this happen by using the `swapDepths()` method to swap the stacking order of movie clips dynamically. `swapDepths()` can switch the stacking order of movie clips either by swapping two named movie clips or by swapping a named movie clip with whatever movie clip is in a designated depth. Higher depth-level numbers overlap lower ones, much like levels of loaded movies.

The amazing thing about `swapDepths()` is that it works across layers, so a movie clip in the bottom layer can swap with a movie clip in the top layer.

Knowing where a movie clip lies in the stacking order can also be useful. The MovieClip class's `getDepth()` method, which returns the depth level of the movie clip instance, is the logical companion to the `swapDepths()` method.

You can use `swapDepths()` anywhere, but in this task, you'll link it to a `startDrag()` method to see the effects on depth levels.

To swap a movie clip with another movie clip:

1. Create two draggable movie clips on the Stage, as outlined earlier in this chapter.

   Your script should look similar to **Figure 7.29**.

2. In the Script pane, place your pointer after the first `startDrag` statement (inside the first movie clip's `onPress` handler), and press Enter to go to the next line.

3. Enter the keyword `this` followed by a period.

4. Choose ActionScript 2.0 Classes > Movie > MovieClip > Methods > swapDepths.

5. For the parameter of the `swapDepths` method, enter the target path for the second movie clip.

   When you click the first draggable movie clip, it will swap its stacking order with that of the other movie clip.

6. Place your pointer after the `startDrag` statement in the second movie clip's `onPress` event handler; on the next line, add the word `this` and a `swapDepths` statement.

7. Between the parentheses for the second `swapDepths` statement, enter the target path of the first movie clip.

   The completed scripts should look like the one in **Figure 7.30**.

8. Test your movie.

   When you drag the first movie clip, it swaps its stacking order with that of the second movie clip and vice versa.

```
puzzle1_mc.onPress = function() {
    this.startDrag();
};
puzzle1_mc.onRelease = function() {
    stopDrag();
};
puzzle2_mc.onPress = function() {
    this.startDrag();
};
puzzle2_mc.onRelease = function() {
    stopDrag();
};
```

Figure 7.29 The ActionScript to make the movie clips `puzzle1_mc` and `puzzle2_mc` draggable.

```
puzzle1_mc.onPress = function() {
    this.startDrag();
    this.swapDepths(puzzle2_mc);
};
puzzle1_mc.onRelease = function() {
    stopDrag();
};
puzzle2_mc.onPress = function() {
    this.startDrag();
    this.swapDepths(puzzle1_mc);
};
puzzle2_mc.onRelease = function() {
    stopDrag();
};
```

Figure 7.30 Each `swapDepths()` method is associated with a `startDrag()` method. When you click `puzzle1_mc`, it swaps with `puzzle2_mc`. When you click `puzzle2_mc`, it swaps with `puzzle1_mc`.

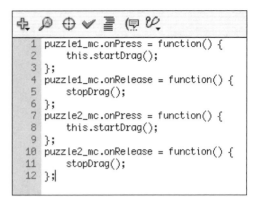

```
puzzle1_mc.onPress = function() {
    this.startDrag();
    this.swapDepths(2);
};
puzzle1_mc.onRelease = function() {
    stopDrag();
};
puzzle2_mc.onPress = function() {
    this.startDrag();
    this.swapDepths(2);
};
puzzle2_mc.onRelease = function() {
    stopDrag();
};
```

Figure 7.31 The current movie clip swaps with the one in depth level 2.

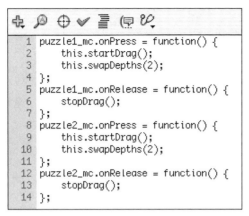

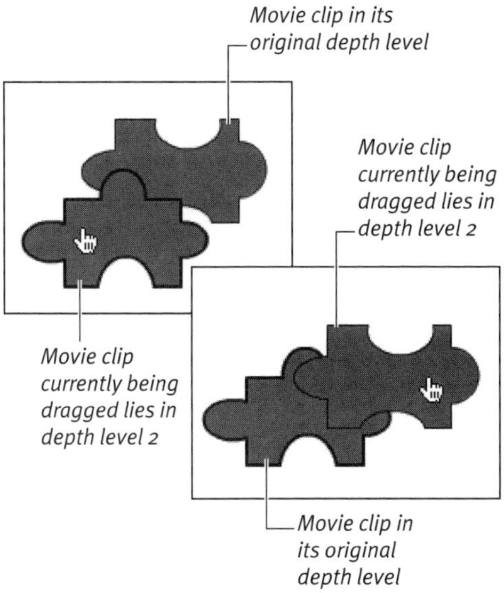
Movie clip in its original depth level
Movie clip currently being dragged lies in depth level 2
Movie clip currently being dragged lies in depth level 2
Movie clip in its original depth level

Figure 7.32 Swapping depth levels is ideal for dealing with multiple draggable movie clips, such as these puzzle pieces.

To swap the depth level of a movie clip:

1. Continuing with the same file you created in the preceding task, place your pointer inside the parentheses for the first `swapDepths` statement.
2. Replace the target path with a number specifying the depth level (**Figure 7.31**).
3. Select the second `swapDepths` statement, and replace its `Parameters` field with the same depth-level number.
4. Test your movie.

   The first movie clip you drag is put into the specified depth level. The second movie clip you drag is swapped with whatever is currently in that depth level (**Figure 7.32**).

✔ Tip

- The difference between using a target path and using a depth number as the `swapDepths()` parameter depends on your needs. Use a target path to swap the two named movie clips so the movie clip that is overlapping the other movie clip is sent behind it. To keep a draggable movie clip above all other movie clips, use depth level to send it to the top of the stacking order.

To determine the depth level of a movie clip:

1. Using the file from the preceding task, place your pointer after the first `swapDepths` statement, and press Enter to go to the next line. Choose Global Functions > Miscellaneous Functions > trace.

   The `trace` command will display information in the Output window when you test your movie. You'll add the `getDepths()` method to the `trace` command to see the depth level of your movie clip.

2. With your pointer between the parentheses for the `trace` statement, choose ActionScript 2.0 Classes > Movie > MovieClip > Methods > getDepth.

3. Select and replace the placeholder `not_set_yet` with the target path to the first draggable movie clip (**Figure 7.33**).

4. Select the second `swapDepths` statement, and add another `trace` command with a `getDepth()` method for the second draggable movie clip.

5. Test your movie.

   When you drag the first movie clip, the Output window appears and displays the movie clip's depth level. When you drag the second movie clip, its depth level displays in the Output window (**Figure 7.34**).

✔ Tip

- The `getDepth()` method is also a method of the `Button` class and the `TextField` class; you can use it in the same way to determine the stacking order of those objects.

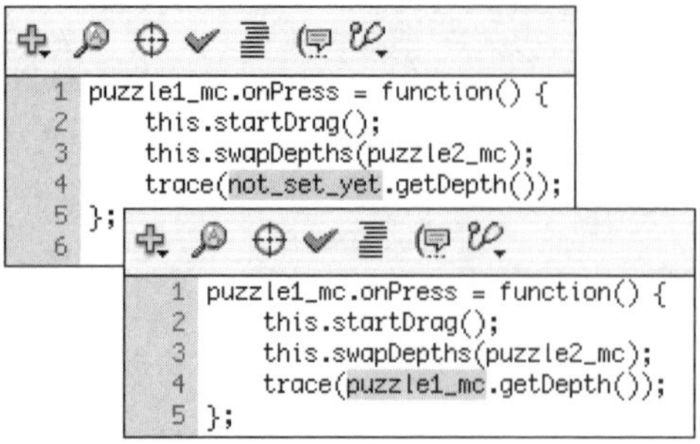
puzzle1_mc.onPress = function() {
this.startDrag();
this.swapDepths(puzzle2_mc);
trace(not_set_yet.getDepth());
};
puzzle1_mc.onPress = function() {
this.startDrag();
this.swapDepths(puzzle2_mc);
trace(puzzle1_mc.getDepth());
};

Figure 7.33 Replace the default placeholder `not_set_yet` with the target path to the draggable movie clip, shown here as `puzzle1_mc`.

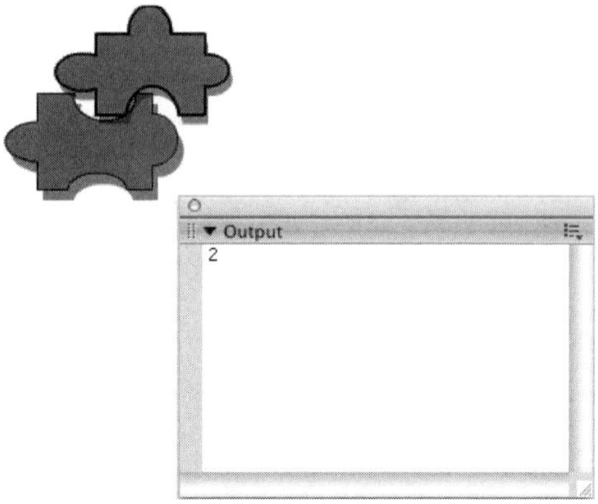
Output
2

Figure 7.34 The `trace` command shows in the Output window that the currently dragged movie clip is in depth level 2. The Output window appears only when you test your Flash movie. It doesn't appear in your final SWF file.

Detecting Movie Clip Collisions

Now that you can make a movie clip that can be dragged around the Stage, you'll want to know where the user drops it. If the movie clips are puzzle pieces, for example, you need to know whether those pieces are dragged and dropped on the correct spots.

It's also valuable to check whether a movie clip intersects another movie clip. The game of Pong, for example, detects collisions between the ball, the paddles, and the wall, all of which are movie clips. Detecting movie clip collisions can be useful on sophisticated e-commerce sites as well. Suppose you develop an online shopping site that lets your customers drag merchandise into a shopping cart. You can detect when the object intersects with the shopping cart and provide interaction such as highlighting the shopping cart or displaying the product price before the user drops the object.

To detect dropped movie clips or colliding movie clips, use the movie clip method `hitTest()`. You can use `hitTest()` two ways. First, you can check whether the bounding boxes of any two movie clips intersect. The *bounding box* of a movie clip is the minimum rectangular area that contains the graphics. This method is ideal for graphics colliding with other graphics, such as a ball with a paddle, a ship with an asteroid, or a puzzle piece with its correct resting spot. In this case, you enter the target path of the movie clip as the parameter—for example, `hitTest(_root.target)`.

The second way to use hitTest() is to check whether a certain x-y coordinate intersects with a movie clip. This method is point specific, which makes it ideal for checking whether only the registration point of a graphic or the mouse pointer intersects with a movie clip. In this case, the hitTest() parameters are an x value, a y value, and the shapeflag parameter, as in hitTest(x, y, shapeflag). The shapeflag parameter is either true or false. This parameter indicates whether Flash should use the bounding box of a movie clip (false) or the shape of the graphics it contains (true) in deciding if the point is in contact with the movie clip (**Figure 7.35**).

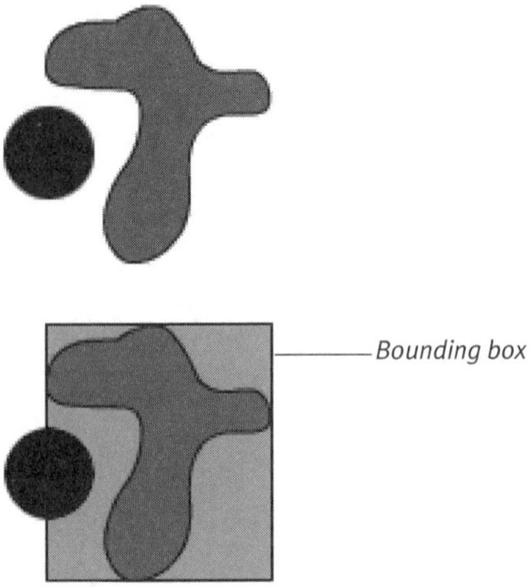

Figure 7.35 When the shapeflag parameter is true (top), then according to Flash, the two objects aren't intersecting; only the shapes are considered. When the shapeflag parameter is false (bottom), the two objects are intersecting according to Flash; the bounding box is considered.

To detect an intersection between two movie clips:

1. Create a movie clip, place an instance of it on the Stage, and name it in the Property inspector.
2. Create another movie clip, place an instance of it on the Stage, and name it in the Property inspector.
3. Select the first frame of the main Timeline, and open the Actions panel; assign actions to make the second movie clip instance draggable.
4. Create a new line in the Script pane at the end of the current script, and choose ActionScript 2.0 Classes > Movie > MovieClip > Event Handlers > onEnterFrame.
5. Select the placeholder text not_set_yet and replace it with _root.

   The onEnterFrame event handler for the root Timeline is established. This event occurs at the frame rate of the movie, which makes it ideal for checking the hitTest condition continuously.
6. Inside the curly braces of the onEnterFrame handler, choose Statements > Conditions/Loops > if.

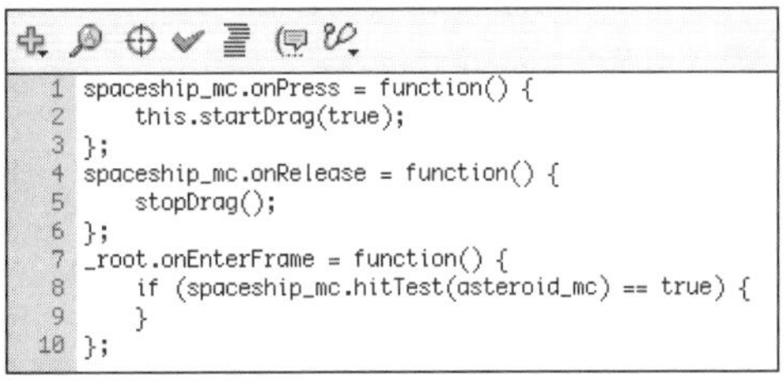

```
spaceship_mc.onPress = function() {
    this.startDrag(true);
};
spaceship_mc.onRelease = function() {
    stopDrag();
};
_root.onEnterFrame = function() {
    if (spaceship_mc.hitTest(asteroid_mc) == true) {
    }
};
```

Figure 7.36 This condition checks whether the spaceship_mc movie clip intersects the asteroid_mc movie clip.

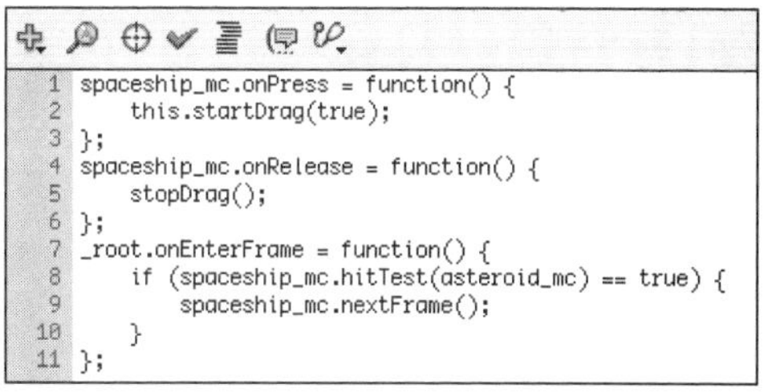

```
spaceship_mc.onPress = function() {
    this.startDrag(true);
};
spaceship_mc.onRelease = function() {
    stopDrag();
};
_root.onEnterFrame = function() {
    if (spaceship_mc.hitTest(asteroid_mc) == true) {
        spaceship_mc.nextFrame();
    }
};
```

Figure 7.37 The consequence of an intersection is the `nextFrame` action.

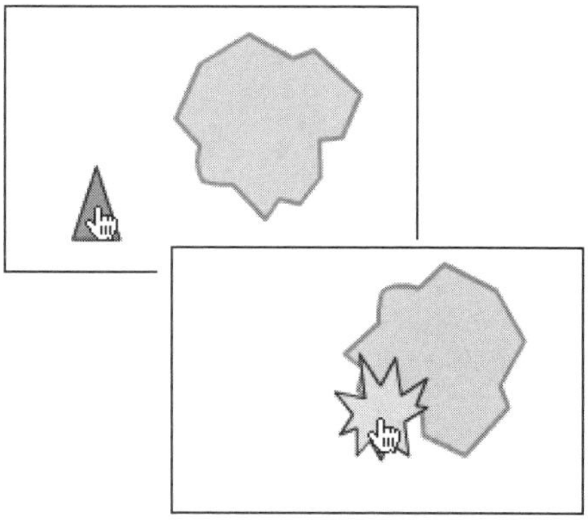

Figure 7.38 Dragging the `spaceship_mc` movie clip into the bounding box of the `asteroid_mc` movie clip advances the spaceship movie clip to the next frame, which displays an explosion.

- To detect a dropped movie clip, set the alpha value of the stationary (target) movie clip to 0 so it's invisible. Assign the `hitTest()` method to an `if` statement immediately after the `stopDrag()` method, like this:

```
eyes_mc.onRelease = function() {
    stopDrag();
    if (this.hitTest(hiddenClip_mc)) {
        //drop successful
    }
};
```

In this example, when the draggable movie clip `eyes_mc` is dropped, Flash checks to see whether it's dropped on the movie clip `hiddenClip_mc`.

7. For the condition (between the parentheses), enter the name of the draggable movie clip followed by a period.

8. Select `hitTest` from the code hint pull-down menu.

   or

   Choose ActionScript 2.0 Classes > Movie > MovieClip > Methods > hitTest.

9. Within the parentheses of the `hitTest` method, enter the path of the stationary movie clip.

10. Immediately after the `hitTest` call's parentheses, enter two equals signs followed by the Boolean value `true` (**Figure 7.36**).

11. Choose an action to be performed when this condition is met, and add it between the curly braces of the `if` statement.

    The final script should look like **Figure 7.37**.

12. Test your movie (**Figure 7.38**).

✔ Tips

- When you're checking `true`/`false` values (known as *Boolean values*) in an `if` statement as you do in this task, you can test the value and leave out the last part, `== true`. Flash returns true or a false when you call the `hitTest()` method, and the `if` statement tests `true` and `false` values. You'll learn more about conditional statements in Part V.
- It doesn't matter whether you test the moving movie clip to the target or the target to the moving movie clip. The following two statements detect the same collision:

```
spaceship_mc.hitTest(asteroid_mc)
asteroid_mc.hitTest(spaceship_mc)
```

To detect an intersection between a point and a movie clip:

1. Continuing with the same file you created in the preceding task, select the first frame of the root Timeline, and open the Actions panel.
2. Place your pointer within the parentheses of the if statement.
3. Change the condition so it reads as follows:

   `asteroid_mc.hitTest(spaceship_mc._x, spaceship_mc._y, true)`

   The `hitTest()` method now checks whether the x and y positions of the draggable movie clip `spaceship_mc` intersect with the shape of the movie clip `asteroid_mc` (**Figure 7.39**).
4. Test your movie.

✔ Tip

- The MovieClip class's properties `_xmouse` and `_ymouse` are values of the current x and y positions of the pointer on the screen. You can use these properties in the parameters of the `hitTest()` method to check whether the pointer intersects a movie clip. This expression returns true if the pointer intersects the movie clip `asteroid_mc`:

```
asteroid_mc.hitTest(_root._xmouse,
_root._ymouse, true)
```

```
spaceship_mc.onPress = function() {
    this.startDrag(true);
};
spaceship_mc.onRelease = function() {
    stopDrag();
};
_root.onEnterFrame = function() {
    if (asteroid_mc.hitTest(spaceship_mc._x, spaceship_mc._y, true) == true) {
        spaceship_mc.nextFrame();
    }
};
```

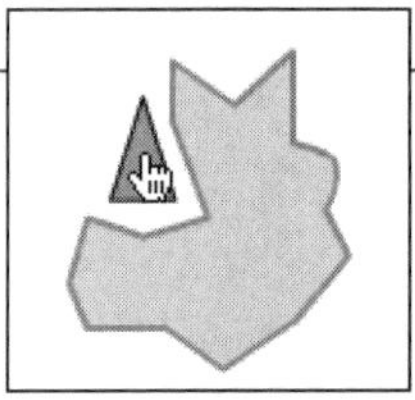

Figure 7.39 The ActionScript (above) tests whether the registration point of the `spaceship_mc` movie clip intersects with any shape in the `asteroid_mc` movie clip. Notice that the spaceship is safe from collision because its registration point is within the crevice and clear of the asteroid.

Detecting Dropped Movie Clips with _droptarget

Another way to detect whether a draggable movie clip has been dropped onto another is to use the movie clip property `_droptarget`. This property retrieves the absolute target path of another movie clip where the draggable movie clip was dropped. The second movie clip is the destination for the draggable movie clip. Use a conditional statement to compare whether the `_droptarget` value of the draggable movie clip is the same as the target path of the destination movie clip. Perform any actions based on whether the condition is true or false.

A word of caution: the `_droptarget` property returns the absolute target path in slash syntax. This property originated in Flash 4, which supported only the slash syntax. (ActionScript 2.0 does *not* support slash syntax.) However, you can get the target path of a movie clip in slash syntax by accessing that clip's `_target` property. For example, to test whether the `_droptarget` property matches the target path of a destination movie clip, you construct a conditional statement that looks like the following:

```
draggableMovieClip_mc._droptarget ==
destinationMovieClip_mc._target
```

Using the methods you learned in the preceding task, create a draggable movie clip (**Figure 7.40**).

Test the `_droptarget` property in a conditional statement after the `stopDrag()` statement.

Figure 7.41 is a completed script that makes `burger_mc` invisible when it's dropped on `trashCan_mc`.

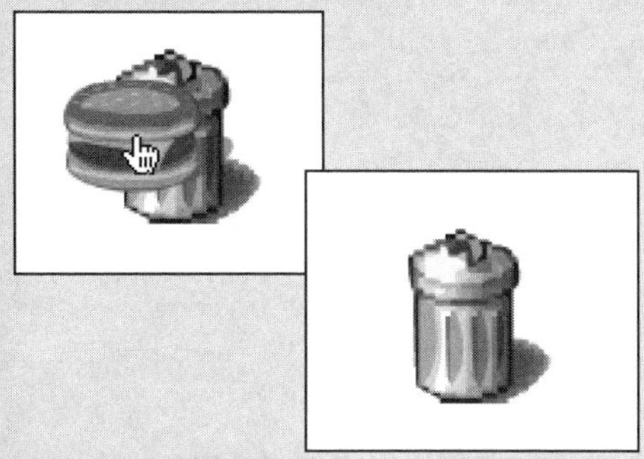

Figure 7.40 The hamburger disappears when it's dropped on the trash can.

```
burger_mc.onPress = function() {
    // begin dragging this movie clip
    this.startDrag();
};
burger_mc.onRelease = function() {
    // stop dragging this movie clip
    stopDrag();
    // check to see if this movie clip
    // is dropped on the destination movie clip
    if (this._droptarget == trashCan_mc._target) {
        // if it's true, then make it invisible
        this._visible = false;
    }
};
```

Figure 7.41 If the draggable movie clip is dropped on the movie clip `trashCan_mc`, its visibility is set to false.

Getting the Boundaries of Movie Clips

Often, when you're changing the dimensions and location of a movie clip dynamically, you need to know its boundaries to keep limitations on those changes. You can create a map that your viewer can move around or zoom in on for more details by setting the _x, _y, _xscale, and _yscale properties of the map movie clip. But you also want to know where the edges of the map are so you can make sure they're never exposed. The method to use to do this is getBounds(). This method gets the minimum and maximum dimensions of a movie clip's bounding box and puts the information in a generic object containing the properties xMin, xMax, yMin, and yMax. If you call your bounding box object myBounds, the value of the movie clip's left edge is myBounds.xMin, the right edge is myBounds.xMax, the top edge is myBounds.yMin, and the bottom edge is myBounds.yMax (**Figure 7.42**).

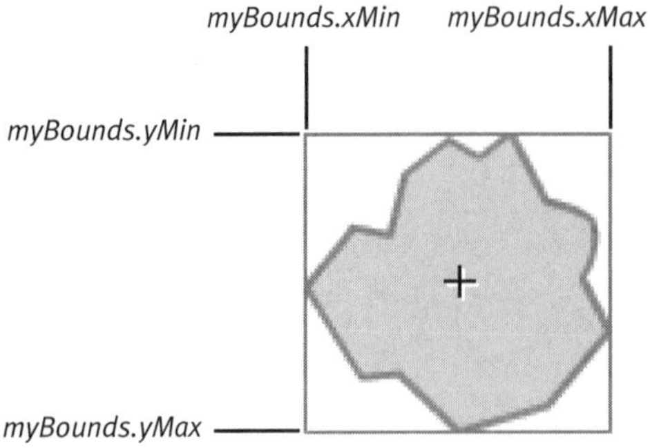

Figure 7.42 The xMin, xMax, yMin, and yMax properties of a boundary object refer to the edges of a movie clip whose boundaries have been retrieved.

To get the boundaries of a movie clip:

1. Create a movie clip symbol, place an instance of it on the Stage, and give it a name in the Property inspector.
   This clip will be the movie clip whose boundaries you'll determine.
2. Select the first frame on the root Timeline, and open the Actions panel.
3. Declare a generic object (data type Object) that will hold the boundary information, and enter an equals sign.
4. Choose ActionScript 2.0 Classes > Movie > MovieClip > Methods > getBounds.

```
var myBounds:Object = square_mc.getBounds()
```

Figure 7.43 myBounds is the boundary object, and square_mc is the movie clip whose boundaries you're interested in finding.

```
var myBounds:Object = square_mc.getBounds(_root);
```

Figure 7.44 getBounds() retrieves the minimum x (xMin), minimum y (yMin), maximum x (xMax), and maximum y (xMax) values of the movie clip square_mc relative to the _root clip's coordinates and stores that information in the object myBounds.

```
Output
Level #0:
Variable _level0.$version = "MAC 8,0,0,450"
Variable _level0.myBounds = [object #1] {
    xMin:47.9,
    xMax:268.05,
    yMin:28.4,
    yMax:178.6
  }
Movie Clip: Target="_level0.square_mc"
Movie Clip: Target="_level0.ship_mc"
```

Figure 7.45 The myBounds object and its properties are listed in the Output window when you choose List Variables in test mode.

5. Replace the default placeholder `not_set_yet` with the target path to the movie clip whose boundary box you want to retrieve (**Figure 7.43**).

   The results of the `getBounds()` method will be assigned to the name of your object. The method, however, still needs a `targetCoordinateSpace` parameter.

6. Between the parentheses of the `getBounds()` method, enter a target path to the Timeline whose x-y coordinate space you want to use as the reference for the boundary information (**Figure 7.44**).

   Flash gets the boundaries of the movie clip on the Stage. The boundaries are made relative to the root Timeline. All this information is put in an object whose properties contain the minimum and maximum x and y values.

7. Test your movie.

   Choose Debug > List Variables to verify the boundaries of the movie clip (**Figure 7.45**). Use the object properties `xMin`, `yMin`, `xMax`, and `yMax` as constraints on other interactivity. Use the boundary properties to constrain a draggable movie clip, for example (**Figure 7.46**).

```
var myBounds:Object = square_mc.getBounds(_root);
ship_mc.startDrag(true, myBounds.xMin, myBounds.yMin, myBounds.xMax, myBounds.yMax);
```

Figure 7.46 Using the boundary information as the parameters for the startDrag() method constrains a draggable movie clip to the edges of the square_mc movie clip.

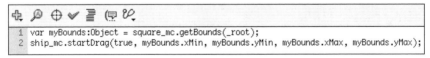

Generating Movie Clips Dynamically

Creating movie clips on the fly—that is, during playback—opens a new world of exciting interactive possibilities. Imagine a game of Asteroids in which enemy spaceships appear as the game progresses. You can store those enemy spaceships as movie clip symbols in your Library and create instances on the Stage with ActionScript as you need them. Or, if you want an infinite supply of a certain draggable item (such as merchandise) to be pulled off the shelf of an online store, you can make a duplicate of the movie clip each time the viewer drags it away from its original spot. Or create afterimages of a movie clip's motion, much like onion skinning, by duplicating a movie clip and making it lag as it moves across the screen. All the while, you maintain the power to modify properties, control the position of the playhead in those Timelines, and use the clips as you would any other movie clips.

Flash has many methods that enable dynamically generated movie clips. Among them are the `MovieClip` class's `duplicateMovieClip()`, `attachMovie()`, and `createEmptyMovieClip()` methods.

Duplicating movie clips

When you use the `duplicateMovieClip()` method, an exact replica of the instance that calls the method is created in the same position as the original. Duplicate movie clip instances are given their own unique names as well as a specific depth level for each instance. This depth level determines stacking order, as described in the earlier discussion of the movie clip method `swapDepths()`.

It's common practice to duplicate movie clips by using looping functions to store movie clip instances in an `Array` and assign depth levels automatically. For example, duplicating a movie clip `asteroid_mc` in this manner can produce duplicates in depth level 1, 2, 3, and so on, and store them all in an `Array` where they can be accessed any time. Check out Chapter 10 to learn about the looping actions that complement the duplication of movie clips.

To duplicate a movie clip instance:

1. Create a movie clip symbol, place an instance of it on the Stage, and name it in the Property inspector.
2. Create a button symbol, place an instance of it on the Stage, and name it in the Property inspector.
3. Select the first frame of the root Timeline, and open the Actions panel.
4. Enter the name of your button in the Script pane followed by a period.
5. Choose ActionScript 2.0 Classes > Movie > Button > Event Handlers > onRelease. (**Figure 7.47**).
6. On the next line, declare a new variable with its type defined as `MovieClip`; enter an equals sign.

   This variable will be used to refer to your new movie clip once it's created.
7. Following the equals sign, enter the name of your original movie clip; then choose ActionScript 2.0 Classes > Movie > MovieClip > Methods > duplicateMovieClip.

   The `duplicateMovieClip` method appears within the `onRelease` event handler in the Script pane.
8. With your pointer between the parentheses, enter the name for the new (duplicate) movie clip, followed by a comma.

   Make sure the new name is surrounded by quotation marks.

9. Enter a number to specify the stacking order for your duplicate movie clip (**Figure 7.48**).

   At this point, when you play your movie, the actions assigned to your button duplicate the `nerd_mc` movie clip; but the new instance appears right above the original, so you can't see whether anything happened. To see the duplicate, you need to move or change it in some way to make it stand out from the original.

10. On a new line, enter the name of the `MovieClip` variable you declared in step 6; add a period and the `_x` property followed by `+= 40`.

    This expression adds 40 to the x position of the original movie clip. The assignment operator += tells Flash to move the object 40 pixels to the right.

11. Add more statements to transform the duplicate movie clip.

12. Test the movie (**Figure 7.49**).

```
duplicateButton_btn.onRelease = function() {

};
```

Figure 7.47 The `onRelease` event handler for the button `duplicateButton_btn` is created.

```
duplicateButton_btn.onRelease = function() {
    var nerdCopy_mc:MovieClip = nerd_mc.duplicateMovieClip("nerdCopy_mc", 2);
};
```

Figure 7.48 The duplicate movie clip `nerdCopy_mc` is made in depth level 2 from the movie clip `nerd_mc`.

```
duplicateButton_btn.onRelease = function() {
    var nerdCopy_mc:MovieClip = nerd_mc.duplicateMovieClip("nerdCopy_mc", 2);
    nerdCopy_mc._x += 40;
    nerdCopy_mc._xscale = 75;
    nerdCopy_mc._yscale = 110;
};
```

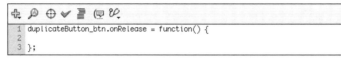

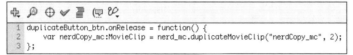

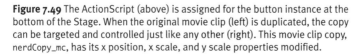

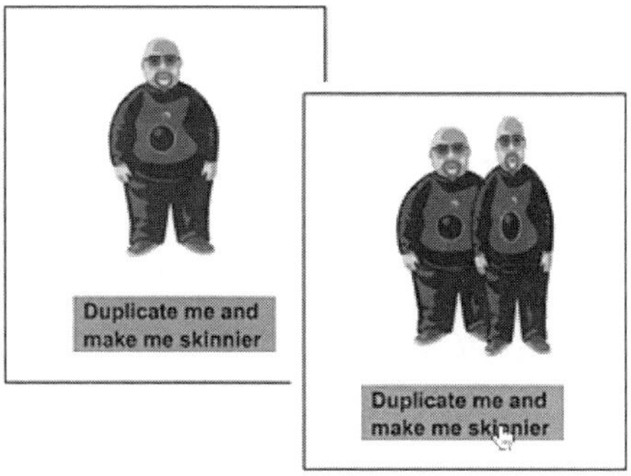

Figure 7.49 The ActionScript (above) is assigned for the button instance at the bottom of the Stage. When the original movie clip (left) is duplicated, the copy can be targeted and controlled just like any other (right). This movie clip copy, `nerdCopy_mc`, has its x position, x scale, and y scale properties modified.

✔ Tips

- You can have only one movie clip instance per depth level. If you duplicate another instance in a level that's already occupied, that instance replaces the first one.
- Duplicate movie clips inherit the properties of the original instance. If the original instance has an alpha transparency of 50 percent, for example, the duplicate movie clip instance also has an alpha transparency of 50 percent. Duplicate instances always start in frame 1, however, even if the original movie clip instance is in a different frame when it's duplicated.
- Duplicate movie clips also take on any ActionScript that may be assigned to the original instance. If the original instance contains ActionScript that makes it a draggable movie clip, for example, the duplicate is also draggable.
- The depth level corresponds to the same depth level in the movie clip method `swapDepths()`. Use `swapDepths()` to change the stacking order of duplicated movie clips.

Attaching movie clips

The technique of duplicating movie clips is useful for existing movie clips, but what if you need to dynamically place a *new* movie clip on the Stage from the Library? In this situation, you turn to the `attachMovie()` method. This method lets you create new instances of movie clips from the Library and attach them to existing movie clip instances already on the Stage or to the root Timeline. The attached movie clip doesn't replace the original but becomes part of the movie clip object in a parent/child relationship. If the original instance on the Stage is `parentClip_mc`, the target path for the attached movie clip will be something like

```
_root.parentClip_mc.attachedClip_mc
```

If a movie clip attaches to the root Timeline, the target path is

```
_root.attachedClip_mc
```

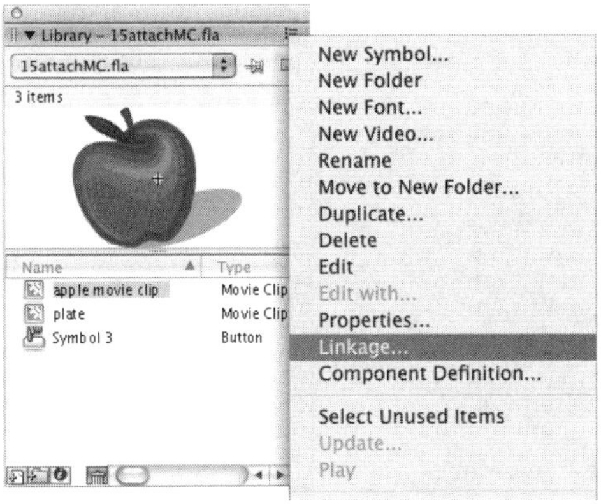

Figure 7.50 The Linkage option in the Library panel's Options menu.

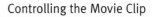

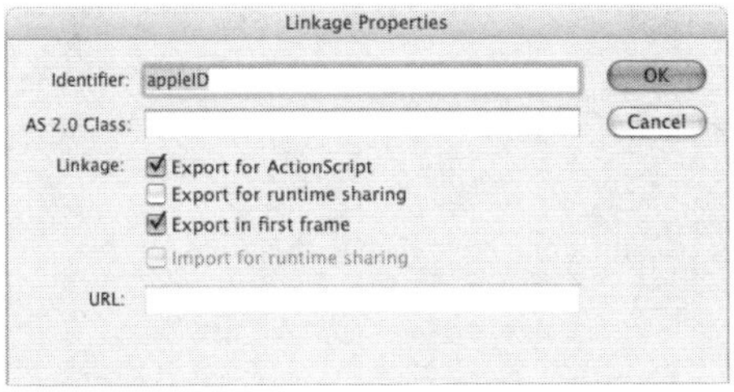

Figure 7.51 The Linkage Properties dialog box.

To attach a movie clip from the Library:

1. Create a movie clip symbol, place an instance of it from the Library on the Stage, and give it a name in the Property inspector.

   This instance will be the original, parent instance to which you'll attach another movie clip.

2. Create another movie clip symbol, and select it in the Library.

3. From the Library Options menu, choose Linkage (**Figure 7.50**).

   The Linkage Properties dialog box appears.

4. In the Linkage section, select Export for ActionScript and leave "Export in first frame" selected; in the Identifier field, enter a unique name for your movie clip; then, click OK (**Figure 7.51**).

   The identifier allows you to call on this movie clip by name from ActionScript and attach it to an instance on the Stage.

5. Create a button, drag an instance of it to the Stage, and name it in the Property inspector.

6. Select the first frame of the root Timeline, and open the Actions panel.

7. Create an `onRelease` event handler for your button.

8. Inside the event handler function, enter the target path of the movie clip instance on the Stage, followed by a period.

   This instance is the one to which you'll attach the new instance.

9. Choose ActionScript 2.0 Classes > Movie > MovieClip > attachMovie.

continues on next page

10. With your pointer between the parentheses, enter the identifier of the movie clip symbol in the Library, a name for the newly attached instance, and a depth level, separating your parameters with commas (**Figure 7.52**).

    The identifier and new name must be in quotation marks.

11. Test your movie.

    When you click the button that you created, the movie clip identified in the Library attaches to the instance on Stage and overlaps it. The registration point of the attached movie clip lines up with the registration point of the parent instance (**Figure 7.53**).

    You need to keep several names straight when you use the `attachMovie()` method. In this example, the name of the movie clip symbol in the Library is apple movie clip. The name of the identifier is `appleID`. The name of the attached instance is `attachedApple_mc`.

✔ Tips

- You can always attach movie clips to the root Timeline by calling the method `attachMovie()` on _root. The registration point of the attached instance is aligned with the top-left corner (x = 0, y = 0) of the Stage.
- An attached movie clip takes on the properties of the movie clip instance to which it attaches. If the original movie clip instance is rotated 45 degrees, the attached movie clip is also rotated 45 degrees.

```
appleButton_btn.onRelease = function() {
    plate_mc.attachMovie("appleID", "attachedApple_mc", 1);
};
```

Figure 7.52 The `attachMovie()` method requires the parameters `idName`, `newName`, and `depth`. This `attachMovie()` method attaches the movie clip identified as `appleID` to the instance `plate_mc` in depth level 1 and names the attached instance `attachedApple_mc`.

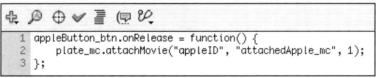

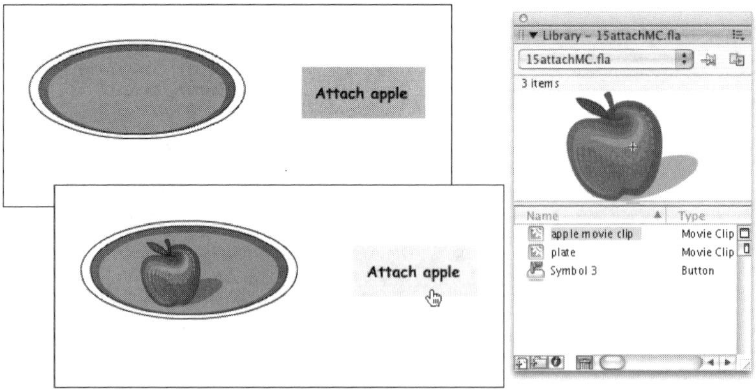

Figure 7.53 The movie clip instance `plate_mc` sits on the Stage (top). The actions assigned for the button attach an instance of the `apple_mc` movie clip from the Library (right) to the `plate_mc` instance (bottom).

- You can attach multiple movie clips to the same parent instance as long as you specify different depth levels. Each depth level can hold only one movie clip.
- You can attach movie clips to a recently attached movie clip. The target path for the first attached movie clip becomes `_root.parentClip_mc.attachedClip1_mc`, the target path for another attached movie clip becomes `_root.parentClip_mc.attachedClip1_mc.attachedClip2_mc`, and so on.
- Just as you did with the method `duplicateMovieClip()` in an earlier task, you can assign a movie clip created with the `attachMovie()` method to a variable (the value returned by the `attachMovie()` method is the newly created movie clip). You can then use that variable to refer to the dynamically created movie clip.
- You can't attach a movie clip to another movie clip that has an external file loaded into it (see Chapter 6 for the `loadMovie` action and the files that can be dynamically loaded using `loadMovie`).

Creating empty movie clips

When you use `attachMovieClip()`, you need to prepare a movie clip symbol in your Library by creating it at author time, assigning an identifier, and marking it to export for ActionScript. If you need an empty movie clip—a movie clip without graphics, animations, or attached scripts—use the method `createEmptyMovieClip()`. This method is similar to `attachMovie()` in that it attaches a movie clip dynamically to another movie clip already on the Stage. But instead of attaching a movie clip symbol from the Library, it creates and attaches a new, empty movie clip. As with `attachMovie()` and `duplicateMovieClip()`, you give each newly created empty movie clip a unique name and depth level.

Use empty movie clips as shells in preparation for additional content that may be loaded into your Flash movie. Create an empty movie clip on the root Timeline, and modify its x and y properties to position it anywhere on the Stage. Then you can use `loadMovie()` to load external SWF files or images into your empty movie clip. Or, use empty movie clips as the parent clip for the `attachMovie()` method.

Empty movie clips are also important for movie clip drawing methods. You'll learn to draw lines, curves, fills, and gradients just by using ActionScript. An empty movie clip provides a canvas on which to draw with these drawing methods.

To create an empty movie clip on the root Timeline:

1. Select the first frame of the root Timeline, and open the Actions panel.
2. In the Script pane, enter `_root`, followed by a period.
3. Choose ActionScript 2.0 Classes > Movie > MovieClip > Methods > createEmptyMovieClip.

   An empty movie clip is created and attached to the root Timeline.
4. Between the parentheses, enter a unique name for your empty movie clip as well as a unique depth level.

   Separate your parameters with commas, and make sure your movie clip's name is in quotation marks (**Figure 7.54**).

   A movie clip with the name you've chosen is created on the root Timeline at the specified depth level.

✔ Tip

- The `createEmptyMovieClip` method returns a reference to the newly created clip, which can be assigned to a variable. You can then use the variable to manipulate the movie clip rather than needing to use the full target path.

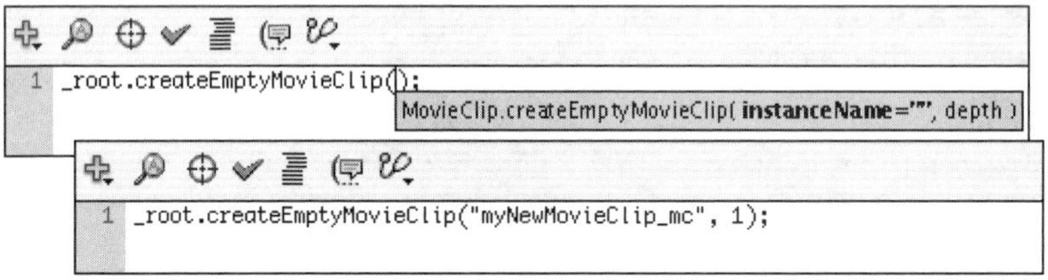

Figure 7.54 Code hints in the Script pane indicate the parameters to use (top) to create a new empty movie clip `myNewMovieClip_mc` on the root Timeline in depth level 1 (bottom).

Removing Movie Clips Dynamically

Just as you can generate movie clips dynamically, you can remove them dynamically. You can delete movie clip instances that have been duplicated or attached, delete empty movie clips, and even delete movie clip instances that were put on the Stage at author time.

To remove a movie clip created dynamically:

1. Choose ActionScript 2.0 Classes > Movie > MovieClip > Methods > removeMovieClip.
2. Replace the placeholder text `not_set_yet` with the target path of the movie clip to remove (**Figure 7.55**).

✔ Tip

- A similar (older) movie clip method, `unloadMovie()`, also removes movie clips from the Stage. However, `unloadMovie()` doesn't delete the movie clip from the computer's memory—just from the Stage—so `removeMovieClip()` is the preferred way to delete movie clips.

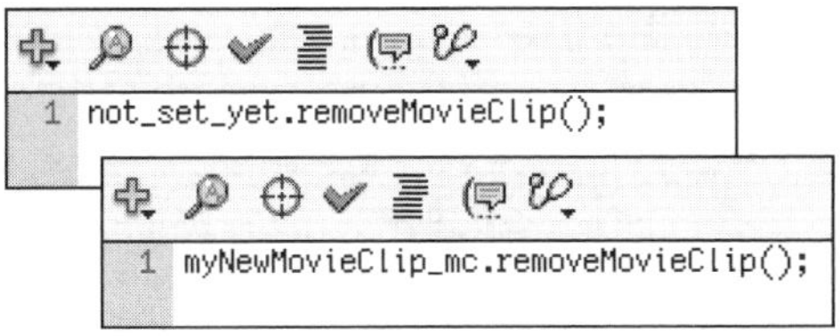

Figure 7.55 Use `removeMovieClip` to remove dynamically generated movie clips. This statement removes the `myNewMovieClip_mc` movie clip from the Stage.

Removing movie clips placed on the Stage

Unlike dynamically created movie clips, movie clips placed on the Stage at author time usually can't be deleted using `removeMovieClip()`. However, this limitation is easy to get around.

When a SWF file is published, any movie clips created at author time are given a depth that is negative (less than 0). When the `removeMovieClip()` method is called on a movie clip with a negative depth, the Flash Player ignores the method. However, by using the `swapDepths()` method with a numeric depth as the parameter, you can shift a movie clip created in the authoring tool from the negative depth it was assigned by Flash to a positive depth—essentially turning it into a dynamically created movie clip from the Flash Player's perspective. At that point, you can call the `removeMovieClip()` method on that movie clip, and it will be removed as expected.

To remove a movie clip placed on the Stage at author time:

1. Enter the target path of the movie clip, and choose ActionScript 2.0 Classes > Movie > MovieClip > Methods > swapDepths.
2. In the parentheses, enter a positive number that isn't the depth of any movie clips on the Stage.
3. On the next line, enter the target path of the movie clip; choose ActionScript 2.0 Classes > Movie > MovieClip > Methods > removeMovieClip.

Getting Movie Clip Depth Levels

When you're working with a movie clip, you may need to control the depth level at which an instance shows up at run time. As you've learned so far, every movie clip has an associated depth level, which determines whether it displays in front of or behind another object.

When you create a new movie clip using the `createEmptyMovieClip()` method, you're required to define the new object's depth level as a parameter. But how do you know what depth level to choose? After all, if you've already been generating movie clips dynamically, you may not know the depth levels for each of them. The method `getNextHighestDepth()` can tell you the next available depth value.

On the other hand, if you want to manipulate the movie clip that is occupying a certain depth level, you can use the `getInstanceAtDepth()` method. This method helps you target and manipulate particular movie clips that have been generated at run time.

In addition, you can use the combination of `getInstanceAtDepth()` and `getNextHighestDepth()` to control the placement of a movie clip at a specific depth level and even x and y positioning.

To position dynamically attached movie clips:

1. Create two movie clip symbols in the Library (Insert > New Symbol). Give each a unique ID name in the Linkage Properties dialog box.
   Don't add instances of these symbols to the Stage.
2. Select the first frame of the root Timeline, and open the Actions panel.
3. Enter the target path `_root`, followed by a period.
4. Choose ActionScript 2.0 Classes > Movie > MovieClip > createEmptyMovieClip.
5. Within the parentheses, enter an instance name and depth level for your new movie clip (**Figure 7.56**).
   An empty movie clip is generated on the main Stage.
6. On the next line, enter the instance name of your newly created movie clip followed by a period, the `_x` property and an equals sign, and a value for the x position.
7. Repeat step 6 for the y position of your movie clip (**Figure 7.57**).
   Your empty movie clip is positioned at the specified x and y coordinates.
8. On the next line, enter the instance name of your movie clip, followed by a period.
9. Choose ActionScript 2.0 Classes > Movie > MovieClip > methods > attachMovie.
10. Enter the ID name for the first movie clip instance in your Library followed by a new instance name and a depth level of 10.
    The ID name and new instance name must be surrounded by quotation marks.
11. Repeat step 10 to attach the second movie clip at a depth level of 20.
12. On the next line, enter the instance name of your movie clip followed by a period.
13. Choose ActionScript 2.0 Classes > Movie > MovieClip > Methods > getInstanceAtDepth.

```
_root.createEmptyMovieClip("myClip_mc", 1);
```

Figure 7.56 An empty movie clip named `myClip_mc` has been created and placed on level 1.

```
_root.createEmptyMovieClip("myClip_mc", 1);
myClip_mc._x = 15;
myClip_mc._y = 50;
```

Figure 7.57 At run time, the empty movie clip `myClip_mc` will position itself at the x position 15 and the y position 50.

```
_root.createEmptyMovieClip("myClip_mc", 1);
myClip_mc._x = 15;
myClip_mc._y = 50;

myClip_mc.attachMovie("girl1", "girl1_mc", 10);
myClip_mc.attachMovie("girl2", "girl2_mc", 20);

myClip_mc.getInstanceAtDepth(20)._x = 134;
myClip_mc.getInstanceAtDepth(20)._y = 42;
```

Figure 7.58 The movie clip at depth level 20 is moved to the x position 134 and the y position 42.

14. Enter a depth level of 20 inside of the parentheses. Place your pointer to the right of the closing parenthesis; enter a period followed by the _x property, an equals sign, and then a value for the x position.

Flash retrieves the name of the instance at depth level 20 and assigns it a specific x position.

15. Repeat step 14 to define the y position for the attached movie clip in level 20 (**Figure 7.58**).

16. Test your movie.

At run time, Flash initially attaches the two movie clip instances to the empty movie clip. The instance at depth level 20 is then placed at the exact x and y positions that you define (**Figure 7.59**).

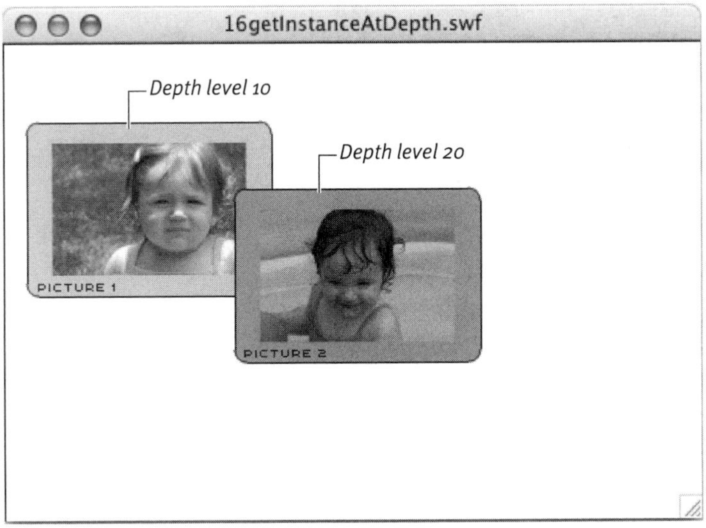

Figure 7.59 At run time, Flash places `girl1_mc` at the x position 15 and the y position 50 and `girl2_mc` at the x position 134 and the y position 42.

To control the depth level and positioning of a dynamically placed movie clip:

1. Continuing with the file you used in the preceding task, place a button instance on the root Timeline. In the Property inspector, assign an instance name (**Figure 7.60**).

   This button will add a dynamically placed movie clip at a depth level it obtains using the `getNextHighestDepth()` method.

2. Select the first frame of the main Timeline, and open the Actions panel.

3. Create a new line after your last line of code from the preceding task.

4. Assign an `onRelease` handler to the button.

5. Inside the event handler function, choose Statements > Variables > var.

6. Enter the variable name `newDepth` and then `:Number`, followed by an equals sign. Enter the name of the empty movie clip created in the preceding task, followed by a period. Choose ActionScript 2.0 Classes > Movie > MovieClip > Methods > getNextHighestDepth (**Figure 7.61**).

   A new variable named `newDepth` is created and will store the next available depth level of movie clips attached to your empty movie clip.

7. On the next line, enter the instance name of the empty movie clip followed by a period.

8. Choose ActionScript 2.0 Classes > Movie > MovieClip > Methods > attachMovie.

9. With your pointer between the parentheses, enter an ID name, a new name, and a depth level of `newDepth`.

   The new movie clip is attached to the empty movie clip at depth `newDepth`.

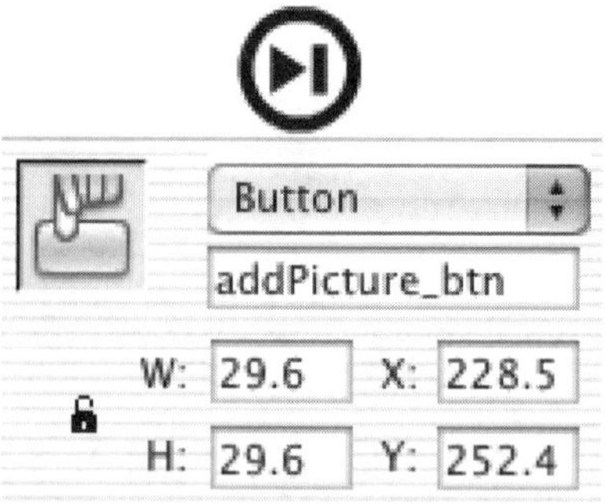

Figure 7.60 A new button is placed on the root Timeline and given an instance name of `addPicture_btn` in the Property inspector.

```

addPicture_btn.onRelease = function() {
    var newDepth:Number = myClip_mc.getNextHighestDepth();
};
```

Figure 7.61 A variable named `newDepth` has been created within the `onRelease` event, which will contain the next highest depth for the empty movie clip.

```
addPicture_btn.onRelease = function() {
    var newDepth:Number = myClip_mc.getNextHighestDepth();
    myClip_mc.attachMovie("girl3", "girl3_mc", newDepth);
    myClip_mc.getInstanceAtDepth(newDepth)._x = 261;
    myClip_mc.getInstanceAtDepth(newDepth)._y = 91;
};
```

Figure 7.62 The movie clip girl3 is assigned an x position of 261 and a y position of 91.

```
_root.createEmptyMovieClip("myClip_mc", 1);
myClip_mc._x = 15;
myClip_mc._y = 50;

myClip_mc.attachMovie("girl1", "girl1_mc", 10);
myClip_mc.attachMovie("girl2", "girl2_mc", 20);

myClip_mc.getInstanceAtDepth(20)._x = 134;
myClip_mc.getInstanceAtDepth(20)._y = 42;

addPicture_btn.onRelease = function() {
    var newDepth:Number = myClip_mc.getNextHighestDepth();
    myClip_mc.attachMovie("girl3", "girl3_mc", newDepth);
    myClip_mc.getInstanceAtDepth(newDepth)._x = 261;
    myClip_mc.getInstanceAtDepth(newDepth)._y = 91;
    trace("A new movie clip was placed at level " + newDepth);
};
```

Figure 7.63 The `trace` statement is added to the `onPress` event and will display the current depth level of the new movie clip when the button is clicked.

10. Using the `getInstanceAtDepth()` method, assign x and y values to the new movie clip (**Figure 7.62**).

11. On the next line, choose Global Functions > Miscellaneous Functions > trace.

12. Concatenate text and the variable `newDepth` to display a message in the Output window (**Figure 7.63**).

13. Test your movie.

    When you click your button, a new movie clip is attached to the next highest level. The Output window displays the depth level information (**Figure 7.64**).

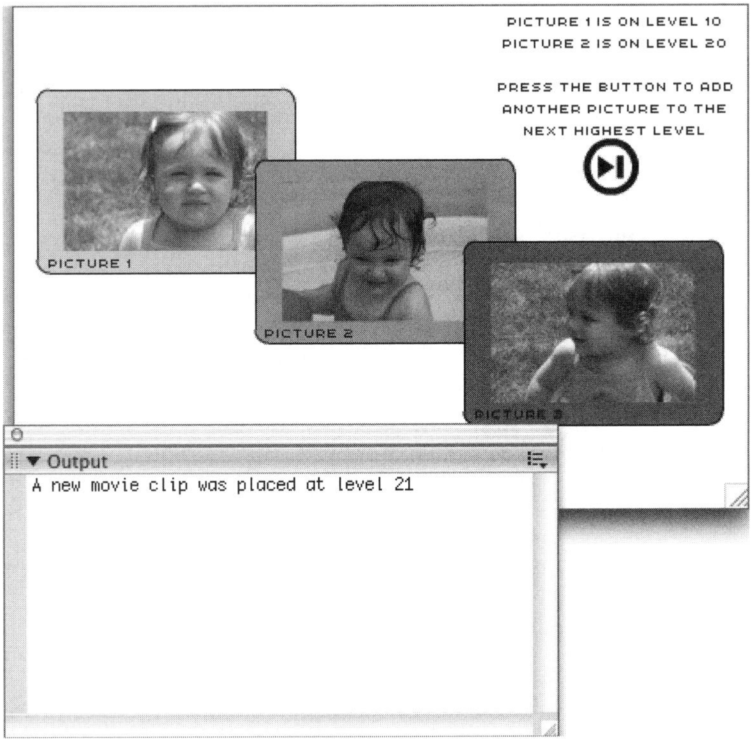

Figure 7.64 When the button is clicked, a new movie clip is placed at the next available level. The output window displays the level at which the movie clip is placed.

GETTING MOVIE CLIP DEPTH LEVELS

Creating Shapes Dynamically

A special category of movie clip methods is reserved for creating lines, curves, fills, and gradients. These methods are the drawing methods of the movie clip, known in Flash as the *Drawing API*. With these methods, you can create your own shapes and control their color, transparency, stroke width, and even the kind and placement of gradient strokes and fills. You can use the drawing methods to create your own simple paint and coloring application, or you can draw bar graphs or pie charts or connect data points to visualize numerical data that your viewer inputs.

To use the drawing methods, you must start with a movie clip. The movie clip acts as the canvas that holds the drawing you create. It also acts as the point of reference for all your drawing coordinates. If your movie clip is anchored at the top-left corner of the Stage (at x = 0, y = 0), all the drawing coordinates are relative to that registration point. The movie clip also keeps track of the current drawing point, like a pen tip, anchoring the start of a line or curve and keeping track of its end point as you tell it to draw. The movie clip doesn't move; it just remembers the location of its virtual pen tip.

Although you can use any movie clip to begin drawing, the most common way is to use the method `createEmptyMovieClip()` to create an empty movie clip on the root Timeline. The new movie clip is positioned at the top-left corner of the Stage automatically, so its drawing coordinates are identical to the Stage coordinates. Use **Figure 7.65** to review the Stage coordinates.

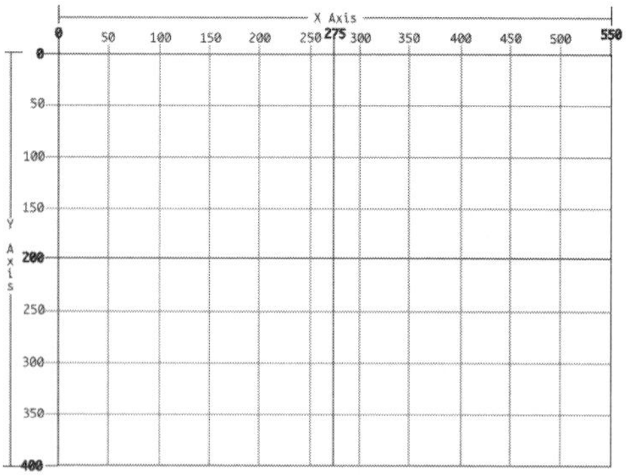

Figure 7.65 An overview of the default Stage size, 550 pixels in width by 400 pixels in height. The upper-left corner is x = 0 and y = 0, and the lower-right corner is x = 550 and y = 400.

Creating lines and curves

Three of the `MovieClip` class's methods are used to draw lines and curves: `moveTo()`, `lineTo()`, and `curveTo()`. The `moveTo()` method sets the beginning point of your line or curve, like placing a pen on paper. The `lineTo()` and `curveTo()` methods set the end point and, in the case of curves, determine its curvature.

The `lineStyle()` method changes the characteristics of your stroke, such as its point size, color, and transparency. The `clear()` method erases all the drawing on a movie clip.

Color, line width, and transparency are just the beginning of the ways you can style lines you draw in ActionScript. Flash 8 provides additional line-style properties to control how lines scale and the style of the corners (*joins*) and ends (*caps*) of the lines you draw. You can also create lines that use a gradient rather than a solid color. All these techniques are demonstrated in the next several tasks.

To create lines:

1. Select the first frame of the root Timeline, and open the Actions panel.
2. Declare a variable with the data type `MovieClip`, and enter an equals sign.
3. Enter `_root`, followed by a period.
4. Choose ActionScript 2.0 Classes > Movie > MovieClip > Methods > createEmptyMovieClip.
5. For the method's parameters, enter a name for this movie clip and a depth level, making sure that your instance name is in quotation marks (**Figure 7.66**).

   An empty movie clip is created on the root Timeline at the top-left corner of the Stage, and the variable is given a reference to it.

continues on next page

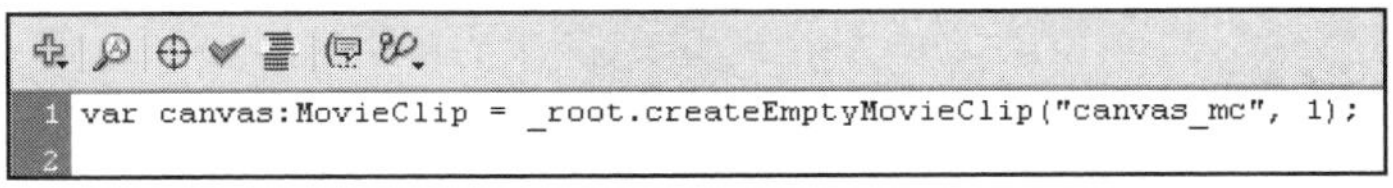

Figure 7.66 The empty movie clip canvas_mc will be the coordinate space for the drawing and will track the virtual pen.

6. On the next line, enter the name of your `MovieClip` variable, followed by a period.
7. Choose ActionScript 2.0 Classes > Movie > MovieClip > Drawing Methods > lineStyle.
8. With your pointer between the parentheses, enter the thickness of the line, the RGB color in hex code, and its transparency, separating your parameters with commas (**Figure 7.67**).

   The thickness is a number from 0 to 255; 0 is hairline thickness, and 255 is the maximum point thickness.

   The RGB parameter is the hex code referring to the color of the line. You can find the hex code for any color in the Color Mixer panel next to the color swatch. Red, for example, is `0xFF0000`.

   The transparency is a number from 0 to 100 for the line's alpha value; 0 is completely transparent, and 100 is completely opaque.
9. On the next line, enter your `MovieClip` variable's name followed by a period.
10. Choose ActionScript 2.0 Classes > Movie > MovieClip > Drawing Methods > moveTo.
11. With your pointer between the parentheses, enter the x- and y-coordinates where you want your line to start, separating the parameters with a comma (**Figure 7.68**).
12. On the next line, enter your variable's name followed by a period.
13. Choose ActionScript 2.0 Classes > Movie > MovieClip > Drawing Methods > lineTo.
14. With your pointer between the parentheses, enter the x- and y-coordinates of the end point of your line, separating the parameters with a comma (**Figure 7.69**).

    The end point of your line segment automatically becomes the beginning point for the next, so you don't need to use the `moveTo()` method to move the coordinates.
15. Continue adding more `lineTo()` methods to draw more line segments.

```
var canvas:MovieClip = _root.createEmptyMovieClip("canvas_mc", 1);
canvas.lineStyle(2, 0xFF0000, 100);
```

Figure 7.67 Define the line style (stroke thickness, color, and transparency) before you begin drawing.

```
var canvas:MovieClip = _root.createEmptyMovieClip("canvas_mc", 1);
canvas.lineStyle(2, 0xFF0000, 100);
canvas.moveTo(200, 200);
```

Figure 7.68 The beginning of this line is at x = 200, y = 200.

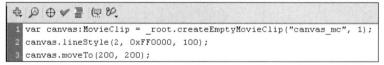

✔ Tips

- You can change the line style at any time, so multiple line segments can have different thicknesses, colors, transparencies, and so forth. Add a `lineStyle()` method before the `lineTo()` method whose line you want to modify.
- After you finish your drawing, you can modify its properties by modifying the properties of the movie clip. Or, you can affect the behavior of your drawing by calling a method of the movie clip. The drawing still belongs to the movie clip it was drawn in, so whatever you do to the clip affects the drawing. You can duplicate your drawing, for example, by using the `duplicateMovieClip()` method on the movie clip, or even make your drawing draggable by assigning a `startDrag()` method to the movie clip!
- Instead of creating an empty movie clip to control the drawing methods, you can use the root Timeline. But you don't have as much control of the root Timeline as you do a separate movie clip.

To create paths with square corners and ends:

1. Select the first frame of the root Timeline, and open the Actions panel.
2. Add code to declare a `MovieClip` variable, and assign it a new empty movie clip created on `_root`, as in the previous task.
3. On the next line, enter the name of your `MovieClip` variable followed by a period; choose ActionScript 2.0 Classes > Movie > MovieClip > Drawing Methods > lineStyle.
4. With your pointer between the parentheses, enter the thickness of the line, the RGB color in hex code, and its transparency, separating your parameters with commas.

   Choose a thickness large enough that you can see the shape of corners and ends.

continues on next page

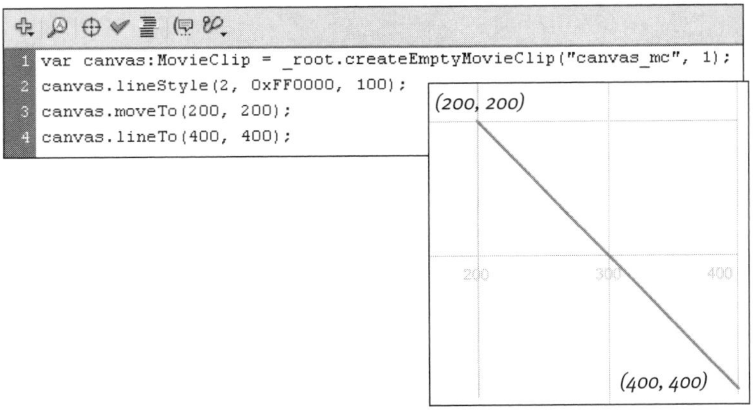

Figure 7.69 This diagonal line is drawn with a 2-point red stroke. The virtual pen tip is now positioned at x = 400, y = 400 and ready for a new `lineTo()` method.

5. Add additional parameters to the `lineStyle()` call for pixel hinting, scaling behavior, cap style, join style, and miter limit (**Figure 7.70**).

   Pixel hinting takes a `true/false` value. With pixel hinting on, Flash draws anchor and curve points on exact pixels rather than fractions of pixels, leading to smoother curves.

   Scaling behavior determines what happens to the line when the movie clip's size is scaled up or down. It can be one of four string values: `normal` means lines scale normally; `none` means line thickness doesn't scale; `vertical` means line thickness doesn't scale in the vertical direction; and `horizontal` means line thickness doesn't scale horizontally.

   The remaining three parameters, cap style, join style, and miter limit, are described in the sidebar "Cap and Join Styles."

6. Starting on the next line, add `moveTo()` and `lineTo()` method calls to draw line segments with corners (**Figure 7.71**).

```
var canvas:MovieClip = _root.createEmptyMovieClip("canvas_mc", 1);
canvas.lineStyle(8, 0xFF0000, 100, true, "none", "square", "miter");
```

Figure 7.70 Additional parameters added to the `lineStyle()` method call control the cap and join style and scaling of the lines. Here the line doesn't scale and has square caps and mitered joints.

```
var canvas:MovieClip = _root.createEmptyMovieClip("canvas_mc", 1);
canvas.lineStyle(8, 0xFF0000, 100, true, "none", "square", "miter");
canvas.moveTo(200, 200);
canvas.lineTo(300, 300);
canvas.lineTo(200, 400);
```

Figure 7.71 The complete code draws line segments with corners, which makes the cap and join styles apparent.

Cap and Join Styles

One common complaint with versions of Flash prior to Flash 8 was that the corners and ends of lines were rounded off, a problem that became noticeable when the line thickness was large. Consequently, Flash 8 has three new parameters for the `lineStyle` method to allow greater control over this aspect of line styling.

Figure 7.72 The three cap styles are (l-r) no caps, round, and square, drawn here with a thick line. The overlaid thin line shows the actual end point.

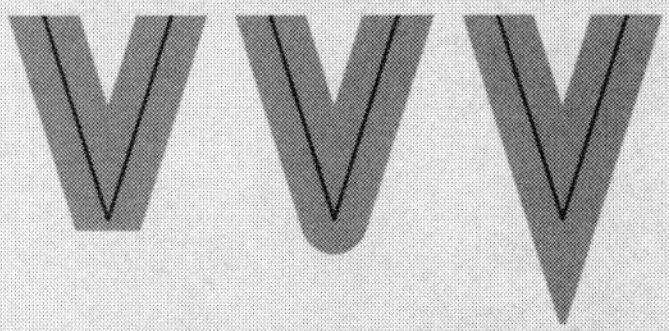

Figure 7.73 The three join styles, bevel (left), round (middle), and miter (right).

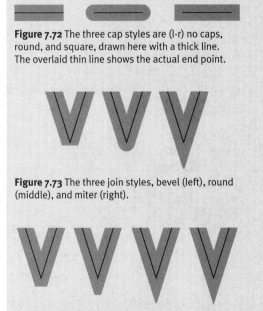

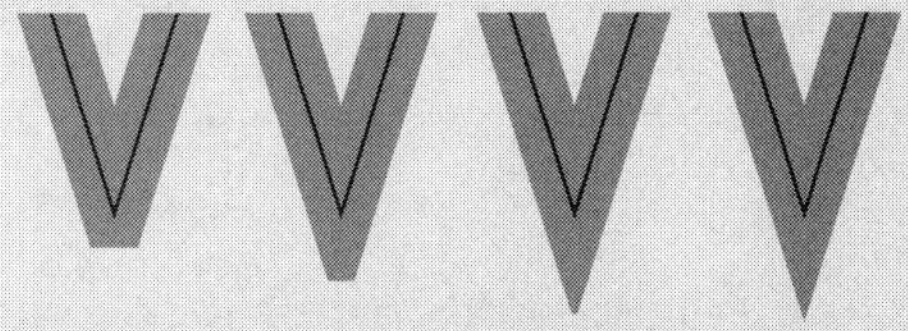

Figure 7.74 This small angle is chopped off with miter limits of 1, 2, and 3 but extends fully with a limit of 4 or greater.

The **cap style** parameter controls what the start and end of the lines will look like. The three options are (**Figure 7.72**) as follows:

- No cap (`"none"`): The end falls exactly at the end coordinate, resulting in a squared-off end.
- Round (`"round"`): The end is squared off and extends slightly beyond the end x, y coordinate to add thickness to the end.
- Square (`"square"`): The end is rounded and extends slightly beyond the end x, y coordinate to add thickness to the end.

The **join style** parameter determines the appearance of corners where two line segments are joined. These are the three options are (**Figure 7.73**):

- Bevel (`"bevel"`): The corner is flattened off perpendicular to the center of the angle and extends only slightly beyond the corner x, y coordinate.
- Round (`"round"`): The corner is rounded off and extends beyond the corner x, y coordinate.
- Miter (`"miter"`): The lines continue to a point beyond the corner coordinate. The point may be chopped short depending on the miter limit setting.

The **miter limit**, which is used only when the join style is set to Miter, determines how far an angle extends beyond the true corner point before it's chopped short. For small angles, without some sort of limit, the miter joint could extend across the width of the Stage or farther; the miter limit sets constraints on the joint.

The value you set is a number between 1 and 255. How this value translates into the actual distance that the angle extends before being cut short depends on the angle of the corner and the line thickness. In general, with small angles (smaller than 45 degrees), the default limit of 3 causes some trimming. It's a good idea to experiment with the specific line thickness and angle before using miter limits in a Flash movie. **Figure 7.74** shows some examples of different miter limits.

Creating gradient lines

Creating a solid colored line is simple: specify the color and alpha parameters in the `lineStyle()` method. To create a line that is drawn with a *gradient* color (a color that smoothly blends between two or more colors) is more involved. To create a gradient, after calling `lineStyle()` to indicate the line thickness, you then call the `lineGradientStyle` movie clip method, which takes various parameters that control the gradient's appearance:

Gradient type is either the string `"radial"` or the string `"linear"`. You must include the quotation marks. A radial gradient's colors are defined in rings from the inside to the outside. With a linear gradient, the colors are defined from left to right.

Colors takes an `Array` object of numeric color values. You must create an `Array` object and put the hex codes for the gradient colors into the array in the order in which you want them to appear. If you want blue on the left side of a linear gradient and red on the right side, for example, your array is created like this:

```
var colors:Array;
colors = new Array(0x0000FF,0xFF0000);
```

Alphas is also an `Array` object and contains the alpha values (0 through 100) corresponding to the colors in the order in which you want them to appear. If you want your blue on one side to be 50 percent transparent, you create an array like this:

```
var alphas:Array;
alphas = new Array (50,100);
```

Ratios is an array object containing values (0 through 255) that correspond to the colors, determining how they mix. The ratio value defines the point along the gradient where the color is at 100 percent. An array like `ratios = new Array(0, 127)` means that the blue is 100 percent at the left side and the red is 100 percent starting at the middle (**Figure 7.75**).

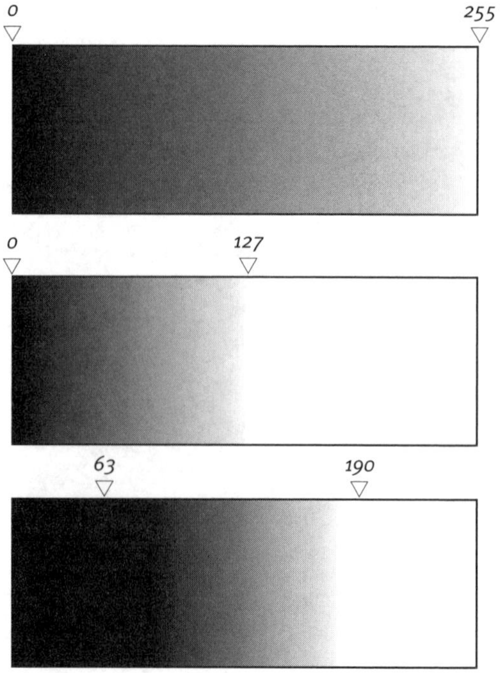

Figure 7.75 Ratios determine the mixing of colors for your gradient. The entire width of your gradient (or radius, for a radial gradient) is represented on a range from 0 through 255. Ratio values of (0,255) represent the typical gradient where each color is at one of the far sides (top). Ratio values of (0,127) create a tighter mixing in the first half of the gradient (middle). Ratio values of (63,190) create a tighter mixing in the middle of the gradient (bottom).

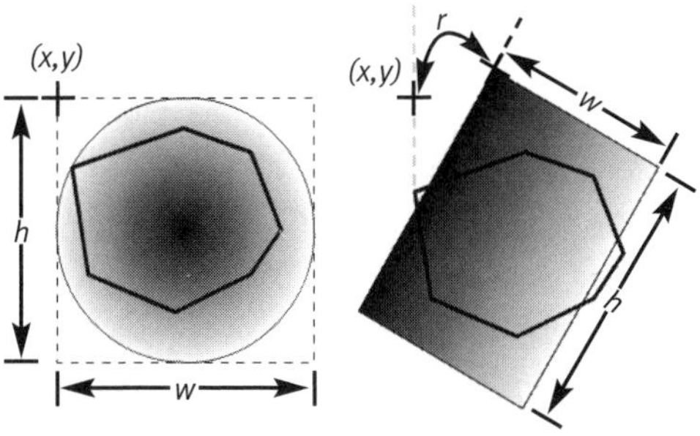

Figure 7.76 Parameters for the matrix type. A radial gradient (left) and a linear gradient (right) are shown superimposed on a shape they would fill. w and h are its width and height. r is the clockwise angle that it makes from the vertical. x and y are the position offset coordinates for the top-left corner of the gradient.

Matrix type is an object that represents size, position, scale, and rotation information. You can define properties that determine the size, position, and orientation of your gradient. You can use any of three matrix types: a `flash.geom.Matrix` object or a generic object in either box or matrix style. Using the `Matrix` class is a straightforward and powerful way to create the gradient. You create a matrix and specify width and height properties (in pixels), an angle property (in radians), and x and y offset (position) coordinates (**Figure 7.76**).

Spread method determines how the gradient behaves when the shape is larger than the gradient matrix. The parameter takes a string with one of three values: `"pad"` fills out the shape with solid color, using the end color of the gradient; `"repeat"` causes the gradient pattern to repeat; and `"reflect"` causes the pattern to repeat in a mirror image of itself.

Interpolation method instructs Flash how to calculate the blend between colors. The two string values are `"RGB"`, which blends colors more directly, resulting in a less spread-out appearance; and `"linearRGB"`, which includes intermediate colors as part of blending colors, resulting in a more spread-out gradient.

Focal point ratio controls the *focal point* (center point) of a radial gradient and takes a number between -1 and 1. Normally, the focal point is the center of the gradient (0); a value between 0 and 1 (or -1) shifts the center toward one or the other edge by that percentage. For instance, a value of .5 shifts the focal point 50 percent between the center and the positive edge.

To create gradient lines:

1. Add an `import` statement for the `flash.geom.Matrix` class.
2. As you did in the previous tasks, create a new, empty movie clip to serve as the drawing space, and assign it to a `MovieClip` variable.
3. On the next line, enter the name of your `MovieClip` variable; choose ActionScript 2.0 Classes > Movie > MovieClip > Methods > lineStyle, and enter the line thickness parameter between the parentheses.

   The other parameters are optional and don't apply when creating gradient lines.
4. Declare and instantiate a new `Array` object to hold your gradient's colors. In the parentheses of the constructor function, enter the numeric color values (**Figure 7.77**).
5. Create a similar `Array` object, adding the alpha value corresponding to each color as a parameter.

   The constructor function call for this `Array` objects should have the same number of parameters as the colors `Array` (**Figure 7.78**).
6. Add a third `Array` object, entering ratio values defining the distribution of the colors in the gradient.
7. To declare and instantiate a new `Matrix` object, enter `var` then the name, followed by `:Matrix`. Enter an equals sign and choose ActionScript 2.0 Classes > "flash.geom package" > Matrix > "new Matrix". Don't enter any parameters in the constructor function call.
8. On the next line, enter the name of your `Matrix` object. Choose ActionScript 2.0 Classes > "flash.geom package" > Matrix > Methods > createGradientBox.

   The `Matrix` class's `createGradientBox` method is specially designed for creating `Matrix` objects to use when drawing gradients. The parameters you enter in this method call determine the size and position of the gradient.

```
import flash.geom.Matrix;
var canvas:MovieClip = _root.createEmptyMovieClip("canvas_mc", 1);
canvas.lineStyle(8);
var colors:Array = new Array(0x009900, 0xCC0066, 0x999999);
```

Figure 7.77 The `Array` holds the set of color values that will make up the gradient.

```
import flash.geom.Matrix;
var canvas:MovieClip = _root.createEmptyMovieClip("canvas_mc", 1);
canvas.lineStyle(8);
var colors:Array = new Array(0x009900, 0xCC0066, 0x999999);
var alphas:Array = new Array(100, 100, 100);
```

Figure 7.78 For each value in the colors `Array`, there is a corresponding value in the alphas `Array`.

9. Inside the parentheses of the `createGradientBox()` method call, enter parameters for width, height, rotation, x offset position, and y offset position (**Figure 7.79**):

   Width and **height** (numbers in pixels) determine the size of the gradient. Outside those dimensions, the colors will end or repeat according to the spread method you choose.

   Rotation (number in radians) indicates how much to rotate the gradient—by default, linear gradients go from left to right, so if you want the gradient to go from top to bottom or at an angle, you must specify a rotation parameter. Otherwise, use 0.

   X and y offset (numbers in pixels) indicate at what coordinate (relative to the movie clip's registration point) to begin the gradient.

10. On the following line, enter your movie clip's name, and choose ActionScript 2.0 Classes > Movie > MovieClip > Methods > lineGradientStyle.

    The gradient properties you've specified will be added as parameters to this method.

11. In the parentheses, add the following parameters: the gradient type (`"linear"` or `"radial"`), your colors `Array`, your alphas `Array`; your ratios `Array`, and your `Matrix` object. Be sure to separate the parameters with commas.

12. Still in the parentheses, if you wish to do so, enter a gradient spread method, interpolation method, and focal point ratio.

13. Add `moveTo` and `lineTo` method calls to draw lines on your MovieClip variable (**Figure 7.80**).

```
var colors:Array = new Array(0x009900, 0xCC0066, 0x999999);
var alphas:Array = new Array(100, 100, 100);
var ratios:Array = new Array(0, 127, 255);
var matrix:Matrix = new Matrix();
matrix.createGradientBox(150, 150, 0, 10, 10);
```

Figure 7.79 The `Matrix` class's `createGradientBox()` method takes parameters that control the gradient's position and rotation properties.

```
import flash.geom.Matrix;
var canvas:MovieClip = _root.createEmptyMovieClip("canvas_mc", 1);
canvas.lineStyle(8);
var colors:Array = new Array(0x009900, 0xCC0066, 0x999999);
var alphas:Array = new Array(100, 100, 100);
var ratios:Array = new Array(0, 127, 255);
var matrix:Matrix = new Matrix();
matrix.createGradientBox(150, 150, 0, 10, 10);
canvas.lineGradientStyle("linear", colors, alphas, ratios, matrix, "reflect", "linearRGB");
canvas.moveTo(0, 200);
canvas.lineTo(300, 300);
canvas.lineTo(0, 400);
```

Figure 7.80 The complete script creates a gradient line style and uses it to color the lines that are drawn.

To create curved lines:

1. Add ActionScript to create an empty movie clip on the root Timeline, and assign it to a variable as described in the preceding tasks.
2. Enter your `MovieClip` variable's name, and then choose ActionScript 2.0 Classes > Movie > MovieClip > Drawing Methods > lineStyle.
3. Add parameters to define the line style to be used for your curve, as described in the preceding tasks.
4. On the next line, enter your movie clip's name, and then choose ActionScript 2.0 Classes > Movie > MovieClip > Drawing Methods > moveTo.
5. Move the starting point of your curve as described in the preceding tasks.
6. On the next line, enter the name of your movie clip.
7. Choose ActionScript 2.0 Classes > Movie > MovieClip > Drawing Methods > curveTo.
8. With your pointer between the parentheses, enter x- and y-coordinates for the control point and x- and y-coordinates for the end of the curve (**Figure 7.81**).

   The *control point* is a point that determines the amount of curvature. If you were to extend a straight line from the control point to the end point of the curve, you would see that it functions much like the handle of a curve (**Figure 7.82**). Check out the sample file in this section on the accompanying CD-ROM to see how the control point affects your curve in real time.

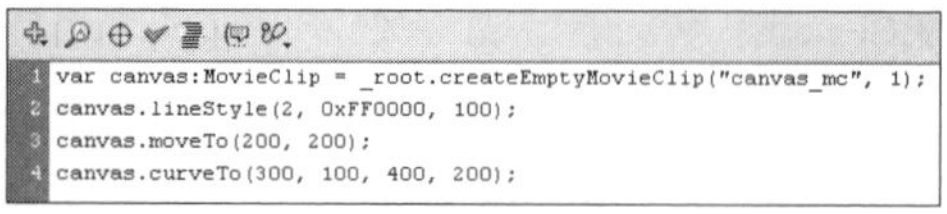

```
var canvas:MovieClip = _root.createEmptyMovieClip("canvas_mc", 1);
canvas.lineStyle(2, 0xFF0000, 100);
canvas.moveTo(200, 200);
canvas.curveTo(300, 100, 400, 200);
```

Figure 7.81 The curveTo() method requires x- and y-coordinates for its control point and for its end point. This curve starts at (200,200) and ends at (400,200), with the control point at (300,100) (see Figure 7.82).

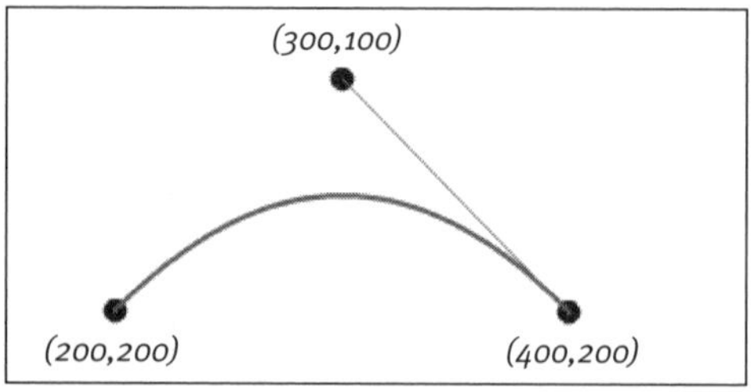

Figure 7.82 By drawing a straight line from the control point to the end point, you can visualize the curve's Bézier handle. The dots have been added to show the two anchor points and the control point.

✔ Tip

- To reduce the repetition of writing the canvas movie clip's name, use a `with` statement to change the scope temporarily. For example, the statement

```
_root.createEmptyMovieClip("canvas", 1);
with (canvas) {
    lineStyle(5, 0xff0000, 100);
    moveTo(200, 100);
    curveTo(300, 100, 300, 200);
    curveTo(300, 300, 200, 300);
    curveTo(100, 300, 100, 200);
    curveTo(100, 100, 200, 100);
}
```

is the same as

```
_root.createEmptyMovieClip("canvas", 1);
canvas.lineStyle(5, 0xff0000, 100);
canvas.moveTo(200, 100);
canvas.curveTo(300, 100, 300, 200);
canvas.curveTo(300, 300, 200, 300);
canvas.curveTo(100, 300, 100, 200);
canvas.curveTo(100, 100, 200, 100);
```

Quadratic Bézier Curves

If you were to try to draw a circle with the curveTo() method using four segments, you might be surprised by the results. The following script doesn't produce a perfect circle, as you might expect (**Figure 7.83**):

```
_root.createEmptyMovieClip("canvas", 1);
with (canvas) {
    lineStyle(5, 0xff0000, 100);
    moveTo(200, 100);
    curveTo(300, 100, 300, 200);
    curveTo(300, 300, 200, 300);
    curveTo(100, 300, 100, 200);
    curveTo(100, 100, 200, 100);
}
```

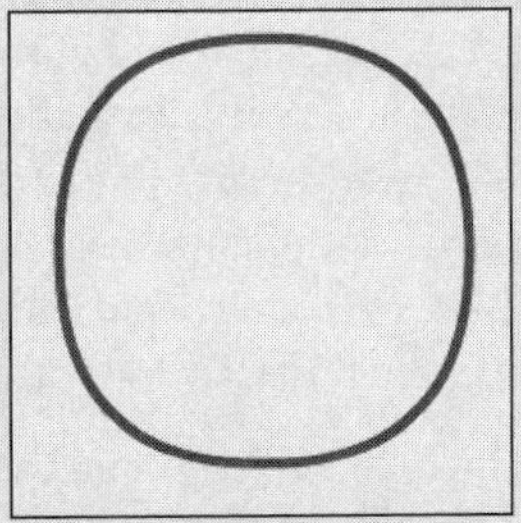

Figure 7.83 An imperfect circle drawn with four curveTo() statements.

The curveTo() method uses what are called *quadratic Bézier curves*—the same kind used for the Oval tool in the Tools panel. Four segments don't produce a perfect circle because Flash needs eight (**Figure 7.84**). How do you determine their anchor points and control points? The answer involves a fair bit of math and trigonometry (which you'll explore in Chapter 12), but the code to produce a perfect circle in eight segments is presented here. Essentially, the start and end points of each curve lie on a circle of a certain radius (r). The x-coordinate is r * cos(theta), and the y-coordinate is r * sin(theta). *Theta* is the angle that one segment covers; so, for eight segments, theta is 45 degrees. The control points lie exactly between the start and end anchor points at a distance of r / cos(0.5 * theta):

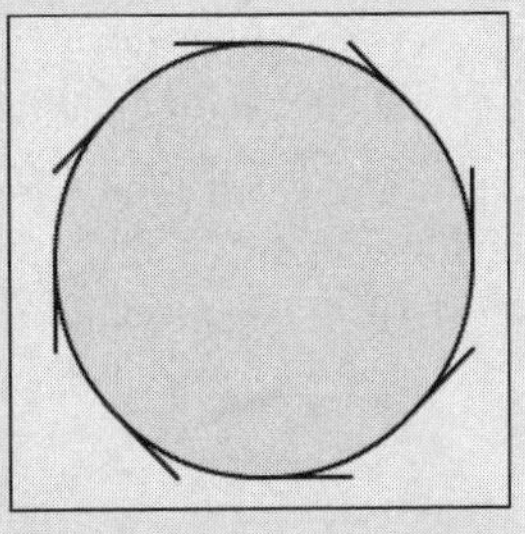

Figure 7.84 A perfect circle drawn with eight curveTo() statements. Line segments from the control points to the end points have been added to show the eight curves.

```
function degToRadians(degrees:Number):Number {
    return (Math.PI / 180) * degrees;
}
var theta:Number = 45;
var r:Number = 100;
var d:Number = r / Math.cos(degToRadians(0.5 * theta));
var canvas:MovieClip;
canvas = this.createEmptyMovieClip("canvas_mc", 1);
canvas.lineStyle(1, 0x000000, 100);
canvas.moveTo(r, 0);
for (var k:Number = (theta / 2); k < 361; k += theta) {
    var xControl:Number = d * Math.cos(degToRadians(k));
    var yControl:Number = d * Math.sin(degToRadians(k));
    var xAnchor:Number = r * Math.cos(degToRadians(k + (theta / 2)));
    var yAnchor:Number = r * Math.sin(degToRadians(k + (theta / 2)));
    canvas.curveTo(xControl, yControl, xAnchor, yAnchor);
}
```

Updating a drawing

The `clear()` method erases the drawings made with the movie clip drawing methods. In conjunction with an `onEnterFrame` event or a `setInterval()` function, you can make Flash continually erase a drawing and redraw itself. This is how you can create curves and lines that aren't static, but change.

The following task shows the dynamic updates you can make in a drawing by moving vertices with draggable movie clips.

To use clear to update a drawing dynamically:

1. Create four small movie clips; give each one an instance name in the Property inspector.
2. Select the first keyframe on the root Timeline, and open the Actions panel.
3. Add `onPress` and `onRelease` event handlers for each movie clip to make the movie clips draggable.

   The code for each instance should look like this:

   ```
   instanceName.onPress = function() {
        this.startDrag();
   };
   instanceName.onRelease = function() {
        stopDrag();
   };
   ```

4. On the next line, add ActionScript to create an empty movie clip on the root Timeline, as described in the previous tasks.
5. On the next line, enter `_root`, followed by a period.
6. Choose ActionScript 2.0 Classes > Movie > MovieClip > Event Handlers > onEnterFrame (**Figure 7.85**).

   The `onEnterFrame` event handler is created. This event happens at the frame rate of the movie, providing a way to perform actions continuously.

7. On the next line, enter the name of your empty movie clip, followed by a period.
8. Choose ActionScript 2.0 Classes > Movie > MovieClip > Drawing Methods > clear (**Figure 7.86**).

   The `clear()` method erases the previous drawings made on your empty movie clip.

9. On the next line, enter the movie clip variable's name followed by a period.
10. Choose ActionScript 2.0 Classes > Movie > MovieClip > Drawing Methods > lineStyle.
11. With your pointer between the parentheses, enter the line thickness, hex code for its color, and its alpha value.

```
var canvas:MovieClip = _root.createEmptyMovieClip("canvas_mc", 1);
_root.onEnterFrame = function() {
};
```

Figure 7.85 The `onEnterFrame` event handler is created for the root Timeline.

```
var canvas:MovieClip = _root.createEmptyMovieClip("canvas_mc", 1);
_root.onEnterFrame = function() {
    canvas.clear();
};
```

Figure 7.86 All drawings created on the canvas movie clip are cleared continuously.

12. On the next line, enter the movie clip variable's name, followed by a period.

13. Choose ActionScript 2.0 Classes > Movie > MovieClip > Drawing Methods > moveTo.

14. With your pointer between the parentheses, enter the _x property and the _y property for one of your draggable movie clips (**Figure 7.87**).

15. Continue adding `lineTo()` methods whose x- and y-coordinates correspond to the x and y properties of the draggable movie clips.

    The final script should look like **Figure 7.88**.

16. Test your movie.

    Flash continuously erases the line segments with the `clear()` method and redraws them according to where the draggable movie clips lie. You can drag the movie clips around the Stage to change the shape dynamically (**Figure 7.89**).

```
var canvas:MovieClip = _root.createEmptyMovieClip("canvas_mc", 1);
_root.onEnterFrame = function() {
    canvas.clear();
    canvas.lineStyle(2, 0xff00ff, 100);
    canvas.moveTo(circle1_mc._x, circle1_mc._y);
};
```

Figure 7.87 The first line segment begins where the registration point of `circle1_mc` lies.

```
var canvas:MovieClip = _root.createEmptyMovieClip("canvas_mc", 1);
_root.onEnterFrame = function() {
    canvas.clear();
    canvas.lineStyle(2, 0xff00ff, 100);
    canvas.moveTo(circle1_mc._x, circle1_mc._y);
    canvas.lineTo(circle2_mc._x, circle2_mc._y);
    canvas.lineTo(circle3_mc._x, circle3_mc._y);
    canvas.lineTo(circle4_mc._x, circle4_mc._y);
};
```

Figure 7.88 The line segments are drawn to where the draggable movie clips `circle2_mc`, `circle3_mc`, and `circle4_mc` are located.

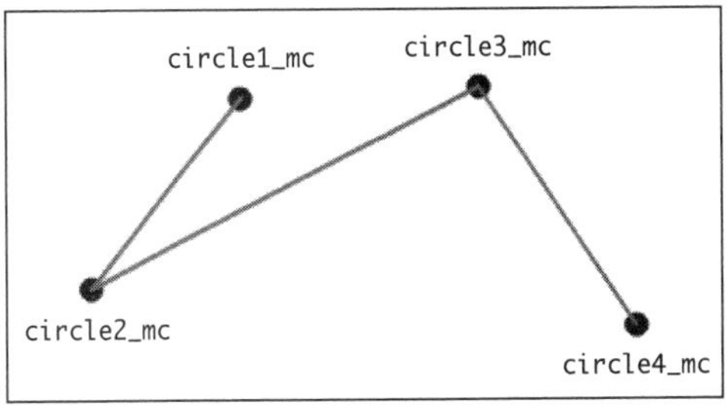

Figure 7.89 The three line segments between the four draggable movie clip circles are redrawn continuously, creating a moveable, Tinker Toys–like shape that moves where you position the vertices.

✔ Tip

- In this example, you can use `onMouseMove` instead of `onEnterFrame` because the only time the drawing needs to be updated is when the viewer is dragging one of the movie clips. If you do use `onMouseMove`, add the `updateAfterEvent()` statement (Global Functions > Movie Clip Control > updateAfterEvent) to force Flash to refresh the screen whenever the mouse pointer moves.

Creating fills and gradients

You can fill shapes with solid colors, transparent colors, or radial or linear gradients by using the methods `beginFill()`, `beginGradientFill()`, and `endFill()`. Begin the shape to be filled by calling either the `beginFill()` or the `beginGradientFill()` method, and mark the end of the shape with `endFill()`. If your path isn't closed (the end points don't match the beginning points), Flash automatically closes it when the `endFill()` method is applied.

Applying solid or transparent fills with `beginFill()` is fairly straightforward; specify a hex code for the color and a value from 0 to 100 for the transparency. Gradients are more complex. You control the gradient by adding up to eight parameters to the `beginGradientFill()` method call. These parameters are the same ones used for creating gradient lines, as described earlier in this chapter:

Gradient type: The string `"radial"` or the string `"linear"`.

Colors: An `Array` object containing the hex codes for the gradient colors

Alphas: An `Array` object containing the alpha values (0 through 100) corresponding to the colors.

Ratios: An `Array` object that contains values (0 through 255) corresponding to the colors that determine how they will mix.

Matrix: An object whose properties determine the size, position, and orientation of your gradient.

Spread method: One of three string values—`"pad"`, `"repeat"`, or `"reflect"`—which controls how the gradient overflows.

Interpolation method: One of two string values—`"RGB"` or `"linearRGB"`—which instructs Flash how to calculate the blend between colors.

Focal point ratio: A number between –1 and 1 that controls the focal point (center point) of a radial gradient.

To fill a shape with a solid color:

1. Create an empty movie clip on the root Timeline.
2. On a new line, enter the name of your empty movie clip and a period. Choose ActionScript 2.0 Classes > Movie > MovieClip > Drawing Methods > lineStyle, and define the style of your line.
3. On the next line, enter the name of the movie clip, followed by a period.
4. Choose ActionScript 2.0 Classes > Movie > MovieClip > Drawing Methods > beginFill.

5. With your pointer between the parentheses, enter the hex code for a color and a value for the alpha, separating your parameters with a comma (**Figure 7.90**).

6. On a new line, enter the name of the drawing movie clip followed by a period. Choose ActionScript 2.0 Classes > Movie > MovieClip > Drawing Methods > moveTo, and add parameters for the starting point of your line.

7. Use the `lineTo()` or `curveTo()` method to draw a closed shape (**Figure 7.91**).

8. When the end point matches the beginning point of your shape, enter the target path of the empty movie clip and a period, and then choose ActionScript 2.0 Classes > Movie > MovieClip > Drawing Methods > endFill.

   No parameters are required for the `endFill()` method. Flash fills the closed shape with the specified color (**Figure 7.92**).

```
var canvas:MovieClip = _root.createEmptyMovieClip("canvas_mc", 1);
canvas.lineStyle(1, 0xFF0000, 100);
canvas.beginFill(0x7E6AE3, 100);
```

Figure 7.90 This fill is light blue at 100 percent opacity.

```
var canvas:MovieClip = _root.createEmptyMovieClip("canvas_mc", 1);
canvas.lineStyle(1, 0xFF0000, 100);
canvas.beginFill(0x7E6AE3, 100);
canvas.moveTo(100, 100);
canvas.lineTo(100, 200);
canvas.lineTo(200, 200);
canvas.lineTo(200, 100);
canvas.lineTo(100, 100);
```

Figure 7.91 The end point of the last `lineTo()` method (100,100) matches the beginning point (100,100), creating a closed shape that can be filled.

```
var canvas:MovieClip = _root.createEmptyMovieClip("canvas_mc", 1);
canvas.lineStyle(1, 0xFF0000, 100);
canvas.beginFill(0x7E6AE3, 100);
canvas.moveTo(100, 100);
canvas.lineTo(100, 200);
canvas.lineTo(200, 200);
canvas.lineTo(200, 100);
canvas.lineTo(100, 100);
canvas.endFill();
```

Figure 7.92 A blue box appears as a result of this code. The box was drawn counterclockwise from its top-left corner, but the order of line segments is irrelevant.

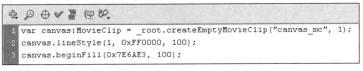

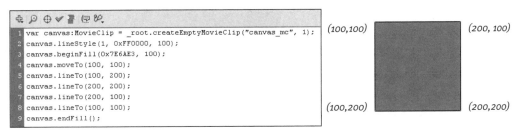

To fill a shape with a gradient:

1. Add an `import` statement for the class `flash.geom.Matrix`.
2. Add the action to create an empty movie clip on the root Timeline, and assign it to a variable.
3. On the next line, enter `var colors:Array` followed by an equals sign.
4. Choose ActionScript 2.0 Classes > Core > Array > "new Array".

   The constructor function creates a new `Array` object.
5. Between the parentheses of the `new Array()` statement, enter the colors of your gradient in hex code, separating your hex codes with commas (**Figure 7.93**).

   By adding parameters to the `new Array()` statement, you instantiate a new array object and populate the array at the same time. The first color refers to the left side of a linear gradient or the center of a radial gradient.
6. On the next line, declare an `alphas Array` variable, and enter an equals sign.
7. Choose ActionScript 2.0 Classes > Core > Array > "new Array".
8. Between the parentheses of this `new Array()` statement, enter the alpha values that correspond to each color.
9. On the next line, declare a `ratios Array`, followed by an equals sign; choose ActionScript 2.0 Classes > Core > Array > "new Array".
10. Between the parentheses of this `new Array()` statement, enter the ratio values that correspond to each color (**Figure 7.94**).
11. On the next line, enter `var matrix:Matrix`, followed by an equals sign.
12. Choose ActionScript 2.0 Classes > "flash.geom package" > Matrix > "new Matrix".

```
import flash.geom.Matrix;
var canvas:MovieClip = _root.createEmptyMovieClip("canvas_mc", 1);
var colors:Array = new Array(0xFF0000, 0x0000FF);
```

Figure 7.93 The colors array is created with blue on one side and red on the other. If this gradient will be a linear gradient, blue (`0x0000FF`) will be on the left. If it will be a radial gradient, blue will be in the center.

```
import flash.geom.Matrix;
var canvas:MovieClip = _root.createEmptyMovieClip("canvas_mc", 1);
var colors:Array = new Array(0xFF0000, 0x0000FF);
var alphas:Array = new Array(100, 100);
var ratios:Array = new Array(0, 255);
```

Figure 7.94 The `alphas` array is created with 100 percent opacity for both the blue and the red. The `ratios` array is created with blue on the far left side (or the center, in the case of a radial gradient) and with red on the far right side (or the edge of a radial gradient).

13. Enter the name of your `Matrix` object; choose ActionScript 2.0 Classes > "flash.geom package" > Matrix > Methods > createGradientBox, and add parameters to define the size, rotation, and position of your gradient (**Figure 7.95**).

14. Enter the name of your canvas movie clip, followed by a period. Choose ActionScript 2.0 Classes > Movie > MovieClip > Drawing Methods > lineStyle, and define the style of your line.

15. On the next line, enter the name of your movie clip, followed by a period. Choose ActionScript 2.0 Classes > Movie > MovieClip > beginGradientFill.

16. For the parameters of the `beginGradientFill` method, enter the string `"linear"` or `"radial"` to choose your gradient type; then enter the name of your `colors` array, `alphas` array, `ratios` array, and `Matrix` object.

    Separate the parameters with commas.

    All the information about your gradient that you defined in your arrays and `Matrix` object is fed into the parameters of the `beginGradientFill()` method.

17. On the next line, enter the name of your empty movie clip, followed by a period.

18. Choose ActionScript 2.0 Classes > Movie > MovieClip > Drawing Methods > moveTo, and enter starting coordinates for your shape.

continues on next page

```
import flash.geom.Matrix;
var canvas:MovieClip = _root.createEmptyMovieClip("canvas_mc", 1);
var colors:Array = new Array(0xFF0000, 0x0000FF);
var alphas:Array = new Array(100, 100);
var ratios:Array = new Array(0, 255);
var matrix:Matrix = new Matrix();
matrix.createGradientBox(100, 100, 0, 100, 100);
```

Figure 7.95 The width, height, rotation, and x, y coordinates of the gradient are defined as parameters of the `createGradientBox` method call.

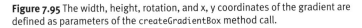

19. Create a series of lines or curves with `lineTo()` or `curveTo()` to create a closed path.

20. On a new line, enter the name of your empty movie clip and a period, and then choose ActionScript 2.0 Classes > Movie > MovieClip > Drawing Methods > endFill.

Flash fills your shape with the gradient (**Figure 7.96**).

✔ Tip

- The `rotation` parameter of the `createGradientBox` method takes radians, not degrees. Using radians is a way to measure angles using the mathematical constant pi. To convert degrees to radians, multiply by the number pi and then divide by 180. Using the `Math` class for pi (`Math.PI`), you can use the formula:

  `radians = degrees * (Math.PI / 180)`

```
import flash.geom.Matrix;
var canvas:MovieClip = _root.createEmptyMovieClip("canvas_mc", 1);
var colors:Array = new Array(0xFF0000, 0x0000FF);
var alphas:Array = new Array(100, 100);
var ratios:Array = new Array(0, 255);
var matrix:Matrix = new Matrix();
matrix.createGradientBox(100, 100, 0, 100, 100);
canvas.lineStyle(5, 0xFF0000, 100);
canvas.beginGradientFill("linear", colors, alphas, ratios, matrix);
canvas.moveTo(100, 100);
canvas.lineTo(100, 200);
canvas.lineTo(200, 200);
canvas.lineTo(200, 100);
canvas.lineTo(100, 100);
canvas.endFill();
```

Figure 7.96 The complete ActionScript code creates a box with a linear gradient from blue to red.

Figure 7.97 This speech bubble movie clip (top) becomes distorted when it's scaled (bottom).

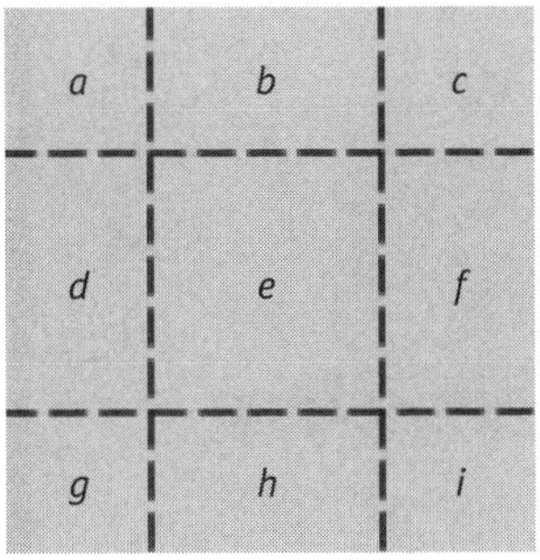

Figure 7.98 The nine segments of a movie clip with 9-slice scaling enabled. The four corners (a, c, g, i) don't scale at all. The four edges (b, d, f, h) scale in only one direction. The center region (e) scales in both directions.

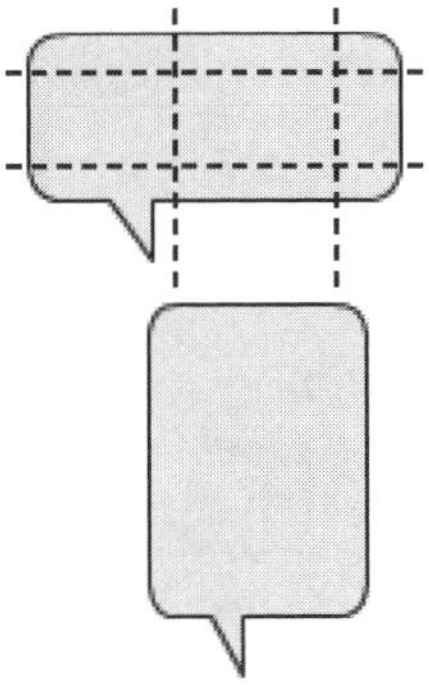

Figure 7.99 By including the corners and point of the speech bubble in corner segments with 9-slice scaling enabled, they don't become distorted when the clip is scaled. The slices are shown by overlaid dashed lines.

Movie Clip Scaling and Distortion

Flash's drawing tools and the movie clip drawing methods work with vector graphics—lines and shapes that are designed to scale up and down and maintain their relative sizes. However, sometimes you don't want all the parts of a movie clip to scale the same way. Imagine, for example, a movie clip symbol of a speech bubble with rounded corners. To accommodate different amounts of text, the speech bubble needs to be scaled larger and smaller. When the speech bubble is scaled, the rounded corners are distorted, making it look bad (**Figure 7.97**).

Flash 8 provides a mechanism known as *9-slice scaling*, which allows you to control how different parts of the movie clip scale. When a movie clip has 9-slice scaling enabled, the clip is divided into nine regions, each of which has a specific behavior when scaled (**Figure 7.98**). The four corner regions don't scale at all—their content always stays the same size. The center regions on the top and bottom scale horizontally but not vertically, whereas the left and right regions on the middle row scale vertically but not horizontally. The center region scales normally; that is, it scales in both directions.

If there are certain parts of the movie clip that you don't want to distort when the movie clip is scaled, be sure to include them in one of the corner regions (**Figure 7.99**).

9-slice scaling can be enabled for movie clips in the movie clip symbol properties in the Library panel. When it's enabled, guides appear in symbol-editing mode for that movie clip, which let you define the scaling regions. You can also enable 9-slice scaling using ActionScript by assigning a value to the `scale9Grid` property of the `MovieClip` object.

To define how a movie clip will scale:

1. Create a movie clip symbol that you want to use. It should have portions that you want to protect from being distorted when scaling.
2. In the Library panel, select your movie clip symbol. From the Library panel's Options menu, choose Properties.

   or

   Right-click or Cmd-click (Mac) the symbol in the Library panel, and choose Properties from the context menu (**Figure 7.100**).

   The Symbol Properties dialog box appears.
3. If necessary, click the Advanced button to see all the movie clip properties.
4. Select the "Enable guides for 9-slice scaling" check box (**Figure 7.101**), and click OK.

   In the preview window in the Library panel, dashed lines appear indicating the placement of the scaling guides.

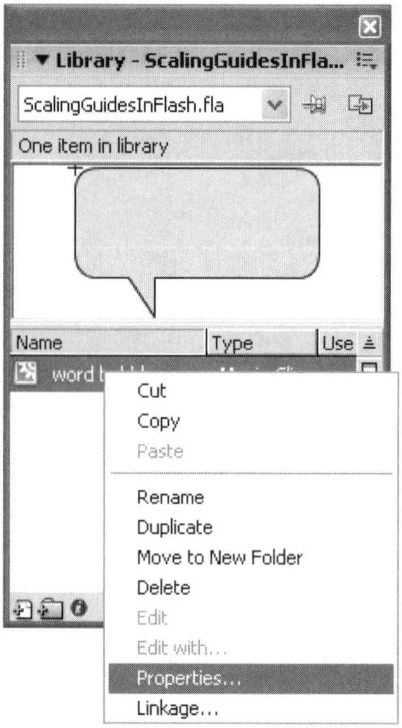

Figure 7.100 Choose Properties to edit a movie clip symbol's properties.

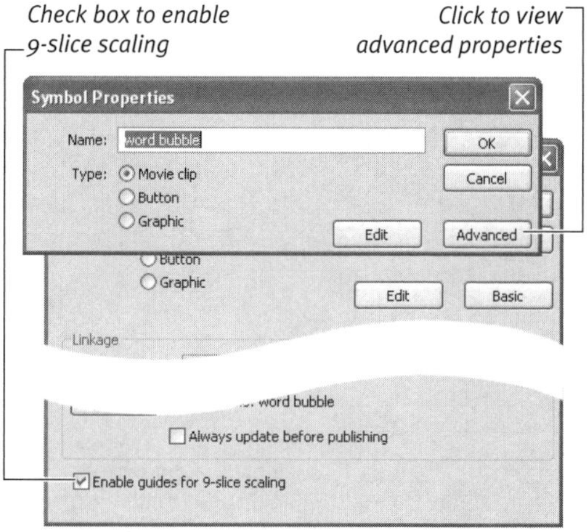

Figure 7.101 To enable 9-slice scaling, select the appropriate check box in the movie clip symbol's Advanced properties.

5. Double-click the icon next to your movie clip symbol's name in the Library to open the clip in symbol-editing mode.

   In addition to the movie clip's content, you'll see scaling guides on the Stage (**Figure 7.102**).

6. Click and drag the scaling guides to define the scaling regions for your movie clip. Exit symbol-editing mode.

7. Place an instance of your movie clip on the Stage, and use the Free Transform tool to adjust its size.

   When you test your movie, it will scale and distort (or not distort) according to the scaling regions you defined.

✔ Tip

- When you scale a movie clip on the Stage, the preview on the Stage distorts as though 9-slice scaling isn't applied. However, when you test your movie, the 9-slice scaling will be applied.

9-slice scaling in ActionScript

When you're dynamically defining 9-slice scaling regions for a movie clip using ActionScript, you create an instance of the `flash.geom.Rectangle` class and assign it to the movie clip's `scale9Grid` property. A `Rectangle` object has four important properties: the x and y positions and a width and height. The Flash Player uses those properties of your `Rectangle` object to calculate the locations of the scaling guides. Each corner of the `Rectangle` object indicates an intersection of two scaling guides; that is all the information Flash needs to figure out the guides' positions and control the movie clip's scaling (**Figure 7.103**).

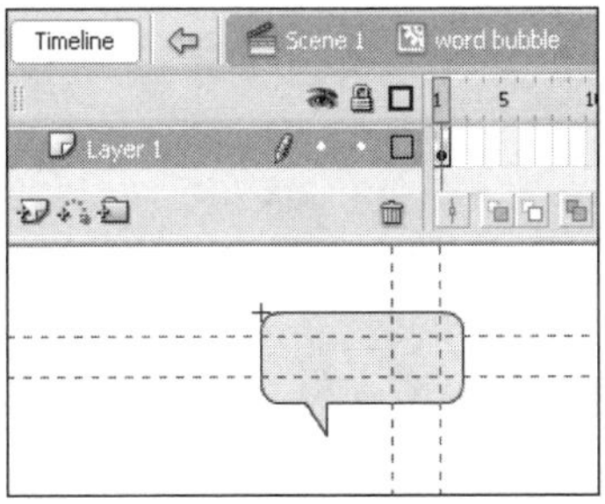
Timeline
Scene 1
word bubble
Layer 1
5

Figure 7.102 Drag the scaling guides to designate regions that will or won't scale.

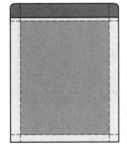

Figure 7.103 The `Rectangle` object assigned to the `scale9Grid` property (overlaid here) gives Flash the information to calculate the scaling guides (shown as dashed lines).

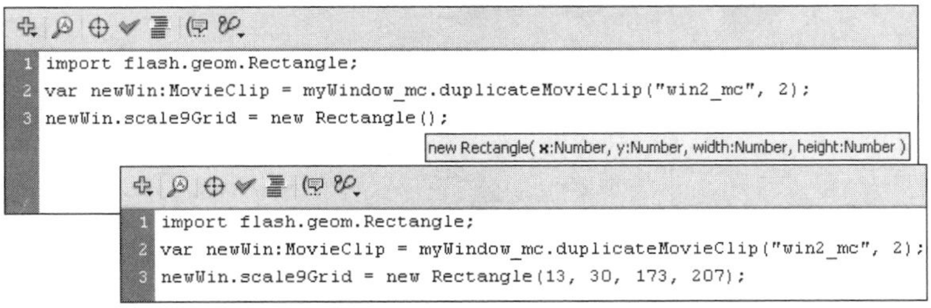
import flash.geom.Rectangle;
var newWin:MovieClip = myWindow_mc.duplicateMovieClip("win2_mc", 2);
newWin.scale9Grid = new Rectangle();
new Rectangle(x:Number, y:Number, width:Number, height:Number)
import flash.geom.Rectangle;
var newWin:MovieClip = myWindow_mc.duplicateMovieClip("win2_mc", 2);
newWin.scale9Grid = new Rectangle(13, 30, 173, 207);

Figure 7.104 The parameters of the `Rectangle` object's constructor define its position and size.

To define movie clip scaling using ActionScript:

1. Create a movie clip symbol; place it on the Stage, and give it an instance name.

   or

   Add ActionScript to dynamically add a movie clip to the Stage.

   or

   Add ActionScript to create an empty movie clip, and use the drawing methods to draw a shape.

2. Select the first keyframe, and open the Actions panel.

3. Add the following `import` statement to the Script pane:

   `import flash.geom.Rectangle;`

4. Enter the target path of the movie clip that will be scaled.

5. Choose ActionScript 2.0 Classes > Movie > MovieClip > Properties > scale9Grid.

6. On the same line, enter an equals sign; choose ActionScript 2.0 Classes > "flash.geom package" > Rectangle > "new Rectangle".

   The constructor function for a new `Rectangle` object is added to the script.

7. Inside the parentheses of the `Rectangle` constructor function, enter four `Number` parameters, separated by commas (**Figure 7.104** on previous page).

   The four parameters are the x position, y position, width, and height of the `Rectangle` object. The x and y position are relative to the movie clip's registration point.

8. Add statements to scale the movie clip symbol (using the `_xscale`, `_yscale`, `_width`, and/or `_height` movie clip properties).

   In this example, the duplicate clip is scaled to 75 percent on the x-axis and 60 percent on the y-axis (**Figure 7.105**).

   When you test your movie, the movie clip scales but the corner regions maintain their original size.

```
import flash.geom.Rectangle;
var newWin:MovieClip = myWindow_mc.duplicateMovieClip("win2_mc", 2);
newWin.scale9Grid = new Rectangle(13, 30, 173, 207);
newWin._x = 250;
newWin._y = 50;
newWin._xscale = 75;
newWin._yscale = 60;
```

Figure 7.105 The completed script (top) creates a duplicate movie clip that is scaled (bottom), but the corners and title bar of the window aren't distorted by the scaling.

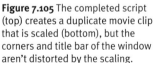

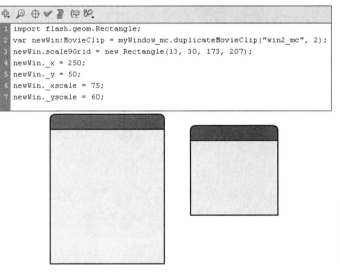

Unwrap this Season's
Latest Looks

Figure 7.106 Combining draggable movie clips (the vertices), drawing methods (the lines connecting the vertices), and dynamic masking (uncovering the image behind the wrapping paper).

Figure 7.107 A movie clip containing a cityscape image will be the masked movie clip.

Using Dynamic Masks

You can turn any movie clip into a mask and specify the movie clip to be masked with the method `setMask()`. To do so, you define the movie clip you want to be masked as the movie clip that calls the method and then specify the movie clip you want to act as a mask as its parameter: `masked_mc.setMask(mask_mc)`. Because you can control all the properties of movie clips, you can make your mask move or grow and shrink in response to viewer interaction. You can even combine the `setMask()` method with the movie clip drawing methods to create masks that change shape (**Figure 7.106**).

An effective combination assigns `startDrag()` and `stopDrag()` methods to the movie clip mask and creates a draggable mask. When you add `startDrag()` to an `onPress` handler and `stopDrag()` to an `onRelease` handler, your viewer can control the position of the movie clip mask.

To set a movie clip as a mask:

1. Create a movie clip, place an instance on the Stage, and name it in the Property inspector (**Figure 7.107**).

   This movie clip will be masked.

continues on next page

2. Create another movie clip, place an instance on the Stage, and name it in the Property inspector (**Figure 7.108**).

   This movie clip will act as a mask.

3. Select the first frame of the root Timeline, and open the Actions panel.

4. Enter the target path to the movie clip you want to be masked, followed by a period.

5. Choose ActionScript 2.0 Classes > Movie > MovieClip > Methods > setMask.

6. With your pointer between the parentheses for the `setMask` method, enter the name of the target path to the movie clip you want to use as a mask (**Figure 7.109**).

7. Test your movie.

   The opaque shapes of the mask movie clip reveal the masked movie clip (**Figure 7.110**).

Figure 7.108 A movie clip of vertical shapes will be the mask.

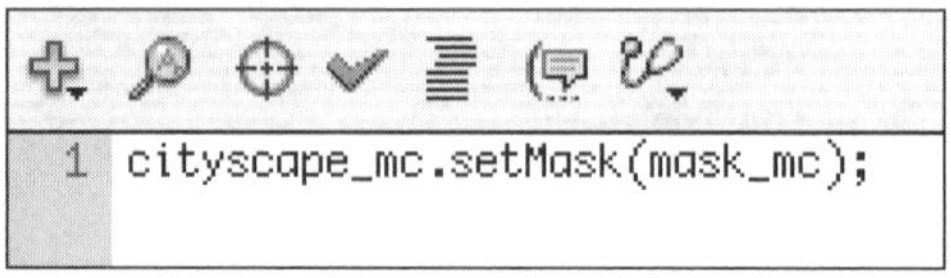
1 cityscape_mc.setMask(mask_mc);

Figure 7.109 The `mask_mc` movie clip will mask the `cityscape_mc` movie clip.

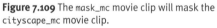

Figure 7.110 The result of the `setMask()` method.

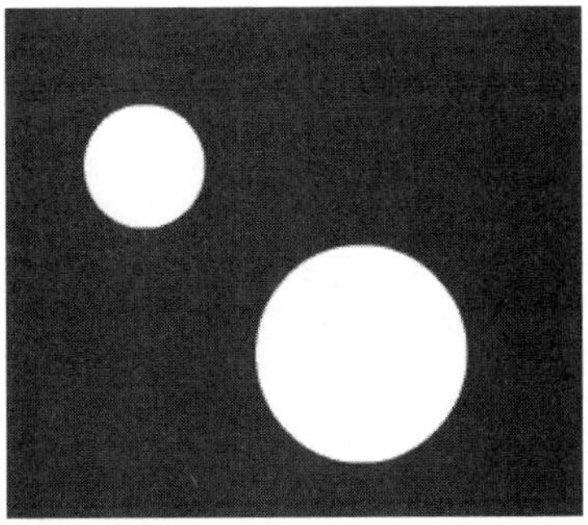

Figure 7.111 If this shape were to be used in a movie clip for the `setMask()` method, Flash would recognize only a square for the mask unless runtime bitmap caching was enabled for the clips.

Figure 7.112 You'll create a draggable mask to uncover this movie clip to make the viewer look for the monkey in the bush.

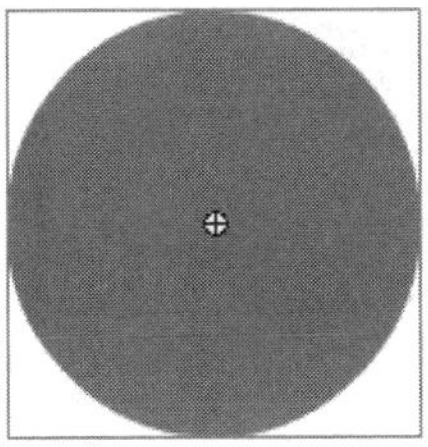

Figure 7.113 A simple circle will be the mask.

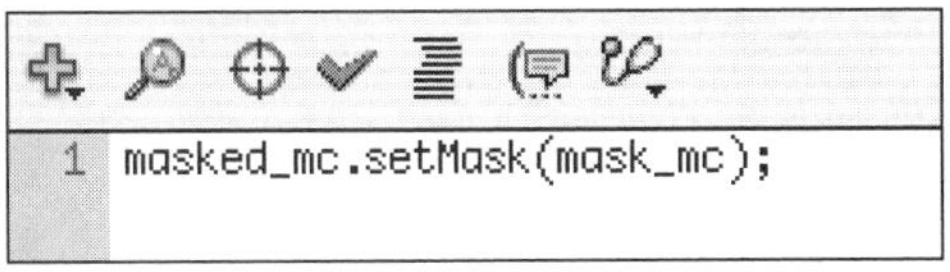
1 masked_mc.setMask(mask_mc);

Figure 7.114 Create the mask of the circle over the masked image (the monkey in the bush).

✔ Tips

- You can specify the root Timeline as the movie clip to be masked, and all the graphics on the main Timeline (including movie clips on the Stage) will be masked. To do so, enter `_root` as the target path that calls the `setMask()` method.
- Holes and areas with alpha transparency in the opaque shapes of your mask movie clip aren't recognized and don't normally affect the mask (**Figure 7.111**). To make the mask function with holes and/or alpha, you must set both masked and mask movie clips to use runtime bitmap caching, either by selecting the "Use runtime bitmap caching" check box in the Property inspector or by setting the `cacheAsBitmap` property to `true` in ActionScript.
- To undo a `setMask()` method, use the `null` keyword for its parameter, as follows:

  `masked_mc.setMask(null).`

To create a draggable mask:

1. Create a movie clip, put an instance of it on the Stage, and name it in the Property inspector.

   This movie clip will be masked (**Figure 7.112**).
2. Create another movie clip, put an instance of it on the Stage, and name it in the Property inspector.

   This movie clip will act as a mask (**Figure 7.113**).
3. Select the first frame of the root Timeline, and open the Actions panel.
4. Enter the target path of the movie clip to be masked, followed by a period.

continues on next page

5. Choose ActionScript 2.0 Classes > Movie > MovieClip > Methods > setMask.
6. With your pointer between the parentheses, enter the target path of the mask movie clip (**Figure 7.114**).
7. On the next line, enter the target path of the mask movie clip, followed by a period.
8. Choose ActionScript 2.0 Classes > Movie > MovieClip > Event Handlers > onPress. (**Figure 7.115**).
9. With your pointer between the curly braces for the `onPress` function, enter the target path of your mask movie clip followed by a period.
10. Choose ActionScript 2.0 Classes > Movie > MovieClip > Methods > startDrag (**Figure 7.116**).
11. On the next line, after the closing curly brace of the `onPress` event handler, enter the target path of the mask movie clip, followed by a period.
12. Choose ActionScript 2.0 Classes > Movie > MovieClip > Events > onRelease.
13. Choose Global Functions > Movie Clip Control > stopDrag.
14. Test your movie.

    The movie clip acts as a mask, and the `onPress` and `onRelease` handlers provide the drag-and-drop interactivity (**Figure 7.117**).

```
masked_mc.setMask(mask_mc);
mask_mc.onPress = function() {

};
```

Figure 7.115 The `onPress` event handler is created for the movie clip `mask_mc`.

```
masked_mc.setMask(mask_mc);
mask_mc.onPress = function() {
    mask_mc.startDrag();
};
```

Figure 7.116 A new `startDrag` action has been created within the `onPress` event handler.

```
masked_mc.setMask(mask_mc);
mask_mc.onPress = function() {
    mask_mc.startDrag();
};
mask_mc.onRelease = function() {
    stopDrag();
};
```

Figure 7.117 The final ActionScript code (top) assigns interactivity to create a dynamic mask as well as a draggable movie clip.

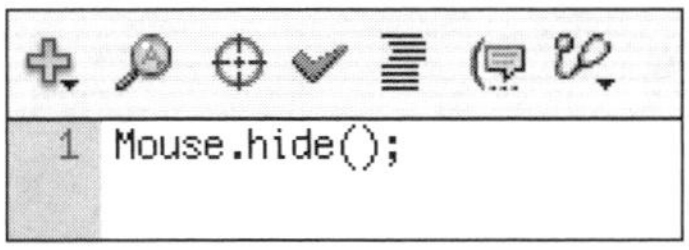
1 Mouse.hide();

Figure 7.118 The `hide()` method of the `Mouse` object doesn't require an instance.

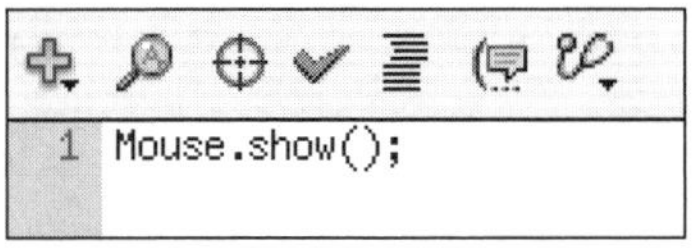
1 Mouse.show();

Figure 7.119 The `show()` method of the `Mouse` object makes a hidden mouse pointer visible again.

Customizing Your Pointer

When you understand how to control the movie clip, you can build your own custom mouse pointer. Think about all the different pointers you use in Flash. As you choose different tools in the Tools palette—the Paint Bucket, the Eyedropper, the Pencil—your pointer changes to help you understand and apply them. Similarly, you can tailor the pointer's form to match its function in your Flash projects.

Customizing the pointer involves first hiding the default mouse pointer. Then you must match the location of your new graphic to the location of the hidden (but still functional) pointer. To do this, set the `X Position` and `Y Position` properties of a movie clip to the x and y positions of the mouse pointer. The x and y positions of the mouse pointer are defined by the `MovieClip` class's properties `_xmouse` and `_ymouse`.

To hide the mouse pointer:

1. Select the first frame, and open the Actions panel.
2. Choose ActionScript 2.0 Classes > Movie > Mouse > Methods > hide (**Figure 7.118**).

   When you test your movie, the mouse pointer becomes invisible.

To show the mouse pointer:

- From the Actions panel, choose ActionScript 2.0 Classes > Movie > Mouse > Methods > show (**Figure 7.119**).

To create your own mouse pointer:

1. Create a movie clip symbol, place an instance of it on the Stage, and name it in the Property inspector.

   This movie clip will become your pointer.

2. Select the first frame of the root Timeline, and open the Actions panel.

3. Choose ActionScript 2.0 Classes > Movie > Mouse > Methods > hide.

   The `Mouse.hide()` method appears. When this movie begins, the mouse pointer disappears.

4. On the next line, enter the instance name for your mouse pointer movie clip.

5. Choose ActionScript 2.0 Classes > Movie > MovieClip > Event Handlers > onMouseMove.

6. Inside the curly braces of the `onMouseMove` event handler function, enter the word `this`, followed by a period.

   In an event handler function, the word `this` refers to the movie clip that is assigned the event handler—your mouse pointer movie clip, in this case.

7. Choose ActionScript 2.0 Classes > Movie > MovieClip > Properties > _x, and add an equals sign.

8. Enter `_root`, followed by a period. Choose ActionScript 2.0 Classes > Movie > MovieClip > Properties > _xmouse (**Figure 7.120**).

9. On the next line, enter the word `this`, followed by a period.

```
Mouse.hide();
cursor_mc.onMouseMove = function() {
    this._x = _root._xmouse;
    this._y = _root._ymouse;
};
```

Figure 7.121 The y property for the movie clip `cursor_mc` follows the mouse pointer's y position as well.

```
Mouse.hide();
cursor_mc.onMouseMove = function() {
    this._x = _root._xmouse;
    this._y = _root._ymouse;
    updateAfterEvent();
};
```

Figure 7.122 Add the `updateAfterEvent` function to force Flash to refresh the display and create smoother motion.

Figure 7.123 This magnifying glass is a movie clip that matches the x and y positions of the pointer. Create helpful pointers like this one with an appearance that matches function.

10. Choose ActionScript 2.0 Classes > Movie > MovieClip > Properties > _y, and add an equals sign.
11. Enter `_root` followed by a period. Choose ActionScript 2.0 Classes > Movie > MovieClip > Properties > _ymouse (**Figure 7.121**).
12. Choose Global Functions > Movie Clip Control > updateAfterEvent (**Figure 7.122**).

    The `updateAfterEvent` function appears in the Script pane. Flash updates the graphics on the screen each time the pointer moves, creating smoother motion.
13. Test your movie (**Figure 7.123**).

✔ Tips

- Explore using multiple movie clips that track the location of your pointer. A vertical line that follows `_xmouse` and a horizontal line that follows `_ymouse` create a moving crosshair.
- To reactivate the hand cursor when rolling over buttons or movie clips, you must create new event handlers that set the visibility of your custom cursor to `false` for each button. The statement `Mouse.show()` can then reactivate the hand cursor. Use an `onRollOut` event handler to restore your original settings. For example, if you have a custom cursor `cursor_mc` but still want the hand cursor to appear over a button `button1_btn`, use the following code:

```
button1_btn.onRollOver = function() {
    cursor_mc._visible = false;
    Mouse.show()
};
button1_btn.onRollOut = function() {
    cursor_mc._visible = true;
    Mouse.hide();
};
```

Beginning to Animate with ActionScript

The actions and methods discussed so far in this chapter—scripts that let you control and test virtually all aspects of the movie clip (appearance, position, draggability, collisions, depth level, duplication and creation, drawing capability, and masking capability)—are the basic tools for animating entirely with ActionScript. Whereas motion tweens and shape tweens are created before playback, ActionScript animation is generated during playback, so it can respond to and change according to your viewer's actions. You can use the mouse properties `_xmouse` and `_ymouse` as parameters in movie clip methods or to control movie clip properties so that the location of your viewer's pointer determines the behavior and appearance of graphics onscreen.

The following tasks show how to use the mouse properties `_xmouse` and `_ymouse` to create responsive animations. The first task is a simple game of tag. You create a movie clip that follows your pointer, and if the movie clip catches up to you, you lose the game. The second task combines `_xmouse` and `_ymouse` with the movie clip drawing methods so you can draw with the pointer. The third task is a scrolling menu that moves according to the pointer's location.

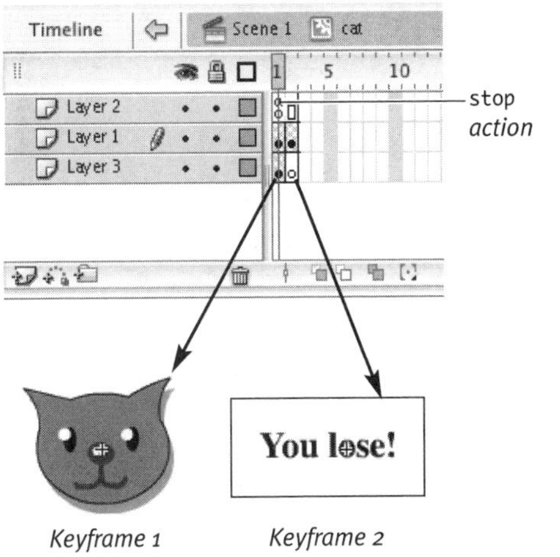

Figure 7.124 This cat movie clip displays a cat graphic in keyframe 1 when it chases your pointer and a different graphic in keyframe 2 when you lose the game.

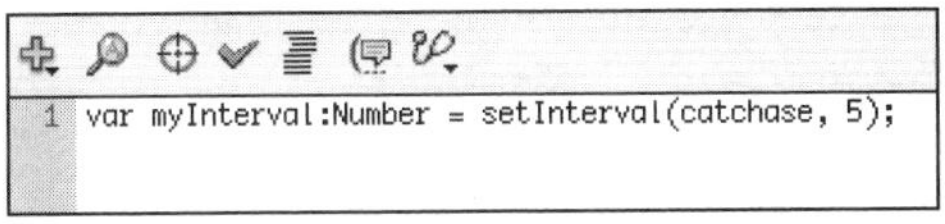

Figure 7.125 The action `setInterval`, like the event handler `onEnterFrame`, is a good way to execute ActionScript statements continuously. This `setInterval` is identified with the variable name `myInterval`.

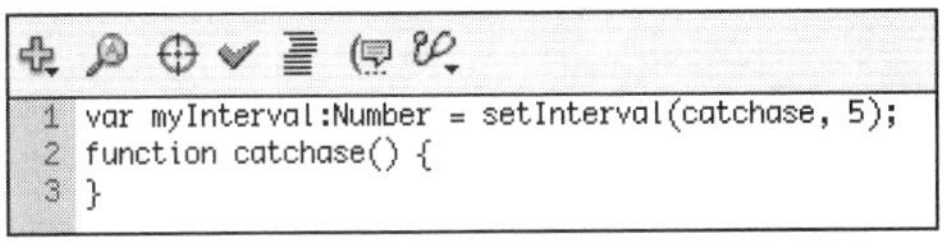

Figure 7.126 The function `catchase` will be called every 5 milliseconds.

To create a mouse-tracking game:

1. Create a movie clip symbol with two keyframes.

   The first keyframe contains a graphic and a `stop` action, and the second keyframe contains a "You lose!" message (**Figure 7.124**).

2. Place an instance of the movie clip on the Stage, and name it in the Property inspector.

   In this example, the clip is called `cat_mc`.

3. Select the first frame of the root Timeline, and open the Actions panel.

4. Declare a `Number` variable, enter an equals sign, and then choose Global Functions > Miscellaneous Actions > setInterval.

5. With your pointer between the parentheses, enter the name of a function followed by a comma and then `5` (**Figure 7.125**).

   The function you specify in the `setInterval` statement will be called every 5 milliseconds.

6. On a new line, choose Statements > User-Defined Functions > function.

7. Enter the name of the function you used in step 5 (**Figure 7.126**).

8. On the next line, enter the target path of the movie clip, followed by a period and the property _x. Then enter an equals sign.

   The statement should look like this:

   ```
   cat_mc._x =
   ```

continues on next page

9. On the same line, enter the following after the equals sign:

```
cat_mc._x + (_root._xmouse - cat_mc._x)
 / 100;
```

This statement starts with the x position of the cat movie clip and adds the difference between the mouse pointer position and the cat position. If the mouse pointer is to the right of the cat, the statement adds a positive value. If the mouse pointer is to the left of the cat, the statement adds a negative value. In either case, the cat gets closer to the mouse. The division by 100 makes sure that the cat doesn't jump on the mouse immediately. The increment is small (one-hundredth of the distance), so the cat lags behind the position of the mouse pointer.

10. On the next line, enter the same information for the y coordinate (**Figure 7.127**).

11. Still inside the function, on a new line, choose Statements > Conditions/ Loops > if.

12. For the condition inside the parentheses of the `if` statement, enter the following:

```
cat_mc.hitTest(_root._xmouse,
_root._ymouse, true)
```

This statement uses the `hitTest()` method to test whether the x and y positions of the mouse pointer intersect the cat movie clip. The `shapeflag` parameter (the third parameter) is set to `true` so that only the graphics of the cat movie clip are considered rather than the entire bounding box (**Figure 7.128**).

13. In between the curly braces of the `if` statement, enter the target path for the cat movie clip followed by a period.

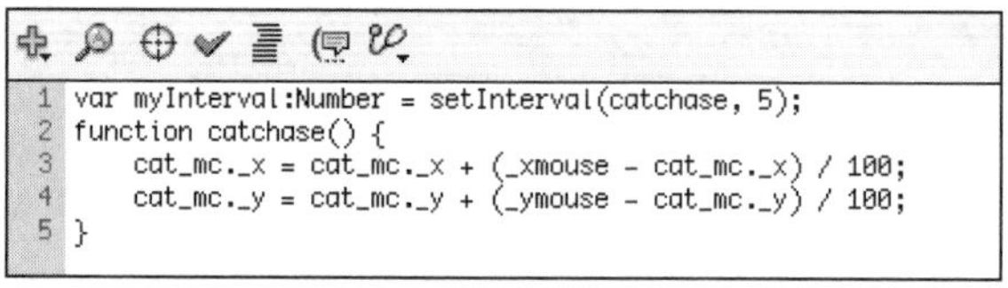

```
var myInterval:Number = setInterval(catchase, 5);
function catchase() {
    cat_mc._x = cat_mc._x + (_xmouse - cat_mc._x) / 100;
    cat_mc._y = cat_mc._y + (_ymouse - cat_mc._y) / 100;
}
```

Figure 7.127 The x and y positions of the cat movie clip instance change according to the position of the pointer.

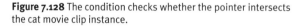

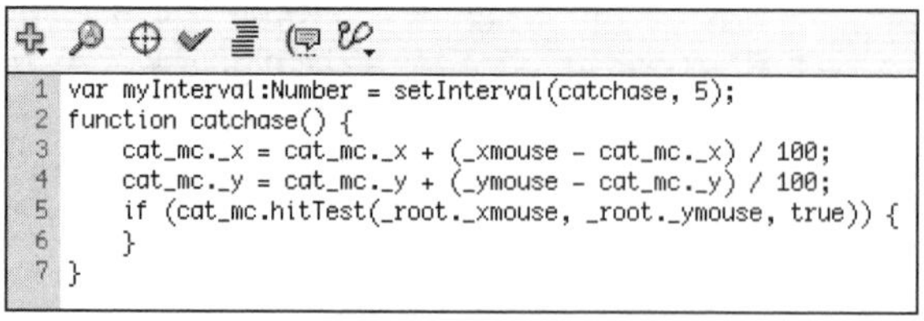

```
var myInterval:Number = setInterval(catchase, 5);
function catchase() {
    cat_mc._x = cat_mc._x + (_xmouse - cat_mc._x) / 100;
    cat_mc._y = cat_mc._y + (_ymouse - cat_mc._y) / 100;
    if (cat_mc.hitTest(_root._xmouse, _root._ymouse, true)) {
    }
}
```

Figure 7.128 The condition checks whether the pointer intersects the cat movie clip instance.

```
var myInterval:Number = setInterval(catchase, 5);
function catchase() {
    cat_mc._x = cat_mc._x + (_xmouse - cat_mc._x) / 100;
    cat_mc._y = cat_mc._y + (_ymouse - cat_mc._y) / 100;
    if (cat_mc.hitTest(_root._xmouse, _root._ymouse, true)) {
        cat_mc.nextFrame();
    }
}
```

Figure 7.129 The cat movie clip advances to the next frame in its Timeline.

```
var myInterval:Number = setInterval(catchase, 5);
function catchase() {
    cat_mc._x = cat_mc._x + (_xmouse - cat_mc._x) / 100;
    cat_mc._y = cat_mc._y + (_ymouse - cat_mc._y) / 100;
    if (cat_mc.hitTest(_root._xmouse, _root._ymouse, true)) {
        cat_mc.nextFrame();
        clearInterval(myInterval);
    }
}
```

Figure 7.130 The interval is cleared.

```
var myInterval:Number = setInterval(catchase, 5);
function catchase() {
    cat_mc._x = cat_mc._x + (_xmouse - cat_mc._x) / 100;
    cat_mc._y = cat_mc._y + (_ymouse - cat_mc._y) / 100;
    if (cat_mc.hitTest(_root._xmouse, _root._ymouse, true)) {
        cat_mc.nextFrame();
        clearInterval(myInterval);
    }
    updateAfterEvent();
}
```

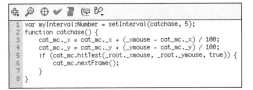

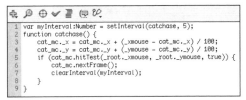

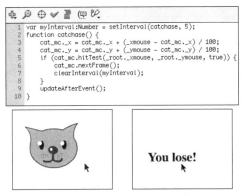

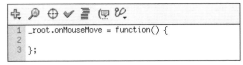

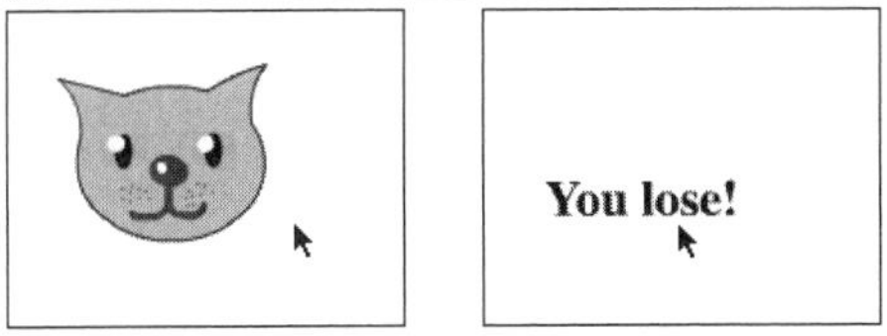

Figure 7.131 The ActionScript assigned to the catchase function (top) provides all the interactivity for the mouse-chasing game. The cat movie clip chases the pointer (left) and displays a message that was hidden on frame 2 of its Timeline when it intersects with the pointer (right).

```
_root.onMouseMove = function() {

};
```

Figure 7.132 The onMouseMove event handler is created for the root Timeline.

14. Choose ActionScript 2.0 Classes > Movie > MovieClip > Methods > nextFrame.

When `hitTest()` returns `true`, the cat movie clip advances to the next frame, displaying the "You lose!" message (**Figure 7.129**).

15. On the next line, choose Global Functions > Miscellaneous Functions > clearInterval.

16. For the parameter of the action `clearInterval()` x, enter the name of the variable that is storing the ID of your `setInterval` statement in step 4 (**Figure 7.130**).

The interval created by `setInterval` is cleared, preventing the `catChase` function from being invoked, which stops the cat movie clip from following the mouse pointer.

17. Create a new line after the closing brace of the `if` statement, and choose Global Functions > Movie Clip Control > updateAfterEvent.

18. Test your movie (**Figure 7.131**).

To draw with the pointer:

1. Select the first frame of the root Timeline, and open the Actions panel.
2. Enter `_root` followed by a period.
3. Choose ActionScript 2.0 Classes > Movie > MovieClip > Event Handlers > onMouseMove (**Figure 7.132**).
4. On the next line, inside the `onMouseMove` event, enter `_root`, followed by a period.
5. Choose ActionScript 2.0 Classes > Movie > MovieClip > Drawing Methods > lineStyle.

continues on next page

6. With your pointer between the parentheses, enter a thickness, a hex-code value, and an alpha value (**Figure 7.133**).
7. On the next line, enter `_root`, followed by a period.
8. Choose ActionScript 2.0 Classes > Movie > MovieClip > Drawing Methods > lineTo.
9. With your pointer between the parentheses, enter `_root._xmouse`, a comma, and `_root._ymouse` (**Figure 7.134**).

   Whenever the pointer moves, Flash draws a line segment from the previous position to the current position of the pointer.
10. On a new line but still within the `onMouseMove` event handler, choose Global Functions > Movie Clip Control > updateAfterEvent.
11. Test your movie (**Figure 7.135**).

```
_root.onMouseMove = function() {
    _root.lineStyle(1, 0xFF0000, 100);
};
```

Figure 7.133 This line style is defined as a 1-point red line.

```
_root.onMouseMove = function() {
    _root.lineStyle(1, 0xFF0000, 100);
    _root.lineTo(_root._xmouse, _root._ymouse);
};
```

Figure 7.134 The `lineTo()` method draws a segment to the x, y position of the mouse pointer.

```
_root.onMouseMove = function() {
    _root.lineStyle(1, 0xFF0000, 100);
    _root.lineTo(_root._xmouse, _root._ymouse);
    updateAfterEvent();
};
```

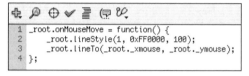

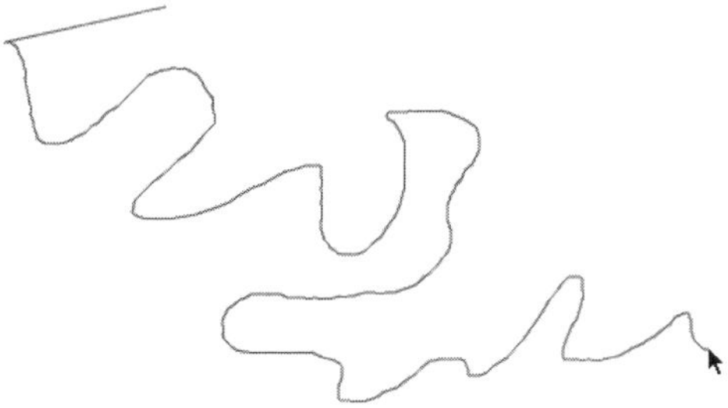

Figure 7.135 Whenever your mouse pointer moves, a new line segment is drawn, creating a simple drawing program.

To create a scrolling menu that responds to the mouse pointer:

1. Create a movie clip that contains a long row of buttons or graphics (**Figure 7.136**), put it on the Stage, and name it in the Property inspector.
2. Select the first frame of the root Timeline, and open the Actions panel.
3. Enter `_root`, followed by a period.
4. Choose Objects > Movie > MovieClip > Event Handlers > onEnterFrame (**Figure 7.137**).
5. On the next line of the `onEnterFrame` event, enter the name of your movie clip, followed by a period and then `_x` for its *x* property.
6. Enter an equals sign, the name of your movie clip, a period, and _x; then enter this expression:

   ```
   + (.5 * Stage.width - _root._xmouse)
    / 10
   ```

   When you subtract the horizontal position of the mouse pointer from half of the Stage width, you get a number that is positive if the pointer is on the left or negative if the pointer is on the right. Use this value to move the x position of your movie clip. The division by 10 makes the increments smaller and, hence, the movement of the movie clip slower (**Figure 7.138**).
7. Test your movie.

✔ Tip

■ The next step for this scrolling menu would be to script boundaries so the movie clip can't scroll off the screen. You'll learn about creating `if` statements in Chapter 10.

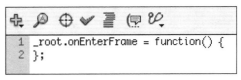

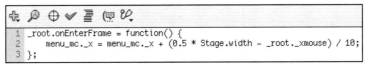

Figure 7.136 A movie clip with a long row of buttons extends off the Stage. To provide access to the buttons, the movie clip will scroll to the right or to the left, depending on where the mouse pointer is located.

```
_root.onEnterFrame = function() {
};
```

Figure 7.137 The `onEnterFrame` event handler is created on the root Timeline.

```
_root.onEnterFrame = function() {
    menu_mc._x = menu_mc._x + (0.5 * Stage.width - _root._xmouse) / 10;
};
```

Figure 7.138 The horizontal position of the mouse pointer is used to calculate the new position of the movie clip `menu_mc`.

CONTROLLING BITMAP GRAPHICS

8

One of the hallmark characteristics of Flash is that the images you create are vector images, whether you use the drawing tools in the authoring environment or the drawing methods of the `MovieClip` class. For computer-based drawing, vectors are convenient because they allow you to deal with lines, shapes, text, and other objects as a single unit rather than as a collection of pixels that must be controlled individually. However, as part of the process of displaying the Flash movie on a computer screen, the Flash Player has always converted those vectors to bitmap images behind the scenes.

In Flash 8, the curtain has been lifted, and you can now manipulate bitmap images through ActionScript. You've already seen some of the power of bitmap manipulation in the previous chapter when you learned to apply filters to movie clips. Filters are a bitmap manipulation technique, and inside the Flash Player a vector-based movie clip is converted to a bitmap before any filter effect is applied to it. In addition to the filter effects, Flash 8 includes the new `flash.display.BitmapData` class, which makes it possible to manipulate a bitmap image directly. Using the properties and methods of the `BitmapData` class, you can create your own filters and graphical effects to enhance your Flash projects. You can add subtle touches, like converting an image to grayscale or fading two images together. Add textures and static to give it a worn look. Or go wild, invert images, chop them into pieces like a puzzle, and envelop them in a cloud of flame! With the bitmap manipulation capabilities in Flash 8, the possibilities are literally unlimited.

Creating and Accessing Images

A bitmap image consists of a series of rows and columns of colored dots known as *pixels*. Each pixel is assigned a single color value containing a mix of red, green, blue, and possibly alpha (transparency) values. Although the image's pixels often form shapes that humans recognize, such as a rectangle, a sweeping landscape, or a person's smiling face, the computer is only aware of the individual pixel values and knows nothing about what the content of the bitmap represents. When you use the `BitmapData` class to manipulate image information, all the changes are made to the individual pixel's color values.

The first step to manipulating a bitmap image is to create an instance of the `BitmapData` class. Sometimes you'll want to start with a new, blank image, and many times you'll want to manipulate an existing image such as a digital photo.

As with most objects in ActionScript, to create a new `BitmapData` object you declare a variable with its data type set to `BitmapData`, and then you create a new instance by calling the `BitmapData` constructor function. The `BitmapData` constructor takes up to four parameters. You must use the first two parameters, a width and height for the image. You can optionally add two more parameters to specify whether the image will use transparency (alpha channel) information and what color to fill the image with initially.

In previous chapters, you used hexadecimal numbers to specify color values in the form 0xRRGGBB, where *RR* is a two-digit value for the amount of red in the image, *GG* for the amount of green, and *BB* for the amount of blue. Several of the `BitmapData` methods require you to provide a numeric color parameter. For a `BitmapData` object with no alpha channel, the six-digit hexadecimal format is still used. If the `BitmapData` object has an alpha channel, you use a similar format, with eight digits instead of six, like this: 0x*AARRGGBB*. In this case, you add two extra digits that represent the alpha value after the 0x prefix but before the two red digits. These two digits indicate the amount of transparency the color will have. As with the other color values, the possible alpha values range from 0 (00) to 255 (FF). Note that this is different than the `MovieClip` class's `_alpha` property, which uses a percentage from 0 to 100.

Finally, one important idea to keep in mind is that by itself, a `BitmapData` object doesn't have a visible representation on the Stage. If you want to see a `BitmapData` object, you must attach it to a movie clip on the Stage using the `MovieClip` class's `attachBitmap()` method. In the next two tasks, you'll see how to create a `BitmapData` object with a solid color or by loading an image into the object. The task "To display a `BitmapData` object on the Stage" shows how to make the object visible to the user.

To create a new BitmapData object:

1. In the Script pane, enter an `import` statement for the `flash.display.BitmapData` class.

2. On the next line, declare a variable using the `var` statement followed by the variable name and then `:BitmapData` for the variable's type.

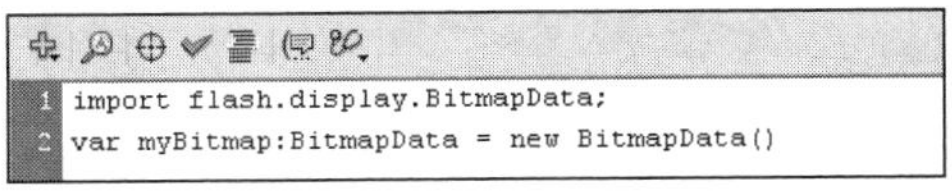

Figure 8.1 The constructor function new `BitmapData()` creates a `BitmapData` object.

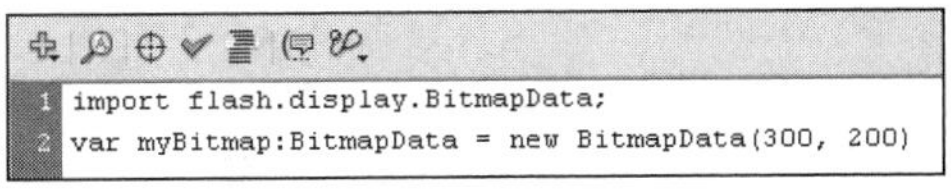

import flash.display.BitmapData;
var myBitmap:BitmapData = new BitmapData(300, 200)

Figure 8.2 The first two parameters of the `BitmapData` constructor specify the width and height of the bitmap.

3. On the same line, enter an equals sign, and then choose ActionScript 2.0 Classes > "flash.display package" > BitmapData > new BitmapData (**Figure 8.1**).

4. Inside the parentheses of the `BitmapData` constructor function, enter two number parameters for the width and height of the bitmap image in pixels (**Figure 8.2**).

   Remember to separate the parameters with a comma.

5. If you don't want the `BitmapData` object to use alpha information, enter the value `false` for the third parameter.

   If you don't specify a value, the value `true` is used automatically.

6. To specify the initial color for the bitmap, enter a six- or eight-digit numeric color value as the fourth parameter in the constructor.

   If you set the third parameter to false, you should use a six-digit number; otherwise, use an eight-digit number (**Figure 8.3**).

   If you leave off this parameter, the `BitmapData` object is filled with solid white pixels by default.

   At this point, the `BitmapData` object only exists in the computer's memory and isn't displayed on the Stage.

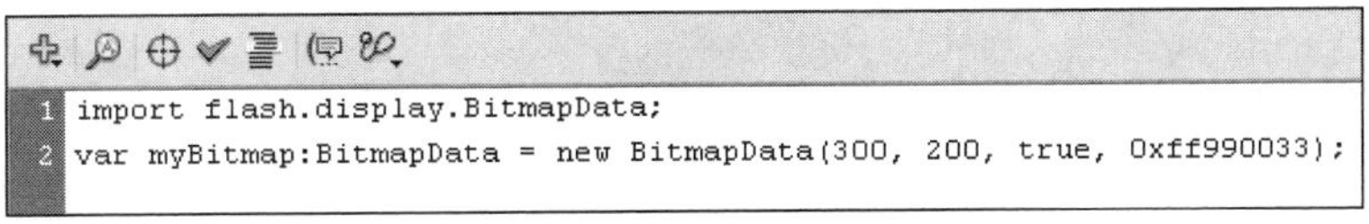

import flash.display.BitmapData;
var myBitmap:BitmapData = new BitmapData(300, 200, true, 0xff990033);

Figure 8.3 A new `BitmapData` object is created that is 300 pixels wide and 200 pixels high. The pixels contain alpha channel information (indicated by the `true` parameter), and they're all set to the same color. In order, the four pairs of hexadecimal numbers define this color with alpha `ff` (fully opaque), lots of red (99), no green (`00`), and a small amount of blue (33).

Accessing images dynamically

In addition to creating an image filled with a single color, as in the previous task, you can prepopulate your `BitmapData` object with image information. You can use the `loadImage()` method to retrieve an image from the Library and turn it into a `BitmapData` object. You can also copy a snapshot of a movie clip into a `BitmapData` object using the `draw()` method. Using this approach, you can load an external image file using any of the techniques for loading content into a movie clip and then copy that image into a `BitmapData` object to manipulate it.

Figure 8.4 After you import an image into Flash, it appears in the Library as a Bitmap item.

To access a Library image:

1. In your Flash document, add an image to the Library by choosing File > Import > Import to Library, browsing to your image file in the dialog box, and clicking OK.

   Your image appears in the Library, identified as a Bitmap item (**Figure 8.4**).

2. Select the bitmap in the Library panel. In the Library panel's Options menu, choose Linkage to open the Linkage Properties dialog box.

3. Select the Export for ActionScript check box, and enter a value in the Identifier field (**Figure 8.5**). Click OK to close the dialog box.

   As you did with movie clip symbols in the previous chapter, you must give the Library image a linkage identifier in order to be able to access it dynamically with ActionScript.

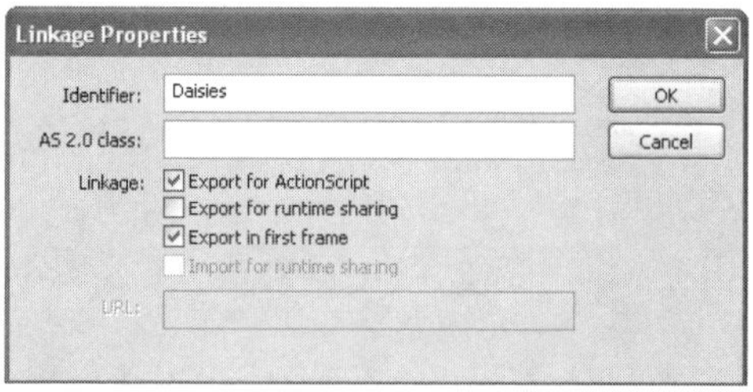

Figure 8.5 To access the Bitmap Library item, you must export it for ActionScript and give it a linkage identifier.

4. Select the first keyframe of the main Timeline, and open the Actions panel.

5. In the Script pane, add an `import` statement for the `flash.display.BitmapData` class.

6. On the next line, declare a variable using the `var` statement followed by the variable name and then `:BitmapData` for the variable's type.

7. On the same line, enter an equals sign followed by `BitmapData.loadBitmap()` (**Figure 8.6**).

   Like the methods of the `Mouse` class or the `Key` class, the `loadBitmap` method is a *static method*, meaning it's called using the name of the class rather than requiring an object instance of the class. The `loadBitmap` method is the only static method of the `BitmapData` class; all the other methods require you to create a `BitmapData` object as you did in the previous task and call the methods on that instance.

8. In the parentheses of the `loadBitmap` method, enter the linkage identifier of your Library image, surrounded by quotation marks (**Figure 8.7**).

   The bitmap image from the Library is now stored in the `BitmapData` object.

To display a bitmap on the Stage:

1. Continuing with the previous task, on a new line, create an empty movie clip by calling the `createEmptyMovieClip` method on the `_root` movie clip, as described in the Chapter 7.

2. On the next line, enter the name of your movie clip and then a period. Choose ActionScript 2.0 Classes > Movie > MovieClip > Methods > attachBitmap.

continues on next page

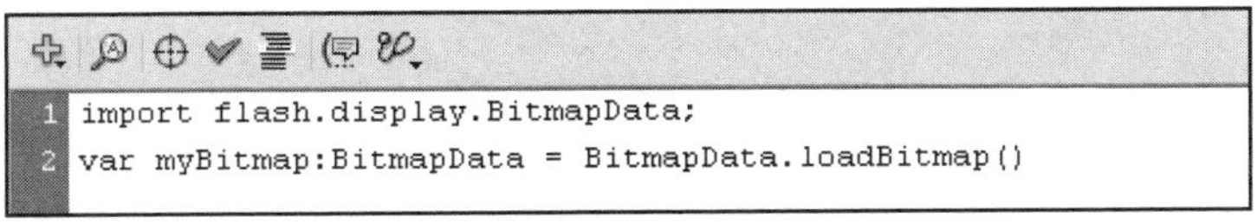
import flash.display.BitmapData;
var myBitmap:BitmapData = BitmapData.loadBitmap()

Figure 8.6 To retrieve an image from the Library and assign it to a `BitmapData` object, use the static method `BitmapData.loadBitmap()`.

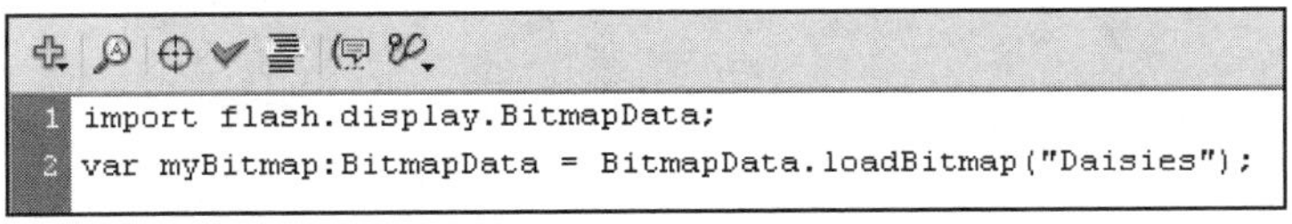
import flash.display.BitmapData;
var myBitmap:BitmapData = BitmapData.loadBitmap("Daisies");

Figure 8.7 The `loadBitmap` method's linkage ID parameter (`"Daisies"` in this example) tells Flash which image to load from the Library.

3. Between the parentheses, enter the name of your `BitmapData` object, a comma, and then a number for the depth level where the `BitmapData` object should be placed (**Figure 8.8**).

   Like dynamically created movie clips, `BitmapData` objects must be placed on a unique depth level within their container movie clip.

4. Test your movie.

   The movie clip containing your `BitmapData` object appears on the Stage. The top-left corner of the bitmap is placed at the registration point of the movie clip, which in this example is at the top-left corner of the Stage (**Figure 8.9**).

To copy a movie clip's contents into a bitmap:

1. Create a movie clip symbol, place an instance on the Stage, and give it an instance name in the Property inspector (**Figure 8.10**).

   or

   Use ActionScript to dynamically create or attach a movie clip to the Stage.

2. Select the first keyframe on the Timeline, and open the Actions panel.

3. In the Script pane, enter an `import` statement for the `flash.display.BitmapData` class.

```
import flash.display.BitmapData;
var myBitmap:BitmapData = BitmapData.loadBitmap("Daisies");
var content:MovieClip = _root.createEmptyMovieClip("content_mc", 1);
content.attachBitmap(myBitmap, 1);
```

Figure 8.8 Use the `MovieClip` class's `attachBitmap` method to add a `BitmapData` object to a movie clip on the Stage.

Figure 8.9 The final result is an image dynamically loaded from the Library and displayed in a movie clip on the Stage.

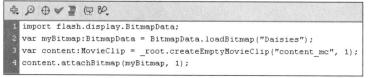

Figure 8.10 A snapshot, or single frame, of this movie clip animation, named `source_mc`, will be copied into a `BitmapData` object.

4. Declare a variable with the data type `BitmapData`, followed by an equals sign. Choose ActionScript 2.0 Classes > "flash.display package" > BitmapData > "new BitmapData".

5. Inside the parentheses, enter your movie clip's name, a period and `_width`, followed by a comma, then your movie clip's name, a period, and `_height`.

   This sets the `BitmapData` object's width and height to match the movie clip's width and height (**Figure 8.11**).

6. On the next line, enter your `BitmapData` object's name followed by a period. Choose ActionScript 2.0 Classes > "flash.display package" > BitmapData > Methods > draw.

7. Between the parentheses, enter the name of your movie clip (**Figure 8.12**).

   The `draw` method copies (*draws*) a snapshot of the current frame of the movie clip onto the `BitmapData` object.

continues on next page

```
import flash.display.BitmapData;
var bmp:BitmapData = new BitmapData(source_mc._width, source_mc._height);
```

Figure 8.11 Set the width and height equal to the `_width` and `_height` properties of your movie clip.

```
import flash.display.BitmapData;
var bmp:BitmapData = new BitmapData(source_mc._width, source_mc._height);
bmp.draw(source_mc);
```

Figure 8.12 As the parameter of the `draw` method, enter the name of the movie clip to be copied.

8. To view the contents of your `BitmapData` object, enter code to attach it to a movie clip on the Stage, as described in the previous task (**Figure 8.13**).

✔ Tips

- If the movie clip is an animation or video with more than one frame, you can put the `draw` method inside an `onEnterFrame` event handler function to continuously update the `BitmapData` object to match the current frame of the movie clip.
- You can't load an external image file into a `BitmapData` object directly. However, there are several methods (described in Chapter 6) to load an external image into a movie clip. Once the image has loaded into a movie clip, use the `draw` method to copy it into a `BitmapData` object.

  This may seem like a limitation, but it has significant benefits. For example, you can use all the image-loading capabilities available to movie clip objects, such as using the `MovieClipLoader` class to preload an external image, and you can then manipulate the image as a `BitmapData` object.

```
import flash.display.BitmapData;
var bmp:BitmapData = new BitmapData(source_mc._width, source_mc._height);
bmp.draw(source_mc);
var target:MovieClip = _root.createEmptyMovieClip("target_mc", 1);
target._x = 265;
target._y = 220;
target.attachBitmap(bmp, 1);
```

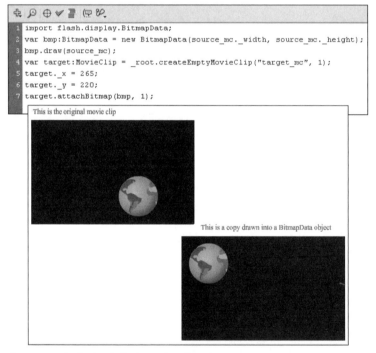

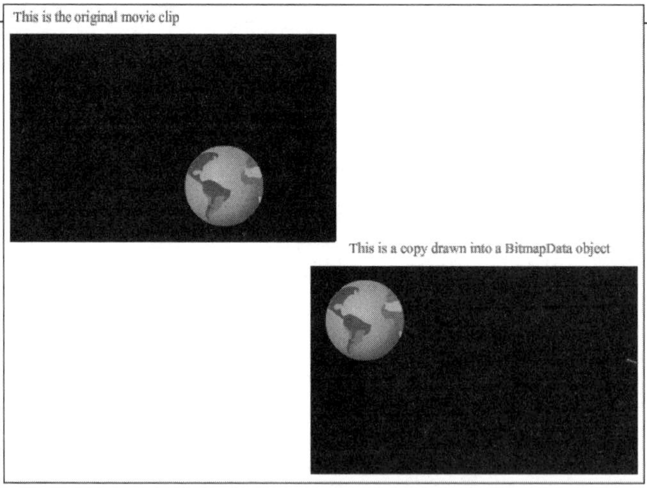
This is the original movie clip
This is a copy drawn into a BitmapData object

Figure 8.13 The final code (top) attaches the `BitmapData` snapshot to a movie clip on the Stage (bottom). While the movie clip continues to animate, the `BitmapData` object contains a static image.

```
7  myBitmap.dispose();
8  delete myBitmap;
```

Figure 8.14 Use the BitmapData class's dispose method in conjunction with the delete statement to let Flash know you're finished with a BitmapData object, to free up memory.

- You can hide the source movie clip by setting its _x and _y properties so that it's off the Stage. Only your bitmap duplicate, modified with whatever effects you choose, will appear on the Stage.

- The movie clip you copy into the BitmapData object doesn't have to contain an animation. For instance, if you want to overlay text on an image, you can create a new empty movie clip, attach text to it (as described in Chapter 11), and then use the draw method to copy the movie clip's contents into the BitmapData object.

 This approach saves you the trouble of creating the text image outside of Flash and makes it possible to use dynamic text entered by the user.

To remove a BitmapData image:

1. In the Script pane, enter the name of your BitmapData object. Choose Action-Script 2.0 Classes > "flash.display package" > BitmapData > Methods > dispose. Because BitmapData objects potentially require a large amount of the computer's memory, this step helps the Flash Player know that it's safe to clear out the BitmapData object.

2. Enter delete followed by the BitmapData object's name to completely remove the object from the Flash Player's memory (**Figure 8.14**).

✔ Tips

- Calling the dispose method on a BitmapData object that is attached to a movie clip causes the BitmapData object to disappear from the Stage (although its parent movie clip remains).

- Be careful not to try to manipulate or access a BitmapData object once you have called its dispose method; at that point, its width and height are set to 0, and its methods and properties won't work.

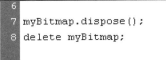

Drawing on a BitmapData Object

There is little use in creating a `BitmapData` object just to hold an image. The `BitmapData` class's real strength is in manipulating the image's pixels. The most basic way to do this is to draw color onto the bitmap.

You can change the color of a single pixel at a time using the `setPixel` and `setPixel32` methods. To cover a larger area, use the `fillRect` method to set all the pixels in a rectangular portion of a `BitmapData` object to the same color; the `floodFill` method lets you fill in a region of color with a different color, similar to the Paint Bucket tool in many graphics programs. Finally, using the `getPixel` and `getPixel32` methods, you can identify the color of a pixel in a `BitmapData` object, much like the Eyedropper tool that is common in image-editing programs.

To draw single pixels:

1. Create a movie clip symbol that will be used to display your `BitmapData` object, and place an instance on the Stage. Give it an instance name in the Property inspector.

2. Select the first keyframe on the Timeline, and open the Actions panel.

3. As you have done in the previous tasks, declare and instantiate a new `BitmapData` variable with `width` and `height` parameters equal to the width and height of your movie clip, and use the `attachBitmap` method to attach the `BitmapData` object to your movie clip (**Figure 8.15**).

   Remember to either add an `import` statement for the `flash.display.BitmapData` class or use the full name of the class when declaring and instantiating your `BitmapData` object.

```
import flash.display.BitmapData;
var myBitmap:BitmapData = new BitmapData(300, 300);
frame_mc.attachBitmap(myBitmap, 1);
```

Figure 8.15 A new `BitmapData` object called `myBitmap` is created, which is 300 pixels square. It's attached to a movie clip called `frame_mc` on the Stage.

```
import flash.display.BitmapData;
var myBitmap:BitmapData = new BitmapData(300, 300);
frame_mc.attachBitmap(myBitmap, 1);
frame_mc.onPress = function() {
    myBitmap.setPixel()
};
```

Figure 8.16 When the mouse button is pressed over the movie clip called `frame_mc`, the `setPixel` method will be called.

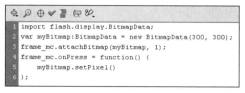

4. On a new line, create an `onPress` event handler function for your movie clip.
5. Between the curly braces of the event handler function, enter the name of your `BitmapData` object. Choose ActionScript 2.0 Classes > "flash.display package" > BitmapData > Methods > setPixel.

   The `setPixel` method is called on your `BitmapData` object (**Figure 8.16**).
6. Inside the parentheses of the `setPixel` method, enter three number parameters separated by commas.

   The first and second parameters indicate the x- and y-coordinates of the pixel whose color should be set, and the third parameter is the numeric color value to apply to the pixel.

   In this example, the `_xmouse` property of the movie clip is used as the x-coordinate, and the `_ymouse` property is used as the y-coordinate, so that the color is applied to the pixel directly below the mouse pointer (**Figure 8.17**).
7. Test your movie.

   As you click different places on the movie clip, those pixels are set to the designated color (**Figure 8.18**).

```
import flash.display.BitmapData;
var myBitmap:BitmapData = new BitmapData(300, 300);
frame_mc.attachBitmap(myBitmap, 1);
frame_mc.onPress = function() {
    myBitmap.setPixel(frame_mc._xmouse, frame_mc._ymouse, 0x990000);
};
```

Figure 8.17 The three parameters of the `setPixel` method set the color of the pixel at the x, y coordinate matching the mouse cursor's position to crimson red.

```
import flash.display.BitmapData;
var myBitmap:BitmapData = new BitmapData(300, 300);
frame_mc.attachBitmap(myBitmap, 1);
frame_mc.onPress = function() {
    myBitmap.setPixel(frame_mc._xmouse, frame_mc._ymouse, 0x990000);
};
frame_mc.useHandCursor = false;
```

Figure 8.18 The final code (top) draws a red pixel every time the mouse is clicked over the movie clip (bottom). The movie clip's `useHandCursor` property is set to false so that Flash uses an arrow pointer rather than the hand that appears by default.

✔ Tips

- The `setPixel` method only accepts color values without an alpha channel; that is, color values specified as six-digit hexadecimal values. To change a pixel's color to a color that is partially transparent, use the `setPixel32` method instead.
- To create a more conventional drawing behavior, use a Boolean variable to track whether the mouse is pressed, and then use an `onMouseMove` event handler to continue to draw pixels as long as the mouse button is held down. This technique, known as a *continuous-feedback button*, is explained in Chapter 10.

To fill a rectangle with a color:

1. Select the first keyframe, and open the Actions panel.
2. Add two `import` statements, one for the `flash.display.BitmapData` class and another on the next line for the `flash.geom.Rectangle` class.
3. As you have done in previous tasks, enter the ActionScript to declare and instantiate a `BitmapData` object, and then add the code to create an empty movie clip and attach the `BitmapData` object to that clip (**Figure 8.19**).
4. On a new line, declare a variable using the `var` statement, giving it the data type `Rectangle`.

```
import flash.display.BitmapData;
import flash.geom.Rectangle;
var bmp:BitmapData = new BitmapData(280, 180, false, 0x000000);
var clip:MovieClip = _root.createEmptyMovieClip("clip_mc", 1);
clip.attachBitmap(bmp, 1);
```

Figure 8.19 A new `BitmapData` object called `bmp` is created and attached to a movie clip. The `BitmapData` object is 280 pixels wide by 180 pixels high and is filled with black pixels.

```
var rect:Rectangle = new Rectangle(10, 12, 101, 88);
```

Figure 8.20 A new `Rectangle` object called `rect` is created. This object represents a rectangular region at the coordinate *(10, 12)* that is 101 pixels wide and 88 pixels high.

```
bmp.fillRect(rect, 0x990000);
```

Figure 8.21 The `fillRect` method fills the region defined by a `Rectangle` object named `rect` with the color `0x990000` (crimson).

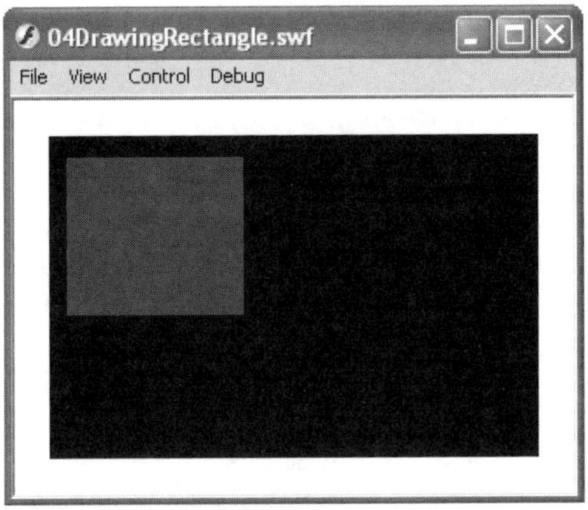

Figure 8.22 A rectangular portion of the `BitmapData` object is filled with a color.

5. On the same line, enter an equals sign, and choose ActionScript 2.0 Classes > "flash.geom package" > Rectangle > "new Rectangle".

6. In the parentheses of the `Rectangle` constructor, enter the following four `Number` parameters: `x-coordinate`, `y-coordinate`, `width`, and `height` (**Figure 8.20**).

   A `Rectangle` object represents a rectangular region. The x- and y-coordinates represent the top left corner of the rectangle, which has the width and height specified in the parameters.

7. On the next line, enter the name of your `BitmapData` object followed by a period. Choose ActionScript 2.0 Classes > "flash.display package" > BitmapData > Methods > fillRect.

   The `fillRect` method is added to the script. This method fills a rectangular region with a solid color.

8. Inside the parentheses of the `fillRect` method, enter two parameters separated by a comma (**Figure 8.21**).

   For the first parameter, enter the name of your `Rectangle` object, indicating the section of the `BitmapData` objects that should be colored.

   For the second parameter, enter a numeric color value indicating what color to set the pixels in the rectangle.

9. Test your movie.

   The `BitmapData` object is drawn on the Stage, and the rectangular region is filled in with the color you chose (**Figure 8.22**).

To fill a region with a color:

1. Import an image that has one or more regions of solid color into the Library using the File > Import > Import to Library command. Give the image a linkage identifier, as described earlier in this chapter.
2. Select the first keyframe, and open the Actions panel.
3. In the Script pane, enter an `import` statement for the `flash.display.BitmapData` class.
4. On the next line, declare a `BitmapData` variable, and add the code to load your Library image into the `BitmapData` object (using the `BitmapData.loadBitmap()` method).
5. Add the code to create an empty movie clip on the `_root` object, and attach your `BitmapData` object to that movie clip (**Figure 8.23**).

   Up to this point, these are all things you have seen in previous tasks.
6. On the next line, create an `onPress` event handler function for your movie clip.
7. Inside the `onPress` event handler's curly braces, enter the name of your `BitmapData` object followed by a period, and then choose ActionScript 2.0 Classes > "flash.display package" > BitmapData > Methods > floodFill.

```
import flash.display.BitmapData;
var bmp:BitmapData = BitmapData.loadBitmap("mouse");
var clip:MovieClip = _root.createEmptyMovieClip("clip_mc", 1);
clip.attachBitmap(bmp, 1);
```

Figure 8.23 This code creates a new `BitmapData` object named `bmp` and a new movie clip named `clip`, and places the `BitmapData` object inside the movie clip on the Stage.

```
clip.onPress = function() {
    bmp.floodFill()
};              flash.display.BitmapData.floodFill( x:Number, y:Number, color:Number )
```

Figure 8.24 The `BitmapData` class's `floodFill` method takes three parameters: the x and y location of the starting point of the fill and the fill color.

8. Enter the following three parameters in the parentheses of the `floodFill` method call (**Figure 8.24**):

   x: The x-coordinate of the pixel to use as the starting point for the fill operation

   y: The y-coordinate of the starting pixel

   color: The numeric color to set as the color for the affected pixels

   In this example, enter the mouse pointer's x and y position, determined using the movie clip's `_xmouse` and `_ymouse` properties, as the starting point for the fill (**Figure 8.25**).

9. Test your movie.

   As you click in regions of solid color, those regions are filled with the color you chose in the `floodFill` method (**Figure 8.26**).

✔ Tip

- Unlike many image-editing programs, which allow you to specify a tolerance level for filling a region, the `floodFill` method only fills pixels whose color is exactly the same as the starting pixel.

```
clip.onPress = function() {
    bmp.floodFill(clip._xmouse, clip._ymouse, 0xcccccc);
};
```

Figure 8.25 In this example, the values passed as parameters are the _xmouse and _ymouse properties of the movie clip and the color oxcccccc (light gray).

```
import flash.display.BitmapData;
var bmp:BitmapData = BitmapData.loadBitmap("mouse");
var clip:MovieClip = _root.createEmptyMovieClip("clip_mc", 1);
clip.attachBitmap(bmp, 1);
clip.onPress = function() {
    bmp.floodFill(clip._xmouse, clip._ymouse, 0xcccccc);
};
```

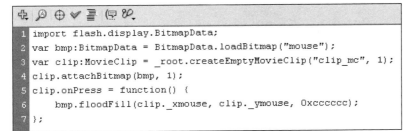

Figure 8.26 The final code (left) fills continuous regions of color with a new color (right) when you click in those spaces.

To get a color from an image:

1. Create a BitmapData object using any of the methods described in the previous tasks.
2. On a new line, declare a Number variable, which will be used to store the color value of the pixel you choose.
3. At the end of the same line, enter an equals sign followed by the name of your BitmapData object. Choose ActionScript 2.0 Classes > "flash.display package" > BitmapData > Methods > getPixel.
4. Inside the parentheses of the getPixel method, enter two parameters: the x- and y-coordinates for the pixel whose color you want to know (**Figure 8.27**).

   The color of the selected pixel is stored in the Number variable.

✔ Tip

- The color value provided by the getPixel method only includes the red, green, and blue color information for the chosen pixel. If you want to know the alpha channel value as well, you must use the getPixel32 method instead.

```
var color:Number = img.getPixel(xCoord, yCoord);
```

Figure 8.27 The BitmapData class's getPixel method targets a pixel and returns a number that is the numeric color value at that pixel.

Copying image information

In addition to setting colors directly on an image, a common image-manipulation task is to incorporate part or all of one image into another image. Perhaps you want to duplicate an image in multiple places on the screen. Or maybe you want to copy a `BitmapData` object so that you can make changes to it without modifying the original. The `BitmapData` class offers several ways to accomplish the task of copying image data.

You have already used the `draw` method to copy a movie clip to a `BitmapData` object; that same method can be used to copy all or part of a `BitmapData` object onto another, optionally applying one of the blending modes described in Chapter 7.

In addition, there are methods to make an exact copy of a `BitmapData` object (the `clone` method), to copy all the colors (`copyPixels`) or just a single color channel (`copyChannel`) from one `BitmapData` object into another, and even a method to combine the colors of two `BitmapData` objects (the `merge` method). The following tasks demonstrate the use of these methods.

To make an exact copy of a bitmap:

1. Declare a `BitmapData` variable, and load an image into it using any of the techniques described earlier.

   Don't forget to include an `import` statement for the `flash.display.BitmapData` class (**Figure 8.28**).

2. On a new line, declare another `BitmapData` variable, and enter an equals sign at the end of the line.

3. On the same line, enter the name of your first `BitmapData` object and a period. Choose ActionScript 2.0 Classes > "flash.display package" > BitmapData > Methods > clone (**Figure 8.29**).

   This method doesn't need any parameters, but it still requires the parentheses. It creates a new `BitmapData` object that is an exact duplicate of the original (the one calling the `clone` method) and assigns it to the second `BitmapData` object.

4. To display your `BitmapData` objects, attach them to movie clip instances as you have done in previous tasks.

```
import flash.display.BitmapData;
var orig:BitmapData = BitmapData.loadBitmap("daisies");
```

Figure 8.28 The `BitmapData` class is imported, and an image is loaded into a `BitmapData` object called `orig`. This is the original image that will be duplicated.

```
import flash.display.BitmapData;
var orig:BitmapData = BitmapData.loadBitmap("daisies");
var copy:BitmapData = orig.clone();
```

Figure 8.29 The `clone` method creates an exact copy of a `BitmapData` object and places it in a new `BitmapData` object.

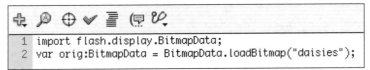

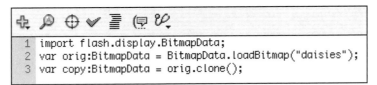

To copy part of an image onto another image:

1. Enter `import` statements for the following three classes (**Figure 8.30**):
   - ▲ `flash.display.BitmapData`
   - ▲ `flash.geom.Point`
   - ▲ `flash.geom.Rectangle`
2. As described previously, create a `BitmapData` object that will be the source for the copying operation.
3. Create a second `BitmapData` object that the image will be copied onto. This `BitmapData` object can contain an image, a solid color, or any other bitmap information (**Figure 8.31**).
4. Declare a `Rectangle` object followed by an equals sign, and choose ActionScript 2.0 Classes > "flash.geom package" > Rectangle > "new Rectangle". Between the parentheses, enter four parameters: the x, y, width, and height values corresponding to the rectangular portion of the source `BitmapData` object that you want to copy.
5. Declare a new `Point` variable, enter an equals sign, and choose ActionScript 2.0 Classes > "flash.geom package" > Point > "new Point". Between the parentheses for the `Point` constructor, enter two `Number` parameters x and y, which are the x- and y-coordinates of the pixel in the destination `BitmapData` object where you want the top-left corner of the copied pixels to be placed (**Figure 8.32**).

```
import flash.display.BitmapData;
import flash.geom.Rectangle;
import flash.geom.Point;
```

Figure 8.30 These `import` statements make it possible to use the `BitmapData`, `Rectangle`, and `Point` class names without specifying their full package names.

```
var src:BitmapData = BitmapData.loadBitmap("daisies");
var dest:BitmapData = new BitmapData(290, 212, false, 0x000000);
```

Figure 8.31 Two `BitmapData` objects, the source and the destination for the copying, have been created. In this case, the source image is a photo of two flowers, and the destination object is filled with solid black pixels. The source image will be cropped, so the black pixels will create a matte-like border around the image.

```
var cropping:Rectangle = new Rectangle(75, 35, 204, 126);
var destPoint:Point = new Point(43, 43);
```

Figure 8.32 The source `Rectangle` and destination `Point` objects are created, with values entered in their constructor functions.

```
dest.copyPixels(src, cropping, destPoint);
```

Figure 8.33 Using the source bitmap, source rectangle, and destination point parameters for the `copyPixels` method gives you fine-tuned control over the copying and pasting of image data.

6. Enter the name of your destination `BitmapData` object followed by a period. Choose ActionScript 2.0 Classes > "flash.display package" > BitmapData > Methods > copyPixels.

   Like the `clone` method, the `copyPixels` method copies information from one `BitmapData` object into the pixels of another `BitmapData` object. However, with `copyPixels`, the object calling the method (that is, the one to the left of the period) is the destination image.

7. Inside the parentheses for the `copyPixels` method, enter the following three parameters, separated by commas, to control how the image information is copied (**Figure 8.33**):

   `sourceBitmap`: The `BitmapData` object from which to copy pixel information (the name of the source `BitmapData` object)

   `sourceRect`: The `Rectangle` object designating the portion of the source bitmap to copy

   `destPoint`: The `Point` object designating the x- and y-coordinates on the destination image where the top-left corner of the copied rectangle should be positioned

continues on next page

8. To display the final image on the Stage, create an empty movie clip and attach the destination `BitmapData` object to it (**Figure 8.34**).

✔ Tips

- If you want to copy the entire source image, the easiest way to indicate this is to use the source `BitmapData` object's `rectangle` property as the second parameter, like this: `sourceImage.rectangle`.

  Any `BitmapData` object's `rectangle` property contains a `Rectangle` object whose size and boundaries match those of the `BitmapData` object.

- To place the copied pixels at the top-left corner of the destination image, use the `topLeft` property of the destination `BitmapData` object's `rectangle` property for the third parameter, like this: `destImage.rectangle.topLeft`.

```
import flash.display.BitmapData;
import flash.geom.Rectangle;
import flash.geom.Point;

var src:BitmapData = BitmapData.loadBitmap("daisies");
var dest:BitmapData = new BitmapData(290, 212, false, 0x000000);

var cropping:Rectangle = new Rectangle(75, 35, 204, 126);
var destPoint:Point = new Point(43, 43);

dest.copyPixels(src, cropping, destPoint);

var clip:MovieClip = _root.createEmptyMovieClip("clip_mc", 1);
clip.attachBitmap(dest, 1);
clip._x = 30;
clip._y = 85;
```

Figure 8.34 The final code (top) copies a cropped portion of the original image and places it at a point 43 pixels over and 43 pixels down from the top-left corner of the destination image, creating a frame effect (bottom).

To copy one color channel of an image onto another image:

1. Continue working with the same document from the previous task.
2. In the line with the `copyPixels` method call, change the word `copyPixels` to `copyChannel`.

   The `copyChannel` method works like the `copyPixels` method, except that it copies only one of the source image's color channels (red, green, blue, or alpha) onto a single channel of the destination image. This is similar to the command in some image manipulation programs that allows you to separate an image into its component channels.
3. Inside the parentheses of the `copyChannel` method call, add two additional parameters after the three parameters that are currently there (**Figure 8.35**). These two parameters are as follows:

   `sourceChannel`: A `Number` indicating which color channel should be copied from the source image. The value must be 1 (red), 2 (green), 4 (blue), or 8 (alpha).

   `destChannel`: A `Number` indicating the color channel in the destination image into which the copied pixels should be placed. The possible values are the same as for the `sourceChannel` parameter (1, 2, 4, or 8).
4. Test your movie.

   This time, instead of copying the entire image, only one of the color channels is copied onto the destination image.

```
dest.copyChannel(src, cropping, destPoint, 1, 1);
```

Figure 8.35 The `copyChannel` method works like the `copyPixels` method, but it copies only a single color channel from the source image (1 for red, in this case) onto a single channel of the destination image.

✔ Tips

- The copied color channel is still only one of four channels in the destination image. Any color that was already present in the other channels of the destination image will be used together with the copied channel to determine the actual color displayed. If you want the destination image to show only the copied channel, create the destination image as solid black, which has a value of 0 in all color channels.
- For an interesting effect, try using the same image as the source and destination, and copy one channel (for example, red) into a different channel (such as green). Depending on the selected color channels and the brightness of the colors in the original image, this can create a muted effect or a wildly vivid one.
- To create a grayscale representation of a single color channel from the source `BitmapData` object, call the `copyChannel` method three times. Use the same source channel for all three method calls, and use a different destination channel (1, 2, and 4) in each. For example, to create a grayscale image of the red channel, copy channel 1 to destination channel 1, copy channel 1 to destination channel 2, and finally, copy channel 1 to destination channel 4.

To blend an image onto another image:

1. As in the previous tasks, enter `import` statements for the `flash.display.BitmapData` class, the `flash.geom.Point` class, and the `flash.geom.Rectangle` class.
2. As in previous tasks, create two `BitmapData` objects that will be blended together into a single image.

   The source image will be combined onto the destination image. The dimensions of the destination image will be used for the final image.
3. Declare and instantiate a `Rectangle` object with parameters indicating the portion of the source image to copy onto the destination image.
4. Declare and instantiate a `Point` object with parameters indicating the x- and y-coordinates where the source image should be placed in the destination image (**Figure 8.36**).
5. On a new line, enter the name of the destination `BitmapData` object followed by a period. Choose ActionScript 2.0 Classes > "flash.display package" > BitmapData > Methods > merge.

```
import flash.display.BitmapData;
import flash.geom.Rectangle;
import flash.geom.Point;

var src:BitmapData = BitmapData.loadBitmap("daisies");
var dest:BitmapData = BitmapData.loadBitmap("cowboy");

var cropping:Rectangle = src.rectangle;
var destPoint:Point = dest.rectangle.topLeft;
```

Figure 8.36 To use the `merge` method, you must create two `BitmapData` objects and define the source rectangle and destination points.

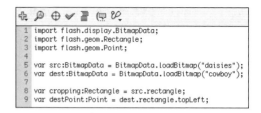

```
dest.merge(src, cropping, destPoint, 128, 128, 128, 128);
```

Figure 8.37 Entering `128` for the `merge` method's final four (multiplier) parameters creates an even blend between the two `BitmapData` objects.

Figure 8.38 Using the `merge` method, the flower image is overlaid onto the cowboy image. Because the cowboy image is the destination image, its size determines the final image size; the flower image is cropped.

6. Inside the parentheses of the `merge` method, enter seven parameters to control how the `BitmapData` objects will be blended together.

   The first three parameters, `sourceBitmap`, `sourceRect`, and `destPoint`, are equivalent to those parameters in the `copyPixels` and `copyChannel` methods, as explained in the previous tasks.

   The last four parameters are multiplier numbers between 0 and 255, which control the balance of the colors between the two images. Each parameter represents the color balance of a single channel (in the order red, green, blue, and alpha). The larger the value, the more the balance favors the source image. For instance, entering `255` for all the values shows only the source image. For an even blend between the two images, enter `128` for each parameter (**Figure 8.37**).

7. To display the result, enter code to create an empty movie clip, and attach the destination `BitmapData` object to it.

   When you test your movie, you see a new image composed of the two original images blended together (**Figure 8.38**).

Using Filters to Alter Images

In the previous chapter, you learned how filters can be applied to movie clips to add visual interest. The same filters can be applied to bitmap graphics as well, using the `BitmapData` class's `applyFilter` method. There are a few important differences between applying filters to a movie clip and applying them to a `BitmapData` object.

First, with a movie clip, the filters are just an enhancement; they can be added or removed at any time without altering the underlying movie clip. However, when a filter is applied to a `BitmapData` object, the object itself (that is, the information it contains about pixels and color values) is directly modified; there is no way to undo the change or remove a filter from a `BitmapData` object.

However, you have a greater degree of control over the end result when you apply a filter to a `BitmapData` object versus applying a filter to a movie clip. Because the filter modifies the pixels of the `BitmapData` object directly, any rotation, scaling, or other transformations applied to the `BitmapData` object are reflected in the filtered result—something that isn't done when applying filters to movie clips.

The `applyFilter` method takes four parameters. The first three parameters are the source bitmap, the source rectangle, and the destination point; these are the same three parameters you used in the `copyPixels` method and the related methods you learned about in the previous tasks. The fourth parameter is the filter object that is to be applied to the `BitmapData` object.

```
import flash.display.BitmapData;
import flash.filters.GlowFilter;
import flash.geom.Point;
import flash.geom.Rectangle;

var src:BitmapData = BitmapData.loadBitmap("elephant");

var dest:BitmapData = new BitmapData(src.width, src.height, true);
```

Figure 8.39 A source bitmap (which will be filtered) and a destination bitmap (where the filter's result will be placed) are created.

```
var cropping:Rectangle = src.rectangle;
var destPoint:Point = new Point(0, 0);
```

Figure 8.40 In this example the filter will be applied to the entire source bitmap, and it will be placed in the top left corner (0, 0) of the destination bitmap.

```
var glow:GlowFilter = new GlowFilter(0x009900);
glow.inner = true;
glow.blurX = 20;
glow.blurY = 20;
```

Figure 8.41 A glow filter (`GlowFilter` class) object is created. It will be a green (`0x009900`) inner glow, blurred 20 pixels in each direction.

To apply a filter to a bitmap:

1. In the Actions panel, enter `import` statements for these four classes:
   - `flash.display.BitmapData`
   - `flash.geom.Rectangle`
   - `flash.geom.Point`
   - The filter class you'll use (`flash.filters.[`*`class name`*`]`)
2. Using any of the techniques described previously, create your source `BitmapData` object (the one that contains the bitmap to which the filter will be applied).
3. On the next line, declare and instantiate a destination `BitmapData` object, into which the output of the filter operation will be placed (**Figure 8.39**).

   If you don't need to preserve the original image, you can use the source `BitmapData` object as the destination object as well.

   Whether you're using the source `BitmapData` object or a new `BitmapData` object as the destination object, there are a few important details to keep in mind—see the Tips following this task.
4. As you did in previous tasks, create a `Rectangle` object to define the region of the source bitmap to which the filter will be applied and a `Point` object defining the point where the result will be placed within the destination `BitmapData` object (**Figure 8.40**).
5. On the following line, declare and instantiate the filter object that will be used to alter the bitmap. Enter parameters in the constructor function to set the filter's properties, or set the properties directly (**Figure 8.41**).

continues on next page

6. On a new line, enter the name of your destination `BitmapData` object followed by a period. Choose ActionScript 2.0 Classes > “flash.display package” > BitmapData > Methods > applyFilter.
7. As parameters for the `applyFilter` method, enter the name of your source `BitmapData` object, the name of your source `Rectangle` object, the name of your destination `Point` object, and the name of your filter object (**Figure 8.42**).
8. To display the result on the Stage, enter code to attach the destination `BitmapData` object to a movie clip.
9. Test your movie.

   The destination `BitmapData` object, which contains a copy of the source `BitmapData` object with the filter applied to it, appears on the Stage (**Figure 8.43**).

```
dest.applyFilter(src, cropping, destPoint, glow);
```

Figure 8.42 The `applyFilter` method applies a filter to a source `BitmapData` object and copies the result into the destination bitmap.

Figure 8.43 The resulting image has a glow filter applied to it, giving it a colored halo look.

✔ Tips

- Several of the filters (bevel, gradient bevel, glow, gradient glow, blur, and drop shadow) use alpha channel values; consequently, the destination `BitmapData` object must be able to store alpha channel values (its `transparency` property must be `true`). If your source `BitmapData` object doesn't have alpha channel information (its `transparency` is `false`), you must create a new `BitmapData` object rather than using the source object as the destination object.
- Often, the output of a filter such as an outer glow or drop shadow is larger than the size of the `BitmapData` object (or the designated `Rectangle`). If the destination `BitmapData` object isn't large enough (for example, if its dimensions are identical to the source bitmap's dimensions), then the filter will be cropped and may not be displayed.

  In order to know the output size of the filter beforehand, use the `generateFilterRect` method on the source bitmap. It takes two parameters—the cropping rectangle and the filter object that will be used—and returns a `Rectangle` object whose dimensions match the size of the output from the filter. Use those dimensions to define the size of your destination `BitmapData` object and the destination point in order to prevent the filter's result from being cropped.

Bitmap images and noise

Graphics created in a computer are perfect—they don't have blemishes or scratches. However, in the real world, dust, dirt, and wear and tear make it so few things are flawless for long. One image effect provided in the `BitmapData` class adds *noise*—random discolored pixels—that you can use to create realistic textures such as a dirty or worn effect or to simulate an imperfect image like static on a television set.

In the next task, you'll use the `BitmapData` class's `noise` method to create a randomly generated noise effect that looks somewhat like television static. Calling the `noise` method on a `BitmapData` object fills the entire bitmap with noise information. The noise pixels aren't applied on top of the existing image data—they replace it. You won't want to use the `noise` method on a `BitmapData` object that already contains image information you want to display. Instead, create a new `BitmapData` object and fill it with noise. Then you can either copy the noise information onto your original image using one of the copying methods described earlier, such as `copyChannel` or `merge`, or overlay a noise image that is partially transparent on top of the original image on the Stage.

When you use the `noise` method, several parameters control the range of colors and color channels that fill the image:

`randomSeed`: A number used as the basis for the noise pattern. The assumption is that this number is created randomly. If you reuse the same random seed when calling the method multiple times, the noise pattern will be identical each time.

`low`: A number between 0 and 255 indicating the low end (minimum value) of the range of color values used in the noise image.

`high`: A number between 0 and 255 indicating the maximum color value that will appear in the noise image.

`channelOptions`: A number indicating which color channel or channels the generated noise will populate. The channel values are the same ones you have seen in previous tasks: 1 (red), 2 (green), 4 (blue), and 8 (alpha). With this method, unlike others discussed previously, you can combine values to create more than one color of noise. For instance, if you use 1 as the `channelOptions` parameter, all the noise will be shades of red. However, if you use 3 (1 + 2), noise will be created in both the red and green channels, so the noise will be shades of red and green combined; if you use 9 (1 + 8), the noise will be shades of red with varying alpha (transparency) levels.

`grayScale`: A Boolean (true or false) value. If the value is `true`, the generated noise pixels are all shades of gray rather than different colors.

To create noise in a bitmap:

1. Create a movie clip or graphic on the Stage to serve as the background over which the noise image will be placed.
2. Select the first keyframe, and open the Actions panel.
3. In the Script pane, enter an `import` statement for the `flash.display.BitmapData` package.

continues on next page

4. Declare and instantiate a new `BitmapData` object. Enter width and height parameter values equal to the width and height of your background movie clip (**Figure 8.44**). The transparency and color parameters can be left off, which will set them to their default values.

```
import flash.display.BitmapData;

var noiseBmp:BitmapData = new BitmapData(212, 320);
```

Figure 8.44 The TV static `BitmapData` object is created with the same width and height as the image it will appear over.

5. On the next line, enter `_root`, and then choose ActionScript 2.0 Classes > Movie > MovieClip > Event Handlers > onEnterFrame (**Figure 8.45**).

   This `onEnterFrame` event handler is used to animate the noise effect.

```
_root.onEnterFrame = function() {

};
```

Figure 8.45 The `onEnterFrame` event handler will be called repeatedly, animating the TV static image.

6. Inside the curly braces of the `onEnterFrame` event handler, declare a new `Number` variable followed by an equals sign.

7. At the end of that line, choose ActionScript 2.0 Classes > Core > Math > Methods > random, and then enter `* 10000` after the parentheses (**Figure 8.46**).

   The `Math.random` method creates a random number between 0 and 1. Multiplying that value times 10,000 makes it a random number between 0 and 10,000. This random number is the random seed that the `noise` method uses to determine the distribution of the random noise pattern. Because a new random seed is created each time the function is called, the noise pattern on the Stage will change continuously.

```
_root.onEnterFrame = function() {
    var seed:Number = Math.random() * 10000;
};
```

Figure 8.46 The `Math.random() * 10000` statement creates a random number between 0 and 10,000 to be used as the seed value for the noise pattern.

```
_root.onEnterFrame = function() {
    var seed:Number = Math.random() * 10000;
    noiseBmp.noise(seed, 0, 150, 8);
};
```

Figure 8.47 This `noise` method call will fill the `BitmapData` object named `noiseBmp` with random noise. The pixels will all have an alpha value (indicated by the number 8) between 0 and 150.

8. On the next line, inside the `onEnterFrame` event handler, enter the name of your `BitmapData` object followed by a period. Choose ActionScript 2.0 Classes > "flash.display package" > BitmapData > Methods > noise.

9. Inside the parentheses of the `noise` method, enter the name of your random number variable, and then enter values for the other parameters as described previously (**Figure 8.47**).

   In this example, where the noise will be overlaid on top of another image on the Stage, keep the `low` and `high` parameter values fairly small (for example, `low`: 0 and `high`: 150), and set the `channelOptions` parameter to 8 (for alpha). The pixels in the noise image will all be white (the default color for a `BitmapData` object) and will have an alpha channel value between 0 (completely transparent) and 150 (a little more than halfway opaque). Use a smaller `high` value for even less noise.

continues on next page

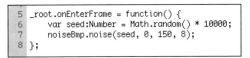

10. After the onEnterFrame event handler function, enter actions that create an empty movie clip, attach the noise BitmapData object to that clip, and set its _x and _y properties to position it over the background movie clip on the Stage.

11. Test your movie.

    The background image is displayed with a shifting pattern of noise pixels over it (**Figure 8.48**).

```
import flash.display.BitmapData;

var noiseBmp:BitmapData = new BitmapData(212, 320);

_root.onEnterFrame = function() {
    var seed:Number = Math.random() * 10000;
    noiseBmp.noise(seed, 0, 150, 8);
};

var clip:MovieClip = _root.createEmptyMovieClip("clip_mc", 1);
clip.attachBitmap(noiseBmp, 1);
clip._x = 18;
clip._y = 18;
```

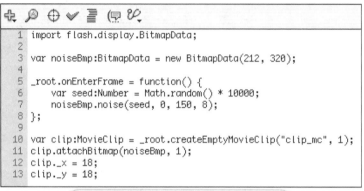

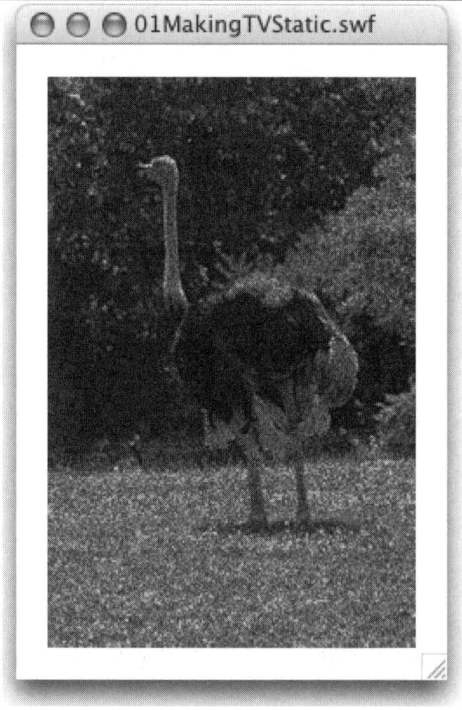

Figure 8.48 The final code (top) creates an animated noise image that can be placed over another image (bottom) to simulate a fuzzy picture.

Animating with Bitmap Images

Throughout this chapter, you've seen ways that bitmap images can be created, drawn onto, copied, combined, and changed. These techniques allow for interesting and exciting effects. But this is Flash—it's an animated, interactive medium, and bitmap images can animate and be part of interactivity just like any Flash elements.

As you explore the bitmap manipulation capabilities of Flash, chances are you'll continue to be impressed not only by their power but also by how quickly they perform. Not only can you blend images and apply a filter effect to them, but you can also do it in real time, over and over again.

To help give your creativity a head start, here are two ideas for animation projects you can build using the bitmap manipulation capabilities of Flash 8: an animated dissolve transition, and an animated flame that follows the mouse pointer.

The first task that follows shows how to create an animated dissolve transition between two images. This task uses the `pixelDissolve` method, which hasn't been presented yet in this chapter. Like many of the methods you've seen, with the `pixelDissolve` method, you set parameters including a source bitmap, source rectangle, and destination point; the method takes pixels from the source, manipulates them, and places them into the destination `BitmapData` object. In this case, each time you call the method, it extracts a specified number of randomly chosen pixels from the source image and pastes them into the destination image. By calling the method repeatedly, more and more pixels are copied over to the destination image until eventually the entire source image is copied over, completing the transition effect.

To dissolve an image into another image:

1. As described previously, import two images that have the same width and height into the Library, and give each one a linkage identifier.
2. Select the first keyframe, and open the Actions panel.
3. Enter three `import` statements, one for each of the following classes:
   - `flash.display.BitmapData`
   - `flash.geom.Point`
   - `flash.geom.Rectangle`
4. Declare a `BitmapData` variable, followed by an equals sign and the method call `BitmapData.loadBitmap()`. Between the parentheses, enter the linkage identifier for your first Library image surrounded by quotation marks.

   This serves as the destination image (the one that is displayed first, onto which pixels from the other image will be copied).
5. Repeat the previous step, declaring a new variable and using the linkage identifier of your second image (**Figure 8.49**).
6. Declare and create a new, empty movie clip on the `_root` movie clip. On the next line, enter that movie clip's name with an `attachBitmap` method call, using your first `BitmapData` object as the parameter (**Figure 8.50**).
7. On the next line, declare a `Number` variable that will be used as the interval ID for a `setInterval` action. You don't need to assign a value to the variable in this step.

```
var img1:BitmapData = BitmapData.loadBitmap("elephant");
var img2:BitmapData = BitmapData.loadBitmap("giraffes");
```

Figure 8.49 Two images named `img1` and `img2` are loaded from the Library. The first (`img1`) is the destination image into which `img2` will be dissolved.

```
var clip:MovieClip = _root.createEmptyMovieClip("clip_mc", 1);
clip.attachBitmap(img1, 1);
```

Figure 8.50 The destination image (`img1`) is attached to a movie clip called `clip` on the Stage at depth level 1.

8. Declare a `Number` variable to contain the random seed used by the `pixelDissolve` method. Enter an equals sign followed by `Math.random() * 1000` (**Figure 8.51**).

9. Declare another `Number` variable, followed by an equals sign.

10. After the equals sign, enter a statement multiplying the first `BitmapData` object's `width` property times its `height` property.

    The expression to the right of the equals sign should look similar to this:

    `img1.width * img1.height`

    As the pixel dissolve proceeds, the code must be able to check when all the pixels have been dissolved and, hence, the transition has finished. This variable contains the total number of pixels (width times height) in the destination image, to which the progress will be compared.

11. On a new line, declare a fourth `Number` variable, and then enter an equals sign and `0` to set the variable's initial value (**Figure 8.52**).

    This variable will be used to keep track of how many pixels have transitioned as the animation progresses; eventually this number will equal the total number of pixels and the code will instruct Flash to stop the animation.

12. Enter the name of the movie clip that has the `BitmapData` object attached to it. Choose ActionScript 2.0 Classes > Movie > MovieClip > Event Handlers > onPress to add an `onPress` event handler function for the movie clip.

13. Within the `onPress` event handler function, enter the name of the interval ID variable you declared in step 7, followed by an equals sign. Choose Global Functions > Miscellaneous Functions > setInterval to add a `setInterval` action.

continues on next page

```
var myInterval:Number;
var seed:Number = Math.random() * 1000;
```

Figure 8.51 Two `Number` variables are added, one (`myInterval`) to track the interval ID for the `setInterval` action and another (`seed`) to serve as the random seed value for the `pixelDissolve` method.

```
var totalPixels:Number = img1.width * img1.height;
var changedPixels:Number = 0;
```

Figure 8.52 Two more `Number` variables are added. The first (`totalPixels`) stores the total number of pixels in `img1`, and the second (`changedPixels`) keeps track of how many pixels have been dissolved as the animation progresses (initially zero).

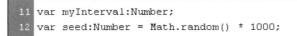

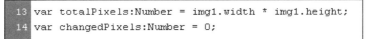

14. Inside the parentheses of the `setInterval` function, enter a name for a function that will be called at a regular interval (you'll define it in the next step), then a comma, and the number `10` for how often (every 10 milliseconds) the function will be called by the Flash Player (**Figure 8.53**).

```
clip.onPress = function() {
    myInterval = setInterval(dissolve, 10);
};
```

Figure 8.53 This onPress event handler function is defined so that when the movie clip is clicked, the `setInterval` action calls the `dissolve` function every 10 milliseconds. This repeated action creates the animation.

15. On a new line outside the `onPress` event handler function, choose Statements > User-Defined Functions > function. With the cursor between the word `function` and the parentheses, enter the function name you used in the `setInterval` action in the previous step (**Figure 8.54**).

This function will call the `pixelDissolve` method. Because this function was entered as a parameter of the `setInterval` action, it will be called regularly, creating the animation effect.

```
function dissolve() {
}
```

Figure 8.54 The `dissolve` function will call the `pixelDissolve` method and track the progress of the pixel dissolve animation.

16. Inside the function body, declare a `Rectangle` object, followed by an equals sign and the `rectangle` property of your second `BitmapData` object. The code is similar to this:

```
var crop:Rectangle = img2.rectangle;
```

As in previous tasks, this variable indicates the portion of the source image to copy into the destination image (in this case, the entire image).

17. On the next line, declare a `Point` object, followed by an equals sign and the code `new Point(0, 0)` (**Figure 8.55**).

As in previous tasks, this `Point` object specifies the point in the destination image that will be the top-left corner of the area into which the source pixels will be copied. In this case, this is the top-left corner of the destination image.

```
    var crop:Rectangle = img2.rectangle;
    var destPoint:Point = new Point(0, 0);
```

Figure 8.55 The source rectangle (in this case, the `Rectangle` corresponding to the entire source image) and destination point (the top-left point of the destination image) are defined.

18. On the next line, enter the name of the random seed variable created in step 8 followed by an equals sign. Choose ActionScript 2.0 Classes > "flash.display package" > BitmapData > Methods > pixelDissolve.

19. Inside the parentheses of the `pixelDissolve` method, enter the following five parameters separated by commas (**Figure 8.56**):

`sourceBitmap`: The name of your source `BitmapData` object (your second image).

`sourceRect`: The `Rectangle` object defined in step 16.

`destPoint`: The `Point` object defined in step 17.

`randomSeed`: The name of your random seed variable (again). This parameter controls the distribution of the pixels that dissolve into the image. The first time the `pixelDissolve` method is called, the random value created earlier is passed in, and the `pixelDissolve` method returns a new seed that must be used the next time to ensure a smooth transition. This is why the random seed variable is placed to the left of the equals sign as well as used as a parameter for the method. On subsequent calls to `pixelDissolve`, the new seed value is passed in and then replaced in turn.

`numberOfPixels`: A number indicating how many pixels should be dissolved each time the `pixelDissolve` method is called. You can play with this value to make the transition smooth but not too slow.

continues on next page

```
seed = img1.pixelDissolve(img2, crop, destPoint, seed, 500);
```

Figure 8.56 The `pixelDissolve` method determines which pixels should be copied and moves them onto the destination image. The parameters indicate the source image, the source rectangle, the destination point, the random seed to control the pixel distribution, and the number of pixels to dissolve in each iteration. The value returned by the method is stored in the `seed` variable to be used as the random seed input for the next iteration.

20. On the next line, enter the name of the variable declared in step 11, then an equals sign, and then the variable's name again, followed by a plus sign and the number entered for the `numberOfPixels` parameter in the previous step. This line looks something like this:

```
changedPixels = changedPixels + 500;
```

As mentioned, this variable keeps track of the number of pixels that have been dissolved to track the progress of the transition.

21. On the next line, choose Statements > Conditions/Loops > if.

```
changedPixels = changedPixels + 500;
if (changedPixels >= totalPixels) {
}
```

Figure 8.57 The variable that contains the current number of dissolved pixels (`changedPixels`) has 500 added to its value. It's then compared to the variable `totalPixels`, which holds the total number of pixels in the destination image, to see whether the pixel dissolve transition has completed.

```
if (changedPixels >= totalPixels) {
    clearInterval(myInterval);
}
```

Figure 8.58 When the transition has finished, the `clearInterval` action is used to turn off the animation, because it isn't needed any more.

```
import flash.display.BitmapData;
import flash.geom.Point;
import flash.geom.Rectangle;

var img1:BitmapData = BitmapData.loadBitmap("elephant");
var img2:BitmapData = BitmapData.loadBitmap("giraffes");

var clip:MovieClip = _root.createEmptyMovieClip("clip_mc", 1);
clip.attachBitmap(img1, 1);

var myInterval:Number;
var seed:Number = Math.random() * 1000;
var totalPixels:Number = img1.width * img1.height;
var changedPixels:Number = 0;

clip.onPress = function() {
    myInterval = setInterval(dissolve, 10);
};

function dissolve() {
    var crop:Rectangle = img2.rectangle;
    var destPoint:Point = new Point(0, 0);
    seed = img1.pixelDissolve(img2, crop, destPoint, seed, 500);
    changedPixels = changedPixels + 500;
    if (changedPixels >= totalPixels) {
        clearInterval(myInterval);
    }
}
```

Figure 8.59 The final code causes one image to dissolve into another one when clicked.

Figure 8.60 In this example, the code animates a transition from an image of an elephant into an image of two giraffes.

22. Inside the parentheses of the `if` statement, enter the variable whose value is increased on the previous line of code (step 20), a greater-than or equal sign (>=), and then the name of the variable that contains the total number of pixels in the `BitmapData` object (defined in step 10). The code in the parentheses looks something like this:

```
changedPixels >= totalPixels
```

The Flash Player checks whether the number of pixels that has been copied is equal to or greater than the total number of pixels in the image (**Figure 8.57**). If it is, the Flash Player carries out the actions between the curly braces of the `if` statement (which you'll add in the next step). In this example, it stops the `setInterval` action and consequently stops the dissolve animation.

23. Inside the curly braces of the `if` statement, choose Global Functions > Miscellaneous Functions > clearInterval.

24. Inside the parentheses of the `clearInterval` action, enter the name of the variable that contains the interval ID, assigned to it in step 13 (**Figure 8.58**).

25. That's all! Test your movie (**Figure 8.59**).

The first image appears on the Stage. When you click the image, it dissolves into the second image (**Figure 8.60**).

Creating animated flame

This task uses several of the techniques you have learned in this chapter. First, the `draw` method copies a movie clip, the source of the fire color and shape, into a `BitmapData` object. By default, the `draw` method copies the pixels into the top-left corner of the destination bitmap. In this case, the copied pixels should be placed at the mouse pointer, so an additional parameter is used with the `draw` method to control the positioning. Unlike many methods that accept a `Point` object to indicate the destination point, the `draw` method requires a `Matrix` object for that purpose.

Once the initial fire colors are drawn into the bitmap, the `copyPixels` method animates the flame moving upward. To do this, the image is copied onto itself, but the destination point is set to (0, -3), which copies the image three pixels above its current location and creates the illusion of upward movement.

Finally, a blur filter is applied to the entire image. As the image is blurred, the orange of the flame blends with the black background, making the flame gradually blend into the black and disappear.

These three tasks—drawing the flame color, shifting the pixels upward, and blurring the image—are placed in an `onEnterFrame` event handler function that is called repeatedly, creating the animation.

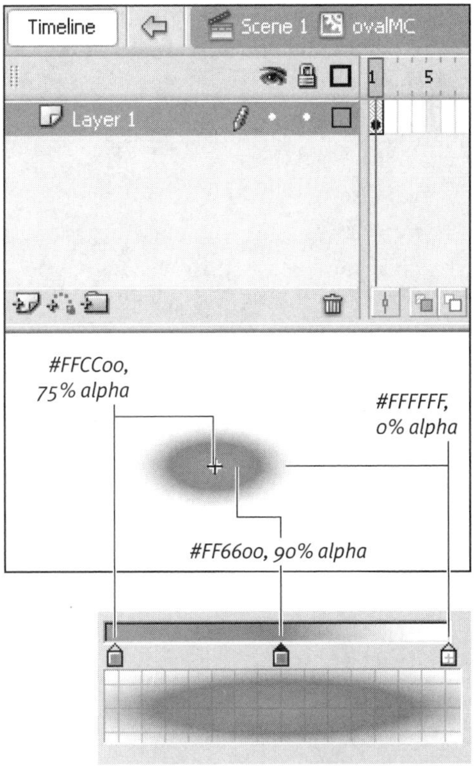

Figure 8.61 A radial gradient with shades of yellow and orange is used to fill an oval shape.

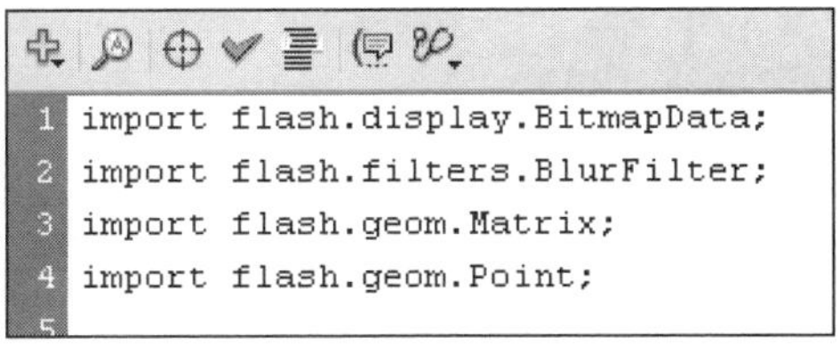

Figure 8.62 These classes are imported to allow you to refer to them by their class name only.

To create an animated flame:

1. Choose Insert > New Symbol to create a new movie clip symbol that will provide the initial color and shape for the fire.

2. In symbol-editing mode, activate the Oval tool and draw a small oval shape. Give the shape a radial gradient fill.

   In this example, the three gradient colors are `FFCC00` (75% alpha) on the left, `FF6600` (90% alpha) in the middle, and `FFFFFF` (0% alpha) on the right. These values create a radial gradient that is yellow in the center and then dark orange fading to transparent (**Figure 8.61**).

3. Using the Align panel, center the oval over the registration point.

4. Exit symbol-editing mode.

5. Right-click (Cmd-click on Mac) your oval symbol in the Library. Choose Linkage, select Export for ActionScript, and give your movie clip a linkage identifier. Click OK.

6. Select the first keyframe, and open the Actions panel.

7. Enter `import` statements for the following classes (**Figure 8.62**):
   - ▲ `flash.display.BitmapData`
   - ▲ `flash.filters.BlurFilter`
   - ▲ `flash.geom.Matrix`
   - ▲ `flash.geom.Point`

8. Declare a `MovieClip` variable, followed by an equals sign. Enter `_root`, and then choose ActionScript 2.0 Classes > Movie > MovieClip > attachMovie.

   The `attachMovie` method will load the movie clip out of the Library and place an instance of it on the Stage.

continues on next page

9. Inside the parentheses of the `attachMovie` method, enter the following three parameters: the linkage identifier of your movie clip symbol (in quotes), a new name for the movie clip instance (also in quotes), and the number 1 (the depth level).

10. On the next two lines, enter statements to set your movie clip's _x property to 10 and to set its _y property to 10 (**Figure 8.63**).

11. On a new line, declare a `BitmapData` variable followed by an equals sign. Choose ActionScript 2.0 Classes > "flash.display package" > BitmapData > "new BitmapData".

12. In the `BitmapData` constructor, enter these four parameters, separated by commas:
    - `Stage.width`
    - `Stage.height`
    - `false`
    - `0x000000`

    This constructor creates a new `BitmapData` object with a width and height that match the Stage's dimensions, no transparency, and a black background.

13. Enter code to create an empty movie clip on the `_root` movie clip, and attach the `BitmapData` object to it (**Figure 8.64**). The new movie clip's depth should be larger than 1 so that it will be placed above the movie clip created earlier, hiding it.

```
var circle:MovieClip = _root.attachMovie("circle", "circle_mc", 1);
circle._x = 10;
circle._y = 10;
```

Figure 8.63 An instance of the gradient oval movie clip is attached to the Stage and positioned. This will be the source for the flame's colors.

```
var img:BitmapData = new BitmapData(Stage.width, Stage.height, false, 0x000000);
var clip:MovieClip = _root.createEmptyMovieClip("clip_mc", 10);
clip.attachBitmap(img, 0);
```

Figure 8.64 A new bitmap the size of the Stage is created with a solid black background. It's then attached to a movie clip on the Stage.

14. On a new line, enter this new movie clip's name. Choose ActionScript 2.0 Classes > Movie > MovieClip > Event Handlers > onEnterFrame (**Figure 8.65**).

15. Between the curly braces of the `onEnterFrame` event handler, enter a `var` statement to declare a new `Matrix` object, followed by an equals sign and the `Matrix` constructor function `new Matrix()`.

A `Matrix` object contains information about transformations (position and size changes) that have been or will be applied to an object. In this case, it will define the destination position where the fire movie clip is copied into the `BitmapData` object.

16. On the following line, enter the name of the `Matrix` object. Choose ActionScript 2.0 Classes > "flash.geom package" > Matrix > Methods > translate.

The `translate` method adds a position change to the transformations in the `Matrix` object.

17. Inside the parentheses of the `translate` method, enter two parameters separated by commas: `this._xmouse` and `this._ymouse + 3` (**Figure 8.66**).

The `Matrix` object is assigned the instruction to change position to the x- and y-coordinates of the mouse pointer. Whatever object the `Matrix` object is applied to will have that position change applied to it.

The extra three pixels on the y-axis compensate for the three pixel upward motion that will be applied later to keep the flame centered on the mouse pointer.

18. On the next line, enter the name of your `BitmapData` object. Choose ActionScript 2.0 Classes > "flash.display package" > BitmapData > Methods > draw.

continues on next page

```
clip.onEnterFrame = function() {
};
```

Figure 8.65 A new `onEnterFrame` event handler is created. The repeated calling of this event handler will drive the animation.

```
clip.onEnterFrame = function() {
    var matrix:Matrix = new Matrix();
    matrix.translate(this._xmouse, this._ymouse + 3);

};
```

Figure 8.66 A new `Matrix` object is created, and its `translate` method is called. The chosen parameters cause a copy of the oval movie clip to be placed at the mouse pointer's coordinates.

19. For the parameters of the `draw` method, enter the name of your gradient movie clip (the color source) followed by the name of your `Matrix` object (**Figure 8.67**).

20. On the following line, declare a `BlurFilter` object followed by an equals sign and the `BlurFilter` constructor call `new BlurFilter(2, 2, 2)`.

This constructor creates a new `BlurFilter` object that blurs two pixels in each direction and has a quality setting of 2.

21. Enter the name of your `BitmapData` object. Choose ActionScript 2.0 Classes > "flash.display package" > BitmapData > Methods > applyFilter.

22. Inside the parentheses of the `applyFilter` method, enter these four parameters (**Figure 8.68**):

- ▲ The `BitmapData` object
- ▲ The `BitmapData` object's `rectangle` property
- ▲ The `BitmapData` object's `rectangle` property object's `topLeft` property
- ▲ The `BlurFilter` object

The parameters look something like this:

```
img, img.rectangle,
img.rectangle.topLeft, blur
```

23. On the next line, declare a `Point` object followed by an equals sign and `new Point(0, -3)`.

This point will be used by the `copyPixels` method to copy the image over itself, three pixels higher than before.

```
img.draw(circle, matrix);
```

Figure 8.67 The `draw` method is used to copy the gradient oval into the `BitmapData` object. The transformations in the `Matrix` object (a position change in this example) determine the placement of the copied pixels.

```
var blur:BlurFilter = new BlurFilter(2, 2, 2);
img.applyFilter(img, img.rectangle, img.rectangle.topLeft, blur);
```

Figure 8.68 A blur filter is created and applied to the `BitmapData` object. This causes the color to fade away as it moves upward.

```
var shiftPoint:Point = new Point(0, -3);
img.copyPixels(img, img.rectangle, shiftPoint);
```

Figure 8.69 The copyPixels method, using a destination Point object of (0, -3), copies the image onto itself, shifted three pixels upward.

24. On the following line, enter the name of the `BitmapData` object. Choose Action-Script 2.0 Classes, > "flash.display package" > BitmapData > Methods > copyPixels.

25. Enter the following parameters for the `copyPixels` method call (**Figure 8.69**):
- ▲ The `BitmapData` object
- ▲ The `BitmapData` object's `rectangle` property
- ▲ The `Point` object declared on the previous line

26. Test your movie.

With each passing frame, the movie clip is copied onto the bitmap at the point beneath the mouse cursor, blurred, and shifted upward three pixels (**Figure 8.70**).

```
import flash.display.BitmapData;
import flash.filters.BlurFilter;
import flash.geom.Matrix;
import flash.geom.Point;

var circle:MovieClip = _root.attachMovie("circle", "circle_mc", 1);
circle._x = 10;
circle._y = 10;

var img:BitmapData = new BitmapData(Stage.width, Stage.height, false, 0x000000);

var clip:MovieClip = _root.createEmptyMovieClip("clip_mc", 10);
clip.attachBitmap(img, 0);

clip.onEnterFrame = function() {
    var matrix:Matrix = new Matrix();
    matrix.translate(this._xmouse, this._ymouse + 3);
    img.draw(circle, matrix);
    var blur:BlurFilter = new BlurFilter(2, 2, 2);
    img.applyFilter(img, img.rectangle, img.rectangle.topLeft, blur);
    var shiftPoint:Point = new Point(0, -3);
    img.copyPixels(img, img.rectangle, shiftPoint);
};
```

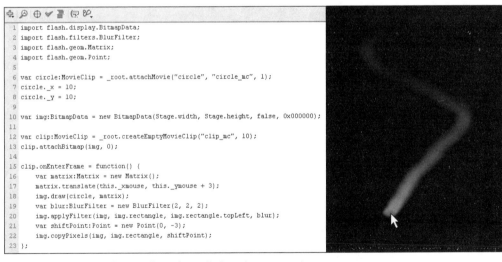

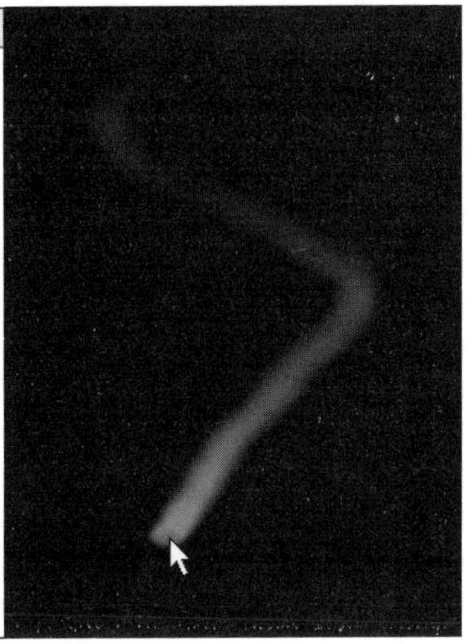

Figure 8.70 The final product is a flame that trails from the mouse pointer.

Controlling Sound

9

Incorporating sound into your Flash movie can enhance the animation and interactivity and add excitement to even the simplest project by engaging more of the user's senses. You can play background music to establish the mood of your movie, use narration to accompany a story, or give audible feedback to interactions such as button clicks and drag-and-drop actions. Flash supports several audio formats for import, including WAV, AIF, and MP3, which enables you to work with a broad spectrum of sounds. Flash also gives you many options for sound export, from speech-quality compression to high-quality MP3 compression, to help keep your Flash file size to a minimum.

This chapter explores the Sound class—the Flash class that lets you control sound with ActionScript. You should already be familiar with basic sound handling in Flash, such as importing sounds and assigning them to keyframes with the Event, Start, Stop, and Stream Sync options. If you're unsure about some of these techniques, review the tutorials and the Help files that accompany Flash for additional information. Moving forward, you'll learn how to use the Sound class to play sounds from the Library dynamically without having to assign them to keyframes. You'll learn how to load sounds that reside outside your movie, enabling efficient management of your Flash and sound content. Using ActionScript, you can start, stop, and adjust the sound volume or its stereo effect, giving you control based on user interactions or movie conditions. You'll learn to use the Sound class's properties and events to time your sounds with animations or with other sounds. You'll also learn how to retrieve and display information about an MP3 file using its ID3 tag, which can tell you file information like song title, artist, or genre.

All these methods, properties, and events of the Sound class give you the flexibility and power to integrate sounds into your movies creatively. You can create a slider bar that lets your viewers change the volume, for example, or add sounds to an arcade game that are customized to the game play. Develop dynamic slide shows synchronized to music or narration, or even make your own jukebox to play MP3 tunes.

Using the Sound Class

Attaching a sound file to a keyframe in the Timeline is an easy way to incorporate sounds into your movie. Two common ways to integrate sound on the Timeline are to use the Event Sync option to play a clicking sound in the Down state of a button symbol and to use the Stream Sync option to synchronize dialogue with an animation. But if you need to control when a sound plays at run time, change its volume and playback through the left and right speakers dynamically, or retrieve information about the number of seconds it has been playing, turn to the Sound class.

The methods of the Sound class control a sound's playback behavior, and the properties of the Sound class can help you control its timing and gather MP3 file information. You need to instantiate the Sound class by using a constructor function and assigning it to a variable, just as you did with the ColorTransform class in Chapter 7. When a Sound object is named, you'll be able to use it to play and modify sound files that you associate with it.

To create a global Sound object:

1. Select the first frame of the main Timeline, and open the Actions panel.
2. Enter var and then a name for your new Sound object followed by :Sound to indicate the data type. At the end of the line, enter an equals sign.
3. Choose ActionScript 2.0 Classes > Media > Sound > "new Sound" (**Figure 9.1**).

   The new Sound() constructor function appears in the Script pane. The constructor can optionally take a MovieClip object as a parameter. In that case, the Sound object controls the sounds in that movie clip. By not specifying a movie clip, you create a Sound object that controls all the sounds in the Flash document.

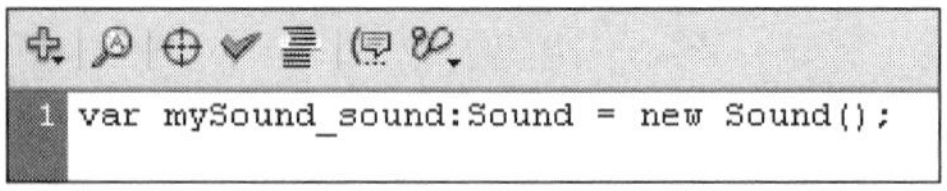
var mySound_sound:Sound = new Sound();

Figure 9.1 The completed statement in the Script pane creates the Sound object called mySound_sound.

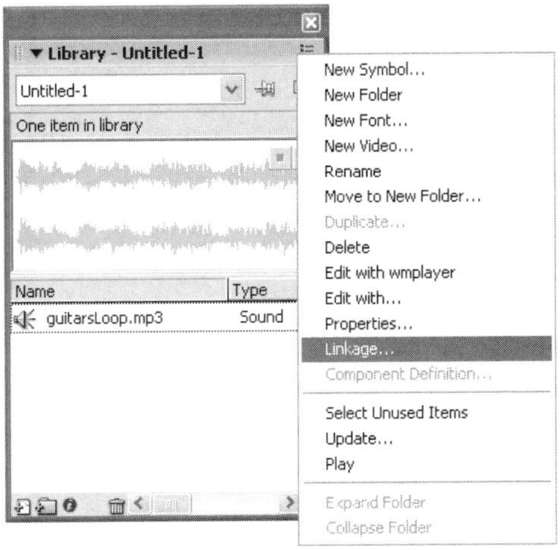

Figure 9.2 Choose the Linkage option from the Library for each sound you want to attach.

Attaching Sounds

After your new Sound object is instantiated, you must associate a sound with it. You can load an external MP3 file into your Sound object (which is covered later in this chapter), or you can attach a sound from the Library. When you have multiple imported sounds in your Library, you have to convey to the Sound object which one to play and control. You identify sounds in the Library by using the Linkage option, just as you did in Chapter 7 when you attached a movie clip symbol from the Library to a movie clip instance on the Stage. In addition to identifying your sound, setting the Linkage option causes the sound file to be embedded into the SWF file so that it will be available when called by the Sound object. When an imported sound is given a linkage identifier, you attach it to a Sound object using the attachSound() method.

To attach a Library sound to the Sound object:

1. Continuing with the file you created in the preceding task, import a sound file by choosing File > Import > Import to Library and selecting an audio file.

   Your selected audio file appears in the Library. You may import these sound formats: AIF (Mac), WAV (Windows), and MP3 (Mac and Win). More formats may be available if QuickTime is installed on your system.

2. Select the sound symbol in your Library.

3. From the Options menu, choose Linkage (**Figure 9.2**).

   The Linkage Properties dialog box appears.

continues on next page

4. In the Linkage section, select the Export for ActionScript check box. Leave "Export in first frame" selected.
5. In the Identifier field, enter a name to identify your sound (**Figure 9.3**).
6. Click OK.

   Flash exports the selected sound in the SWF file with the unique identifier so that it's available to be attached to the `Sound` object.
7. Select the first frame of the main Timeline, and open the Actions panel.
8. On the next line, after the `new Sound` constructor function, enter the name of your `Sound` object followed by a period.
9. Choose ActionScript 2.0 Classes > Media > Sound > Methods > attachSound.

   or

   From the code hint drop-down menu, choose `attachSound`.
10. With your pointer between the parentheses, enter the linkage identifier of your Library sound within quotation marks (**Figure 9.4**).

    Your Library sound is attached to the `Sound` object.

    It's very important that you specify the linkage identifier within quotation marks. This tells Flash that the word is the literal name of the identifier and not an expression that it must evaluate to determine the name of the identifier.

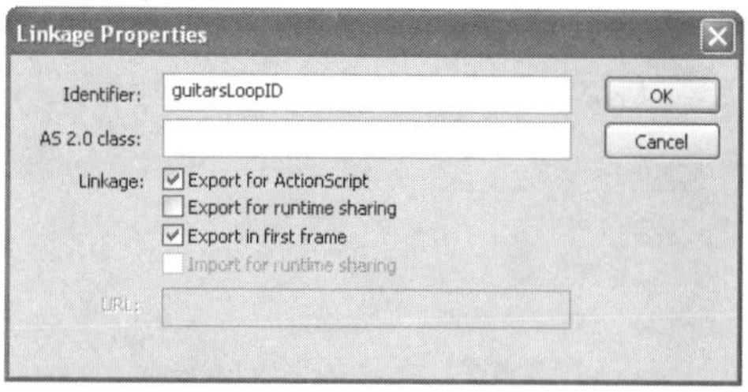

Figure 9.3 This sound is called `guitarsLoopID` and will be included in the exported SWF file.

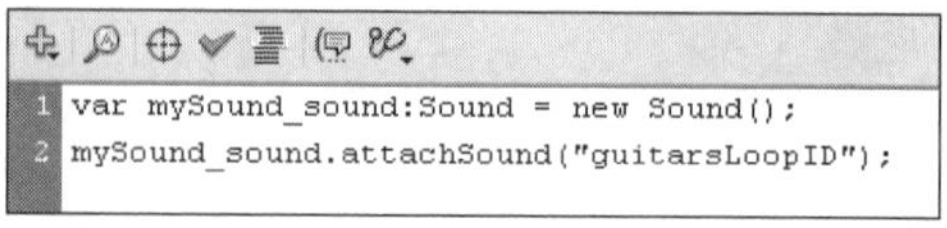

var mySound_sound:Sound = new Sound();
mySound_sound.attachSound("guitarsLoopID");

Figure 9.4 The `attachSound()` method attaches a sound from the Library (`"guitarsLoopID"`) to the `Sound` object (`mySound_sound`).

Playing Sounds

After you have created a new `Sound` object and attached a sound to it from the Library, you can play the sound. Use the `start()` method to play a sound from your `Sound` object. The `start()` method takes two parameters: `secondsOffset` and `loops`.

The `secondsOffset` parameter is a number that determines how many seconds into the sound it should begin playing. You can set the sound to start from the beginning or at some later point. If you have a 20-second sound attached to your `Sound` object, for example, a `secondsOffset` setting of 10 makes the sound play from the middle. It doesn't delay the sound for 10 seconds but begins immediately at the 10-second mark.

The `loops` parameter is a number that determines how many times the sound plays. A `loops` setting of 2 plays the entire sound two times with no delay in between.

If no parameters are defined for the `start()` method, Flash plays the sound from the beginning and plays one loop.

To play a sound:

1. Continuing with the file you used in the preceding task, create a button symbol, place an instance of it on the Stage, and give it a name in the Property inspector.

   You'll assign actions to this button to start playing your sound.

2. Select the first frame of the main Timeline, and open the Actions panel.

3. At the end of the current script, assign an `onRelease` event handler to your button.

4. Within the event handler function, enter the name of your `Sound` object followed by a period.

continues on next page

5. Choose ActionScript 2.0 Classes > Media > Sound > Methods > start.

6. With your pointer between the parentheses, enter `0` followed by a comma and then 5 (**Figure 9.5**).

   The `secondsOffset` parameter is set to `0`, and the `loops` parameter is set to 5.

7. Test your movie.

   When your viewer clicks the button, the sound plays from the beginning and loops five times.

```
startButton_btn.onRelease = function() {
    mySound_sound.start(0,5);
};
```

Figure 9.5 A portion of the Script pane shows just the `onRelease` handler for the button called `startButton_btn`. This `start()` method call plays the sound that is attached to `mySound_sound` 5 times.

✔ Tips

- Unfortunately, you have no way of telling the `start()` method to loop a sound indefinitely. Instead, set the `loops` parameter to a ridiculously high number, such as 99999.

- The `start()` method plays the attached sound whenever it's called, even when the sound is already playing. This situation can produce multiple, overlapping sounds. For example, when the viewer clicks the button created in the preceding task multiple times, the sounds play over one another. To prevent overlaps of this type, insert a `stop()` method (as outlined in the following task) right before the `start()` method. This technique ensures that a sound always stops before it plays again.

- The `start()` method always plays the current sound attached to the `Sound` object. This means you can attach more sounds from the Library to the same `Sound` object, and the `start()` method plays the most current sound. You can create three buttons and assign the following script:

```
var:my_sound:Sound = new Sound();
firstButton_btn.onRelease = function() {
    my_sound.attachSound
    ("Hawaiian");
};
secondButton_btn.onRelease = function() {
    my_sound.attachSound ("Jazz");
};
startButton_btn.onRelease = function() {
    my_sound.start(0, 1);
};
```

  When you click `firstButton_btn` and then `startButton_btn`, you'll hear the Hawaiian sound. When you click `secondButton_btn` and then `startButton_btn`, you'll hear the Jazz sound. If you begin playing the Jazz sound before the Hawaiian sound finishes, you'll hear overlapping sounds.

```
stopButton_btn.onRelease = function() {
    mySound_sound.stop();
};
```

Figure 9.6 A portion of the Script pane shows just the `onRelease` handler for the button called `stopButton_btn`. This `stop` method call stops playing the sound attached to the `mySound_sound` Sound object. The `stop` method has no parameters.

To stop a sound:

1. Continuing with the file you used in the preceding task, place another instance of the button symbol on the Stage, and give it an instance name in the Property inspector.
2. Select the first frame of the main Timeline, and open the Actions panel.
3. Assign an `onRelease` event handler to your new button instance.
4. Enter the name of your Sound object followed by a period.
5. Choose ActionScript 2.0 Classes > Media > Sound > Methods > stop (**Figure 9.6**).
6. Test your movie.

   When your viewer clicks this button, any sound attached to the Sound object that is playing stops.

To stop all sounds:

- Choose Global Functions > Timeline Control > stopAllSounds (Esc + ss).

  When this action is performed, Flash stops all sounds, whether they are attached to a Sound object or playing from the Timeline.

Modifying Sounds

When you use the Sound class, Flash gives you full control of its volume and its output through either the left or right speaker, known as *pan control*. With this level of sound control, you can let your users set the volume to their own preferences, and you can create environments that are more realistic. In a car game, for example, you can vary the volume of the sound of cars as they approach or pass you. Playing with the pan controls, you can embellish the classic Pong game by making the sounds of the ball hitting the paddles and the walls play from the appropriate sides.

The two methods for modifying sounds are `setVolume()` and `setPan()`. The method `setVolume()` takes a number from 0 to 100 as its parameter, representing the percentage of full volume; 100 represents the maximum volume, and 0 is silence. The method `setPan()` takes a number from −100 to 100. The setting −100 plays the sound completely through the left speaker, 100 plays the sound completely through the right speaker, and 0 plays the sound through both speakers equally.

To set the volume of a sound:

1. Continuing with the file you used in the preceding task, place another instance of the button symbol on the Stage, and give it an instance name in the Property inspector.
2. Select the first frame of the main Timeline, and open the Actions panel.
3. At the end of the current script, assign an `onRelease` event handler to your new button.
4. Within the event handler function, enter the name of your Sound object followed by a period.
5. Choose ActionScript 2.0 Classes > Media > Sound > Methods > setVolume.
6. With your pointer between the parentheses, enter a number from 0 to 100 (**Figure 9.7**).
7. Test your movie.

   First, play your sound. When you click the new button, the volume changes according to the volume parameter.

```
volUp_btn.onRelease = function() {
    mySound_sound.setVolume(100);
};
volDown_btn.onRelease = function() {
    mySound_sound.setVolume(20);
};
```

Figure 9.7 A portion of the Script pane shows the `onRelease` handler for a button called `volUp_btn`. This `setVolume()` method call restores the volume for the Sound object `mySound_sound` to 100 percent. Also listed in the Script pane is an `onRelease` handler for a button called `volDown_btn`. This `setVolume()` method call reduces the volume for the Sound object `mySound_sound` to 20 percent.

```
leftSpeaker_btn.onRelease = function() {
    mySound_sound.setPan(-100);
};
rightSpeaker_btn.onRelease = function() {
    mySound_sound.setPan(100);
};
bothSpeakers_btn.onRelease = function() {
    mySound_sound.setPan(0);
};
```

Figure 9.8 A portion of the Script pane shows the `onRelease` handlers for `rightSpeaker_btn`, `leftSpeaker_btn`, and `bothSpeakers_btn`.

To set the right and left balance of a sound:

1. Continuing with the file you used in the preceding task, place another instance of the button symbol on the Stage, and give it an instance name in the Property inspector.
2. Select the first frame of the main Timeline, and open the Actions panel.
3. At the end of the current script, assign an `onRelease` event handler to your new button.
4. Within the curly braces of the event handler, enter the name of your Sound object followed by a period.
5. Choose ActionScript 2.0 Classes > Media > Sound > Methods > setPan.
6. With your pointer between the parentheses, enter a number from –100 to 100 (**Figure 9.8**).

   This single number controls the balance between the left and right speakers.
7. Test your movie.

   First, play your sound. When you click this button, the left-right balance changes according to the `pan` parameter.

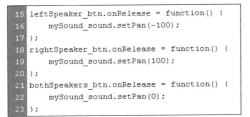

Modifying Independent Sounds

When you instantiate your Sound object and don't specify a movie clip for its parameter, like `var mySound_sound:Sound = new Sound()`, the `setVolume()` and `setPan()` methods have a global effect, controlling all the sounds in the root Timeline. Even if you create two separate Sound objects like the following

```
var mySound1_sound:Sound = new Sound();
var mySound2_sound:Sound = new Sound();
```

you can't use the `setPan()` method to play `mySound1_sound` through the left speaker and `mySound2_sound` through the right speaker.

To modify sounds independently, you must create your Sound objects with parameters that target specific movie clips. Thereafter, Sound objects will be applied to different movie clips, and you can use the `setVolume()` and `setPan()` methods to control the two sounds separately.

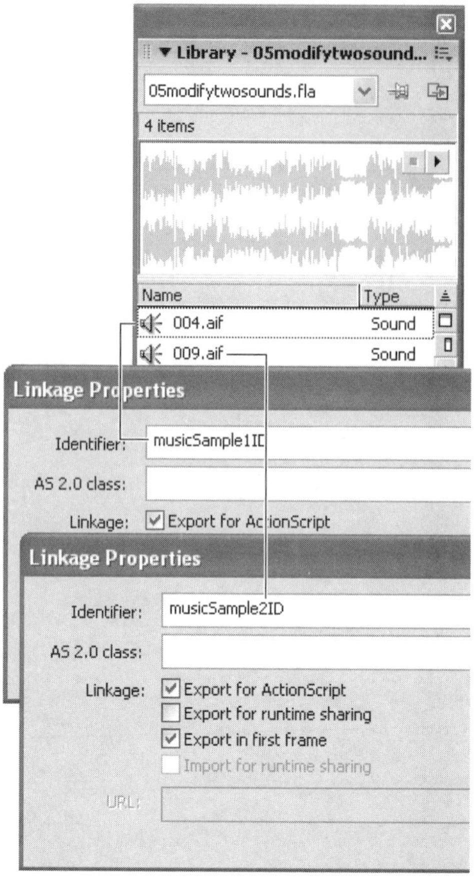

Figure 9.9 Give each imported sound a different identifier in the Linkage Properties dialog box.

To modify two sounds independently:

1. Import two sound files into Flash.
2. Select one sound in the Library. From the Options menu in the Library window, choose Linkage.

   The Linkage Properties dialog box opens.
3. Select the Export for ActionScript check box, and give the sound a linkage identifier.
4. Repeat steps 2–3 for the other Library sound (**Figure 9.9**).

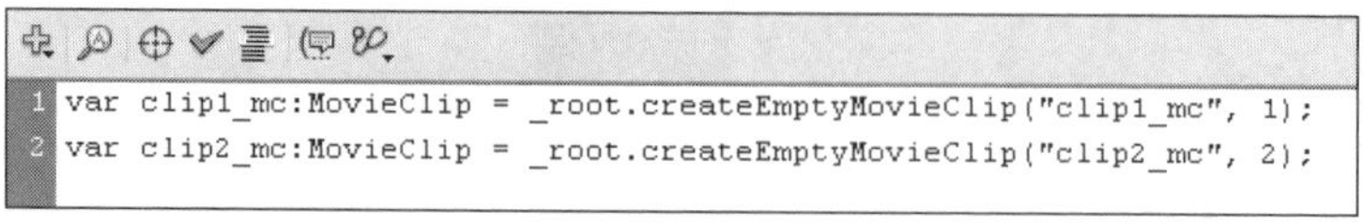

Figure 9.10 Create two empty movie clip instances on the main Timeline to act as targets for the new Sound objects. The two movie clip instances here are called `clip1_mc` and `clip2_mc`.

```
var mySound1_sound:Sound = new Sound(clip1_mc);
var mySound2_sound:Sound = new Sound(clip2_mc);
```

Figure 9.11 The mySound1_sound Sound object is created; it targets clip1_mc. The mySound2_sound Sound object is created; it targets clip2_mc.

```
mySound1_sound.attachSound("musicSample1ID");
mySound2_sound.attachSound("musicSample2ID");
```

Figure 9.12 Attach the two sounds from the Library to the two Sound objects.

```
start1Button_btn.onRelease = function() {
    mySound1_sound.start(0, 1);
};
```

Figure 9.13 This onRelease handler is for the button called start1Button_btn. This start() method plays the mySound1_sound object. Notice that although mySound1_sound targets clip1_mc, clip1_mc isn't referenced at all in the target paths of mySound1_sound's methods. The methods attachSound() and start() refer to the Sound object, not to the targeted movie clip instance.

5. Select the first frame of the main Timeline, and open the Actions panel.
6. Using the createEmptyMovieClip() method (ActionScript 2.0 Classes > Movie > MovieClip > Methods > createEmptyMovieClip), create two movie clip instances on the root Timeline, using unique names and different depth levels (**Figure 9.10**).

   Flash creates two movie clips dynamically. You'll use these movie clips as targets for your Sound objects. (See Chapter 7 for more information about the createEmptyMovieClip() method.)
7. On the next lines, instantiate two new Sound objects as you did earlier in this chapter.
8. Between the parentheses of each constructor function, enter the names of the empty movie clips (**Figure 9.11**).

   Now each Sound object is associated with its own movie clip.
9. Use the attachSound() method to attach the two sounds from the Library to each of your Sound objects (**Figure 9.12**).
10. Create a button symbol, place an instance of it on the Stage, and name it in the Property inspector.
11. Select the first frame of the main Timeline, and open the Actions panel.
12. At the end of the script, assign an onRelease event handler to the button.
13. Assign the start() method for the first Sound object (**Figure 9.13**).

continues on next page

14. Repeat steps 9–12 to create a button that starts to play the second Sound object (**Figure 9.14**).

15. Place two more instances of button symbols on the Stage, and name them in the Property inspector.

16. For the first button instance, assign the `setPan()` method to the first Sound object with a pan parameter of –100 (**Figure 9.15**).

This button plays the first Sound object in the left speaker.

17. For the second button instance, assign the `setPan()` method to the second Sound object with a pan parameter of 100 (**Figure 9.16**).

This button plays the second Sound object in the right speaker.

18. Test your movie.

When this movie starts, two empty movie clips are created. Then two Sound objects are created, associated with the newly created movie clips. Finally, a different Library sound is attached to each Sound object. This technique enables you to control the left-right balance of each sound separately with the buttons called `leftButton_btn` and `rightButton_btn`.

```
start2Button_btn.onRelease = function() {
    mySound2_sound.start(0, 1);
};
```

Figure 9.14 In the onRelease handler for the button called `start2Button_btn`, this `start()` method plays the mySound2_sound object.

```
leftButton_btn.onRelease = function() {
    mySound1_sound.setPan(-100);
};
```

Figure 9.15 In the onRelease handler for the button called `leftButton_btn`, the `setPan()` method for mySound1_sound plays that sound in the left speaker.

```
rightButton_btn.onRelease = function() {
    mySound2_sound.setPan(100);
};
```

Figure 9.16 In the onRelease handler for the button called `rightButton_btn`, the `setPan()` method for mySound2_sound plays that sound in the right speaker.

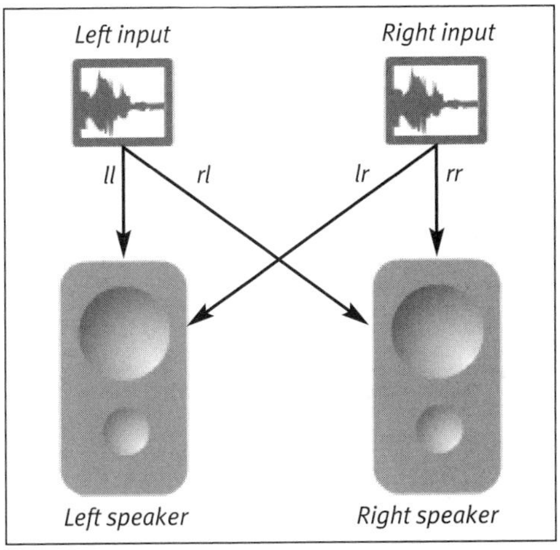

Figure 9.17 The properties of the object passed to the `setTransform()` method determine distribution of sounds between the left and right speakers. The first letter refers to the output speaker; the second letter refers to the input sound.

Transforming Sounds

For cases where you want more precise control of how a sound is playing through the left and right speakers, the Sound class includes the method `setTransform()`. This method allows you to set percentages that determine how much of the right or left channel plays through the right and left speakers. Using this method, you can make your sound switch speakers from left to right dynamically or switch from stereo to mono.

To use `setTransform()` with the Sound class, you create a generic object and add properties to it that hold the information specifying the distribution of left and right sounds. The properties of the sound transformation object are `ll`, `lr`, `rr`, and `rl` (**Figure 9.17**). **Table 9.1** summarizes the purpose of these properties.

Table 9.1

Properties for the Sound Transform Object (setTransform Parameter)

Parameter	Value
`ll`	Percentage value specifying how much of the left input plays in the left speaker
`lr`	Percentage value specifying how much of the right input plays in the left speaker
`rr`	Percentage value specifying how much of the right input plays in the right speaker
`rl`	Percentage value specifying how much of the left input plays in the right speaker

To switch the left and right speakers:

1. Import a sound file into Flash.
2. With the sound selected in the Library, from the Options menu in the Library panel, choose Linkage.

   The Linkage Properties dialog box opens.
3. Select the Export for ActionScript check box, and give the sound a linkage identifier (**Figure 9.18**).
4. Create a button symbol, place an instance of it on the Stage, and give it a name in the Property inspector.
5. Select the first frame of the main Timeline, and open the Actions panel.
6. Instantiate a new `Sound` object, as you did earlier in this chapter (**Figure 9.19**).

   Don't specify a target movie clip for the parameter.
7. Attach the sound to this `Sound` object with the method `attachSound()`.
8. Create an `onRelease` event handler for your button.
9. Choose the `start()` method for your `Sound` object (**Figure 9.20**).

   This button plays your sound.
10. Place another instance of the button symbol on the Stage, and give it a name in the Property inspector.
11. In the Actions panel, assign an `onRelease` event handler to the second button.
12. Inside the event handler function, declare your transformation object by entering `var`, a name, and `:Object` followed by an equals sign.

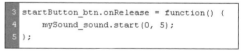

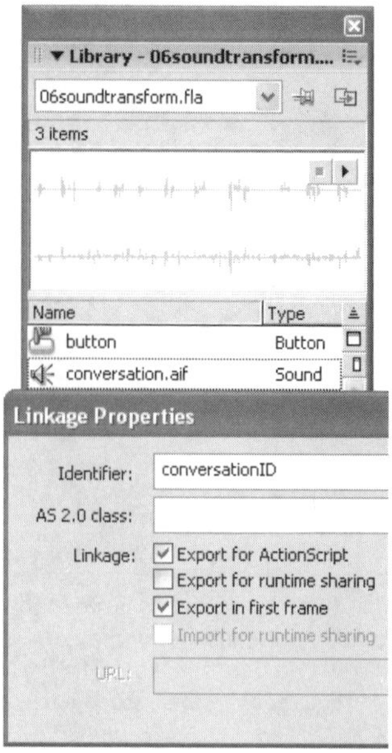

Figure 9.18 This sound is identified in the Library as `conversationID`.

```
var mySound_sound:Sound = new Sound();
```

Figure 9.19 The `mySound_sound` `Sound` object is created.

```
startButton_btn.onRelease = function() {
    mySound_sound.start(0, 5);
};
```

Figure 9.20 The sound called `conversationID` plays five times when the button called `startButton_btn` is clicked.

```
transformButton_btn.onRelease = function() {
    var mySoundTransform:Object = new Object();
};
```

Figure 9.21 Within the onRelease handler for the button called transformButton_btn, the object mySoundTransform is created as an instance of the generic Object class.

```
transformButton_btn.onRelease = function() {
    var mySoundTransform:Object = new Object();
    mySoundTransform.ll = 0;
    mySoundTransform.lr = 100;
    mySoundTransform.rl = 100;
    mySoundTransform.rr = 0;
};
```

Figure 9.22 In the onRelease handler for the button called transformButton_btn, the four properties to be used by the setTransform() method are defined as properties of the object mySoundTransform.

```
transformButton_btn.onRelease = function() {
    var mySoundTransform:Object = new Object();
    mySoundTransform.ll = 0;
    mySoundTransform.lr = 100;
    mySoundTransform.rl = 100;
    mySoundTransform.rr = 0;
    mySound_sound.setTransform(mySoundTransform);
};
```

Figure 9.23 In the onRelease handler for the button called transformButton_btn, add the setTransform() method with the object mySoundTransform as its parameter. The four properties of the mySoundTransform object supply the method with the information required to distribute the sound to the left and right speakers.

13. Choose ActionScript 2.0 Classes > Core > Object > "new Object".

    Your new sound transformation object is instantiated (**Figure 9.21**).

14. On the next line of the `onRelease` event, enter the name of your sound transformation object followed by a period and then one of the properties. Enter an equals sign and then a number representing the percentage for that property. Do this for all four properties (**Figure 9.22**).

    The properties of your sound transformation object are defined. These properties will be used by the `setTransform()` method.

15. On the next line, still inside the `onRelease` event, enter the name of your `Sound` object followed by a period.

16. Choose ActionScript 2.0 Classes > Media > Sound > Methods > setTransform.

17. With your pointer between the parentheses, enter the name of your sound transformation object (**Figure 9.23**).

18. Test your movie.

    When you click the second button, Flash creates a generic object whose properties (`mySoundTransform.ll`, `mySoundTransform.lr`, and so on) hold the sound transformation information. This information is then used by the `setTransform()` method to change the distribution of sound in the left and right speakers.

Creating Dynamic Sound Controls

One of the most effective uses of the Sound class and its methods is to create dynamic controls that allow the user to set the desired volume level or speaker balance. A common strategy is to create a draggable movie clip that acts as a sliding controller. By correlating the position of the draggable movie clip with the volume parameter of the setVolume() method, you can make the volume change dynamically as the viewer moves the movie clip.

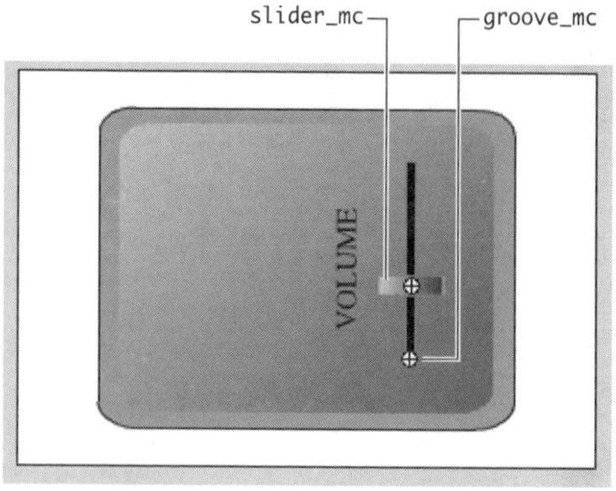

Figure 9.24 The components of a volume control are the slider that moves up and down and the groove.

For a vertical slider bar that controls volume, you must create two elements: the handle or slider and the track or groove it runs along (**Figure 9.24**). First, you create a movie clip called groove_mc. To make things easy, make the groove_mc movie clip 100 pixels high with its registration point at the bottom of the rectangle. Making the groove_mc 100 pixels high will make it simpler to correlate the position of the slider on the groove_mc with the setVolume() parameter. To create the draggable slider, create a movie clip called slider_mc and assign the startDrag() action with constraints on the motion relative to the groove_mc movie clip.

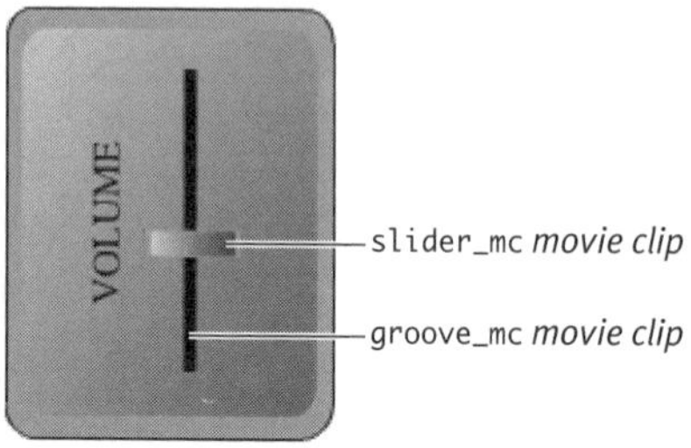

Figure 9.25 The movie clip instance called groove_mc will limit the motion of the draggable movie clip called slider_mc. Make sure that the registration point of the groove_mc movie clip lies at its bottom edge.

To constrain a slider over a groove for a volume-control interface:

1. Create a movie clip of a tall rectangle that is 100 pixels high and whose registration point lies at the bottom edge.
2. Place an instance of the clip on the Stage, and name it groove_mc in the Property inspector.
3. Create another movie clip of a slider.
4. Place the slider clip on the groove_mc movie clip, and name it slider_mc in the Property inspector (**Figure 9.25**).

```
slider_mc.onPress = function() {
    this.startDrag(false,
                   _root.groove_mc._x,
                   _root.groove_mc._y - 100,
                   _root.groove_mc._x,
                   _root.groove_mc._y);
};
```

Figure 9.26 In the onPress handler for the slider movie clip, the startDrag() method's second through fifth parameters constrain the slider_mc movie clip from the center point to 100 pixels above the center point of the groove_mc movie clip. Here the method has been split onto five lines, but it works the same written out as one line.

```
slider_mc.onPress = function() {
    this.startDrag(false,
                   _root.groove_mc._x,
                   _root.groove_mc._y - 100,
                   _root.groove_mc._x,
                   _root.groove_mc._y);
};
slider_mc.onRelease = function() {
    stopDrag();
};
```

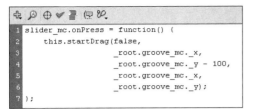

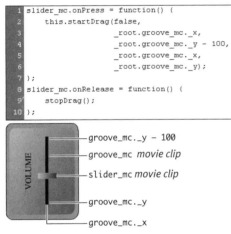

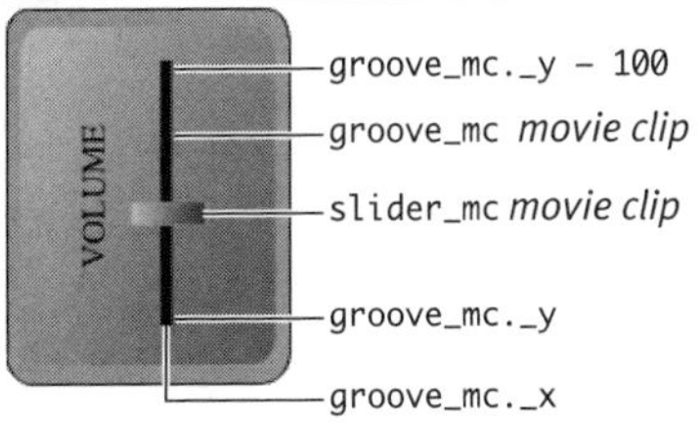

Figure 9.27 The full script. The slider movie clip can be dragged along the groove movie clip.

5. Select the first frame of the main Timeline, and open the Actions panel.
6. Assign an `onPress` event handler to the `slider_mc` movie clip.
7. Enter the keyword `this` followed by a period.
8. Choose Global Functions > Movie Clip Control > startDrag.
9. With your pointer between the parentheses, enter the Boolean value `false` followed by a comma.

   The `lockCenter` parameter tells Flash to drag the object from wherever the mouse pointer clicks it.
10. Enter the following parameters for the left, top, right, and bottom constraints, respectively:

    ```
    _root.groove_mc._x
    _root.groove_mc._y - 100
    _root.groove_mc._x
    _root.groove._y
    ```

    These parameter values constrain the left and right sides to the center of the `groove_mc` movie clip. The top is constrained to 100 pixels above the lower edge of the `groove_mc` movie clip, and the bottom is constrained to the lower edge of `groove_mc` (**Figure 9.26**).
11. Assign an `onRelease` event handler to the slider movie clip.
12. In the `onRelease` event handler, choose Global Functions > Movie Clip Control > stopDrag.
13. Test your movie (**Figure 9.27**).

The globalToLocal movie clip method

The second part of creating a dynamic sound control for volume is correlating the y position of the slider bar with the parameter for the `setVolume()` method. You want the top of the groove to correspond to a volume of 100 and the bottom of `groove_mc` to correspond to a volume of 0 (**Figure 9.28**).

But how do you get the y-coordinates of the moving slider to match up with a number from 0 to 100? One way is to use the movie clip method `globalToLocal()`, which can convert the coordinates of the slider bar to coordinates that are relative to the groove movie clip. Because the groove movie clip is 100 pixels high and the slider bar is constrained to the groove movie clip's height, the groove movie clip's local coordinates provide a convenient correlation with the volume settings (**Figure 9.29**).

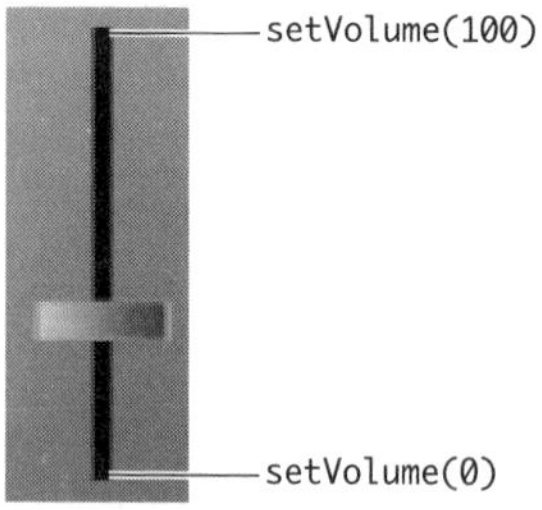

Figure 9.28 The `setVolume()` parameters need to correspond with the position of the `slider_mc` movie clip on top of the `groove_mc` movie clip.

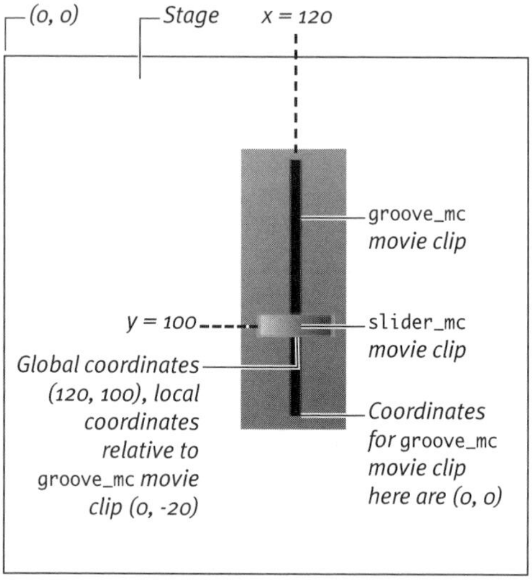

Figure 9.29 The global coordinates of the `slider_mc` movie clip are determined by the root Timeline's Stage. The local coordinates are relative to the `groove_mc` movie clip.

```
slider_mc.onMouseMove = function() {
    var myPoint:Object = new Object();
};
```

Figure 9.30 This is the onMouseMove handler for the `slider_mc` movie clip. The object `myPoint` is created with the data type `Object`.

```
slider_mc.onMouseMove = function() {
    var myPoint:Object = new Object();
    myPoint.x = this._x;
};
```

Figure 9.31 In the onMouseMove handler for the `slider_mc` movie clip, the current x position of the slider movie clip is assigned to `myPoint.x`.

To transform global coordinates to local coordinates:

1. Continuing with the file you used in the preceding task, select the first frame of the main Timeline, and open the Actions panel.
2. On a new line, enter the name of your slider movie clip followed by a period.
3. Choose ActionScript 2.0 Classes > Movie > MovieClip > Events > onMouseMove.

   While being dragged, the slider moves whenever the pointer moves, so the `onMouseMove` event provides a good way to trigger a volume change based on the slider position.
4. Declare a generic object (a variable with the data type `Object`) that will hold the x and y information to be transformed from global to local coordinates.
5. Enter an equals sign, and then choose ActionScript 2.0 Classes > Core > Object > "new Object".

   This is your point object (**Figure 9.30**).
6. Enter the name of your point object followed by a period, the property `x`, and an equals sign.
7. Enter `this._x` (**Figure 9.31**).

   This step sets the `x` property of your point object to the x position of the slider movie clip.
8. On the next line, enter the name of your point object followed by a period, the property `y`, and an equals sign.
9. Enter `this._y`.

   This step sets the `y` property of your point object to the y position of the draggable movie clip.

continues on next page

10. On the next line, enter the target path of the movie clip whose coordinate system you want to use (in this example, the groove movie clip) followed by a period.

11. Choose ActionScript 2.0 Classes > Movie > MovieClip > Methods > globalToLocal.

12. With your pointer between the parentheses, enter the name of your point object (**Figure 9.32**).

    Flash transforms the coordinates of your point object (relative to the Stage) to the coordinates of the targeted movie clip (the groove movie clip's registration point).

```
slider_mc.onMouseMove = function() {
    var myPoint:Object = new Object();
    myPoint.x = this._x;
    myPoint.y = this._y;
    _root.groove_mc.globalToLocal(myPoint);
};
```

Figure 9.32 The final onMouseMove handler for the `slider_mc` movie clip. The global coordinates currently assigned to `myPoint` (`myPoint.x` and `myPoint.y`) are changed to the local coordinates of the `groove_mc` movie clip.

✔ Tip

- Instead of using a generic object, you can use a `flash.geom.Point` object if you're publishing your movie for Flash Player 8. In that case, steps 4-9 could be collapsed into a single statement:

  ```
  var myPoint:Point =
  new Point(this._x, this._y);
  ```

  If you use a `Point` object, remember to add the appropriate `import` statement to the top of the script:

  ```
  import flash.geom.Point;
  ```

To link the slider position to the volume setting:

1. Continuing with the file you used in the preceding task, import a sound file into Flash.

2. From the Options menu in the Library panel, choose Linkage.

   The Linkage Properties dialog box opens.

3. Select the Export for ActionScript check box, and give the sound a linkage identifier.

```
var myMusic_sound:Sound = new Sound();
myMusic_sound.attachSound("musicSampleID");
startButton_btn.onRelease = function() {
    myMusic_sound.start(0, 10);
};
```

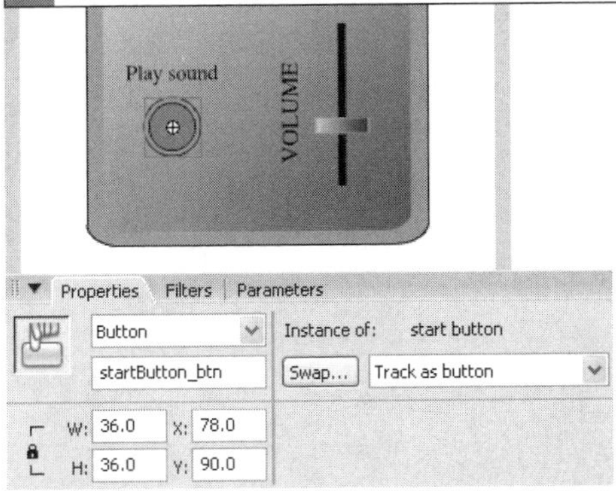

Figure 9.33 The code creates a Sound object and attaches a sound from the Library, and the event handler for `startButton_btn` plays the sound.

```
slider_mc.onMouseMove = function() {
    var myPoint:Object = new Object();
    myPoint.x = this._x;
    myPoint.y = this._y;
    _root.groove_mc.globalToLocal(myPoint);
    myMusic_sound.setVolume(-myPoint.y);
};
```

Figure 9.34 The onMouseMove handler for the `slider_mc` movie clip with a `setVolume` method call added to it. The `groove_mc` movie clip symbol is 100 pixels tall, with its center point at the bottom edge. Hence, the local coordinates of the `groove_mc` movie clip range from –100 to 0. To change this range, add a negative sign (–). The result is a range from 100 at the top to 0 at the bottom that can be used as the `setVolume()` method's parameter.

4. Create a button symbol, place an instance of it on the Stage, and give it an instance name in the Property inspector.
5. Select the first keyframe of the main Timeline, and open the Actions panel.
6. At the top of the script, enter actions to create a new Sound object and to attach the sound from the Library to the Sound object, as you did in the preceding tasks.
7. On the next line, assign an `onRelease` event handler to your button. Within this function, enter your Sound object's name, a period, and a `start()` method to start the sound (**Figure 9.33**).
8. Create a new line within the onMouseMove event handler and enter the target path of your Sound object followed by a period.
9. Choose ActionScript 2.0 Classes > Media > Sound > Methods > setVolume.
10. With your pointer between the parentheses, enter `-myPoint.y`.

    The y position of your slider moves from –100 to 0. By adding the minus (negative) sign, you convert the range of values from 100 to 0 (**Figure 9.34**).
11. Choose Global Functions > Movie Clip Control > updateAfterEvent.
12. Test your movie.

    When you drag the slider up or down in the groove, you change the sound volume dynamically.

Loading External Sounds

Each time you use the Linkage Properties dialog box to identify a sound in the Library and mark it for export, that sound is added to your SWF file, increasing its size. Sounds take up an enormous amount of space, even with MP3 compression, so you have to be judicious with your inclusion of sounds. One way to manage sounds so that your file stays small is to keep sounds as separate files outside your Flash movie. Use the method `loadSound()` to bring MP3 audio files into Flash and associate them with a `Sound` object only when you need them. (MP3 is the only allowable format.) This method also allows you to change the sound file easily without having to edit your Flash movie. For example, you can maintain several background music tracks that users can choose among. To turn on the music, you use the method `loadSound()`. To choose a different track, you call the method again and load a different sound file.

The method `loadSound()` requires two parameters. The first parameter is the path to the MP3 file. The second parameter determines whether you want the sound to be a streaming or an event sound. Enter `true` for streaming or `false` for not streaming (event). Streaming sounds begin to play as soon as enough data downloads. For this reason, streaming sounds don't need the `start()` method. Event sounds, however, must download in their entirety and do require the `start()` method to begin playing.

Event or Streaming: Sound-Sync Options

Sounds behave differently depending on their sync options. The method `loadSound()` requires that a sound have a Stream or an Event sync option. (Two additional sync options, Start and Stop, are available only to sounds that are assigned to a keyframe.) Understanding the differences between the two sync options will help you decide when to use one or the other:

- Streaming sounds begin playing before they have downloaded completely. You can have only one stream per `Sound` object, so overlapping sounds aren't possible (unless you instantiate more `Sound` objects). Streaming sounds are ideal for long passages of music or narration. To stop a streaming sound, call the `stop()` method; to start a streaming sound, call the `loadSound()` method again.
- Event sounds must be downloaded completely before they can play. Event sounds play when you call the `start()` method. If you call the `start()` method again before the first sound has finished, another instance begins, creating overlapping sounds. To stop an event sound, call the `stop()` method. Event sounds are appropriate for short sounds and sound effects for user-interface elements such as button rollovers and mouse clicks.

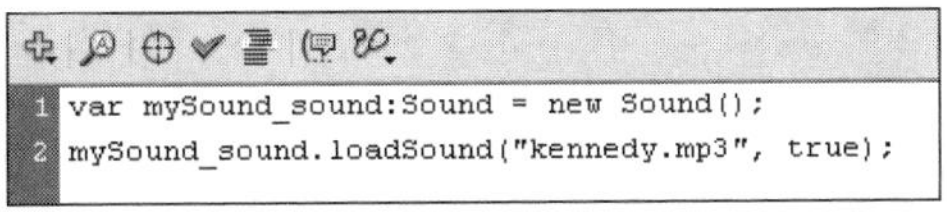

1 var mySound_sound:Sound = new Sound();
2 mySound_sound.loadSound("kennedy.mp3", true);

Figure 9.35 The `loadSound()` method streams the MP3 file called kennedy.mp3 that resides in the same directory as the Flash movie. The sound plays as soon as enough data has downloaded.

To load and play an external sound:

1. Declare and instantiate a `Sound` object with the constructor function `new Sound()`.
2. Enter the name of your `Sound` object followed by a period.
3. Choose ActionScript 2.0 Classes > Media > Sound > Methods > loadSound.
4. With your pointer between the parentheses, enter the path to your MP3 file.

   If the file resides in the same directory as your Flash movie, you can enter just the name of the file. Put the path or filename in quotation marks. Enter a comma; then enter `true` for a streaming sound (**Figure 9.35**).
5. Test your movie.

   As soon as your movie begins, it creates a `Sound` object, loads an MP3 file into it, and plays.

To stop a loaded sound:

- Use the `stop()` method.

  The loaded sound associated with your `Sound` object stops playing.

✔ Tip

- After you stop a loaded sound, you have two ways to make it play again, depending on whether your sound is a streaming sound or an event sound. If your sound is a streaming sound, you must reload it with `loadSound()` to begin playing it again. If your sound is an event sound, you must use the `start()` method.

Reading Sound Properties

The Sound class provides two properties that you can use to find out more about the lengths of sounds. The `position` property measures the number of milliseconds a sound has been playing. The `duration` property measures the total number of milliseconds of the sound. Both properties are read-only (**Table 9.2**).

Use `position` and `duration` to time your animations to your sounds. In the following task, you'll modify an image according to the length of time a sound has been playing. As the sound plays, the image slowly reveals itself. When the sound ends, the image is revealed completely.

To use the position and duration properties:

1. Continuing with the file you used in the preceding task, import an image, convert it to a movie clip, place the movie clip instance on the Stage, and name it in the Property inspector.

   You'll modify the scale and the alpha of this movie clip according to the length of time your sound plays.

2. Select the first frame of the main Timeline, and open the Actions panel.
3. Enter `_root` followed by a period.
4. Choose ActionScript 2.0 Classes > Movie > MovieClip > Events > onEnterFrame.

   The `onEnterFrame` event handler is created (**Figure 9.36**).

5. Inside the event handler function, enter the name of your movie clip followed by a period, the property `_alpha`, and an equals sign.

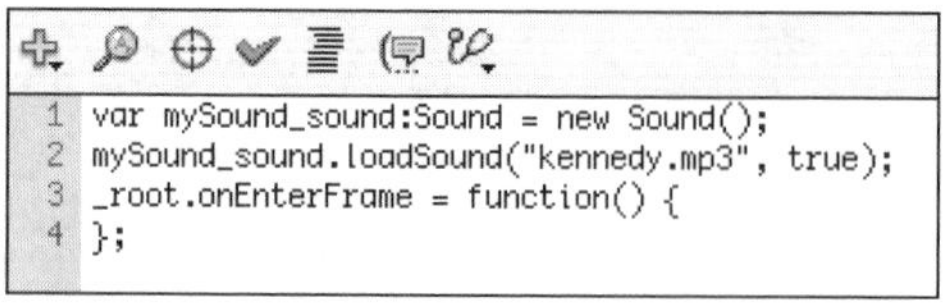
var mySound_sound:Sound = new Sound();
mySound_sound.loadSound("kennedy.mp3", true);
_root.onEnterFrame = function() {
};

Figure 9.36 Assign the `onEnterFrame` event handler to the root Timeline.

Table 9.2

Sound Properties	
Property	**Description**
`position`	Length of time a sound has been playing (in milliseconds)
`duration`	Total length of a sound (in milliseconds)

6. Enter the following after the equals sign:

```
(mySound_sound.position /
mySound_sound.duration) * 100
```

mySound_sound is the name of your Sound object. mySound_sound.position is the number of milliseconds that the sound has been playing. mySound_sound.duration is the total duration of the sound, in milliseconds. Dividing these values and multiplying by 100, you get a value that represents the percentage of the sound that has downloaded (**Figure 9.37**).

The complete statement increases the alpha value of the movie clip as the sound plays so that the movie clip begins completely transparent and ends completely opaque when the sound stops.

7. Create two more statements that use the duration and position properties of the Sound object to modify the _xscale and _yscale properties of the movie clip.

The statements should look like the following:

```
image_mc._xscale = 50 +
((mySound_sound.position /
mySound_sound.duration) * 50);
image_mc._yscale = 50 +
((mySound_sound.position /
mySound_sound.duration) * 50);
```

The movie clip called image_mc slowly increases from 50 percent of its size to 100 percent of its size.

continues on next page

```
_root.onEnterFrame = function() {
    image_mc._alpha = (mySound_sound.position / mySound_sound.duration) * 100;
};
```

Figure 9.37 The position and duration properties of the mySound_sound object modify the _alpha property of the movie clip called image_mc. As the value of position reaches duration, the opacity of the image increases.

8. Test your movie.

In this example, as you hear the words spoken by Senator Ted Kennedy at his brother's funeral, an image of Robert Kennedy slowly appears. The `duration` and `position` properties of the `Sound` object enable you to synchronize the sound to the transparency and size of the image (**Figure 9.38**).

✔ Tip

- The `position` property behaves a little differently when you use `loadSound()` set to streaming. When you load several streaming sounds, the `Sound` object doesn't recognize the start of each new sound, so the `position` property doesn't reset. In this case, the position measures the cumulative length of time your sounds have played.

```
var mySound_sound:Sound = new Sound();
mySound_sound.loadSound("kennedy.mp3", true);
_root.onEnterFrame = function() {
    image_mc._alpha = (mySound_sound.position / mySound_sound.duration) * 100;
    image_mc._xscale = 50 + ((mySound_sound.position / mySound_sound.duration) * 50);
    image_mc._yscale = 50 + ((mySound_sound.position / mySound_sound.duration) * 50);
};
```

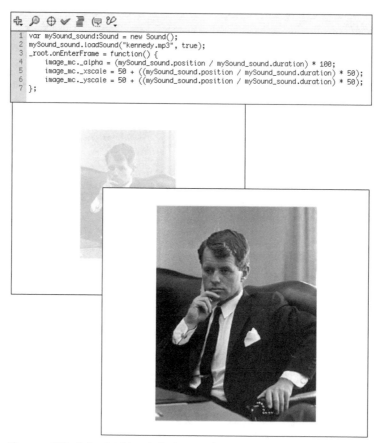

Figure 9.38 The full script (above). As the sound progresses, the image slowly appears (middle). When the sound is complete (`position` equals `duration`), the image is opaque and full-size. (Photo courtesy U.S. Senate.)

```
mySound_sound.onSoundComplete = function() {
};
```

Figure 9.39 Create the onSoundComplete event handler for your Sound object called mySound_sound.

Detecting Sound Events

You can detect when a sound loads with the event `onLoad` or detect when a sound ends with `onSoundComplete`. Assign an anonymous function to the event to build the event handler. For example, consider the following script:

```
mySound_sound.onSoundComplete = function() {
    gotoAndStop(10);
};
```

In this script, when the sound assigned to `mySound_sound` is complete, Flash goes to frame 10.

The `onSoundComplete` event lets you control and integrate your sounds in several powerful ways. Imagine creating a jukebox that randomly plays selections from a bank of songs. When one song finishes, Flash knows to load a new song. Or you could build a business presentation in which the slides are timed to the end of the narration. In the following task, the completion of the sound triggers a graphic to appear on the Stage, providing a visual cue for the end of the sound.

To detect the completion of a sound:

1. Continuing with the file you used in the preceding task, select the first frame of the main Timeline, and open the Actions panel.
2. Enter the name of your `Sound` object followed by a period.
3. Choose ActionScript 2.0 Classes > Media > Sound > Event Handlers > onSoundComplete (**Figure 9.39**).

   Your `onSoundComplete` event handler detects when the sound associated with the `Sound` object ends. When that happens, the function is triggered.

continues on next page

4. Within the event handler, add actions to be performed when the sound ends (**Figure 9.40**).

5. Test your movie (**Figure 9.41**).

✔ Tip

- If a sound is looping, the onSoundComplete event is triggered when all the loops have finished.

```
mySound_sound.onSoundComplete = function() {
    image_mc.attachMovie("endQuoteID", "ending_mc", 1);
};
```

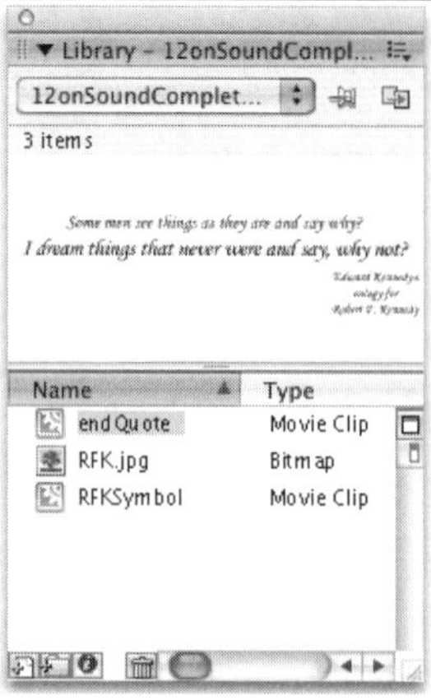

Figure 9.40 The statement within the onSoundComplete event handler (above) attaches a movie clip from the Library to the image_mc movie clip.

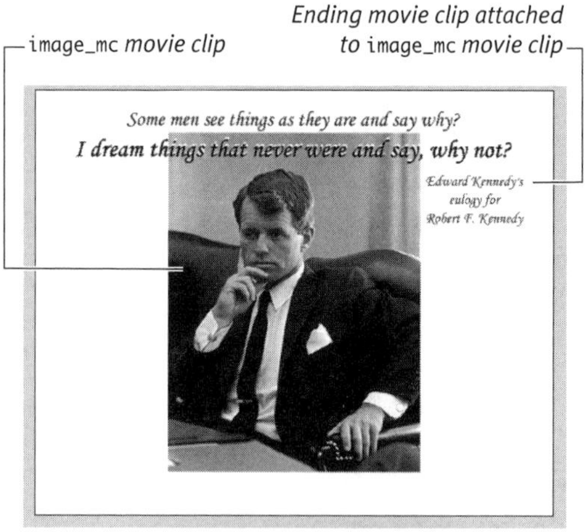

Figure 9.41 When the onSoundComplete event is triggered, a movie clip containing a quote from the sound attaches to the image_mc movie clip. The registration point of the attached movie clip was modified so that when it appears, it's positioned correctly. (Photo courtesy U.S. Senate.)

Table 9.3

ID3v2 Sound Properties

Property	Description
id3.COMM	Comment
id3.TALB	Album/movie/show title
id3.TBPM	Beats per minute
id3.TCOM	Composer
id3.TCOP	Copyright message
id3.TDAT	Date
id3.TDLY	Playlist delay
id3.TENC	Encoded by
id3.TEXT	Lyricist/text writer
id3.TFLT	File type
id3.TIME	Time
id3.TIT1	Content group description
id3.TIT2	Title/song name/description
id3.TIT3	Subtitle/description refinement
id3.TKEY	Initial key
id3.TLAN	Languages
id3.TLEN	Length
id3.TMED	Media type
id3.TOAL	Original album/movie/show title
id3.TOFN	Original filename
id3.TOLY	Original lyricists/text writer
id3.TOPE	Original artists/performers
id3.TORY	Original release year
id3.TOWN	File owner/licensee
id3.TPE1	Lead performers/soloists
id3.TPE2	Band/orchestra/accompaniment
id3.TPE3	Conductor/performer refinement
id3.TPE4	Interpreted, remixed, or otherwise modified by
id3.TPOS	Part of a set
id3.TPUB	Publisher
id3.TRCK	Track number/position in set
id3.TRDA	Recording dates
id3.TRSN	Internet radio station name
id3.TRSO	Internet radio station owner
id3.TSIZ	Size
id3.TSRC	International Standard Recording Code (ISRC)
id3.TSSE	Software/hardware and settings used for encoding
id3.TYER	Year
id3.WXXX	URL link frame

Working with MP3 Song Information

MP3 files are the most popular format for storing and playing digital music. The MP3 compression gives a dramatic decrease in file size, yet the quality is maintained at near-CD levels. Another virtue of MP3 files is that they are capable of carrying simple information about the audio file itself. This *metadata* (descriptive information about data) tag was originally appended to the end of an MP3 file and called ID3 version 1. Information about the music file (such as song title, artist, album, year, comment, and genre) could be stored at the end of the song file in the ID3 tag and then detected and read by decoders.

Over time and slight version upgrades, ID3 is currently at version 2. One of the more notable improvements was moving the data to the beginning of the song file to better support streaming. It now also supports several new fields, such as composer, conductor, media type, copyright message, and recording date.

Flash can read the ID3v2 data of an MP3 file. Each bit of information about the song, or *tag*, corresponds to a property of the `id3` object of the `Sound` object. So, for example, `mySound_sound.id3.TALB` refers to the album name of the MP3 file. **Table 9.3** covers all of the ID3 version 2 `Sound` properties.

How do you retrieve these ID3 properties? First, you must create an event handler that is triggered when available ID3 tags are present after a `loadSound()` or an `attachSound()` method is called. Using the event handler `onID3` is the only way you can access the ID3 data.

Sometimes an MP3 file may contain both ID3v1 and ID3v2 tags. The older Flash player, Flash Player 6, supports a few of the version 1 tags. **Table 9.4** covers the supported ID3v2 properties for the Flash Player 6 and their corresponding ID3v1 properties.

In the following task, you'll load an external MP3 file and display the track information in the Output window.

To retrieve ID3 information about an MP3 file:

1. Declare a new Sound object and instantiate it with the constructor function new Sound().
2. On the next line, enter the name for your new Sound object followed by a period.
3. Choose ActionScript 2.0 Classes > Media > Sound > Methods > loadSound.
4. With your pointer between the parentheses, enter the path to your MP3 file, and then enter true (**Figure 9.42**).

   Make sure that the MP3 path and name are surrounded by quotation marks and a comma separates the two parameters.
5. On a new line, enter the name of your Sound object followed by a period.
6. Choose ActionScript 2.0 Classes > Media > Sound > Event Handlers > onID3.

   An anonymous function is created as the onID3 event handler (**Figure 9.43**).
7. On a new line inside the event handler, choose Global Functions > Miscellaneous Functions > trace.
8. With your pointer between the parentheses, enter the name of your Sound object followed by a period.

```
var mySound_sound:Sound = new Sound();
mySound_sound.loadSound("jazz1.mp3", true);
```

Figure 9.42 The loadSound() method streams the MP3 file named jazz1.mp3 that resides in the same directory as the Flash movie. The sound plays as soon as enough data has downloaded.

```
var mySound_sound:Sound = new Sound();
mySound_sound.loadSound("jazz1.mp3", true);
mySound_sound.onID3 = function() {
};
```

Figure 9.43 The onID3 event handler is attached to the Sound object named mySound_sound. The onID3 event handler is triggered when ID3 tags are available from an attached or loaded MP3.

Table 9.4

Flash Player 6 Supported ID3 Tags

ID3v2 Property	Corresponding ID3v1 Property
id3.COMM	id3.comment
id3.TALB	id3.album
id3.TCON	id3.genre
id3.TIT2	id3.songname
id3.TPE1	id3.artist
id3.TRCK	id3.track
id3.TYER	id3.year

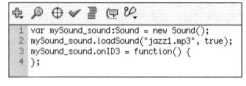

```
var mySound_sound:Sound = new Sound();
mySound_sound.loadSound("jazz1.mp3", true);
mySound_sound.onID3 = function() {
    trace("Artist: " + mySound_sound.id3.TPE1);
    trace("Album: " + mySound_sound.id3.TALB);
    trace("SongName: " + mySound_sound.id3.TIT2);
    trace("Released: " + mySound_sound.id3.TYER);
};
```

Figure 9.44 Use the `trace` statement to display the ID3 information in the Output window.

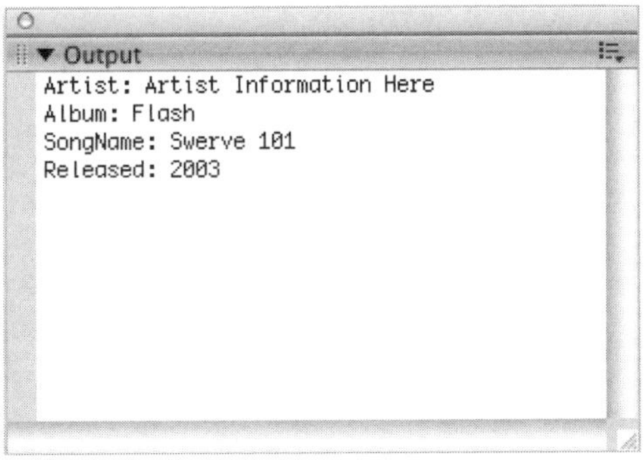

Figure 9.45 The Output window displays the ID3 information about the MP3 file that has been loaded into Flash.

9. Choose ActionScript 2.0 Classes > Media > Sound > Objects > id3 > Properties > TPE1.

   The performer's name will appear in the Output window during testing mode in Flash.

10. Repeat steps 6–8 to retrieve all the ID3 information you want (**Figure 9.44**).

11. Save your FLA file in the location where it can find your MP3 file based on the target path you entered in step 4.

    When you test your movie in the Flash authoring environment, the Output window displays the ID3 information (**Figure 9.45**).

✔ Tips

- Using dynamic text fields, you can have Flash dynamically populate text fields and display the ID3 information on the Stage (rather than in the Output window). You'll learn more about dynamic text fields in Chapter 11.
- When an MP3 file contains a mix of ID3v2 and ID3v1 tags, the event handler `onID3` is triggered twice.
- To view the ID3 files of your MP3 files outside of Flash:

  In Windows XP: Right-click the MP3 file, and select Properties > Summary > Advanced.

  Using Mac OS X: In iTunes, select the song in your playlist, and press Command-I.

Part V: Working with Information

10 Controlling Information Flow

As your Flash movie displays graphics and animation and plays sounds, a lot can be happening behind the scenes, unapparent to the viewer. Your Flash document may be tracking many bits of information, such as the number of lives a player has left in a game, a user's login name and password, or the items a customer has placed in a shopping cart. Getting and storing this information requires *variables,* which are containers for information. Variables are essential in any Flash movie that involves complex interactivity because they let you create scenarios based on information that changes. You can modify variables and use them in *expressions*—formulas that can combine variables with other variables and values—and then test the information against certain conditions to determine how the Flash movie will unfold. This testing is done in *conditional statements,* which control the flow of information. Conditional statements are the decision makers of your Flash movie; they evaluate information that comes in and then tell Flash what to do based on that information. You can use conditional statements to make a ball bounce back if it collides with a wall, for example, or to increase the speed of the ball if the game time exceeds 1 minute.

This chapter is about managing information by using variables, expressions, and conditional statements. You've dealt with all three in earlier chapters, but here, you'll learn how to work with them in more detail. When you understand how to get, modify, and evaluate information, you can direct your Flash movie and change the graphics, animation, and sound in dynamic fashion.

Using Variables and Expressions

In Chapter 3, you learned the basics of variables—how to declare them, assign values to them, and combine them in expressions. Now that you have more experience with variables in different contexts, this chapter takes another, more refined look at using variables and expressions in ActionScript.

You use variables and expressions as placeholders for parameters within your ActionScript. In virtually every action or method that requires you to enter a parameter, you can place a variable or an expression instead of a fixed value. For example, you can enter an expression instead of a frame number as the parameter for the basic action `gotoAndStop`. This expression may be a variable `myCard` that holds a number from 1 to 52. Frames 1 through 52 in the Timeline can contain graphics of the 52 playing cards, so changing the variable `myCard` in the `gotoAndStop` action makes Flash display different cards.

The parameter in the action `getURL` can be an expression rather than a fixed Internet address. The expression may be a string concatenated with a variable such as `"http://" + yourWebSite`. Changing the variable `yourWebSite` makes Flash load a different URL with the `getURL` action.

You can also use a variable as a simple counter. Rather than taking the place of a parameter, a counter variable keeps track of how many times certain things occur for later retrieval and testing. A player's score can be stored in a variable so that Flash knows when the player reaches enough points to win the game. Or a variable can keep track of a certain state. You can set the variable `myShield = true` if a character's force field is turned on, for example, and change the variable to `myShield = false` if the force field is turned off.

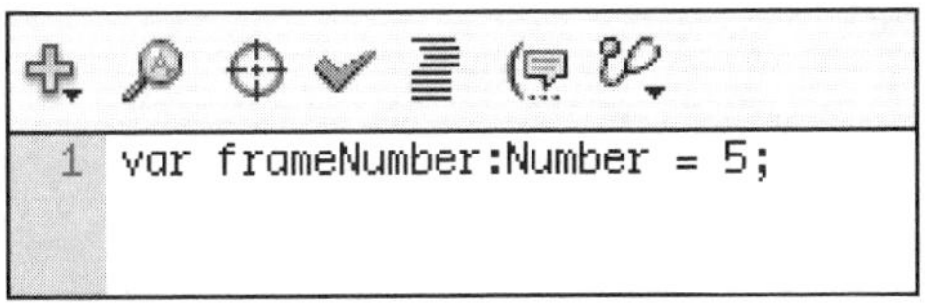

Figure 10.1 The variable `frameNumber` is initialized to 5.

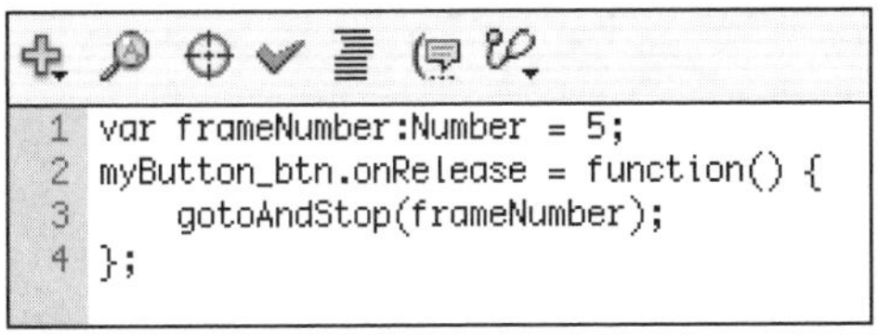

Figure 10.2 The variable `frameNumber` is the parameter for the `gotoAndStop()` action. Instead of a predefined number, the `gotoAndStop()` action will use the value of the variable.

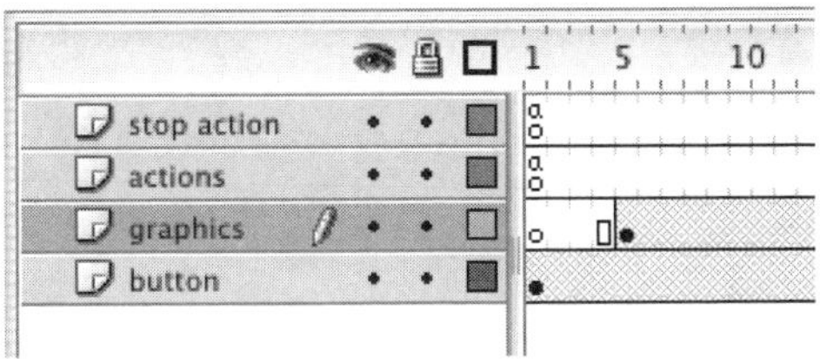

Figure 10.3 When the user clicks the button in the bottom layer, Flash goes to the value of `frameNumber`, which is 5.

To use a variable:

1. In the first keyframe of the root Timeline, declare a variable as described in Chapter 3, using the `var` statement and specifying the data type `Number`. Assign a numerical value to your variable (**Figure 10.1**).
2. Create a button symbol, drag an instance of it to the Stage, and give it an instance name in the Property inspector.
3. Select the first frame of the root Timeline again, and open the Actions panel.
4. Assign an `onRelease` event handler to your button.
5. Between the curly braces of the event handler, enter the action `gotoAndStop()`. For its parameter, enter the name of the variable you initialized in the root Timeline (**Figure 10.2**).
6. Provide additional frames so the playhead has somewhere to go.
7. Test your movie (**Figure 10.3**).

   Your variable contains a number. When Flash performs the `gotoAndStop` action, it uses the information contained in the variable as the frame to go to. If you change the value of the variable, Flash will go to a different frame. This strategy lets you change parameters in code that may be spread throughout your movie by just changing variables initialized on the first keyframe.

✔ Tip

- To use a frame label instead of a frame number to identify the frame you want Flash to go to, declare your variable with the `String` data type. Assign the string `"Conclusion"` to the variable `myFrameLabel`, for example. By using `myFrameLabel` as the parameter in the `gotoAndPlay` action, you can have Flash go to the frame labeled `Conclusion`.

The scope of variables

When you initialize variables, they belong to the Timeline where you create them. This is known as the *scope* of a variable. Variables have their own scope, just as you learned in Chapter 5 that functions and event handlers have a scope. If you initialize a variable on the root Timeline, the variable is scoped to the root Timeline. If you initialize a variable inside a movie clip's event handler, the variable is scoped to that movie clip.

Think of a variable's scope as being its home. Variables live on certain Timelines, and if you want to use the information inside a variable, first you must find it with a target path. This process is analogous to targeting movie clips and other objects. To access either a movie clip or a variable, you identify it with a target path. When you construct a target path for a variable, you can use the absolute term `_root` or the relative terms `this` and `_parent`.

In the following task, you'll build a pull-down menu that loads a Web site by using the `getURL` action. The URL for the action is stored in a variable that is initialized and scoped to the main Timeline. Because the `getURL` action resides in a movie clip, the variable and the action that uses the variable have different scopes. Use a target path to tell Flash how to get from the movie clip's Timeline to the main Timeline to identify the variable.

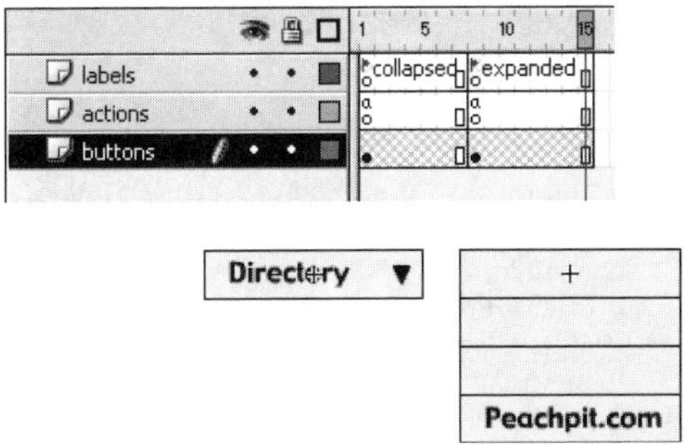

Figure 10.4 A movie clip of a pull-down menu has two states—collapsed and expanded—that toggle back and forth.

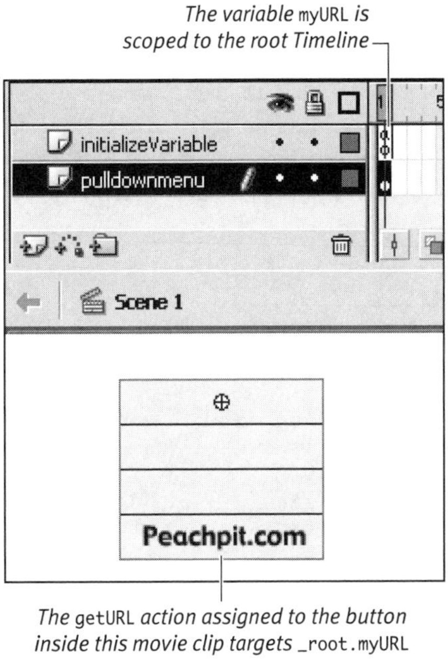


```
button4_btn.onRelease = function() {
    gotoAndStop(1);
    getURL(_root.myURL);
};
```

Figure 10.5 For the last button of the pull-down menu, assign _root.myURL as the parameter of the getURL action. Because this action is inside the movie clip of the pull-down menu, _root is necessary to target the variable myURL in the root Timeline.

To target a variable with a different scope:

1. Create a movie clip of a pull-down menu, as demonstrated in Chapter 4 in the section "Complex Buttons."
2. Drag an instance of the movie clip from the Library to the Stage (**Figure 10.4**), and give the instance a name in the Property inspector.
3. Select the first frame of the root Timeline, and open the Actions panel.
4. Declare a `String` variable, and assign an Internet address as its value:
   ```
   var myURL:String =
   "http://www.peachpit.com";
   ```
   This variable is initialized in the root Timeline.
5. Enter symbol-editing mode for your movie clip, and select the first keyframe of the Timeline.
6. Within the `onRelease` event handler of one of your buttons, choose Global Functions > Browser/ Network > getURL.
7. As the parameter for the `getURL` action, enter `_root` followed by a dot and then the name of the variable you initialized in the root Timeline (**Figure 10.5**).
8. Test your movie.

   When you click your pull-down menu to expand it and then choose the button to which you assigned the `getURL` action, Flash retrieves the information stored in the variable on the root Timeline. If you hadn't specified the root Timeline in the URL field of the `getURL` action, Flash would look within the movie clip for that variable and wouldn't be able to find it.

Global variables

If you want to have access to a variable no matter where you are, you can initialize a *global variable*. A global variable belongs to a special scope that makes it available to all timelines.

To initialize a global variable, precede it with the identifier `_global`. In this case, you don't use the ActionScript term `var` because it applies only to local variables. After the variable is initialized, you can read its contents from anywhere in your Flash movie with just the variable name. To modify the contents of your global variable, use the `_global` identifier with the variable name, and assign new values.

To initialize a variable with a global scope:

1. Select the first frame of the main Timeline, and open the Actions panel.
2. In the Script pane, enter `_global` (or choose Global Properties > Identifiers > global).
3. Enter a dot following the `_global` identifier, and then enter a name for your variable.
4. Complete the statement by entering an equals sign followed by a value (**Figure 10.6**).

   Your global variable is established. Although the variable is initialized in the root Timeline, you can access its contents from anywhere in your Flash movie without having to specify a target path (**Figure 10.7**).

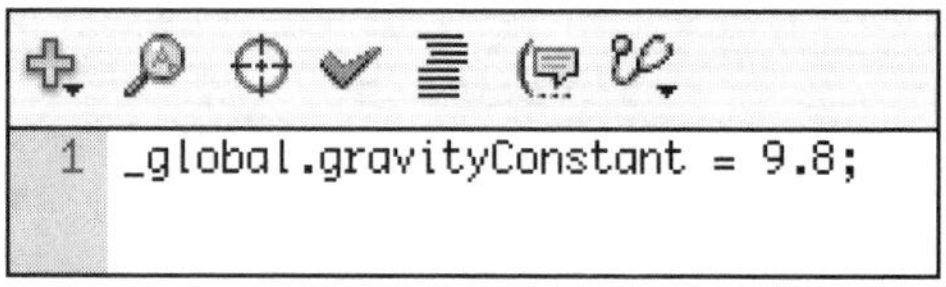

Figure 10.6 The global variable `gravityConstant` contains the value 9.8. You can use this variable from any Timeline in the movie just by referencing its name, `gravityConstant`.

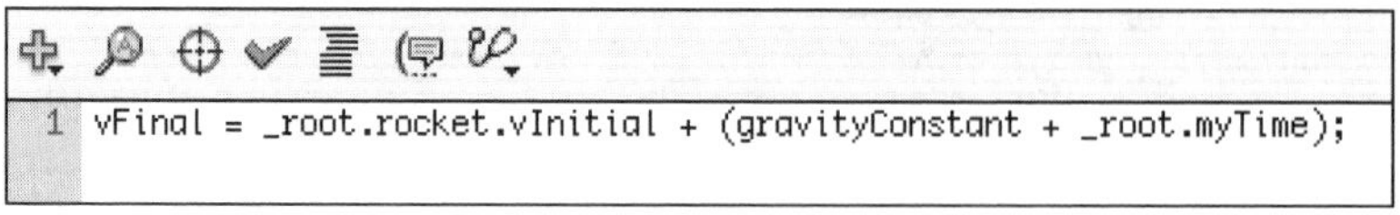

Figure 10.7 After a global variable is initialized, you can use it anywhere. Notice that in the example statement, which calculates the final velocity (`vFinal`) based on `gravityConstant` and two more variables (`vInitial` and `myTime`), no target path is necessary for `gravityConstant`.

Loading External Variables

You don't have to store the initial value of a variable inside your movie. Flash lets you keep variables outside your Flash movie in a text document that you can load whenever you need the variables. This way, you can change the variables in the text document easily and thereby change the Flash movie without having to edit the movie. Build a quiz, for example, with variables holding the questions and answers. Keep the variables in a text document, and when you want to change the quiz, edit the text document. You can also set up the variables in the text document to be generated automatically with server-side scripts based on other external data. Then your Flash movie can read the variables in the text document with only the most recent or user-customized values.

The external text document can contain as many variables as you want; but its contents need to be written in the Multipurpose Internet Mail Extensions (MIME) url-encoded format, which is a standard format that HTML forms and CGI scripts use. In the MIME url-encoded format, variables are written in the following form:

variable1=value1&variable2=value2&variable3=value3

Each variable/value pair is separated from the next by a single ampersand (&) symbol.

To load variables a single time when the SWF file loads, add the variables to the HTML page that contains the Flash movie. This approach is useful for small amounts of data that won't change during the course of the SWF. For instance, you can create a generic video player SWF with playback controls; when the SWF file is loaded in the HTML page, the variable will indicate which video to play.

To send and load variables between the Flash Player and a server, or to load variables from an external text file, use the `LoadVars` class, which lets you load data multiple times and send data as well.

The LoadVars class

When you want to have control over the loading of external variables or data, use the `LoadVars` class. It provides properties, methods, and events to handle and manage incoming (and outgoing) data. You can test how much of the external data has loaded with the method `getBytesLoaded()`, for example, or define actions to take when external data finishes loading (or fails to load) with the `onLoad` event handler.

To use the `LoadVars` class, you must create an instance using the class's constructor function. After the `LoadVars` object is instantiated, use the `load()` method to bring variables from an external file into the object. As mentioned previously, the variables must be in url-encoded format.

To load external variables with the LoadVars class:

1. Launch a text editor, and create a new document.
2. Write your variable names and their values in the standard MIME url-encoded format (**Figure 10.8**).
3. Save your text document in the same directory where your Flash movie will be saved.

   It doesn't matter what you name your file, but it helps to keep the name simple and to stick to a standard three-letter extension.
4. In Flash, open a new document.
5. Create a button on the Stage, and give it an instance name in the Property inspector.

   When this button is clicked, the `LoadVars` object will load the external data from the text file.
6. Select the first keyframe of the root Timeline, and open the Actions panel.
7. In the Script pane, declare a `LoadVars` object, followed by an equals sign, and instantiate the object with the constructor function `new LoadVars()` (choose ActionScript 2.0 Classes > Client/Server and XML > LoadVars > "new LoadVars") (**Figure 10.9**).
8. On a new line of the Script pane, create an `onRelease` event handler function for your button.

```
myRotation=45&mySize=150
```

Figure 10.8 Two variables and their values written in MIME format. In this example, the variables are saved in a text document called data.txt.

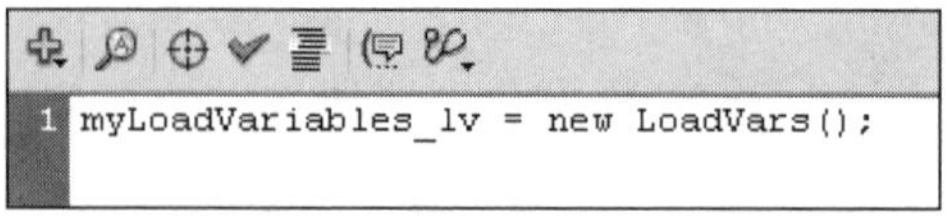
1 myLoadVariables_lv = new LoadVars();

Figure 10.9 The new `LoadVars` instance `myLoadVariables_lv` is created.

```
molecule_mc.onRelease = function() {
    myLoadVariables_lv.load("data.txt");
};
```

Figure 10.10 The `load()` method loads the data.txt file from the same directory as the Flash movie and puts the variables in the `myLoadVariables_lv` object.

9. Inside the curly braces of the `onRelease` event handler, enter the name of your `LoadVars` object, followed by a period.

10. In the code hint pull-down menu that appears, select `load` (or choose Action-Script 2.0 Classes > Client/Server and XML > LoadVars > Methods > load).

11. As a parameter of the `load()` method, enter the path to the text file that contains your variables.

    If your SWF file and the text file will reside in the same directory, you can enter just the text file's name. Enclose the path or filename in quotation marks (**Figure 10.10**).

    Flash calls the `load()` method, which loads the variable and value pairs from the external text file into the `LoadVars` object.

12. Use the loaded external variables within your Flash movie (see the next task).

Receiving the LoadVars result

After you call the `load()` method for your `LoadVars` object, the data isn't always immediately available to the Flash Player. For instance, the data is often loaded from a Web server, meaning it has to travel across the Internet to reach the Flash Player. You can detect when the data is loaded using the `onLoad` event handler of the `LoadVars` object. Always wait for the `onLoad` event handler to be called before attempting to use the loaded data. Typically, this means that you place the actions that use the loaded data within the `onLoad` event handler function.

In addition, the onLoad event handler tells you whether the data loaded successfully. In this handler, you specify a Boolean variable as a parameter; when the onLoad function is called, the variable is assigned a true or false value indicating whether the loading succeeded or failed. Here is one example:

```
my_lv.onLoad = function(success:Boolean) {
    trace("load successful: " + success);
};
```

Once you're finished with loaded data, it's good practice to delete the LoadVars object using the delete command. For example:

```
delete my_lv;
```

Otherwise, the data will persist and take up memory until the movie ends.

To detect the completion of loaded data:

1. Continuing with the file you used in the preceding task, select the first frame of the main Timeline, and open the Actions panel.
2. On a new line at the end of the current script, enter the name of your LoadVars object, followed by a period.
3. In the code hint pull-down menu that appears, select the onLoad event (or choose ActionScript 2.0 Classes > Client/Server and XML > LoadVars > Event Handlers > onLoad).

   The onLoad event handler appears. This event handler is triggered when an attempt to load data completes.
4. For the parameter of the onLoad event handler, enter success:Boolean. This defines a variable as though you had declared it with the var statement (**Figure 10.11**).

   When the Flash Player calls your onLoad event handler, this variable's value will be set to true or false, indicating whether the data loaded successfully.
5. Choose actions to be performed using the loaded data, and place them between the curly braces of the event handler when the loaded variables arrive at the Flash Player.

   The loaded variables are added as properties on the LoadVars object, so to access them you must enter the LoadVars object's name, a period, and then the loaded variable's name (**Figure 10.12**).

```
myLoadVariables_lv.onLoad = function(success:Boolean) {
};
```

Figure 10.11 The onLoad event handler for the myLoadVariables_lv object will be triggered when the loading operation completes. Nothing is written inside the event handler yet.

✔ Tips

- The variables you specify in an external text file are loaded into Flash as strings, making quotation marks around string values unnecessary. Flash automatically converts strings to numbers for certain operations and actions. In the preceding example, Flash knows to use a number for the `_rotation`, `_xscale`, and `_yscale` properties. The string values `"45"` and `"150"` are automatically converted to number values `45` and `150`. To tell Flash explicitly to use a number, use the `Number` function. Choose Global Functions > Conversion Functions > Number, and enter your variable's name as a parameter (**Figure 10.13**).
- Write your variable and value pairs in an external text file without any line breaks, spaces, or other punctuation except the ampersand. Although you may have a harder time reading the file, Flash will have an easier time understanding it.
- In addition to loading data using the `LoadVars` object, you can also send variables to the Web server, which can be used to customize the values that are returned. To send variables, define them as properties of your `LoadVars` object, and then call the `sendAndLoad()` method instead of the `load()` method to send the variables to the server and start the loading operation.

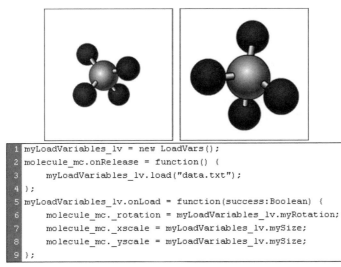

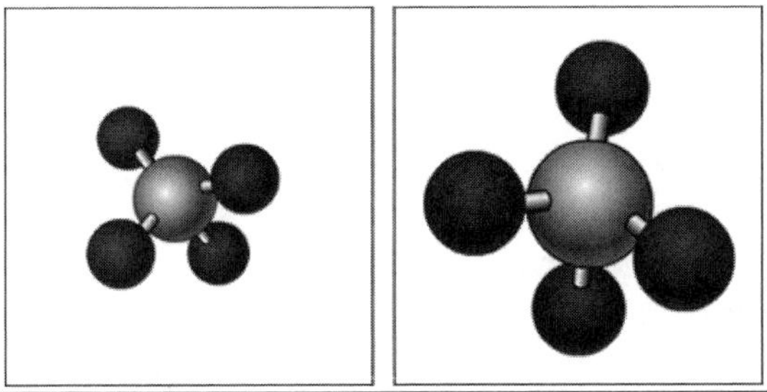

```
myLoadVariables_lv = new LoadVars();
molecule_mc.onRelease = function() {
    myLoadVariables_lv.load("data.txt");
};
myLoadVariables_lv.onLoad = function(success:Boolean) {
    molecule_mc._rotation = myLoadVariables_lv.myRotation;
    molecule_mc._xscale = myLoadVariables_lv.mySize;
    molecule_mc._yscale = myLoadVariables_lv.mySize;
};
```

Figure 10.12 The variables that were loaded into the `myLoadVariables_lv` object are used to change the rotation and scale of the movie clip `molecule_mc`.

```
myLoadVariables_lv.onLoad = function(success:Boolean) {
    molecule_mc._rotation = Number(myLoadVariables_lv.myRotation);
    molecule_mc._xscale = Number(myLoadVariables_lv.mySize);
    molecule_mc._yscale = Number(myLoadVariables_lv.mySize);
};
```

Figure 10.13 Use the `Number` function to convert the contents of a variable to the `Number` data type. If the value of the variable `mySize` is a string `"150"`, the `Number` function converts it to the numerical value `150`.

Loading variables from the HTML page

Using the LoadVars class, you can load variables from external text files into your movie. However, as an alternative approach to loading external data, you can access variables that are placed in the HTML page containing your SWF file. If you place those variables in the <object> and <embed> tags (the tags that indicate to the browser that the Web page contains a Flash Player movie), the variables are loaded into the SWF automatically. Putting variables in the HTML is a useful alternative to using a LoadVars object if you have only a small amount of data to load and if the data only needs to be loaded into the SWF file one time.

To load a variable from the HTML page:

1. Open the HTML document that is created with your SWF file when you publish your movie.

2. Find the <object> tag, which should be followed by a series of <param name="" value=""> tags that tell the browser how to display the movie.

3. Insert a variable as follows:

   ```
   <param name="FlashVars"
   value="myRotationVariable=45">
   ```

   FlashVars is the name of the attribute of the param HTML tag, and its value is a string of variable name/value pairs in MIME url-encoded format. If you have multiple variables, use ampersands to connect them, like this "myRotationVariable=45&mySizeVariable=150".

4. Find the <embed> tag, which should contain a series of attributes that tell the browser how to display the movie.
5. Add your variable in an additional attribute within the <embed> tag, as follows:

   `flashvars="myRotationVariable=45"`

   You must add both the FlashVars <param> tag and <embed> tag attribute for cross-browser compatibility (**Figure 10.14**).
6. Save the modified HTML document, and open it in a browser.

   When the SWF file loads in the HTML page, the variables are automatically created in the SWF file; no action is necessary to load them. The variables are defined in the scope of the _root Timeline.

✔ Tips

- You can't test the result of variables loaded with FlashVars in Flash's Test Movie mode; you must load the SWF file in a Web browser in order to see the result.
- Once you've modified your HTML file by adding the FlashVars parameters, if you publish your Flash movie again, the HTML file is overwritten. To prevent this, after you've modified the HTML file, choose File > Publish Settings and, on the Formats tab, deselect the HTML check box.
- The FlashVars parameter containing the variable name/value pairs loaded from the <object> and <embed> tags has a size limit of 64 KB.

```
<object classid="clsid:d27cdb6e-ae6d-11cf-96b8-444553540000"
        codebase="http://fpdownload.macromedia.com/pub/shockwave/cabs/flash/swflash.
        width="400" height="300" id="05variablesInHTML" align="middle">
        <param name="allowScriptAccess" value="sameDomain" />
        <param name="movie" value="05variablesInHTML.swf" />
        <param name="FlashVars" value="myRotationVariable=45" />
        <param name="quality" value="high" />
        <param name="bgcolor" value="#ffffff" />
        <embed src="05variablesInHTML.swf"
                quality="high"
                bgcolor="#ffffff"
                flashvars="myRotationVariable=45"
                width="400"
                height="300"
                name="05variablesInHTML"
                align="middle"
                allowScriptAccess="sameDomain"
                type="application/x-shockwave-flash"
                pluginspage="http://www.macromedia.com/go/getflashplayer" />
</object>
```

Figure 10.14 A portion of the HTML page shows where the FlashVars parameters are inserted.

Communicating with XML Objects

In addition to loading url-encoded variables from the HTML page or using the `LoadVars` class, Flash supports loading and using data in XML format. Although it's beyond the scope of this book to cover XML in depth, this short discussion will help you understand the exciting possibilities Flash brings to XML.

XML is similar to a traditional markup language such as HTML, which contains content surrounded by tags that are meant to be understood by a computer. XML is more generic than HTML, in that it lets you define content according to its meaning and its audience. The structure and meaning of the content are defined by tags that are easy to read and understand:

```
<invoice>
<vendorname>Big Tents</vendorname>
<vendorID>MYBDAY021570</vendorID>
<vendorLogo>03SUIRAUQA.GIF</vendorLogo>
<productdescription>
    <name>All-Weather Tent</name>
    <packageDimensions>
        <height>7.25</height>
        <width>7.25</width>
        <depth>48.5</depth>
        <weight>8lbs.</weight>
    </packageDimensions>
    <wholesale>$75.43</wholesale>
    <retail>$135.99</retail>
</productdescription>
</invoice>
```

In Flash, the XML object lets you load XML data from a server, read and manipulate that data, and send XML data to a server. The way you use the XML class to load data is nearly identical to the way you load variables with the `LoadVars` class; you use the XML class's `load()` method to start loading an XML file, and you define an `onLoad` event handler for the XML object that is called when the XML data is loaded. Once the data is loaded, you can use additional methods of the XML object to navigate through the XML data to retrieve the values. Using XML in Flash provides an alternative way to communicate with a server from Flash, using more complex information than can be easily contained in individual variables.

To learn more about Flash's XML object, refer to the Flash Help that comes with the software.

Storing and Sharing Information

Although variables enable you to keep track of information, they do so only within a single playing of a Flash movie. When your viewer quits the movie, all the information in variables is lost. When the viewer returns to the movie, the variables are again initialized to their starting values or are loaded from external sources.

You can have Flash remember the current values of your variables even after a viewer quits the movie, however. The solution is to use the `SharedObject` class. `SharedObject` instances save information on a viewer's computer, much like browsers save information in cookies. When a viewer returns to a movie that has saved a `SharedObject`, that object can be loaded back in and the variables from the previous visit can be used.

You can use the `SharedObject` class in a variety of ways to make your Flash site more convenient for repeat visitors. Store visitors' high scores in a game, or store their login names so they don't have to type them again. If you've created a complex puzzle game, you can store the positions of the pieces for completion at a later date; for a long animated story, you can store the user's current location.

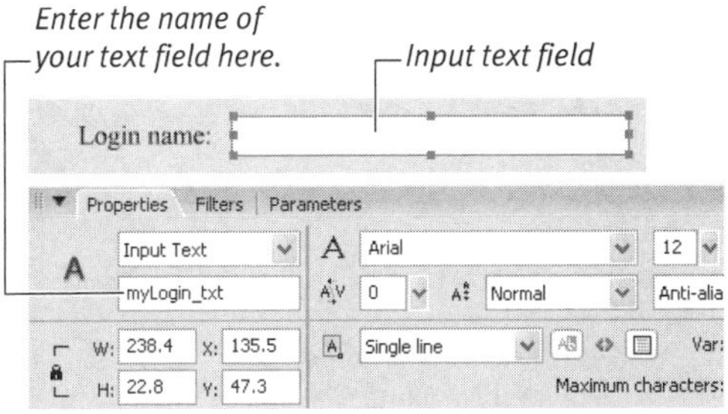

Figure 10.15 Create an input text field with the Text tool, and give it a name in the Property inspector.

To store information in a `SharedObject` instance, add a new property to the `SharedObject`'s `data` property object. You then store the information that you want to keep in your new property. The statement `mySO_so.data.highscore = 200` stores the high score information in the `mySO_so` `SharedObject` instance. The static method `getLocal()` creates or retrieves a `SharedObject`, and the method `flush()` causes the `data` properties to be written to the computer's hard disk. In the following task, you'll save a login name from a text field (you'll learn more about text fields in the next chapter). When you quit and then return to the movie, your login name is retrieved and displayed.

To store information on a user's computer:

1. Select the Text tool, and drag a text field onto the Stage.
2. In the Property inspector, select Input Text, and give the text field the instance name `myLogin_txt` (**Figure 10.15**).

   This input text field allows users to enter information via the keyboard.
3. Create a button, place an instance of it on the Stage, and give it an instance name in the Property inspector.

   You'll assign actions to this button to save the information in your text field in a `SharedObject`.
4. Select the first frame of the main Timeline, and open the Actions panel.
5. In the Script pane, declare a new `SharedObject` by entering `var mySO_so: SharedObject`, followed by an equals sign.

continues on next page

6. On the right side of the equals sign, enter `SharedObject.getLocal("myCookie")` (**Figure 10.16**).

   Flash creates a `SharedObject` instance that will be stored on the user's local hard drive. You can reference this object with the variable `mySO_so`. If the `SharedObject` already exists from a previous visit, Flash retrieves the object instead of creating one.

7. On the next line, create an `onRelease` event handler for your button.

8. Between the curly braces of the event handler, enter the following:

   `mySO_so.data.loginData = myLogin_txt.text`.

   The content of your text field on the Stage is saved in a property named `loginData` on the `data` property of your `SharedObject`.

9. On the next line, enter `mySO_so.flush()` (**Figure 10.17**).

   Calling the `flush()` method saves all the information in the `data` property of your `SharedObject` on the viewer's computer.

✔ Tips

- If the `flush()` method isn't called explicitly, the information in the `data` object of your `SharedObject` is saved automatically when the viewer quits the movie. The `flush()` method lets you choose when to save information.
- Many kinds of information can be stored in the `data` object of a `SharedObject`, such as numbers, strings, and even objects such as an array.

  Just remember to assign the information to the `data` object of a `SharedObject`, as in

  `mySO_so.data.name = "Russell"`

  rather than

  `mySO_so.data = "Russell"`

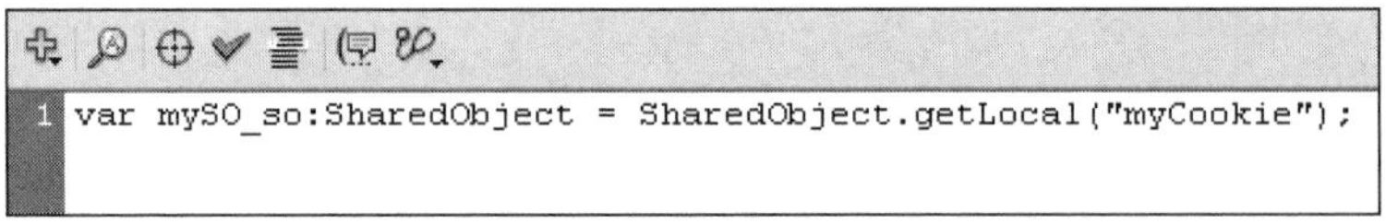
var mySO_so:SharedObject = SharedObject.getLocal("myCookie");

Figure 10.16 The `getLocal()` method creates a `SharedObject` that will be stored on the user's computer.

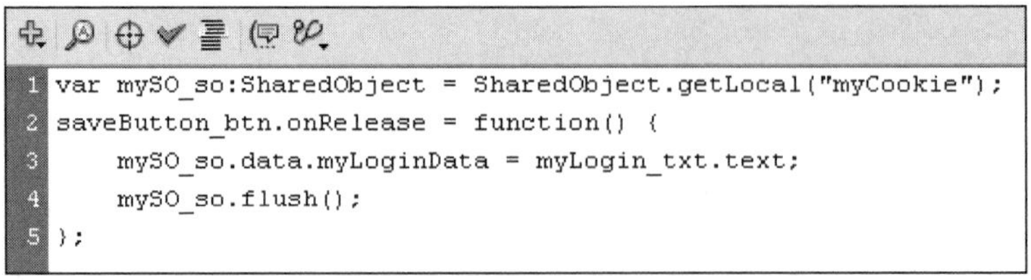
var mySO_so:SharedObject = SharedObject.getLocal("myCookie");
saveButton_btn.onRelease = function() {
mySO_so.data.myLoginData = myLogin_txt.text;
mySO_so.flush();
};

Figure 10.17 The `onRelease` handler for the button `saveButton_btn` puts the contents of the input text field in the `myLoginData` property of the `data` property of your `SharedObject` and saves it on the user's computer.

To retrieve information from a user's computer:

1. Continuing with the file you used in the preceding task, create a second button, place an instance of it on the Stage, and give it a name in the Property inspector.

   You'll assign actions to this second button, which will retrieve `mySO_so.data` and the most recently saved contents of your text field.

2. Select the main Timeline, and, in the Actions panel, assign an `onRelease` handler to this second button.

3. Between the curly braces of the event handler, enter the following statement:

   ```
   myLogin_txt.text =
   mySO_so.data.myLoginData;
   ```

   This statement retrieves the information in `myLoginData` that was saved on the viewer's computer in a `SharedObject`. That information is used to change the contents of your text field (**Figure 10.18**).

4. Test your movie.

   Enter your name in the text field on the Stage, and then click the button to save the information into a `SharedObject`. Quit the movie. When you open up the movie again and click the second button, your name appears in the text field because Flash retrieved the information from your previous session (**Figure 10.19**).

```
var mySO_so:SharedObject = SharedObject.getLocal("myCookie");
saveButton_btn.onRelease = function() {
    mySO_so.data.myLoginData = myLogin_txt.text;
    mySO_so.flush();
};
loadButton_btn.onRelease = function() {
    myLogin_txt.text = mySO_so.data.myLoginData;
};
```

Figure 10.18 The `onRelease` handler for the button `loadButton_btn` puts the saved data into the input text field.

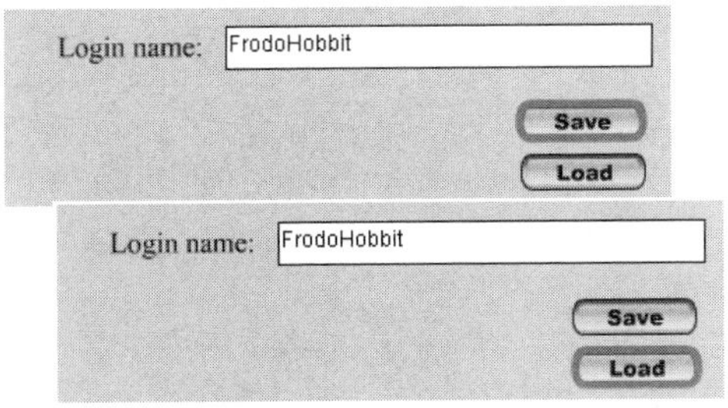

Figure 10.19 Enter your login name in the input text field, and click the button `saveButton_btn`. Close the movie, and then return to it. When you click the button `loadButton_btn`, your login name appears again so you don't have to retype it.

To clear information on a user's computer:

- Use the `delete` statement to clear information saved in a `SharedObject`.

  The statement

  `delete mySO_so.data.myLoginData;`

  removes the `myLoginData` property.

Sharing information among multiple movies

Flash keeps track of a `SharedObject` saved on the viewer's computer by remembering the name of the object as well as the location of the movie in which it was created.
The location of the movie is known as the `SharedObject`'s *local path*. By default, the local path is the relative path from the domain name to the filename. If your movie is at www.myDomain.com/flash/myMovie.swf, the local path is /flash/myMovie.swf. Flash lets you specify a different local path when you use the `getLocal()` method so that you can store a `SharedObject` in a different place. Why would you do this? If you have multiple movies, you can define one `SharedObject` and a common local path, allowing all the movies to access the same `SharedObject` and share its information.

Valid local paths for a `SharedObject` include the directory in which your movie sits or any of its parent directories. Don't include the domain name, and don't specify any other directories in the domain. Remember, you aren't telling Flash to store information on the server; you're telling Flash to store information locally on the viewer's computer (the host), and the local path helps Flash keep track of the `SharedObject`. Because local paths are relative to a single domain, a `SharedObject` can be shared only with multiple movies in the same domain.

To store information that multiple movies can share:

1. Continuing with the file that you created in the preceding task, in the Actions panel, add a forward slash as the second parameter to the `getLocal()` method. Make sure the forward slash is between quotation marks (**Figure 10.20**).

   Flash will save the `SharedObject` `mySharedObject_so` with the local path `"/"`. This entry represents the top-level directory.

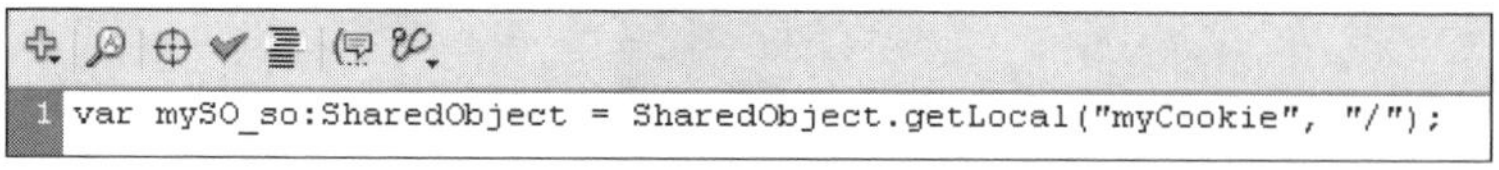
var mySO_so:SharedObject = SharedObject.getLocal("myCookie", "/");

Figure 10.20 The second parameter of the `getLocal()` method determines the local path of the `SharedObject` and its location on the viewer's computer. The single slash indicates the top-level directory of the domain where the Flash movie resides.

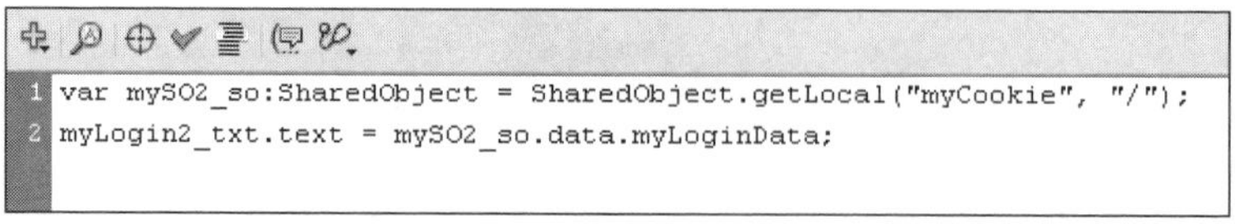
var mySO2_so:SharedObject = SharedObject.getLocal("myCookie", "/");
myLogin2_txt.text = mySO2_so.data.myLoginData;

Figure 10.21 In this second Flash movie, the `getLocal()` method retrieves the same `SharedObject` that was saved in the first Flash movie, because the same name and local path are given in its parameters for both movies.

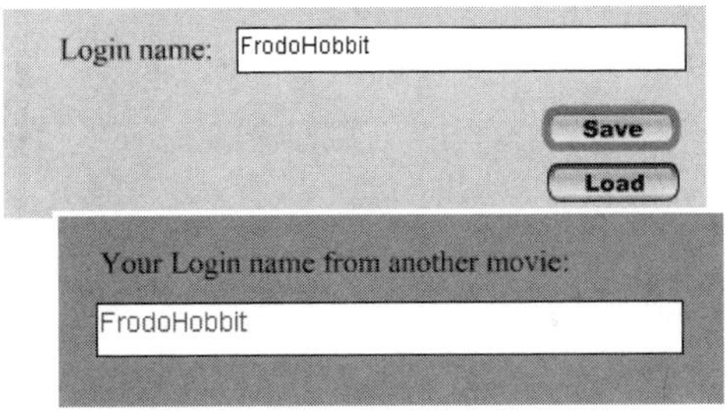

Figure 10.22 When the login name in the first Flash movie is saved, you can open the second Flash movie, and its input text field displays the same login name. Both movies access the same `SharedObject` on the user's hard drive.

2. In a new Flash document, create an input text field on the Stage, and give it the name `myLogin2_txt` in the Property inspector.

   This input text field will display information stored in the `SharedObject` you created in your first movie.

3. Select the first frame of the main Timeline, and open the Actions panel.

4. In the Script pane, enter the following statement:

   ```
   var mySO2_so:SharedObject =
   SharedObject.getLocal("myCookie", "/");
   ```

   Flash retrieves the `SharedObject` with the local path `"/"` from the viewer's computer. Notice that the parameter `"myCookie"` must be identical to the one used in the first Flash movie, but the `SharedObject` variable's name `mySO2_so` can be different (**Figure 10.21**).

5. On a new line of the Script pane, assign the property `myLoginData` in the `data` property of the `SharedObject` to the contents of your input text field with the following statement:

   ```
   myLogin2_txt.text =
   mySO2_so.data.myLoginData;
   ```

   This statement retrieves the `myLoginData` information from the `SharedObject` and displays it in the text field.

6. Test your movies.

   Play the first movie, enter your name in the text field, click the first button to save its position in a `SharedObject`, and close the movie. Now open your second movie. Flash reads the information in the `SharedObject` created by the first movie and displays your name (**Figure 10.22**).

SharedObjects, Permission, and Local Disk Space

The default amount of information that Flash Player allows a single domain to store on a viewer's computer is set at 100 KB, and users can configure the amount of space they allow to be used by `SharedObject` data. When you call the `flush()` method, depending on the amount of data you're trying to store and the viewer's settings, different things happen. If the new data doesn't exceed the amount the viewer allows, the `SharedObject` is saved and `flush()` returns `true`. If the new data exceeds the allowable amount and the viewer's Flash Player is set to block requests for more space, the `SharedObject` isn't saved and `flush()` returns a value of `false`. Finally, if the `SharedObject` data exceeds the amount the user has allowed and the Flash Player isn't set to block requests for more space, a dialog box appears over the Stage asking the viewer for permission to store information (**Figure 10.23**). In that case, the `flush()` method returns the string `"pending"`. The viewer can allow the request or deny it.

Viewers can change their local storage settings at any time by right-clicking or Control-clicking (Mac) the movie and then choosing Settings from the contextual menu (**Figure 10.24**). The viewer can choose never to accept information from a particular domain or to accept varying amounts (10 KB, 100 KB, 1 MB, 10 MB, or unlimited). Local storage permission is specific to the domain (which appears in the dialog box), so future movies from the same domain can save `SharedObjects` according to the same settings.

If you know that the information you save to a viewer's computer will grow, you can request more space ahead of time by defining a minimum disk space for the `flush()` method. Calling the method `mySO_so.flush(1000000)` saves the `SharedObject` and reserves 1,000,000 bytes (1 MB) for the information. If Flash asks the viewer to allow disk space for the `SharedObject`, it will ask for 1 MB. After the permission is given, Flash won't ask for more space until the data in all that domain's `SharedObject` exceeds 1 MB or the viewer changes their local storage settings.

Figure 10.23 Flash asks to store more information than the viewer currently allows. This request comes from local, which is the viewer's computer.

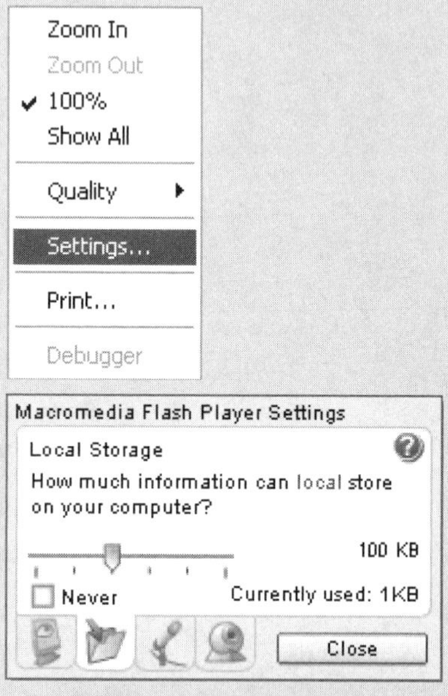

Figure 10.24 From the Flash Player contextual menu, access the Settings dialog box. You can decide how much information a particular domain can save on your computer. This setting is for local, which is the viewer's computer.

Table 10.1

Common Operators

Symbol	Description
+	Addition
-	Subtraction
*	Multiplication
/	Division
%	Modulo division; calculates the remainder of the first number divided by the second number. 7 % 2 results in 1.
++	Increases the value by 1. x++ is equivalent to x = x + 1.
--	Decreases the value by 1. x-- is equivalent to x = x - 1.
+=	Adds a value to and assigns the result to the variable. x += 5 is equivalent to x = x + 5.
-=	Subtracts a value from and assigns the result to the variable. x -= 5 is equivalent to x = x - 5.
*=	Multiplies by a value and assigns the result to the variable. x *= 5 is equivalent to x = x * 5.
/=	Divides by a value and assigns it to the variable. x /= 5 is equivalent to x = x / 5.

Modifying Variables

Variables are useful because you can always change their contents with updated information about the status of the movie or your viewer. Sometimes, this change involves assigning a new value to the variable. At other times, the change means adding, subtracting, multiplying, or dividing the variable's numeric values or modifying a string by adding characters. The variable `myScore`, for example, may be initialized at 0. Then, for every goal a player makes, the `myScore` variable changes in increments of 1. The job of modifying information contained in variables falls upon *operators*—symbols that operate on data.

Assignment and arithmetic operators

The assignment operator (=) is a single equals sign that assigns a value to a variable. You've already used this operator in initializing variables and creating new objects. **Table 10.1** lists the other common operators.

Operators are the workhorses of Flash interactivity. You'll use them often to perform calculations behind the scenes—adding the value of one variable to another or changing the property of one object by adding or subtracting the value of a variable, for example. The following task is a simple example of how you can use operators to modify a variable that affects the graphics in a movie. You'll create a button that increases the value of a variable each time the button is clicked. That variable is used to set the rotation of a movie clip.

To incrementally change a variable that affects a movie clip property:

1. Create a movie clip symbol, place an instance of it on the Stage, and give it an instance name in the Property inspector.
2. In the first keyframe of the root Timeline, initialize a `Number` variable `myRotation` to 0.
3. Create a button symbol, place an instance of it on the Stage, and give it an instance name.
4. Select the first keyframe again, and, in the Actions panel, create an `onRelease` event handler for the button.
5. Between the curly braces of the event handler, enter `myRotation += 10` (**Figure 10.25**).

   The statement adds 10 to the current value and reassigns the sum to the variable `myRotation`.
6. On a new line after the event handler, create an `onEnterFrame` event handler for the main Timeline (`_root`).
7. Between the curly braces of the `onEnterFrame` event handler, enter the name of your movie clip, a period, and then `_rotation`.
8. On the same line, enter an equals sign and then the name of your variable, `myRotation` (**Figure 10.26**).

   The `onEnterFrame` event handler makes the statement on line 6 in the example run continuously. This code assigns the rotation of the movie clip to the value of the `myRotation` variable, which the user can increase by clicking the button.
9. Place another instance of the button on the Stage.

```
1 var myRotation:Number = 0;
2 right_btn.onRelease = function() {
3     myRotation += 10;
4 };
```

Figure 10.25 Each time the button is clicked, its actions increase the `myRotation` variable by 10.

```
5 _root.onEnterFrame = function() {
6     cannon_mc._rotation = myRotation;
7 };
```

Figure 10.26 The rotation of the `cannon_mc` movie clip is updated continually to the value of the `myRotation` variable in the root Timeline.

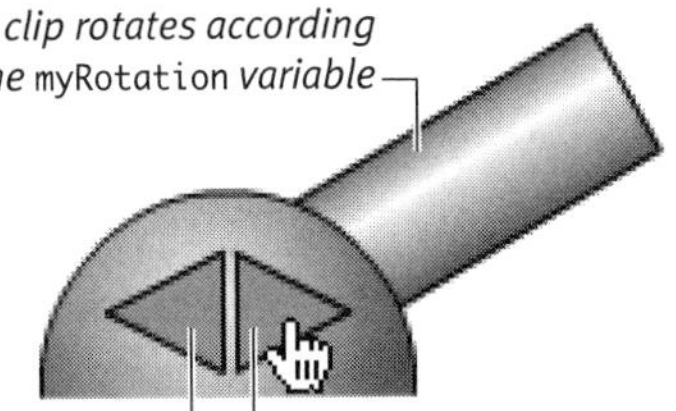
Movie clip rotates according to the myRotation variable
Button decreases the myRotation variable
Button increases the myRotation variable

Figure 10.27 The turret of this cannon is the movie clip whose rotation property changes according to the `myRotation` variable.

10. Use a subtraction assignment operator (`-=`) with the `myRotation` variable to decrease the variable's value each time the button is clicked.

    This code controls the rotation of the movie clip in the opposite direction (**Figure 10.27**).

✔ Tips

- To perform more complicated mathematical calculations (such as square root, sine, and cosine) or string manipulations on your variables and values, you must use the `Math` class or the `String` class. You'll learn about these objects in Chapters 11 and 12.
- The arithmetic rules of precedence (remember them from math class?) apply when Flash evaluates expressions, which means that certain operators take priority over others. The most important rule is that multiplication and division are performed before addition and subtraction. `3 + 4 * 2`, for example, gives a very different result than `3 * 4 + 2`.
- Use parentheses to group variables and operators so those portions are calculated before other parts of the expression are evaluated. `(3 + 2) * 4` returns a value of 20; but without the parentheses, `3 + 2 * 4` returns a value of 11.
- Use the modulo division operator (`%`) to check whether a variable is an even or an odd number. The statement `myNumber % 2` returns 0 if `myNumber` is even and 1 if `myNumber` is odd. Use this logic to create toggling functionality. You can count the number of times a viewer clicks a light switch, for example. If the count is even, you can turn on the light; if the count is odd, you turn off the light.

Concatenating Variables and Dynamic Referencing

The addition operator (+) adds the values of numeric data types. But it can also put together string data types. The expression "Hello " + "world", for example, results in the string "Hello world". This kind of operation is called *concatenation.*

One use of concatenation is to mix strings, numbers, and variables to create expressions that allow you to dynamically create and access objects or variables. For example, you can name duplicate movie clip instances by concatenating a variable with the name of the original movie clip. The variable is a counter that increases by 1 each time a duplicate is made. If the movie clip name is mushroom_mc and the variable name is counter, you can concatenate a new name with the following expression:

```
"mushroom_mc" + counter
```

The result is something like mushroom_mc1 or mushroom_mc2, depending on the value of counter. The new names of the duplicated movie clips are assigned dynamically with a concatenation expression (**Figure 10.28**).

This kind of concatenation to reference an object dynamically works because the concatenated string is used as a parameter of a method. Flash knows to resolve the expression before using it as the parameter. What happens in other cases? Consider this statement in the Script pane of the Actions panel:

```
var "myVariable" + counter = 5;
```

This statement doesn't make sense to Flash and causes an error. To construct a dynamic variable name and assign a value to that variable, you must instruct Flash to resolve the left side first and then treat the result as a concatenated variable name before assigning a value to it. The way to do that is to use the array access operators.

```
addMushroom_btn.onRelease = function() {
    duplicateMovieClip("musroom_mc", "mushroom_mc" + counter, counter);
    counter++;
};
```

Figure 10.28 The duplicateMovieClip action makes a copy of the movie clip mushroom_mc. The name of the copy is assigned dynamically, based on the concatenation of "mushroom_mc" and the value of the variable counter. The first click creates a movie clip mushroom_mc1, the second click creates mushroom_mc2, and so on.

Array access operators

To reference a variable or an object dynamically, use the *array access operators*. The array access operators are the square brackets (`[]`, located on the same keys as the curly braces). They're called array access operators because they're usually used to access the contents of an `Array` object, but they can also be used to dynamically access the contents of other objects.

What does this capability mean? Think of the main Timeline as being a `_root` or a `_level0` movie clip object; variables and objects sitting in the main Timeline are its contents. A variable `myVariable` initialized in the main Timeline can be targeted with the array access operators as follows:

```
_root["myVariable"]
```

Notice that there is no dot between the object (`_root`) and the square brackets. The array access operators automatically resolve concatenated expressions within the square brackets. For example, the following statement puts together a single variable name based on the value of `counter` and then assigns the numeric value of 5 to the variable:

```
_root["myVariable" + counter] = 5;
```

If the value of `counter` is 7, Flash creates or accesses the variable named `_root.myVariable7` and assigns the value 5 to that variable.

Using the array access operators also enables you to call methods and change the properties of dynamically referenced objects with dot syntax. For example, you can modify an object's transparency this way:

```
_root["mushroom_mc" + counter]._alpha = 50
```

If the value of `counter` is 3, the movie clip in the root Timeline named `_root.mushroom_mc3` becomes 50 percent transparent. To make the movie clip play, call the designated method like this:

```
_root["myClip_mc" + counter].play()
```

To reference a variable dynamically and assign a value:

- In the Script pane of the Actions panel, enter the parent of the variable followed by an opening square bracket, an expression, a closing square bracket, an equals sign, and a value.

  Flash resolves the expression within the square brackets and assigns the value to the variable with that name (**Figure 10.29**).

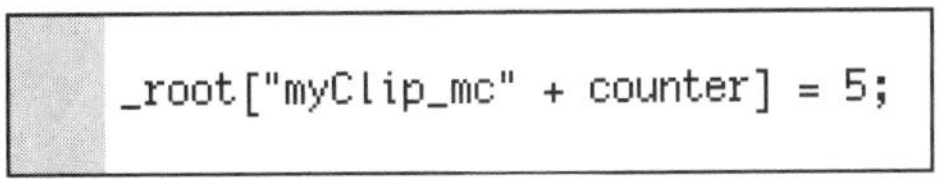
_root["myClip_mc" + counter] = 5;

Figure 10.29 Use the square brackets (array access operators) to dynamically reference a variable. In this example, if `counter` is equal to 1, the result of this assignment will be to initialize a variable `myClip_mc1` to the value 5. The parent object here is `_root`, the main Timeline.

To reference an object dynamically and call a method:

1. In the Script pane of the Actions panel, enter the parent of the object followed by an opening square bracket, an expression, and a closing square bracket.
2. On the same line, enter a period, and then enter the method name (**Figure 10.30**).
   Flash resolves the expression between the square brackets and calls the method on that object.

To reference an object dynamically and change a property:

- In the Script pane of the Actions panel, enter the parent of the object followed by an opening square bracket, an expression, a closing square bracket, a dot, a property, an equals sign, and a value (**Figure 10.31**).
  Flash resolves the expression between the square brackets and assigns the value on the right of the equals sign to the object.

```
_root["myClip_mc" + counter].play();
```

Figure 10.30 Use the array access operators to dynamically reference an object and then call one of its methods. If `counter` equals 1, this statement targets the movie clip `myClip_mc1` in the main Timeline and then makes it play.

```
_root["myClip_mc" + counter]._alpha = 50;
```

Figure 10.31 Use the array access operators to dynamically reference an object and then evaluate or modify one of its properties. If `counter` equals 1, this statement targets the movie clip `myClip_mc1` in the main Timeline and changes its transparency to 50 percent.

Dynamic Referencing with the eval Function

You can also resolve an expression for dynamic referencing using the `eval` function, which reads an expression and returns the value as a single string. You can modify an object's transparency with the following statement:

```
eval("mushroom_mc" + counter)._alpha = 50
```

Or, call a method of an object like this:

```
eval("mushroom_mc" + counter).play()
```

Notice that the `eval` function accomplishes the same task as the array access operators. Which technique should you use? Learn and use the array access operators for dynamic referencing. The `eval` function is an older function that was useful before recent ActionScript objects and syntax made it redundant. The array access operators are preferable because they're less taxing on the processor and result in more compact code that's easier to read.

In addition, in some cases, the `eval` function fails to give predictable results. You can't use `eval` to assign values directly to variables, for example. The statement `eval("myVariable" + counter) = 5` fails.

```
if (condition) {
 consequence1;
 consequence2;
 consequence3;
}
```

Figure 10.32 If, and only if, the condition within the parentheses is true, consequence1, consequence2, and consequence3 are all performed. If the condition is false, all three consequences are ignored.

Testing Information with Conditional Statements

Variables and expressions go hand in hand with conditional statements. The information you retrieve, store in variables, and modify in expressions is useful only when you can compare it with other pieces of information. Conditional statements let you do this kind of comparison and carry out instructions based on the results. The logic of conditional statements is the same as the logic in the sentence "If abc is true, then do xyz," and in Flash, you define abc (the condition) and xyz (the consequence).

Conditional statements begin with the statement `if()`. The statement that goes between the parentheses is the *condition*—a statement that can be resolved to a true or false value, usually by comparing one thing with another. Is the variable `myScore` greater than the variable `alltimeHighScore`? Does the `_currentframe` property of the root Timeline equal 10? These are typical examples of the types of things that are compared in conditions.

How do you compare values? You use comparison operators.

Comparison operators

A *comparison operator* evaluates the expressions on both sides of itself and returns a value of `true` or `false`. **Table 10.2** summarizes the comparison operators.

When the statement is evaluated and the condition holds true, Flash performs the consequences within the `if` statement's curly braces. If the condition turns out to be false, all the actions within the curly braces are ignored (**Figure 10.32**).

Table 10.2

Comparison Operators

Symbol	Description
==	Equality
===	Strict equality (value and data type must be equal)
<	Less than
>	Greater than
<=	Less than or equal to
>=	Greater than or equal to
!=	Not equal to
!==	Strict inequality

In the following task, you'll use the same file you created to rotate a cannon turret in the section "Modifying Variables" earlier in this chapter. You want to constrain the rotation of the turret to a maximum of 90 degrees, so you'll construct a conditional statement to have Flash test whether the value of its rotation is greater than 90. If it is, you'll keep its rotation at 90, preventing the turret from rotating past the horizontal plane.

To create a conditional statement:

1. Continuing with the task that demonstrates the rotation of a movie clip (see "Modifying Variables," earlier in this chapter), select the keyframe containing the ActionScript, and open the Actions panel.
2. In the right arrow button's `onRelease` event handler, after the line that increases the variable's value by 10, add a conditional statement by choosing Statements > Conditions/Loops > if (Esc + if).
3. For the condition, enter the name of the rotation variable (`myRotation`, in this example), followed by the > symbol and then `90` (**Figure 10.33**).

   Flash tests to see whether the variable is greater than 90.
4. Between the curly braces of the `if` statement, enter your variable name and then an equals sign followed by the number `90` (**Figure 10.34**).

   If the variable exceeds 90, Flash resets it to 90. This setting prevents the cannon turret from rotating past the horizontal plane.
5. Choose the other button, which decreases the rotation variable, and create a similar conditional statement to test whether the variable is less than –90.
6. If the condition is true, set the variable to –90.

```
right_btn.onRelease = function() {
    myRotation += 10;
    if (myRotation > 90) {
    }
};
```

Figure 10.33 Add a condition that tests the `myRotation` variable to see if its value exceeds 90.

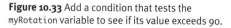

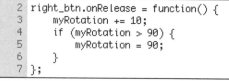

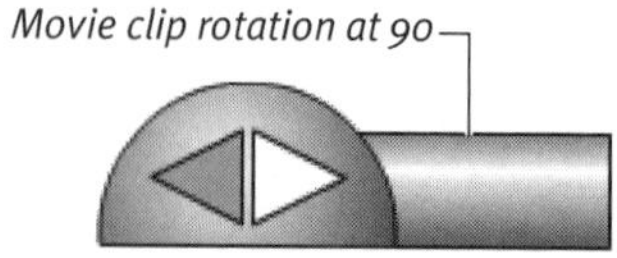


```
right_btn.onRelease = function() {
    myRotation += 10;
    if (myRotation > 90) {
        myRotation = 90;
    }
};
```

Figure 10.34 The cannon turret can't rotate past 90 degrees because the `if` statement won't allow the variable `myRotation` to increase in value beyond 90.

✔ Tips

- Any action residing outside the `if` statement is performed regardless of whether the condition in the `if` statement is true or false. Consider the following script:

```
if (myVariable == 10) {
    myVariable = 20;
}
myVariable = 30;
```

  After Flash runs this block of code, `myVariable` is always set to 30, even if the condition `myVariable == 10` is true. The last statement is executed no matter what.

- A common mistake is to mix up the assignment operator (=) and the comparison operator for equality (==). The single equals sign assigns whatever is on the right side of it to whatever is on the left side. Use the single equals sign when you're setting and modifying properties and variables. The double equals sign compares the equality of two things; use it in conditional statements.

Creating a continuous-feedback button

A simple but powerful and widely applicable use of the `if` statement is to monitor the state of a button click and provide continuous actions as long as the button is held down. A button that provides this kind of functionality is sometimes called a *continuous-feedback button.* A continuous-feedback button causes change even when it's held down at a constant state. When you click and hold down a button, for example, you can increase the sound volume (like a television remote control) until you let go. A simple button event can't accomplish this functionality.

The solution requires you to toggle the value of a variable based on the state of the button. When the button is depressed, the toggle variable is set to `true`. When the button is released or the pointer is moved away from the button, the variable is set to `false`. Within an `onEnterFrame` handler, you can monitor the status of the variable continuously with an `if` statement. If the toggle variable is `true`, the code performs an action. As long as the toggle variable remains `true` (the button continues to be held down), those actions continue to be executed.

When you build your continuous-feedback button, you'll use a movie clip. Doing so lets you assign both button events (`onPress` and `onRelease`) as well as clip events (`onEnterFrame`) to the instance.

To create a continuous-feedback button:

1. Create a movie clip symbol, place an instance of it on the Stage, and give it an instance name in the Property inspector.
2. Select the first frame of the main Timeline, and open the Actions panel.
3. Declare a Boolean variable, and set its initial value to `false`.

   This will be the toggle variable that tracks whether the button is being held down.
4. Choose ActionScript 2.0 Classes > Movie > MovieClip > Event Handlers > onPress.
5. Replace the placeholder `not_set_yet` with the name of your movie clip instance.
6. Between the curly braces of the `onPress` event handler, enter the name of your toggle variable, an equals sign, and then the word `true` (**Figure 10.35**).

   The variable is set to `true` whenever the movie clip is pressed. Note that there are no quotation marks around the word `true`, so `true` is treated correctly as a `Boolean` data type, not a `string` data type.
7. On a new line of the Script pane, choose ActionScript 2.0 Classes > Movie > MovieClip > Event Handlers > onRelease.
8. Replace the placeholder `not_set_yet` with the name of your movie clip instance.
9. Between the curly braces of the `onRelease` event handler, enter the name of your toggle variable, an equals sign, and then the word `false` (**Figure 10.36**).

   The variable is set to `false` whenever the movie clip is released.
10. On a new line of the Script pane, choose ActionScript 2.0 Classes > Movie > MovieClip > Event Handlers > onEnterFrame.

```
var pressing:Boolean = false;
continuousFeedback_mc.onPress = function() {
    pressing = true;
};
```

Figure 10.35 The variable `pressing` keeps track of whether the movie clip `continuousFeedback_mc` is being pressed or released. When the movie clip is pressed, `pressing` is set to `true`.

```
continuousFeedback_mc.onRelease = function() {
    pressing = false;
};
```

Figure 10.36 When the movie clip is released, `pressing` is set to `false`.

```
continuousFeedback_mc.onEnterFrame = function() {
    if (pressing == true) {
        // put actions that you want to be performed
        // continuously, as long as the movie clip is
        // being pressed
    }
};
```

Figure 10.37 The status of the `pressing` variable can be monitored continuously by an `if` statement inside an `onEnterFrame` handler.

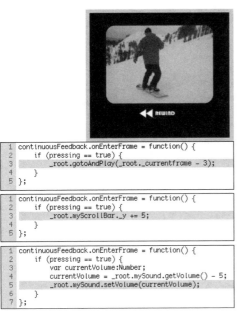

```
continuousFeedback.onEnterFrame = function() {
    if (pressing == true) {
        _root.gotoAndPlay(_root._currentframe - 3);
    }
};
```

```
continuousFeedback.onEnterFrame = function() {
    if (pressing == true) {
        _root.myScrollBar._y += 5;
    }
};
```

```
continuousFeedback.onEnterFrame = function() {
    if (pressing == true) {
        var currentVolume:Number;
        currentVolume = _root.mySound.getVolume() - 5;
        _root.mySound.setVolume(currentVolume);
    }
};
```

Figure 10.38 Three examples of how a continuous-feedback button can affect a movie. At top, when the button is held down, Flash moves the playhead three frames behind the current frame, creating a rewind button like the one shown here that controls a snowboard video. In the middle, when the button is held down, a movie clip `myScrollbar` moves down the Stage like a regular scroll bar. At the bottom, when the button is held down, the volume of the sound object `mySound` decreases.

11. Replace the placeholder `not_set_yet` with the name of your movie clip instance.

12. Between the curly braces of the `onEnterFrame` event handler, choose Statements > Conditions/Loops > if.

13. For the condition, enter the toggle variable name followed by two equals signs and then `true` (**Figure 10.37**).

The condition tests whether the movie clip is being pressed.

14. Choose an action as a consequence that you want to be performed as long as the button is held down (**Figure 10.38**).

✔ Tips

- To refine the continuous-feedback interaction, add an `onDragOut` event to your `onRelease` handler, as follows:

```
continuousFeedback.onRelease =
continuousFeedback.onDragOut =
function() { }
```

  Now if your viewer releases the movie clip or if the pointer wanders off the movie clip, the continuous actions will stop.

- You can use a shorthand way of testing whether a variable is true or false by eliminating the comparison operator (==). The `if` statement automatically tests whether its condition is true, so you can test whether a variable is true by entering the variable name within the parentheses of the `if` statement, like this:

```
if (myVariable) {
    // myVariable is true
}
```

  You can test whether a variable is false by preceding the variable name with an exclamation point, which means "not," like so:

```
if (!myVariable) {
    // myVariable is not true
}
```

Providing Alternatives to Conditions

In many cases, you need to provide an alternative response to the conditional statement. The `else` statement lets you create consequences when the condition in the `if` statement is `false`. The `else` statement takes care of any condition that the `if` statement doesn't cover.

The `else` statement must be used in conjunction with the `if` statement and follows the syntax and logic of this hypothetical example:

```
if (daytime) {
    goToWork();
} else {
    goToSleep();
}
```

Use `else` for either-or conditions—something that can be just one of two options. In the preceding example, there are only two possibilities: It's either daytime or nighttime. Situations in which the `else` statement can be useful include collision detection, true/false or right/wrong answer checking, and password verification.

For this task, you'll build an `if-else` statement to detect the keyboard input given to the question "Is the earth round?" The answer can be only right or wrong—there are no other alternatives.

To use else for the false condition:

1. Select the first frame of the main Timeline, and open the Actions panel. In the Script pane, create a listener object (see Chapter 4).
2. On the next line, create an onKeyDown event handler for your listener object (**Figure 10.39**).

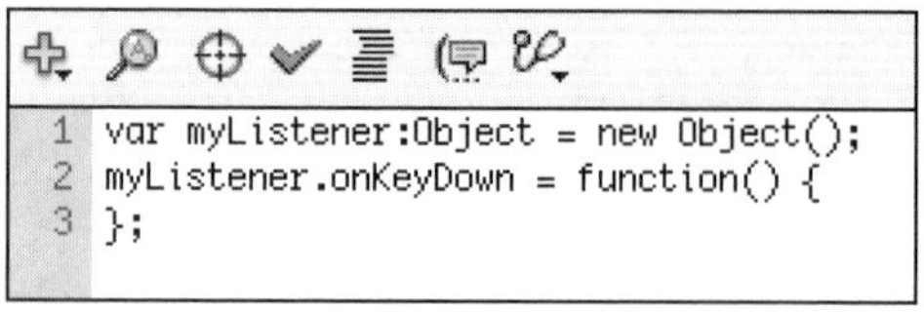
var myListener:Object = new Object();
myListener.onKeyDown = function() {
};

Figure 10.39 The onKeyDown event handler will detect a keypress on the keyboard.

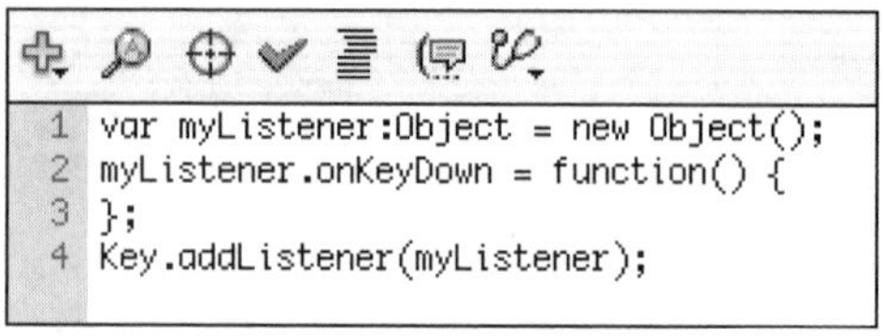
var myListener:Object = new Object();
myListener.onKeyDown = function() {
};
Key.addListener(myListener);

Figure 10.40 Register your listener object to the Key class.

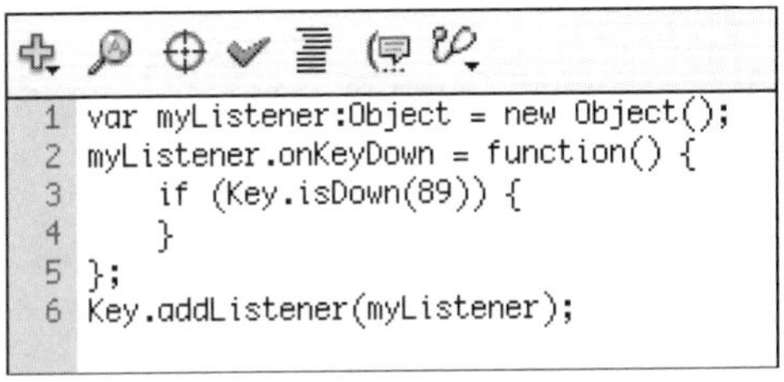
var myListener:Object = new Object();
myListener.onKeyDown = function() {
if (Key.isDown(89)) {
}
};
Key.addListener(myListener);

Figure 10.41 The `if` statement within the onKeyDown event handler checks whether the Y key, which corresponds to the key code value of 89, is being pressed.

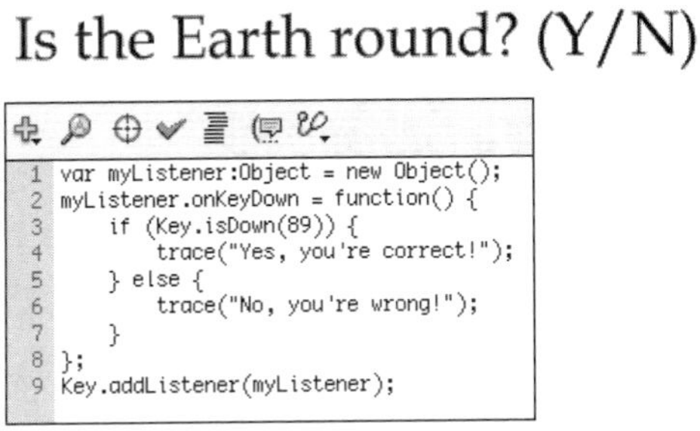
Is the Earth round? (Y/N)
var myListener:Object = new Object();
myListener.onKeyDown = function() {
if (Key.isDown(89)) {
trace("Yes, you're correct!");
} else {
trace("No, you're wrong!");
}
};
Key.addListener(myListener);

Figure 10.42 The `else` statement triggers the "No, you're wrong" `trace` action if a key other than the Y key is pressed. Note how the `else` statement is commonly written in a group with the `if` statement, beginning on the same line as the ending curly brace of the `if` statement.

- The conditions for this task don't include the comparison operator for equality (==). For Boolean data types and methods that return Boolean values, you don't need to compare them explicitly to the value `true`. The following two expressions are equivalent:

```
if (Key.isDown(89))
if (Key.isDown(89) == true)
```

3. On a new line after your completed event handler, register your listener with the Key class (**Figure 10.40**).
4. Between the curly braces of the onKeyDown event handler, create an `if` statement by choosing Statements > Conditions/Loops > if.
5. As the condition, enter `Key.isDown (89)`, which tests whether the Y key is pressed down (**Figure 10.41**).
6. Choose an action as a response to this condition.
7. On the same line as the closing curly brace of the `if` statement, enter `else` followed by an opening curly brace.
8. On the next line, choose another action as a response to the `false` condition, and then close the `else` statement with a closing curly brace (**Figure 10.42**).

   In this example, Flash listens for a key being pressed. If the key is the Y key, then the correct-answer message is sent. Otherwise, the incorrect-answer message is sent. The `else` statement covers any key other than the Y key.

✔ Tips

- You can add an `else` statement by choosing Statements > Conditions/Loops > else or by pressing Esc + el, but doing so adds a closing brace behind the `else` statement.
- By convention, the `else` statement cuddles the closing brace of the `if` statement to show that they belong together. In the Auto Format options, however, you can change the Script pane's formatting to put the `else` statement on its own line.

Branching Conditional Statements

If you have multiple possible conditions and just as many consequences, you need to use more complicated branching conditional statements that provide functionality a single `else` statement can't. If you create an interface to a Web site or a game that requires keyboard input, for example, you need to test which keys are pressed and respond appropriately to each keypress. Flash gives you the `else if` statement, which lets you construct multiple responses, as in the following hypothetical example:

```
if (sunny) {
    bringSunglasses();
} else if (raining) {
    bringUmbrella();
} else if (snowing) {
    bringSkis();
}
```

Each `else if` statement has its own condition that it evaluates and its own set of consequences to perform if that condition returns `true`. Only one condition in the entire `if-else if` code block can be true. If more than one condition is true, Flash performs the consequences for the first true condition it encounters and ignores the rest. In the preceding example, even if it's both sunny *and* snowing, Flash can perform the consequence only for the sunny condition (`bringSunglasses()`) because it appears before the snowing condition. If you want the possibility of multiple conditions to be true, you must construct separate `if` statements that are independent, like the following:

```
if (sunny) {
    bringSunglasses();
}
if (raining) {
    bringUmbrella();
}
if (snowing) {
    bringSkis();
}
```

The following example uses the `Key` class and branching conditional statements to move and rotate a movie clip according to different keypresses.

To use else if for branching alternatives:

1. Create a movie clip symbol, place an instance of it on the Stage, and give it an instance name in the Property inspector.
2. Select the first frame of the main Timeline, and open the Actions panel.
3. Choose ActionScript 2.0 Classes > Movie > MovieClip > Event Handlers > onEnterFrame.
4. Replace the placeholder `not_set_yet` with the name of the movie clip instance.
5. Between the curly braces of the event handler, choose Statements > Conditions/Loops > if.
6. Enter `Key.isDown(Key.UP)` as the condition.

   The first condition uses the `isDown()` method of the `Key` class to test whether the up arrow key is pressed.

```
beetle_mc.onEnterFrame = function() {
    if (Key.isDown(Key.UP)) {
        this._rotation = 0;
        this._y -=30;
    }
};
```

Figure 10.43 If the up arrow key is pressed, this movie clip is rotated to 0 degrees and is repositioned 30 pixels up the Stage.

```
beetle_mc.onEnterFrame = function() {
    if (Key.isDown(Key.UP)) {
        this._rotation = 0;
        this._y -=30;
    } else if (Key.isDown(Key.LEFT)) {
        this._rotation = -90;
        this._x -=30;
    }
};
```

Figure 10.44 The `else if` statement provides another alternative to the first condition. Pressing either the up arrow key or the left arrow key can now trigger actions.

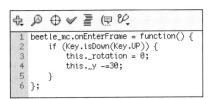

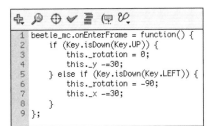

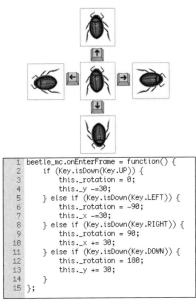

```
beetle_mc.onEnterFrame = function() {
    if (Key.isDown(Key.UP)) {
        this._rotation = 0;
        this._y -=30;
    } else if (Key.isDown(Key.LEFT)) {
        this._rotation = -90;
        this._x -=30;
    } else if (Key.isDown(Key.RIGHT)) {
        this._rotation = 90;
        this._x += 30;
    } else if (Key.isDown(Key.DOWN)) {
        this._rotation = 180;
        this._y += 30;
    }
};
```

Figure 10.45 The complete script has four conditions that use `if` and `else if` to test whether the up, left, right, or down arrow key is pressed. The rotation and position of the movie clip change depending on which condition holds true.

7. On the next line, between the curly braces of the `if` statement, enter `this` followed by a dot, the property `_rotation`, an equals sign, and `0`.

8. On the next line, enter `this` followed by a dot, the property _y, a minus sign and equals sign (-=), and `30`.

   The two statements within the `if` statement rotate the movie clip so that the head faces the top and subtract 30 pixels from its current y position, making it move up the Stage. Recall that the operator -= means "subtract this amount and assign the result to myself" (**Figure 10.43**).

9. On the same line as the closing curly brace of the `if` statement, enter `else if` and an opening parenthesis. Enter `Key.isDown(Key.LEFT)` and then a closing parenthesis.

10. On the same line, enter an opening curly brace.

11. On the next line, create two more statements to set the rotation of the movie clip to 90 and add 30 pixels to its x position, and then close the `else if` statement with a closing curly brace (**Figure 10.44**).

12. Add two more `else if` statements in the manner described earlier to test whether `Key.DOWN` is being pressed and whether `Key.RIGHT` is being pressed. Change the rotation and position of the movie clip accordingly.

13. Test your movie.

    Your series of `if` and `else if` statements tests whether the user presses the arrow keys and moves the movie clip accordingly (**Figure 10.45**). Now you have the beginnings of a game of Frogger!

The switch, case, and default actions

Another way to create alternatives to conditions is to use the switch, case, and default actions instead of the if statement. These actions provide a different way to test the equality of an expression. The syntax and logic can be seen in this hypothetical example:

```
switch (weather) {
    case sun :
        bringSunglasses();
        break;
    case rain :
        bringUmbrella();
        break;
    case snow :
        bringSkis();
        break;
    default :
        stayHome();
        break;
}
```

Flash compares the expression in the switch statement's parentheses to each of the expressions in the case statements. If the two expressions are equal, the actions after the colon are performed (for example, if weather is equal to sun, bringSunglasses happens). The break action is necessary to break out of the switch code block after a case has matched. Without it, Flash runs through all the actions. The default action, which is optional, provides the actions to be performed if no case matches the switch expression.

A subtlety to keep in mind is that the switch and case statements test for a *strict equality*. A strict equality is represented by three equals signs (===); it compares both the value and the data type of two expressions.

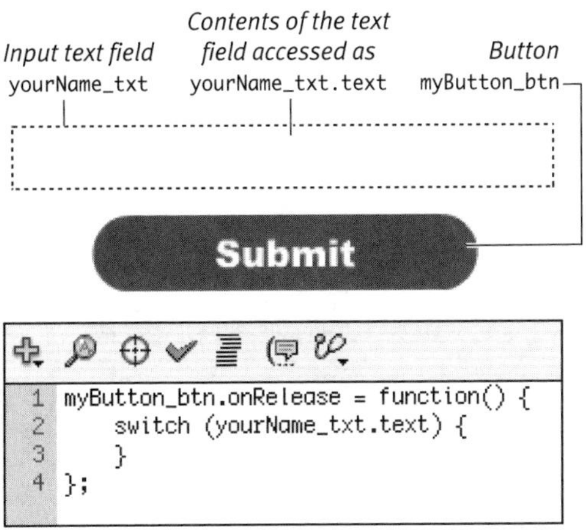

Figure 10.46 Enter `yourName_txt.text` as the condition of the `switch` statement.

In the following example, you'll create an input text field for your viewers to enter their names. When viewers click a button, the `switch` and `case` statements will compare what they typed in the text field with some known users.

To use switch and case for branching alternatives:

1. Select the Text tool, and drag a text field onto the Stage.
2. In the Property inspector, select Input Text, and give the text field an instance name.
3. Create a button, place an instance below the text field, and give your button instance a name in the Property inspector.
4. Select the first frame of the main Timeline, and open the Actions panel.
5. Create an `onRelease` event handler for your button.
6. Inside the event handler, choose Statements > Conditions/Loops > switch (Esc + sw).
7. As the condition for the `switch` statement, enter the name of your input text field followed by a dot and then `text` (**Figure 10.46**).

   The `switch` statement will compare the contents of the input text field with the expressions in the `case` statements.
8. On a new line between the curly braces of the `switch` statement, choose Statements > Conditions/Loops > case (Esc + ce).

continues on next page

9. Replace the placeholder `condition` with the string "Adam" (**Figure 10.47**).

10. On a new line after the colon, choose an action to be performed when the contents of the text field match "Adam" (**Figure 10.48**).

11. On a new line, choose Statements > Conditions/Loops > break (Esc + br).

    The `break` action discontinues the current code block and makes Flash go on to any ActionScript after the `switch` statement.

12. Repeat steps 8–11, but replace "Adam" with a different user's name (**Figure 10.49**).

```
myButton_btn.onRelease = function() {
    switch (yourName_txt.text) {
        case "Adam" :

    }
};
```

Figure 10.47 Flash will test whether `yourName_txt.text` is equal to the string "Adam".

```
myButton_btn.onRelease = function() {
    switch (yourName_txt.text) {
        case "Adam" :
            AdamFunction();
    }
};
```

Figure 10.48 If `yourName_txt.text==="Adam"`, the function `AdamFunction` is triggered.

```
myButton_btn.onRelease = function() {
    switch (yourName_txt.text) {
        case "Adam" :
            AdamFunction();
            break;
        case "Betty" :
            BettyFunction();
            break;
    }
};
```

Figure 10.49 Create additional cases to test against the `switch` expression.

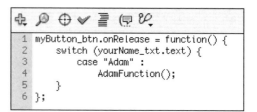

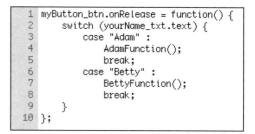

```
myButton_btn.onRelease = function() {
    switch (yourName_txt.text) {
        case "Adam" :
            AdamFunction();
            break;
        case "Betty" :
            BettyFunction();
            break;
        default :
            errorFunction();
            break;
    }
};
```

Figure 10.50 If the expression in the `switch` statement doesn't match either "`Adam`" or "`Betty`", the `default` action will be performed. It may help to think of the `default` action as being like the `else` action. Both statements define the consequences when none of the conditions match.

```
beetle_mc.onEnterFrame = function() {
    switch (true) {
        case Key.isDown(Key.UP):
            this._y -= 30;
            this._rotation = 0;
            break;
        case Key.isDown(Key.LEFT):
            this._x -= 30;
            this._rotation = -90;
            break;
        case Key.isDown(Key.RIGHT):
            this._x += 30;
            this._rotation = 90;
            break;
        case Key.isDown(Key.DOWN):
            this._y += 30;
            this._rotation = 180;
    }
};
```

Figure 10.51 The full script to move a beetle movie clip with the arrow keys, using `switch` and `case` instead of the `if` statement.

13. On a new line, choose Statements > Conditions/Loops > default (Esc + dt).

14. Choose an action to be performed when the contents of the text field don't match any of the `case` statements (**Figure 10.50**).

15. Test your movie.

✔ Tip

- What would the `switch` and `case` statements look like for the keyboard-controlled beetle in the preceding example? To create identical interactivity, enter the value `true` for the `switch` parameter and test it against each keypress in separate `case` statements (**Figure 10.51**). It may look backward, but it works!

Combining Conditions with Logical Operators

You can create compound conditions with the logical operators && (AND), || (OR), and ! (NOT). These operators combine two or more conditions in one `if` statement to test scenarios involving combinations of conditions. You can test whether the up arrow key and the right arrow key are pressed together to make a movie clip move diagonally, for example. Or, test whether a draggable movie clip is dropped on one valid target or another. You can use the NOT operator to test whether a variable contains a valid email address whose domain isn't restricted.

The following task uses the same file that you created to move a movie clip using the keyboard. You'll combine conditions to have Flash test for combination keypresses to move the movie clip diagonally.

To combine conditions:

1. Continuing with the file from the task "To use else if for branching alternatives," select the first frame of the main Timeline, and open the Actions panel.
2. Select the first `if` statement.
3. Place your pointer at the end of the existing condition (inside the closing parenthesis).
4. Choose Operators > Logical Operators > &&.
5. Enter your second condition after the two ampersands (**Figure 10.52**).

   Both conditions appear within the parentheses of the `if` statement separated by the && operator.
6. Change the actions within the `if` statement to rotate and move the movie clip diagonally (**Figure 10.53**).

```
if (Key.isDown(Key.UP) && Key.isDown(Key.RIGHT)) {
```

Figure 10.52 The logical && operator joins these two expressions so that both the up and right arrow keys must be pressed for the whole condition to be true.

```
if (Key.isDown(Key.UP) && Key.isDown(Key.RIGHT)) {
    this._rotation = 45;
    this._y -= 15;
    this._x += 15;
}
```

Figure 10.53 The first portion of the script shows that when both up and right arrow keys are pressed, the beetle rotates 45 degrees and moves diagonally top and right.

7. Continue to add `else if` statements with combined conditions for the other three diagonal keypresses while keeping the four conditions for the cardinal directions (**Figure 10.54**).

   Using the && logical operator to combine two conditions, Flash checks whether the user presses two keys in combination.

✔ Tip

- You can nest `if` statements within other `if` statements, which is equivalent to using the logical && operator in a single `if` statement. These two scripts test whether both conditions are true before setting a new variable:

```
if (yourAge >= 12) {
    if (yourAge <= 20) {
        status = "teenager";
    }
}
```

or

```
if (yourAge >= 12 && yourAge <= 20) {
    status = "teenager";
}
```

```
beetle_mc.onEnterFrame = function() {
    if (Key.isDown(Key.UP) && Key.isDown(Key.RIGHT)) {
        this._rotation = 45;
        this._y -= 15;
        this._x += 15;
    } else if (Key.isDown(Key.DOWN) && Key.isDown(Key.RIGHT)) {
        this._rotation = 135;
        this._y += 15;
        this._x += 15;
    } else if (Key.isDown(Key.UP) && Key.isDown(Key.LEFT)) {
        this._rotation = -45;
        this._y -= 15;
        this._x -= 15;
    } else if (Key.isDown(Key.DOWN) && Key.isDown(Key.LEFT)) {
        this._rotation = -135;
        this._y += 15;
        this._x -= 15;
    } else if (Key.isDown(Key.UP)) {
        this._rotation = 0;
        this._y -= 30;
    } else if (Key.isDown(Key.LEFT)) {
        this._rotation = -90;
        this._x -= 30;
    } else if (Key.isDown(Key.RIGHT)) {
        this._rotation = 90;
        this._x += 30;
    } else if (Key.isDown(Key.DOWN)) {
        this._rotation = 180;
        this._y += 30;
    }
};
```

Figure 10.54 The complete script contains combined conditions for two keypresses as well as conditions for single keypresses.

Looping Statements

With looping statements, you can create an action or set of actions that repeats. For example, you may have actions repeat a certain number of times or as long as a certain condition holds true. Repeating actions are often used together with an *array,* which is a special kind of variable that holds multiple values in a structured, easily accessible way. Using a looping action lets you add or retrieve the pieces of data in a particular order. You'll learn more about arrays in Chapter 12.

In general, use looping statements to execute actions automatically a specific number of times by using an incrementing counter variable. The counter variable is used in parameters of methods called in the loop or to modify properties of objects that are created. For example, you can generate intricate patterns by duplicating movie clips or dynamically drawing lines and shapes with looping statements. Use looping statements to change the properties of a whole series of movie clips, modify multiple sound settings, or alter the values of a set of variables.

There are three kinds of looping statements—the `while`, `do while`, and `for` statements—but they all accomplish the same task. The first two loop types repeat as long as a certain condition holds true. The third statement repeats using a counter variable and a condition that is checked each time the loop repeats.

To use the while statement to duplicate movie clips:

1. Create a movie clip symbol, place an instance of it on the Stage, and give it a name in the Property inspector.
2. Select the first frame of the main Timeline, and open the Actions panel.
3. Declare a `Number` variable named `i`, and initialize it to `0`.

   The names `i`, `j`, `k`, and so forth are often used as loop counter variables.
4. On the next line, choose Statements > Conditions/Loops > while (Esc + wh).
5. In the parentheses, enter `i < 361` (**Figure 10.55**).

   This expression acts as a condition, like the condition of an `if` statement. As long as the condition works out to `true`, the actions in the curly braces of the loop will repeat; but once it's `false`, the Flash Player will stop looping.

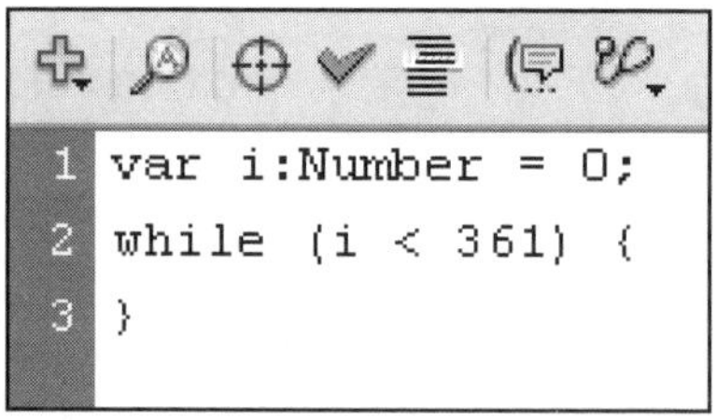
var i:Number = 0;
while (i < 361) {
}

Figure 10.55 Initialize the variable `i`, and create the condition that must be true for the loop to continue. As long as the variable `i` is less than 361, this loop will run.

6. Assign any actions that you want to run while the condition remains true (while `i` is less than 361).

   For this example, add a call to your movie clip's `duplicateMovieClip` method, and two statements that rotate and modify the transparency of the duplicate clip (**Figure 10.56**).

7. On the next line, enter `i += 10`, or the equivalent statement `i = i + 10`.

   Each time the loop runs, the variable `i` will increase by an increment of 10. When it exceeds 361, the condition that the `while` statement checks at each pass will become `false`, and Flash will end the loop (**Figure 10.57**).

```
var i:Number = 0;
while (i < 361) {
    var clip:MovieClip = oval_mc.duplicateMovieClip("oval_mc" + i, i);
    clip._rotation = i;
    clip._alpha = (i / 360) * 100;
}
```

Figure 10.56 The `oval_mc` movie clip is duplicated, and its duplicate is rotated and changed in transparency.

```
var i:Number = 0;
while (i < 361) {
    var clip:MovieClip = oval_mc.duplicateMovieClip("oval_mc" + i, i);
    clip._rotation = i;
    clip._alpha = (i / 360) * 100;
    i += 10;
}
```

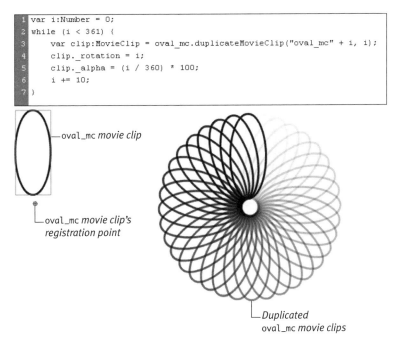

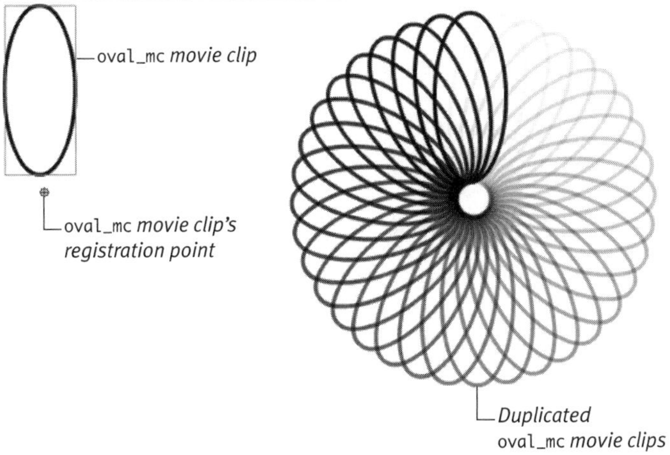

Figure 10.57 At the end of each loop, the variable `i` increases by 10. This loop will run 37 times. The `oval_mc` movie clip (left) is the basis for the pattern (right) made with the looping statement.

The do while statement

The do while (Esc + do) statement is similar to the while statement, except that the condition is checked at the end of the loop rather than the beginning. This means the actions in the loop are always executed at least once. The script in the preceding task can be written with the do while statement, as shown in **Figure 10.58**.

The for statement

The for (Esc + fr) statement provides built-in places to define a counter variable, condition, and operation to increment or decrement the counter, so you don't have to write separate statements. The three statements that go in the parentheses of the for statement are init, where you can initialize a counter variable; condition, which is the expression that is tested before each iteration of the loop; and next, which defines a statement to increment or decrement the counter variable. The preceding task's script can be written with a for loop, as shown in **Figure 10.59**.

```
var i:Number = 0;
do {
    var clip:MovieClip = oval_mc.duplicateMovieClip("oval_mc" + i, i);
    clip._rotation = i;
    clip._alpha = (i / 360) * 100;
    i += 10;
} while (i < 361);
```

Figure 10.58 The equivalent do while statement.

```
for (var i:Number = 0; i < 361; i += 10) {
    var clip:MovieClip = oval_mc.duplicateMovieClip("oval_mc" + i, i);
    clip._rotation = i;
    clip._alpha = (i / 360) * 100;
}
```

Figure 10.59 The equivalent for loop. You can read the statements in the parentheses this way: Start my counter at 0; before each loop, check the condition, and as long as it's smaller than 361, perform the loop actions; after each loop, add 10 to my counter and repeat.

✔ Tips

- Don't use looping statements to build continuous routines to check a certain condition over time. Real-time testing should be done using an `if` statement in an `onEnterFrame` event handler or from a `setInterval` function call. When Flash executes looping statements, the display remains frozen, and no mouse or keyboard events can be detected.
- With the `while` and `do while` statements, make sure the statement that modifies the variable checked in the condition is inside the curly braces. If it isn't, the condition will never be met, and Flash will be stuck executing the loop infinitely. Fortunately, Flash warns you about this problem when it detects a problem in your script that causes it to stall (**Figure 10.60**).
- Note that the statements within the parentheses of the `for` statement are separatedby semicolons, and *not* by commas.

The for..in loop

Another kind of loop, called the `for..in` loop, is used specifically to look through the properties or elements of an object. You don't use a counter variable as you do for the other kinds of loops. Instead, you use a variable called an *iterator*, which is given a new value (the name of one of the object's properties) each time the loop repeats. You can use the iterator in expressions within the `for..in` loop to access each of the properties. If a movie clip `parent_mc` contains many child movie clips, you can use the `for..in` loop to reference each child this way:

```
for (var iterator:String in parent_mc) {
    parent_mc[iterator]._rotation = 90;
}
```

This `for..in` statement looks inside `parent_mc` and loops through its child properties, putting a different property's name (as a string) in the variable `iterator` on each round of the loop. In the example, the expression within the curly braces uses the `iterator` variable with the array access operator to dynamically access each property, rotating every child movie clip inside the parent movie clip.

The built-in `MovieClip` class properties of the parent movie clip are hidden from the `for..in` loop—only properties that you define on the movie clip, such as child movie clips or variables declared on that movie clip's Timeline, are accessed in the loop.

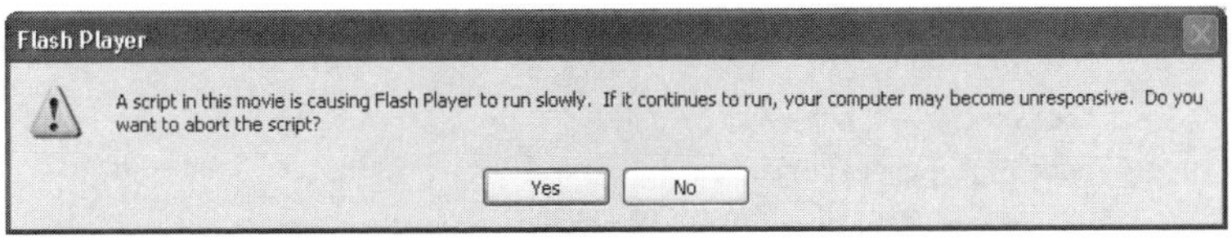

Figure 10.60 This warning dialog box appears when you inadvertently cause an infinite loop.

To use the for..in loop to reference elements inside a movie clip:

1. Create a movie clip symbol that contains many child movie clips.
2. Drag an instance of the parent movie clip to the main Stage, and give it a name in the Property inspector.
3. Select the first frame of the main Timeline, and open the Actions panel.
4. Choose Statements > Conditions/Loops > for . . in (Esc + fi).
5. Inside the parentheses of the `for..in` loop, declare an `iterator` variable with the data type `String`; then, enter `in` and the name of your parent movie clip instance (**Figure 10.61**).
6. Between the curly braces of the `for..in` loop, enter an expression that references each child movie clip with the iterator and modifies its property (**Figure 10.62**).

   In this example, all the child movie clips rotate the same amount.

```
for (var iterator:String in flowers_mc) {
}
```

Figure 10.61 The variable `iterator` will loop through the objects inside the movie clip `flowers_mc`.

```
for (var iterator:String in flowers_mc) {
    flowers_mc[iterator]._rotation = 15;
}
```

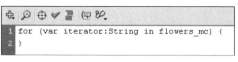

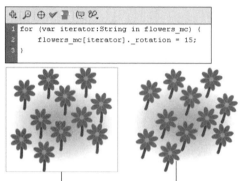

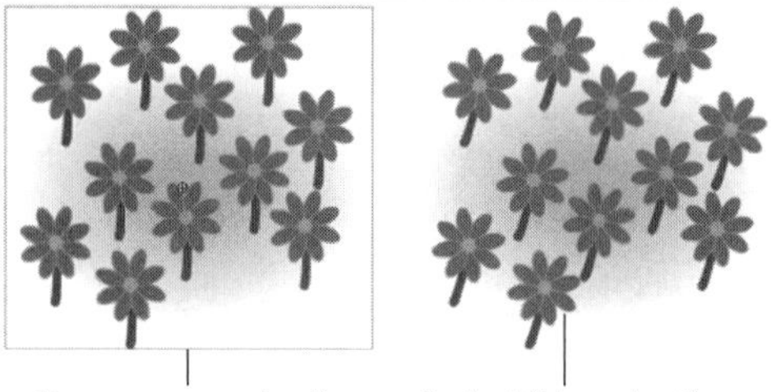
flowers_mc movie clip
Each child movie clip rotates on its own axis

Figure 10.62 Using the array access operators, dynamically reference each child movie clip within `flowers_mc` and modify the rotation of those clips.

✔ Tips

- Enter `_root` as the target object for the `for..in` statement, and you can reference all the objects (buttons, text fields, and movie clips) that sit on the main Stage.
- To modify only child properties of a certain type (such as only child movie clips or only child text fields), use an `if` statement in the `for..in` loop. For the `if` statement's condition, check the data type of the child property like this:

```
for (var iterator:String in parent_mc) {
   if (typeof(parent_mc[iterator]) ==
"movieclip") {
        parent_mc[iterator]._rotation =
90;
   }
}
```

11

Controlling Text

You know that Flash lets you create visually engaging text elements—such as titles, labels, and descriptions—to accompany your graphics, animation, and sound. But did you know that you can do more with text than just set the style, color, and size? Flash text can be *live*, meaning that your viewers can enter text in the Flash movie as it plays, as well as select and edit the text. And Flash text can be dynamic, so it can update during playback. A text field in which viewers can enter text is called an *input text field*, and a text field that you can update during playback is called a *dynamic text field*. Both input and dynamic text fields are controlled in ActionScript using the `TextField` class. Input and dynamic text fields provide a way to receive complex information from the viewer and tailor your Flash movie by using that information.

During author time, you use the Text tool and the Property inspector to create your text fields. But you can also create text fields at run time, dynamically defining their properties (such as background color) or formatting (such as font size and style, set with the `TextFormat` class). This control of text fields' content and appearance lets you animate text purely through ActionScript, making it responsive to the viewer and to different events.

Two additional classes—the `Selection` class and the `String` class—help control the information within text fields. You'll use these classes to analyze and manipulate the text or the placement of the insertion point within the text. You can catch a viewer's misspellings or incorrectly entered information, for example, before using the text in your Flash movie or passing it on to an outside application for processing.

This chapter explores some of the many possibilities of the `TextField`, `TextFormat`, `Selection`, and `String` classes and introduces the tools you can use to integrate text and control the information exchange between your Flash movie and your audience.

Input Text

You can build your Flash project to gather information directly from the viewer—information such as a login name and password, personal information for a survey, answers to quiz questions, requests for an online purchase, or responses in an Internet chat room. The text a user inputs into a text field is assigned to the `text` property of the text field. You can retrieve it from that property and pass it along to other parts of the Flash movie for further processing or send it to a server-side application through the CGI `GET` or `POST` method.

The following task demonstrates how you can incorporate user-input text to let your user control the parameters of an action. In this case, you'll accept information from the viewer in an input text field and use that information to load a URL.

To use user input to request a URL:

1. Choose the Text tool in the Tools panel, and drag out a text field on the Stage (**Figure 11.1**).
2. In the Property inspector, choose Input Text from the pull-down menu.

   Your selected text field becomes an input text field, allowing text entry during playback.
3. In the Instance Name field of the Property inspector, enter the name for your text field. Use the suffix `_txt` in order to trigger code hints in the Actions panel.
4. Click the Show Border button in the Property inspector.

   Your text field is drawn with a black border and a white background (**Figure 11.2**).

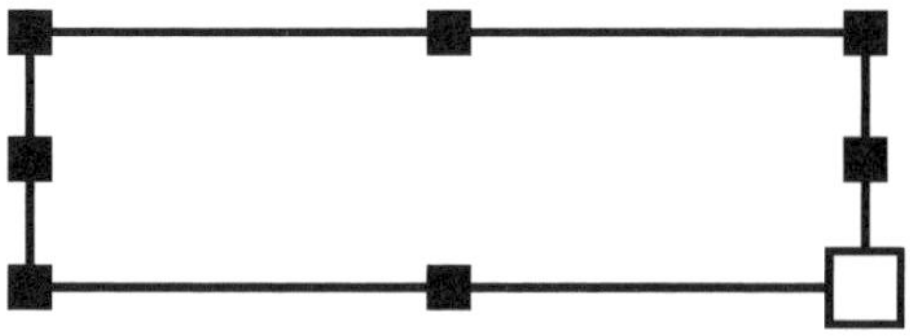

Figure 11.1 A text field is created with the Text tool. You can resize the text field with any of its handles (the black and white squares around its edges).

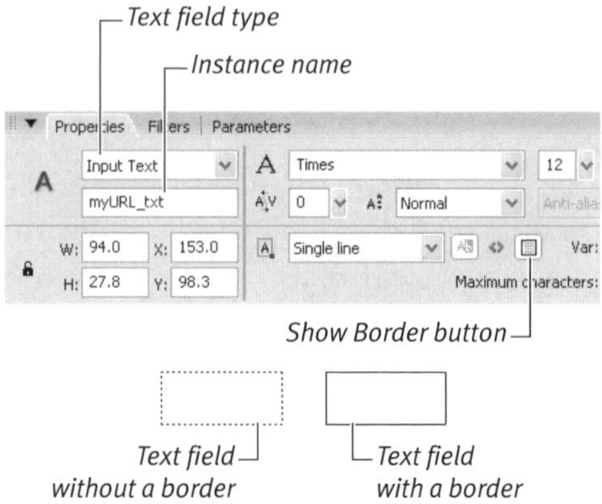

Figure 11.2 The Property inspector defines the text field's type as input text. The instance name is `myURL_txt`, and the Show Border button is selected. A text field without a border (bottom left) appears on your Stage in authoring mode with a dotted border. A text field with a border (bottom right) appears with a solid black border and a white background.

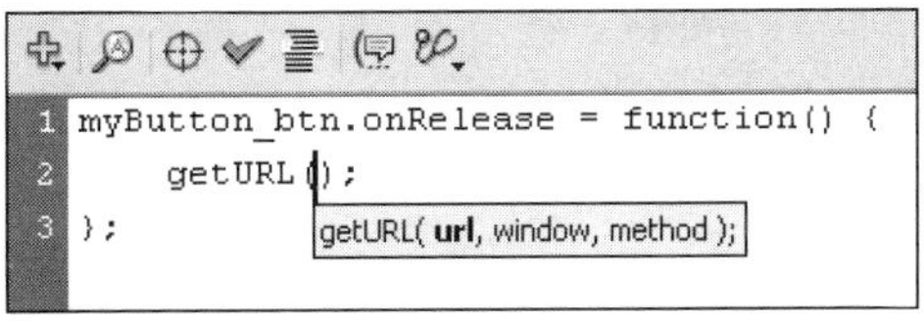

Figure 11.3 The code hint tooltip shows the parameters of the `getURL` action.

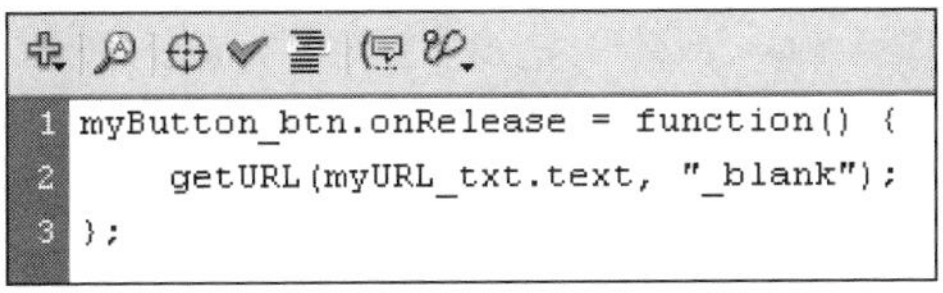

Figure 11.4 The actions assigned to the button `myButton_btn` load the URL entered in the text field `myURL_txt` in a new browser window.

Figure 11.5 The contents of the input text field are used as the URL for the `getURL` action. Note that the user must include the protocol http:// in the input text field.

5. Create a button symbol, place an instance of the button on the Stage below the text field, and name the button instance in the Property inspector.

6. Select the first frame of the main Timeline, and open the Actions panel.

7. On the first line of the Script pane, create an `onRelease` event handler for your button.

8. Between the opening and closing curly braces of the event handler function, choose Global Functions > Browser/Network > getURL (**Figure 11.3**).

9. As the first parameter of the `getURL` method, enter the instance name of your input text field, followed by a period (`.`) and the word `text`. Enter a comma and then `"_blank"` for the second parameter (**Figure 11.4**).

10. Test your movie.

    When the user enters a URL in the text field, the URL is put into the `text` property of the text field. Then, when the user clicks the button, Flash opens a new browser window and loads the specified Web site (**Figure 11.5**).

✔ Tip

- You can put initial text in an input text field to instruct viewers what to enter. Put `Enter Web site address here` in your text field, for example, so that users know to replace that text with their Web site address. Or, start them off by putting `http://` in the text field.

Dynamic Text

For text that you control—such as scores in an arcade game, the display of a calculator, or the percentage-of-download progress of your Flash movie—take advantage of Flash's dynamic text option. Whereas input text fields accept information from the viewer, dynamic text fields output information to the viewer. As with input text, the contents of the text field are assigned to its `text` property.

In the following task, you'll create an input text field and a dynamic text field. When viewers enter the temperature in Celsius in the input text field, Flash will convert the value to Fahrenheit and display it in the dynamic text field.

To use dynamic text to output expressions:

1. Choose the Text tool in the Tools panel, and drag out a text field onto the Stage.
2. In the Property inspector, choose Input Text from the pull-down menu.
3. In the Instance Name field, enter the name of your input text field. Use the suffix `_txt` to activate code hints in the Actions panel (**Figure 11.6**).

   Your selected text field becomes an input text field, allowing text entry during playback.
4. Again, choose the Text tool, and drag out another text field on the Stage.
5. In the Property inspector, this time choose Dynamic Text from the pull-down menu.

   Your selected text field becomes a dynamic text field, allowing you to display and update text in that field.
6. In the Instance Name field of the Property inspector, enter the name for the dynamic text field (**Figure 11.7**).

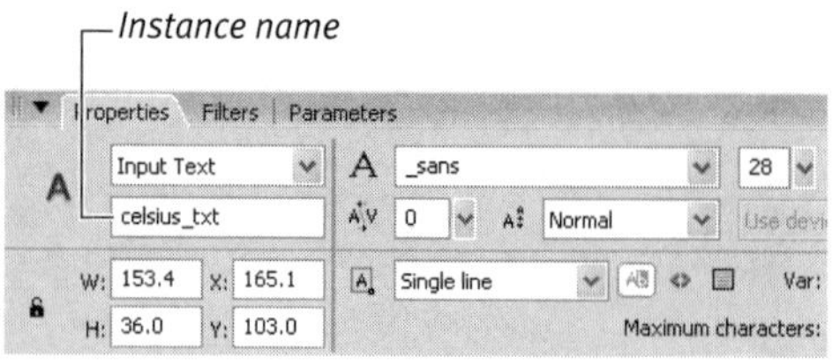

Figure 11.6 The instance name for this input field is `celsius_txt`.

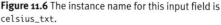

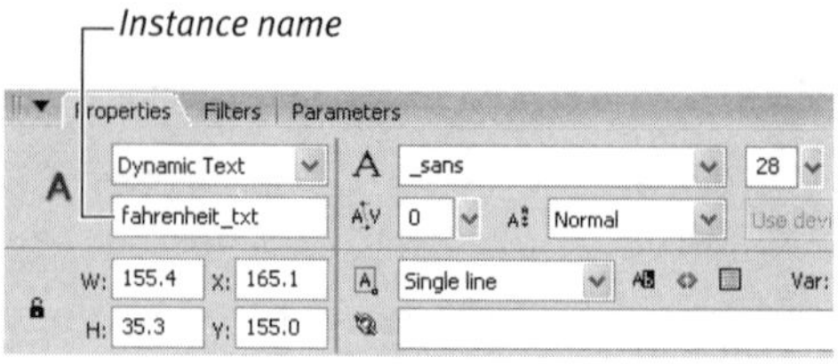

Figure 11.7 The instance name for the dynamic text field is `fahrenheit_txt`.

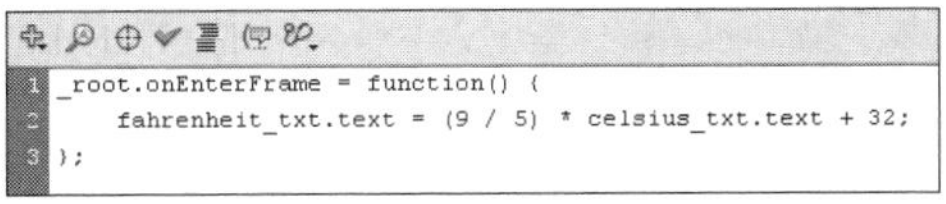

Figure 11.8 This statement calculates the Fahrenheit value from the expression on the right side of the equals sign.

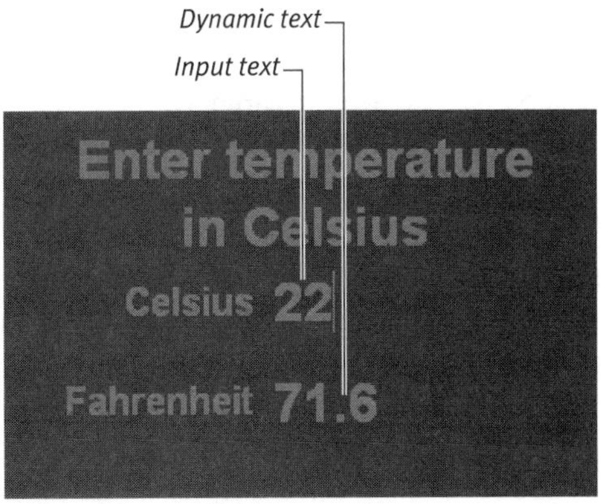

Figure 11.9 The contents of the dynamic text field (`fahrenheit_txt.text`) updates itself when new input text (`celsius_txt.text`) is entered.

7. Select the first frame of the main Timeline, and open the Actions panel.

8. In the Script Pane, enter `_root`. Choose ActionScript 2.0 Classes > Movie > Movie Clip > Events > onEnterFrame.

   The `onEnterFrame` event is triggered continuously, providing a way to do the conversion of Celsius to Fahrenheit in real time.

9. Between the curly braces of the `onEnterFrame` event handler, enter the name of your dynamic text field, followed by a period, the word `text`, and an equals sign. Continue by entering a formula that incorporates the input text field's `text` property (**Figure 11.8**).

10. Test your movie.

    Flash sets the contents of the dynamic text field based on the information the viewer enters in the input text field (**Figure 11.9**). The calculation is done in real time, and the display is updated any time the input text changes.

✔ Tip

- Use dynamic text as a debugging tool to show the contents of variables. If you're developing a complicated Flash movie involving multiple variables, you can create a dynamic text field to display the variables' current values so you know how Flash is processing the information. In Chapter 13, you'll learn other ways to track variables, but this way you can integrate the display of variables into your movie.

Selecting Text Field Options

The Property inspector offers many options for an input or dynamic text field (**Figure 11.10**). The most important field to fill is Instance Name. The Instance Name field contains the instance name of your text field, which you use in ActionScript to refer to the text field to modify its properties and call its methods. The other options let you modify the way text appears:

The **Line Type pull-down menu** defines how text fits into the text field:

- Single Line forces entered text to stay on one row in the text field. If text goes beyond the limits of the text field, the text begins to scroll horizontally.
- Multiline No Wrap allows entered text to appear on more than one row in the text field if the viewer presses the Enter key (Windows) or Return key (Macintosh) for a carriage return.
- Multiline automatically causes the text to wrap when it reaches the edge of the text field.
- Password disguises the letters entered in the text field with asterisks; use this option to hide sensitive information such as a password from people looking over your viewer's shoulder.

The **Selectable button** allows your viewers to select the text inside the text field. (This button isn't available for input text because input text is—by nature—always selectable.)

The **Render as HTML button** allows text to preserve rich formatting using a few basic HTML tags, including `a`, `b`, `font color`, `font face`, `font size`, `i`, `p`, and `u`.

The **Show Border button** draws your text field with a black border and white background. Deselect this option to leave the text field invisible, but be sure to draw your own background or border if you want your viewers to find your text field on the Stage.

The **Maximum Characters field** puts a limit on the amount of text your viewer can enter. If you want the viewer to enter their home state by using only the two-digit abbreviation, for example, enter `2` in this field. (This option is available only for input text.)

The **Embed button** brings up the Character Embedding dialog box, where you can choose to embed font outlines with your exported SWF so that your text field displays anti-aliased type in the font of your choice. Keep in mind that this option increases your file size.

The **Format button** (paragraph sign) brings up the Format Options dialog box, where you can choose paragraph spacing and alignment options.

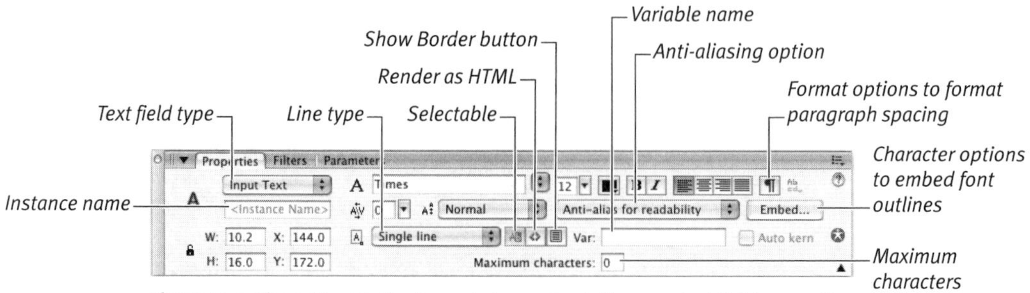

Figure 11.10 The options in the Property inspector define your text field properties and formatting.

The **Anti-aliasing options pull-down menu** allows you to choose the style of anti-aliasing (edge smoothing) to apply to your text. You can choose to have anti-aliasing that is optimized for readability or for animation:

- For very small font sizes, choose "Bitmap text (no anti-alias)" to create crisp and legible text optimized for small size representation.
- If the text will be animated to move, choose "Anti-alias for animation." The text won't be as smooth looking in general, but it will remain more readable while moving. However, the file size of the final SWF will be larger as a result.
- If ease of reading is the priority, choose "Anti-alias for readability," which makes small to medium-sized text look more attractive and easier to read.
- For ultimate control, choose "Custom anti-alias," which opens the Custom Anti-Aliasing dialog box, allowing you to specify thickness and sharpness values for your text.

✔ Tips

- "Anti-alias for readability" and "Custom anti-alias" are only available when publishing your document for Flash Player 8 or later. These settings utilize a new technology known as FlashType, which is specifically designed for easier on-screen reading.
- Unfortunately, dynamic and input text fields don't support vertical text. Vertical text is allowed only for static text.

Embedding Fonts and Device Fonts

Embedding font outlines via the Character Options dialog box ensures that the font you use in the authoring environment is the same one your audience sees during playback. This operation is done by default for static text, but you must choose the option when you create input text or dynamic text. When you don't embed fonts in your movie, Flash uses the closest font available on your viewer's computer and displays it as aliased text (**Figure 11.11**).

Why wouldn't you choose to embed font outlines all the time? Embedding fonts dramatically increases the size of your exported SWF file, because the information needed to render the fonts is included. You can keep the file size down by embedding only the characters your viewers use in the text field. If you ask viewers to enter numeric information in an input text field, for example, you can embed just the numbers of the font outline. All the numbers are available during movie playback; the other characters are disabled and won't display.

Another way to maintain small file sizes and eliminate the problem caused by viewers not having the matching font is to use *device fonts*. Device fonts appear at the beginning (Windows) or in alphabetical order (Mac) of your Font Style pull-down menu. The three device fonts are _sans, _serif, and _typewriter. This option finds the fonts on a viewer's system that most closely resemble the specified device font. Following are the corresponding fonts for the device fonts.

On the Mac:

- _sans maps to Helvetica.
- _serif maps to Times.
- _typewriter maps to Courier.

In Windows:

- _sans maps to Arial.
- _serif maps to Times New Roman.
- _typewriter maps to Courier New.

When you use device fonts, you can be assured that your viewer sees text that is very similar to the text you see in the authoring environment. Be aware of two warnings about device fonts, however: They don't display anti-aliased, and they can't be tweened or masked on the Timeline (device fonts can, however, be masked if you use ActionScript to set your mask).

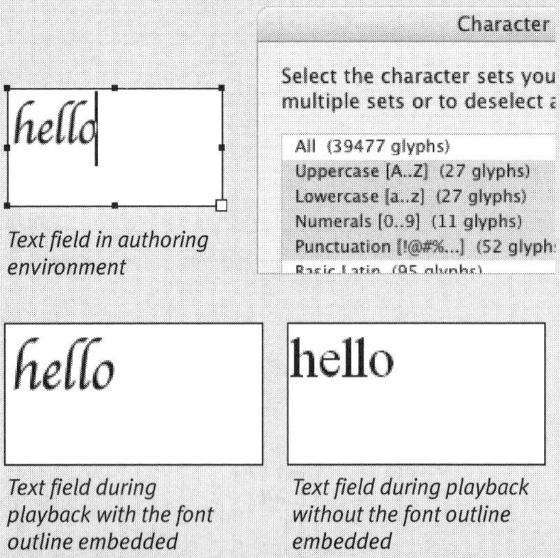

Figure 11.11 A text field using a font in authoring mode (top) displays differently during playback on a computer that doesn't have the font, depending on whether the font outlines are embedded (bottom).

Concatenating Text

Using dynamic text to *concatenate*, or connect, input text with other variables and strings lets you work with expressions in more flexible ways and also allows you to create more-personalized Flash interactions with your viewers. You can have viewers first enter their names in an input text field `yourName_txt`; and in a dynamic text field, you can set its `text` property to this:

```
"Hello, " + yourName_txt.text +
", welcome to Flash!"
```

Your viewers will see their own names concatenated with your message.

In an earlier task in this chapter, you created a Flash movie that loads a URL based on input text. By concatenating the contents of the input text `myURL_txt` in the expression `"http://" + myURL_txt.text`, you eliminate the requirement that your viewer type the Internet protocol scheme before the Web site address.

Use this strategy in combination with other Flash actions to develop flexible, customizable functions and interfaces. In the following task, you concatenate input text from a customer to compile the information in the correct layout automatically and then use the methods of the `PrintJob` class to print a complete receipt or order form.

To concatenate text fields for custom printing:

1. Choose the Text tool in the Tools panel, create several input text fields, and give each of them a unique instance name in the Property inspector (**Figure 11.12**).
2. Create a movie-clip symbol, and enter symbol-editing mode for that movie clip.
3. In the first keyframe of the movie clip, create a large dynamic text field.

continues on next page

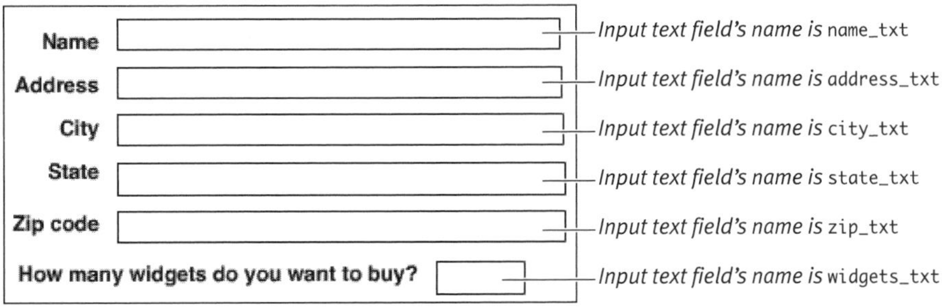

Figure 11.12 Define six input text fields with unique instance names.

4. In the Property inspector, choose Multiline from the Line Type pull-down menu, enter an instance name, embed the entire font outline through the Character Options dialog box, and add graphics you want to include in the printed piece (**Figure 11.13**).

   The dynamic text field will display the concatenated information.

5. Return to the root Timeline, drag an instance of the movie clip you just created to the Stage, and give it a name in the Property inspector.

6. Create a button symbol, drag an instance of it to the Stage, and give it an instance name in the Property inspector. Place it between your input text fields and the movie clip that contains your dynamic text field (**Figure 11.14**).

7. Select the first keyframe on the main Timeline, and open the Actions panel.

8. Create an `onRelease` event handler function for your button (ActionScript 2.0 Classes > Movie > Button > Event Handlers > onRelease).

9. Inside the curly braces of the event handler function, enter the target path to the dynamic text field's `text` property, followed by an equals sign.

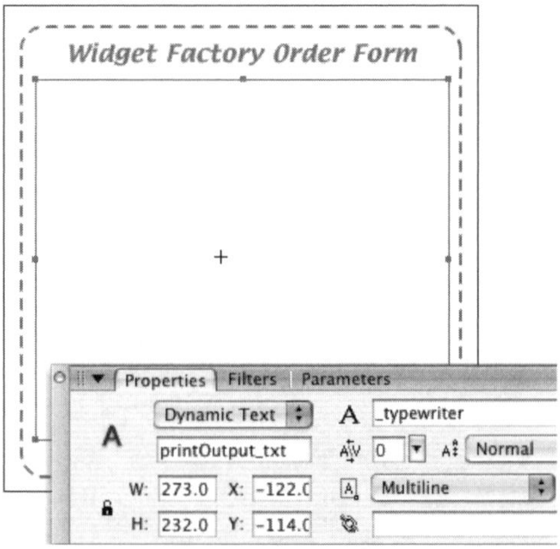

Figure 11.13 The dynamic text field is laid out with surrounding graphics, ready to print.

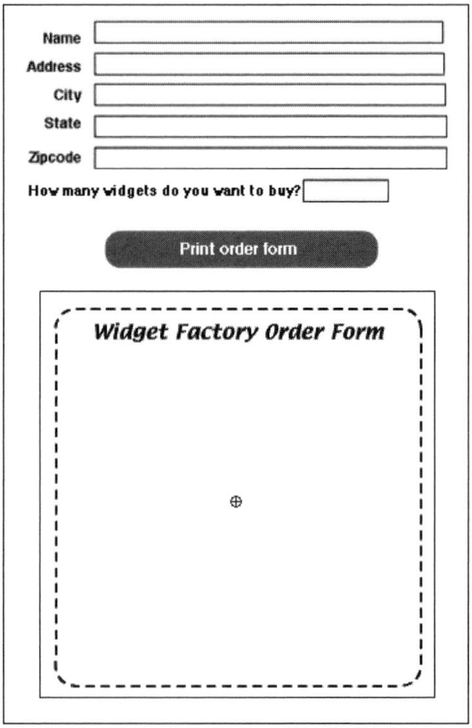

Figure 11.14 The button lies between the input text fields above and the dynamic text field below.

10. Directly following the equals sign, enter a combination of strings and the input text field's `text` properties to concatenate the user-entered information into a compact, printable form (**Figure 11.15**).

Use the escape sequence `\n` to add a line break.

11. On a new line, declare and instantiate a new `PrintJob` variable (ActionScript 2.0 Classes > Movie > PrintJob > "new PrintJob").

12. On the next line, declare a `Boolean` variable followed by an equals sign. Enter the name of your `PrintJob` object and a period, and then choose ActionScript 2.0 Classes > Movie > PrintJob > Methods > start.

13. Add a new `if` statement (Statements > Conditions/Loops > if). In the parentheses, enter the name of your `Boolean` variable.

14. Inside the curly braces of the `if` statement, enter the name of your `PrintJob` object, and then choose ActionScript 2.0 Classes > Movie > PrintJob > Methods > addPage. In the parentheses of the `addPage` method, enter the name of the movie clip that contains the concatenated text output.

15. On the next line, enter the name of your `PrintJob` object, and then choose ActionScript 2.0 Classes > Movie > PrintJob > Methods > send.

continues on next page

```
print_btn.onRelease = function() {
    orderform_mc.printOutput_txt.text = "Hello, " + name_txt.text + "
thanks for your order! \nDelivery to: \n" + name_txt.text + "\n" +
address_txt.text + "\n" + city_txt.text + ", " + state_txt.text + " " +
zip_txt.text + "\n\nWidgets: " + widgets_txt.text + "\nTOTAL COST: $ " +
(Number(widgets_txt.text) * 5);
};
```

Figure 11.15 The target path to the dynamic text field `printOutput_txt` includes the movie clip `orderform_mc`. A string is constructed by concatenating the contents of the input text fields as well as the total cost of ordered widgets obtained by multiplying the ordered quantity by 5.

16. On the line following the closing curly brace of the if statement, enter `delete` followed by the name of your `PrintJob` object (**Figure 11.16**).

    This code creates a `PrintJob` object, starts the printing process, adds the output movie clip to a page and sends it to the printer, and finally deletes the `PrintJob` object to conserve computer resources.

17. Test your movie.

    When the viewer enters information into the input text fields and then clicks the button, the dynamic text in the movie clip concatenates the input text and displays the information. Then the `PrintJob` object prints the movie clip (**Figure 11.17**).

✔ Tips

- You can hide a movie clip that's on the Stage from the viewer but still have it available for printing by setting the `_visible` property to `false`. Changing the visibility property of a movie clip doesn't affect how it prints.
- For long lines of code like the one in this task, choose Word Wrap from the Actions panel's Options menu to see all the code within the Script pane.
- It's important that you embed fonts for dynamic text fields sent to the printer. Embedding fonts for a text field results in a much better-quality print, but it also increases the file size of your exported movie.

```
var print_pj:PrintJob = new PrintJob();
var canPrint:Boolean = print_pj.start();
if (canPrint) {
    print_pj.addPage(orderform_mc);
    print_pj.send();
}
delete print_pj;
```

Figure 11.16 The `PrintJob` object sends the contents of the movie clip to the printer.

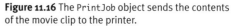

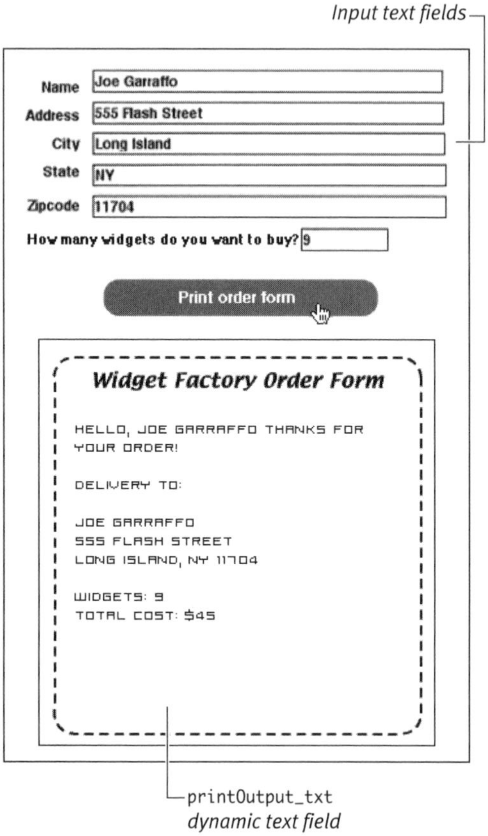

Figure 11.17 The Flash movie gathers information from input text fields, compiles the entered information in a dynamic text field, and prints it.

Displaying HTML

Flash can display HTML 1.0–formatted text in dynamic text fields. When you mark up text with HTML tags and assign the text to a dynamic text field, Flash interprets the tags and preserves the formatting. This means you can integrate HTML content inside your Flash movie, maintaining the styles and links.

The following common HTML tags are supported by text fields:

- `<a href>`: Anchor tag to create hot links
- `<b>`: Bold style
- `<font color>`: Font-color style
- `<font face>`: Font-face style
- `<font size>`: Font-size style
- `<i>`: Italics style
- `<p>`: Paragraph
- `<u>`: Underline style

A useful combination is to load HTML-formatted text into dynamic text fields with the `LoadVars` class. By changing the HTML that resides outside the Flash file, you can update the information that displays during playback of your movie. This feature can be convenient because you don't have to open the Flash file to make periodic edits, and a server-side script (or even a user unfamiliar with Flash) can make the necessary updates.

Flash also allows you to write your HTML code directly into the Script pane for display in a dynamic text field, as you'll see in the task "To populate a dynamic text field with HTML code from the Script pane." For that approach, it isn't necessary to include the `<html>`, `<head>`, or `<body>` tag.

To load and display HTML in a dynamic text field:

1. Open a text-editing application or a WYSIWYG HTML editor, and create your HTML document.
2. At the very beginning of the HTML text, add a variable name and the assignment operator (the equals sign) (**Figure 11.18**).

continues on next page

```
HTMLpage=<html><body><p><b>This is an HTML page</b></p><p>This contains
<i>simple</i> HTML 1.0 tags that <font face="Arial">Flash</font> can
understand. Flash will display HTML formatted text when the HTML option
is checked in Dynamic Text in the Property Inspector.</p><p><font
face="Courier">a href</font> will also work to create links to Web
sites! For example, if you <font color="#0000FF"><u><a
href="http://www.macromedia.com">click here</a></u></font>, you will be
sent to Macromedia's Web site.</p></body></html>
```

Figure 11.18 The HTML text is assigned to the variable `HTMLpage` and saved as a separate document.

3. Save the file in the same directory where you'll create your Flash document.

4. In Flash, choose the Text tool, and drag out a large text field that nearly covers the Stage.

5. In the Property inspector, choose Dynamic Text and Multiline, and click the Render as HTML button.

   The Render as HTML button lets Flash know to treat the contents of the text field as HTML-formatted text.

6. Give the text field an instance name (**Figure 11.19**).

7. Create a button symbol, and place an instance of it on the Stage. In the Property inspector, give your button an instance name.

8. Select the first frame of the main Timeline, and open the Actions panel.

9. Declare and instantiate a new `LoadVars` object (ActionScript 2.0 Classes > Client/Server and XML > LoadVars > "new LoadVars").

10. On the next available line, create an `onRelease` event handler for your button.

11. Within the `onRelease` event handler, enter the instance name of your text field, followed by a period.

12. Enter the name of the `LoadVars` object. Choose ActionScript 2.0 Classes > Client/Server and XML > LoadVars > Methods > load, and enter the name of the HTML file (in quotation marks) in the parentheses of the `load` method (**Figure 11.20**).

    When the button is clicked, Flash loads the text file that contains the variable into the `LoadVars` object.

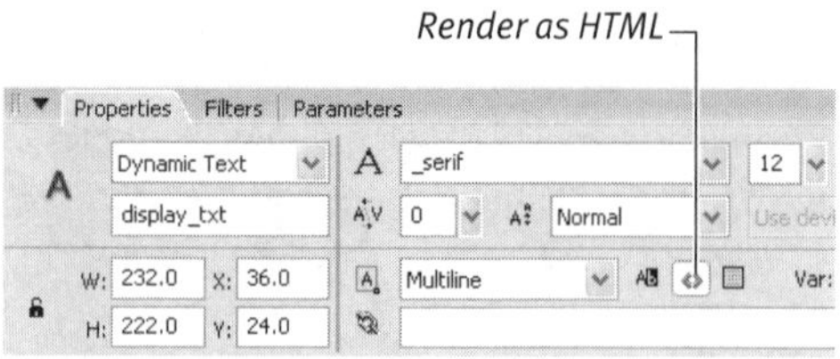

Figure 11.19 Enter `display_txt` as the instance name for your dynamic text field, and click the Render as HTML button.

```
var loader_lv:LoadVars = new LoadVars();
load_btn.onRelease = function() {
    loader_lv.load("variables.txt");
};
```

Figure 11.20 In the button's `onRelease` handler, enter code that loads the file variables.txt, which contains the variable holding HTML text.

```
loader_lv.onLoad = function(success:Boolean) {
    display_txt.htmlText = this.HTMLpage;
};
```

Figure 11.21 The dynamic text field instance `display_txt` is assigned the contents of the variable `HTMLpage`.

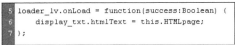

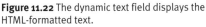

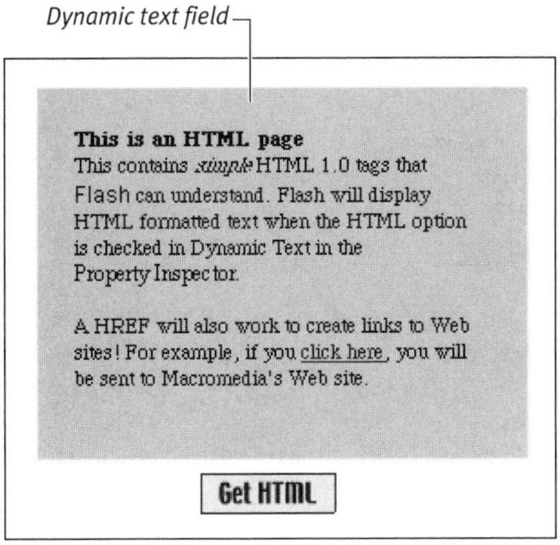

Dynamic text field
This is an HTML page
This contains simple HTML 1.0 tags that Flash can understand. Flash will display HTML formatted text when the HTML option is checked in Dynamic Text in the Property Inspector.
A HREF will also work to create links to Web sites! For example, if you click here, you will be sent to Macromedia's Web site.
Get HTML

Figure 11.22 The dynamic text field displays the HTML-formatted text.

- The anchor tag (<a>) normally appears underlined and in a different color in browser environments. In Flash, however, the hot link is indicated only by the pointer changing to a finger. To create the underline and color style for hot links manually, apply the underline tag (<u>) and the font-color tag (<font color="#0000FF">).
- The HTML tags override any style settings you assign in the Property inspector for your dynamic text. If you choose red for your dynamic text, when you display HTML text in the field, the <font color> tag will modify the text to a different color.

13. On the line following the `onRelease` event handler's closing curly brace, enter the name of the `LoadVars` object. Choose ActionScript 2.0 Classes > Client/Server and XML > LoadVars > Event Handlers > onLoad.

The `onLoad` event handler function will be called when the text file finishes loading into the `LoadVars` object.

14. Inside the curly braces of the `onLoad` event handler, enter the instance name of the text field, followed by a period.

15. From the code hint pull-down menu, select `htmlText`. Enter an equals sign, followed by the word `this`, a period, and then the variable you assigned in the text file (**Figure 11.21**).

The contents of the external variable are put into the `htmlText` property of your dynamic text field. The `htmlText` property displays HTML-tagged text correctly, as would a browser.

16. Test your movie.

When the user clicks the button, the variable in the external text file is loaded into the `LoadVars` object. When the file has completely loaded, Flash sets the `htmlText` property of the dynamic text to the variable, which holds HTML-formatted text. The dynamic text field displays the information, preserving all the style and format tags (**Figure 11.22**).

✔ Tips

- Because only a limited number of HTML tags are supported by dynamic text, you should do a fair amount of testing to see how the information displays. When Flash doesn't understand a tag, it ignores it.

To populate a dynamic text field with HTML code from the Script pane:

1. Choose the Text tool, and drag out a large text field that nearly covers the Stage.
2. In the Property inspector, choose Dynamic Text and Multiline, and click the Render as HTML button.

   The Render as HTML button lets Flash know to treat the contents of the text field as HTML-formatted text.
3. Give your text field an instance name (**Figure 11.23**).
4. Select the first keyframe in the root Timeline, and open the Actions panel.
5. Enter the instance name you assigned to your text field, followed by a period and then `htmlText`.

   The `htmlText` property contains the HTML-formatted contents of the dynamic text field.

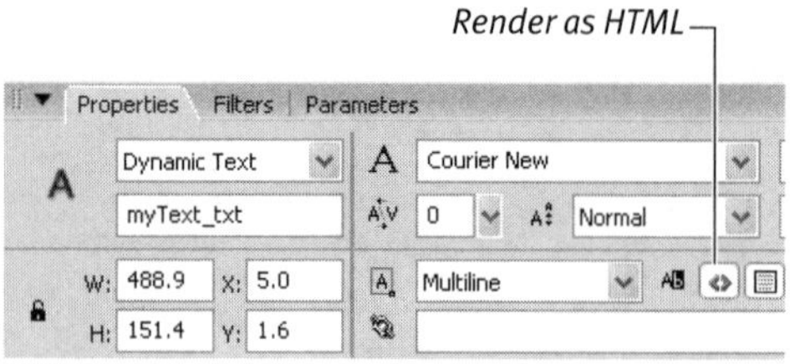

Figure 11.23 Enter `myText_txt` as the instance name for your dynamic text field, and be sure to click the Render as HTML button.

6. Enter an equals sign, followed by your HTML code in quotation marks (**Figure 11.24**).
7. Test your movie.

   All the HTML-formatted text assigned to your text field displays correctly, as it would in a browser (**Figure 11.25**).

✔ Tip

- You can also set your dynamic text field to support HTML-formatted text with ActionScript instead of clicking the Render as HTML button in the Property inspector (as you did in step 2). Set the `html` property of your text field to `true`, and your text field will display HTML code correctly. For example, enter the statement `myText_txt.html = true`.

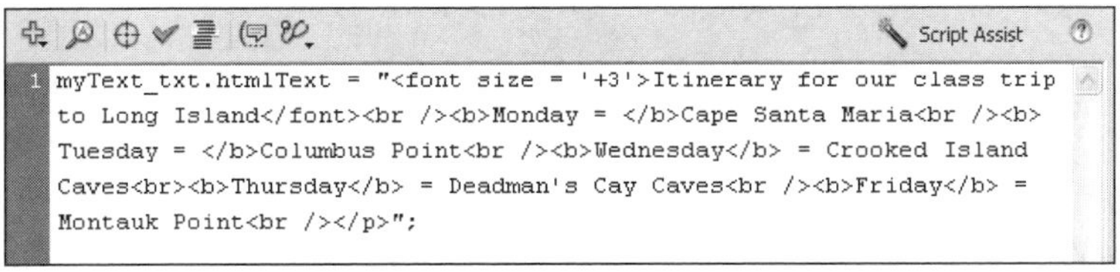

Figure 11.24 The completed code.

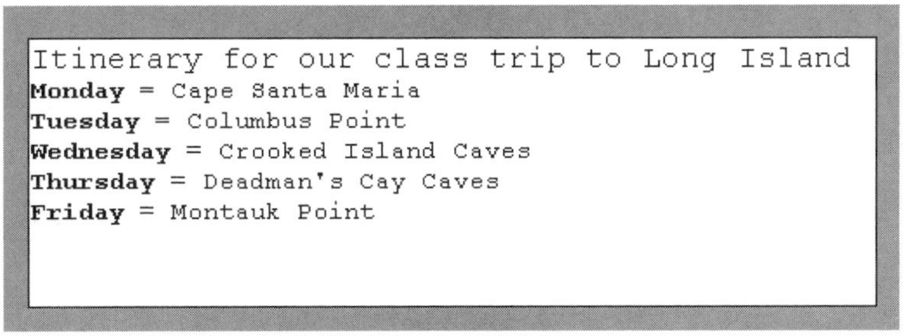

Itinerary for our class trip to Long Island
Monday = Cape Santa Maria
Tuesday = Columbus Point
Wednesday = Crooked Island Caves
Thursday = Deadman's Cay Caves
Friday = Montauk Point

Figure 11.25 At run time, Flash displays all the HTML code in the dynamic text field `myText_txt`.

Tweening Text Fields

If you place text fields in movie clip symbols, you can apply motion tweens to them just as you can with other symbol instances. This technique lets you create titles and banners that not only can be updated dynamically, but also can move across the screen, rotate, and shrink or grow. Imagine a blimp traveling across the Stage with a giant scoreboard attached to its side. By using a dynamic text field as the scoreboard on the blimp graphic, you can update scores or have messages appear as the blimp floats. You can use the same method to create a stock ticker-tape monitor, with the stock prices moving across the screen. Or, create a game that displays the current status of an individual player next to the player's icon as it moves around the Stage.

Eventually, you'll learn to animate text fields just with ActionScript. Even so, keep in mind that you'll still rely on tweens, or a combination of tweens and ActionScript, for many kinds of motions. Making text follow a path, for example, is a challenge better solved with tweens than with ActionScript alone.

To create a moving dynamic text field:

1. Select the Text tool, and drag out a text field on the Stage.
2. In the Property inspector, choose Dynamic Text and Single Line, give the text field an instance name, and embed the entire font outline through the Character Options dialog box (**Figure 11.26**).
3. Select your text field, and choose Modify > Convert to Symbol (F8) from the main toolbar.

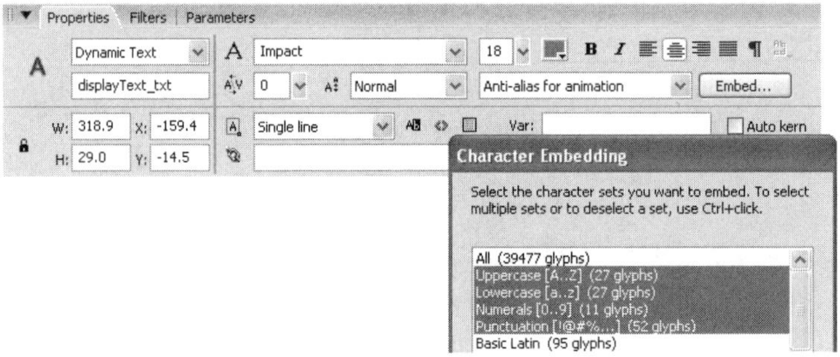

Figure 11.26 Enter `displayText_txt` as the instance name for your dynamic text field, and embed all font outlines by clicking the Embed button in the Property inspector and Shift-selecting the range of characters in the dialog box that appears.

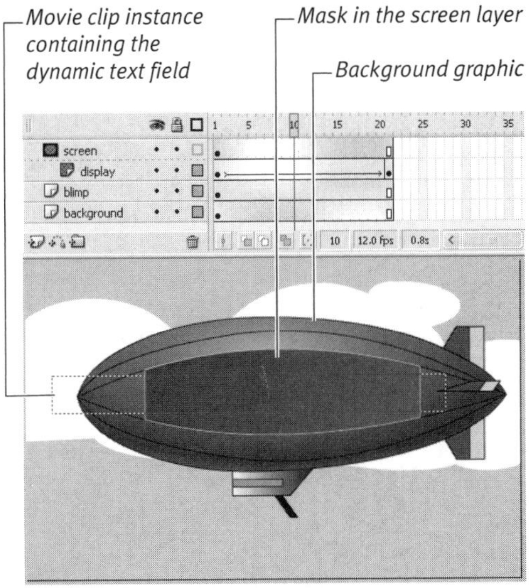

Figure 11.27 On the main Timeline, tween the movie clip instance that contains the dynamic text field. This movie clip instance (the dotted-line rectangle) moves across the Stage behind a mask of the scoreboard on the blimp.

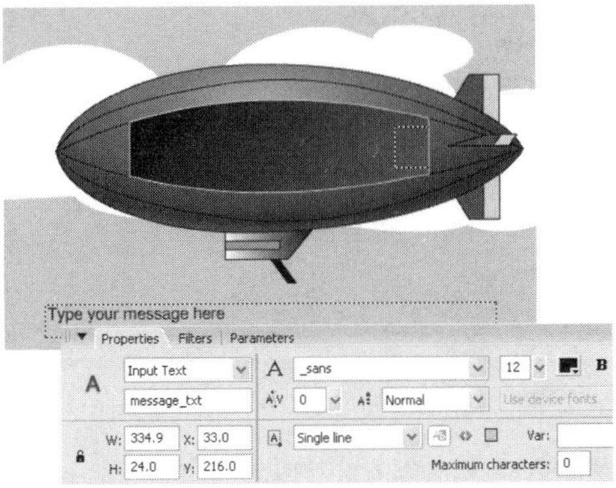

Figure 11.28 Enter `message_txt` as the instance name for the input text field.

4. In the dialog box that appears, name your symbol and choose Movie Clip as the behavior; then click OK.

   Flash puts your dynamic text field inside a movie clip symbol and places an instance on the Stage.

5. In the Property inspector, give the movie clip an instance name.

6. Create a motion tween of the movie clip instance moving across the Stage (**Figure 11.27**).

7. Select the Text tool, and drag out another text field below the tween of the movie clip instance in a separate layer.

8. In the Property inspector, choose Input Text and Single Line, and give this text field an instance name (**Figure 11.28**).

9. Select the main Timeline, and open the Actions panel.

10. Enter `_root`, followed by a period, and then choose ActionScript 2.0 Classes > Movie > Movie Clip > Event Handlers > onEnterFrame.

11. Within the `onEnterFrame` event handler, enter the target path to your dynamic text field (the instance name of your movie clip, followed by a period, and then the instance name of the dynamic text field inside the movie clip), followed by a period.

12. Enter a period, followed by `text` and an equals sign.

    Flash now understands that whatever follows the equals sign will be the text that is displayed in the dynamic text field inside of your movie clip.

continues on next page

13. After the equals sign, enter the name of your input text field, a period, and the word `text` (**Figure 11.29**).

    The dynamic text field inside the movie clip is updated continuously with the contents of the input text field.

14. Test your movie.

    When the viewer enters information in the input text field, that information is assigned to the dynamic text field inside the movie clip, and the updated text moves across the screen (**Figure 11.30**).

✔ Tip

- It's important to include the entire font outline in a dynamic text field when you tween it (change its rotation and alpha, especially) or when it's part of a masked layer. If the font outline isn't included, the text field won't tween properly or show up behind the mask.

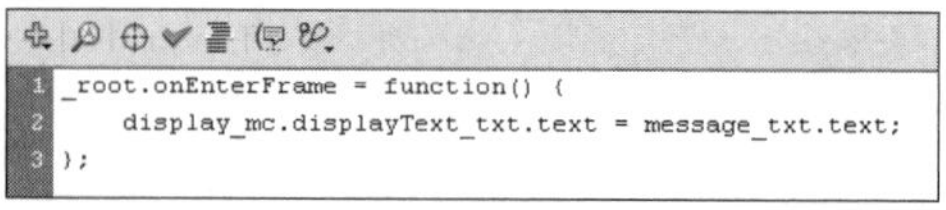

```
_root.onEnterFrame = function() {
    display_mc.displayText_txt.text = message_txt.text;
};
```

Figure 11.29 Assign the `text` property of the input text field `message_txt` to the `text` property of the dynamic text field `displayText_txt`. Because the dynamic text field is inside a movie clip, the target path is `display_mc.displayText_txt`.

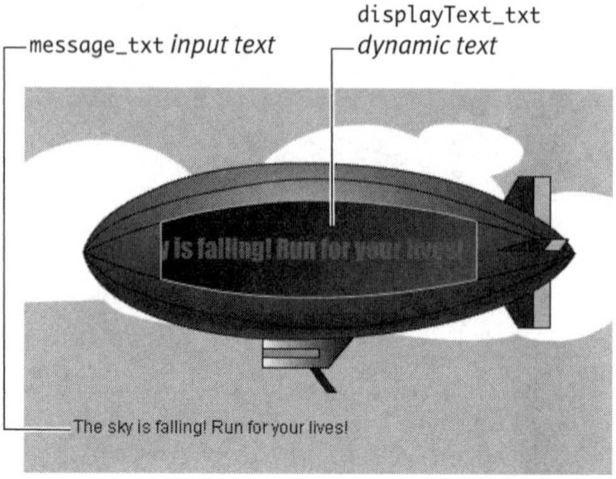

message_txt *input text*
displayText_txt *dynamic text*
The sky is falling! Run for your lives!

Figure 11.30 Flash tweens the dynamic text field containing any message your viewer enters in the input text field.

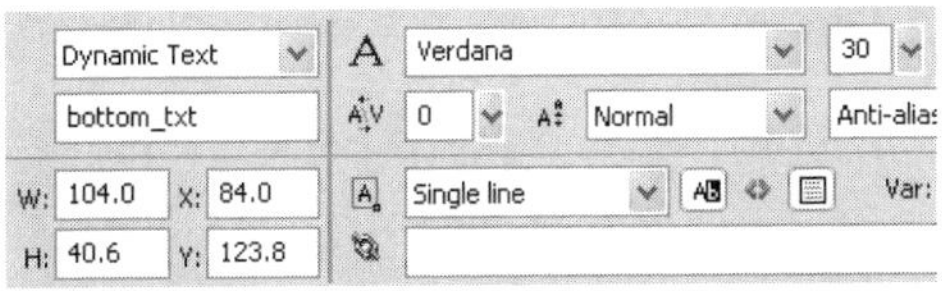

Figure 11.31 The instance name of a text field (highlighted with a rectangle) allows you to access its properties using ActionScript.

TextField Properties

When you drag an input or dynamic text field on the Stage with the Text tool, you're creating an instance of the `TextField` class. Before you can access its methods and properties, however, you must name your text field in the Property inspector so that you can identify it with ActionScript (**Figure 11.31**).

The instance name identifies the text field for targeting purposes. When you can target the text field, you can evaluate or modify its many properties. These properties determine the kind and display of the text field. You've already used the `text` property to get and set the contents of text fields. The `text` property holds the current contents of a text field: The statement `myTextField_txt.text = "Congratulations!"` displays the string `Congratulations!` in the text field `myTextField_txt`. There are many other properties. For example, you've encountered the `htmlText` and `html` properties, as well. Other properties include `type`, which defines an input or dynamic text field; `border`, which determines whether the text field has one; and `_rotation`, which controls the angle of the text field.

Table 11.1 (next page) summarizes many of the properties of the `TextField` class. Most of them are identical to the properties you can set in authoring mode in the Property inspector. In addition, you can use the properties common to the `MovieClip` and `Button` classes, such as `_rotation`, `_alpha`, `_x`, `_y`, `_width`, `_height`, `_xscale`, `_yscale`, `_name`, `_visible`, `filters`, and `menu`.

Table 11.1

TextField Properties		
Property	**Value**	**Description**
text	A string	Contents of the text field.
type	"dynamic" or "input"	Specifies a dynamic or input text field.
autosize	"none", "left", "center", or "right"	Controls automatic alignment and sizing so that a text field shrinks or grows to accommodate text.
background	true or false	Specifies whether the text field has a background fill.
backgroundColor	A hex code	Specifies the color of the background (visible only when border is true).
border	true or false	Specifies whether the text field has a border.
borderColor	A hex code	Specifies the color of the border.
textColor	A hex code	Specifies the color of the text.
styleSheet	A TextField.StyleSheet object	Defines style rules to be applied to the text field.
antiAliasType	"normal" or "advanced"	Indicates whether regular anti-aliasing or FlashType (advanced) anti-aliasing is used.
sharpness	A number, -400 to 400	Specifies the level of sharpness to apply to character edges.
thickness	A number, -200 to 200	Specifies the thickness to be applied to character edges.
gridFitType	"none", "pixel", or "subpixel"	Indicates whether character lines are fit to exact pixels, fit to subpixels (fractional pixels on an LCD monitor), or not fit to any grid.
textWidth	A number, in pixels	Specifies the width of the text (read-only).
textHeight	A number, in pixels	Specifies the height of the text (read-only).
length	A number	Specifies the number of characters in a text field (read-only).
scroll	A number	Specifies the top line visible in the text field.
bottomscroll	A number	Specifies the bottom line visible in the text field (read-only).
hscroll	A number, in pixels	Specifies the horizontal scrolling position of a text field. 0 defines the position where there is no scrolling.
maxscroll	A number	Specifies the maximum value for the scroll property (read-only).
maxhscroll	A number	Specifies the maximum value for the hscroll property (read-only).
mouseWheelEnabled	true or false	Specifies whether the user's mouse wheel can scroll multiline text fields.
restrict	A string	Specifies the allowable characters in the text field.
maxChars	A number	Specifies the maximum number of characters allowable.
variable	A string	Specifies the name of the text field variable.
embedFonts	true or false	Specifies whether fonts are embedded. You must create a font symbol and export it for ActionScript in its Linkage properties.
html	true or false	Specifies whether the text field renders HTML tags.
htmlText	A string	Specifies the contents of a text field when html is true.
condenseWhite	true or false	Specifies whether extra white space in an HTML text field should be removed.
multiline	true or false	Specifies whether the text field can display more than one line.
wordWrap	true or false	Specifies whether the text field breaks lines automatically.
selectable	true or false	Specifies whether the contents of the text field are selectable.
password	true or false	Specifies whether input text is disguised.
tabEnabled	true or false	Specifies whether the text field can receive focus when the Tab key is used.
tabIndex	A number	Specifies the order of focus when the Tab key is used.

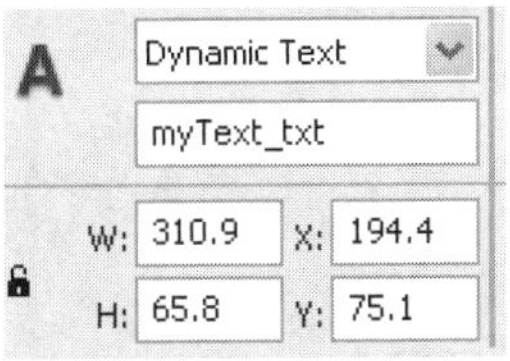
Dynamic Text
myText_txt
W: 310.9 X: 194.4
H: 65.8 Y: 75.1

Figure 11.32 The dynamic text field is called `myText_txt`.

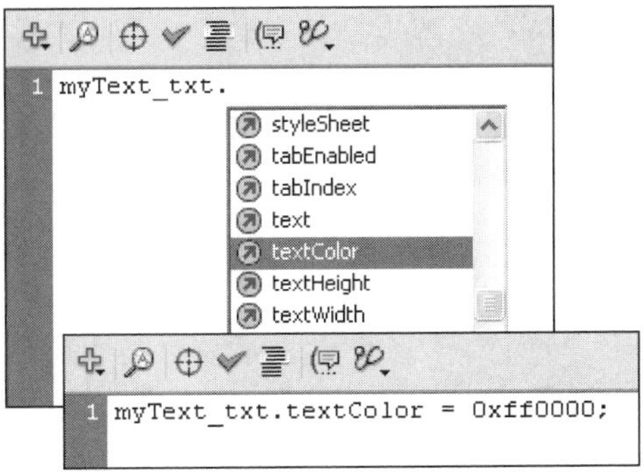
myText_txt.
styleSheet
tabEnabled
tabIndex
text
textColor
textHeight
textWidth
myText_txt.textColor = 0xff0000;

Figure 11.33 Select the property `textColor` from the code hint pull- down menu for the text field named `myText_txt`. In this example, the `textColor` property of the text field `myText_txt` is set to red.

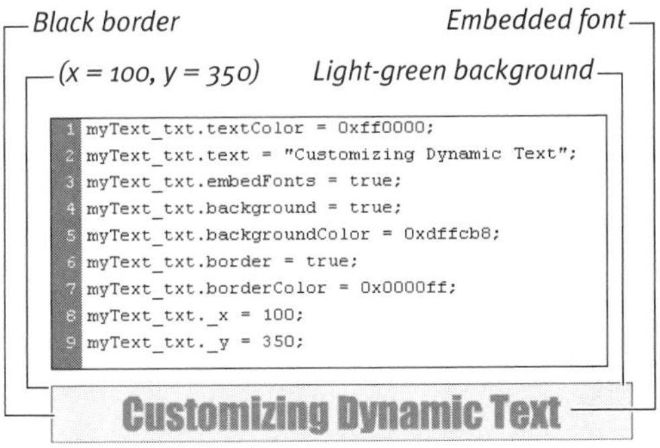
Black border
Embedded font
(x = 100, y = 350)
Light-green background
myText_txt.textColor = 0xff0000;
myText_txt.text = "Customizing Dynamic Text";
myText_txt.embedFonts = true;
myText_txt.background = true;
myText_txt.backgroundColor = 0xdffcb8;
myText_txt.border = true;
myText_txt.borderColor = 0x0000ff;
myText_txt._x = 100;
myText_txt._y = 350;
Customizing Dynamic Text

Figure 11.34 The script modifies many properties of the text field `myTextField_txt`, resulting in the text below.

To modify the properties of the text field:

1. Select the Text tool in the Tools panel, and drag out a text field on the Stage.
2. In the Property inspector, select Dynamic Text, give the text field an instance name, and leave all other options at their default settings (**Figure 11.32**).
3. Select the first frame of the main Timeline, and open the Actions panel.
4. In the Script pane, enter the instance name of your text field, followed by a period.
5. From the code hint pull-down menu, select a property. For this example, choose `textColor`, and enter an equals sign.
6. After the equals sign, enter `0xff0000`.

   The completed statement changes the color of the text to red (**Figure 11.33**).
7. Repeat steps 5 and 6, choosing different properties and values to modify your text field (**Figure 11.34**).

✔ Tips

- To modify the font, font size, and other characteristics of the text, you must use the `TextFormat` class, discussed later in this chapter.
- If you modify the properties `_alpha` and `_rotation`, you must embed the font outlines for your text field. If you don't, the text won't be modified correctly.
- The properties `_x` and `_y` refer to the top-left corner of the text field.
- The properties `_width` and `_height` change the pixel dimensions of the text field but don't change the size of the text inside the text field. The properties `_xscale` and `_yscale`, on the other hand, scale the text.

Embedding Fonts: Creating Font Symbols for ActionScript Export

When you set the `embedFonts` property of a text field to `true`, you must provide the font outline in the exported SWF. This process involves creating a font symbol in the Library and marking it for ActionScript export. If you don't, Flash won't know to make the font available when it publishes your movie. In the Library, choose New Font from the Options menu. In the Font Symbol Properties dialog box that appears, select the font in the list (**Figure 11.35**). Click OK, and you'll have a new font symbol in your Library. Select the symbol, and choose Linkage from the Options menu. In the Linkage Properties dialog box that appears, select Export for ActionScript, and choose an identifier for your font symbol (**Figure 11.36**). Click OK. Your font symbol will be exported to the SWF. When you set the `embedFonts` property to `true` via ActionScript, the font symbol will be available.

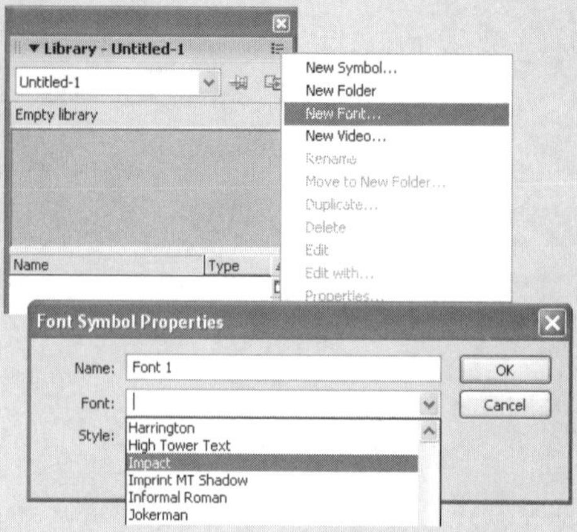

Figure 11.35 Choose New Font from the Library window's Options menu to create a font symbol. Choose your font in the Font Symbol Properties dialog box. The Name field contains the name of the symbol that will appear in the Library.

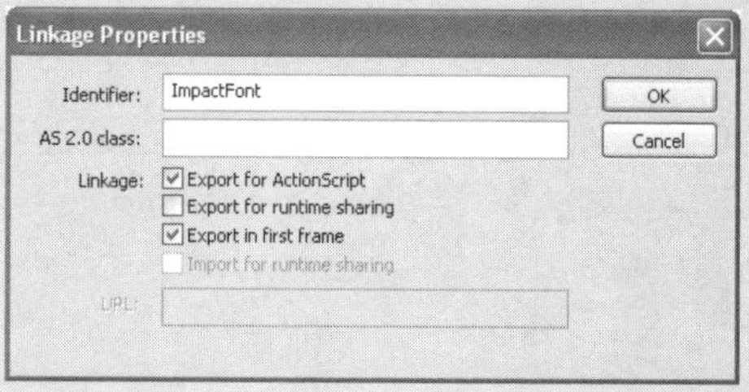

Figure 11.36 The Linkage Properties dialog box enables you to export your font symbol for use in ActionScript. The Identifier field contains the name that you'll use in ActionScript to refer to this font.

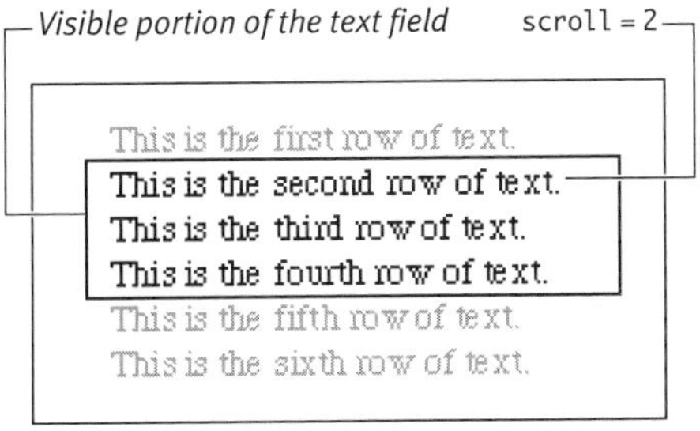
Visible portion of the text field
scroll = 2
This is the first row of text.
This is the second row of text.
This is the third row of text.
This is the fourth row of text.
This is the fifth row of text.
This is the sixth row of text.

Figure 11.37 The `scroll` property is the first visible row of text within a text field.

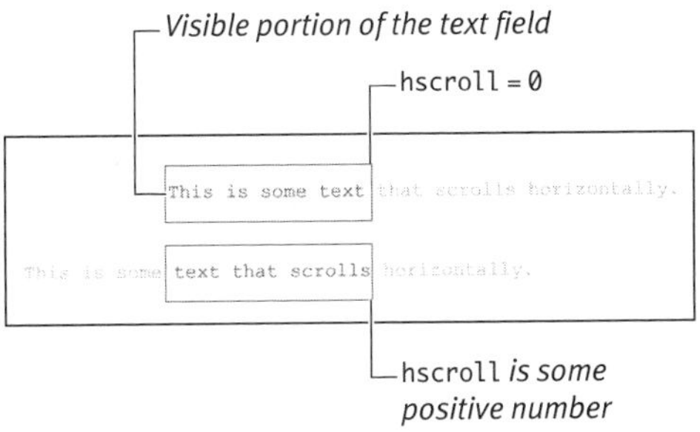
Visible portion of the text field
hscroll = 0
This is some text that scrolls horizontally.
This is some text that scrolls horizontally.
hscroll is some positive number

Figure 11.38 The `hscroll` property is relative to the point at which there is no scrolling. The value of `hscroll` increases as horizontal scrolling occurs.

Controlling text field scrolling

If a text field is too small to display its text content, you can use the `TextField` properties `scroll`, `maxscroll`, `hscroll`, `maxhscroll`, and `bottomscroll`, all of which give information about the position of the text within the text field.

When the information in a multiline text field exceeds its defined boundaries, Flash displays only the current text (unless you set the `autosize` property to fit the information). Text that can't fit within the text field is hidden from view but is still accessible if the viewer clicks inside the text field and drags up or down. You can display different portions of the hidden text dynamically by defining the properties `scroll` and `hscroll`.

Think of the text field as being a window that shows only a portion of a larger piece of text. Each row of text has an index value. The top row is 1, the second row is 2, and so on. The `scroll` property refers to the topmost visible row. The `bottomScroll` property refers to the bottommost visible row. The visible portion of a text field is the rows from `scroll` to `bottomscroll`, and as new lines of text scroll up or down, those properties change (**Figure 11.37**).

If a line of text exceeds the width of its text field, you can use `hscroll` to display different portions of its horizontal scrolling. The point on the right edge of the text field where the initial text is visible has an `hscroll` value of `0`. The value of `hscroll` is measured in pixels; as `hscroll` increases, the text scrolls to reveal more of itself (**Figure 11.38**).

You can retrieve the values of `scroll` and `hscroll` so you know exactly which portion of the text your viewer is currently looking at, or you can modify their values to force your viewer to look at a particular portion. It's common to provide interface controls so that viewers can control the scrolling of text, just as they control the scroll bars in a Web browser or any window on the computer screen. In the following task, you'll create interface controls of this kind.

To create a vertical scrolling text field:

1. Select the Text tool in the Tools panel, and drag out a text field onto the Stage.
2. In the Property inspector, choose Input Text, enter an instance name, choose Multiline from the pull-down menu, and click the Show Border button (**Figure 11.39**).
3. Create a button symbol of an arrow pointing up, place an instance of the button on the Stage, and give it a name in the Property inspector.
4. Place a second instance of the button on the Stage, choose Modify > Transform > Flip Vertical to make the second button point down, and give the down arrow button a name in the Property inspector.
5. Align both buttons vertically next to the input text field (**Figure 11.40**).
6. Select the first frame of the main Timeline, and open the Actions panel.
7. Declare a `Boolean` variable, and set its value to `false`.

   This variable will track whether one of the scrolling buttons is being clicked at a given time.

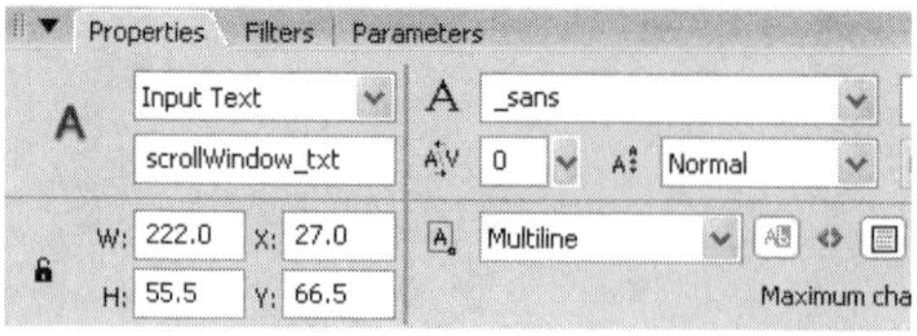

Figure 11.39 Enter `scrollWindow_txt` as the instance name of your text field.

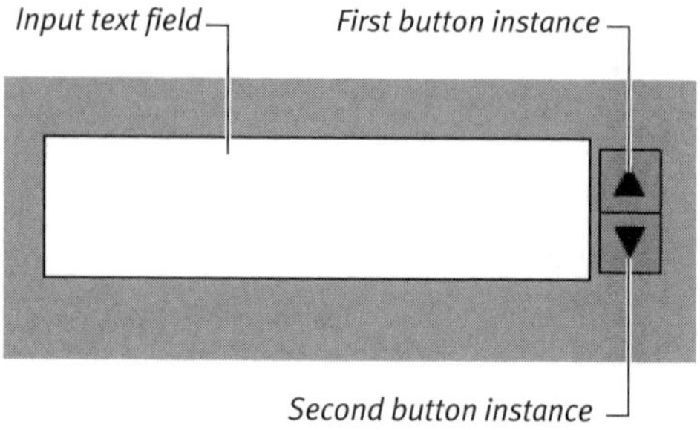

Figure 11.40 Place two buttons next to the input text field.

TEXTFIELD PROPERTIES

```
var pressing:Boolean = false;
var movement:Number = 0;
upButton_btn.onPress = function() {
    pressing = true;
    movement = -1;
};
```

Figure 11.41 Clicking the upButton_btn button sets the variable pressing to true and the variable movement to -1.

```
var pressing:Boolean = false;
var movement:Number = 0;
upButton_btn.onPress = function() {
    pressing = true;
    movement = -1;
};
upButton_btn.onRelease = function() {
    pressing = false;
};
```

Figure 11.42 Releasing the upButton_btn button sets the variable pressing to false.

```
downButton_btn.onPress = function() {
    pressing = true;
    movement = 1;
};
downButton_btn.onRelease = function() {
    pressing = false;
};
```

Figure 11.43 Add onRelease and onPress event handlers for the button downButton_btn.

8. Declare a variable with the data type `Number`, and assign it the value `0`.

   This variable will track the direction of scrolling movement (negative or positive).

9. Create an `onPress` event handler for the up arrow button.

10. On a new line inside the `onPress` event handler, enter the name of your `Boolean` variable, followed by an equals sign and the value `true`.

11. On the next line, enter the name of your `Number` variable, and give it a value of -1 (**Figure 11.41**).

12. Assign an `onRelease` event handler to the up arrow button.

13. On a new line inside the `onRelease` event handler, enter the name of your `Boolean` variable, and assign it the value `false` (**Figure 11.42**).

14. Create similar `onPress` and `onRelease` event handlers for your down arrow button, and enter the same statements in the Script pane of the Actions panel, except assign the `Number` variable to change to 1 when the mouse button is pressed (**Figure 11.43**).

15. Create an `onEnterFrame` event handler assigned to the root Timeline.

16. On a new line inside the `onEnterFrame` event handler, choose Statements > Conditions/Loops > if.

17. For the condition of the `if` statement, enter the name of your `Boolean` variable, followed by `== true`.

continues on next page

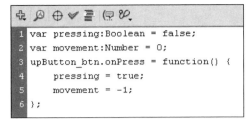

18. With your cursor between the opening and closing curly braces of the `if` statement, enter the name of the input text field, followed by a period. Select the property `scroll` from the code hint pull-down menu, and enter an equals sign.

19. Directly following the equals sign, enter the name of your input text field, followed by a period and then the property `scroll`; add the value of your `Number` variable (**Figure 11.44**).

    Flash continuously checks to see whether one of the buttons is pressed. If so, Flash adds the value of the `Number` variable to the current `scroll` property. If the up arrow button is pressed, the `scroll` value is decreased by 1. If the down arrow button is pressed, the `scroll` value is increased by 1 (**Figure 11.45**).

Determining the maximum scrolling position

Whereas the `scroll` property defines the first visible text row in a text field, the `maxscroll` property defines the maximum allowable value for `scroll` in that text field. This row appears at the top of the text field when the last line of text is visible (**Figure 11.46**). You can't change the value of `maxscroll`, because it's defined by the amount of text and the size of the text field itself, but you can read its value. Assign the value of `maxscroll` to `scroll`, and you can scroll the text to the bottom of the text field automatically. Or you can calculate the value of `scroll` proportionally to `maxscroll` and build a draggable scroll bar that reflects and controls the text's position within the text field.

```
var pressing:Boolean = false;
var movement:Number = 0;
upButton_btn.onPress = function() {
    pressing = true;
    movement = -1;
};
upButton_btn.onRelease = function() {
    pressing = false;
};
downButton_btn.onPress = function() {
    pressing = true;
    movement = 1;
};
downButton_btn.onRelease = function() {
    pressing = false;
};
_root.onEnterFrame = function() {
    if (pressing == true) {
        scrollWindow_txt.scroll = scrollWindow_txt.scroll + movement;
    }
};
```

Figure 11.44 The actions assigned to the `onEnterFrame` handler continuously add the value of the variable `movement` to the `scroll` property of `scrollwindow_txt` when `pressing` is `true`.

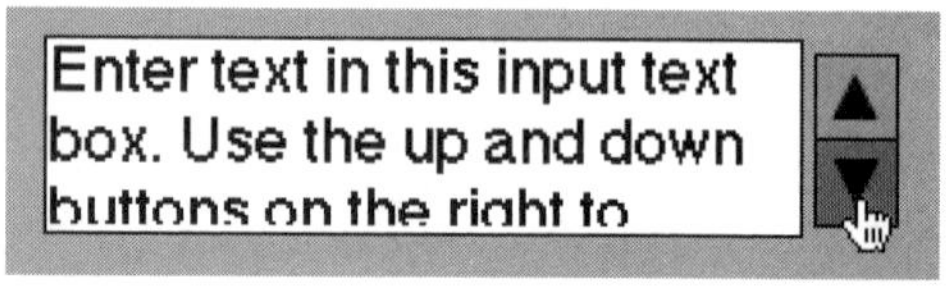
Enter text in this input text box. Use the up and down buttons on the right to

Figure 11.45 The buttons on the right increase or decrease the value of the `scroll` property of the input text field.

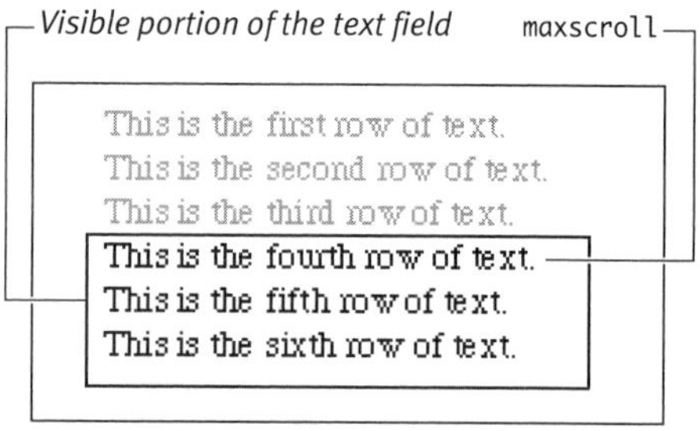
Visible portion of the text field
maxscroll
This is the first row of text.
This is the second row of text.
This is the third row of text.
This is the fourth row of text.
This is the fifth row of text.
This is the sixth row of text.

Figure 11.46 The `maxscroll` property refers to the maximum value of the `scroll` property. This value is the value of `scroll` when the last line of text is visible. In this example, `maxscroll` is 4.

```
skipToEndButton_btn.onRelease = function() {
    scrollWindow_txt.scroll = scrollWindow_txt.maxscroll;
};
```

Figure 11.47 A portion of the Script pane shows the `onRelease` handler for a button `skipToEndButton_btn`. The property `maxscroll` is assigned to the `scroll` property of `scrollwindow_txt`.

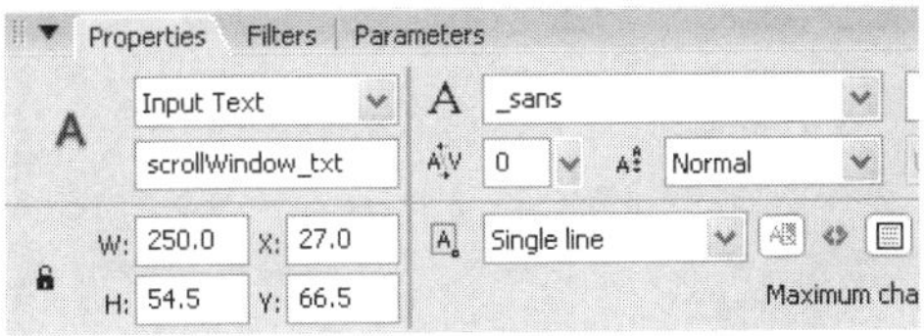

Figure 11.48 Enter `scrollWindow_txt` as the instance name of your input text field.

To scroll to the end of a text field:

1. Continuing with the preceding task, create a new button symbol, drag an instance of it to the Stage, and give it a name in the Property inspector.
2. Select the first frame of the main Timeline, and open the Actions panel.
3. Assign an `onRelease` event handler to the new button.
4. Enter the name of the text field, followed by a period and then the property `scroll`.
5. After the `scroll` property, enter an equals sign, the name of the text field, a period, and then the property `maxscroll` (**Figure 11.47**).

   When the viewer clicks this button, the current value of `maxscroll` for the text field is assigned to `scroll`. The text automatically moves so that the last line is visible.

To create a horizontal scrolling text field:

1. Select the Text tool in the Tools panel, and drag out a text field onto the Stage.
2. In the Property inspector, choose Input Text, enter an instance name, choose Single Line from the pull-down menu, and click the Show Border button (**Figure 11.48**).
3. Create a button symbol of a right-pointing arrow, place an instance of the button on the Stage, and give it a name in the Property inspector.
4. Place a second instance of the button on the Stage, choose Modify > Transform > Flip Horizontal to make the second button point left, and give the left arrow button a name in the Property inspector.

continues on next page

5. Align both buttons horizontally above the input text field (**Figure 11.49**).

6. Select the first frame of the main Timeline, and open the Actions panel.

7. Declare a `Boolean` and a `Number` variable, and assign code to the right and left arrow buttons as you did to the down and up arrow buttons in the preceding task.

   Your code should look similar to this:

```
var pressing:Boolean = false;
var movement:Number = 0;
rightButton_btn.onPress=function(){
    pressing = true;
    movement = 20;
};
rightButton_btn.onRelease=function(){
    pressing = false;
};
leftButton_btn.onPress=function(){
    pressing = true;
    movement = -20;
};
leftButton_btn.onRelease=function(){
    pressing = false;
};
```

8. Assign an `onEnterFrame` event handler to the root Timeline.

9. On a new line within the `onEnterFrame` event handler, choose Statements > Conditions/Loops > if.

10. For the condition of the `if` statement, enter `pressing == true`.

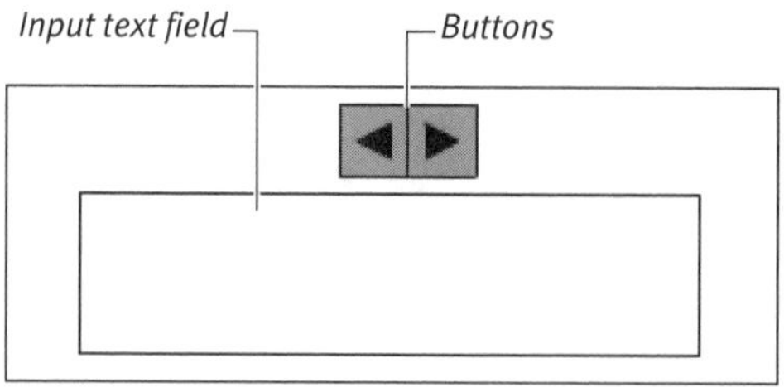

Figure 11.49 Align two buttons above your input text field.

```
var pressing:Boolean = false;
var movement:Number = 0;
rightButton_btn.onPress = function() {
    pressing = true;
    movement = 20;
};
rightButton_btn.onRelease = function() {
    pressing = false;
};
leftButton_btn.onPress = function() {
    pressing = true;
    movement = -20;
};
leftButton_btn.onRelease = function() {
    pressing = false;
};
_root.onEnterFrame = function() {
    if (pressing == true) {
        scrollWindow_txt.hscroll = scrollWindow_txt.hscroll + movement;
    }
};
```

Figure 11.50 The actions assigned to the `onEnterFrame` handler continuously add the value of the variable `movement` to the `hscroll` property of `scrollwindow_txt` when `pressing` is `true`.

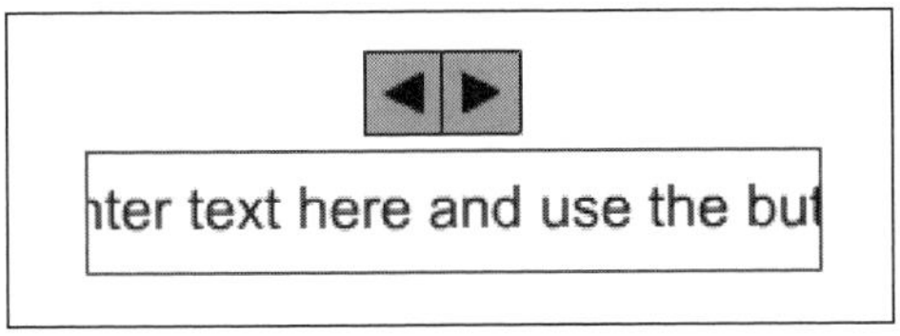
nter text here and use the bu

Figure 11.51 The buttons above the input text field increase or decrease the value of the `hscroll` property of the input text field.

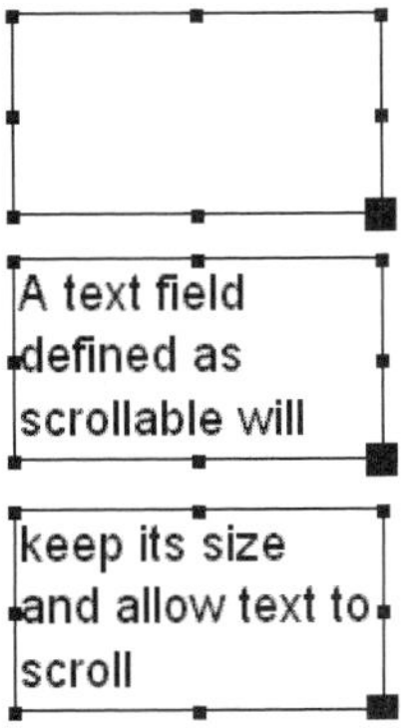
A text field
defined as
scrollable will
keep its size
and allow text to
scroll

Figure 11.52 When you define a text field as scrollable in authoring mode, the resizing handle turns black (top). You can enter text in authoring mode, but the size of the text field remains constant, hiding text that can't fit and allowing scrolling (bottom).

11. Within the curly braces of the `if` statement, enter the name of the input text field, followed by a period and then the property `hscroll`; add the value of the variable `movement` (**Figure 11.50**).

    Flash continuously checks to see whether one of the buttons is clicked. If so, Flash adds the value of `movement` to the current `hscroll` property. If the right arrow button is clicked, the `hscroll` value increases by 20, moving the text to the left by 1 pixel. If the down arrow button is clicked, the `hscroll` value decreases by 20, moving the text to the right by 1 pixel (**Figure 11.51**).

Constraining text field height in authoring mode

Sometimes, in authoring mode, you'll want to restrict the size of your text field so that its contents are scrollable. By defining your text field as scrollable, you can keep much of the text it contains hidden from view.

To define a scrollable text field in authoring mode:

1. Select the Text tool in the Tools panel, and drag out a text field on the Stage.

2. Choose Text > Scrollable from the main menu's toolbar.

   The resizing handle at the bottom-right corner of your text field fills in with black, indicating that the text field is scrollable. Although your text field remains resizable, any text that doesn't fit in the text field will begin to scroll (**Figure 11.52**).

   or

   Shift-double-click the resizing handle of the text field.

   The handle turns black, and the text field becomes scrollable.

TEXTFIELD PROPERTIES

Generating Text Fields Dynamically

If you need to have text appear in your movie based on a viewer's interaction, you must be able to create a text field during run time. You can generate text fields dynamically with the MovieClip class's createTextField() method. The method creates a new text field attached to the movie clip that calls the method. For instance, if you choose the root Timeline as the movie clip to which it's attached, your text field is placed on the main Stage. You also must specify an instance name, depth level, x and y positions, and width and height in pixels for the new text field. For example, the following statement creates a new text field with the instance name newTF_txt on the main Stage in depth level 1. Its top-left corner is positioned at x = 100, y = 100, and it's 200 pixels wide by 50 pixels tall:

```
var myTF:TextField = _root.createTextField
("newTF_txt", 1, 100, 100, 200, 50);
```

A reference to the new text field is assigned to the variable myTF, so you can use that variable to access the text field without needing to specify the full target path.

To create a text field on the main Stage:

1. Select the first frame of the main Timeline, and open the Actions panel.
2. Declare a variable using the `var` statement, and assign it the data type `TextField`.

   Your statement looks something like `var myText:TextField`.
3. On the same line, enter an equals sign and then `_root`, and choose ActionScript 2.0 Classes > Movie > MovieClip > Methods > createTextField.

   The new text field will be attached to the root Timeline (the main Stage).
4. As parameters in the parentheses of the `createTextField` method, enter an instance name (in quotation marks), depth level, x position, y position, width, and height, separating the parameters with commas (**Figure 11.53**).

   A text field is created on the main Stage. To see it, assign text to it with the `text` property (**Figure 11.54**).

```
var myText:TextField = _root.createTextField("myText_txt", 1, 50, 50, 300, 100);
```

Figure 11.53 This code defines a text field assigned to the variable `myText` that is 300 pixels wide by 100 pixels tall, attached to the root Timeline at x = 50, y = 50, in depth level 1.

```
var myText:TextField = _root.createTextField("myText_txt", 1, 50, 50, 300, 100);
myText.text = "Fun with Text";
myText.border = true;
```

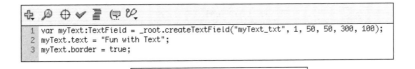

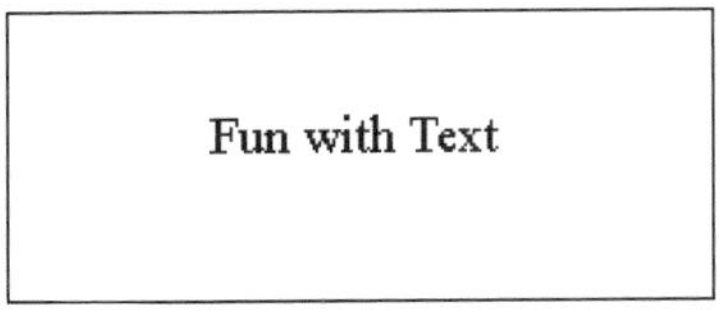

Figure 11.54 The contents of the `text` property of `myText` appear on the Stage. The default format for a dynamically created text field is black 12-point Times New Roman (Windows) or Times (Mac).

To remove a text field that was created dynamically:

1. In the Script pane of the Actions panel, enter the instance name of the text field you want to remove.
2. Choose ActionScript 2.0 Classes > Movie > TextField > Methods > removeTextField (**Figure 11.55**).

   The text field deletes itself when this method is called. You can only use this method to remove text fields created by the `MovieClip` method `createTextField()`.

```
myText.removeTextField();
```

Figure 11.55 The dynamically generated text field `myText` is removed.

The Default Text Field Appearance

When you create a text field dynamically with the `createTextField()` method, it has the following default properties:

`type = dynamic`	`html = false`
`selectable = true`	`embedFonts = false`
`multiline = false`	`restrict = null`
`password = false`	`maxChars = null`
`wordWrap = false`	`variable = null`
`background = false`	`autoSize = none`
`border = false`	

The text field also has the following default format properties (which you can change with a `TextFormat` object):

`font = Times New Roman` (Windows)	`leftMargin = 0`
`font = Times` (Mac)	`rightMargin = 0`
`size = 12`	`indent = 0`
`textColor = 0x000000`	`leading = 0`
`bold = false`	`URL = ""`
`italic = false`	`target = ""`
`underline = false`	`bullet = false`
`align = "left"`	

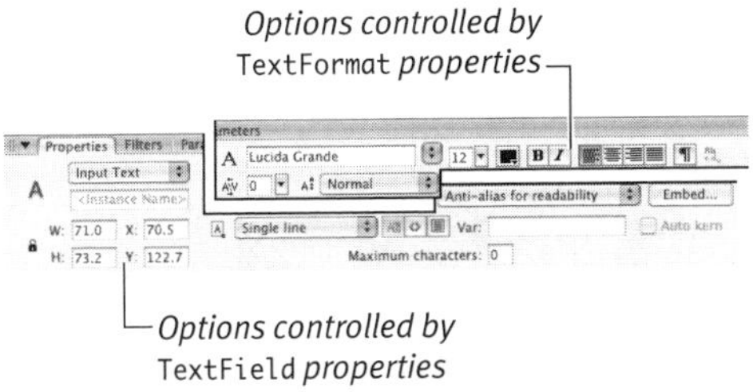

Figure 11.56 The Property inspector can be divided into sections of options controlled by `TextFormat` properties and options controlled by `TextField` properties.

Modifying Text in Text Fields

Although the properties of a text field can define the way text behaves and the way the text field itself appears, the properties don't control the formatting of the text the text field contains. For that task, you need to use the `TextFormat` class. The `TextFormat` class controls character and paragraph formatting, which are also options available in authoring mode in the Property inspector. Notice that the Property inspector is divided into sections of options that are controlled by the `TextField` class and those that are controlled by the `TextFormat` class (**Figure 11.56**). **Table 11.2** summarizes the properties of the `TextFormat` class.

Table 11.2

TextFormat Properties

PROPERTY	VALUE	DESCRIPTION
`size`	A number	Specifies the point size of the text.
`font`	A string	Specifies the font of the text. You must create a font symbol and choose Export for ActionScript in its Linkage properties. Use the Linkage Identifier for this property. Works only when `embedFonts = true`.
`color`	A hex number	Specifies the color of the text.
`underline`	`true` or `false`	Specifies whether the text is underlined.
`italic`	`true` or `false`	Specifies whether the text is italicized.
`bold`	`true` or `false`	Specifies whether the text is bold.
`bullet`	`true` or `false`	Specifies whether text is in a bulleted list.
`align`	`"left"`, `"center"`, or `"right"`	Specifies the alignment of text within the text field.
`leading`	A number in pixels	Specifies the space between lines.
`indent`	A number	Specifies the indentation of the first line of paragraphs, in points.
`blockIndent`	A number	Specifies the indentation of the entire text, in points.
`rightMargin`	A number	Specifies the space between the text and the right edge, in points.
`leftMargin`	A number	Specifies the space between the text and the left edge, in points.
`tabStops`	An array of numbers	Specifies the placement (in pixels) of custom tab stops.
`URL`	A string	Specifies the URL that the text links to.
`target`	A string	Specifies the target window where the hyperlink opens.

To change the formatting of text in a text field, first create a new instance of the TextFormat class, like so:

```
var myFormat_fmt:TextFormat =
new TextFormat();
```

Then assign values to the properties of your TextFormat object:

```
myFormat_fmt.size = 48;
```

Finally, call the setTextFormat() method for your text field. This method is a method of the TextField class, not of the TextFormat class:

```
myTextField_txt.setTextFormat
(myFormat_fmt);
```

This statement applies the formatting in the TextFormat object to the text in the text field. In this example, it changes the size of the text in the text field myTextField_txt to 48 points.

To modify the text formatting of a text field:

1. As described earlier in this chapter, create a new font symbol in the Library, and export it for ActionScript in the Linkage Properties dialog box (**Figure 11.57**).
2. Select the Text tool, and drag out a text field on the Stage.
3. In the Property inspector, choose Input Text or Dynamic Text, enter an instance name, choose a different font than the one you marked for export in step 1, and embed its font outline.
4. Enter some text in the text field (**Figure 11.58**).

   You'll use a TextFormat object to modify this text field.
5. Select the first frame of the main Timeline, and open the Actions panel.
6. Declare a TextFormat object using the var statement followed by an equals sign.

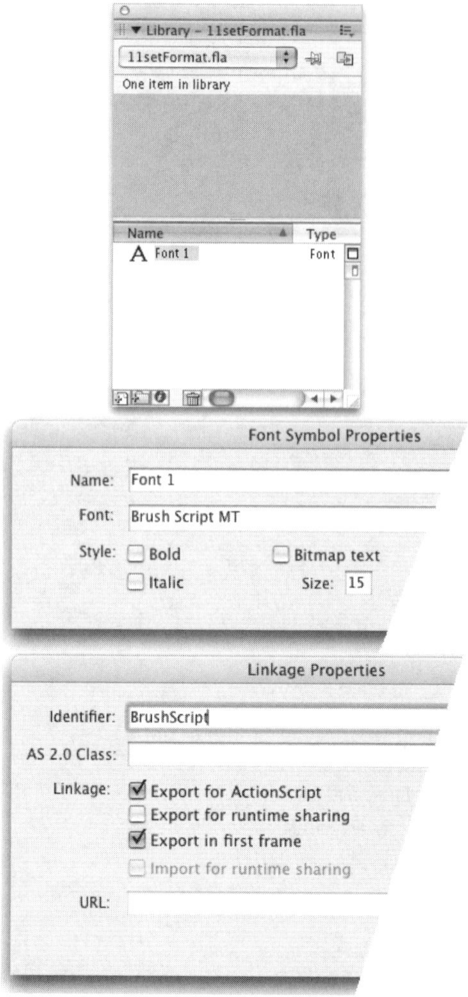

Figure 11.57 Create a font symbol, and export it for ActionScript. This font is identified as BrushScript.

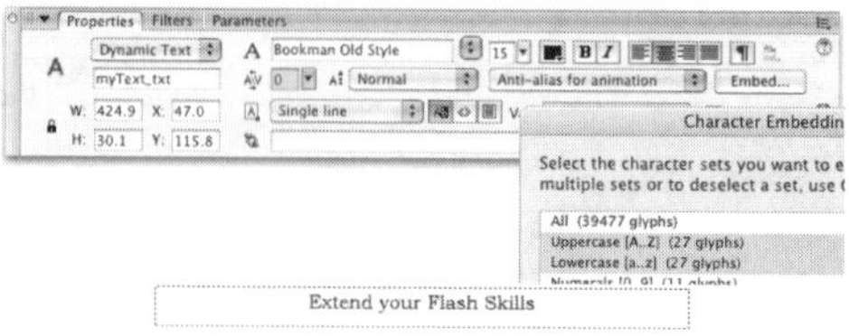

Figure 11.58 Create a text field called myText_txt. The outline for this text field's font (Bookman Old Style) is embedded.

```
var myFormat_fmt:TextFormat = new TextFormat();
```

Figure 11.59 Instantiate a `TextFormat` object called `myFormat_fmt`.

```
var myFormat_fmt:TextFormat = new TextFormat();
myFormat_fmt.font = "BrushScript";
```

Figure 11.60 Assign the outline font that you've marked for export.

```
var myFormat_fmt:TextFormat = new TextFormat();
myFormat_fmt.font = "BrushScript";
myFormat_fmt.size = 30;
myFormat_fmt.color = 0xFF0000;
myText_txt.setTextFormat(myFormat_fmt);
```

Figure 11.61 Assign the new format to the text field `myText_txt`.

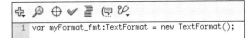

Figure 11.62 The original text (in Figure 11.58) changes to red 30-point Brush Script.

✔ Tips

- The `setTextFormat()` method modifies only existing text in the text field. If you add more text after `setTextFormat()` is called, that text will have its original formatting.
- You can also use a variant: the `setNewTextFormat()` method. This method modifies any new text that appears in the text field. Existing text is unaffected. Use `setNewTextFormat()` when you want to distinguish existing text from new text with different formatting.

7. Choose ActionScript 2.0 Classes > Movie > TextFormat > newTextFormat (**Figure 11.59**).
8. On the next line, enter the name of your `TextFormat` object, followed by a period. In the code hint pull-down menu that appears, choose "font".

   or

   Choose ActionScript 2.0 Classes > Movie > TextFormat > Properties > font.
9. Assign a value to the `font` property by entering an equals sign followed by the linkage identifier of the exported font symbol (**Figure 11.60**).
10. Enter additional statements to assign values to the properties of your `TextFormat` object.
11. On a new line, enter the name of your input or dynamic text field, followed by a period. Choose `setTextFormat` from the code hint pull-down menu.

    or

    Choose ActionScript 2.0 Classes > Movie > TextField > Methods > setTextFormat.
12. For the parameter of the `setTextFormat` method, enter the name of your `TextFormat` object (**Figure 11.61**).

    The `TextFormat` object is used as the parameter for the `setTextFormat()` method and changes the formatting of the text field.
13. Test your movie.

    Flash creates a `TextFormat` object. The properties of the object are passed through the `setTextFormat()` method and modify the existing contents of the text field (**Figure 11.62**).

Formatting segments of text

The `setTextFormat()` method enables you to format the entire text field, a single character, or a span of characters. In order to do so, you must specify the portion of the text that you want to format. The position of any given character in a `String` (such as the `text` property of a text field) is known as the character's *index*. The index of the first character is 0, the index of the second character is 1, and so on. If you use an index as the first parameter of the `setTextFormat()` method, only that single character is affected. If you use a beginning index and an ending index as the first and second parameters, the span of characters between the two indexes, including the beginning character, is affected.

To modify the text formatting of a single character:

1. Continuing with the file you created in the preceding example, select the first frame of the main Timeline, and open the Actions panel.
2. Place your pointer inside of the parentheses of the `setTextFormat` method.
3. Before the `TextFormat` object's name, enter a number index, followed by a comma to separate the two parameters (**Figure 11.63**).
4. Test your movie.

   Flash modifies the format of a single character (**Figure 11.64**).

```
var myFormat_fmt:TextFormat = new TextFormat();
myFormat_fmt.font = "BrushScript";
myFormat_fmt.size = 30;
myFormat_fmt.color = 0xFF0000;
myText_txt.setTextFormat(9, myFormat_fmt);
```

Figure 11.63 The character at index (position) 9 in the text field will be formatted.

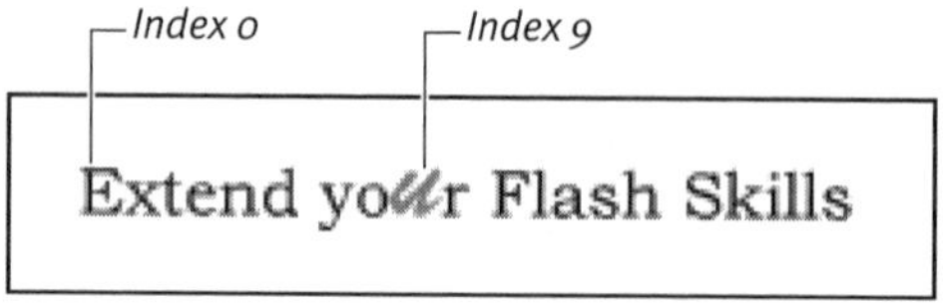

Figure 11.64 Although the rest of the text stays the same, the *u* character at index 9 changes to red 30-point Brush Script.

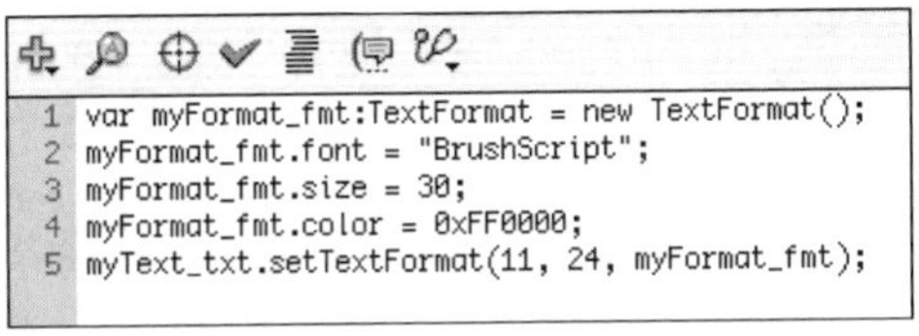

```
var myFormat_fmt:TextFormat = new TextFormat();
myFormat_fmt.font = "BrushScript";
myFormat_fmt.size = 30;
myFormat_fmt.color = 0xFF0000;
myText_txt.setTextFormat(11, 24, myFormat_fmt);
```

Figure 11.65 The characters beginning at index 11 and up to, but not including, index 24 will change formats.

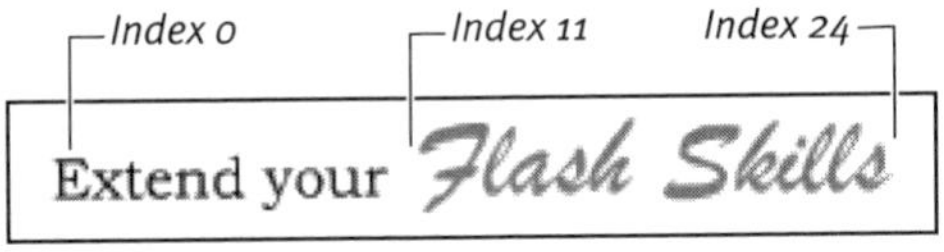

Figure 11.66 The rest of the text stays the same, but the words *Flash Skills,* from index 11 to index 24, change to red 30-point Brush Script. Although the parameters specify the indexes 11 and 24, the last index isn't included in the selection.

To modify the text formatting of a span of characters:

1. Continuing with the file you used in the preceding example, select the first frame of the main Timeline, and open the Actions panel.
2. Place your pointer inside of the parentheses of the `setTextFormat` method.
3. Before the `TextFormat` object's name (in place of the single `Number` index parameter), enter a beginning index and an ending index, separating the three parameters with commas (**Figure 11.65**).
4. Test your movie.

   Flash modifies the format of the span of characters (**Figure 11.66**).

Creating dynamic text animations

Using a combination of `TextFormat` properties and `TextField` properties, you can animate text entirely with ActionScript to make its motion respond dynamically to run-time events or to viewer interaction. You can also use ActionScript to do things to text that are difficult, if not impossible, to do with normal tweens, such as swapping characters' styles or animating the color of the text independently of the color of its background.

In the following demonstration, a text field is generated and animated dynamically by being modified with `setInterval` statements and an `onEnterFrame` event handler.

To animate text:

1. Enter the action to create a text field on the root Timeline (use the `createTextField()` method), and place it at depth level 1 on the center of the Stage.

 The size of the text field doesn't matter.

2. Assign text to the text field's `text` property, set `autosize` to "center", and set `embedFonts` to true.

 The code should look like **Figure 11.67**.

3. Because you're embedding the font, make sure you create a font symbol in the Library.

4. Select your newly created font symbol in the Library, and choose Linkage from the Options menu. In the Linkage Properties dialog box, select the Export for ActionScript check box, and enter a linkage identifier in the Identifier field (**Figure 11.68**).

5. On a new line in the Script pane of the Actions panel, declare and instantiate a new `TextFormat` object, and set the `font` property of the object to the font you marked for export (**Figure 11.69**).

```
1  var sign:TextField = _root.createTextField("blink_txt", 1, 200, 150, 10, 10);
2  sign.text = "Open 24 hours! Visit us!";
3  sign.autoSize = "center";
4  sign.embedFonts = true;
```

Figure 11.67 Create the text field assigned to the variable `sign`, and set its `text`, `autosize`, and `embedFonts` properties.

Linkage Properties

Identifier: dreamer

AS 2.0 Class:

Linkage: ☑ Export for ActionScript
☐ Export for runtime sharing
☑ Export in first frame
☐ Import for runtime sharing

URL:

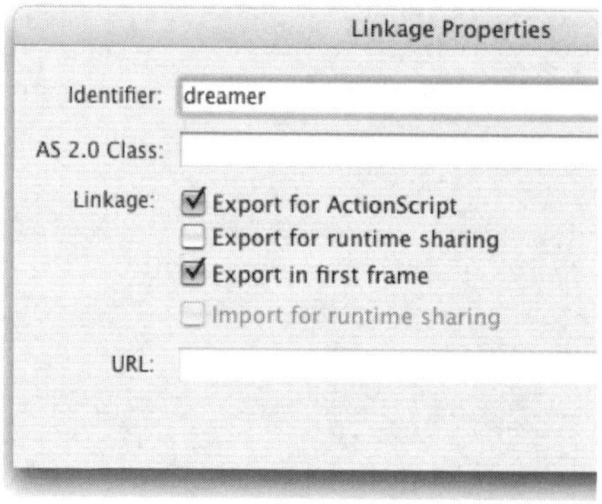

Figure 11.68 This font symbol is marked for export and identified as dreamer.

```
1  var sign:TextField = _root.createTextField("blink_txt", 1, 200, 150, 10, 10);
2  sign.text = "Open 24 hours! Visit us!";
3  sign.autoSize = "center";
4  sign.embedFonts = true;
5  var myFormat_fmt:TextFormat = new TextFormat();
6  myFormat_fmt.font = "dreamer";
```

Figure 11.69 A new TextFormat object is created, and "dreamer" is used as the new font.

```

function makeRed() {
    myFormat_fmt.color = 0xff0000;
    sign.setTextFormat(myFormat_fmt);
}

```

Figure 11.70 The function makeRed, which changes the text field sign to a red Dreamer font.

6. On a new line, choose Global Functions > Miscellaneous Functions > setInterval.
7. For the parameters of the `setInterval` statement, enter `makeRed`, followed by a comma and then 100.

   The function `makeRed` will be invoked every 100 milliseconds.
8. On a new line again, choose Global Functions > Miscellaneous Functions > setInterval.
9. For the parameters of this `setInterval` statement, enter `makeBlue`, followed by a comma and then 200.

   The function `makeBlue` will be invoked every 200 milliseconds.
10. On a new line, choose Statements > User-Defined Functions > function. Enter the name `makeRed`.

    Your `makeRed` function is created.
11. Within the function, add a statement to assign the value `0xff0000` to the `color` property of your `TextFormat` object.
12. On the next line within the function, enter the name of your text field, followed by a period. Choose ActionScript 2.0 Classes > Movie > TextField > Methods > setTextFormat.

    For the parameter of the method `setTextFormat()`, enter the name of your `TextFormat` object.

    When the `makeRed` function is invoked, your text field turns red (**Figure 11.70**).
13. Repeat steps 10–12 to create the function `makeBlue`. For the `color` property of the `TextFormat` object, use the hex code `0x0000FF`.

    When the `makeBlue` function is invoked, your text field turns blue.

continues on next page

14. On a new line, enter `_root`. Choose ActionScript 2.0 Classes > Movie > MovieClip > Event Handlers > onEnterFrame.

15. Within the curly braces of the `onEnterFrame` event handler, enter a statement to increase the `size` property of the `TextFormat` object by 1, and then call the `setTextFormat()` method again (**Figure 11.71**).

    The `onEnterFrame` handler continuously increases the font size of your text field.

16. Test your movie (**Figure 11.72**).

```
var sign:TextField = _root.createTextField("blink_txt", 1, 200, 150, 10, 10);
sign.text = "Open 24 hours! Visit us!";
sign.autoSize = "center";
sign.embedFonts = true;
var myFormat_fmt:TextFormat = new TextFormat();
myFormat_fmt.font = "dreamer";

setInterval(makeRed, 100);
setInterval(makeBlue, 200);

function makeRed() {
    myFormat_fmt.color = 0xff0000;
    sign.setTextFormat(myFormat_fmt);
}

function makeBlue() {
    myFormat_fmt.color = 0x0000ff;
    sign.setTextFormat(myFormat_fmt);
}

_root.onEnterFrame = function() {
    myFormat_fmt.size++;
    sign.setTextFormat(myFormat_fmt);
};
```

Figure 11.71 The full script. The functions `makeRed` and `makeBlue` are invoked alternately by the `setInterval` actions, which change the formatting to make the text blink. At the same time, the `onEnterFrame` handler continuously increases the size of the text.

Open 24 hours! Visit us!
Open 24 hours! Visit us!

Figure 11.72 The text field animates by growing and blinking red and blue.

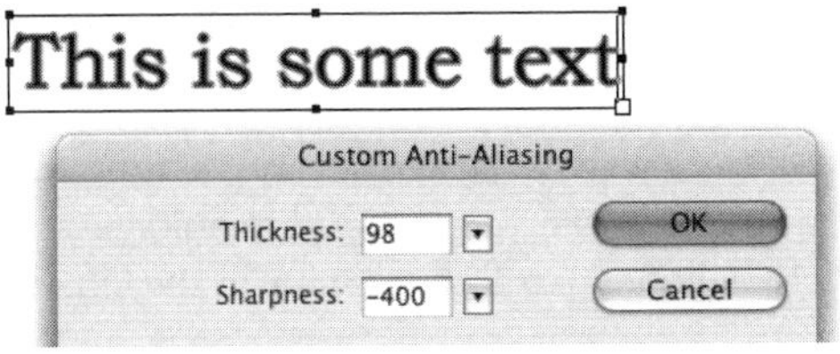

Figure 11.73 The Custom Anti-Aliasing dialog box allows you to experiment to find the best values to use for the `thickness` and `sharpness` properties of your text field.

Text field anti-aliasing

Putting text on a computer screen involves two key things—you want the text to look good, to have smooth edges and not look jagged or pixelated, and you also want the text to be easy to read. *Anti-aliasing* is a technique that is used to make text look smooth and to maintain readability by modifying the edges of the characters.

Flash 8 includes a new anti-aliasing technology known as FlashType that provides industry-leading text-rendering capabilities; it yields smooth-looking text that's also easy to read on the computer screen. In ActionScript, you can turn on FlashType text rendering for your text field by setting its `antiAliasType` property to `"advanced"`. To use advanced anti-aliasing, you must embed the font outlines for text fields placed on the Stage during authoring. For text fields that are created dynamically, you must create a Font symbol in the Library and set the `embedFonts` property of your `TextField` object to `true`.

With FlashType turned on, the quality of the text in your text field will probably improve; but depending on the font and size you're using, you may want to make small adjustments to how Flash displays your text. Two additional properties of the `TextField` class, `sharpness` and `thickness`, give you precise control over the anti-aliasing of your text so you can adjust it to match your needs.

How do you know what values to use for `sharpness` and `thickness`? To avoid tedious trial and error, experiment in the Flash authoring tool. With a text field selected on the Stage, choose Custom in the "Anti-aliasing option" pull-down menu. In the dialog box, adjust the Thickness and Sharpness values. As you do so, you can see a real-time preview of your text on the Stage, allowing you to easily find values that suit your text (**Figure 11.73**).

To set anti-aliasing for a text field:

1. As described in previous tasks, choose a font and add it to the Library as a font symbol. Make sure to choose Export for ActionScript and give it a linkage identifier.
2. Select the first keyframe, and open the Actions panel.
3. In the Script pane, enter code to create a text field using a `createTextField()` method call on the root Timeline.
4. Enter code to add text to your `TextField` object by assigning a value to its `text` property.
5. Add a statement to set the `embedFonts` property of your `TextField` object to `true`.

   The text field is created and is ready to be formatted (**Figure 11.74**).
6. On a new line, declare and instantiate a new `TextFormat` object.
7. Enter a statement to set the `TextFormat` object's `font` property to the linkage identifier of the font symbol in the Library.
8. Enter additional statements to set other formatting properties for your text, as desired.
9. On a new line, assign the `TextFormat` object to the text field by calling the `setTextFormat()` method on the text field (**Figure 11.75**).

   Remember to use your `TextFormat` object as the parameter of the `setTextFormat` method.

```
var myTF:TextField = _root.createTextField("myTF_txt", 1, 100, 100, 350, 50);
myTF.text = "This is a message from Flash";
myTF.embedFonts = true;
```

Figure 11.74 A new text field is created, assigned text, and set to use an embedded font.

```

var myFormat_fmt:TextFormat = new TextFormat();
myFormat_fmt.font = "Bookman24";
myFormat_fmt.size = 24;
myTF.setTextFormat(myFormat_fmt);
```

Figure 11.75 This example creates a `TextFormat` object, sets its `font` property to the Library font Bookman24, sets the `size` to 24 point, and assigns the `TextFormat` object to the text field named `myTF`.

```
myTF.antiAliasType = "advanced";
myTF.sharpness = 50;
```

Figure 11.76 The text field's `antiAliasType` is set to `"advanced"`, enabling FlashType anti-aliasing, and its `sharpness` is increased to 50.

10. On the next line, enter the name of your text field, followed by a period. Choose ActionScript 2.0 Classes > Movie > TextField > Properties > antiAliasType.

11. On the same line, enter an equals sign and the text `"advanced"`.

    This statement sets the `antiAliasType` property to advanced anti-aliasing (FlashType).

12. If desired, add statements to set the thickness and sharpness properties of the `TextField` object, to alter the anti-aliasing of the text (**Figure 11.76**).

13. Test your movie.

    The text field appears on the Stage, formatted according to the settings you gave, and rendered using the advanced (FlashType) anti-aliasing technology.

Formatting Text Fields from an External Style Sheet

External Cascading Style Sheets (CSS) help designers and developers maintain consistency across multiple HTML documents. Flash also allows you to tap into this resource to help maintain the same formatting rules—such as font size, color, and other formatting styles—across all associated dynamic or input text fields. You can even apply styles defined by the style sheet to a text field that contains text structured as HTML or XML.

First, you must create a new style sheet object from the `StyleSheet` class, which is a child or *inner class* of the `TextField` class:

```
import TextField.StyleSheet;
var myStyle:StyleSheet = new StyleSheet();
```

Next, load an external CSS document containing the style rules to apply to your text using the `StyleSheet` class's `load()` method:

```
myStyle.load("mystyles.css");
```

You can determine when the external style sheet has loaded by assigning an `onLoad` event handler function to the `StyleSheet` object.

Finally, apply those styles to your text field by assigning your style sheet object to the text field's `styleSheet` property:

```
myTextField_txt.styleSheet = myStyle;
```

The following common CSS tags are supported by text fields:

- `font-family` specifies the font to be used.
- `font-size` sets the size of the font.
- `font-weight` sets the weight of the font.
- `font-style` sets the style of the font (normal, italic, or oblique).
- `text-align` aligns the text.
- `text-indent` indents the first line of text in a text field.

By writing HTML-formatted text in the Script pane and assigning a `StyleSheet` object to the `styleSheet` property of the text field object, you can control its format options through an external CSS document. This feature can be very convenient; you don't have to open the Flash file to make text style changes because it can all be done inside one CSS document. In addition, the CSS document applies the same styles to both your HTML pages and your Flash movies.

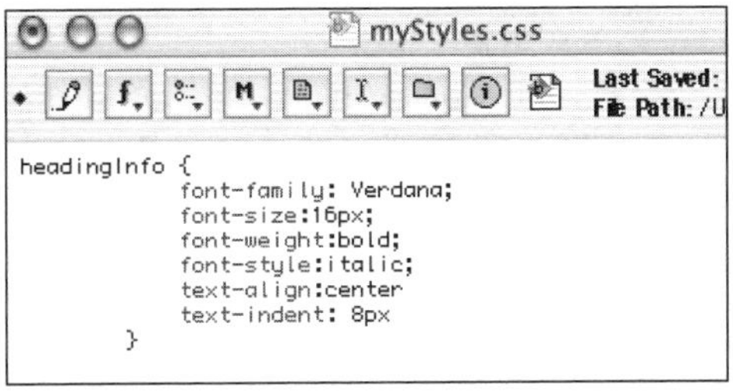
myStyles.css
Last Saved:
File Path: /U
headingInfo {
font-family: Verdana;
font-size:16px;
font-weight:bold;
font-style:italic;
text-align:center
text-indent: 8px
}

Figure 11.77 In an external cascading style sheet, a selector is defined with the name of `headingInfo`.

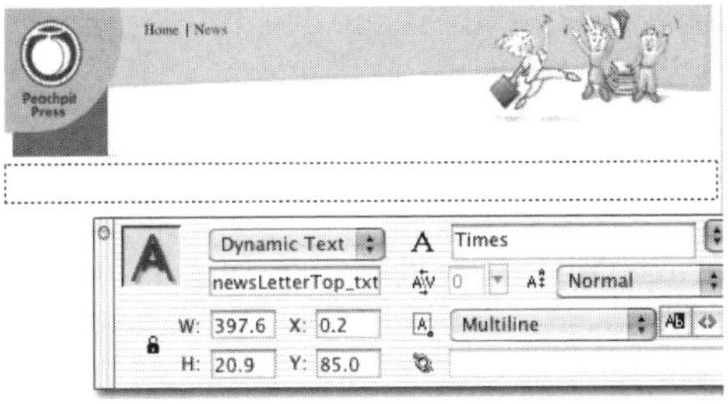
Dynamic Text
newsLetterTop_txt
Times
Normal
Multiline
W: 397.6
X: 0.2
H: 20.9
Y: 85.0

Figure 11.78 An instance of `newsLetterTop_txt` dynamic text field is defined.

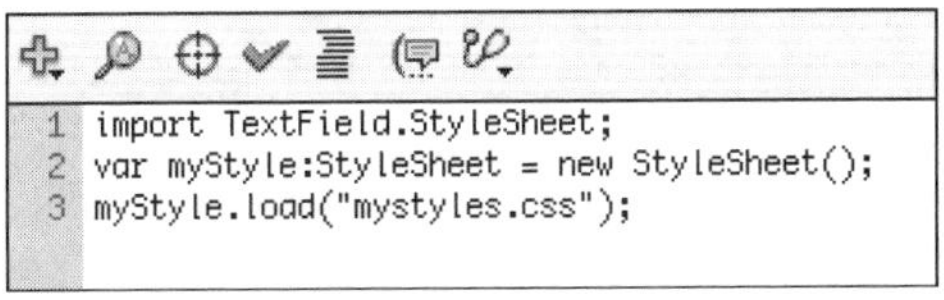
import TextField.StyleSheet;
var myStyle:StyleSheet = new StyleSheet();
myStyle.load("mystyles.css");

Figure 11.79 Load the external style sheet document called mystyles.css into the new style sheet object. The mystyles.css document in this example must reside in the same folder as the Flash movie.

To display HTML text with CSS formatting:

1. Open a text-editing application or a WYSIWYG HTML editor, and create your CSS document.
2. Save the text file (**Figure 11.77**).

   For external Cascading Style Sheet files, use a .css extension.
3. In Flash, choose the Text tool, and drag out a large text field.
4. In the Property inspector, choose Dynamic Text, and enter an instance name (**Figure 11.78**).
5. Select the first keyframe in the root Timeline, and open the Actions panel.
6. Enter an `import` statement for the `TextField.StyleSheet` class.
7. On the next line, declare a variable with the data type `StyleSheet`, followed by an equals sign. Choose ActionScript 2.0 Classes > Movie > TextField > StyleSheet > "new StyleSheet".
8. On the next line, enter the name of your style sheet object, and then choose ActionScript 2.0 Classes > Movie > TextField > StyleSheet > Methods > load.
9. For the parameter of the `load` method, enter the path to the filename of your external CSS document. Make sure that the path is surrounded by quotation marks (**Figure 11.79**).

   The external CSS begins loading into the style sheet object.

continues on next page

10. On the next line, enter the name of your dynamic text field, followed by a period. Choose ActionScript 2.0 Classes > TextField > StyleSheet > Event Handlers > onLoad.

11. Between the curly braces of the `onLoad` event handler, assign your `StyleSheet` object to the text field's `styleSheet` property, assign the value `true` to its `html` property, and assign XML-formatted text to its `text` property (**Figure 11.80**).

12. Test your movie.

Flash loads and applies the style defined in the external CSS to the HTML-formatted text in your dynamic text (**Figure 11.81**).

✔ Tip

- To utilize the formatting created in the external CSS, you must begin and end your XML-formatted text with an element (tag) whose name matches the selector name that was used in the style sheet. In this example, the selector name is `headingInfo` (see Figures 11.77 and 11.80).

```
import TextField.StyleSheet;
var myStyle:StyleSheet = new StyleSheet();
myStyle.load("mystyles.css");
myStyle.onLoad = function(success:Boolean) {
    newsLetterTop_txt.styleSheet = myStyle;
    newsLetterTop_txt.html = true;
    newsLetterTop_txt.text = "<headingInfo>Welcome to the Peachpit Press Newsletter</headingInfo>";
};
```

Figure 11.80 Assign the `myStyle` style sheet object to the `styleSheet` property of your dynamic text field. Set the `html` property to `true`, and assign XML-formatted text to the `text` property.

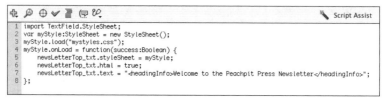

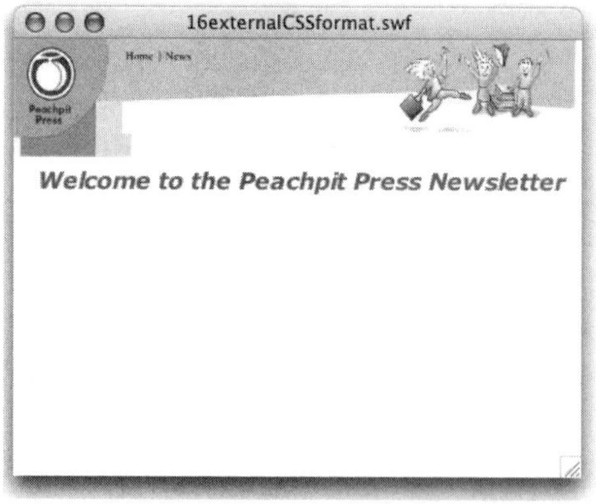

Figure 11.81 The text displays in the style defined in the external CSS.

Manipulating Text Field Contents

When you define a text field as an input text field, you give your viewers the freedom to enter and edit information. You've seen how this information can be used in expressions with other actions or concatenated and displayed in dynamic text fields. Often, however, you need to analyze the text entered by the viewer before using it. You may want to tease out certain words or identify the location of a particular character or sequence of characters. If you require viewers to enter an email address in an input field, for example, you can check to see whether that address is in the correct format by looking for the @ symbol. Or check a customer's telephone number, find out the area code based on the first three digits, and personalize a directory or news listing with local interests.

This kind of parsing, manipulation, and control of the information within text fields is done with a combination of the `Selection` class and the `String` class. The `Selection` class lets you control the focus of multiple text fields and the position of the insertion point within a focused text field. The `String` class lets you retrieve and change the characters inside a `String` object, such as the `text` property of a text field.

The Selection Class

The `Selection` class controls the selection of characters in text fields. You don't need to create an instance of the `Selection` class to use its methods. Because there can be only one insertion-point position or selection in a Flash movie at a time, the `Selection` class always refers to that one position or selection.

Using the methods of the `Selection` class, you can affect a text field in two ways: You can control which text field is currently active, or *focused*, and you can control where the insertion point is positioned within that text field. **Table 11.3** summarizes important methods of the `Selection` class.

Table 11.3

Methods of the Selection Class

Method	Description
`getBeginIndex()`	Retrieves the index of the character at the beginning of the selection
`getEndIndex()`	Retrieves the index of the character at the end of the selection
`getCaretIndex()`	Retrieves the index of the insertion-point position
`setSelection (`*`beginIndex`*`,` *`endIndex`*`)`	Positions the selection at a specified *`beginIndex`* and *`endIndex`*
`getFocus()`	Retrieves the instance name of the active text field
`setFocus (`*`instanceName`*`)`	Sets the focus on the text field specified in *`instanceName`*

Controlling the Focus of Text Fields

You can have only one focused object on the Stage at any time. If you have multiple text fields on the Stage, you must be able to control which one is focused before you can retrieve or assign the insertion-point location or selection. The `getFocus()` and `setFocus()` methods of the `Selection` class let you do this.

The method `getFocus()` returns a string containing the absolute path to the text field starting with the level. If the selected text field `yourName_txt` is on the root Timeline, for example, and you call the `getFocus()` method, the returned value is `"_level0.yourName_txt"`.

It's important to remember that the returned value is a string and that the `_level0` term is used. If you compare the `getFocus()` method with a pathname using `_root` or `this`, or if you forget the quotation marks, then Flash won't recognize the path. The `getFocus()` method returns a value of `null` if there is no focused text field on the Stage.

The `setFocus()` method takes one parameter, which is the text field you want to give focus to. You can use a string containing the path of the text field, or you can pass the actual object. `setFocus(scoreboard_txt)`, for example, makes the text field `scoreboard_txt` active.

To set the focus of a text field:

1. Select the Text tool in the Tools panel, and drag out two separate text fields on the Stage.
2. In the Property inspector, for each text field choose Input Text, give the text field an instance name, and click the Show Border button.
3. Select the first frame of the main Timeline, and open the Actions panel.
4. Declare and instantiate a new Object variable to use as a listener object (**Figure 11.82**).
5. Define an `onKeyDown` method on your listener.
6. Within the `onKeyDown` event handler, choose Statements > Conditions/Loops > if.
7. For the condition of the `if` statement, enter `Key.isDown(Key.LEFT)`.
8. With your pointer between the curly braces of the `if` statement, choose ActionScript 2.0 Classes > Movie > Selection > Methods > setFocus.

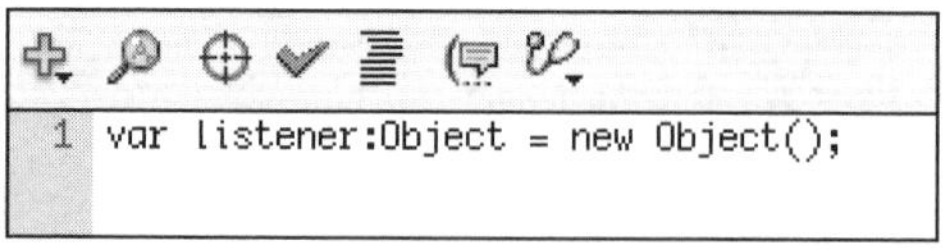

Figure 11.82 Create the listener object called `listener`.

```
var listener:Object = new Object();
listener.onKeyDown = function() {
    if (Key.isDown(Key.LEFT)) {
        Selection.setFocus(displayLeft_txt);
    }
};
```

Figure 11.83 When the left arrow key is pressed, Flash focuses the first input text field, `displayLeft_txt`.

```
    if (Key.isDown(Key.RIGHT)) {
        Selection.setFocus(displayRight_txt);
    }
```

Figure 11.84 When the right arrow key is pressed, Flash focuses the second input text field, `displayRIght_txt`.

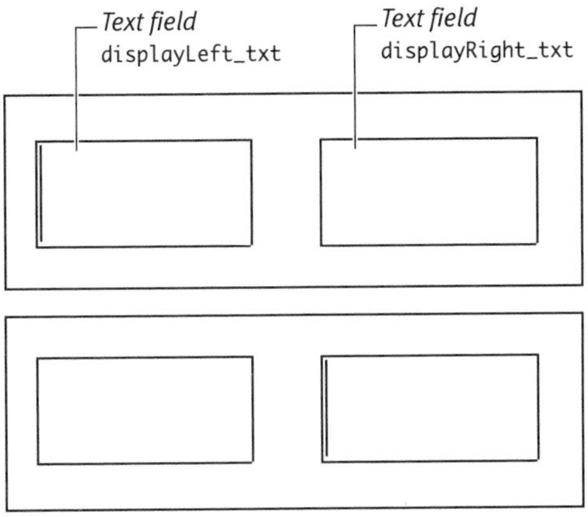

Figure 11.85 The focus of text fields is controlled by the left arrow and right arrow keys. At top, the left text field is focused (the blinking insertion point is visible inside the text field). At bottom, the right text field is focused.

9. For the parameter of the `setFocus` method, enter the name of the first input text field (**Figure 11.83**).

   When the left arrow key is pressed, Flash focuses the first input text field.

10. Place your pointer on a new line outside the closing brace of your `if` statement, and choose Statements > Conditions/Loops > if.

11. For the condition of your second `if` statement, enter `Key.isDown(Key.RIGHT)`.

12. Between the curly braces of the second `if` statement, choose ActionScript 2.0 Classes > Movie > Selection > Methods > setFocus.

13. For the parameter of the second `setFocus` method, enter the name of the second input text field (**Figure 11.84**).

    When the right arrow key is pressed, Flash focuses the second input text field.

14. On the line following the event handler method, add a call to the `Key` class's `addListener()` method to register your listener.

15. Test your movie.

    Flash detects when the right arrow or the left arrow key is pressed on the keyboard and changes the selected text field (**Figure 11.85**). If you disable the automatic focusing with the Tab key, you can build your own way to navigate and select multiple text fields.

To get the focus of a text field:

1. Continuing with the file you created in the preceding task, place your pointer on a new line after the closing brace of the second `if` statement (inside the event handler function).
2. Choose Global Functions > Miscellaneous Functions > trace.
3. With your pointer between the parentheses of the `trace` statement, choose ActionScript 2.0 Classes > Movie > Selection > Methods > getFocus (**Figure 11.86**).
4. Test your movie.

   When you use the right and left keys to change the focus of the text fields, Flash displays their target paths in the Output panel (**Figure 11.87**).

```
    }
    trace(Selection.getFocus());
};
```

Figure 11.86 Add a `trace` statement to display the name of the focused text field.

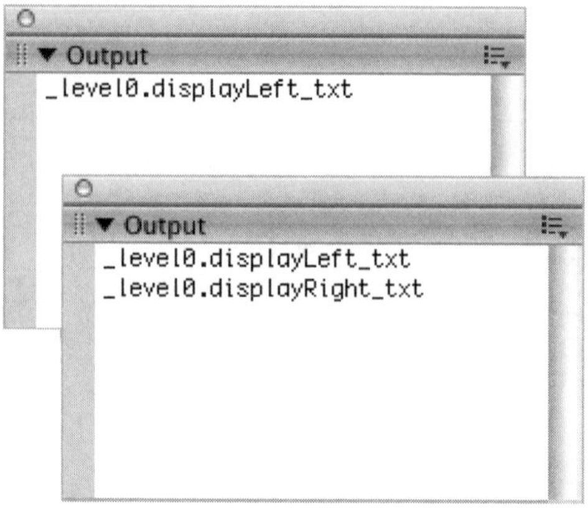

Figure 11.87 The Output panel when the left arrow key is pressed (top) and when the right arrow key is pressed immediately afterward (bottom).

Controlling the Selection Within Text Fields

When you have a focused text field, either by using ActionScript or by a viewer's clicking it with the pointer, you can control the selection or insertion-point position inside it. This technique lets you direct your viewers' attention to particular characters or words they've entered, perhaps to point out errors or misspellings. It also lets you keep track of the insertion-point position, much as the `_xmouse` and `_ymouse` properties let you keep track of the location of the viewer's mouse pointer. You can also select certain parts of the text field and replace just those portions with different text.

The index or position of each character in a string is numbered and used in the methods of the `Selection` class, just as index values are used in the `setTextFormat()` method. The first character in a `String` is assigned the index of 0, the second character is 1, and so on. If you retrieve the selection index for a text field that doesn't have focus (the insertion point isn't positioned within the text field), Flash returns a value of -1.

The task "To identify the position of the insertion point in a text field" demonstrates how the `getCaretIndex()` method of the `Selection` class retrieves the position of the user's cursor (known as the *caret*) within a text field.

In addition to identifying the location of the insertion point, you can cause a portion of the text field's contents to be selected with `Selection.setSelection()` and can replace a selected set of text with the `TextField` method `replaceSel()`. In the task "To change the selection in a text field," you'll replace a portion of the text field with different text when you click a button.

To identify the position of the insertion point in a text field:

1. Select the Text tool, and drag out a text field on the Stage.
2. In the Property inspector, choose Input Text and Multiline from the pull-down menus, give the input text field an instance name, and click the Show Border button (**Figure 11.88**).
3. Select the Text tool, and drag out a second text field on the Stage.
4. In the Property inspector, choose Dynamic Text and Multiline from the pull-down menus, give the dynamic text field an instance name, and click the Show Border button (**Figure 11.89**).
5. Select the first frame of the main Timeline, and open the Actions panel.
6. Enter `_root`, and choose ActionScript 2.0 Classes > Movie > MovieClip > Event Handlers > onEnterFrame.
7. Within the `onEnterFrame` event handler, enter the instance name of your dynamic text field, followed by a period and the property `text`.
8. On the same line, enter an equals sign, and then choose ActionScript 2.0 Classes > Movie > Selection > Methods > getCaretIndex (**Figure 11.90**).
9. Test your movie.

   Initially, the dynamic text field displays –1 because the input text field isn't focused. When your viewer begins to type in the input text field, Flash updates the dynamic text field to display the insertion point's position (**Figure 11.91**).

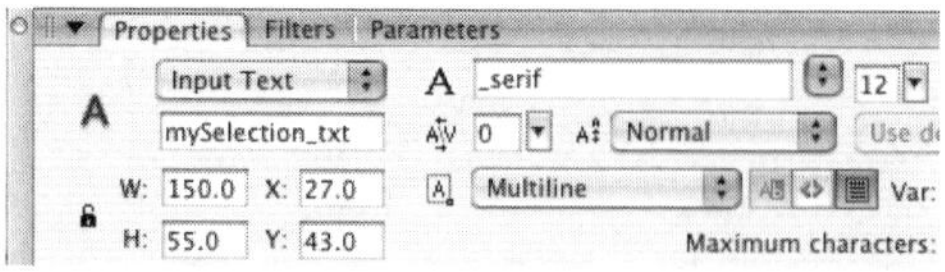

Figure 11.88 Enter `mySelection_txt` as the instance name for your input text field.

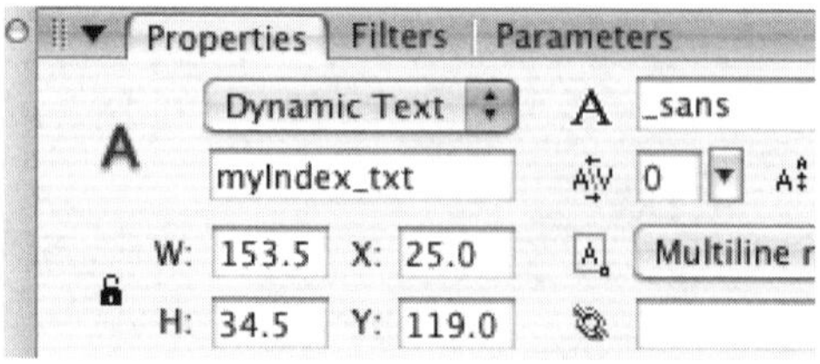

Figure 11.89 Enter `myIndex_txt` as the instance name for your dynamic text field.

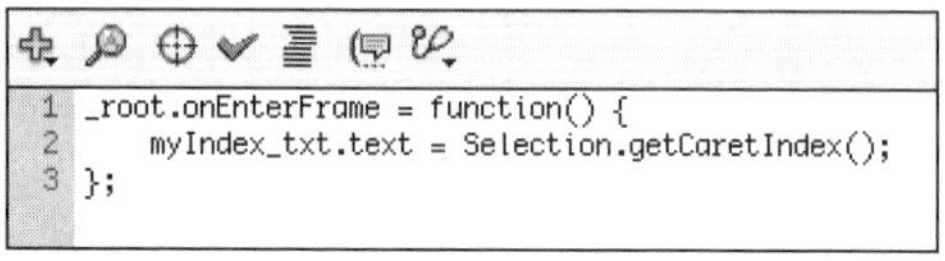

_root.onEnterFrame = function() {
myIndex_txt.text = Selection.getCaretIndex();
};

Figure 11.90 Flash assigns the position of the insertion point, or caret, to the contents of the text field `myIndex_txt`.

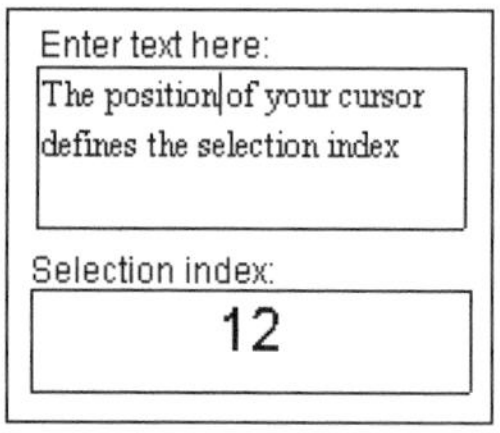

Figure 11.91 The current index of the insertion point is 12. The first letter, *T*, is 0. The space between *position* and *of* is 12.

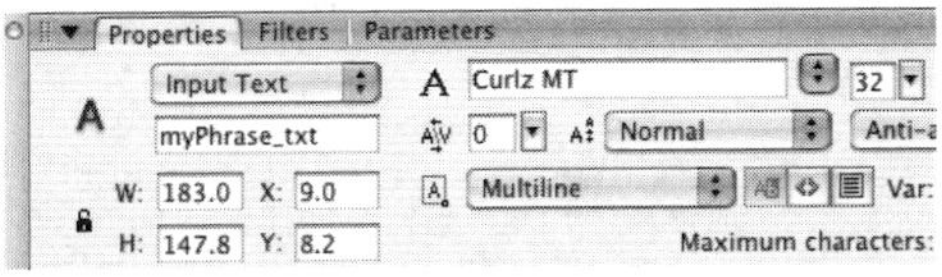

Figure 11.92 Create the text field called `myPhrase_txt`.

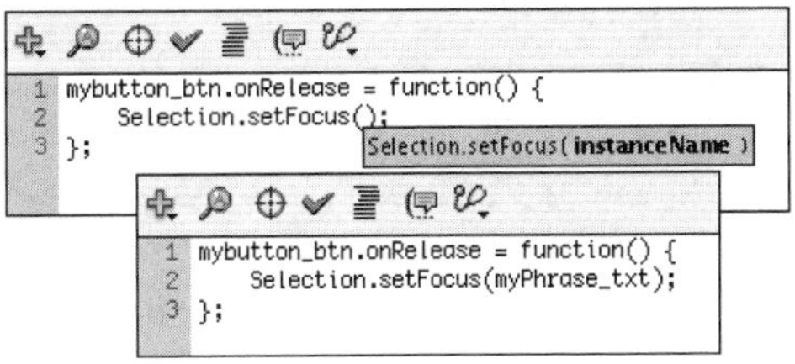

Figure 11.93 Set the focus to the text field `myPhrase_txt`.

To change the selection in a text field:

1. Select the Text tool in the Tools panel, and drag out a text field on the Stage.
2. Enter the text `Carrots are good to eat.`
3. In the Property inspector, choose Input Text and Multiline, enter an instance name, and embed the font that you want to use (**Figure 11.92**).
4. Create a button symbol, place an instance on the Stage, and give it a name in the Property inspector.
5. Select the first frame of the main Timeline, and open the Actions panel.
6. Create an `onRelease` event handler assigned to your button.
7. Within the `onRelease` event handler, choose ActionScript 2.0 Classes > Movie > Selection > Methods > setFocus.
8. For the parameter of the `setFocus` method, enter the instance name of your text field (**Figure 11.93**).

   When you click this button, Flash focuses the text field. (The focus moves from your button to the text field.)
9. On a new line, choose ActionScript 2.0 Classes > Movie > Selection > Methods > setSelection.

continues on next page

10. For the parameter of the `setSelection` method, enter `0`, followed by a comma and then 7 (**Figure 11.94**).

    The `setSelection()` method selects all the characters between the indexes of its first parameter and its second parameter, including the character whose index is the first parameter. This `setSelection()` statement selects the first seven characters (index 0 to index 6) of the text field.

11. On the next line, enter the name of your text field, followed by a period. Choose ActionScript 2.0 Classes > Movie > TextField > Methods > replaceSel.

12. For the parameter of the `replaceSel` method, enter text to replace the selected text (**Figure 11.95**).

    In this example, the replacement word is *Burritos*. Make sure the replacement word is in quotation marks.

13. Test your movie.

    When you click the button, the `setSelection()` method selects the word *Carrots*, and the `replaceSel()` method replaces it with the word *Burritos* (**Figure 11.96**).

```
mybutton_btn.onRelease = function() {
    Selection.setFocus(myPhrase_txt);
    Selection.setSelection(0, 7);
};
```

Figure 11.94 Select everything between index 0 (inclusive) and index 7. The word *Carrots* is selected.

```
mybutton_btn.onRelease = function() {
    Selection.setFocus(myPhrase_txt);
    Selection.setSelection(0, 7);
    myPhrase_txt.replaceSel("Burritos");
};
```

Figure 11.95 Replace the selection with the word *Burritos*.

Figure 11.96 The original text field (top) and the text field after the selection is replaced (bottom). Notice that the insertion point is positioned just after the new selection.

Table 11.4

Selection and TextField Events

Event	Description
onSetFocus	A new text field receives focus. When onSetFocus is used as a TextField event, the handler can take one parameter: oldFocus. When onSetFocus is used as a Selection event, the handler can take two parameters—oldFocus and newFocus—and requires a listener.
onChanged	The contents of a text field change. This TextField event can also be assigned to a listener.
onScroller	One of the text field properties—scroll or hscroll—changes. This TextField event can also be assigned to a listener.
onKillFocus	A text field loses focus. The handler for this TextField event can take one parameter: newFocus.

Detecting Changes in the Text Field

Often, you want to capture information from a text field only when the viewer has entered something new. Or you want to respond when a viewer has selected a particular text field. You can detect these changes in a text field with event handlers and listeners. Flash provides a variety of them through the Selection class and the TextField class (**Table 11.4**).

In this section, you'll look at two important TextField events: onSetFocus and onChanged.

The onSetFocus event happens when a text field receives focus because a viewer clicks inside the text field or presses the Tab key to activate the text field. It's also triggered when the setFocus() ActionScript command sets focus in the text field. Each text field has its own onSetFocus event handler. You can use an optional parameter in an onSetFocus event handler that can tell you what the previously focused text field was, as in this example:

```
myTF_txt.onSetFocus =
function(oldFocus:Object) {
    trace ("you came from" + oldFocus);
};
```

In this handler, when you focus the text field myTF_txt, the Output window displays a message telling you which object was previously focused. If no object was previously focused, oldFocus contains null.

The onChanged event handler happens when the viewer changes the contents of a text field. A viewer can click inside a text field and select portions of the text, but the onChanged event handler is triggered only when the viewer adds to, deletes, or changes its contents.

In the following task, you'll create multiple input text fields. You'll detect which text field your viewer selects and display a customized message in a dynamic text field.

To detect the focus of a text field:

1. Select the Text tool, and drag out three text fields on the Stage.
2. In the Property inspector, set each text field as Input Text and Single Line, and enter an instance name for each text field.
3. Select the Text tool, and drag out a fourth text field on the Stage.
4. In the Property inspector, choose Dynamic Text and Multiline from the pull-down menus, and enter an instance name for this dynamic text field (**Figure 11.97**).
5. Select the first frame of the main Timeline, and open the Actions panel.
6. Enter the name of your first input text field. Choose ActionScript 2.0 Classes > Movie > TextField > Event Handlers > onSetFocus.
7. Within the `onSetFocus` event handler, assign a message to the `text` property of your dynamic text field that gives instructions to the viewer for the selected text field (**Figure 11.98**).

   Make sure the message to be displayed is in quotation marks.
8. On a new line, create another `onSetFocus` event handler for your second input text field, as you did in step 6.
9. Within the second `onSetFocus` event handler, assign a message to the `text` property of the dynamic text field, giving instructions to the viewer (**Figure 11.99**).

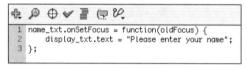

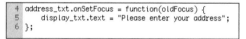

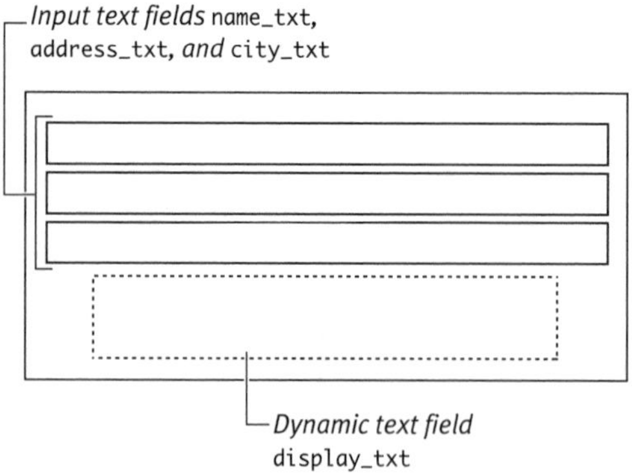

Figure 11.97 Create three input text fields (top) and one dynamic text field (bottom).

```
name_txt.onSetFocus = function(oldFocus) {
    display_txt.text = "Please enter your name";
};
```

Figure 11.98 When the input text field `name_txt` is focused, the bottom dynamic text field tells viewers to enter their name.

```
address_txt.onSetFocus = function(oldFocus) {
    display_txt.text = "Please enter your address";
};
```

Figure 11.99 When the input text field `address_txt` is focused, the bottom dynamic text field tells viewers to enter their address.

```
name_txt.onSetFocus = function(oldFocus) {
    display_txt.text = "Please enter your name";
};
address_txt.onSetFocus = function(oldFocus) {
    display_txt.text = "Please enter your address";
};
city_txt.onSetFocus = function(oldFocus) {
    display_txt.text = "Please enter your city";
};
display_txt.text = "Please select a text field";
```

Figure 11.100 The full script. A different message appears for each focused input text field, and another message initially appears before any text field is selected.

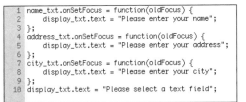

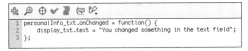

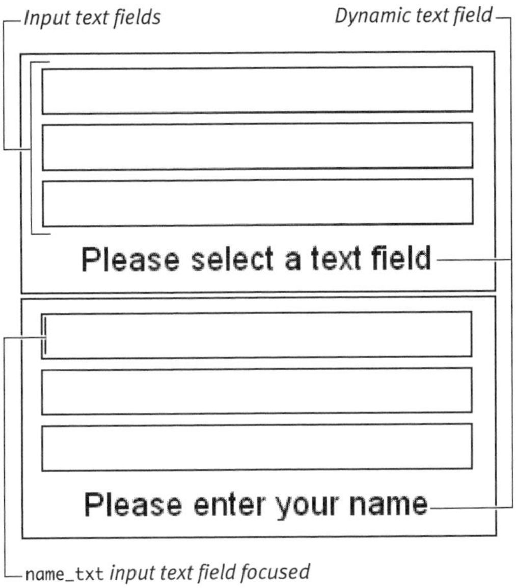

Figure 11.101 This example shows how the movie appears initially (top) and after the first text field is focused (bottom).

```
personalInfo_txt.onChanged = function() {
    display_txt.text = "You changed something in the text field";
};
```

Figure 11.102 When the contents of the text field `personalInfo_txt` change, this event handler will be triggered.

10. Add a third `onSetFocus` handler to detect when the third input text field has received focus, and have the dynamic text field change in response.
11. Add a statement outside all the `onSetFocus` handlers that gives initial instructions to the viewer before any of the text fields receive focus.

    The final script looks like **Figure 11.100**.
12. Test your movie.

    When the viewer first sees your Flash movie, none of the text fields is focused, so the message in the dynamic text field tells the viewer what to do. When the viewer selects a text field, Flash detects which one it is and displays a custom message (**Figure 11.101**).

To detect a change in the contents of a text field:

1. Select the Text tool, and drag out a text field on the Stage.
2. In the Property inspector, choose Input Text and Single Line from the pull-down menus, and enter an instance name for this input text field.
3. Select the first frame of the main Timeline, and open the Actions panel.
4. Enter the name of your text field, followed by a period. Choose ActionScript 2.0 Classes > Movie > TextField > Event Handlers > onChanged.
5. Assign actions within the curly braces of the onChanged handler (**Figure 11.102**).

   Any additions, deletions, or changes in the contents of this text field will trigger the actions within this handler.

✔ Tip

- The onChanged event doesn't detect changes in a text field via ActionScript. Only user-entered changes trigger the event.

The String Class

You can apply the methods and properties of the String class to analyze and manipulate string data types. The String class can tell you the position of a certain character, for example, or what character occupies a certain position. You can also dissect just a portion of the string and put that part, called a *substring*, into a new string, or you can concatenate substrings and strings. You can even change the lowercase and uppercase styles of different parts of the string. **Table 11.5** summarizes several methods and properties of the String class.

When you're working with the contents of a text field, you can easily perform all this parsing and shuffling of Strings because the text property of the TextField class is an instance of the String class.

Like those of the Selection and TextField class, the indexes of the String class are based on the positions of the characters in the string; the first character is assigned an index of 0.

✔ Tip

- Flash also includes a built-in String() function to convert the value of any variable, expression, or object to a String object before applying the methods of the String class. If your variable radioButton is a Boolean data type, the statement String(radioButton) returns a String object with the value "true" or "false". Now you can manipulate the actual characters with the methods of the String class.

Table 11.5

String Class Methods and Properties

Method or Property	Description
indexOf(*searchString*, *fromIndex*)	Searches the String and returns the index of the first occurrence of a substring specified in the parameter *searchString*. The optional *fromIndex* parameter sets the starting position of the search.
lastIndexOf(*searchString*, *fromIndex*)	Searches the String and returns the index of the last occurrence of a substring specified in the parameter *searchString*. The optional *fromIndex* parameter sets the starting position of the search.
charAt(*index*)	Returns the character at the specified index position.
substring(*indexA*, *indexB*)	Returns a String that is the portion of the original String between positions *indexA* and *indexB*.
substr(*start*, *length*)	Returns a String containing the portion of the original String with the specified length from the start index.
concat(*string1*,...,*stringN*)	Concatenates the specified Strings.
toLowerCase()	Returns a copy of the original String that contains all lowercase characters.
toUpperCase()	Returns a copy of the original String that contains all uppercase characters.
length	A property that returns the length (number of characters) of the String.

Analyzing Strings

Use the methods of the `String` class to identify a character or characters in a `String`. The following tasks analyze input text fields to verify that the viewer has entered the required information.

To identify the position of a character:

1. Select the Text tool in the Tools panel, and drag out a text field on the Stage.
2. In the Property inspector, choose Input Text and Single Line from the pull-down menus, and enter an instance name for this input text field.
3. Create a button symbol, place an instance of it on the Stage, and give it a name in the Property inspector.
4. Select the first frame of the main Timeline, and open the Actions panel.
5. Assign an `onRelease` event handler to your button.
6. Within the `onRelease` event handler, declare a `Number` variable, and enter an equals sign.
7. On the same line, enter the name of your input text field, followed by a period and then the `text` property.
8. With your pointer next to the `text` property, choose ActionScript 2.0 Classes > Core > String > Methods > indexOf.
9. Between the parentheses of the `indexOf()` method, enter the character you want to find, surrounded by quotation marks (**Figure 11.103**).

   The `indexOf` method takes two parameters: `searchString` and `fromIndex`. The parameter `searchString` is the specific character you want to identify in the `String`. The parameter `fromIndex`, which is optional, is a `Number` representing the starting position for the search within the `String`.
10. Test your movie.

    When the user enters information in the input text field and clicks the button, Flash searches the contents of the input text field for the specified character and assigns its position to your variable. You can use this variable in the methods of the `Selection`, `TextField`, and `String` objects to modify the information further.


```
myButton_btn.onRelease = function() {
    var charPosition:Number = myString_txt.text.indexOf("%");
};
```

Figure 11.103 Call the `indexOf("%")` method of the `String` object `myString_txt.text` to search its contents for the % character. If that character is found, the index of its position within the text is assigned to the variable `charPosition`. If that character isn't found, –1 is assigned to the variable.

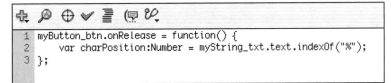

✔ Tips

- The opposite of the method `indexOf()` is `charAt()`. This method returns the character that occupies the index position you specify for a string. You could use this method to verify that the first, second, and third characters correspond to numbers for a certain area code of a telephone number, for example.
- If the character you search for with `indexOf()` occurs more than once in the string, Flash returns the index of only the first occurrence. Use the method `lastIndexOf()` to retrieve the last occurrence of the character.
- To retrieve all the occurrences of a certain character, you must use several iterations of the method `indexOf()`. Use its optional second parameter, `fromIndex`, which begins the search at a specific index. For example, if the text field `my_txt` contains the string `"home/images/vacation"`, consider this script:

  ```
  slash1 = my_txt.text.indexOf ("/")
  slash2 = my_txt.text.indexOf ("/",
  slash1 + 1)
  ```

  The first statement assigns the variable `slash1` to the first occurrence of the slash symbol in the string input (`slash1` is 4). The second statement searches for the slash symbol again but starts the search at the next character after the first slash (at index 5, or the *i* in *images*). By constructing a `while` or a `do while` loop, you can make Flash march down the string, starting new searches as it finds occurrences of the character. Do this until the returned value of the `indexOf()` method equals the value of the `lastIndexOf()` method.

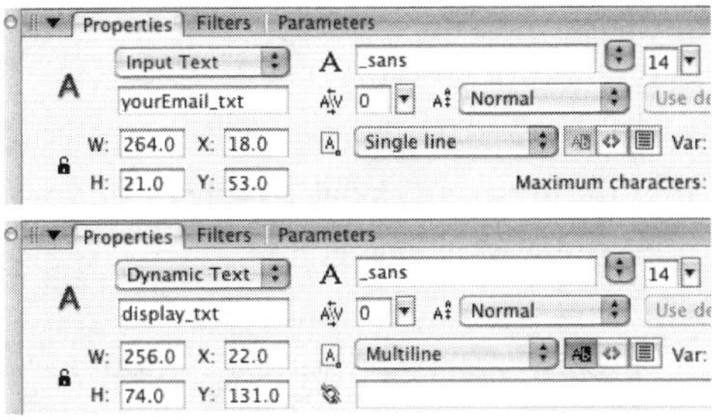

Figure 11.104 Enter `yourEmail_txt` as the instance name for your input text field, and enter `display_txt` as the instance name for your dynamic text field.

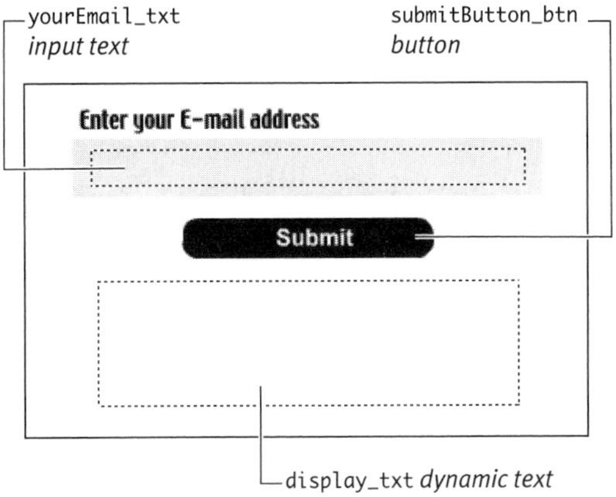

Figure 11.105 Place the input text field at the top, the button in the middle, and the dynamic text field at the bottom.

When a character isn't found in a String

If Flash searches a `String` with the `indexOf()` or `lastIndexOf()` method and doesn't find the specified character, it returns a value of –1. You can use this fact to check for missing characters within a string. For example, if `indexOf("%") == -1`, you know that the percent symbol is missing from the string. In the next task, you'll search an input text field for the @ symbol and the period to check whether an email address has been entered correctly.

To check for a missing character:

1. Select the Text tool, and drag out a text field on the Stage.
2. In the Property inspector, choose Input Text and Single Line from the pull-down menus, and enter an instance name for this input text field.

   The user will enter an e-mail address in this input text field.
3. Select the Text tool again, and drag out another text field on the Stage.
4. In the Property inspector, choose Dynamic Text and Multiline from the pull-down menus, and enter an instance name for this dynamic text field (**Figure 11.104**).

   You'll display feedback to the user in this dynamic text field.
5. Create a button symbol, place an instance of the button on the Stage between the input text field and the dynamic text field, and give the button a name in the Property inspector (**Figure 11.105**).

continues on next page

6. Select the first frame of the main Timeline, and open the Actions panel.
7. Assign an `onRelease` handler to the button.
8. Within the `onRelease` event handler, choose Statements > Conditions/ Loops > if.
9. For the condition of the `if` statement, enter the name of the input text field, followed by a period and then the property `text`.
10. With your insertion point immediately after the word `text`, choose ActionScript 2.0 Classes > Core > String > Methods > indexOf.
11. Between the parentheses of the `indexOf()` method, enter `"@"`.

    Make sure you include the quotation marks.

    Flash searches the input text field for the @ symbol.
12. Complete the rest of the condition so that the whole statement looks like the following:

    `yourEmail_txt.text.indexOf ("@") == -1`

    This condition is true if the @ symbol in the string within `yourEmail_txt.text` isn't present (**Figure 11.106**).
13. After the conditional statement, enter the logical `OR` operator, `||`.
14. Add a second condition that checks whether a period (.) isn't present in this string:

    `yourEmail_txt.text.indexOf (".") == -1`
15. Between the curly braces of the `if` statement, enter the name of your dynamic text field, followed by a period and then the `text` property.
16. Following the `text` property, enter an equals sign and a message that notifies your viewer of a problem with the input (**Figure 11.107**).
17. With your pointer positioned after the closing curly brace for the `if` statement, enter `else { }`.

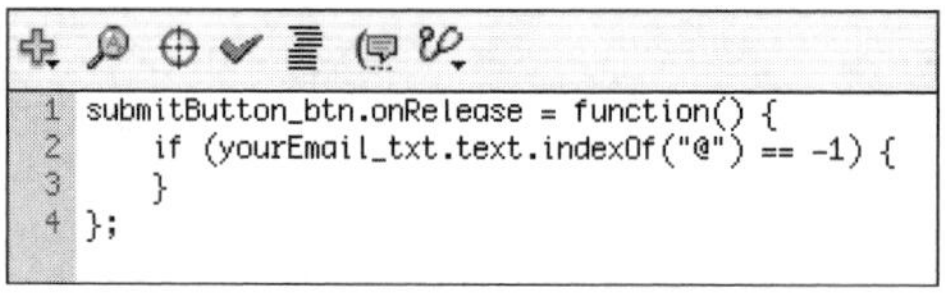

```
submitButton_btn.onRelease = function() {
    if (yourEmail_txt.text.indexOf("@") == -1) {
    }
};
```

Figure 11.106 If the @ symbol is missing from the string inside `yourEmail_txt.text`, this condition is true.

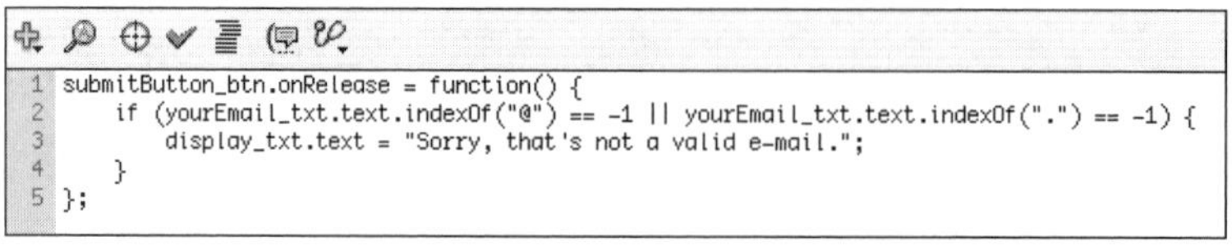

```
submitButton_btn.onRelease = function() {
    if (yourEmail_txt.text.indexOf("@") == -1 || yourEmail_txt.text.indexOf(".") == -1) {
        display_txt.text = "Sorry, that's not a valid e-mail.";
    }
};
```

Figure 11.107 The message in quotation marks appears in the dynamic text field `display_txt`.

18. Between the curly braces of the `else` statement, add a statement to assign an alternate message to the contents of the dynamic text field that thanks your viewer for submitting an email address (**Figure 11.108**).

19. Test your movie.

    When the viewer clicks the button after entering an email address in the input text field, Flash checks the string for both the @ symbol and a period and returns the indexes of those symbols. If either index is –1, the viewer receives a message that the input is incorrect. Otherwise, the viewer receives a thank-you message (**Figure 11.109**).

✔ Tip

- Use the `indexOf()` or `lastIndexOf()` method to check for a character or sequence of characters. If you specify a string as the parameter, such as `indexOf(".org")`, Flash returns the index of the first occurrence of the sequence ".org" that appears in the string.


```
    } else {
        display_txt.text = "Thank you, " + yourEmail_txt.text + ", we'll contact you soon.";
    }
```

Figure 11.108 This message appears in the dynamic text field `display_txt` when the condition is false.

```
submitButton_btn.onRelease = function() {
    if (yourEmail_txt.text.indexOf("@") == -1 || yourEmail_txt.text.indexOf(".") == -1) {
        display_txt.text = "Sorry, that's not a valid e-mail.";
    } else {
        display_txt.text = "Thank you, " + yourEmail_txt.text + ", we'll contact you soon.";
    }
};
```

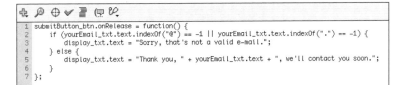

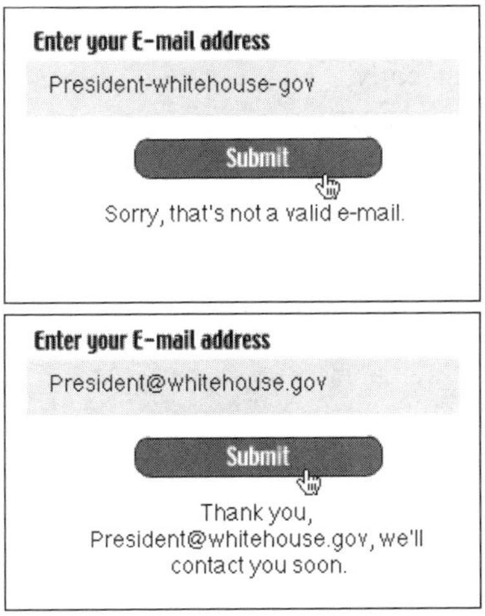

Figure 11.109 The full script (top). Entering an incorrect email address in the input text field results in a warning displayed in the dynamic text field (middle). Entering an email address with an @ sign and a period results in a thank-you message displayed in the dynamic text field (bottom).

Determining a String's size

The `String` class has one property, `length`, that tells you value of the number of characters in the `String`. This is a read-only property that is useful for checking the relative positions of characters. If you're building an online purchasing interface with input text fields for prices, you can check the input text to see whether a period character is three positions from the end of the input string using the following expression:

```
input.text.indexOf (".") ==
input.text.length - 3
```

If this condition is true, you can treat the last two digits as a decimal.

The following task refines the preceding example of verifying an email address. You'll have Flash make sure that the length of the input isn't 0 (meaning that the viewer hasn't entered anything).

To check the length of a String:

1. Continuing with the file you used in the preceding task, select the main Timeline, and open the Actions panel.
2. On a new line after the closing curly brace of the `else` statement, add another `if` statement.
3. For the condition, check the length of the string.

   The expression should look like the following:

   `yourEmail_txt.text.length == 0`
4. Within the curly braces of the `if` statement, assign text to the dynamic text field to notify the viewer that the input text field is empty.

   When your viewer clicks the button, Flash also checks the length of the input text field to see whether anything has been entered (**Figure 11.110**).

```
if (yourEmail_txt.text.length == 0) {
    display_txt.text = "Please enter something";
}
```

Figure 11.110 Flash checks whether the string inside `yourEmail_txt.text` is empty and displays an appropriate message.

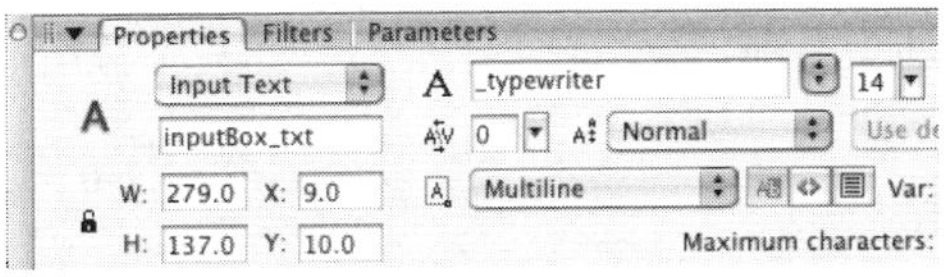

Figure 11.111 Enter `inputBox_txt` as the instance name for your input text field.

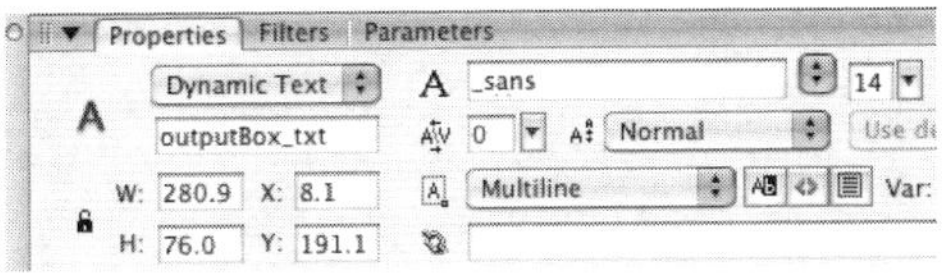

Figure 11.112 Enter `outputBox_txt` as the instance name for your dynamic text field.

Figure 11.113 Place the input text field at the top, the button in the middle, and the dynamic text field at the bottom.

Rearranging Strings

When you have information about the position of certain characters and the length of a `String`, you can select a portion of the `String` and put it in a new variable. Flash provides tools to get specific selections from a `String` and put them together with other `Strings` using methods such as `concat()`, `fromCharCode()`, `slice()`, `split()`, `substr()`, and `substring()`. Many of these methods are similar. This section discusses only `substring()`, to get a specific portion of a string, and `concat()`, to put several strings together. You can use a combination of these two methods to control the information that flows from input text fields into the rest of your Flash movie and back out into dynamic text fields.

The following task uses `Selection` and `String` methods to copy the current selection that the viewer has made and paste it into a dynamic text field.

To get selected portions of Strings:

1. Select the Text tool, and drag out a text field on the Stage.
2. In the Property inspector, choose Input Text and Multiline from the pull-down menus, and enter an instance name for this input text field (**Figure 11.111**).
3. Drag out another text field on the Stage.
4. In the Property inspector, choose Dynamic Text and Multiline from the pull-down menus, and enter an instance name for this dynamic text field (**Figure 11.112**).
5. Create a button symbol, place an instance of it on the Stage between the input text field and the dynamic text field (**Figure 11.113**), and give it an instance name.

continues on next page

6. Select the first keyframe on the root Timeline, and open the Actions panel.

7. Declare a `String` variable. This variable will be used to temporarily store the copied text.

8. Enter the name of your button. Choose ActionScript 2.0 Classes > Movie > Button > Event Handlers > onRollOver.

9. Within the curly braces of the `onRollOver` event handler, declare a `Number` variable, followed by an equals sign.

10. Choose ActionScript 2.0 Classes > Movie > Selection > Methods > getBeginIndex.

    The position of the start of the selection is assigned to this variable (**Figure 11.114**).

11. On the next line, declare another `Number` variable, followed by an equals sign.

12. Choose ActionScript 2.0 Classes > Movie > Selection > Methods > getEndIndex (**Figure 11.115**).

    The index position of the end of the selection is assigned to this variable.

13. On the next line, enter the name of the `String` variable declared in step 7, followed by an equals sign.

14. For its value, enter the name of the input text field, followed by a period and then the `text` property.

15. Choose ActionScript 2.0 Classes > Core > String > Methods > substring.

    The `substring()` method appears after your `text` property. This method takes two parameters: `indexA` and `indexB`. `indexA` defines the start of the sequence of characters you want to grab, and `indexB` defines the end of the sequence.

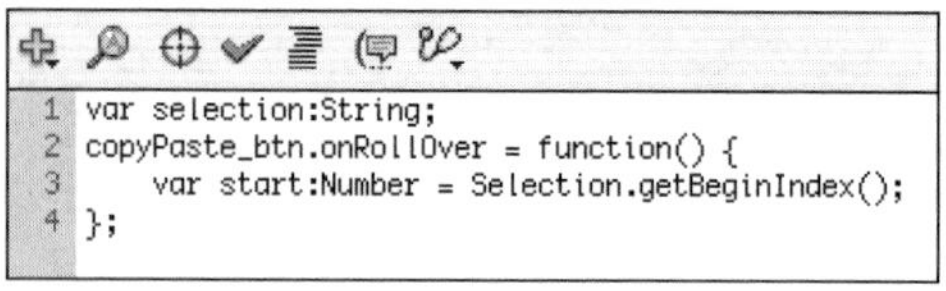

var selection:String;
copyPaste_btn.onRollOver = function() {
var start:Number = Selection.getBeginIndex();
};

Figure 11.114 The variable `start` contains the position of the start of the selection.

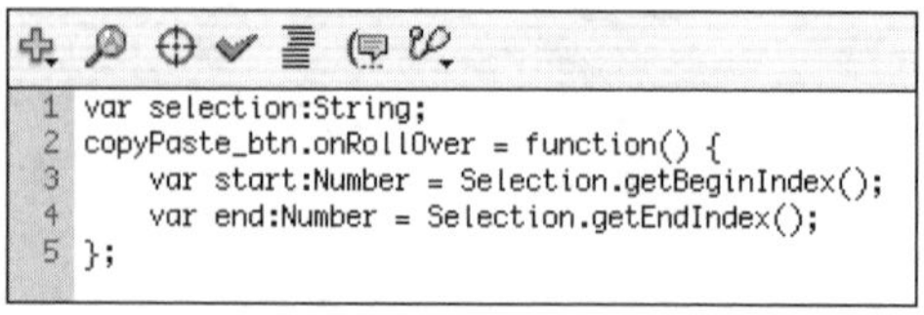

var selection:String;
copyPaste_btn.onRollOver = function() {
var start:Number = Selection.getBeginIndex();
var end:Number = Selection.getEndIndex();
};

Figure 11.115 The variable end contains the position of the end of the selection.

```
var selection:String;
copyPaste_btn.onRollOver = function() {
    var start:Number = Selection.getBeginIndex();
    var end:Number = Selection.getEndIndex();
    selection = inputBox_txt.text.substring(start, end);
};
```

Figure 11.116 The `substring()` method creates a substring out of the string inside `inputBox_txt.text` between the indexes `start` and `end`.

```
var selection:String;
copyPaste_btn.onRollOver = function() {
    var start:Number = Selection.getBeginIndex();
    var end:Number = Selection.getEndIndex();
    selection = inputBox_txt.text.substring(start, end);
};
copyPaste_btn.onRelease = function() {
    outputBox_txt.text = selection;
};
```

Figure 11.117 The contents of `outputBox_txt` display the contents of the variable `selection`.

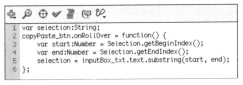

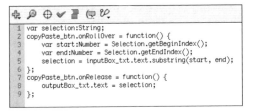

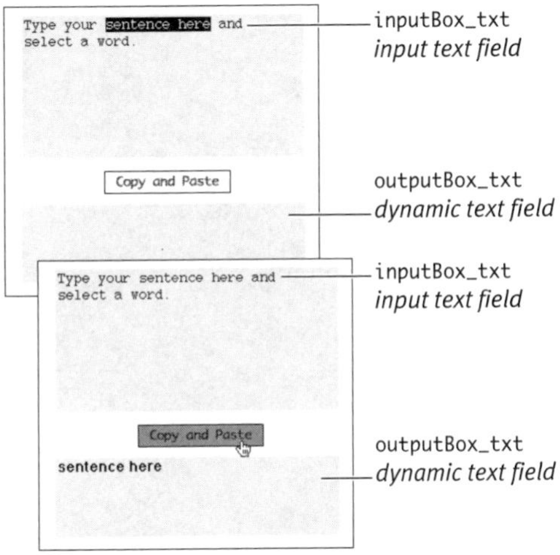

Figure 11.118 The selection *sentence here* (top) is put in a substring and displayed in the dynamic text field below the button (bottom).

16. Between the parentheses of the `substring()` method, enter the name of your first `Number` variable (the starting index of the selection) and then the second `Number` variable (the ending index of the selection), separated by commas (**Figure 11.116**).

17. On a new line outside the `onRollOver` event handler, create a new `onRelease` event handler assigned to the button.

18. Within the `onRelease` event handler, enter a statement to assign the `String` variable (which holds the selected substring) to the `text` property of the dynamic text field (**Figure 11.117**).

The user can enter information in the input text field and select portions of the text. When the user's mouse rolls over the button that you created, Flash captures the position of the selection and puts the substring into another variable. When the user clicks the button, the substring appears in the dynamic text field (**Figure 11.118**).

✔ Tip

- You may wonder why the `Selection` methods are assigned to the `onRollOver` event rather than the `onRelease` event. It's because Flash must maintain the focus of a text field to capture information about the position of the insertion point or the selection. When the viewer clicks a button, the text field loses focus and the selection disappears. By capturing the information about the selection in the `onRollOver` event, you ensure that the selection is captured before the text field loses focus.

Joining Strings

With the method concat(), you can put together strings you've dissected in an order that's more useful. The parameters of the concat() method are individual String objects or expressions, separated by commas, that you want to combine. The concat() method accomplishes the same thing as the addition operator (+), which is discussed in Chapter 10. In the following statements, result1 and result2 contain the same text:

```
var greeting:String = "Hello, ";
var result1:String;
var result2:String;
result1 = greeting.concat(firstName,
" ", lastName);
result2 = greeting + firstName + " " +
lastName;
```

Note that in the line that assigns a value to result1, the variable greeting calls the concat method with other variables as parameters, joining those values to the end of the value in greeting.

To combine multiple Strings:

1. Select the Text tool, and drag out a text field on the Stage.
2. In the Property inspector, choose Input Text and Multiline from the pull-down menus, and enter an instance name for this input text field.
3. Select the Text tool again, and drag out two more input text fields with the same settings as the first.
4. In the Property inspector, give these input text fields different instance names (**Figure 11.119**).
5. Select the Text tool, and drag out a fourth text field on the Stage.

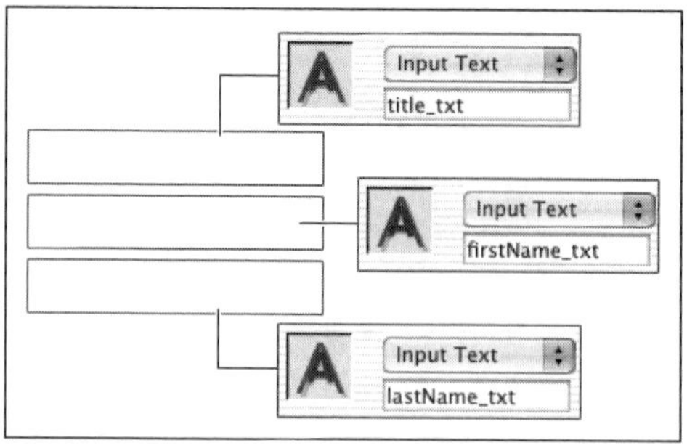

Figure 11.119 Create three input text fields.

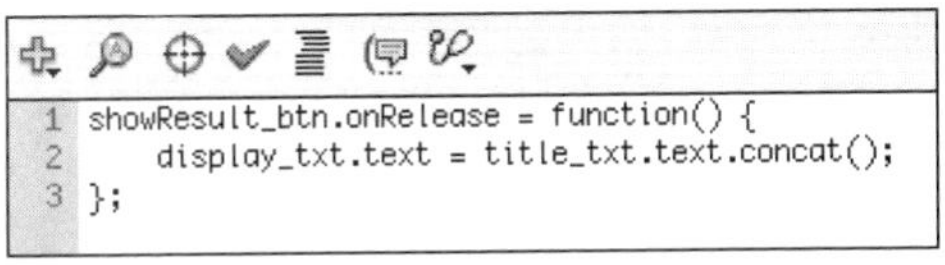

showResult_btn.onRelease = function() {
display_txt.text = title_txt.text.concat();
};

Figure 11.120 The concat() method combines the values specified in its parameters, which haven't yet been defined here, with the string inside title_txt.text.

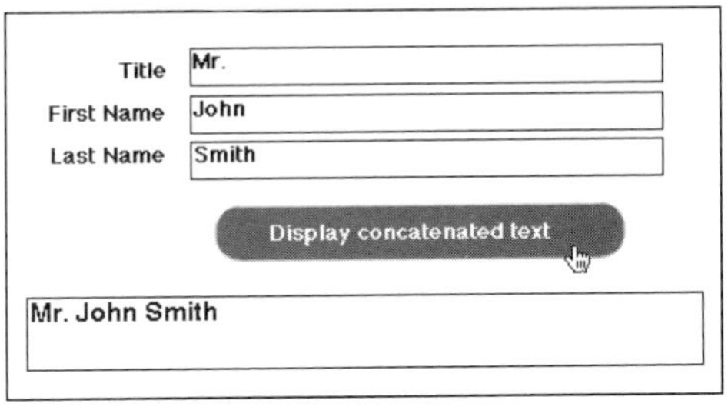

Figure 11.121 Flash concatenates the top three input text fields into one string in the bottom dynamic text field.

6. In the Property inspector, choose Dynamic Text and Multiline from the pull-down menus, and enter an instance name for this dynamic text field.

   You'll use this dynamic text field to display concatenated text from the first three input text fields.

7. Create a button symbol, place an instance of it on the Stage, and give it an instance name.

8. Select the first keyframe on the root Timeline, and open the Actions panel.

9. Enter your button's instance name. Choose ActionScript 2.0 Classes > Movie > Button > Event Handlers > onRelease.

10. Within the `onRelease` event handler, enter the name of your dynamic text field, followed by a period and then the `text` property.

11. On the same line, enter an equals sign. Enter the name of your first input text field, followed by a period and the `text` property. Choose ActionScript 2.0 Classes > Core > String > Methods > concat.

    The `concat()` method appears. You still need to supply the method's parameters, which are values that will be concatenated (**Figure 11.120**).

12. For the parameters of the `concat()` method, enter the `text` properties of the second and third input text fields, separating all your parameters with commas.

13. Test your movie.

    When the viewer enters information in the input text fields and then clicks the button, Flash concatenates the contents of the three input text fields and displays them in the dynamic text field (**Figure 11.121**).

Modifying Strings

You can perform two simple methods on a string to modify the case of its characters: `toUpperCase()` and `toLowerCase()`. Both methods return a `String` that is a copy of the original `String` with all uppercase letters or all lowercase letters. Importantly, these methods don't alter the content of the original `String`—they only return the modified copy. If you want to modify only certain letters to uppercase or lowercase, first you need to create substrings of those specific characters, as discussed in the preceding section. Modify the substrings to uppercase or lowercase; then put the `String` back together with `concat()`.

To change the case of characters in strings:

1. Select the Text tool, and drag out a text field on the Stage.
2. In the Property inspector, choose Input Text and Single Line from the pull-down menus, and enter an instance name for this input text field.

   The user will enter text in this input text field.
3. Select the Text tool, and drag out another text field on the Stage.
4. In the Property inspector, choose Dynamic Text and Single line from the pull-down menus, and enter an instance name for this dynamic text field.

   You'll change the case of the user-input text and display it in this dynamic text field.
5. Create a button symbol, place an instance of it on the Stage, and give it a name in the Property inspector.
6. Select the first keyframe on the root Timeline, and open the Actions panel.

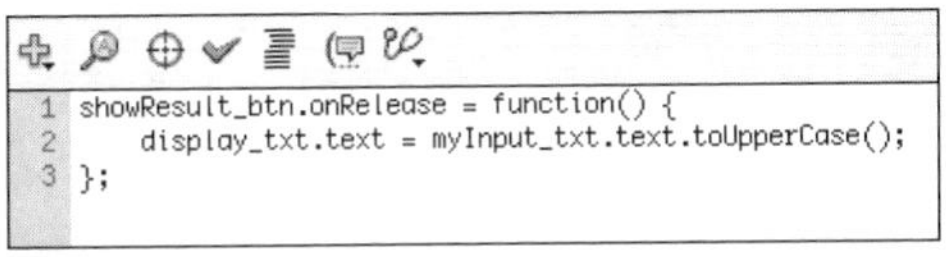

showResult_btn.onRelease = function() {
display_txt.text = myInput_txt.text.toUpperCase();
};

Figure 11.122 The `toUpperCase()` method returns the contents of `myInput_txt` in all uppercase letters.

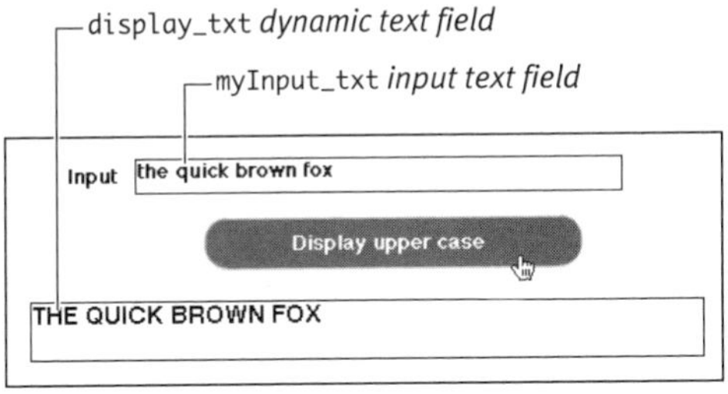

Figure 11.123 The results of the `toUpperCase()` method appear in the dynamic text field `display_txt`.

7. Enter the instance name of the button. Choose ActionScript 2.0 Classes > Movie > Button > Event Handlers > onRelease.

8. Within the `onRelease` event handler, enter the name of your dynamic text field, followed by a period and the `text` property.

9. Enter an equals sign, followed by the name of your input text field, a period, and the `text` property.

10. Choose ActionScript 2.0 Classes > Core > String > Methods > toUpperCase.

    The `toUpperCase()` method doesn't take any parameters (**Figure 11.122**).

11. Test your movie.

    When the user enters text in the input text field and clicks the button, Flash converts the entire string to uppercase and displays the results in the dynamic text field (**Figure 11.123**). Note that the method doesn't change the original string that calls it. In this example, the contents of `myInput_txt` remain as they were originally.

Manipulating Information 12

The information that you store in variables, modify in expressions, and test with conditional statements often needs to be processed and manipulated by mathematical functions such as square roots, sines, cosines, and exponents. Flash can perform these calculations with the `Math` class, which lets you create formulas for complicated interactions between the objects in your movie and your viewer or for sophisticated geometry in your graphics. The `Math` class, for example, allows you to model the correct trajectory of colliding objects or the effects of gravity for a physics tutorial, calculate probabilities for a card game, or generate random numbers to add unpredictable elements to your movie. Much of the information you manipulate sometimes needs to be stored in arrays to give you better control of your data and a more efficient way to retrieve it. You can use the `Array` class to keep track of ordered sets of data such as shopping lists, color tables, and scorecards.

When the information you need depends on the time or the date, you can use the `Date` class to retrieve the current year, month, or even millisecond. Build clocks and timers to use inside your Flash movie, or send the time information (along with a viewer's profile) to a server-side script.

All this information handling and processing is easier when you use functions. Build functions that string together separate actions and methods to accomplish many tasks at the same time. Build a single function, for example, that automatically attaches a sound, plays it, and adjusts the volume level and pan settings based on the parameters you provide. This chapter explores the variety of ways you can manipulate information with added complexity and flexibility and shows you how to integrate the predefined classes you've learned about in previous chapters.

Calculating with the Math Class

The Math class lets you access trigonometric functions such as sine, cosine, and tangent; logarithmic functions; rounding functions; and mathematical constants such as pi and *e*. **Table 12.1** summarizes the methods and properties of the Math class. As with the Key, Mouse, Selection, and Stage classes, the Math class has static methods and properties, so you don't need to create an instance of the Math class to access them. Instead, you precede the method or property with the class name, Math. All the Math class's properties are read-only values that are written in all uppercase letters.

To calculate the square root of 10, for example, you write

```
var myAnswer:Number = Math.sqrt(10);
```

The calculated value is put in the variable myAnswer. To use a constant, use similar syntax:

```
var myCircum:Number = Math.PI * 2 *
myRadius;
```

The mathematical constant pi is multiplied by 2 and the variable myRadius, and the result is put into the variable myCircum.

Table 12.1

Methods and Properties of the Math Class	
abs(number)	Calculates the absolute value. Math.abs(-4) returns 4.
acos(number)	Calculates the arc cosine.
asin(number)	Calculates the arc sine.
atan(number)	Calculates the arc tangent.
atan2(y, x)	Calculates the angle (in radians) from the x-axis to a point on the y-axis.
ceil(number)	Rounds the number up to the nearest integer. Math.ceil(2.34) returns 3.
cos(number)	Calculates the cosine of an angle, in radians.
exp(number)	Calculates the exponent of the constant e.
floor(number)	Rounds the number down to the nearest integer. Math.floor(2.34) returns 2.
log(number)	Calculates the natural logarithm.
max(x, y)	Returns the larger of two values. Math.max(2, 7) returns 7.
min(x, y)	Returns the smaller of two values. Math.min(2, 7) returns 2.
pow(base, exponent)	Calculates the exponent of a number.
random()	Returns a random number between 0 and 1 (including 0 but not including 1).
round(number)	Rounds the number to the nearest integer. Math.round(2.34) returns 2.
sin(number)	Calculates the sine of an angle, in radians.
sqrt(number)	Calculates the square root.
tan(number)	Calculates the tangent of an angle, in radians.
E	Euler's constant *e*; the base of natural logarithms.
LN2	The natural logarithm of 2.
LOG2E	The base-2 logarithm of *e*.
LN10	The natural logarithm of 10.
LOG10E	The base-10 logarithm of *e*.
PI	The circumference of a circle divided by its diameter.
SQRT1_2	The square root of 1/2.
SQRT2	The square root of 2.

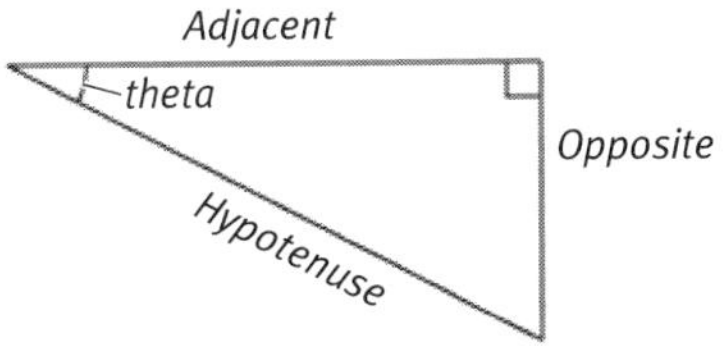

Sin theta = opposite/hypotenuse
Cos theta = adjacent/hypotenuse
Tan theta = opposite/adjacent

Figure 12.1 The angle, theta, of a right triangle is defined by sin, cos, and tan and by the length of the three sides.

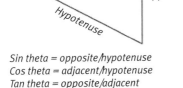

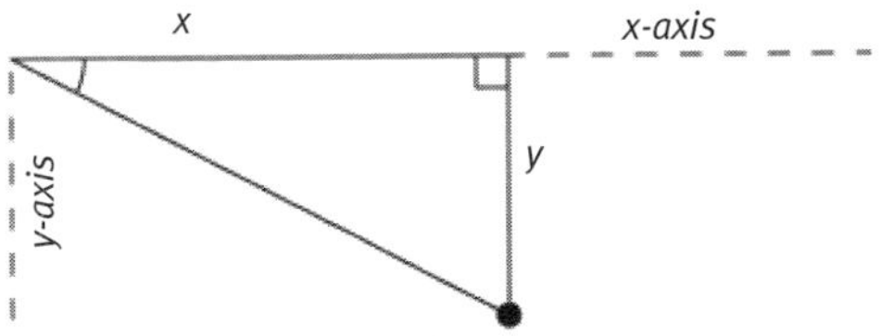

Figure 12.2 A point on the Stage makes a right triangle with x (adjacent side) and y (opposite side).

Calculating Angles with the Math Class

The angle that an object makes relative to the Stage or to another object is useful information for creating many game interactions, as well as for creating dynamic animations and interfaces based purely in ActionScript. To create a dial that controls the sound volume, for example, compute the angle at which your viewer drags the dial relative to the horizontal or vertical axis, and then change the dial's rotation and the sound's volume accordingly. Calculating the angle also requires that you brush up on some of your high-school trigonometry, so a review of some basic principles related to sine, cosine, and tangent is in order.

The mnemonic device *SOH CAH TOA* can help you keep the trigonometric functions straight. This acronym stands for Sine = Opposite over Hypotenuse, Cosine = Adjacent over Hypotenuse, and Tangent = Opposite over Adjacent (**Figure 12.1**). Knowing the length of any two sides of a right triangle is enough information to calculate the other two angles. You'll most likely know the lengths of the opposite and adjacent sides of the triangle because they represent the y- and x-coordinates of a point (**Figure 12.2**). When you have the x- and y-coordinates, you can calculate the angle (theta) by using the following mathematical formulas:

```
tan theta = opposite/adjacent
```

or

```
tan theta = y / x
```

or

```
theta = arctan(y / x)
```

In Flash, you can write this expression by using the `Math` class this way:

```
myTheta = Math.atan(this._y / this._x)
```

Alternatively, Flash provides an even easier method that lets you define the y and x positions without having to do the division. The `atan2()` method accepts the y and x positions as two parameters, so you can write the equivalent statement:

```
myTheta = Math.atan2(this._y, this._x)
```

Unfortunately, the trigonometric methods of the `Math` class require and return angle values in radians, which describe angles in terms of the constant pi—easier mathematically, but not so convenient if you want to use the values to modify the `_rotation` property of an object. You can convert an angle from radians to degrees, and vice versa, by using the following formulas:

```
radians = Math.PI/180 * degrees
degrees = radians * 180/Math.PI
```

The following tasks calculate the angle of a draggable movie clip relative to either the Stage or another point, and display the angle (in degrees) in a dynamic text field.

To calculate the angle relative to the Stage:

1. Create a movie clip symbol, place an instance of it on the Stage, and give the movie clip instance a name in the Property inspector.
   In this example, the movie clip instance is `circle_mc`.
2. Create a dynamic text field on the Stage, choose Single Line in the Property inspector, and give the dynamic text field an instance name.
   In this example, the text field is called `myDegrees_txt`.
3. Select the first frame of the main Timeline, and open the Actions panel.
4. Enter the instance name of the movie clip, followed by a period.
5. Choose ActionScript 2.0 Classes > Movie > MovieClip > Methods > startDrag.
6. With your pointer between the parentheses, enter the `Boolean` value `true` for the `lockcenter` parameter (**Figure 12.3**).
   The center of the movie clip follows the mouse pointer.
7. On the next line, enter `_root`, followed by a period.
8. Choose ActionScript 2.0 Classes > Movie > MovieClip > Event Handlers > onEnterFrame.
9. With your pointer between the curly braces of the `onEnterFrame` event handler, declare a `Number` variable that will hold the angle in radians, followed by an equals sign.
10. Choose ActionScript 2.0 Classes > Core > Math > Methods > atan2.
11. With your pointer between the parentheses of the `atan2()` method, enter `circle_mc._y`, followed by a comma and then `circle_mc._x` (**Figure 12.4**).
    Flash calculates the arc tangent of the y position of the movie clip divided by the x position of the movie clip and returns the value in radians.

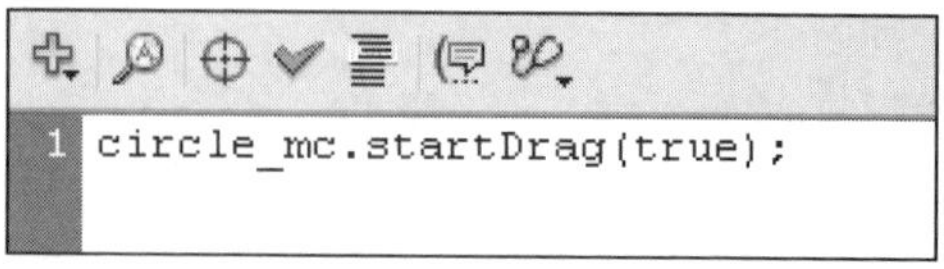
1
circle_mc.startDrag(true);

Figure 12.3 This `startDrag` action makes the movie clip follow the pointer and centers it on the pointer.

12. On the next line within the onEnterFrame event handler, enter myDegrees_txt.text, followed by an equals sign.

13. Enter an expression that multiplies by 180 your variable that holds the radian angle and divides it by the constant pi:

`(myRadians * 180 / Math.PI)`

14. Continuing on the same line, concatenate the string `" degrees"` to the end of the expression.

The angle is converted from radians to degrees and assigned to the contents of the dynamic text field (**Figure 12.5**).

15. Test your movie.

As the viewer moves the pointer around the Stage, the movie clip follows the pointer. Flash calculates the angle that the movie clip makes with the x-axis of the root Timeline and displays the angle (in degrees) in the dynamic text field (**Figure 12.6**).


```
circle_mc.startDrag(true);
_root.onEnterFrame = function() {
    var myRadians:Number = Math.atan2(circle_mc._y, circle_mc._x);
};
```

Figure 12.4 The `Math.atan2()` method calculates the angle that the movie clip `circle_mc` makes with the origin (top-left corner of the Stage).

```
circle_mc.startDrag(true);
_root.onEnterFrame = function() {
    var myRadians:Number = Math.atan2(circle_mc._y, circle_mc._x);
    myDegrees_txt.text = (myRadians * 180 / Math.PI) + " degrees";
};
```

Figure 12.5 The dynamic text field `myDegrees_txt` displays the angle in degrees.

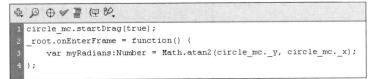

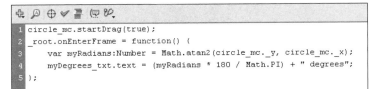

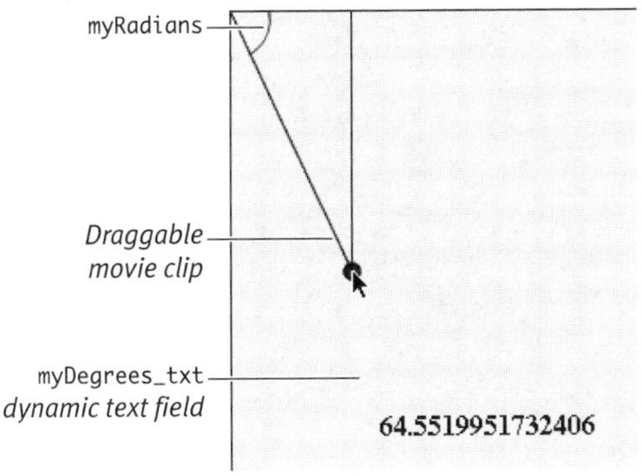

Figure 12.6 The movie clip makes an angle of approximately 65 degrees below the x-axis. The lines have been drawn in to show the right triangle.

To calculate the angle relative to another point:

1. Continuing with the file you used in the preceding task, create another movie clip symbol, place an instance of it on the Stage, and give it a name in the Property inspector.

   In this example, the name is `myReferencePoint_mc`.

2. Select the first frame of the main Timeline, and open the Actions panel.

3. Select the statement that calculates the angle from the `atan2()` method, and change the expression to read as follows:

   ```
   Math.atan2((circle_mc._y -
   myReferencePoint_mc._y),
   (circle_mc._x -
   myReferencePoint_mc._x))
   ```

   By subtracting the y and x positions of the reference point from the draggable movie clip's position, Flash calculates the y and x distances between the two points (**Figure 12.7**).

4. Test your movie.

   As the user moves the pointer around the Stage, the movie clip follows the pointer. Flash calculates the angle that the draggable movie clip makes with the stationary movie clip and displays the angle (in degrees) in the dynamic text field.

```
circle_mc.startDrag(true);
_root.onEnterFrame = function() {
    var myRadians:Number = Math.atan2((circle_mc._y - myReferencePoint_mc._y), (circle_mc._x - myReferencePoint_mc._x));
    myDegrees_txt.text = (myRadians * 180 / Math.PI) + " degrees";
};
```

Figure 12.7 The difference between the y positions of the `circle_mc` movie clip and the `myReferencePoint_mc` movie clip is the y parameter for `Math.atan2()`. The difference between the x positions of the `circle_mc` movie clip and the `myReferencePoint_mc` movie clip is the x parameter for `Math.atan2()`.

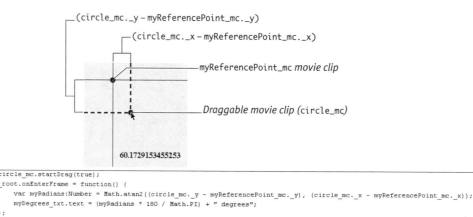

Rounding off decimals

So far, the returned values for your angles have had many decimal places. Often, you need to round those values to the nearest whole number (or integer) so that you can use the values as parameters in methods and properties. Use `Math.round()` to round values to the nearest integer, `Math.ceil()` to round up to the closest integer greater than or equal to the value, and `Math.floor()` to round down to the closest integer less than or equal to the value.

To round a number to an integer:

1. Continuing with the file you used in the preceding task, select the first frame of the main Timeline, and open the Actions panel.
2. Select the statement that converts the angle from radians to degrees.
3. Place your pointer in front of the expression, and enter the method `Math.round` (**Figure 12.8**).

   Flash converts the angle from radians to degrees and then applies the method `Math.round()` to that value, returning an integer.

```
circle_mc.startDrag(true);
_root.onEnterFrame = function() {
    var myRadians:Number = Math.atan2((circle_mc._y - myReferencePoint_mc._y), (circle_mc._x - myReferencePoint_mc._x));
    myDegrees_txt.text = Math.round(myRadians * 180 / Math.PI) + " degrees";
};
```

Figure 12.8 The expression within the parentheses is rounded to the nearest integer and displayed in the dynamic text field `myDegrees_txt`.

Putting it together: Creating a rotating dial

You can apply the methods that calculate angles and round values to create a draggable rotating dial. The approach is to calculate the angle of the mouse's position relative to the center point of the dial and then set the `_rotation` property of the dial to that angle.

To create a rotating dial:

1. Create a movie clip symbol of a dial, place an instance of it on the Stage, and give it a name in the Property inspector.

   In this example, the name is `myDial_mc` (**Figure 12.9**).

2. Select the first frame of the main Timeline, and open the Actions panel.

3. Declare a `Boolean` variable named `pressing`, followed by an equals sign and the value `false`.

   This variable keeps track of whether your viewer is pressing or not pressing this movie clip.

4. On the next line, create an `onPress` event handler function assigned to your movie clip.

5. Within the `onPress` handler, enter `pressing`, followed by an equals sign.

6. Enter the `Boolean` value of `true` (**Figure 12.10**).

7. Create a single event handler for both the `onRelease` event and the `onReleaseOutside` event for your movie clip.

8. Within the `onRelease` and `onReleaseOutside` handler, enter `pressing`, followed by an equals sign.

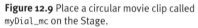

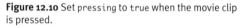

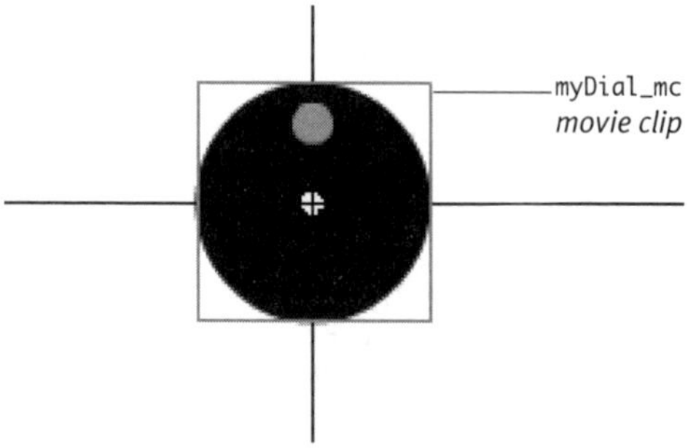

Figure 12.9 Place a circular movie clip called `myDial_mc` on the Stage.

```
var pressing:Boolean = false;
myDial_mc.onPress = function() {
    pressing = true;
};
```

Figure 12.10 Set `pressing` to `true` when the movie clip is pressed.

9. Enter the Boolean value `false` (**Figure 12.11**).

10. On a new line outside the event handlers, enter `_root`, followed by a period.

11. Choose ActionScript 2.0 Classes > Movie > MovieClip > Event Handlers > onEnterFrame.

12. Within the `onEnterFrame` handler, choose Statements > Conditions/Loops > if.

13. For the condition of the `if` statement, enter `pressing == true`.

14. Between the curly braces of the `if` statement, declare a new `Number` variable, followed by an equals sign.

    This variable will be assigned the angle between the mouse pointer and the center of the movie clip, in radians.

15. After the equals sign, enter the following expression:

    `Math.atan2((_ymouse - myDial_mc._y), (_xmouse - myDial_mc._x))`

    Flash calculates the angle between the mouse pointer and the center of the movie clip (**Figure 12.12**).

16. On the next line, declare a new `Number` variable, followed by an equals sign.

    This variable will be assigned the angle value, converted to degrees.

17. After the equals sign, enter an expression to convert radians to degrees and round the result to an integer (**Figure 12.13**).

continues on next page


```
myDial_mc.onRelease = myDial_mc.onReleaseOutside = function () {
    pressing = false;
};
```

Figure 12.11 Set `pressing` to `false` when the movie clip is either released or released outside the movie clip's hit area.

```
_root.onEnterFrame = function() {
    if (pressing == true) {
        var myRadians:Number = Math.atan2((_ymouse - myDial_mc._y), (_xmouse - myDial_mc._x));
    }
};
```

Figure 12.12 The variable `myRadians` contains the calculated angle between the pointer and the movie clip.

```
_root.onEnterFrame = function() {
    if (pressing == true) {
        var myRadians:Number = Math.atan2((_ymouse - myDial_mc._y), (_xmouse - myDial_mc._x));
        var myDegrees:Number = Math.round(myRadians * 180 / Math.PI);
    }
};
```

Figure 12.13 The angle is converted from radians to degrees, rounded to the nearest integer, and assigned to the variable `myDegrees`.

18. Enter `myDial_mc._rotation` on the next line, followed by an equals sign.

19. Enter your variable that holds the angle in degrees, and add 90.

    The rotation of the movie clip is assigned to the calculated angle. The 90 degrees are added to compensate for the difference between the calculated angle and the movie-clip rotation property. A value of `0` for `_rotation` corresponds to the 12 o'clock position of a movie clip, but a calculated arctangent angle value of `0` corresponds to the 3 o'clock position; adding 90 equalizes them (**Figure 12.14**).

20. Test your movie.

    When users press the movie clip in the dial, they can rotate it by dragging it around its center point. When they release the movie clip, the dial stops rotating.

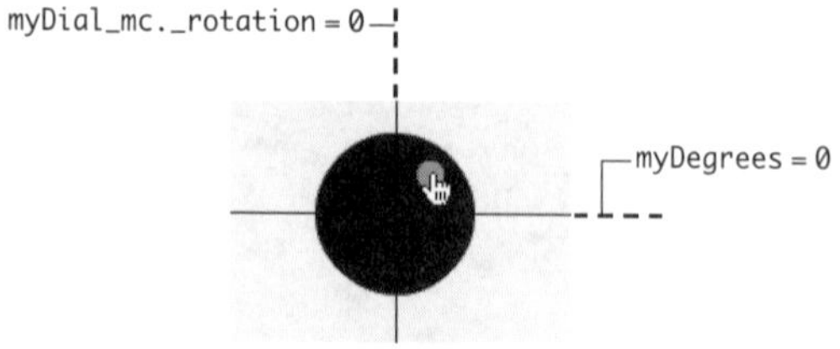


```
var pressing:Boolean = false;
myDial_mc.onPress = function() {
    pressing = true;
};
myDial_mc.onRelease = myDial_mc.onReleaseOutside = function () {
    pressing = false;
};
_root.onEnterFrame = function() {
    if (pressing == true) {
        var myRadians:Number = Math.atan2((_ymouse - myDial_mc._y), (_xmouse - myDial_mc._x));
        var myDegrees:Number = Math.round(myRadians * 180 / Math.PI);
        myDisplay_txt.text = myDegrees + " degrees";
        myDial_mc._rotation = myDegrees + 90;
    }
};
```

Figure 12.14 The final statement within the `if` block modifies the rotation of the `myDial_mc` movie clip. The rotation of `myDial_mc` is set at `myDegrees + 90` to account for the difference between the reference point of the trigonometric functions and Flash's `_rotation` property.

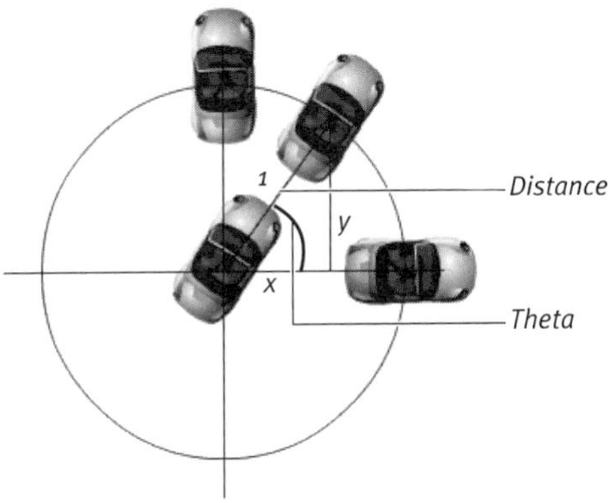

Figure 12.15 The x and y components of this car, which moves a certain distance, are determined by the cosine and sine of its angle, theta.

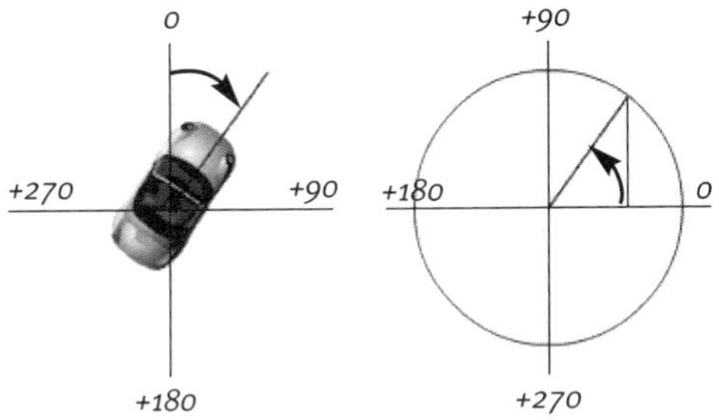

Figure 12.16 The rotation property of a movie clip begins from the vertical axis and increases in the clockwise direction (left). Values for sine and cosine angles begin from the horizontal axis and increase in the counterclockwise direction (right).

Using Sine and Cosine for Directional Movement

To control how far an object on the Stage travels based on its angle, you can use the sine and cosine trigonometric functions. Suppose that you want to create a racing game featuring a car that your viewer moves around a track. The car travels at a certain speed, and it moves according to where the front of the car is pointed.

Calculating how far the car moves in any direction requires the `Math.sin()` and `Math.cos()` methods. The new location of the car is determined by the x and y components of the triangle formed by the angle of the car. When the car is pointing straight up, the y component is 1 and the x component is 0. When the car is pointing to the right, the y component is 0 and the x component is 1. When the car's angle is somewhere between up and right, the sine and cosine of the angle give you the x- and y-coordinates (**Figure 12.15**). The sine of the angle determines the magnitude of the y component, and the cosine of the angle determines the magnitude of the x component.

Sine and cosine are based on angles that begin at 0 degrees from the horizontal axis. The rotation property, on the other hand, is based on angles that begin at 0 degrees from the vertical axis (**Figure 12.16**). Moreover, the y component for the sine function is positive above the origin of the circle and negative below it. When you deal with a movie clip's coordinate space, you must do two transformations: Subtract the rotation property from 90 to get the angle for sine and cosine, and then use the negative value of sine for the change in the y direction:

```
myCar_mc._x += Math.cos(90-rotation);
myCar_mc._y += -Math.sin(90-rotation);
```

In the following task, you'll create a movie clip whose rotation can be controlled by the viewer. The movie clip has a constant velocity, so it will travel in the direction in which it's pointed, just as a car moves according to where it's steered.

To create a controllable object with directional movement:

1. Create a movie clip symbol, place an instance of it on the Stage, and name it in the Property inspector.

   In this example, the name is `car_mc`.

2. Select the first frame of the main Timeline, and open the Actions panel.

3. Enter `_root`, followed by a period.

4. Choose ActionScript 2.0 Classes > Movie > MovieClip > Event Handlers > onEnterFrame.

5. On the next line, choose Statements > Conditions/Loops > if.

6. For the condition of the `if` statement, enter the following:

   `Key.isDown(Key.LEFT)`

   Flash checks to see whether the left arrow key is pressed.

7. On the next line (inside the `if` statement's curly braces), enter `car_mc._rotation -= 10;`.

   Flash subtracts 10 from the current rotation property of the movie clip car when the left arrow key is pressed (**Figure 12.17**).

8. With your pointer after the closing curly brace for the `if` statement, choose Statements > Conditions/Loops > "else if". Delete the extra opening curly brace that's inserted before the `else if` statement.

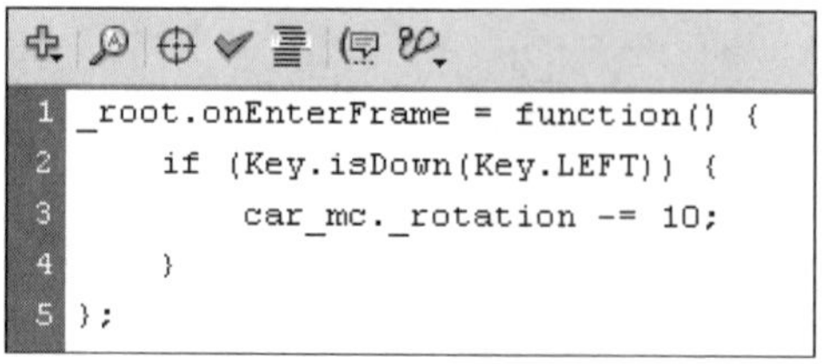
1 _root.onEnterFrame = function() {
2 if (Key.isDown(Key.LEFT)) {
3 car_mc._rotation -= 10;
4 }
5 };

Figure 12.17 The `car_mc` movie clip rotates 10 degrees counterclockwise when the left arrow key is pressed.

9. Between the parentheses of the `else if` statement, enter the following:

   `Key.isDown(Key.RIGHT)`

   Flash checks to see whether the right arrow key is pressed.

10. On the next line of the `else if` statement, enter `car_mc._rotation += 10`.

    Flash adds 10 to the current rotation property of the movie clip car when the right arrow key is pressed (**Figure 12.18**).

11. On a new line, after the closing brace of the `else if` action, declare a new `Number` variable `myAngle`, and enter an equals sign.

12. Enter the following expression: `90 - car_mc._rotation` (**Figure 12.19**).

    When you subtract the rotation property of the movie clip from 90, you get the equivalent angle for use in the sine and cosine functions.

13. On the next line, declare a `Number` variable named `xchange`, followed by an equals sign.

14. Choose ActionScript 2.0 Classes > Core > Math > Methods > cos.

    The `Math.cos()` method appears.

15. Between the parentheses of the `Math.cos()` method, enter an expression to convert `myAngle` from degrees to radians; multiply the entire expression by 5 (**Figure 12.20**).

    The variable `xchange` represents the magnitude of the x component. Multiplying by 5 increases the magnitude of the change so that the movie clip moves a little faster.

continues on next page

```
_root.onEnterFrame = function() {
    if (Key.isDown(Key.LEFT)) {
        car_mc._rotation -= 10;
    } else if (Key.isDown(Key.RIGHT)) {
        car_mc._rotation += 10;
    }
};
```

Figure 12.18 The `car_mc` movie clip rotates 10 degrees clockwise when the right arrow key is pressed.

```
_root.onEnterFrame = function() {
    if (Key.isDown(Key.LEFT)) {
        car_mc._rotation -= 10;
    } else if (Key.isDown(Key.RIGHT)) {
        car_mc._rotation += 10;
    }
    var myAngle:Number = 90 - car_mc._rotation;
};
```

Figure 12.19 The variable `myAngle` will be used as the angle for sine and cosine.

```
_root.onEnterFrame = function() {
    if (Key.isDown(Key.LEFT)) {
        car_mc._rotation -= 10;
    } else if (Key.isDown(Key.RIGHT)) {
        car_mc._rotation += 10;
    }
    var myAngle:Number = 90 - car_mc._rotation;
    var xchange:Number = Math.cos(Math.PI / 180 * myAngle) * 5;
};
```

Figure 12.20 The cosine of the movie clip's angle is calculated and assigned to `xchange`.

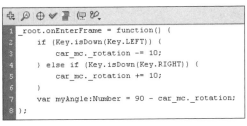

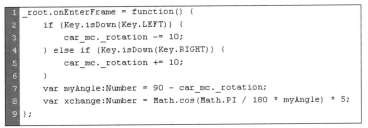

16. On a new line, declare a `Number` variable named `ychange`, followed by an equals sign.

17. Choose ActionScript 2.0 Classes > Core > Math > Methods > sin.

The `Math.sin()` method appears.

18. Between the parentheses of the `Math.sin()` method, enter an expression to convert `myAngle` from degrees to radians; multiply the entire expression by 5 and make it negative by placing a minus sign in front of the expression (**Figure 12.21**).

The variable `ychange` represents the magnitude of the y component. Multiplying by 5 increases the magnitude of the change so that the movie clip moves a little faster. You must use the negative value for the change in the y direction to compensate for the discrepancy between the coordinate space for sine and the coordinate space for the movie clip.

19. On the next line, enter `car_mc._x += xchange;`.

Flash adds the value of `xchange` to the current x position of the movie clip.

20. On the next line, enter `car_mc._y += ychange;`.

Flash adds the value of `ychange` to the current y position of the movie clip.

21. Test your movie.

When the user presses the left or right arrow key, the rotation of the movie clip changes. The x and y positions change continuously as well, calculated from the angle of the movie clip. The movie clip moves according to where the nose of the car is pointed (**Figure 12.22**).

```
_root.onEnterFrame = function() {
    if (Key.isDown(Key.LEFT)) {
        car_mc._rotation -= 10;
    } else if (Key.isDown(Key.RIGHT)) {
        car_mc._rotation += 10;
    }
    var myAngle:Number = 90 - car_mc._rotation;
    var xchange:Number = Math.cos(Math.PI / 180 * myAngle) * 5;
    var ychange:Number = -Math.sin(Math.PI / 180 * myAngle) * 5;
};
```

Figure 12.21 The negative sine of the movie clip's angle is calculated and assigned to ychange.

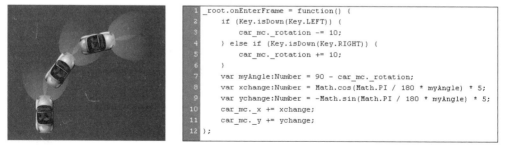

```
_root.onEnterFrame = function() {
    if (Key.isDown(Key.LEFT)) {
        car_mc._rotation -= 10;
    } else if (Key.isDown(Key.RIGHT)) {
        car_mc._rotation += 10;
    }
    var myAngle:Number = 90 - car_mc._rotation;
    var xchange:Number = Math.cos(Math.PI / 180 * myAngle) * 5;
    var ychange:Number = -Math.sin(Math.PI / 180 * myAngle) * 5;
    car_mc._x += xchange;
    car_mc._y += ychange;
};
```

Figure 12.22 The final script is shown at the right. As the movie clip of the car rotates, the x and y components are calculated from cosine and sine, and the car's new position is defined.

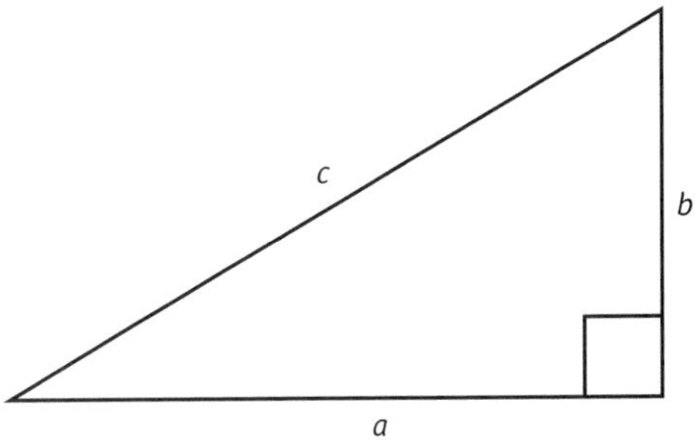

Figure 12.23 This right triangle has sides a, b, and c.

Calculating Distances with the Math Class

Using the Pythagorean theorem, you can calculate the distance between two objects. This technique can be useful for creating novel interactions among interface elements—graphics, buttons, or sounds whose reactions depend on their distance from the viewer's pointer, for example. You can also create games that involve interactions based on the distance between objects and the player. A game in which the player uses a net to catch goldfish in an aquarium, for example, can use the distance between the goldfish and the net to model the behavior of the goldfish. Perhaps the closer the net comes to a goldfish, the quicker the goldfish swims away.

The distance between any two points is defined by the equation

$a^2 + b^2 = c^2$

or

$c = \text{square root } (a^2 + b^2)$

The variables `a` and `b` are the lengths of the sides of a right triangle, and `c` is the length of the hypotenuse (**Figure 12.23**). Using Flash's `Math.sqrt()` and `Math.pow()` methods, you can calculate the distance between the points on the hypotenuse with the following expression:

```
c = Math.sqrt((Math.pow(a, 2)) +
(Math.pow(b, 2)))
```

To calculate the distance between the pointer and another point:

1. Create a movie clip, place an instance of it on the Stage, and give it a name in the Property inspector.

   In this example, the name is `myReference_mc`.

2. Select the first frame of the main Timeline, and open the Actions panel.

3. Enter `_root`, followed by a period.

4. Choose ActionScript 2.0 Classes > Movie > MovieClip > Event Handlers > onMouseMove.

5. Within the `onMouseMove` handler, declare a `Number` variable named `xDistance`, followed by an equals sign.

6. Enter the following on the right side of the equals sign:

   `_xmouse - myReference_mc._x;`

   The distance between the x position of the pointer and the x position of the movie clip is assigned to the variable `xDistance` (**Figure 12.24**).

7. On a new line, declare the `Number` variable `yDistance`, followed by an equals sign.

8. Enter the following:

   `_ymouse - myReference_mc._y;`

   The distance between the y position of the pointer and the y position of the movie clip is assigned to the variable `yDistance` (**Figure 12.25**).

9. On the next line, declare a `Number` variable named `myDistance`, followed by an equals sign.

```
_root.onMouseMove = function() {
    var xDistance:Number = _xmouse - myReference_mc._x;
};
```

Figure 12.24 The difference between the x position of the pointer and the x position of the movie clip `myReference_mc` is the distance between them on the x-axis.

```
_root.onMouseMove = function() {
    var xDistance:Number = _xmouse - myReference_mc._x;
    var yDistance:Number = _ymouse - myReference_mc._y;
};
```

Figure 12.25 The difference between the y position of the pointer and the y position of the movie clip `myReference_mc` is the distance between them on the y-axis.

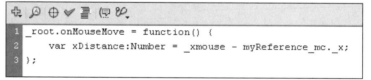

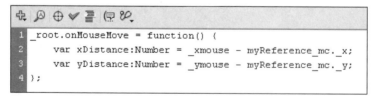

10. Choose ActionScript 2.0 Classes > Core > Math > Methods > sqrt.

    The `Math.sqrt()` method appears.

11. With your pointer between the parentheses of the `Math.sqrt()` method, choose ActionScript 2.0 Classes > Core > Math > Methods > pow.

12. Enter `xDistance` and `2` as the parameters of the `Math.pow()` method.

13. After the closing parenthesis of the `Math.pow` method (but still within the `Math.sqrt` method), enter a plus sign (+), followed by another `Math.pow()` method with the parameters `yDistance` and `2` (**Figure 12.26**).

    Flash calculates the square of `xDistance` and adds it to the square of `yDistance`; then it calculates the square root of that sum.

14. Create a dynamic text field on the Stage, and give it an instance name.

15. On the next line within the `onMouseMove` event handler, assign the value of `myDistance` to the `text` property of the dynamic text field on the Stage (**Figure 12.27**).

16. Test your movie.

    As the pointer moves around the movie clip, Flash calculates the distance between points in pixels.

```
_root.onMouseMove = function() {
    var xDistance:Number = _xmouse - myReference_mc._x;
    var yDistance:Number = _ymouse - myReference_mc._y;
    var myDistance:Number = Math.sqrt(Math.pow(xDistance, 2) + Math.pow(yDistance, 2));
};
```

Figure 12.26 The distance between the two points is calculated from the variables `xDistance` and `yDistance`.

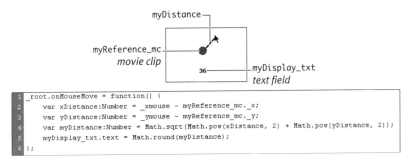

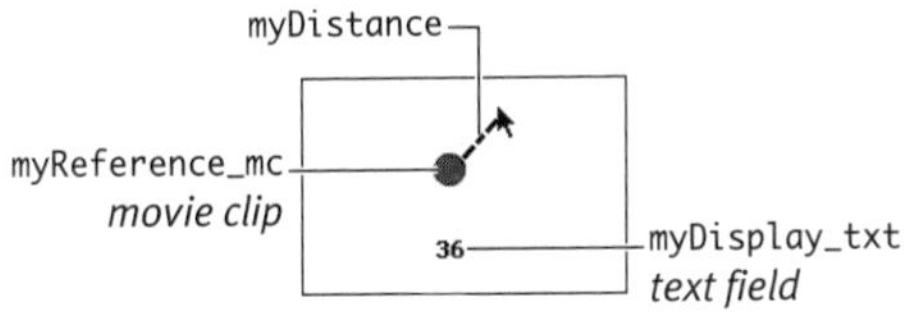


```
_root.onMouseMove = function() {
    var xDistance:Number = _xmouse - myReference_mc._x;
    var yDistance:Number = _ymouse - myReference_mc._y;
    var myDistance:Number = Math.sqrt(Math.pow(xDistance, 2) + Math.pow(yDistance, 2));
    myDisplay_txt.text = Math.round(myDistance);
};
```

Figure 12.27 The full script is shown at the bottom. The dynamic text field `myDisplay_txt` displays an integer of `myDistance`.

A Math Class Alternative: The Point Class

One source of complication when working with trigonometric equations and coordinates is that typically the same calculations must be repeated for both x- and y-coordinates. In addition, common calculations like the Pythagorean theorem often need to be used multiple times.

New in Flash 8, the `flash.geom.Point` class (which you saw several times in Chapter 8) helps minimize the need for this duplicated effort. A `Point` object contains both an x- and a y-coordinate as properties, so any operations on `Point` objects automatically affect both coordinates. In addition, the `Point` class includes properties and methods for commonly needed calculations related to coordinates:

The `Point` class has the following instance properties:

- `x`: A `Number`; the x-coordinate of the `Point` object
- `y`: A `Number`; the y-coordinate of the `Point` object
- `length`: A `Number`; the distance in pixels between the point (0, 0) and this `Point` object

The `Point` class has these instance methods (called on a `Point` object):

- `add(`*`toAdd`*`)`: Adds the x- and y-coordinates of the `Point` object *`toAdd`* to the current `Point` instance
- `subtract(`*`toSubtract`*`)`: Subtracts the x- and y-coordinates of the `Point` object *`toSubtract`* from those of the current instance
- `offset(`*`dx`*`, `*`dy`*`)`: Shifts the `Point` object's x-coordinate by the `Number` value *`dx`* and y-coordinate by the `Number` value *`dy`*
- `normalize(`*`length`*`)`: Shifts the coordinates of the `Point` object so that the distance between (0,0) and the `Point` object is *`length`* (a `Number`) pixels
- `clone()`: Returns a new `Point` object that is an exact copy of the current `Point` object
- `equals(`*`toCompare`*`)`: Compares the coordinates of the current `Point` object to those of the `Point` object *`toCompare`*, and returns `true` if their x- and y-coordinates are both equal

continues on next page

A Math Class Alternative: The Point Class *(continued)*

The `Point` class has the following static methods (called using the class name):

- `Point.distance(`*`pt1`*`, pt2)`: Returns a `Number`, the distance in pixels between the `Point` objects *pt1* and *pt2*.
- `Point.interpolate(`*`pt1`*`, `*`pt2`*`, `*`f`*`)`: Returns a `Point` object that falls on the line between the `Point` objects *pt1* and *pt1*. The parameter *f* (a `Number` between 0 and 1) determines where along the line the new `Point` falls; the smaller the value of *f*, the closer it is to *pt1*.
- `Point.polar(`*`length`*`, `*`angle`*`)`: Returns a `Point` object that is *length* (a `Number`) pixels away from the point (0, 0), in the direction specified by the `Number` *angle* (in radians).

For example, the task "To calculate the distance between the pointer and another point" could be re-created using `Point` objects by replacing the first three lines of the `onMouseMove` event handler.

These lines of code are used in the task to calculate the distance between the mouse pointer and a movie clip:

```
var xDistance:Number = _xmouse - myReference_mc._x;
var yDistance:Number = _ymouse - myReference_mc._y;
var myDistance:Number = Math.sqrt(Math.pow(xDistance, 2) + Math.pow(yDistance, 2));
```

For the equivalent calculation using the `Point` class, add the following line to the top of the script:

```
import flash.geom.Point;
```

Then replace the lines (above) from the `onMouseMove` event handler with these lines:

```
var mousePt:Point = new Point(_xmouse, _ymouse);
var referencePt:Point = new Point(myReference_mc._x, myReference_mc._y);
var myDistance:Number = Point.distance(mousePt, referencePt);
```

As you can see, using the `Point` class removes the need to remember the appropriate equation—it does the work for you.

Generating Random Numbers

When you need to incorporate random elements into your Flash movie, either for a design effect or for game play, you can use the Math class's Math.random() method. The Math.random() method generates random numbers between 0 and 1 (including 0 but not including 1) with up to 15 decimal places in between. Typical return values are

```
0.242343544598273
0.043628738493829
0.7567833408654
```

You can modify the random number by multiplying it or adding to it to get the span of numbers you need. If you need random numbers between 1 and 10, for example, multiply the return value of Math.random() by 9 and then add 1, as in the following statement:

```
Math.random() * 9 + 1
```

You always multiply Math.random() by a number to get your desired range and then add or subtract a number to change the minimum and maximum values of that range. If you need an integer, apply the Math.floor() method to round the number down to the nearest integer.

To generate a random number:

1. Create a button symbol, and place an instance of it on the Stage. In the Property inspector, give it an instance name.
2. Create a dynamic text field, and give it an instance name in the Property inspector.
3. Select the first frame of the main Timeline, and open the Actions panel.
4. Assign an onRelease event handler to your button.
5. With your pointer between the curly braces of the onRelease event handler, enter the name of your text field, followed by a period, the text property, and an equals sign.
6. Choose ActionScript 2.0 Classes > Core > Math > Methods > random.

   The Math.random() method appears (**Figure 12.28**).

   When you click the button, a new random number between 0 and 1 is generated and displayed in the dynamic text field.

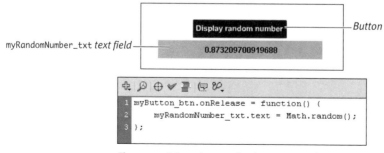

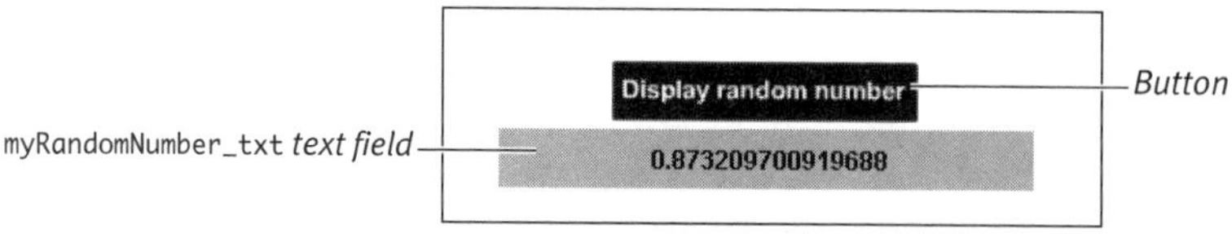


```
myButton_btn.onRelease = function() {
    myRandomNumber_txt.text = Math.random();
};
```

Figure 12.28 A random number between 0 and 1 is displayed in the text field myRandomNumber_txt when the button is clicked.

Using random numbers to modify a movie clip

Use randomly generated numbers to add unpredictable animated elements to your movie. Enemy ships in an arcade game can appear anywhere to attack the player. Make Flash deal random cards from a deck of cards so that every hand is different. Or, for a test, shuffle the order in which the questions appear. The following task demonstrates how random numbers can modify property values by setting the x and y properties of a movie clip.

To use random numbers as property values:

1. Create a movie clip symbol, place an instance of it on the Stage, and give it a name in the Property inspector.
2. Select the first frame of the main Timeline, and open the Actions panel.
3. Enter `_root`, followed by a period.
4. Choose ActionScript 2.0 Classes > Movie > MovieClip > Event Handlers > onEnterFrame.
5. Inside the `onEnterFrame` event handler, declare a `Number` variable, followed by an equals sign.
6. Enter `Math.random() * Stage.width`.
   Flash generates a random number between 0 and the width of the current Stage (**Figure 12.29**).
7. On the next line, declare a second `Number` variable and assign it a random number between 0 and the height of the Stage.
8. On a new line, enter the name of your movie clip, a period, and the _x property, followed by an equals sign.

continues on next page

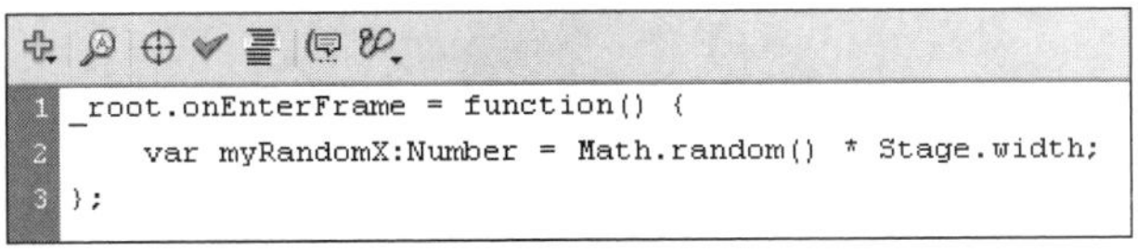

Figure 12.29 A random number between 0 and the width of the Stage is assigned to the variable `myRandomX`.

9. After the equals sign, enter the name and the first randomly generated `Number` variable (**Figure 12.30**).

   The movie clip's x position is set to the first random number.

10. On the next line, enter the movie clip's name, a period, and the _y property. Enter an equals sign, followed by the variable name for the second randomly generated number.

    The movie clip's y position is set to the second random number (**Figure 12.31**).

11. Test your movie.

    The x and y positions of your movie clip are set randomly, making the movie clip jump around the Stage.

✔ Tips

- The `Math.random()` method replaces the `random` action used in earlier versions of Flash. Although the `random` action still works, it's deprecated; stick to using the `Math` class to generate your random numbers.
- Although most properties, such as `_x` and `_y`, can accept non-integer values generated from the `Math.random()` method (as in the preceding task), some properties require integers (numbers without fractions or decimals). The `_currentframe` property, which determines the current frame number of a Timeline, must be set as an integer. Use the `Math.round()` method (or, alternatively, the `Math.floor()` method or `Math.ceil()` method) to convert a decimal number to an integer before assigning it to the `_currentframe` property.

```
_root.onEnterFrame = function() {
    var myRandomX:Number = Math.random() * Stage.width;
    var myRandomY:Number = Math.random() * Stage.height;
    ball_mc._x = myRandomX;
};
```

Figure 12.30 The x position of the movie clip is set to `myRandomX`.

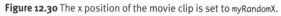

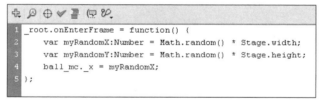

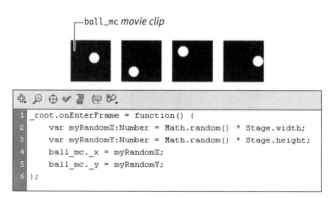

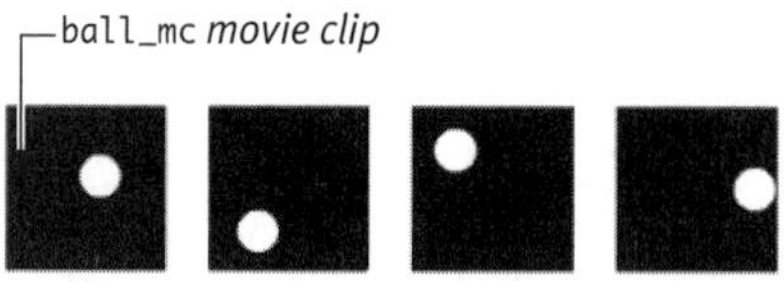


```
_root.onEnterFrame = function() {
    var myRandomX:Number = Math.random() * Stage.width;
    var myRandomY:Number = Math.random() * Stage.height;
    ball_mc._x = myRandomX;
    ball_mc._y = myRandomY;
};
```

Figure 12.31 The y position of the movie clip is set to `myRandomY`. The movie clip changes its position on the Stage randomly.

Index	Value
0	"monitor"
1	"mouse"
2	"keyboard"
3	"CPU"
4	"modem"
5	"speakers"

Figure 12.32 An Array is like a two-column table with an Index column and a corresponding Value column.

Ordering Information with Arrays

When you want to store many pieces of related information as a group, you can use the Array class to help arrange them. *Arrays* are containers that hold data, just as variables do, except that arrays hold multiple pieces of data in a specific sequence. The position of each piece of data is called its *index*. Indexes are numbered sequentially, beginning at 0, so that each piece of data corresponds to an index, as in a two-column table (**Figure 12.32**). Because each piece of data is ordered numerically, you can retrieve and modify the information easily—and, most important, automatically—by referencing its index. Suppose you're building an address book of a list of your important contacts. You can store names in an Array so that index 0 holds your first contact, index 1 holds your second contact, and so on. By using a looping statement, you can check every entry in the Array automatically.

An *element* (individual item) can be accessed using the Array object's name, followed by the element's index in square brackets, like this:

```
myArray[4]
```

The square brackets are known as *array access operators*. This statement accesses the data in index 4 of the array myArray. The number of elements is known as the *length* of the Array; for example, the length of the Array in Figure 12.32 is 6.

It's useful to think of an Array as a set of ordered variables. You can convert the variables myScores0, myScores1, myScores2, and myScores3 to a single Array called myScores of length 4 with indexes from 0 to 3. Because you have to handle only one Array object instead of four separate variables, using Arrays makes information easier to manage.

In ActionScript, the type of data that `Arrays` hold can be mixed. You can have a `Number` in index 0, a `String` in index 1, and a `Boolean` value in index 2. You can change the data in any index in an `Array` at any time. The length of `Arrays` isn't fixed, either, so they can grow or shrink to accommodate new information as needed.

Creating an `Array` involves two steps. The first is to declare an `Array` variable and use the `Array` class's constructor function to instantiate a new `Array` instance, as in this example:

```
var myArray_array:Array = new Array();
```

The second step is to fill, or *populate*, your `Array` with data. One way to populate your `Array` is to assign the data to each index in separate statements, like this:

```
myArray_array[0] = "Russell";
myArray_array[1] = "Rebecca";
myArray_array[2] = "Clint";
myArray_array[3] = "Kathy";
```

Another way to assign the data is to put the information as parameters within the constructor function:

```
var myArray_array:Array = new Array
("Russell", "Rebecca", "Clint", "Kathy")
```

The second is a more compact way of populating your `Array`, but you're restricted to entering the data in sequence.

To create an Array:

1. Select the first keyframe of the Timeline, and open the Actions panel.
2. Declare your `Array` by entering `var`, the object's name, and then `:Array`. On the same line, enter an equals sign.
3. Choose ActionScript 2.0 Classes > Core > Array > "new Array".

   Flash instantiates a new `Array` (**Figure 12.33**).
4. On the next line, enter the name of your new `Array`, an index number between square brackets, and then an equals sign.
5. Enter the data you want to store in the `Array` at that index position (**Figure 12.34**).
6. Continue to assign more data to the `Array`.

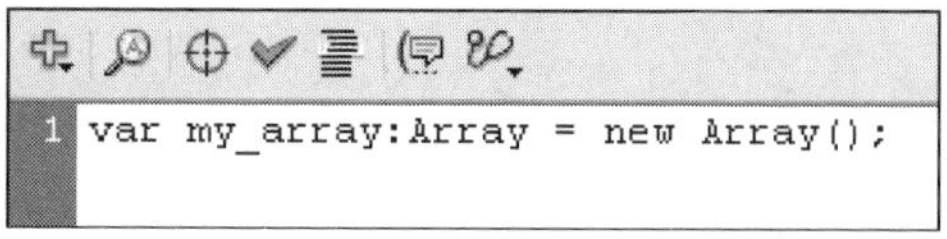

Figure 12.33 A new `Array` called `my_array` is instantiated.

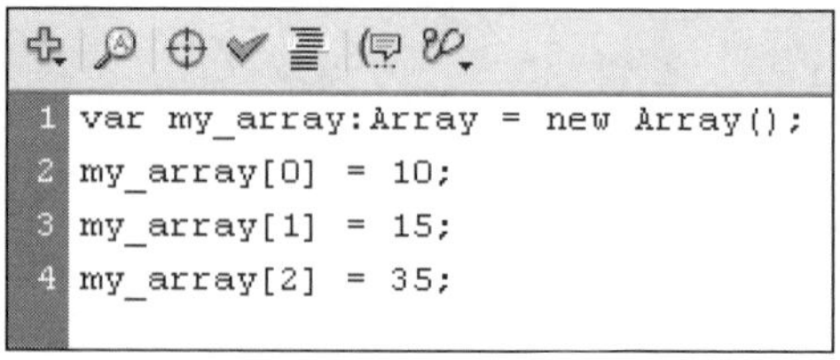

1 var my_array:Array = new Array();
2 my_array[0] = 10;
3 my_array[1] = 15;
4 my_array[2] = 35;

Figure 12.34 This `Array` contains three elements.

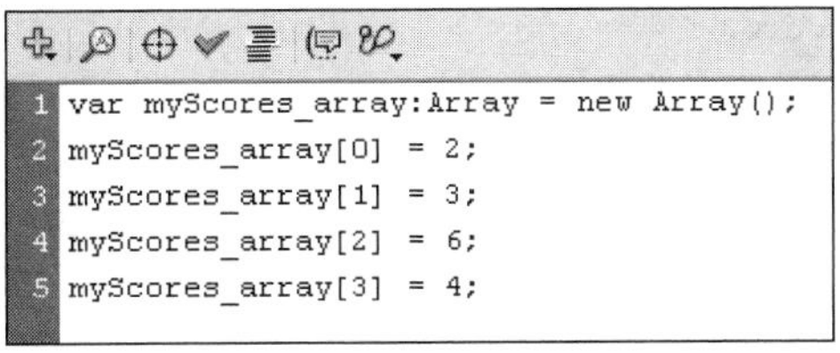

```
var myScores_array:Array = new Array();
myScores_array[0] = 2;
myScores_array[1] = 3;
myScores_array[2] = 6;
myScores_array[3] = 4;
```

Figure 12.35 This Array, called myScores_array, has four elements.

Automating Array operations with loops

Because the elements of an Array are indexed numerically, they lend themselves nicely to looping actions. By using looping actions such as while, do while, and for, you can have Flash go through each index and retrieve or assign new data quickly and automatically. To average the scores of many players in an Array without a looping action, for example, you have to total all their scores and divide by the number of players, like this:

```
mySum = myScores[0] + myScores[1] +
myScores[2] + ...
myAverage = mySum / myScores.length;
```

(The property length defines the number of entries in the Array.)

Using a looping action, however, you can calculate the mySum value this way:

```
for (i=0; I < myScores.length; i++) {
    mySum = mySum + myScores[i];
}
myAverage = mySum / myScores.length;
```

Flash starts at index 0 and adds each indexed entry in the Array to the variable mySum until it reaches the end of the Array.

To loop through an Array:

1. Select the first keyframe of the Timeline, and open the Actions panel.
2. Declare and instantiate a new Array called myScores_array.
3. Populate the myScores_array Array with numbers representing scores (**Figure 12.35**).
4. Create a button symbol, and place an instance of the button on the Stage. In the Property inspector, give the button an instance name.

continues on next page

5. Select the first keyframe of the Timeline. On the next available line in the Actions panel, create an `onRelease` event handler assigned to the button.

6. Within the `onRelease` event handler, declare a `Number` variable called `mySum` and initialize it to `0`.

7. On the next line, choose Statements > Conditions/Loops > for.

8. With your pointer between the parentheses, enter the following:

   `var i:Number = 0; i < myScores_array.length; i++`

   Flash begins with the counter variable `i` set at the value `0`. It increases the variable by increments of 1 until the variable reaches the length of `myScores_array` (**Figure 12.36**).

9. Between the curly braces of the `for` loop, enter `mySum`, followed by an equals sign.

10. Enter `mySum + myScores_array[i]`.

    Rather than using an explicit index, the value of the variable `i` will define the index (and, consequently, which element's value is retrieved and added to `mySum`).

    Flash loops through the `myScores_array`'s elements in turn, adding the value in each element of the `Array` to `mySum`. When the value of `i` reaches the value of `myScores_array.length`, Flash jumps out of the `for` loop and stops retrieving values. Therefore, the last element accessed is `myScores_array[myScores_array.length - 1]`, which is the last element of the `Array` (**Figure 12.37**).

11. On the next line after the ending curly brace of the `for` statement, enter `myAverage_txt.text =`.

12. Enter the expression `mySum / myScores_array.length` (**Figure 12.38**).

```
scores_btn.onRelease = function() {
    var mySum:Number = 0;
    for (var i:Number = 0; i < myScores_array.length; i++) {
    }
};
```

Figure 12.36 This `for` action loops the same number of times as there are elements in the `Array` `myScore_array`.

```
var myScores_array:Array = new Array();
myScores_array[0] = 2;
myScores_array[1] = 3;
myScores_array[2] = 6;
myScores_array[3] = 4;
scores_btn.onRelease = function() {
    var mySum:Number = 0;
    for (var i:Number = 0; i < myScores_array.length; i++) {
        mySum = mySum + myScores_array[i];
    }
};
```

Figure 12.37 The value of each element in the `Array` is added to the variable `mySum`.

```
var myScores_array:Array = new Array();
myScores_array[0] = 2;
myScores_array[1] = 3;
myScores_array[2] = 6;
myScores_array[3] = 4;
scores_btn.onRelease = function() {
    var mySum:Number = 0;
    for (var i:Number = 0; i < myScores_array.length; i++) {
        mySum = mySum + myScores_array[i];
    }
    myAverage_txt.text = mySum / myScores_array.length;
};
```

Figure 12.38 After the `for` loop, the average value of the elements in the `Array` is calculated and displayed in the text field `myAverage_txt`.

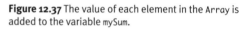

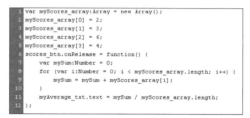

13. Create a dynamic text field on the Stage with the instance name `myAverage_txt`.

14. Test your movie.

    When you click the button on the Stage, Flash loops through the `myScores_array` `Array` to add the values in all the elements, and then it divides the total by the number of elements. The average is displayed in the dynamic text field on the Stage.

The Array class's methods

The methods of the `Array` class let you sort, delete, add, and manipulate the data in an `Array`. **Table 12.2** summarizes the methods of the `Array` class. It's convenient to think of the methods in pairs: `shift()` and `unshift()`, for example, both modify the beginning of an `Array`; `push()` and `pop()` both modify the end of an `Array`; and `slice()` and `splice()` both modify the middle of an `Array`.

Table 12.2

Methods of the Array Object

Method	Description
`concat(`*`array1,...,arrayN`*`)`	Concatenates the specified `Array` objects, and returns a new `Array`.
`join(`*`separator`*`)`	Concatenates the elements of the `Array`, inserts the `String` *`separator`* between the elements, and returns a `String`. The default separator is a comma.
`pop()`	Removes the last element in the `Array`, and returns the value of that element.
`push(`*`value`*`)`	Adds a new element *`value`* to the end of the `Array`, and returns the new length.
`shift()`	Removes the first element in the `Array`, and returns the value of that element.
`unshift(`*`value`*`)`	Adds a new element *`value`* to the beginning of the `Array`, and returns the new length.
`slice(`*`indexA, indexB`*`)`	Returns a new `Array` beginning with element *`indexA`* and ending with element `(`*`indexB`*` - 1)`.
`splice(`*`index, count, elem1,..., elemN`*`)`	Inserts or deletes elements. Set *`count`* to `0` to insert specified values starting at *`index`*. Set *`count`* > `0` to delete the number of elements starting at and including `index`.
`reverse()`	Reverses the order of elements in the `Array`.
`sort()`	Sorts the elements of the `Array`. Numbers are sorted in ascending order, and strings are sorted alphabetically.
`sortOn(`*`fieldName`*`)`	Sorts an `Array` of objects based on the value in each element's *`fieldName`* (a `String`) property.
`toString()`	Returns a `String` with every element concatenated and separated by a comma.

Table 12.3 gives examples of how some of the methods in Table 12.2 operate.

✔ Tips

- It's important to note which methods of the Array class modify the original Array and which ones return a new Array. The methods concat(), join(), slice(), and toString() return a new Array or String and don't alter the original Array. new_array = original_array.concat(8), for example, puts 8 at the end of original_array and assigns the resulting Array to new_array. original_array isn't affected. Also note that some methods modify the Array as well as return a specific value. These two things aren't the same. The statement my_array.pop(), for example, modifies my_array by removing the last element and also returns the value of that last element. At the end of this example, the value of myPop_array is 8, and the value of my_array is 2, 4, 6:

```
my_array = new Array (2, 4, 6, 8);
myPop_array = my_array.pop();
```

- An easy way to remember the duties of some of these methods is to think of the elements of your Array as being components of a stack. (In fact, *stack* is a programming term for a type of array where the last element added is the first element retrieved.) You can think of an Array object as being like a stack of books or a stack of cafeteria trays on a spring-loaded holder. The bottom of the stack is the first element in an Array. When you call the Array's push() method, imagine that you literally push a new tray on top of the stack to add a new element. When you call the pop() method, you pop, or remove, the top tray from the stack (the last element). When you shift an Array, you take out the bottom tray (the first element) so that all the other trays shift down into new positions.

Table 12.3

Examples of Array Methods

Statement	Value of myArray
var myArray:Array = new Array(2, 4, 6, 8)	2, 4, 6, 8
myArray.pop()	2, 4, 6
myArray.push(1, 3)	2, 4, 6, 1, 3
myArray.shift()	4, 6, 1, 3
myArray.unshift(5, 7)	5, 7, 4, 6, 1, 3
myArray.splice(2, 0, 8, 9)	5, 7, 8, 9, 4, 6, 1, 3
myArray.splice(3, 2)	5, 7, 8, 6, 1, 3
myArray.reverse()	3, 1, 6, 8, 7, 5
myArray.sort()	1, 3, 5, 6, 7, 8

Two-Dimensional Arrays

We've compared an `Array` with a two-column table, in which the index is in one column and its contents are in a second column. What if you need to keep track of information stored in more than one row in a table, as in a traditional spreadsheet? The solution is to nest an `Array` inside another one to create what's known as a *two-dimensional Array*. This type of `Array` creates two indexes for every piece of information. To keep track of a checker piece on a checkerboard, for example, you can use a two-dimensional `Array` to reference its rows and its columns (**Figure 12.39**).

For the three rows, create three separate `Arrays` and populate them with numbers:

```
var row0_array:Array = new Array(1,2,3);
var row1_array:Array = new Array(4,5,6);
var row2_array:Array = new Array(7,8,9);
```

Now you can put those three `Arrays` inside another `Array`, like so:

```
var gameBoard_array:Array = new Array();
gameBoard_array[0] = row0_array;
gameBoard_array[1] = row1_array;
gameBoard_array[2] = row2_array;
```

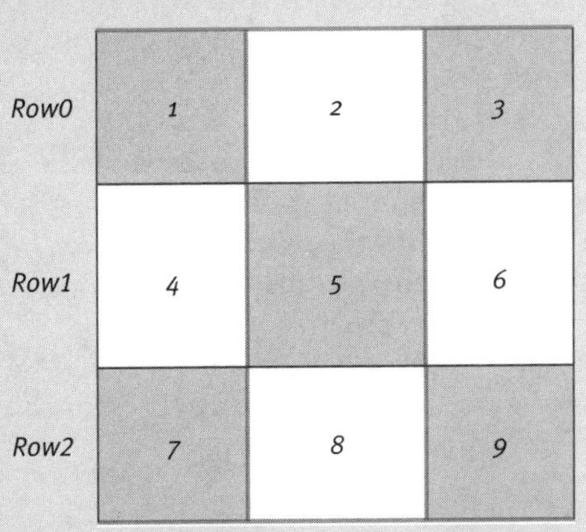

Figure 12.39 You can use a two-dimensional `Array` to map a checkerboard and keep track of what's inside individual squares. Each row is an `Array`. The rows are put inside another `Array`.

To access or modify the information of a checkerboard square, first use one set of square brackets that references the row. The statement `gameBoard_array[2]` references the `Array row2_array`. Then, by using another set of square brackets, you can reference the column within that row. The statement `gameBoard_array[2][0]` accesses the number 7.

Keeping Track of Movie Clips with Arrays

Sometimes, you have to deal with many movie clips on the Stage at the same time. Keeping track of them all and performing actions to modify, test, or evaluate each one can be a nightmare unless you use Arrays to help manage them. Imagine that you're creating a game in which the viewer has to avoid rocks falling from the sky. You can use the hitTest() method to see whether each falling-rock movie clip intersects with the viewer. But if there are 10 rocks on the Stage, that potentially means 10 separate hitTest() statements. You can better manage the multiple falling rocks by putting them in an Array. Doing so allows you to perform the hitTest() in a loop on the elements in the Array instead of in many separate statements.

Put a movie clip into an Array just as you put any other object into the Array, using an assignment statement:

```
rock_array[0]=_root.fallingRock0_mc;
rock_array[1]=_root.fallingRock1_mc;
rock_array[2]=_root.fallingRock2_mc;
```

These statements put the movie clip fallingRock0_mc in element 0 of the Array rock_array, the movie clip fallingRock1_mc in element 1, and the movie clip fallingRock2_mc in element 2. Now you can reference the movie clips through the Array. This statement changes the transparency of the movie clip fallingRock2_mc:

```
rock_array[2]._alpha = 40
```

You can even call methods this way:

```
rock_array[2].hitTest(_xmouse, _ymouse, true)
```

This statement checks to see whether the fallingRock2_mc movie clip intersects with the mouse pointer.

The following tasks use looping statements to populate an Array with movie clips automatically. When the Array is full of movie clips, you can perform the same action, such as modifying a property or calling hitTest(), on all the movie clips by referencing the Array.

To populate an Array with duplicate movie clips:

1. Create a movie clip symbol, place an instance of it on the Stage, and give it a name in the Property inspector.

   In this example, the instance name is block_mc.

2. Select the first frame of the main Timeline, and open the Actions panel.

3. Declare an Array variable, followed by an equals sign.

4. Choose ActionScript 2.0 Classes > Core > Array > "new Array".

   Your Array object is instantiated (**Figure 12.40**).

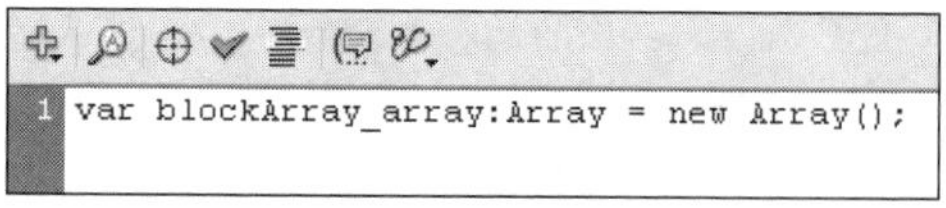
1
var blockArray_array:Array = new Array();

Figure 12.40 A new Array called blockArray_array is instantiated.

5. On the next line, choose Statements > Conditions/Loops > for.
6. With your pointer between the parentheses, enter `var i:Number = 0; i < 15; i++` (**Figure 12.41**).

   This loop will occur 15 times, starting with `i` equal to 0 and ending after `i` equals 14.
7. Inside the `for` statement, declare a new `MovieClip` variable, followed by an equals sign. Enter the instance name of your movie clip, and choose ActionScript 2.0 Classes > Movie > MovieClip > Methods > duplicateMovieClip.
8. For the parameters of the method `duplicateMovieClip`, enter `"block_mc" + i` and `i` (**Figure 12.42**).

   Flash duplicates the `block_mc` movie clip and gives each duplicate a unique name and depth based on the variable `i`. The first duplicate is called `block_mc0`, the second is called `block_mc1`, and so on.

   Each duplicate is stored in the `MovieClip` variable for the duration of the loop, making it easy to access using the variable.
9. On the next line, enter the name of the `Array` object, then the variable `i` in square brackets, followed by an equals sign and the name of the `MovieClip` variable, similar to the following:

   `blockArray_array[i] = clip`

   Each new duplicate is put inside a different element of the `Array` (**Figure 12.43**).

```
var blockArray_array:Array = new Array();
for (var i:Number = 0; i < 15; i++) {
}
```

Figure 12.41 Create a `for` statement that uses a counter that begins at 0 and ends at 14, increasing by 1 with each loop.

```
for (var i:Number = 0; i < 15; i++) {
    var clip:MovieClip = block_mc.duplicateMovieClip("block_mc" + i, i);
}
```

Figure 12.42 The movie clip `block_mc` on the Stage is duplicated and assigned to a `MovieClip` variable.

```
var blockArray_array:Array = new Array();
for (var i:Number = 0; i < 15; i++) {
    var clip:MovieClip = block_mc.duplicateMovieClip("block_mc" + i, i);
    blockArray_array[i] = clip;
}
```

Figure 12.43 Each duplicate is put in `blockArray_array`. The movie clip `block_mc0` is in `blockArray_array[0]`, the movie clip `block_mc1` is in `blockArray_array[1]`, and so on.

Accessing movie clips in an Array

Now that your Array is populated with movie clips, you can reference them easily with just the Array's index value to change their properties or call their methods.

In the next two tasks, you'll first access the movie clips from the Array to move them to random x- and y-coordinates. Then you'll check to see whether the viewer's pointer touches any of the movie clip duplicates. Instead of checking each duplicate separately, you'll loop through the Array again and check all the duplicates with only a few lines of ActionScript.

To reference movie clips inside an Array (part 1, modify properties):

1. Continuing with the file you created in the preceding task, select the main Timeline, and open the Actions panel.
2. Create a new line within the for statement.

   Your next statement will still appear within the for statement, but after the duplicates are made and placed inside the Array.
3. Enter your Array's name, followed by i in square brackets, a period and the _x property. Then add = Math.random() * Stage.width (**Figure 12.44**).

   A different random number between 0 and the width of the current Stage is generated and assigned to the x position of every movie clip inside your Array.
4. On a new line, enter the same statement you entered in step 3, except assign a random number between 0 and the Stage.height property to the _y property of the Array element. Your code will look similar to this:

   blockArray[i]._y = Math.random() * Stage.height (**Figure 12.45**).

   A random number from 0 to the height of the current Stage is generated and assigned to the y position of every movie clip inside the Array.

```
for (var i:Number = 0; i < 15; i++) {
    var clip:MovieClip = block_mc.duplicateMovieClip("block_mc" + i, i);
    blockArray_array[i] = clip;
    blockArray_array[i]._x = Math.random() * Stage.width;
}
```

Figure 12.44 The x position of each movie clip inside blockArray_array is set to a random value.

```
for (var i:Number = 0; i < 15; i++) {
    var clip:MovieClip = block_mc.duplicateMovieClip("block_mc" + i, i);
    blockArray_array[i] = clip;
    blockArray_array[i]._x = Math.random() * Stage.width;
    blockArray_array[i]._y = Math.random() * Stage.height;
}
```

Figure 12.45 The y position of each movie clip inside blockArray_array is assigned a random value.

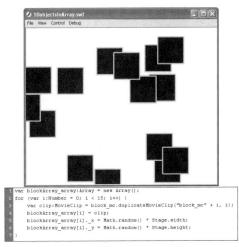

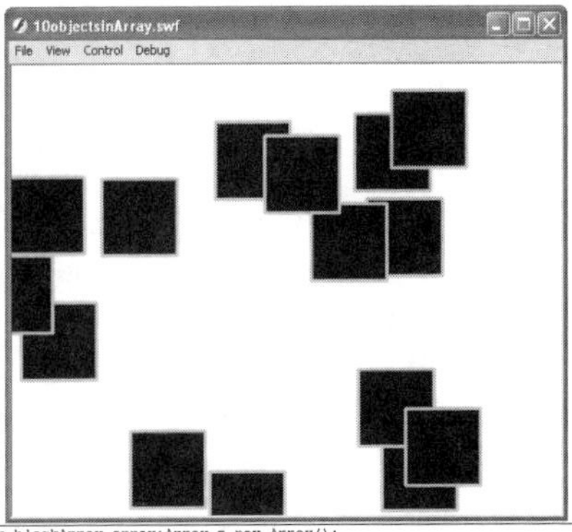


```
var blockArray_array:Array = new Array();
for (var i:Number = 0; i < 15; i++) {
    var clip:MovieClip = block_mc.duplicateMovieClip("block_mc" + i, i);
    blockArray_array[i] = clip;
    blockArray_array[i]._x = Math.random() * Stage.width;
    blockArray_array[i]._y = Math.random() * Stage.height;
}
```

Figure 12.46 The full script is shown at the bottom. The duplicate movie clips scatter randomly within the boundaries of the Stage.

```
_root.onEnterFrame = function() {
    for (var i:Number = 0; i < 15; i++) {
    }
};
```

Figure 12.47 Enter the same loop statements for the `for` loop that you did for the first loop that generated the duplicate movie clips.

```
_root.onEnterFrame = function() {
    for (var i:Number = 0; i < 15; i++) {
        if (blockArray_array[i].hitTest(_xmouse, _ymouse, true)) {
        }
    }
};
```

Figure 12.48 Flash checks every movie clip inside `blockArray_array` to see whether the clips intersect with the mouse pointer.

5. Test your movie.

   The `for` loop generates duplicate movie clips automatically and puts them inside the `Array`. At the same time, it references the movie clips inside the `Array` and changes their x and y positions to random values (**Figure 12.46**).

To reference movie clips inside an Array (part 2, call a method):

1. Continuing with the file you used in the preceding task, select the main Timeline, and open the Actions panel.
2. On a new line after the `for` statement, enter `_root` and create an `onEnterFrame` handler.
3. On a new line inside the `onEnterFrame` event handler, choose Statements > Conditions/Loops > for.
4. With your pointer between the parentheses, enter `var i:Number = 0; i < 15; i++` (**Figure 12.47**).
5. On the next line, choose Statements > Conditions/Loops > if.
6. For the condition, enter the name of your array, followed by `[i]` to reference each movie clip inside the `Array`.
7. Choose ActionScript 2.0 Classes > Movie > MovieClip > Methods > hitTest.
8. Between the parentheses of the `hitTest()` method, enter the parameters `_xmouse`, `_ymouse`, and `true` (**Figure 12.48**).

continues on next page

9. Choose actions to perform when the mouse pointer is over a movie clip, and enter them in the curly braces of the `if` statement.

   For example, enter this expression: `blockArray_array[i]._alpha = 30` (**Figure 12.49**).

10. Test your movie.

    When the `for` loop is performed, all the movie clips inside the `Array` are tested to see whether they intersect with the pointer. Because the `for` loop is within an `onEnterFrame` handler, this check is done continuously. If an intersection occurs, that particular movie clip turns 30 percent opaque (**Figure 12.50**).

```
var blockArray_array:Array = new Array();
for (var i:Number = 0; i < 15; i++) {
    var clip:MovieClip = block_mc.duplicateMovieClip("block_mc" + i, i);
    blockArray_array[i] = clip;
    blockArray_array[i]._x = Math.random() * Stage.width;
    blockArray_array[i]._y = Math.random() * Stage.height;
}

_root.onEnterFrame = function() {
    for (var i:Number = 0; i < 15; i++) {
        if (blockArray_array[i].hitTest(_xmouse, _ymouse, true)) {
            blockArray_array[i]._alpha = 30;
        }
    }
};
```

Figure 12.49 The full script. If Flash detects an intersection between a movie clip and the pointer, that particular movie clip's transparency changes.

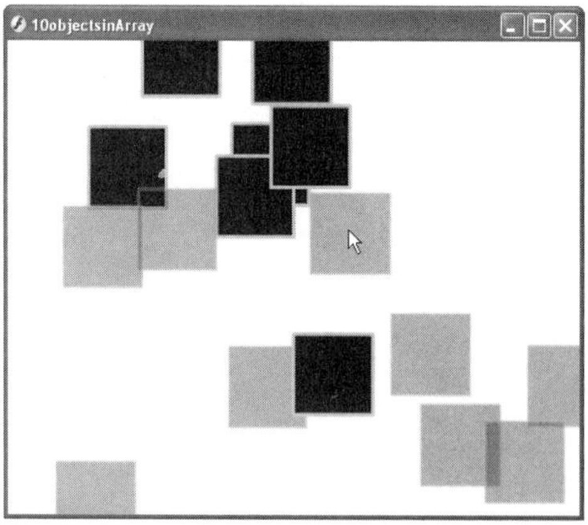

Figure 12.50 The pointer has passed over many of the movie clips, which have turned semi-transparent. Use this technique to manage multiple movie clips for game interactivity.

Table 12.4

Methods of the Date Class

Method	Description
getFullYear()	Returns the year as a four-digit number
getMonth()	Returns the month as a number from 0 (January) to 11 (December)
getDate()	Returns the day of the month as a number from 1 to 31
getDay()	Returns the day of the week as a number from 0 (Sunday) to 6 (Saturday)
getHours()	Returns the hour of the day as a number from 0 to 23
getMinutes()	Returns the minutes as a number from 0 to 59
getSeconds()	Returns the seconds as a number from 0 to 59
getMilliseconds()	Returns the milliseconds

Using the Date and Time

The `Date` class lets you retrieve the local or universal (UTC) date and time information from the clock in your viewer's computer system. Using a `Date` object, you can retrieve the year, month, day of the month, day of the week, hour, minute, second, and millisecond. Use a `Date` object and its methods to create accurate clocks in your movie or to find information about certain days and dates in the past. You can create a `Date` object for your birthday, for example, by specifying the month, day, and year. Using methods of the `Date` class, you can retrieve the day of the week for your `Date` object that tells you what day you were born.

First, you need to instantiate a `Date` object with the constructor function `new Date()`. Then you can call on its methods to retrieve specific time information. **Table 12.4** summarizes the common methods for retrieving the date and time information.

To create a clock:

1. Create a dynamic text field on the Stage, and give it an instance name in the Property inspector.

   The dynamic text field will display the time.

2. Select the first frame of the main Timeline, and open the Actions panel.

3. Enter `_root` and create an `onEnterFrame` handler.

4. Within the `onEnterFrame` event handler, use the `var` statement to declare a `Date` object, followed by an equals sign.

continues on next page

5. Choose ActionScript 2.0 Classes > Core > Date > "new Date".

   The new `Date()` constructor function appears. The `Date` object is instantiated (**Figure 12.51**). If you don't specify any parameters in the constructor, the `Date` object is populated with the current date and time information. You can also specify parameters in the constructor to create an object that references a specific date and time.

6. On a new line, declare a `Number` variable named `currentHour`, followed by an equal sign.

7. Enter the name of your `Date` object, followed by a period.

8. With your pointer next to your `Date` object, choose ActionScript 2.0 Classes > Core > Date > Methods > getHours.

   The `getHours()` method appears after the name of your `Date` object. Flash retrieves the current hour and puts it in the variable `currentHour` (**Figure 12.52**).

9. Repeat step 8 to retrieve the current minute with the `getMinutes()` method and the current second with the `getSeconds()` method, and assign the returned values to variables (**Figure 12.53**).

10. On a new line, choose Statements > Conditions/Loops > if.

11. For the condition, enter `currentHour > 12`.

12. On the next line inside the `if` statement, enter `currentHour = currentHour - 12` (**Figure 12.54**).

```
_root.onEnterFrame = function() {
    var myDate_date:Date = new Date();
};
```

Figure 12.51 The `myDate_date` `Date` object is instantiated inside an `onEnterFrame` handler.

```
_root.onEnterFrame = function() {
    var myDate_date:Date = new Date();
    var currentHour:Number = myDate_date.getHours();
};
```

Figure 12.52 The current hour is assigned to the variable `currentHour`.

```
_root.onEnterFrame = function() {
    var myDate_date:Date = new Date();
    var currentHour:Number = myDate_date.getHours();
    var currentMinute:Number = myDate_date.getMinutes();
    var currentSecond:Number = myDate_date.getSeconds();
};
```

Figure 12.53 The current hour, minute, and second are retrieved from the computer's clock and assigned to different variables.

```
_root.onEnterFrame = function() {
    var myDate_date:Date = new Date();
    var currentHour:Number = myDate_date.getHours();
    var currentMinute:Number = myDate_date.getMinutes();
    var currentSecond:Number = myDate_date.getSeconds();
    if (currentHour > 12) {
        currentHour = currentHour - 12;
    }
};
```

Figure 12.54 The returned value for the method `getHours()` is a number from 0 to 23. To convert the hour to the standard 12-hour cycle, subtract 12 for hours greater than 12.

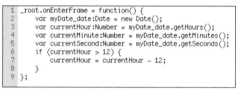

```
_root.onEnterFrame = function() {
    var myDate_date:Date = new Date();
    var currentHour:Number = myDate_date.getHours();
    var currentMinute:Number = myDate_date.getMinutes();
    var currentSecond:Number = myDate_date.getSeconds();
    if (currentHour > 12) {
        currentHour = currentHour - 12;
    } else if (currentHour == 0) {
        currentHour = 12;
    }
};
```

Figure 12.55 Because there is no 0 on a clock, have Flash assign 12 to any hour that has the value 0.

13. Place your pointer after the closing curly brace for the `if` statement, and choose Statements > Conditions/Loops > else if. Delete the extra opening curly brace that's inserted before the `else if` statement.

14. For the condition of the `else if` statement, enter `currentHour == 0`.

15. Inside the `else if` block, enter `currentHour = 12` (**Figure 12.55**).

16. On a new line after the closing curly brace of your `else if` statement, enter the name of your text field, followed by a period, the `text` property, and an equals sign.

17. After the equals sign, create an expression that concatenates the variable names for the hour, the minute, and the second with appropriate spacers between them (**Figure 12.56**).

18. Test your movie.

    The dynamic text field displays the current hour, minute, and second in the 12-hour format.

✔ Tip

- Note that minutes and seconds that are less than 10 display as single digits, such as 1 and 2, rather than as 01 and 02. Refine your clock by adding conditional statements to check the value of the current minutes and seconds and add the appropriate 0 digit.

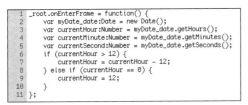

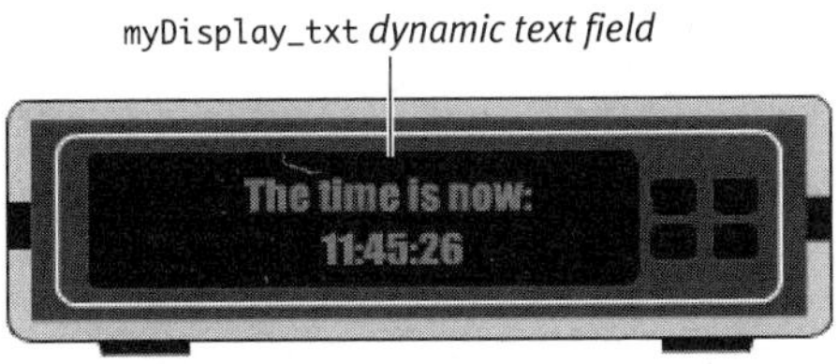


```
myDisplay_txt.text = "The time is now: \n" + currentHour + ":" + currentMinute + ":" + currentSecond;
```

Figure 12.56 The dynamic text field displays the concatenated values for the hour, minute, and second.

Date numbers and names

The values returned by the getMonth() and getDay() methods of a Date object are numbers instead of string data types. The getMonth() method returns values from 0 to 11 (0 = January), and the getDay() method returns values from 0 to 6 (0 = Sunday). To correlate these numeric values with the names of the months or days of the week, you can create Arrays that contain this information. You can create an Array that contains the days of the week with the following statements:

```
var dayNames_array:Array = new Array();
dayNames_array[0] = "Sunday";
dayNames_array[1] = "Monday";
dayNames_array[2] = "Tuesday";
dayNames_array[3] = "Wednesday";
dayNames_array[4] = "Thursday";
dayNames_array[5] = "Friday";
dayNames_array[6] = "Saturday";
```

To create a calendar:

1. Create a dynamic text field on the Stage, and give it an instance name in the Property inspector.

   The dynamic text field will display the date.

2. Select the first keyframe of the Timeline, and open the Actions panel.

3. Declare an Array object that will hold the days of the week, followed by an equals sign.

4. Enter the constructor function new Array().

5. In a series of statements, assign Strings representing the names of the days of the week as elements of your Array (**Figure 12.57**).

6. On a new line, declare a second new Array, followed by an equals sign.

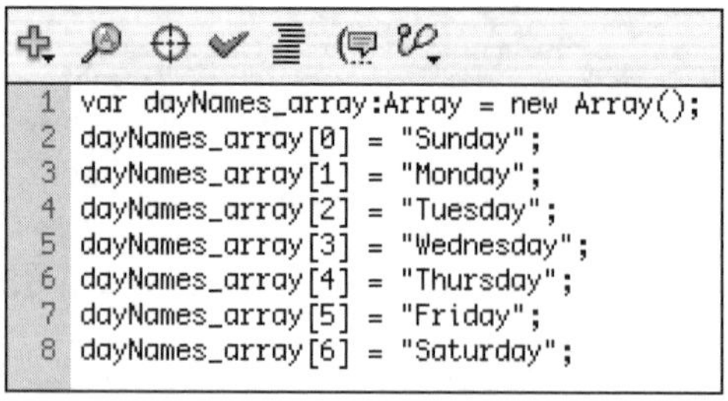
var dayNames_array:Array = new Array();
dayNames_array[0] = "Sunday";
dayNames_array[1] = "Monday";
dayNames_array[2] = "Tuesday";
dayNames_array[3] = "Wednesday";
dayNames_array[4] = "Thursday";
dayNames_array[5] = "Friday";
dayNames_array[6] = "Saturday";

Figure 12.57 The Array dayNames_array contains Strings of all the days of the week.

```
var monthNames_array:Array = new Array();
monthNames_array[0] = "January";
monthNames_array[1] = "February";
monthNames_array[2] = "March";
monthNames_array[3] = "April";
monthNames_array[4] = "May";
monthNames_array[5] = "June";
monthNames_array[6] = "July";
monthNames_array[7] = "August";
monthNames_array[8] = "September";
monthNames_array[9] = "October";
monthNames_array[10] = "November";
monthNames_array[11] = "December";
```

Figure 12.58 The `Array` `monthNames_array` contains `Strings` of all the months.

```
var myDate_date:Date = new Date();
var currentYear:Number = myDate_date.getFullYear();
var currentMonth:Number = myDate_date.getMonth();
var currentDate:Number = myDate_date.getDate();
var currentDay:Number = myDate_date.getDay();
```

Figure 12.59 The current year, month, date, and day are retrieved from the computer's clock and assigned to new variables.

7. Enter the constructor function `new Array()`.

   This `Array` will hold the months of the year.

8. In a series of statements, assign `Strings` representing the names of the months of the year to the elements of this `Array` (**Figure 12.58**).

9. On a new line, declare a new `Date` object, followed by an equals sign.

10. Enter the constructor function `new Date()` without any parameters.

11. In a series of statements, call the `getFullYear()`, `getMonth()`, `getDate()`, and `getDay()` methods, and assign their values to new `Number` variables (**Figure 12.59**).

12. Enter the name of your dynamic text field, followed by a period, the `text` property, and an equals sign.

13. Enter the name of the `Array` that contains the days of the week. As its index, put in the variable containing the value returned by the `getDay()` method.

    The value of this variable is a number from 0 to 6. This number is used to retrieve the correct string in the `Array` corresponding to the current day.

14. Concatenate the `Array` that contains the days of the month, and as its index put the variable containing the value returned by the `getMonth()` method call.

continues on next page

15. Concatenate the other variables that hold the current date and year (**Figure 12.60**).

16. Test your movie.

    Flash gets the day, month, date, and year from the system clock. The names of the specific day and month are retrieved from the `Array` objects, and the information is displayed in the dynamic text field.

Tracking elapsed time

Another way to provide time information to your viewer is to use the Flash function `getTimer`. This function returns the number of milliseconds that have elapsed since the Flash movie started playing. You can compare the returned value of `getTimer` at one instant with the returned value of it at another instant, and the difference gives you the elapsed time between those two instances. Use the elapsed time to create timers for games and activities in your Flash movie. You can time how long it takes for your viewer to answer questions correctly in a test or give your viewer only a certain amount of time to complete the test. Or, award more points in a game if the player successfully completes a mission within an allotted time.

Because `getTimer` is a built-in function and not a method of an object, you call it by using the function name.

To create a timer:

1. Create a dynamic text field on the Stage, and give it an instance name in the Property inspector.

2. Select the first frame of the main Timeline, and open the Actions panel.

3. Declare a `Number` variable named `startTime`, and assign it an initial value of `0`.

4. Enter `_root`, and create an `onMouseDown` event handler.

5. Within the `onMouseDown` event handler, enter `startTime`, followed by an equals sign.

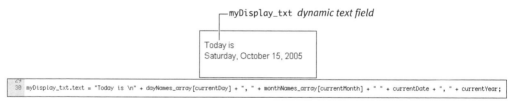

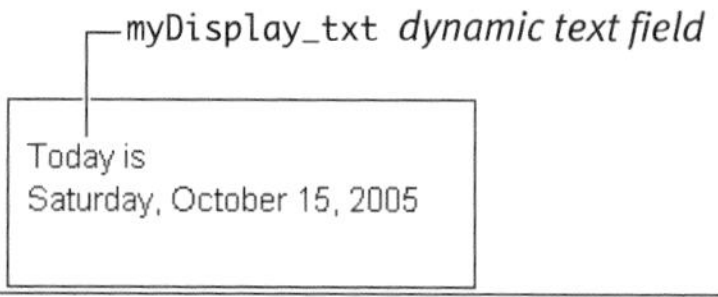


```
myDisplay_txt.text = "Today is \n" + dayNames_array[currentDay] + ", " + monthNames_array[currentMonth] + " " + currentDate + ", " + currentYear;
```

Figure 12.60 The day, month, date, and year information is concatenated and displayed in the `myDisplay` text field.

```
var startTime:Number= 0;
_root.onMouseDown = function() {
    startTime = getTimer();
};
```

Figure 12.61 When the viewer presses the mouse button, the `getTimer` function retrieves the time elapsed since the start of the Flash movie. That time is put in the variable `startTime`.

```
var startTime:Number= 0;
_root.onMouseDown = function() {
    startTime = getTimer();
};

_root.onEnterFrame = function() {
    var currentTime:Number = getTimer();
};
```

Figure 12.62 On an ongoing basis, the `getTimer` function retrieves the time elapsed since the start of the Flash movie. That time is put in the variable `currentTime`.

6. Choose Global Functions > Miscellaneous Functions > getTimer (**Figure 12.61**).

   Whenever the mouse button is pressed, the time that has passed since the movie started playing is assigned to the variable `startTime`.

7. On a new line, enter `_root` and create an `onEnterFrame` handler.

8. Within the `onEnterFrame` event handler, declare a `Number` variable named `currentTime`, followed by an equals sign.

9. Choose Global Functions > Miscellaneous Functions > getTimer.

   The `getTimer` function appears (**Figure 12.62**).

10. On the next line, declare a `Number` variable named `elapsedTime`, followed by an equals sign.

continues on next page

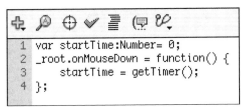

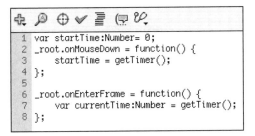

11. Enter `(currentTime - startTime) / 1000`.

    Flash calculates the difference between the current timer and the timer at the instant the mouse button was clicked. The result is divided by 1,000 to convert it to seconds (**Figure 12.63**).

12. On a new line, assign the variable `elapsedTime` to the `text` property of your dynamic text field (**Figure 12.64**).

13. Test your movie.

    Flash displays the time elapsed since the last instant the viewer pressed the mouse button.

✔ Tip

- Experiment with different event handlers to build a stopwatch with Start, Stop, and Lap buttons.

```
var startTime:Number= 0;
_root.onMouseDown = function() {
    startTime = getTimer();
};

_root.onEnterFrame = function() {
    var currentTime:Number = getTimer();
    var elapsedTime:Number = (currentTime - startTime) / 1000;
};
```

Figure 12.63 The variable `elapsedTime` is assigned the difference between the two instances of time recorded in the variables `startTime` and `currentTime`.

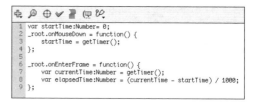

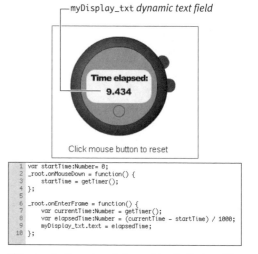

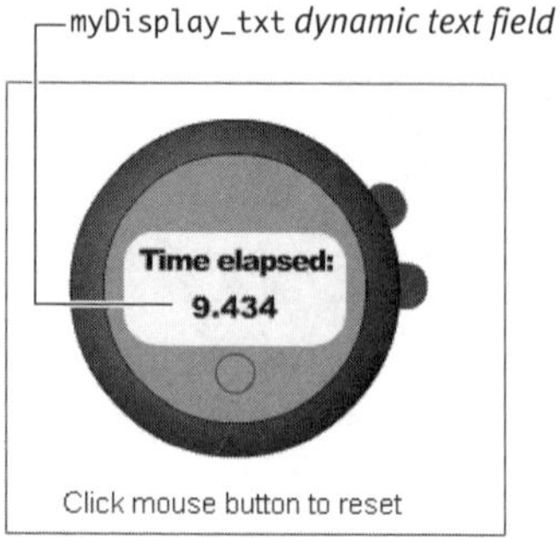


```
var startTime:Number= 0;
_root.onMouseDown = function() {
    startTime = getTimer();
};

_root.onEnterFrame = function() {
    var currentTime:Number = getTimer();
    var elapsedTime:Number = (currentTime - startTime) / 1000;
    myDisplay_txt.text = elapsedTime;
};
```

Figure 12.64 The value of `elapsedTime` is displayed in the text field `myDisplay_txt`.

Building Reusable Scripts

When you need to perform the same kind of manipulation of information multiple times, you can save time and reduce code clutter by building your own functions. You've used functions in previous chapters, mostly as event handlers. When you assign an anonymous function as an object's event handler, for example, that function is triggered whenever the event happens. But whether they're anonymous or named, functions have the same job: They group related statements to perform a task that you can invoke from anywhere at any time. You decide how to mix and match ActionScript statements as needed.

To create a function, use the function command in the Actions toolbox (Statements > User-Defined Functions > function), and give your function a name. Your statement may look something like this:

```
function doExplosion() {
}
```

Any actions within the curly braces of the function are performed when the function is called. You call this function by name, like this: `doExplosion()`.

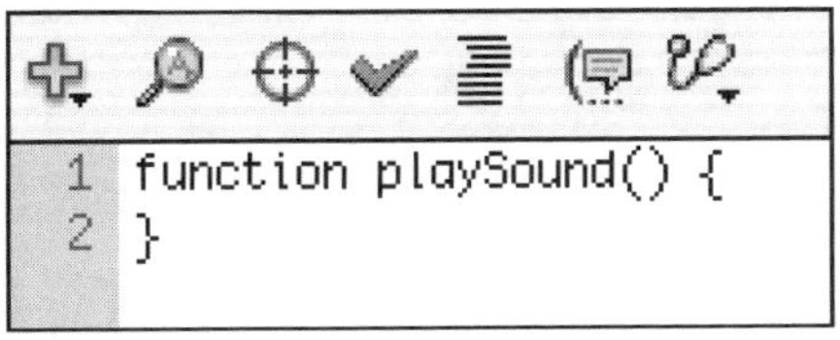
1 function playSound() {
2 }

Figure 12.65 This function is called `playSound` and accepts no parameters.

The following task builds a function that creates a sound object, attaches a sound, starts it, and sets the volume. By consolidating all these methods, you can play the sound with one call to a single function—and do so multiple times from different places in your movie.

To build and call a function:

1. Select the first keyframe of the main Timeline, and open the Actions panel.
2. Choose Statements > User-Defined Functions > function (Esc + fn).
3. Immediately after the word `function`, enter a name for your function.

   The function statement appears in the Script pane with a set of curly braces. All statements included within the curly braces become part of the function; they will be performed when the function is called (**Figure 12.65**).

continues on next page

4. On the next line inside the function, declare a new Sound object, followed by an equals sign.

5. Enter the constructor function new Sound() (**Figure 12.66**).

```
function playSound() {
    var mySound_sound:Sound = new Sound();
}
```

Figure 12.66 The new Sound object mySound_sound is instantiated.

6. Assign the following three methods (replacing mySound_sound with the name of your Sound object). These methods attach the sound, begin playing it, and set its volume (**Figure 12.67**):

```
mySound_sound.attachSound("musicID");
mySound_sound.start(0,2);
mySound_sound.setVolume(50);
```

```
function playSound() {
    var mySound_sound:Sound = new Sound();
    mySound_sound.attachSound("musicID");
    mySound_sound.start(0, 2);
    mySound_sound.setVolume(50);
}
```

Figure 12.67 When the function playSound is called, the sound is attached to the Sound object, it begins playing, and its volume is set.

7. Create a button symbol, and place an instance of the button on the Stage. In the Property inspector, give your button an instance name.

8. Select the first keyframe of the main Timeline, and open the Actions panel.

9. Create an onRelease event handler for your button.

10. With your pointer between the curly braces of the onRelease event handler, enter the name of your function (**Figure 12.68**).

    The function that you created is called when this button is clicked.

```
myButton_btn.onRelease = function() {
    playSound();
};
```

Figure 12.68 Call your function by entering its name and the opening and closing parentheses.

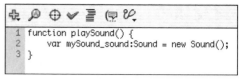

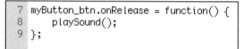

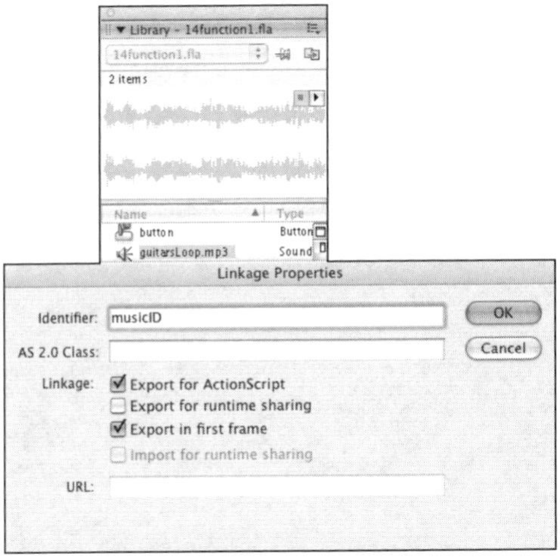

Figure 12.69 The Linkage Properties dialog box for an imported sound. Select Export for ActionScript, and enter a name in the Identifier field.

11. Import a sound clip.

12. In the Linkage Properties dialog box (accessed from the Library Options pull-down menu), select the Export for ActionScript check box and enter a name in the Identifier field (**Figure 12.69**). The name in the Identifier field should be the same name you used in the `attachSound` method in step 6.

13. Test your movie.

Your function is defined in the first keyframe of the main Timeline. When the viewer clicks the button on the Stage, Flash calls the function, which creates a new `Sound` object, attaches the Library sound, and begins playing it at a specified volume level.

✔ Tips

- When you declare a variable using the `var` statement within the body of a function, it's called a *local variable*, because it's scoped only within the function. Local variables expire at the end of the function and don't conflict with variables you've declared elsewhere. Use local variables to keep your functions independent and self-contained. That way, you can copy and paste functions from one project to another easily without having to worry about conflicts with duplicate variable names.
- Remember that the scope of a function is the Timeline on which it's defined. If you call a function that was created on the main Timeline from within a movie clip, the actions from the function still pertain to the main Timeline.

Accepting parameters

When you define a function, you can tell it to perform a certain task based on parameters that you provide, or *pass*, to the function at the time you call on it. This arrangement makes functions more flexible because the work they do is tailored to particular contexts. In the preceding task, for example, you can define the function to accept a parameter for the sound volume. When you call the function, you also provide a value for the sound volume, and the function uses that value in the `setVolume()` method.

To build a function that accepts parameters:

1. Continuing with file you used in the preceding task, select the first keyframe, and open the Actions panel.
2. With your pointer between the parentheses of the function statement, enter `sndLoop:Number` and `sndVolume:Number`, separated by a comma.

   This defines the names and data types of the parameters for your function. You can name your parameters whatever you like (as long as the names conform to the standard naming rules for variables and objects), and you can have any number of parameters (**Figure 12.70**).
3. Select the `start()` method within your function, and replace the `loop` parameter (the second one) with `sndLoop`.
4. Select the `setVolume()` method, and replace the `volume` parameter with `sndVolume`.

   The parameters `sndLoop` and `sndVolume` will be used to play the sound for a certain number of loops and at a certain volume (**Figure 12.71**).

```
function playSound(sndLoop:Number, sndVolume:Number) {
    var mySound_sound:Sound = new Sound();
    mySound_sound.attachSound("musicID");
    mySound_sound.start(0, 2);
    mySound_sound.setVolume(50);
}
```

Figure 12.70 The function `playSound` accepts the parameters `sndLoop` and `sndVolume` and then passes them to the statements within its curly braces (not yet defined).

```
function playSound(sndLoop:Number, sndVolume:Number) {
    var mySound_sound:Sound = new Sound();
    mySound_sound.attachSound("musicID");
    mySound_sound.start(0, sndLoop);
    mySound_sound.setVolume(sndVolume);
}
```

Figure 12.71 The final script for a function that accepts and passes parameters. The parameters of the function `playSound` modify the `start()` method and the `setVolume()` method.

```
function playSound(sndLoop:Number, sndVolume:Number) {
    var mySound_sound:Sound = new Sound();
    mySound_sound.attachSound("musicID");
    mySound_sound.start(0, sndLoop);
    mySound_sound.setVolume(sndVolume);
}
myButton_btn.onRelease = function() {
    playSound(2, 50);
};
```

Figure 12.72 The function `playSound` is called with the parameters 2 and `50`. The sound `"musicID"` begins playing and loops twice at a volume of 50.

```
function myAverage(a:Number, b:Number, c:Number, d:Number) {
}
```

Figure 12.73 The function `myAverage` accepts four `Number` parameters `a`, `b`, `c`, and `d`.

```
function myAverage(a:Number, b:Number, c:Number, d:Number) {
    return (a + b + c + d) / 4;
}
```

Figure 12.74 The `return` statement makes the result of the expression available to a statement that calls the function.

5. Select the line where your function is called (inside the `onRelease` event handler).

6. With your pointer between the parentheses of your function call, enter a value for the `sndLoop` parameter and a value for the `sndVolume` parameter. Separate the two values with a comma (**Figure 12.72**).

7. Test your movie.

   The values of the parameters that are passed to the function are defined when you call the function. Another button can call the same function with different values for the parameters.

Returning a value

When you pass parameters to a function, you often want to know the results of a particular calculation. To make your function report a resulting calculation, use the `return` statement. The `return` statement, which you use within your function's body (between the curly braces), indicates that the value of an expression should be passed back when the function is called.

To build a function that returns a value:

1. Select the first keyframe of the main Timeline, and open the Actions panel.

2. Choose Statements > User-Defined Functions > function.

3. Immediately after the word `function`, enter a name for your function.

4. Between the parentheses of the function, enter `a:Number, b:Number, c:Number, d:Number` (**Figure 12.73**).

5. Between the curly braces for the function, enter the word `return`, followed by an expression to average the four parameters. (**Figure 12.74**).

continues on next page

6. Select the Text tool in the Tools palette, create a dynamic text field on the Stage, and give the text field an instance name in the Property inspector.

7. Create a button symbol, place an instance of it on the Stage, and give the button an instance name in the Property inspector.

8. On a new line in the Actions panel, create an `onRelease` event handler for your button.

9. Inside the `onRelease` event handler function, enter the name of your text field, a period, and then the `text` property, followed by an equals sign.

10. Enter the name of your function and four values for its parameters, separating the values with commas (**Figure 12.75**).

    These four values pass to the function, where they're processed. The function returns a value back to where it was called. The returned value is assigned to the dynamic text field, where it's displayed. Use the `return` statement whenever you need to receive a value from a function.

11. Test your movie.

```
function myAverage(a:Number, b:Number, c:Number, d:Number) {
    return (a + b + c + d) / 4;
}
myButton_btn.onRelease = function() {
    myDisplay_txt.text = myAverage(100, 85, 65, 50);
};
```

Figure 12.75 The function `myAverage` is called, and the returned value appears in the `myDisplay_txt` dynamic text field.

The arguments class

Sometimes, you want to build a function that can accept a variable number of parameters. Building a function that calculates a mathematical average, for example, is much more useful when you can input as many or as few numbers as you want. The `arguments` class can help solve this problem. The `arguments` class is essentially an `Array` that contains all the values of the parameters that are passed to a function. An `arguments` object named `arguments` is available in every function you create.

In the preceding task, you defined a function that accepts four `Number` parameters and returns the average of the parameters. You call the function like this:

```
myAverage(3, 54, 4, 6);
```

The `arguments` object for this function is an `Array` with four elements:

- `arguments[0]` contains 3
- `arguments[1]` contains 54
- `arguments[2]` contains 4
- `arguments[3]` contains 6

The `length` property of the `arguments` object returns the number of parameters passed to the function. For this function, the value of `arguments.length` is 4.

It's important to note that the contents of the `arguments` object are determined by the parameters passed when the function is called—not by the number of parameters in the function definition. If you call the `myAverage()` function with only three parameters, the `arguments` object contains three elements with those three values, and `arguments.length` is 3. Likewise, if you call `myAverage()` with five parameters, the `arguments` object contains all five values, and `arguments.length` is 5.

The following task builds a function that can accept any number of parameters and calculates their average with the `arguments` object. Note that you *must* refer to the `arguments` object using the name `arguments`, with a lowercase *a*.

To use the arguments object to handle a variable number of parameters passed to a function:

1. Select the first frame of the main Timeline, and open the Actions panel.
2. Choose Statements > User-Defined Functions > function.
3. Immediately after the word `function`, enter a name for your function (**Figure 12.76**).

continues on next page

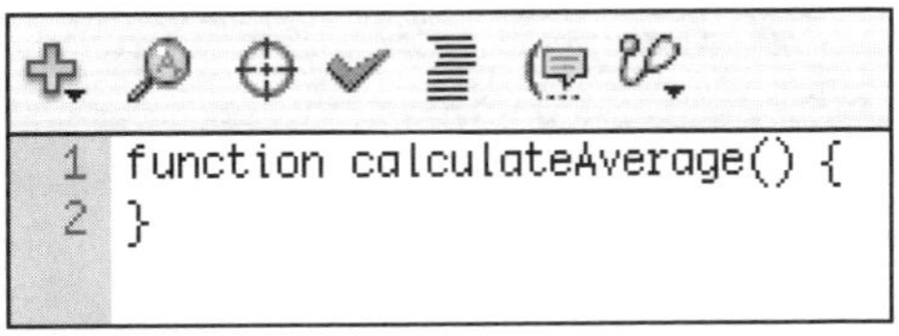

1 function calculateAverage() {
2 }

Figure 12.76 Create the function `calculateAverage`, and don't define any parameters.

4. On the next line, enter `var total:Number = 0`.

   The variable `total` will hold the sum of the numbers you'll pass to this function. Each time this function is called, `total` will be reset to 0.

5. Choose Statements > Conditions/Loops > for.

6. Between the parentheses of the `for` loop, enter `var i:Number = 0; i < arguments.length; i++`.

   This loop statement will be performed as many times as there are elements in the `arguments Array`.

7. On the next line (within the `for` loop), enter `total += arguments[i]`.

   The variable `total` adds the value of each element in the `arguments Array` to itself. This adds up all the parameters passed to the function (**Figure 12.77**).

8. On a new line after the closing brace of the `for` statement, enter `return total / (arguments.length)`.

   The function returns the average of all the parameters that are passed to it (**Figure 12.78**).

```
function calculateAverage() {
    var total:Number = 0;
    for (var i:Number = 0; i < arguments.length; i++) {
        total += arguments[i];
    }
}
```

Figure 12.77 All the parameters passed to this function are stored in the `arguments` object, and the variable `total` adds them up.

```
function calculateAverage() {
    var total:Number = 0;
    for (var i:Number = 0; i < arguments.length; i++) {
        total += arguments[i];
    }
    return total / (arguments.length);
}
```

Figure 12.78 The sum of all the parameters is divided by the number of parameters. The result is returned to the statement that called the function.

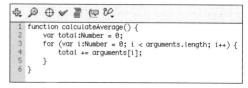

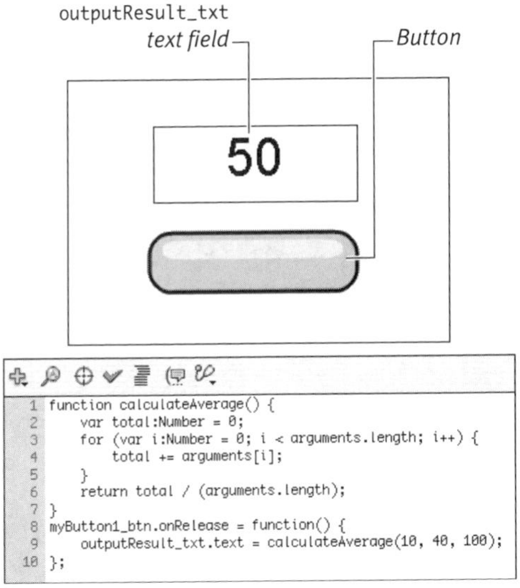
outputResult_txt
text field
Button
50
function calculateAverage() {
    var total:Number = 0;
    for (var i:Number = 0; i < arguments.length; i++) {
        total += arguments[i];
    }
    return total / (arguments.length);
}
myButton1_btn.onRelease = function() {
    outputResult_txt.text = calculateAverage(10, 40, 100);
};

Figure 12.79 Three parameters are passed to the `calculateAverage` function, and the average is displayed in the `outputResult_txt` text field.

9. Create a dynamic text field on the Stage, and give it an instance name in the Property inspector.

   In this example, the instance name is `outputResult_txt`.

10. Create a button symbol, place an instance on the Stage, and give it an instance name in the Property inspector.

11. Select the first frame on the main Timeline, and open the Actions panel.

12. On the next line, after the closing curly brace for the function, create an `onRelease` event handler for the button.

13. Inside the `onRelease` event handler, enter the following:

```
outputResult_txt.text =
calculateAverage(10, 40, 100);
```

   When this button is clicked, the numbers 10, 40, and 100 are passed to the function. The average is calculated and returned, where it's displayed in the dynamic text field `outputResult_txt` (**Figure 12.79**). You can pass any number of parameters to the `calculateAverage` function and still get a mathematical average.

MANAGING CONTENT AND TROUBLESHOOTING

13

As the complexity of your Flash movie increases with the addition of bitmaps, videos, sounds, and animations, as well as the ActionScript that integrates them, you need to keep close track of all the elements so you can make necessary revisions and bug fixes. After all, the most elaborate Flash movie is useless if you can't pinpoint the one variable that's keeping the whole thing from working. Fortunately, Flash provides several tools for troubleshooting and managing Library symbols and code.

This chapter shows you how to create shared Library symbols and external ActionScript files that supply common elements—symbols and code—to a team of Flash developers working on a project. You'll learn about components, which are specialized movie clips containing pre-built functionality that makes interactive applications easy to build. For example, using components that Flash provides, you can quickly build a progressive preloader or a check box and specify parameters to customize it for your own project without having to build your own from scratch. This chapter also delves into the Movie Explorer, Output panel, and Debugger panel, which offer information about the organization and status of your movie. These three panels let you review your ActionScript in context with the other elements in your movie, receive error and warning messages, and monitor the changing values of variables and properties as your movie plays.

Finally, you'll learn some strategies for making your Flash movie leaner and faster—optimizing graphics and code, organizing your work environment, and avoiding some common mistakes—guidelines to help you become a better Flash author and developer.

Sharing Library Symbols

Flash makes it possible for teams of animators and developers to share common Library symbols for a complex project. Each animator might be working on a separate movie that uses the same symbol—the main character in an animated comic book, for example. An identical symbol of this main character needs to reside in the Library of each movie; and if the art director decides to change this character's face, a new symbol has to be copied to all the Libraries—that is, unless you create a shared Library symbol. There are two kinds of shared symbols: runtime shared symbols and author-time shared symbols.

Runtime sharing of symbols

In runtime sharing, one movie provides a symbol for multiple movies to use during runtime. This simplifies the editing process and ensures consistency throughout a Flash project (**Figure 13.1**).

Your viewers also benefit from the shared symbols because they have to download them only once. For example, a main character would be downloaded just once, for the first movie, and all subsequent movies will use that character.

To create a runtime shared Library symbol, mark the symbol for "Export for runtime sharing" in the Linkage Properties dialog box. When you export the SWF file, the symbol will be available to other SWF movies.

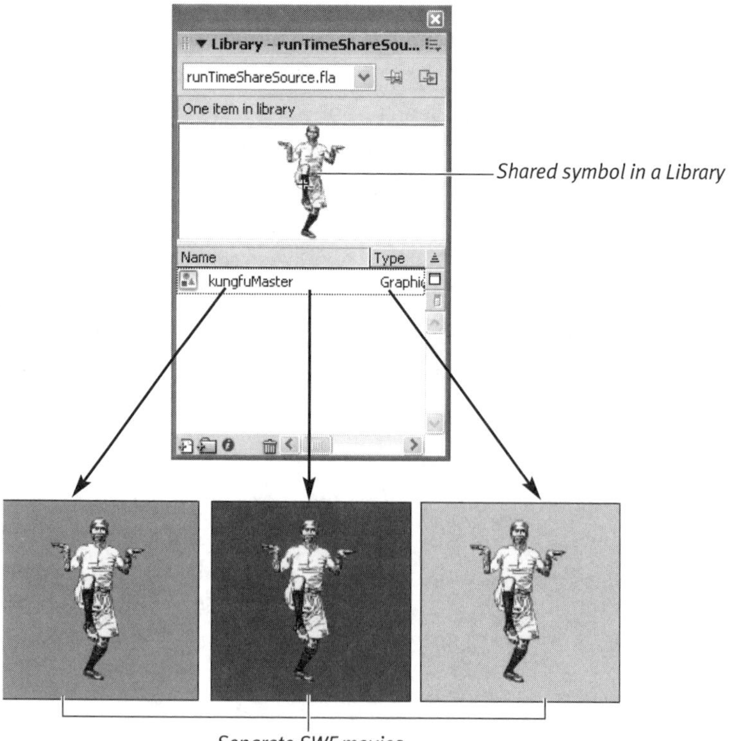

Figure 13.1 A runtime shared symbol (top) can be used by multiple SWF files.

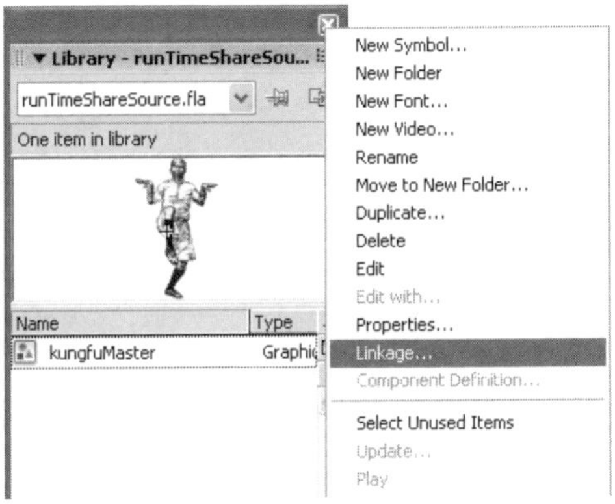

Figure 13.2 Choose Linkage from the Library panel's Options menu.

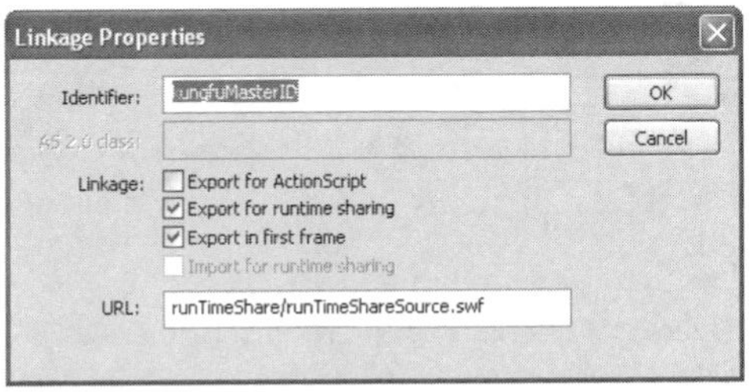

Figure 13.3 To mark a symbol as a shared symbol, give it an identifier in the Linkage Properties dialog box, select it for export, and give a URL where it can be found. This shared symbol will be located in the directory runTimeShare in the file runTimeShareSource.swf.

Once you create a movie that shares a Library symbol, you can create other movies that use it. You do this by opening a new Flash document and creating a symbol. In its Linkage Properties dialog box, mark the symbol to "Import for runtime sharing" and enter the name and location of the source symbol as it appears in the Identifier field of its own Linkage Properties dialog box. At runtime, your new movie finds, imports, and uses the source symbol.

To create a runtime shared symbol:

1. In a new Flash document, create a symbol you want to share.

   The symbol can be a graphic, button, movie clip, font symbol, sound, or bitmap.

2. In the Library panel, select your symbol. From the Library panel's Options menu, choose Linkage (**Figure 13.2**).

   The Linkage Properties dialog box appears.

3. In the Linkage choices, select "Export for runtime sharing". In the Identifier field, enter a unique name for your symbol. In the URL field, enter the relative or absolute path to where the SWF file will be posted. Keep the "Export in first frame" check box selected. Click OK (**Figure 13.3**).

   Your selected symbol is now marked for export and available to be shared by other movies.

4. Export your Flash movie as a SWF file with the name and in the location you specified in the URL field of the Linkage Properties dialog box.

   This is your source movie that shares its symbol.

To use a runtime shared symbol:

1. Open a new Flash document, and create a new symbol.

   It doesn't matter what kind of symbol you create (movie clip, graphic, or button) or what content it holds, because it will be replaced by the shared symbol from the source movie at runtime. This symbol is simply a placeholder.

2. In the Library panel, select your symbol. From the Options menu, choose Linkage.

   The Linkage Properties dialog box appears.

3. From the Linkage choices, select "Import for runtime sharing". In the Identifier field, enter the name for the shared symbol in the source movie (as it appears in the Identifier field of its own Linkage Properties dialog box). In the URL field, enter the path to the source movie. Click OK (**Figure 13.4**).

   Your selected symbol is now marked to find the shared symbol in the source movie and import it.

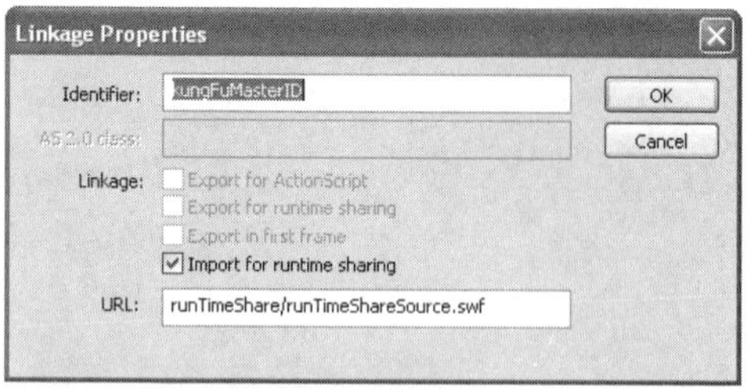

Figure 13.4 In the Linkage Properties dialog box, select the "Import for runtime sharing" check box, and enter the Identifier and location of the shared symbol you wish to use.

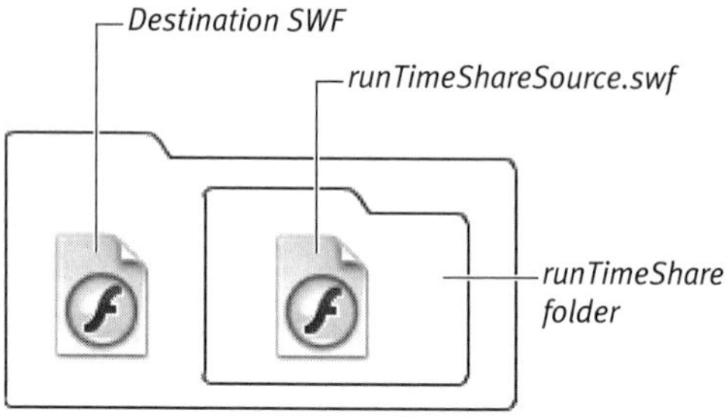

Figure 13.5 The destination SWF imports the shared symbol from the source SWF. The URL fields in Figures 13.3 and 13.4 specify where the source SWF is located relative to the destination SWF.

4. Drag an instance of the symbol onto the Stage, and use it in your movie.
5. Export your Flash movie as a SWF file, and place it in a location where it can find the source movie (**Figure 13.5**).

   When you play the SWF file, it imports the shared symbol from the source movie. The shared symbol takes over the current symbol (**Figure 13.6**).

✔ Tips

- When you make changes and revisions to the shared symbol in the source movie, all the destination movies that use the shared symbol are automatically updated to reflect the change.
- You can also drag the shared symbol from the source movie's Library into the destination movie. The shared symbol is automatically imported into your destination movie with the correct Linkage Properties options selected and field values entered.
- Unfortunately, you can't assign ActionScript that affects runtime shared symbols. For example, you can't use the method `attachMovieClip()` or `attachSound()` to dynamically place a shared symbol from the Library into your movie. The reason is that a symbol can't be marked for both import for runtime sharing and export for ActionScript at the same time.

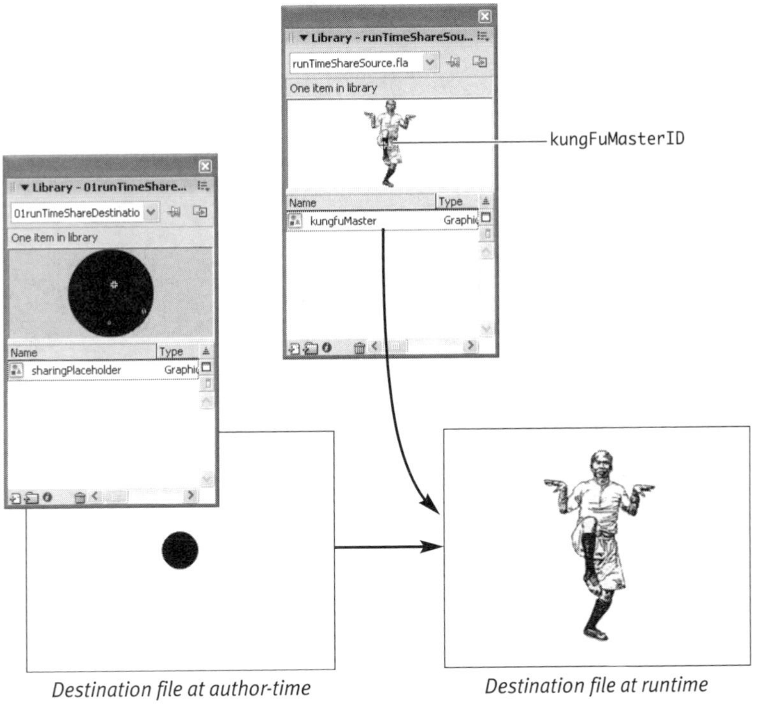

Figure 13.6 The black circle symbol in the destination movie (left) imports the kungFuMasterID shared symbol from the runTimeShareSource.swf at runtime. As a result, the shared symbol appears in the destination SWF file (right).

Author-time sharing of symbols

When you want to share symbols among FLA files instead of SWF files, turn to author-time sharing. Author-time sharing lets you choose a source symbol in a particular FLA file so that another FLA file can reference it and keep its symbol up to date. You only have to worry about modifying one FLA file containing the source symbol instead of multiple FLA files that contain the same symbol. Each movie stores its own copy of the common symbol. You can update the symbol to the source symbol whenever you want, or even make automatic updates before you publish a SWF file.

To update a symbol with another from a different Flash file:

1. Select the symbol you wish to update in the Library panel. From the Options menu, choose Properties.

   The Symbol Properties dialog box appears.

2. Click Advanced.

   The Symbol Properties dialog box expands to display more options (**Figure 13.7**).

3. In the Source section of the dialog box, click Browse. Select the Flash file that contains the symbol you wish to use to update your currently selected symbol. Click OK (Windows) or Open (Mac).

   The Select Source Symbol dialog box appears, showing a list of all the symbols in the selected Flash file's Library.

4. Select a symbol, and click OK (**Figure 13.8**).

   The Select Source Symbol dialog box closes.

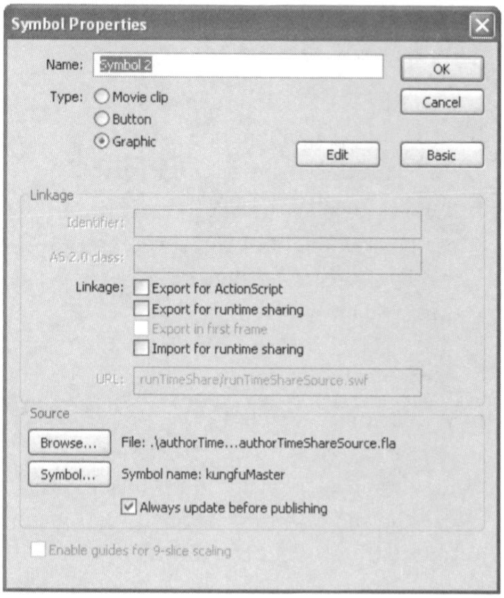

Figure 13.7 The Advanced button in the Symbol Properties dialog box displays more options under Linkage and Source.

Figure 13.8 Select the source symbol for author-time sharing.

Figure 13.9 The Source area of the Symbol Properties dialog box displays the path to the author-time source symbol and the name of the source symbol.

5. In the Symbol Properties dialog box that is still open, note the new source for your symbol (**Figure 13.9**). Click OK.

   The Symbol Properties dialog box closes, and your symbol is updated with the symbol you just chose for its new source. Your symbol retains its name, but its content is updated to the source symbol.

To make automatic updates to a symbol:

- In the Symbol Properties dialog box, select the "Always update before publishing" check box.

  Whenever you export a SWF file from your Flash file, whether by publishing it or by using the Control > Test Movie command, Flash will locate the source symbol and update your symbol.

Runtime Sharing or Author-Time Sharing?

Although they may seem similar, runtime and author-time sharing are two very different ways to work with symbols. Each approach is better suited for different types of projects. Runtime sharing is useful when multiple SWF movies can share common assets, decreasing symbol redundancy, file size, and download times. Publish a single SWF file holding all the common symbols that multiple SWF files can access. Author-time sharing, on the other hand, is useful for organizing your workflow before you publish your SWF movie. You can use author-time sharing to keep different symbols in separate FLA files. A master FLA file can reference all the symbols in the separate files and compile them into a single SWF. Working this way, you can have different members of a Flash development team work on different symbols and rely on author-time sharing to ensure that the final published movie will contain the updated symbols. Compare these two ways of sharing Library symbols in **Figure 13.10**.

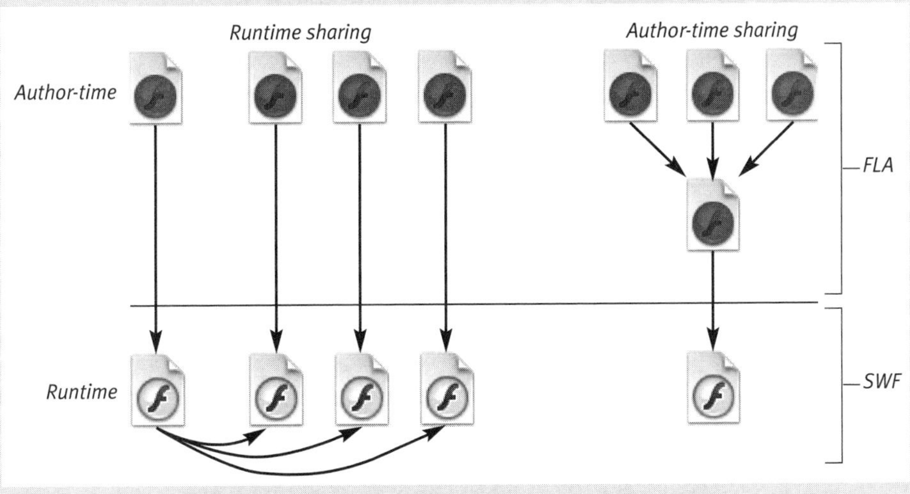

Figure 13.10 During runtime sharing (left), multiple SWF files can share symbols from a single common SWF file. During author-time sharing (right), multiple FLA files can provide updated symbols to a single FLA file that publishes a SWF file to play during runtime.

Sharing Fonts

Just as you can create symbols to share between movies, you can create font symbols and share them. After creating a font symbol, you identify it to be exported using the Linkage identifier in a process similar to the one used to create runtime shared symbols. Use shared fonts to reduce the need to embed the same font outline for multiple movies. When multiple movies share a common font, the font has to be downloaded only once for the first movie, reducing file size and download times for the subsequent movies.

To create a font symbol to share:

1. Open the Library panel. From its Options menu, choose New Font (**Figure 13.11**).

   The Font Symbol Properties dialog box appears.

2. Enter a name for your new font symbol in the Name field. From the Font pull-down menu, select the font you wish to include in your Library as a font symbol. Select the optional check boxes for Style. Click OK (**Figure 13.12**).

   The font symbol appears in your Library.

3. Select your font symbol in the Library panel. From the Options menu, choose Linkage.

   The Linkage Properties dialog box appears.

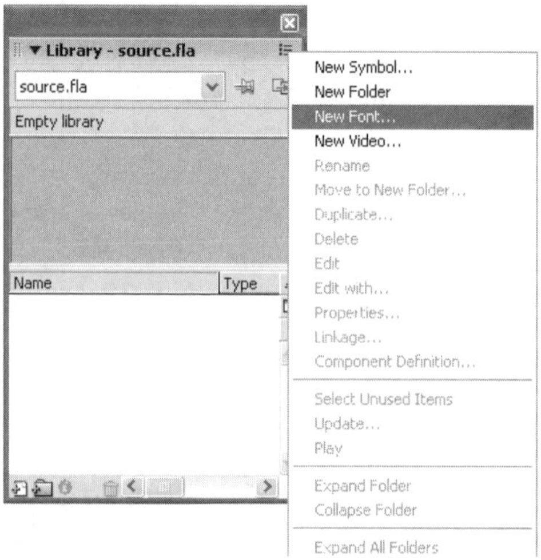

Figure 13.11 Choose New Font from the Library panel's Options menu.

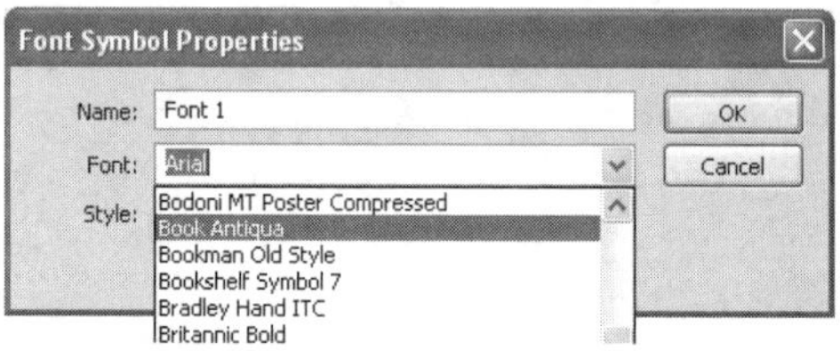

Figure 13.12 Create a font symbol by choosing a font and giving it a name in the Font Symbol Properties dialog box.

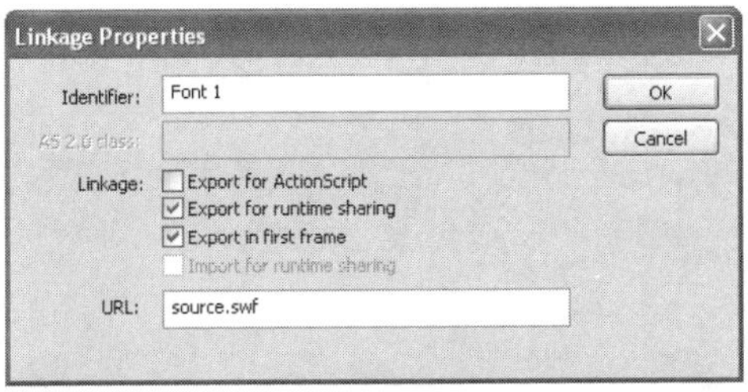

Figure 13.13 In the Linkage Properties dialog box, mark your symbol font for runtime sharing, give it an identifier, and specify the location where this source SWF will be placed. If the destination and source file will reside in the same directory, enter the name of the source file in the URL field, as shown here.

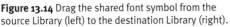

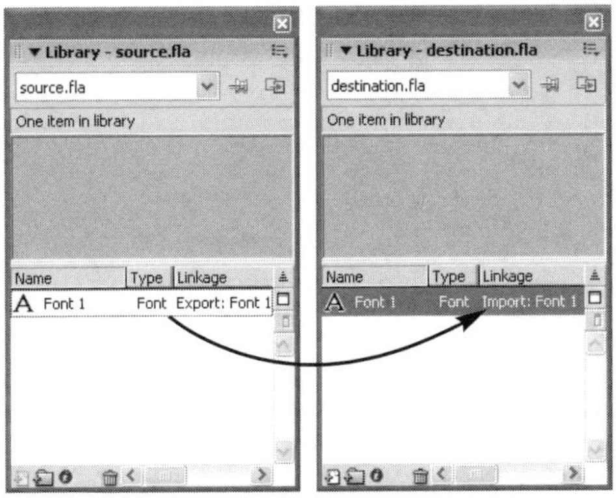

Figure 13.14 Drag the shared font symbol from the source Library (left) to the destination Library (right).

4. From the Linkage choices, select "Export for runtime sharing". In the Identifier field, enter a unique name for your symbol. In the URL field, enter the path where this SWF file will be placed. Click OK (**Figure 13.13**).

   Your selected font symbol is now marked for export and available to be shared by other movies.

5. Export your Flash movie as a SWF file with the name and in the location you specified in the URL field of the Linkage Properties dialog box.

   Your selected font symbol resides in the SWF file. This SWF file provides the shared font to other movies.

To use a shared font symbol:

1. Open a new Flash file (the destination file) where you want to use a shared font symbol.

2. Open the Library of the source file that contains your shared font symbol by choosing File > Import > Open External Library. Drag the shared font symbol from its Library to the Library of the destination Flash file.

   The font symbol appears in the Library of the destination Flash file. The font symbol is automatically marked as "Import for runtime sharing" (**Figure 13.14**).

3. In the destination Flash file, select the font symbol in the Library panel. From the Options menu, choose Linkage.

   The Linkage Properties dialog box appears.

continues on next page

4. Confirm that "Import for runtime sharing" is selected, that the Identifier field contains the name of the shared font symbol in the source movie, and that the URL field contains the path to the source movie (**Figure 13.15**). Click OK.

   Your font symbol in the destination movie is now set to share the font symbol in the source movie.

5. Select the Text tool in the Tools panel. In the Property inspector, choose the shared font symbol from the pull-down list of available fonts (**Figure 13.16**).

   Create input text or dynamic text, and be sure to embed all the font outlines in the Character Options.

6. Publish the destination SWF file and the source SWF file.

   The source SWF shares its font with the destination SWF. The destination SWF displays the shared font correctly and with anti-aliasing, but its file size remains small (**Figure 13.17**).

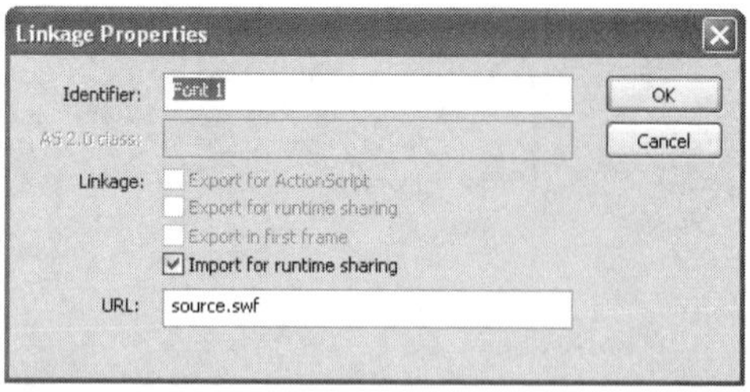

Figure 13.15 The Linkage Properties dialog box for the font symbol in the destination file. This font symbol will import the font called Font 1 from the file source.swf.

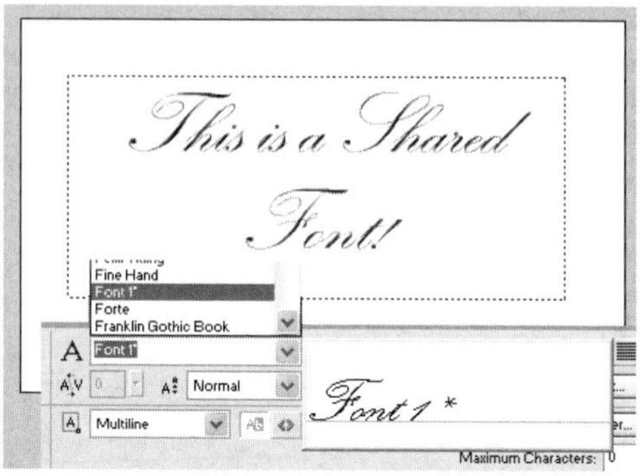

Figure 13.16 Shared fonts are available in the Property inspector and are distinguished by an asterisk after their names.

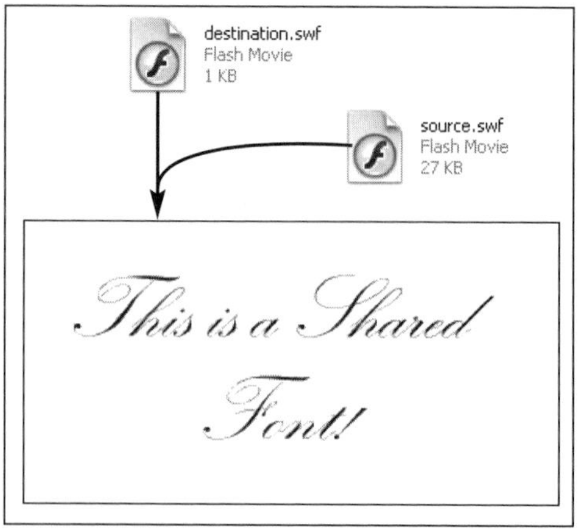

Figure 13.17 The destination SWF file displays the shared font correctly because the font is supplied by the source SWF file. Notice the difference in file size between destination.swf (1 KB) and source.swf (27 KB).

Using Components

Sometimes you create interface elements, like check boxes or pull-down menus, that you want to use in multiple projects but in slightly varying ways. For one movie, you may want your pull-down menu to have three choices; but for another movie, you may want it to have four. Or you may want to hand off your pull-down menu to a designer or animator for their own use but provide them with easy guidelines so they can customize the pull-down menu without recoding your ActionScript. How do you develop this modular piece of interactivity that can be easily customized even by non-ActionScript coders? The solution is to use components. A *component* is a special kind of symbol that has been programmed to be used by developers in multiple contexts, with easily customizable functionality or appearance.

If this sounds very general, it's because components are meant to tackle any sort of task—not just the creation of pull-down menus, check boxes, and other user-interface elements, but data handling, graphics behaviors, sound manipulation, and many other kinds of interactivity. Components are like templates. They provide general functionality as well as parameters to help you make them fit your particular needs.

Flash components

Flash provides a set of components of common user interface elements, located in the Components panel (Window > Components). They are the Button, CheckBox, ComboBox, Label, List, Loader, NumericStepper, ProgressBar, RadioButton, ScrollPane, TextArea, TextInput, UIScrollBar, and Window (**Figure 13.18**). (Flash Professional 8 provides additional components for advanced interactivity and data and media handling.) Each component comes with its own parameters that you define in the Component inspector (Window > Component Inspector) or in the Property inspector. For example, the ComboBox, which works like a pull-down menu, lets you define the number of menu items, their labels, the data to pass when one of the choices is selected, and even an event handler.

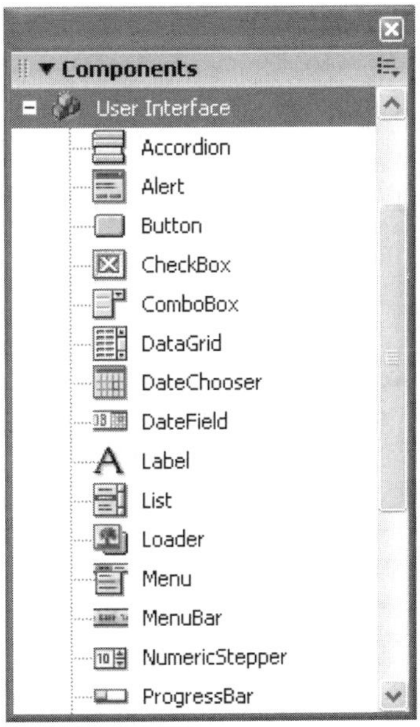

Figure 13.18 The Components panel shows the user-interface components Flash provides to quickly and easily add interactivity to your movie.

You can use the Flash UI components to varying degrees, depending on how much you want to modify them and how willing you are to dig into the custom methods and properties that each component provides. For example, you can change their appearance by calling the custom method `setStyle()`. Consult the Components Language Reference (in the Help panel under Components Language Reference) to learn more about each component's unique methods and properties.

If you don't need anything more than the standard functionality and basic design the Flash UI components provide, they're great resources. In the following task, you'll use the Loader component to quickly create a placeholder in which an external JPG or SWF file can load at run time.

To use the Flash Loader component:

1. Choose Window > Components (Ctrl-F7 for Windows, Command-F7 for Mac). Double-click UI Components to expand the list of available components.

   The Components panel opens and displays the user-interface components that Flash provides (Figure 13.18).

2. Select the Loader component, and drag it to the Stage (**Figure 13.19**).

   A completely transparent placeholder is placed on the stage. The default size is 100 pixels by 100 pixels, but it can be adjusted to whatever size you require. By default, the contents of the external image or SWF movie that will load are scaled to fit the Loader.

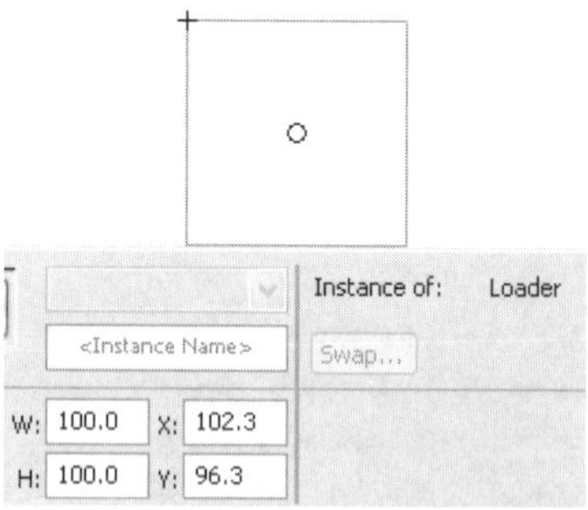

Figure 13.19 The Loader component acts as the placeholder to load external images or SWF movies. By default, the Loader component is 100 x 100 pixels.

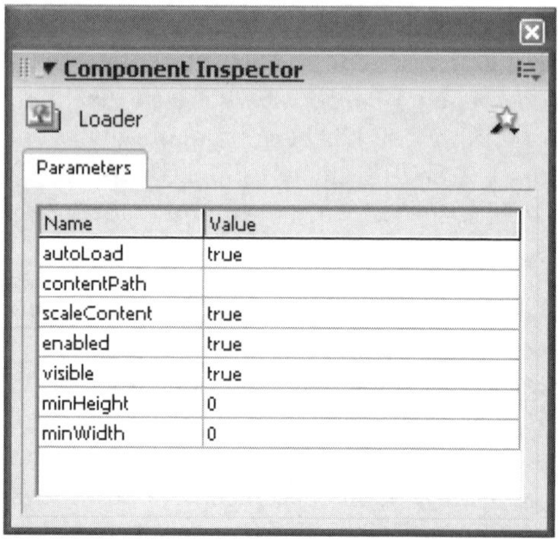

Figure 13.20 The Component inspector displays the parameters and values for the Loader component.

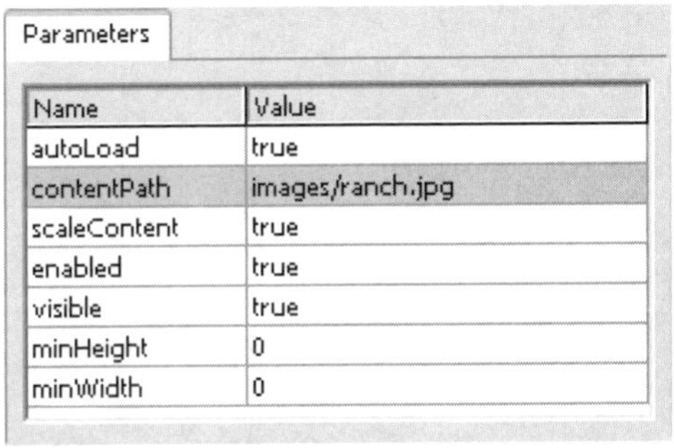

Figure 13.21 The Loader component on the Stage will load the image from the target path next to the `contentPath` parameter. You can use a relative or absolute URL as the `contentPath`.

Figure 13.22 The Stage has four Loader components (top). During playback, external images load in the Flash movie (bottom).

3. With the component selected, choose Window > Component Inspector, and click the Parameters tab.

   The Component inspector opens. The Parameters tab lists the parameters that you can set to customize your Loader component (**Figure 13.20**). You can also view and set some component parameters from the Parameters tab of the Property inspector.

4. In the Value column, click in the field next to the `contentPath` parameter, and enter an absolute or relative path to your SWF or JPG file (**Figure 13.21**).

5. Test your movie.

   At run time, your external movie or image loads into the Loader component (**Figure 13.22**). By default, the contents are scaled to fit the Loader rectangle, but you can change this behavior by changing the component's `scaleContent` parameter.

✔ Tips

- A Loader component can't receive focus, meaning that you can't assign a `startDrag` method or an `onPress` event handler to it. In spite of this, content loaded into the Loader component can receive focus and handle its own interactivity. For more information about controlling focus, check the Loader Components section in the Component Dictionary.
- You can use the Free Transform tool (Q) to adjust the width and height or even skew the Loader component's bounding box.
- If you load an external SWF into a Loader component and the `scaleContent` parameter is set to `true`, off-Stage elements in the external SWF will be visible.

Including External ActionScript

In addition to sharing Library assets between Flash documents, you can also create external ActionScript files to share common code among multiple movies. Create the ActionScript code that appears many times in different movies, and keep that code in a text file outside the Flash movies. If you need to change the code, you only need to change it in one place.

External code can be incorporated into a Flash movie with the action `#include`. This action pulls in an external text file containing ActionScript and includes it as though it were pasted into the existing script in the Script pane.

It's important to know that the `#include` action loads external ActionScript code when the SWF is published, *not* dynamically during run time. If you make changes to the external ActionScript document, you must republish your Flash movie in order for Flash to include the most current ActionScript. This means the `#include` action, although useful, is limited to authoring mode, like author-time shared symbols (**Figure 13.23**).

In the following task, the `#include` action is assigned to the first frame of the main Timeline. A text document contains ActionScript. When you export the SWF file, the code in the external text document is incorporated into the script.

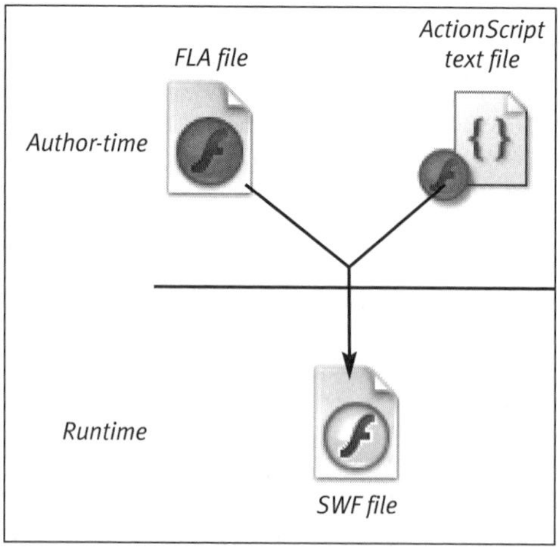

Figure 13.23 The `#include` action integrates ActionScript from an external text file when the FLA file exports a SWF file. The `#include` action doesn't work at run time.

Figure 13.24 This is the ActionScript in a text file saved as myCode.as.

Figure 13.25 When this movie is published, the external text file myCode.as is included in this Script pane.

To include external ActionScript with the #include action:

1. Open a text-editing application such as SimpleText for Mac or Notepad for Windows.
2. Write your ActionScript code, and save it as a text document. Don't include any quotation marks around your script. Use the extension *.as* to identify it as an ActionScript file (**Figure 13.24**).
3. Open a new document in Flash. Create a movie clip symbol, and place an instance of it on the Stage. In the Property inspector, give it a name; for this task, call it `ball_mc`.
4. Select the first frame of the main Timeline, and open the Actions panel.
5. Enter `#include` (Esc + in).
6. On the same line, after the `#include` action and surrounded by quotation marks, enter the name of the text file that contains ActionScript (**Figure 13.25**).
7. Save your FLA file in the same directory as your ActionScript text file.
8. Publish a SWF file from your FLA file.

   Flash integrates the code from the text document. If you change the code in the text file, you must republish the SWF file so that Flash can include the latest changes.

✔ Tips

- Don't include a semicolon at the end of an `#include` statement. Although ActionScript statements are usually separated by semicolons, the `#include` statement is an exception.
- If you want to store your external ActionScript text file separately from you FLA file, you can include a relative or absolute path before the filename.
- If you use the Check Syntax button on a script that contains an `#include` statement, the syntax of the external ActionScript is also selected.

Using the Movie Explorer

To get a bird's-eye view of your whole Flash movie, you can use the Movie Explorer panel (Option-F3 for Mac, Alt-F3 for Windows). You'll notice that the Movie Explorer is very similar to the Script navigator, which is included at bottom left in the Actions panel. Whereas the Script navigator lets you jump from one piece of ActionScript code to another, the Movie Explorer can display all the code in your movie at once. Moreover, the Movie Explorer tracks all the elements of your movie, not just ActionScript code, and it will take you directly to a particular ActionScript, graphic, or frame you want to modify. The Movie Explorer panel can selectively represent the graphical components of a movie and provide information about frames and layers, as well as show ActionScript assigned to buttons, movie clips, and keyframes. The display list is organized hierarchically, letting you see the relationships between elements (**Figure 13.26**).

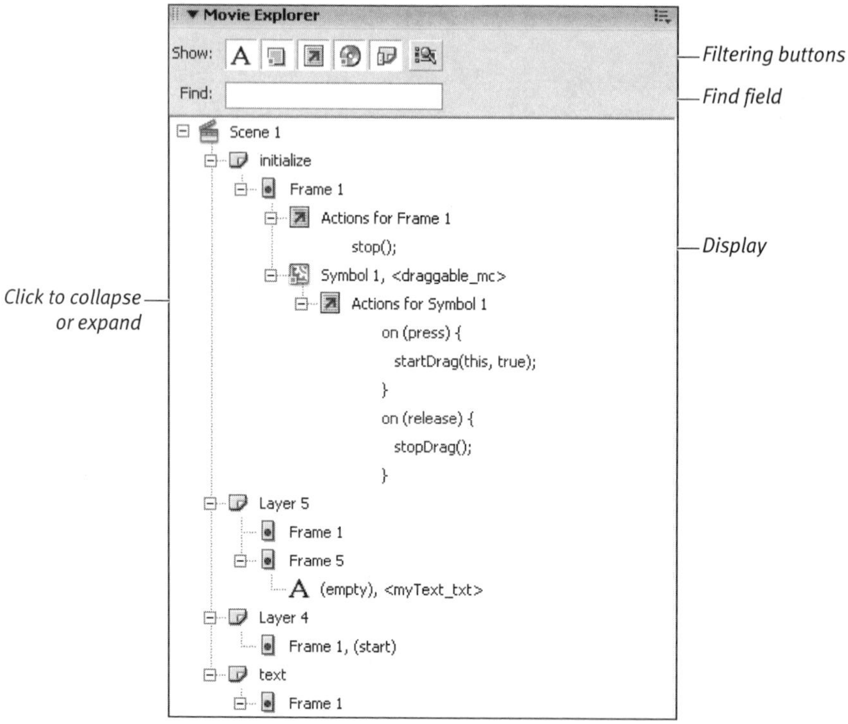

Figure 13.26 A typical display in the Movie Explorer shows various elements of the movie in an expandable hierarchy.

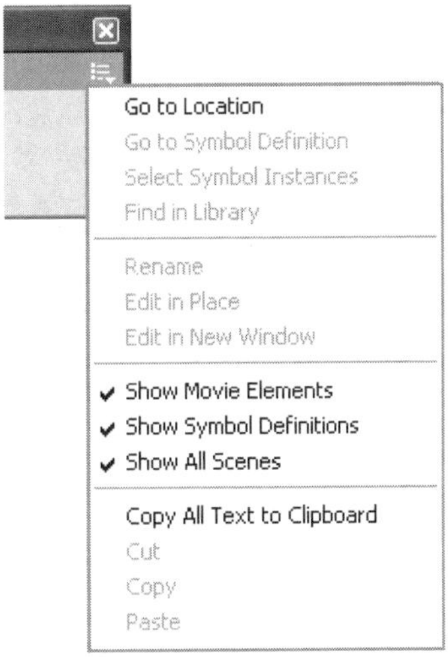

Figure 13.27 The Options menu of the Movie Explorer panel.

The Movie Explorer even updates itself in real time, so as you're authoring a Flash movie, the panel displays the latest modifications. Use the Movie Explorer to find particular elements in your movie. For example, to find all the instances of a movie clip, you can search for them and have Flash display the exact scene, layer, and frame where each instance resides. You can then quickly go to those spots on the Timeline to edit the instances. You can also edit elements within the Movie Explorer panel itself, such as the names of symbols or the contents of a text selection. The customized display and quick navigation capabilities of the Movie Explorer make it much easier to find your way around a complex movie.

To display different categories of elements:

- From the Options menu at the right of the Movie Explorer panel, *select one or more of the following* (**Figure 13.27**):

  Show Movie Elements displays all the elements in your movie and organizes them by scene. Only the current scene is displayed.

  Show Symbol Definitions displays all the elements associated with symbol instances that are on the Stage.

  Show All Scenes displays all the elements in your movie in all scenes.

To filter the categories of elements that are displayed:

- From the row of filtering buttons at the top of the panel, *select one or more* to add categories of elements to display (**Figure 13.28**):

  Show Text displays the actual string in a text selection, the font name and font size, and the instance name and variable name for input and dynamic text.

  Show Buttons, Movie Clips, and Graphics displays the symbol names of buttons, movie clips, and graphics on the Stage, as well as the instance names of movie clips and buttons.

  Show ActionScript displays the actions assigned to buttons, movie clips, and frames.

  Show Video, Sounds, and Bitmaps displays the symbol names of imported video, sounds, and bitmaps on the Stage.

  Show Frames and Layers displays the names of layers, keyframes, and frame labels in the movie.

  Customize Which Items to Show displays a dialog box from which you can choose individual elements to display.

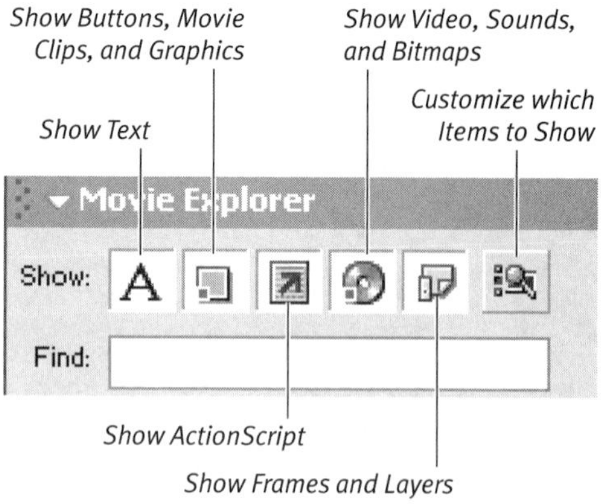

Figure 13.28 The filtering buttons let you selectively display elements.

To find and edit elements in the display:

1. In the Find field at the top of the Movie Explorer panel, enter the name of the element you wish to find (**Figure 13.29**).

   All the elements of the movie that contain that name appear in the display list automatically as you type in the field.

2. Click the desired element to select it.

   The element is also selected on the Timeline and on the Stage. If a scene or keyframe is selected, Flash takes you to that scene or keyframe.

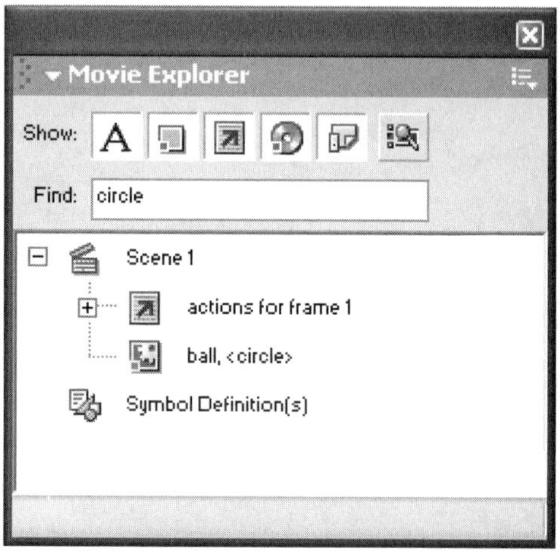

Figure 13.29 Entering a word or phrase in the Find field displays all occurrences of that word or phrase in the Display window. Here, the instance named `circle` of the movie clip symbol `ball` has been found.

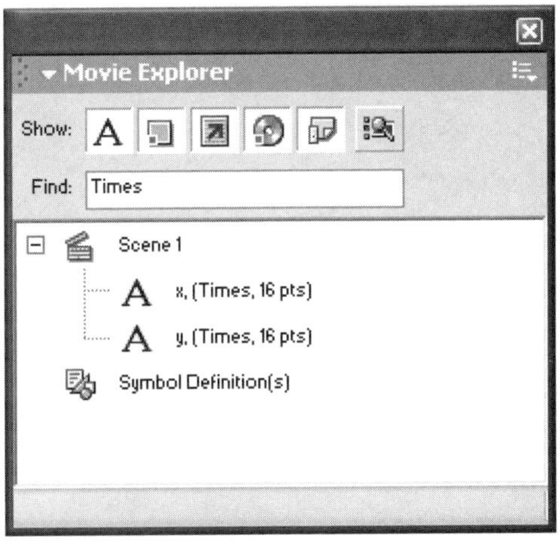

Figure 13.30 All the occurrences of the Times font appear in the Display window.

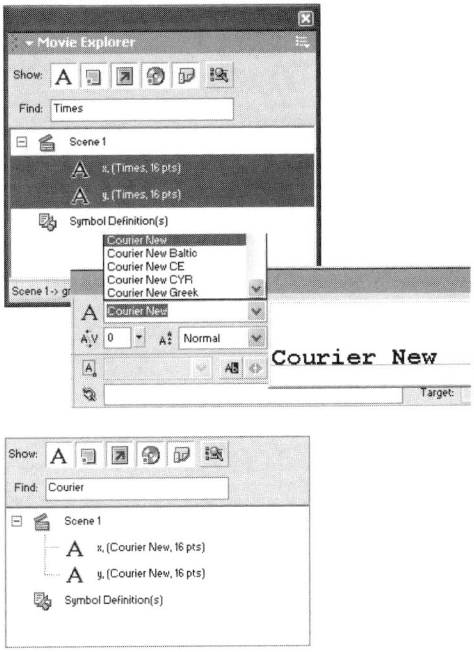

Figure 13.31 With the Times text elements selected, choose a different font, such as Courier New (top) from the Property inspector. Flash changes those text elements from Times to Courier New (bottom).

3. From the Options menu of the Movie Explorer panel, choose Edit in Place or Edit in New Window to go to symbol-editing mode for a selected symbol.

   or

   Choose Rename from the Options menu.

   The name of the element becomes selectable so that you can edit it.

   or

   Double-click the desired element to modify it. Flash makes the element editable or opens an appropriate window, depending on what type of element it is:

   Double-clicking a symbol (except for sound, video, and bitmaps) opens symbol-editing mode.

   Double-clicking ActionScript opens the script in the Actions panel.

   Double-clicking a scene or layer lets you rename it.

   Double-clicking a text selection lets you edit its contents.

To replace all occurrences of a particular font:

1. In the Find field of the Movie Explorer panel, enter the name of the font you wish to replace.

   All occurrences of that font appear in the display (**Figure 13.30**).

2. Select all the text elements, using Shift-click to make multiple selections.

3. In the Property inspector, choose a different font and style for all text elements.

   All the selected text elements change according to your choices in the Property inspector (**Figure 13.31**).

To find all instances of a movie clip symbol:

- In the Find field of the Movie Explorer panel, enter the name of the movie clip symbol whose instances you want to find.

  All instances of that movie clip symbol appear in the display (**Figure 13.32**).

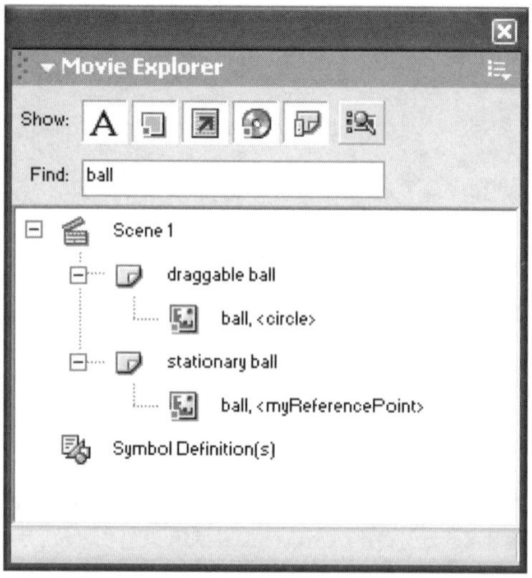

Figure 13.32 Entering the symbol name `ball` in the Find field displays all the instances of the ball symbol. There are two instances listed: one called `circle` in the draggable ball layer, and another called `myReferencePoint` in the stationary ball layer.

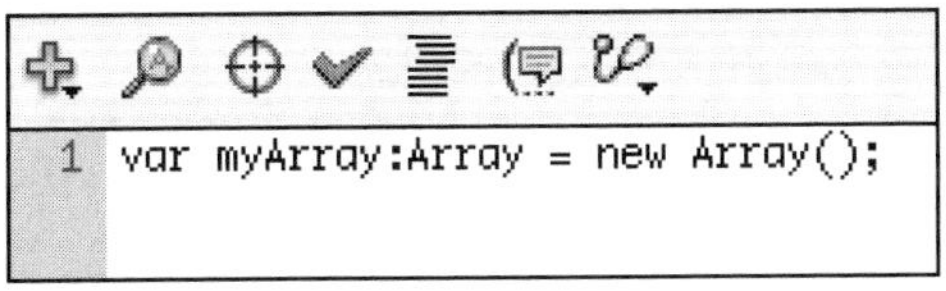
1 var myArray:Array = new Array();

Figure 13.33 The object `myArray` is created using the `new Array` constructor.

Viewing Variables and Objects During Playback

The Movie Explorer represents many of a movie's graphic elements and ActionScript, but it doesn't display variables or object target paths. For this you use the Output panel. Often, while a movie is playing, you want to know the values of your variables and the target paths of movie clips to determine whether Flash is handling the information correctly. This is especially important when your movie is complicated, perhaps involving many parameters passing between functions or having dynamically allocated variables. For example, say you want to initialize and populate an `Array` object in the first frame of the Timeline. After assigning to the frame the ActionScript that does the job, you can test your movie, but you won't really know if Flash has correctly populated the `Array` because there's nothing visual on the Stage. In order to determine whether the `Array` is filled with the correct values, you can list the variables in the Output panel in testing mode. The List Variables command displays all the variables in a movie with their scopes and values.

In the following task, you first create a simple `Array` object and then assign values to it using a looping statement. In testing mode, you list the movie's variables in the Output panel to see the `Array`'s final values.

To list variables in the Output panel:

1. Select the first frame of the main Timeline, and open the Actions panel.
2. Declare and instantiate a new `Array` object called `myArray`, as described in Chapter 12 (**Figure 13.33**).

continues on next page

3. Choose Statements > Conditions/Loops > for. Between the parentheses, enter `var i:Number = 0; i < 5; i++` (**Figure 13.34**).

4. On the next line, enter `myArray[i] = i * 5`.

   Each time the `for` statement loops, the value of `i` increases by 1. Flash assigns each entry in the `myArray Array` the value of its index multiplied by 5. This loop populates the `myArray Array` (**Figure 13.35**).

5. Test your movie (Control > Test Movie). In testing mode, from the main menu, choose Debug > List Variables (Command-Option-V for Mac, Ctrl-Alt-V for Windows).

   The Output panel opens, displaying all the variables in the movie. The first variable listed is `$version`, which contains information about the version of Flash Player and the system platform. The second variable is the `myArray` object. Flash lists its location (`_level0.myArray`), its data type (object of the `Array` class), and all of its values in each index (0, 5, 10, 15, 20). The third variable is the counter variable, `i`, used in the `for` looping statement (**Figure 13.36**).

✔ Tip

- The List Variables command displays all the variables in a movie at the instant you choose the command from the menu. If the variables change as the movie plays, you need to choose List Variables again in order to see the latest values. For real-time display of variables, use the Debugger panel, described later in this chapter.

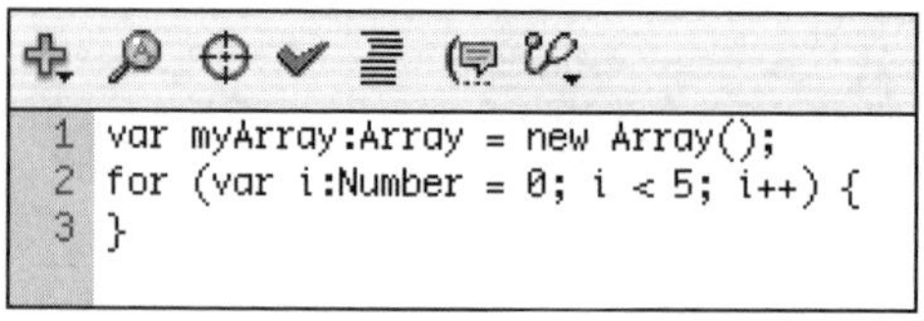

var myArray:Array = new Array();
for (var i:Number = 0; i < 5; i++) {
}

Figure 13.34 Create a loop that begins with `i` equal to 0 and increases by 1 until it reaches 4.

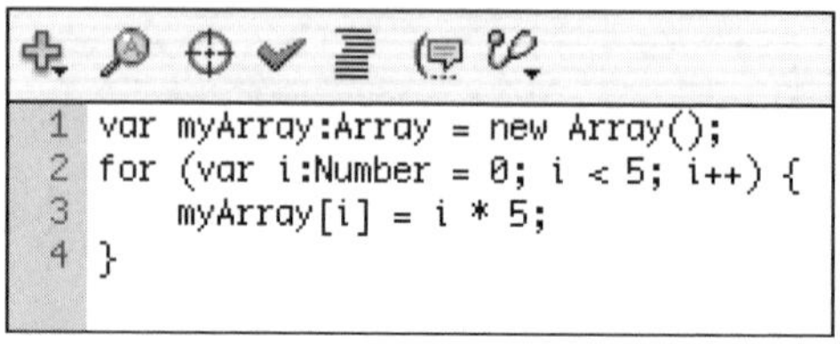

var myArray:Array = new Array();
for (var i:Number = 0; i < 5; i++) {
myArray[i] = i * 5;
}

Figure 13.35 The object `myArray` is automatically filled with the values determined by the looping statement.

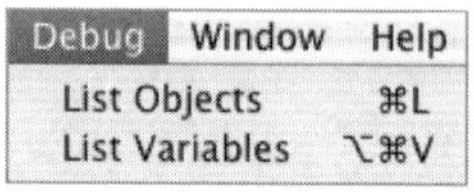

Debug
Window
Help
List Objects ⌘L
List Variables ⌥⌘V

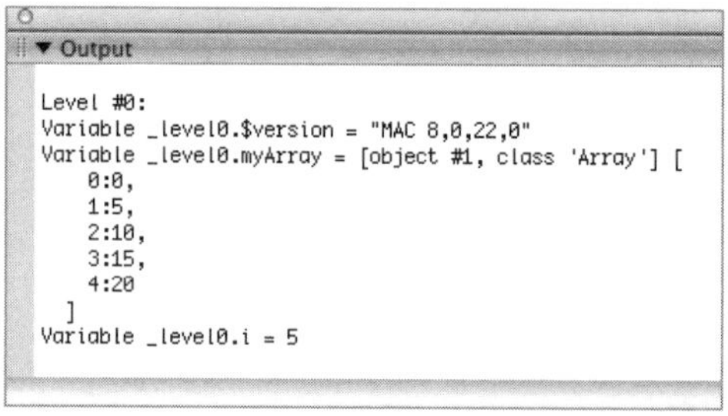

Output
Level #0:
Variable _level0.$version = "MAC 8,0,22,0"
Variable _level0.myArray = [object #1, class 'Array'] [
0:0,
1:5,
2:10,
3:15,
4:20
]
Variable _level0.i = 5

Figure 13.36 Choose Debug > List Variables in testing mode to see all the current variables. The `myArray` object and its values are listed, verifying the results of the looping statement.

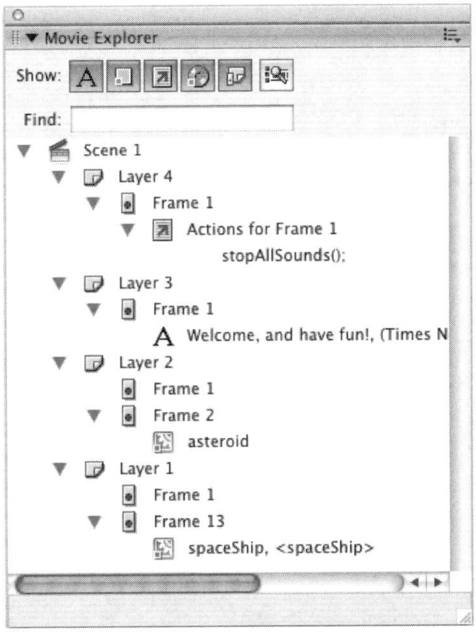

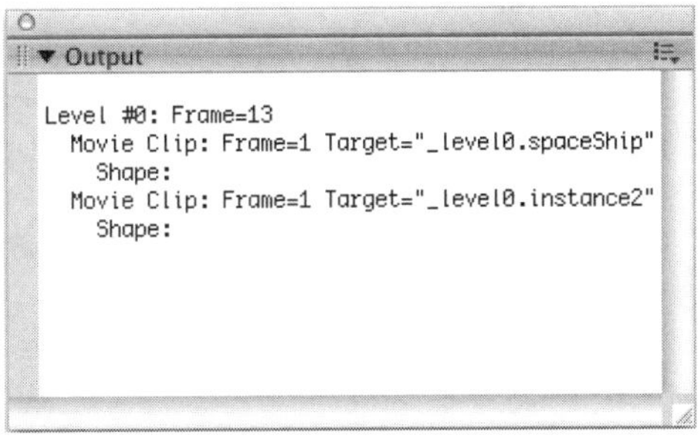

Figure 13.37 Information about the same movie is displayed in the Movie Explorer (top) and the Output panel (bottom). The Movie Explorer visually displays the hierarchy of objects. The Output panel lists the target path of objects and other graphic elements.

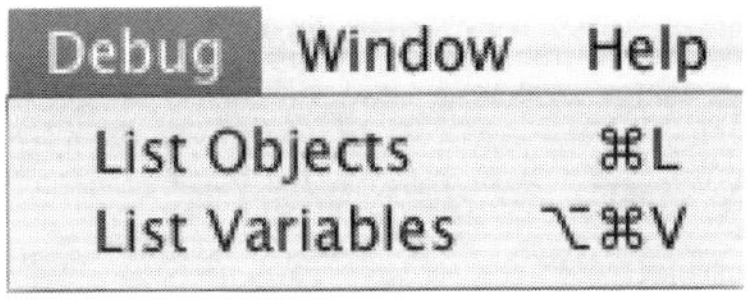

Figure 13.38 Choose Debug > List Objects in testing mode.

Listing objects in the Output panel

You can also use the Output panel to display a list of the objects in the movie. The Output panel's display isn't as graphically appealing as the display in the Movie Explorer, but it gives you information about objects that you can't get from the Movie Explorer. The object information listed in the Output panel includes the object's level, the type of symbol (Movie Clip, Button, Edit Text) or type of graphic (Text, Shape), and the absolute target path of the objects. The target path of objects is the most important bit of information the Output panel can tell you directly, although the Movie Explorer can give that to you indirectly. A comparison of the typical information display for the same movie in the Movie Explorer and in the Output panel is shown in **Figure 13.37**.

To list objects in the Output panel:

- In testing mode, choose Debug > List Objects (Command-L for Mac, Ctrl-L for Windows) (**Figure 13.38**).

  All the objects in the current state of the movie are displayed in the Output panel.

✔ Tip

- Like the List Variables command, the List Objects command displays the movie's current status. If a movie clip disappears from the Timeline as the movie plays, you need to select List Objects again to update the display of objects in the Output panel.

Tracing Variables in the Output Panel

Sometimes you need to know the status of a variable or expression at a particular point during the playback of your movie. For example, imagine that you've created a game of Pong in which a movie clip of a ball bounces between two other movie clips of paddles. You want to find out, for testing purposes, the position of the paddle at the instant of a collision with the ball. The command List Variables is little help because of the rapidly changing variables for the paddle positions. The solution is to use the action `trace`. You can place the action `trace` at any point in the movie to have Flash send a custom message to the Output panel during testing mode. The custom message is an expression you create that gives you tailored information at just the right moment. In the Pong example, you use the `trace` action as follows:

```
trace("paddle X-position is " +
myPaddle_mc._x);
trace("paddle Y-position is " +
myPaddle_mc._y);
```

Place these two `trace` statements in the `if` statement that detects the collision. At the moment of collision, Flash sends the Output panel a message that looks something like this:

```
paddle X-position is 25
paddle Y-position is 89
```

You can also use `trace` to monitor the condition of an expression so you can understand the circumstances that change its value. For example, in the following task, you'll create a simple draggable movie clip and another movie clip that remains stationary. You'll assign a `trace` action to display the value of the draggable movie clip's `hitTest()` method, letting you see when and where the value becomes true or false.

To display an expression in the Output panel:

1. Create a movie clip symbol, place an instance of it on the Stage, and name the instance `myMovieClip_mc`.
2. Create another movie clip symbol, place an instance of it on the Stage, and name the instance `rock_mc`.
3. Select the first frame of the main Timeline, and open the Actions panel.
4. Enter `_root`, and then create an `onEnterFrame` handler.
5. Within the `onEnterFrame` handler, enter `myMovieClip_mc`, followed by a period.

```
_root.onEnterFrame = function() {
    myMovieClip_mc.startDrag(true);
};
```

Figure 13.39 The `startDrag` action will make the movie clip `myMovieClip_mc` follow the pointer.

```
_root.onEnterFrame = function() {
    myMovieClip_mc.startDrag(true);
    trace(myMovieClip_mc.hitTest(rock_mc));
};
```

Figure 13.40 The `trace` action evaluates the expression within its parentheses and displays the value in the Output panel.

6. Choose ActionScript 2.0 Classes > Movie > MovieClip > Methods > startDrag. Enter true for the action's parameter (**Figure 13.39**).

7. On the next line, choose Global Functions > Miscellaneous Functions > trace (Esc + tr).

8. Between the parentheses, enter the following expression (**Figure 13.40**):

   `myMovieClip_mc.hitTest(rock_mc).`

   Flash evaluates the `hitTest()` method to determine whether the draggable movie clip collides with the movie clip `rock_mc`. The returned value is displayed in the Output panel in testing mode.

9. Test your movie.

   The Output panel opens, displaying the result of the `trace` action (**Figure 13.41**).

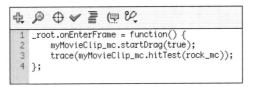

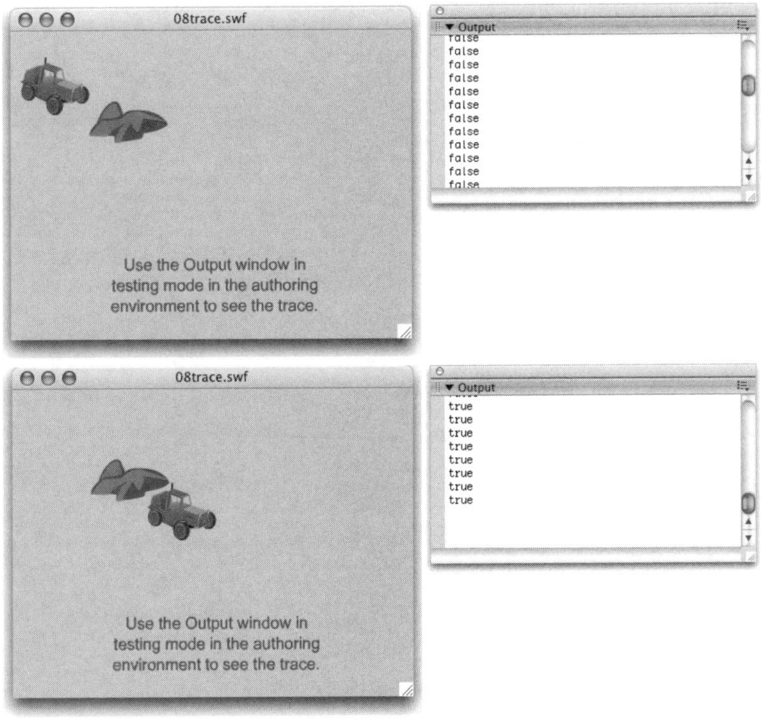

Figure 13.41 The Output panel displays `false` when `myMovieClip_mc` is clear of the `rock_mc` movie clip (top). It displays `true` when there is a collision (bottom).

Determining a Variable's Data Type

You can use the `typeof` operator in conjunction with the `trace` action to display a variable's data type. This information is useful when you begin to encounter problems with unexpected values in your variables. If you suspect that the problem stems from using a variable in ways that are incompatible with its data type, place a `trace` action to display the data type and confirm or disprove your suspicions.

To determine the data type of a variable:

1. Open the file you created in the task "To list variables in the Output panel" earlier in this chapter.

   This is the file in which you created an `Array` and populated the `Array` using a looping statement.

2. Select the first frame, and open the Actions panel.

3. Create a new line after the ending curly brace of the last statement in the Script pane.

4. Choose Global Functions > Miscellaneous Functions > trace.

5. With your pointer between the parentheses, choose Operators > Miscellaneous Operators > typeof.

   The `typeof` operator appears between the parentheses of the `trace` statement.

6. Between the parentheses of the `typeof` operator, enter `myArray` (**Figure 13.42**).

   Flash will evaluate `myArray` and display its data type in the Output panel when you test the movie.

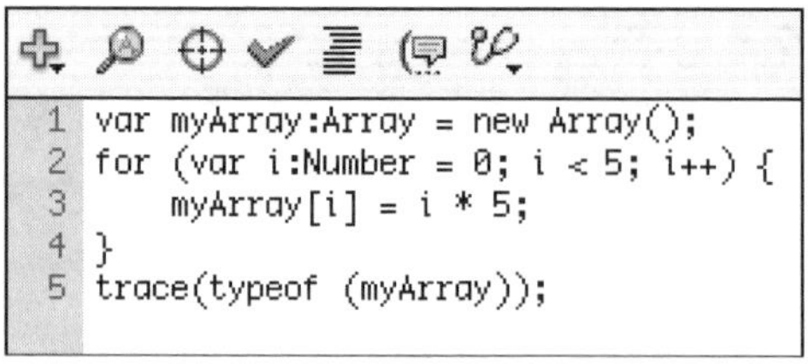
var myArray:Array = new Array();
for (var i:Number = 0; i < 5; i++) {
myArray[i] = i * 5;
}
trace(typeof (myArray));

Figure 13.42 The data type of `myArray` will be determined and displayed in the Output panel.

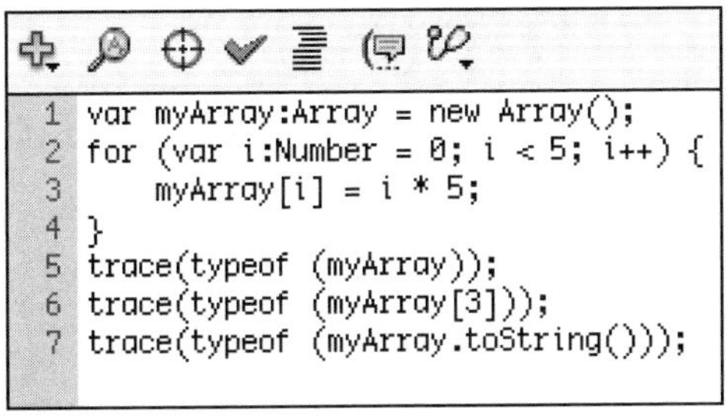

Figure 13.43 Add `trace` actions to evaluate and display the data type of the element with index 3 in `myArray` and the method `toString()` of `myArray`.

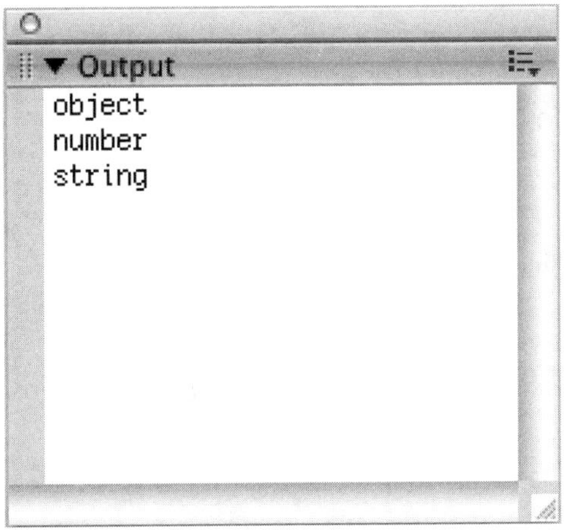

Figure 13.44 The results of the `trace` action in the Output panel.

7. Add two more `trace` actions with the `typeof` operator (**Figure 13.43**).

8. Test your movie.

   Flash displays the results of the three `trace` statements in the Output panel in testing mode. The first trace displays the data type of `myArray`: `object`. The second trace indicates that `myArray[3]` is a `number`, and the third trace shows that `myArray.toString()` is a `string` (**Figure 13.44**).

Debugging

The Debugger panel lets you monitor and modify the values of all the variables and properties in your movie as it plays. You can also examine the values of objects that hold data, such as instances of the Date or Sound class. Use the Debugger to verify that Flash is manipulating the information in variables the way you want it to and to test certain conditions or the effects of certain variables quickly. For example, imagine that you create an animation with the variable `myVelocity` controlling the speed of a spaceship. In the Debugger panel, you can modify the variable `myVelocity` as the movie plays to see how it affects the motion of your spaceship. Increase or decrease the value of `myVelocity` until you're satisfied with the results.

The Debugger panel opens and is active in testing mode when you select Control > Debug Movie. Once open and active, the Debugger displays information in several separate parts: a Display list at the top left; Properties, Variables, Local Variables ("Locals") and Watch lists below it; a Call Stack window at the bottom left; and a Code view on the right (**Figure 13.45**). The Display list shows the root Timeline and the hierarchy of movie clips in that Timeline. You can select the root Timeline or the other movie clips to see the properties belonging to that particular Timeline or to see all the variables within that particular scope. The Code view lets you define breakpoints in your ActionScript so that you can step through the movie line by line to determine where and when a piece of interactivity in your movie is going awry. The Call Stack at bottom left displays the names of your function calls as you step through the code.

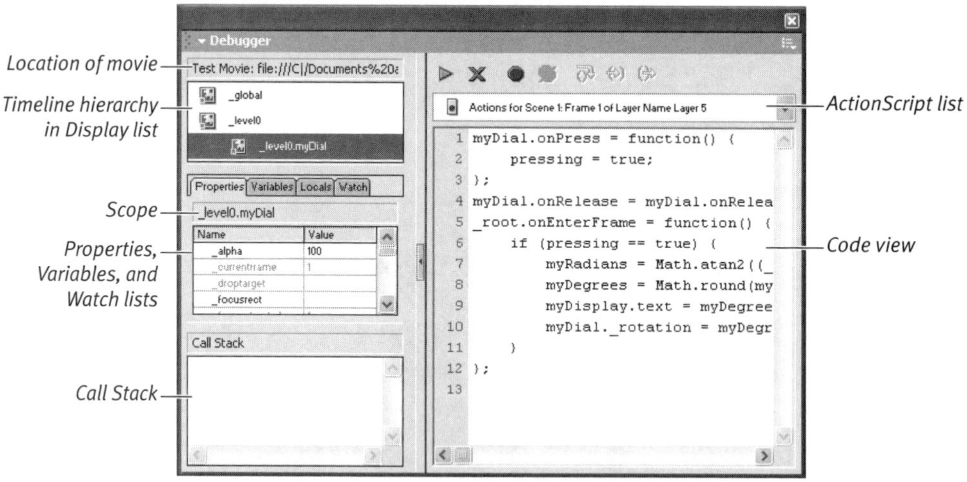

Figure 13.45 The Debugger panel displays a hierarchy of Timelines and their properties and variables on the left side. ActionScript can be displayed on the right side for you to step through the code line by line.

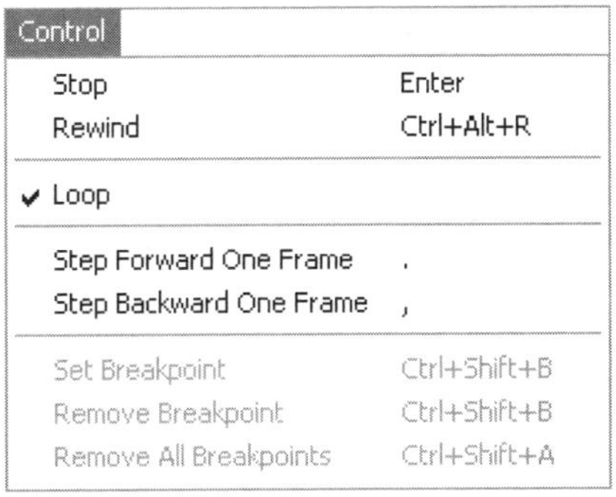

Figure 13.46 Use the Control menu to control the playback of your movie in testing mode.

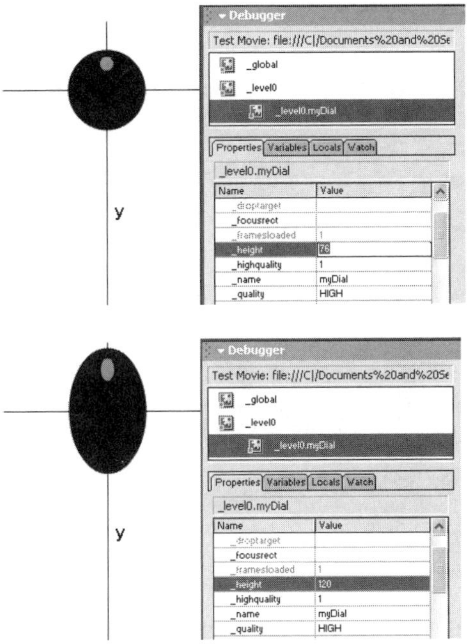

Figure 13.47 The values of properties can be selected (top) and modified (bottom); your movie reflects changes even while it plays.

✔ Tip

- Certain properties are read-only and are grayed out, indicating that they can't be modified. For example, the property `_totalframes` is a fixed value determined by the number of frames in your movie.

Use the Control menu to rewind, play, and step forward or backward through your movie, frame by frame, as necessary, to scrutinize the movie's properties and variables (**Figure 13.46**).

To access the Debugger:

- From the Flash authoring environment, choose Control > Debug Movie (Command-Shift-Return for Mac, Ctrl-Shift-Enter for Windows).

  Flash exports a SWF file and enters testing mode. The Debugger panel opens and is activated. Your movie is initially paused so you can set breakpoints in your code. Click the Continue button (the green right-pointing arrow) to start your movie.

To modify a property or a variable in the Debugger panel:

1. In the Display list of the Debugger panel, select the movie clip whose properties or variables you wish to modify.
2. Click the Properties or the Variables tab. You may have to adjust the moveable divider that separates the Call Stack to see the full list of variables or properties.
3. Double-click the field in the Value column next to the property or variable you wish to modify.
4. Enter a new value.

   The new value must be a constant (a string, number, or boolean value) rather than an expression that refers to another variable or property. For example, it must be `35` instead of `35 + myAlpha`. The movie reflects the new value immediately (**Figure 13.47**).

Watching variables in different scopes

The Variables tab in the Debugger panel lets you watch only the variables within the same scope. To watch variables belonging to different scopes, use the Watch tab to choose the variables you would like to observe. This lets you create a set of critical variables that are displayed in one place for you to watch and modify. The variables in your Watch list are displayed with their absolute target paths.

To add variables to the Watch list:

1. In the Debugger panel, select the root Timeline or a movie clip from the Display list.

2. Select the variable from the Variables tab. From the Options menu at the top-right corner of the Debugger panel, choose Add Watch (**Figure 13.48**).

   A blue dot appears next to the variable, marking it to be displayed on the Watch list.

   or

   Select the variable from the Variables tab. Control-click (Mac) or right-click the variable. Choose Watch from the contextual menu that appears (**Figure 13.49**).

   A blue dot appears next to the variable, marking it to be displayed on the Watch list.

   or

   From the Watch tab, Control-click (Mac) or right-click in the empty list. Choose Add from the contextual menu that appears (**Figure 13.50**). Enter the absolute target path of the variable.

Figure 13.48 The selected variable (myRadians) is added to the Watch list using the Options menu.

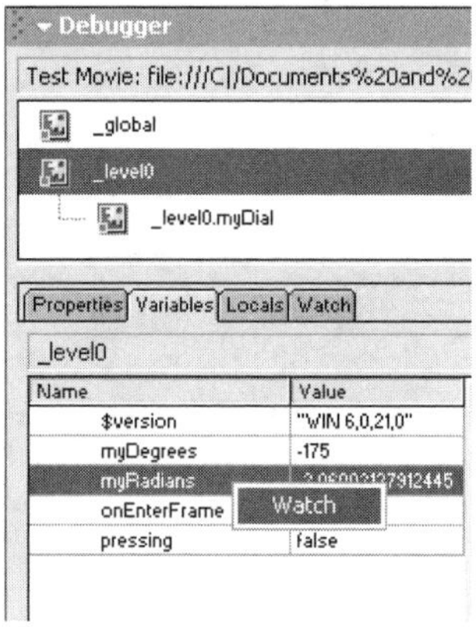

Figure 13.49 The selected variable (myRadians) is added to the Watch list by using the display menu.

Figure 13.50 Choose Add from the display menu on the Watch list to enter a variable by hand.

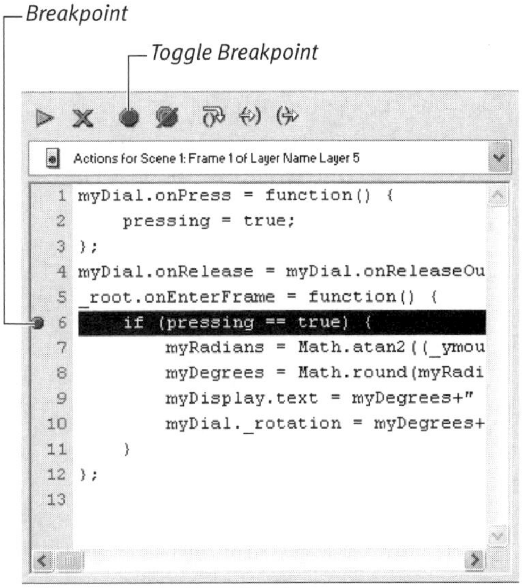
Breakpoint
Toggle Breakpoint
Actions for Scene 1: Frame 1 of Layer Name Layer 5
myDial.onPress = function() {
pressing = true;
};
myDial.onRelease = myDial.onReleaseOu
_root.onEnterFrame = function() {
if (pressing == true) {
myRadians = Math.atan2((_ymou
myDegrees = Math.round(myRadi
myDisplay.text = myDegrees+"
myDial._rotation = myDegrees+
}
};

Figure 13.51 A breakpoint is set at line 6 of this code.

To remove variables from the Watch list:

- *Do one of the following:*
  - ▲ In the Watch list, Control-click (Mac) or right-click the variable, and choose Remove from the contextual menu.
  - ▲ In the Variables list, Control-click (Mac) or right-click the variable, and choose the selected Watch option.
  - ▲ In the Variables or Watch list, select the variable, and then choose Remove Watch from the Debugger panel's Options menu.

Breakpoints and stepping through code

Breakpoints are places in a script where you tell Flash to pause so you can more easily inspect the condition of variables and properties and the status of your movie. You can have multiple breakpoints, and you can set them either in the Debugger panel or in the Actions panel. Once they're set, you can step through the code line by line if you need to. Options let you play through the code or skip function statements as desired.

To set breakpoints in your code:

1. In the active Debugger panel, choose a script from the ActionScript list.

   ActionScript appears in the Code view on the right side of the Debugger panel.

2. Select a line of code where you want to set a breakpoint. Click Toggle Breakpoint.

   or

   Place your pointer to the left of the line number, and click once.

   Flash adds a red stop sign next to the line number (**Figure 13.51**). When the movie plays in the Debugger, it will stop when it reaches the breakpoint so you can inspect the state of the movie and its variables and properties.

To remove a breakpoint:

- In the Debugger panel, select the breakpoint. Click the Toggle Breakpoint button, or Control-click (Mac) or right-click the line of code and select Remove Breakpoint.

  The breakpoint is removed.

  or

  In the Actions panel, select the breakpoint.

  The breakpoint is removed.

To remove all breakpoints:

- In the Debugger panel, click the Remove All Breakpoints button, or Control-click (Mac) or right-click and select Remove All Breakpoints.

  All breakpoint are removed.

To step through code:

- *Do any of the following:*
  - ▲ Click the Continue button to advance the Debugger through ActionScript code until the next breakpoint is encountered (**Figure 13.52**).

    A yellow arrow marks the line of code where the Debugger is paused.
  - ▲ Click the Step Over button to skip over a function you've defined. The Debugger continues to the next line after the function call (**Figure 13.53**).

    Although the Debugger steps over a function, the statements inside the function are still performed.

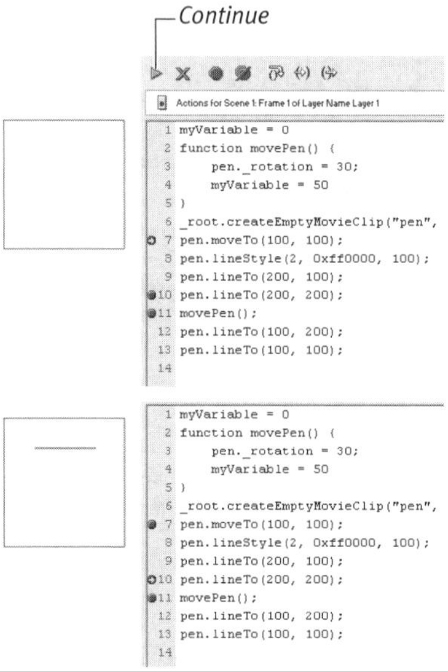

Figure 13.52 The yellow arrow marks the current line where the Debugger is paused. At top, the Debugger is paused at line 7, and the Stage is empty. When you click the Continue button, the Debugger proceeds to the next breakpoint and pauses at line 10 (bottom). The horizontal line segment from (100,100) to (200,100) is drawn. The code at line 10 hasn't yet been performed.

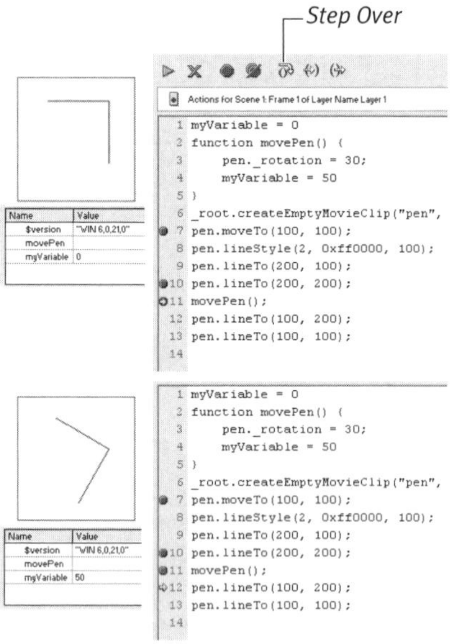

Figure 13.53 At top, the Debugger is paused at line 11, and the Stage shows two line segments. When you click the Step Over button, the Debugger steps over the function `movePen` and stops at the first statement after the function call at line 12 (bottom). The statements inside the function are still performed, as you can see by the rotation and the new value for `myVariable`.

▲ Click the Step In button to perform the statements inside a function (**Figure 13.54**).

▲ Click the Step Out button to break out of a function. The Debugger continues to the next line after the function call (**Figure 13.55**).

Although the Debugger steps out of a function, the rest of the statements inside the function are still performed.

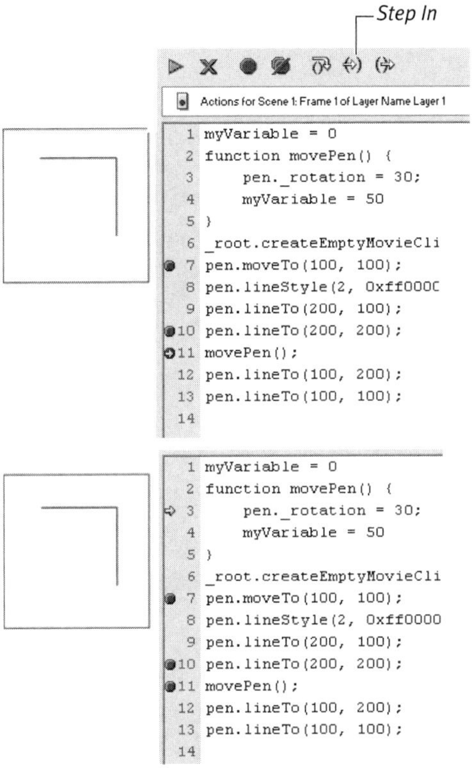

Figure 13.54 At top, the Debugger is paused at line 11, and the Stage shows two line segments. When you click the Step In button, the Debugger proceeds to the next line inside the function movePen (bottom).

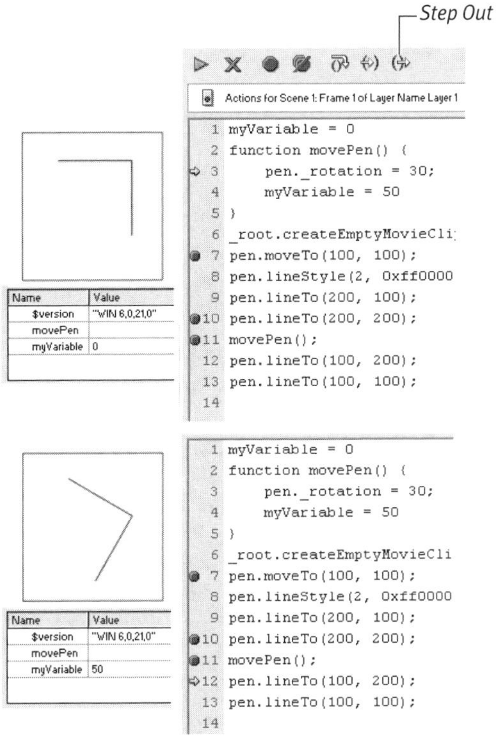

Figure 13.55 At top, the Debugger is paused at line 3, and the Stage shows two line segments. When you click the Step Out button, the Debugger steps out of the function movePen and stops at the first statement after the function call at line 12 (bottom). The statements inside the function are still performed, as you can see by the rotation and the new value for myVariable.

Remote debugging

You can also access the Debugger panel of a SWF movie remotely (outside testing mode). Doing so lets you watch variables and properties and check interactivity when your movie is in a real-life setting, such as when it's uploaded to a Web site.

To enable remote debugging, you must select the Debugging Permitted option in the Flash tab of the Publish Settings dialog box. When you publish your movie, an SWD file is also exported. This file contains debugging information that lets you set breakpoints and step through your code. Keep the SWF and SWD files together in the same directory, and upload them to your Web site. You'll now be able to debug your movie remotely.

To debug remotely:

1. Open the Flash file you want to debug, and choose File > Publish Settings.
2. Click the Flash tab. In the list of options, select the "Debugging permitted" check box. If you wish to protect your movie by limiting debugging access, enter a password in the Password field (**Figure 13.56**).
3. Publish your Flash movie.

   Flash exports an HTML file, a SWF file, and an SWD file. Although the SWD file isn't required for remote debugging, it's required to set breakpoints and step through code.
4. Keep all three files together, and upload them to your Web site or place them in a directory locally on your hard drive.
5. In Flash, choose Window > Debugger.

   The Debugger panel opens.
6. From the Debugger panel's Options menu, choose Enable Remote Debugging (**Figure 13.57**).

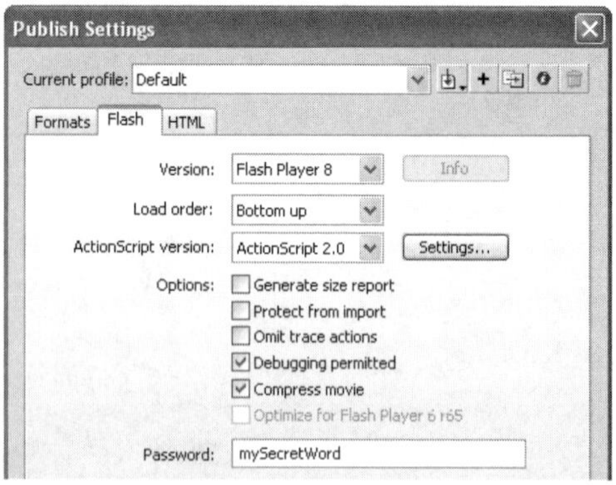

Figure 13.56 To enable remote debugging, select the "Debugging permitted" option in the Flash tab of the Publish Settings dialog box. The password (in this case, `mySecretWord`) gives you access to the Debugger.

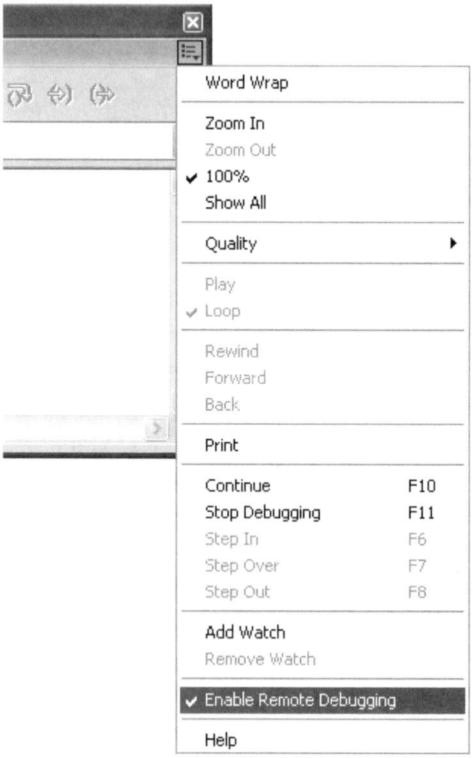

Figure 13.57 Choose Options > Enable Remote Debugging in the Debugger panel.

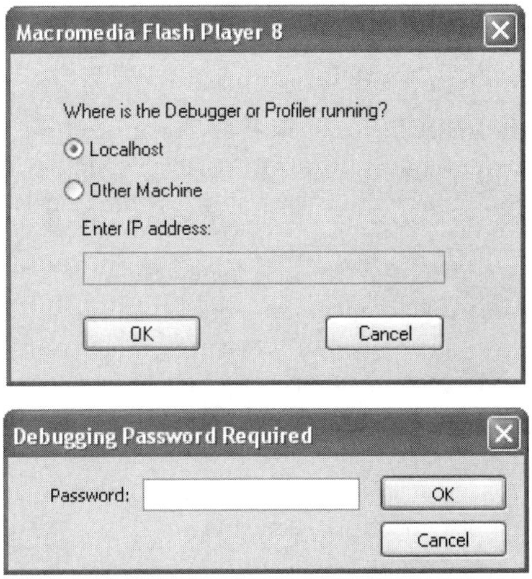

Figure 13.58 When remote debugging has been enabled and the SWD file is in the same directory as the SWF file, the Remote Debug dialog box appears, letting you access the Debugger for the remote movie. If you selected a password in the Publish Settings dialog box when you published your movie, enter it in the second dialog box that appears (bottom).

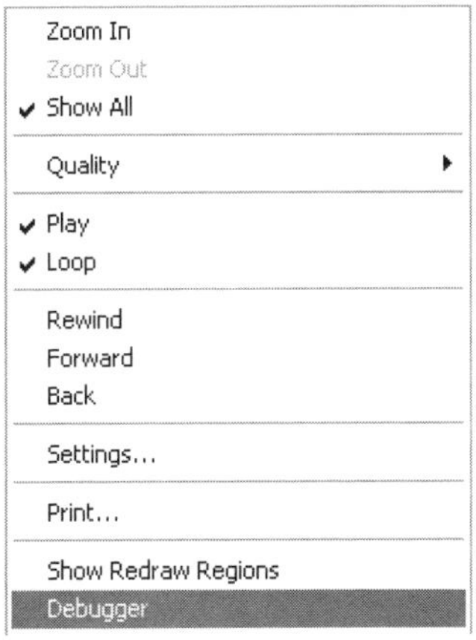

Figure 13.59 You can access the Debugger from the contextual menu.

7. From your browser or from the Flash stand-alone player, open the SWF file that you've either kept on your computer or uploaded to the Web.

   The Remote Debug dialog box appears, requesting information about where the Flash application is running.

8. Select Localhost, because Flash and the Debugger are on the same (local) computer. Click OK. Enter your password if you entered one in the Publish Settings dialog box (**Figure 13.58**).

   The SWF movie opens in the stand-alone player or a Web browser. The Debugger opens in the Flash authoring tool in a paused state with information about the Flash movie you're remotely debugging.

✔ Tip

- If you don't get the Remote Debug dialog box, or if you've closed the Debugger panel, you can open it by right-clicking or Control-clicking (Mac) inside the movie. From the menu that appears, choose Debugger (**Figure 13.59**).

Optimizing Your Movie

Understanding the tools you use to create graphics, animation, sound, and ActionScript is important, but it's equally important to know how best to use them to create streamlined Flash movies. After all, the best-laid designs and animations won't be appreciated if poor construction and clunky code make them too large to download or too inefficient to play easily. To streamline a Flash movie, use optimizations that keep the file size small, the animations smooth, and the revisions simple. Many factors affect the file size and performance of the final exported SWF file. Bitmaps, sounds, complicated shapes, color gradients, alpha transparencies, and embedded fonts all increase the Flash file size and slow the movie's performance.

Only you can weigh the trade-offs between the quality and quantity of Flash content and the size and performance of the movie. Keep in mind the audience to whom you're delivering your Flash movies. Does your audience have Internet connections with DSL or cable lines, or does your audience rely on 56 Kbps modems? Knowing the answer to this question helps you make more informed choices about what to include in your movie and how to build it.

The following strategies can help you work more efficiently and create smaller, more manageable, better-performing Flash movies.

Optimizing your authoring environment

- Use layers to separate and organize your content. For example, place all your actions on one layer, all your frame labels on another layer, and all your sounds in still another layer. By using layers, you'll be able to understand and change different elements of your movie quickly (**Figure 13.60**). Having many layers doesn't increase the size of the final exported SWF file. Use comments in keyframes, as well, to explain the different parts of the Timeline.
- Use dynamic text fields in addition to the `trace` action, Output panel, and Debugger panel to observe variables in your movie. Dynamic text fields and the `trace` action let you display expressions and variables in the context of your movie.
- Avoid using scenes in your movie. Although scenes are a good organizational feature for simple movies, Timelines that contain scenes are more difficult to navigate from movie clips. In addition, movie clip instances aren't continuous between scenes. Use labels to mark different areas of the Timeline, instead, or use movie clips to hold different parts of your animation.

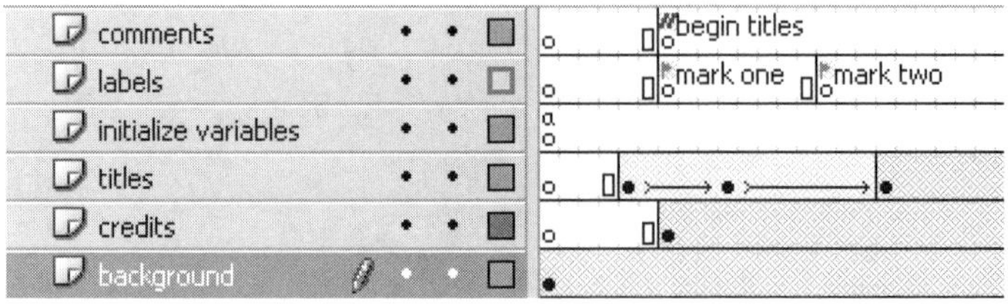

Figure 13.60 Well-organized layers like these are easy to understand and change.

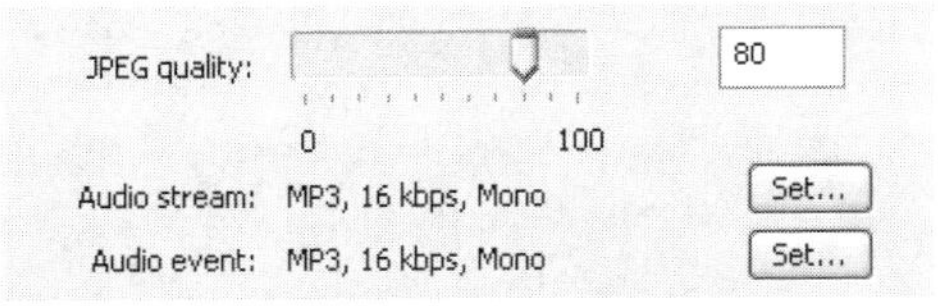

Figure 13.61 The JPEG quality and audio-compression options in the Publish Settings dialog box.

Optimizing bitmaps and sounds for playback performance

- Avoid animating large bitmaps. Keep bitmaps as static background elements if they're large, or make them small for tweening.
- Place streaming sounds on the root Timeline instead of within a movie clip. A movie clip needs to be downloaded in its entirety before playing. A streaming sound on the root Timeline, however, begins playing as the frames download.
- Use the maximum amount of compression tolerable for bitmaps and sounds. You can adjust the JPEG quality level for your exported SWF file in Publish Settings. You can also adjust the compression settings for the stream sync and event sync sounds separately, so you can keep a higher-quality streaming sound for music and narration and a lower-quality event sound for button clicks (**Figure 13.61**).
- Avoid using the Trace Bitmap command to create an overly complex vector image of an imported bitmap. The complexity of a traced bitmap can make the file size larger and the performance significantly slower than if you use the bitmap itself.
- Import bitmaps and sounds at the exact size or length that you want to use them in Flash. Although editing within Flash is possible, you want to import just the information you need to keep the file size small. For example, don't import a bitmap and then reduce it 50 percent to use in your movie. Instead, reduce the bitmap 50 percent first and then import it into Flash.

Optimizing graphics, text, and tweening for playback performance

- Use tweening wherever you can instead of frame-by-frame animation. In an animation, Flash only has to remember the keyframes, making tweening a far less memory-intensive task.
- Tween symbols instead of groups. Groups don't allow you to apply instance effects like tint, brightness, or alpha, and using groups in tweens makes editing difficult because you have to apply the same edit on every group in the tween's keyframes.
- Avoid creating animations that have multiple objects moving at the same time or that have large areas of change. These kinds of animations tax a computer's CPU and slow the movie's performance.
- If you have a large movie clip that isn't animated (such as a background), select the "Use runtime bitmap caching" option in the Property inspector for the instance. This option instructs the Flash Player to not redraw the movie clip's content every frame, reducing the playback computer's workload.
- Break apart groups within symbols to simplify them. Once you're satisfied with an illustration in a symbol, break the groups into shapes to flatten the illustration. Flash will have fewer curves to remember and thus will have an easier time tweening the symbol instance. Alpha effects on the instance also affect the symbol as a whole instead of the individual groups within the symbol (**Figure 13.62**).
- Use color gradients and alpha transparencies sparingly.

Figure 13.62 A symbol defined as separate groups (top left) contains more information (top middle) and can produce undesirable transparency effects (top right). A symbol defined as a shape (bottom left) contains less information (bottom middle) and becomes transparent as one unit (bottom right).

Figure 13.63 Complex curves and shapes can be simplified without losing their detail.

- Use the Property inspector to change the color, tint, and brightness of instances instead of creating separate symbols of different colors.
- Optimize curves by avoiding special line styles (such as dotted lines), by using the Pencil tool rather than the Brush tool, and by reducing the complexity of curves with Modify > Shape > Optimize or Command-Shift-Option-C for Mac, Ctrl-Alt-Shift-C for Windows (**Figure 13.63**).
- Use fewer font styles, and embed only the essential font outlines.

Optimizing ActionScript code

- Try to keep all your code in one place—preferably on the main Timeline—and keep code in just one layer.
- Use a consistent naming convention for variables, movie clips, objects, and other elements that need to be identified. A consistent, simple name makes the job the variable performs more apparent.
- Use comments within your ActionScript to explain the code to yourself and to other developers who may look at your Flash document for future revisions.
- Think about *modularity*. Use smaller, separate components to build your interactivity. For example, use functions to define frequently accessed tasks, use external scripts when possible, and keep large or common assets outside your movie but available through shared symbols, `loadMovie()`, and `loadSound()`. You'll reduce redundancy, save memory, and make revisions easier.

Avoiding Common Mistakes

When you're troubleshooting your Flash movie, there are a few obvious places you should look first to locate common mistakes. These problems usually involve simple but critical elements, such as overlooking quotation marks or a relative path term or forgetting to name an instance. Pay close attention to the following warning list to ensure that all your Flash movies are free of bugs:

- Be mindful of uppercase and lowercase letters. ActionScript 2.0 is case-sensitive, so make sure the names of your variables and objects exactly match. Flash keywords must also match in case. For example, `Key.isDown()` isn't the same as `key.isDown()`.
- Double-check the data types of your values. Review the Script pane to make sure quotation marks appear only around string data types. Movie clip target paths and the keyword `this` should not be within quotation marks.
- Double-check the target paths for your movie clips, variables, and objects.
- Remember to name your movie clip, button, and text field instances in the Property inspector. Be sure your names adhere to the naming rules explained in Chapter 3.
- Check to see whether ActionScript statements are within the correct parentheses or curly braces in the Script pane. For example, verify that statements belonging to an `if` statement or to a function statement are contained within their curly braces.
- Place a `stop` action in the first keyframe of a movie clip to prevent it from playing automatically and looping.
- To test simple actions and simple buttons, choose Enable Simple Frame Actions and Enable Simple Buttons from the Control menu. For more complex button events, you must choose Test Movie from the Control menu.
- Remember that the default setting for your Flash movie in the testing mode is to loop.

For additional help and advice about debugging your movie, check out the vast Flash resources on the Web. Begin your search at Macromedia's Web site, which provides a searchable archive of tech notes, documentation, tutorials, case studies, and more. You'll also find links to other Web sites with articles, FLA source files, bulletin boards, and mailing lists. Check out the CD that accompanies this book for more Flash links and resources.

NAMING SUFFIXES FOR OBJECT TYPES

A

Naming Suffixes for Object Types

OBJECT	SUFFIX
Array	_array
Button	_btn
Camera	_cam
Color	_color
ContextMenu	_cm
ContextMenuItem	_cmi
Date	_date
Error	_err
LoadVars	_lv
LocalConnection	_lc
Microphone	_mic
MovieClip	_mc
MovieClipLoader	_mcl
NetConnection	_nc
NetStream	_ns
PrintJob	_pj
SharedObject	_so
Sound	_sound
String	_str
TextField	_txt
TextFormat	_fmt
Video	_video
XML	_xml
XMLNode	_xmlnode
XMLSocket	_xmlsocket

Keyboard Keys and Matching Key Codes

B

Letters	
Letter Key	Key Code
A	65
B	66
C	67
D	68
E	69
F	70
G	71
H	72
I	73
J	74
K	75
L	76
M	77
N	78
O	79
P	80
Q	81
R	82
S	83
T	84
U	85
V	86
W	87
X	88
Y	89
Z	90

Numbers and Symbols

KEY	KEY CODE	KEY CLASS PROPERTY
0	48	
1	49	
2	50	
3	51	
4	52	
5	53	
6	54	
7	55	
8	56	
9	57	
Numpad 0	96	
Numpad 1	97	
Numpad 2	98	
Numpad 3	99	
Numpad 4	100	
Numpad 5	101	
Numpad 6	102	
Numpad 7	103	
Numpad 8	104	
Numpad 9	105	
Numpad *	106	
Numpad +	107	
Numpad Enter	108	
Numpad -	109	
Numpad .	110	
Numpad /	111	
Backspace	8	BACKSPACE
Tab	9	TAB
Clear	12	
Enter	13	ENTER
Shift	16	SHIFT
Control	17	CONTROL
Alt	18	
Caps Lock	20	CAPSLOCK
Esc	27	ESCAPE
Spacebar	32	SPACE
Page Up	33	PGUP
Page Down	34	PGDN
End	35	END
Home	36	HOME
Left arrow	37	LEFT
Up arrow	38	UP

Numbers and Symbols

KEY	KEY CODE	KEY CLASS PROPERTY
Right arrow	39	RIGHT
Down arrow	40	DOWN
Insert	45	INSERT
Delete	46	DELETEKEY
Help	47	
Num Lock	144	
;:	186	
=+	187	
-_	189	
/?	191	
`~	192	
[{	219	
|	220	
]}	221	
'"	222	

Function Keys

FUNCTION KEY	KEY CODE
F1	112
F2	113
F3	114
F4	115
F5	116
F6	117
F7	118
F8	119
F9	120
F10	121
F11	122
F12	123

INDEX

B

C

INDEX

INDEX

INDEX

INDEX

INDEX

Q

R

S

INDEX

U

V